Hegel's Ethics
of Recognition

Hegel's Ethics
of Recognition

Robert R. Williams

University of California Press
Berkeley / Los Angeles / London

University of California Press
Berkeley and Los Angeles, California

University of California Press
London, England

Library of Congress Cataloging-in-Publication Data

Williams, Robert R., 1939–
    Hegel's ethics of recognition / Robert R. Williams.
       p.   cm.
    Includes bibliographical references and index.
    ISBN 0-520-22492-2 (pbk : alk. paper)
    1. Hegel, Georg Wilhelm Friedrich, 1770–1831. 2. Recognition
(Philosophy)—Moral and ethical aspects—History—19th century.
3. Intersubjectivity—Moral and ethical aspects—History—19th
century. 4. Ethics, Modern—19th century. I. Title.
B2949.E8W55   1997
193—dc21   97-1662
                                             CIP

Printed in the United States of America

09   08   07   06   05   04   03   02   01   00
9 8 7 6 5 4 3 2 1

The paper used in this publication meets the minimum requirements of
ANSI/NISO Z39.48-1992 (R 1997) (Permanence of Paper). ♾

For Irma, Diana, and Daniel

Love is the consciousness of my unity with another so that I am not isolated by myself, but gain my self-consciousness only in the renunciation of my independence, and by knowing myself in relation and union with another.

Hegel, *Philosophy of Right*

Contents

Preface

With over ten thousand books and articles on Hegel, could there possibly be any justification for yet another, long book? I must leave the answer to this question to the reader. But, as far as I know, no one else has done what I propose to do, namely, examine Hegel's concept of recognition, track it from his early manuscripts into his mature thought, including the only recently available transcripts of his lectures on the *Philosophy of Right*, and discern how it informs his philosophy of spirit, especially his ethical and social theory. My thesis is that recognition (*Anerkennung*) is not only the existential phenomenological shape (*Gestalt*) of the concept of freedom but also the general intersubjective structure and pattern of Hegel's concept of spirit. As such it provides the ontological deep structure of his philosophy of spirit, practical philosophy, and account of ethical life (*Sittlichkeit*). Recognition is immanent not merely in Hegel's account of the institutions of abstract right (property, contract, and punishment), of family, civil society, and state, but also in his account of the virtues, such that all virtues are social.

In my opinion the topic and theme of recognition is both important and yet largely ignored, not only in English-speaking Hegel scholarship, but, with few exceptions, in German scholarship as well. Jürgen Habermas asserts that recognition is an important counterdiscourse of modernity in which Hegel presents an inclusive reason open to and mediated by otherness. According to Habermas, inclusion here is more than a disguised form of exclusion. There is much truth in what Habermas says. However, not even Habermas sufficiently appreciates the importance of recognition for Hegel, particularly for understanding his ethics. In my view, recognition is more than a minor theme of the so-called youthful Hegel that later becomes subordinate to metaphysical idealism. I agree with Habermas that recognition is a promising path for ethics and social philosophy, but I deny his contention that it is a path that the "mature Hegel" did not take. I will show that recognition continues as an important operative concept and theme in Hegel's mature philosophy of spirit.

This is not to deny or minimize the importance of the logic or the categorical ordering of the *Philosophy of Right*. Nevertheless, after examining the recently available lecture notes on Hegel's *Philosophy of Spirit* (1825) and the seven different lecture series on the *Philosophy of Right* that Hegel gave between 1817 and 1830, I believe that recognition continues to be an important, largely ignored theme and concept, the existential-empirical dimension of Hegel's concept of freedom. These recently available materials from Hegel's lectures, many of which were previously unpublished, make it possible to understand Hegel's philosophy of spirit better than ever before, and demonstrate the continuing importance of the concept of recognition in Hegel's mature thought. The following study examines the significance of recognition for understanding Fichte's and Hegel's concepts of freedom and their ethical thought. Mutual recognition is a major factor in Hegel's development of a social reason and rationality; it is an operative concept in Hegel's constructive philosophy of spirit and ethical thought. As will be shown, the question and possibility of ethics for Hegel turn on the possibility and significance of reciprocal recognition. This issue remains a controversial one, particularly in the French reception of Hegel and its aftermath.

This project of studying recognition originated on a Fulbright leave in Germany, where I first became acquainted with Ludwig Siep and Edith Düsing and their work on recognition. It continued in my earlier book, *Recognition: Fichte and Hegel on the Other*. That work evoked the interest and criticism of several people, including H. S. Harris and Stephen Houlgate. I am indebted to Houlgate for his criticisms of that earlier work and for the invitation to present a paper on Hegel's theory of punishment at a Hegel conference sponsored by DePaul University in 1994, where I became acquainted with the work of other Chicago Hegelians: Ardis Collins, John McCumber, and Robert Pippen. This paper was an early draft of chapter 8 of the present work. I am further indebted to Houlgate for his criticisms and suggestions concerning the corporations as a possible solution to the problem of poverty (chapter 11).

This book was written while on a sabbatical leave from Hiram College. I also wish to acknowledge the support of a summer fellowship from the National Endowment for the Humanities. I want to express my gratitude to Peter C. Hodgson for his encouragement of work on Hegel and for making available to me a prepublication version of his translation of Hegel's 1817 lectures on the *Philosophy of Right*, which has since been published by the University of California Press as *Hegel's Lectures on Natural Right and Political Science*. I wish to express my appreciation to Daniel Breazeale for his thoughtful, critical review of the manuscript, and for helpful suggestions that stimulated revisions, especially in my account of Hegel's relation to Fichte. I am also grateful to Tom Rockmore and Thomas Bowen for their criticisms and suggestions and to Ludwig Siep for his encouragement of the project. They have all contributed to making the manuscript a better one; none of them is responsible for the defects that remain. A further word of acknowledgment is due to my students, from whom I have learned much. Finally a word of thanks to my family, who patiently endured my apparently endless ordeal of writing and revising, and whose devotion to music provided me not only with aesthetically pleasant background but with more enjoyable times.

Shaker Heights, Ohio
Robert R. Williams

Abbreviations

APP   Ludwig Siep, *Anerkennung als Prinzip der praktische Philoso-phie*. Freiburg: Alber Verlag, 1979.

Difference   *Difference between the Fichtean and Schellingian System of Philosophy* (1800). Trans. W. Cerf and H. S. Harris. Albany: SUNY Press, 1977.

E §—   Hegel, *Encyclopedia Werke*: TWA sk Vols. 8–10. English translation: *Hegel's Logic*, including *Logic, Philosophy of Nature*, and *Philosophy of Spirit. Hegel's Philosophy of Nature, Hegel's Philosophy of Mind*, trans. W. Wallace, together with Zusätze in Boumann's text (1845). Trans. A. V. Miller. Oxford: Clarendon Press, 1971.

ETW   Hegel, *Early Theological Writings*. Trans. T. M. Knox. Chicago: University of Chicago Press, 1948.

FEPW   *Fichte: Early Philosophical Writings*. Trans. and ed. Daniel Breazeale. Ithaca: Cornell University Press, 1988.

GNR   Fichte, *Grundlage des Naturrechts nach Principien der Wissenschaftslehre* (1796). English translation: *The Science of Rights* (*SR*), trans. A. E. Kroeger (1889). Reissued London: Routledge & Kegan Paul, 1970.

HE   Hegel, *Encyclopedia* (1817). Heidelberg. *Sämtliche Werke*, Hrsg. H. Glockner. Stuttgart: Frommann-Holzboog, 1968. Vol 6. English translation: *Hegel: Encyclopedia*, ed. Ernst Behler, trans. S. Taubeneck. *The German Library*. New York: Continuum, 1990.

HET   *Hegel's Ethical Thought*, by Allen W. Wood. Cambridge: Cambridge University Press, 1991.

HHS   *Hegel and the Human Spirit*, a translation with commentary of Hegel's *Jena Philosophie des Geistes 1805/06*, by Leo Rauch. Detroit: Wayne State University Press, 1983.

HTMS   Shlomo Avineri, *Hegel's Theory of the Modern State*. Cambridge: Cambridge University Press, 1972.

MFP   Vincent Descombes, *Modern French Philosophy*. Trans. L. Scott-Fox and J. M. Harding. Cambridge: Cambridge University Press, 1980.

NL   Hegel, *Natural Law*. Trans. T. M. Knox. Philadelphia: University of Pennsylvania Press, 1975.

PhG   *Phänomenologie des Geistes*, Hrsg. Hoffmeister. Hamburg: Felix Meiner Verlag, 1952.

PhS   *Phenomenology of Spirit*. Trans. A. V. Miller. Oxford: Oxford University Press, 1977.

PhM   *Phenomenology of Mind*. Trans. J. B. Baillie. New York: Macmillan, 1910.

PPDI   Ludwig Siep, *Praktische Philosophie im Deutschen Idealismus*. Frankfurt: Suhrkamp, 1992.

PR   Hegel, *Grundlinien der Philosophie des Rechts* (1821). English translation: *Elements of The Philosophy of Right*, trans. H. B. Nisbet. Cambridge: Cambridge University Press, 1991.

PSS   Hegel, *Philosophy of Subjective Spirit*. Ed. and trans. M. J. Petry. 3 vols. Dordrecht: D. Reidel, 1979. Volume 3 contains the Griesheim transcript of the 1825 lectures. This transcript has also been published by Petry as *G. W. F. Hegel: The Berlin Phenomenology*. Dordrecht: D. Reidel, 1981.

SD   Judith Butler, *Subjects of Desire: Hegelian Reflections in Twentieth-Century France*. New York: Columbia University Press, 1987.

SL   Hegel, *Science of Logic*. Trans. A. V. Miller. New York: Humanities Press, 1969.

SR   Fichte, *Science of Rights* (*Grundlage des Naturrechts* [1796]). Trans. A. E. Kroeger (1889). Reissued London: Routledge & Kegan Paul, 1970.

STI   Schelling, *System des Transzendentalen Idealismus*. Hamburg: Felix Meiner, 1962.

TWA   G. W. F. Hegel, *Werke. Theoriewerkausgabe*. Frankfurt: Suhrkamp, 1971.

TI   Emmanuel Levinas, *Totality and Infinity*. Pittsburgh: Duquesne University Press, 1969.

VPR17   *Vorlesungen über Naturrecht und Staatswissenschaft* (Wannenman) (1817 Heidelberg), Hrsg. Staff of the Hegel Archive. Hamburg: Felix Meiner, 1983. English translation: *Lectures on Natural Right and Political Science*, trans. J. M. Stewart and P. C.
Hodgson. Berkeley: University of California Press, 1995.

VPR18   *Vorlesungen ü. Naturrecht* (Homeyer). Berlin, 1818.

VPR19   *Philosophe des Rechts* (1819). Ed. D. Henrich. Frankfurt: Suhrkamp, 1983.

VPR1   Karl-Heinz Ilting and Georg Wilhelm Friedrich Hegel, *Vorlesungen uber Rechtsphilosophie*, 1818–1831. Vol. 1. Stuttgart:
Frommann-Holzboog, 1973.

VPR2   Karl-Heinz Ilting and Georg Wilhelm Friedrich Hegel, *Vorlesungen uber Rechtsphilosophie*, 1818–1831. Vol. 2. Stuttgart:
Frommann-Holzboog, 1973.

VPR3   Karl-Heinz Ilting and Georg Wilhelm Friedrich Hegel, *Vorlesungen uber Rechtsphilosophie,* 1818–1831. Vol. 3. Hotho Nachschrift. Stuttgart: Frommann-Holzboog, 1973.

VPR4   Karl-Heinz Ilting and Georg Wilhelm Friedrich Hegel, *Vorlesungen uber Rechtsphilosophie*, 1818–1831. Vol. 4. Griesheim
Nachschrift. Stuttgart: Frommann-Holzboog, 1973.

WL   Hegel, *Wissenschaft der Logik, Werke*. Vols. 5–6. Theoriewerkausgabe. Frankfurt: Suhrkamp, 1971.

Recognition and Ethics

Introduction

This study focuses on recognition as an operative concept in Hegel's ethics.[1] It builds on and completes the study of the concept of recognition begun in my earlier book, *Recognition: Fichte and Hegel on the Other*, which focuses primarily on Hegel's early thought.[2] The earlier study demonstrates the existence of a concept of intersubjectivity in German idealism and explores convergences between Hegel and Husserlian phenomenology on the topic of intersubjectivity. However, it is restricted to Hegel's Jena writings, including the *Phenomenology of Spirit* (1807), and to defending Hegel against charges that his thought violates intersubjectivity and difference by reducing the other to the same.

In this present work I examine the concept of recognition in Hegel's mature system of practical philosophy, as this system evolves in debate with Fichte's *Foundations of Natural Law* (1796). There are important differences between the account of recognition in the *Phenomenology* and the account in the ma-

---

1. I follow Eugen Fink in distinguishing between thematic concepts and operative concepts. A thematic concept is one that is explicitly coined and thematized by an author. An operative concept is a concept used by an author to explain and elaborate his thematic concept. See Eugen Fink, "Operative Concepts in Husserl's Phenomenology," trans. William McKenna, in *A Priori and World: European Contributions to Husserlian Phenomenology*, ed. W. McKenna, R. M. Harlan, and L. E. Winters (The Hague: Martinus Nijhoff, 1981), 56–70. Some of Hegel's thematic concepts are spirit (*Geist*), freedom, master/slave, and ethical life (*Sittlichkeit*). Recognition (*Anerkennung*) is an operative concept used by Hegel to show and develop his thematic concepts. Thus in his *Phenomenology of Spirit*, spirit originates in reciprocal recognition. Master/slave represent only the particular shape of unequal recognition and fail to exhaust the possibilities inherent in the concept.

2. Robert R. Williams, *Recognition: Fichte and Hegel on the Other* (Albany: State University of New York Press, 1992).

ture system; Hegel does not fundamentally change his position concerning recognition, but he does change its context and develops the concept differently. The *Phenomenology* is a self-accomplishing skepticism that shows that all shapes of consciousness are self-subverting; this self-subversion is clearly demonstrated in the case of master and slave. However, the mature *Philosophy of Spirit* builds on the *Phenomenology* and offers an account of affirmative mutual recognition in other that is central to ethical life. Clearly these differences are relevant to the question of the meaning and possibility of ethics. I propose to track the concept of recognition in Hegel's mature *Encyclopedia Philosophy of Spirit* and its subsequent elaboration in the *Philosophy of Right*. In contrast to my earlier study, the focus here is on the significance of recognition in and for Hegel's ethics, that is, his constructive philosophy of spirit.

There have been other treatments of Hegel's ethics and other treatments of Hegel's concept of recognition, but until now no study has brought these two topics together, much less focused on the importance of recognition as a deep structure in Hegel's account of ethical life. This omission is surprising, for the problematics of freedom and the problematics of recognition are inseparable. This nexus of freedom and recognition—that freedom requires recognition of the other for its self-realization—is part of the legacy Hegel inherits from Fichte. Fichte introduced the concept of recognition as a presupposition of both Rousseau's social contract and Kant's ethics; Fichte developed it as the existential and transcendental foundation of the concept of right and ethics. From Fichte on, the concept of practical subjectivity within German idealism is intersubjective. Recognition and Fichte's related concept of the summons are presuppositions of the consciousness of freedom and its ethical development. For Hegel as for Fichte, right is constituted through recognition, namely, recognition of freedom's presence in the world. Owing to their freedom, human beings may be capable of rights, but these rights remain mere possibilities unless they become actual in the medium of recognition, and in this sense recognition is the foundation of right. For Hegel, recognition mediates the affirmative consciousness of freedom and plays a crucial role in the formation of the ethical sphere, including ethical life (*Sittlichkeit*). Recognition decenters the modern concept of the subject found in Descartes and Kant, not by displacing it as in structuralism, but by transforming and expanding it into intersubjectivity. In short, subjectivity is transformed (*aufgehoben*), expanded, and elevated into intersubjectivity.

The genesis of the consciousness of freedom in mutual recognition establishes the importance of recognition for ethics. For Hegel, the threshold of the ethical is attained when the other ceases to be regarded as a nullity or a mere 'thing,' and comes to count as a self-determining end in itself. Hegel's analysis of recognition constitutes the ethical as a stage in the development of freedom and thus circumscribes narrowly individual interpretations of freedom, that is, nominalism. In contrast to Kant's reflective methodological individualism and *Moralität*, intersubjective recognition is for Hegel the universal shape and pattern of freedom, including all the virtues, and of social institutions from the family through civil society and state. Recognition makes possible Hegel's retrieval of the antirelativist classical social political theories of Plato and Aristotle and their transformation into shapes of intersubjective freedom. Recognition transforms the modern concept of the subject into an ethical intersubjectivity and transforms classical political structures into a historical and social ontology of the conditions of freedom's actualization in the world. Recognition is the medium in which Hegel reconciles Kant with Aristotle and Plato.

Recognition for Hegel is a topic with several levels, aspects, and dimensions in his account of ethical life. First, love and marriage are determinate intersubjectivities constituted through mutual recognition. The unity of the family is a unity of recognition. Hegel's treatment of love and marriage constitutes the interpersonal dimension and level of recognition, wherein he anticipates and influences twentieth-century dialogical philosophy from Buber through Levinas. The second level of recognition is between individuals and institutions, for example, family, property. As we will discover, in abstract right, including property ownership and contract, there is an impersonal formal recognition; similar impersonal forms of recognition are present in civil society. For Hegel, civil society generates inequalities of wealth and poverty and requires the development of ethical institutions to deal with the problems created by such inequalities. These institutions Hegel calls corporations, which are mediating institutions related more to medieval guilds than to modern businesses. As we will see, the corporation is the ethical moment within civil society; it plays a role similar to the family, namely, of recognizing and honoring the human being as a totality and not merely as a worker or consumer. The third level of recognition is the state, which must strive to extend throughout the nation ethical concerns for persons similar to those exhibited by family members for each other. However, despite Hegel's affirmation of reciprocal recognition, recognition retains negative aspects. These underlie his account of conflict, including his famous account of master and slave and his account of transgression and theory of punishment. Moreover, at the level of international relations, Hegel believes that any mutual recognition remains deficient: there is no international 'We,' and international law remains an 'ought to be' (*Sollen*).

Now that I have given a preliminary overview and explanation of Hegel's ethics of recognition, I want to mention some external reasons for this project, which I shall develop in the remainder of this chapter. The first external justification is that recognition either has been entirely overlooked in most previous English-language studies of Hegel's ethics or has been concealed or marginalized in those discussions. However, if English-speaking scholarship has neglected recognition, the opposite is true for the French. Second, the French reception of Hegel, heavily influenced by Alexandre Kojève's lectures, has focused on the struggle for recognition, but in a way that truncates and distorts the meaning of the *concept* of recognition and obscures its ethical significance. Unfortunately Kojève's reading has become almost the standard picture of Hegel that must be overcome if his ethics of recognition is to be understood and appreciated. This will be the topic of the third section. Fourth, recent German philosophy, notably critical theory (Habermas), has appreciated the importance of the concept of recognition for ethics. Habermas identifies Hegel's concept of recognition as an important counterdiscourse of modernity because it provides an inclusive, rather than an exclusive, concept of social rationality. However, Habermas and his followers believe that this social-ethical rationality is a direction that the mature Hegel did not take; instead they believe that Hegel remains a philosopher of the subject. It is ironic that in his interpretation of the "mature Hegel" as a philosopher of the subject, Habermas tends to confirm the interpretation offered by Hegel's French followers—most of whom Habermas disagrees with! In my view, Habermas is correct to identify recognition as a counterdiscourse to modernity but wrong to believe that the mature Hegel closes off or undermines this approach. Fifth, Michael Theunissen supports Habermas's interpretation of Hegel when he seeks to demonstrate what he calls the repression of intersubjectivity in Hegel's *Philosophy of Right*. In contrast, I argue that recognition and intersubjectivity are irrepressible because they constitute the general structure of ethical life. Sixth, my reading of Hegel has been influenced by the recent studies of Ludwig Siep, so I shall summarize some of Siep's contributions to the understanding of the concept of recognition.

The Concealment of Recognition in Hegelian Ethical Studies

A review of the literature on Hegel's ethics reveals a relative paucity of book-length studies: F. H. Bradley's *Ethical Studies* (1876), Bernard Bosanquet's *The Philosophical Theory of the State* (1899), Hugh Reyburn's *Ethical Theory of Hegel* (1921), W. H. Walsh's *Hegelian Ethics* (1969), and most recently, Allen W. Wood's *Hegelian Ethical Theory* (1991).[3] Bradley's work represents a powerful appropriation of portions of Hegel's thought while at the

---

3. See also David Kolb, *The Critique of Pure Modernity: Hegel, Heidegger, and After* (Chicago: University of Chicago Press, 1986). Kolb's book is not a study of Hegel's ethics but of Hegel and Heidegger as critics of modernity. Although Kolb notes the importance of recognition in Hegel's social philosophy (chap. 2), his approach to Hegel and the *Philosophy of Right* is through the logic. Kolb portrays recognition as primarily concerned with right and civil society; however, he also recognizes a deeper sense of recognition implicit in ethical life and the state (p. 32). But since his focus is on the logic and the logical relation between civil society and state, he does not pursue this deeper sense of recognition, which, in my view, is central to Hegel's ethical theory.

same time remaining an independent statement. Reyburn expounds the *Philosophy of Right* in the context of Hegel's mature system and is helpful in interpreting it as an expression of Hegel's logical-categorical analysis. However, with the exception of Wood, none of these mentions Hegel's concept of recognition. Bosanquet uses the term 'recognition', not as a special topic, but as a conceptual vehicle for expounding Hegel's view of rights.[4] Right is a dimension of intersubjective relations. Bosanquet seems to be unaware of both Fichte's and Hegel's independent treatment of recognition, and he passes over Hegel's important discussion of recognition in the *Phenomenology of Spirit*. Nevertheless, he is the only English interpreter who takes recognition seriously as clarifying what Hegel's idealism means in the practical sphere, and the only interpreter who sees recognition as systematically and foundationally related to Hegel's social conception of rights and duties.

In his recent valuable study, Wood acknowledges recent interest in the concept of recognition in both Fichte and Hegel and devotes a helpful chapter to recognition. However, Wood is not sympathetic to or interested in the systematic unity of Hegel's thought. What Hegel considered to be his foundational discipline, speculative logic, Wood pronounces to be a total failure. However, if for Wood Hegel's speculative logic is dead, Hegel's thought is not. He seeks to salvage and expound Hegel's ethical and social thought while jettisoning Hegel's logic and metaphysics and ignoring the influence of the latter on the former.[5] In Wood's approach the unity of Hegel's systematic thought is broken up into a series of discrete themes and arguments, considered in isolation and on their own merit, insofar as these may prove interesting to contemporary philosophers. In such an approach, recognition, instead of providing a unifying concept for Hegel's ethical thought, becomes one discrete theme among others and is considered more or less in isolation from the others, including the themes of self-actualization and freedom. Further, in his piecemeal approach to Hegelian themes and topics, Wood restricts his focus on recognition to Hegel's discussion of abstract right. This restriction of recognition to property

4. Bernard Bosanquet, *The Philosophical Theory of the State* (London: Macmillan, 1899), 192–201. Bosanquet's employment of 'recognition' as an expository term seems purely coincidental, because Bosanquet does not know Hegel's early Jena materials or even mention the German term *Anerkennung* which figures prominently in both Fichte's *Foundations of Natural Law* (1796) and Hegel's Jena writings. However, even if Bosanquet's use of recognition is a coincidence, this fact would constitute an independent confirmation of the importance of recognition for thinking through and understanding Hegel's ethical life and concept of right.

5. For an alternative reading and approach to Hegel's *Philosophy of Right*, see Kolb, *Critique of Pure Modernity*, 59–61. Kolb convincingly demonstrates the importance of Hegel's logic for his political argument and refutes Wood's claim that the logic is dispensable for understanding Hegel's social and political thought. However, in view of Kolb's own criticisms of the logic, it is an open question how far he disagrees with Wood's judgment concerning the failure of Hegel's logic. I suspect that in spite of his criticisms Kolb would deny that the logic is a "total failure." Besides, a "failure" on the part of a Hegel is probably more instructive and interesting than the "successes" (if any) of most other philosophers.

rights resembles Fichte more than Hegel. It threatens to reintroduce Fichte's separation of ethics and politics, duties and rights, which is a target of Hegel's critique. Wood either misses or simply passes over the significance of recognition for morality and conscience and for ethical life and its institutions.

As a consequence Wood analyzes freedom as "being at home with self in an other" in individualistic terms such that otherness must be *subdued* to achieve independence.[6] Such language about coercion and subjugation is more reminiscent of Fichte's account than Hegel's. Wood apparently believes recognition requires no fundamental revisions of the framework of transcendental idealism. Recognition is more nearly like a piece of empirical social psychology, useful for analyzing abstract right, but without any ontological implications for the putative underlying "idealist" concept of subjectivity. Wood fails to take seriously Hegel's phenomenological account of the origin of *Geist* in mutual recognition. *Geist* is not just another term for a transcendental ego, but a universal social We. Whatever Wood says subsequently about recognition, liberation, and the attainment of universal consciousness tends to be filtered through and subordinate to his analysis of freedom as individual self-actualization. This does not mean that what Wood says is false, but he does present a reading of recognition more oriented toward Kant and Fichte than Hegel.[7] This reading overlooks the crucial point that recognition constitutes and results in spirit, the I that is a We. This inclusive teleology of the We constitutes the transition from subjective spirit to objective spirit and is constitutive not only of abstract right but also of ethical life (*Sittlichkeit*) itself. Wood also passes over the fact that for Hegel freedom requires intersubjective mediation and is actual as the state.

As we shall show, the themes of 'freedom,' 'recognition,' and 'ethics' are for Hegel not separable but inextricably intertwined; freedom presupposes and requires recognition. Recognition is the process wherein and whereby freedom becomes both actual and ethical. That is why recognition is central to Hegel's philosophy of spirit (*Geist*). Hegel's account of freedom's becoming actual includes a critique of egoism and individualism, a decentering of the individual 'subject' by the other, that is at the same time a transformation (*Aufhebung*) of subjectivity into ethical intersubjectivity, an expanded or universal self constitutive of ethical life. Although Hegel has a good deal to say about freedom, it is crucial to understand that for Hegel autonomous freedom is intersubjectively mediated. Hegel believes that genuine autonomy is achieved only in relation and community with others. Relation to others does not contradict au-

---

6. Allen W. Wood, *Hegelian Ethical Thought* (Cambridge: Cambridge University Press, 1991), 44–45. Hereafter cited as *HET*.

7. For a similar view of the Fichtean bias of Wood's account of recognition, see Paul Redding, *Hegel's Hermeneutics* (Ithaca: Cornell University Press, 1996), 234–237. Redding's work reached me only after this manuscript was completed and was in production.

tonomy; it is a requirement of autonomy. Genuine autonomy for Hegel is a mediated autonomy.[8] That is why freedom takes the shape of self-recognition in other.

Hegel's story of the social mediation of freedom includes the parochial universality of the family, its dissolution into the self-seeking competitive formal individualism of civil society, and the ethical critique and correction of both by the state. Hegel's important claim that the state must be understood as an ethical institution rests on the critical universalism inherent in reciprocal recognition. This critical universalism means that for Hegel freedom is actual only as ethical community, that is, the state. As far as Hegel is concerned, the state as the realization of freedom constitutes the real refutation of slavery and practices of domination.

In contrast, Wood ignores the existential-ontological implications of recognition and tends to treat it as a theme of empirical social psychology; in this way recognition becomes subordinate to an individualistic concept of selfhood and self-realization. Further, in his piecemeal approach to Hegelian themes and topics, he restricts the focus on recognition to Hegel's discussion of abstract right and misses its significance for the other dimensions and institutions of ethical life, as well as its significance for Hegel's ethics as a whole. It is not surprising, therefore, that Wood believes that Hegel's universal consciousness, Spirit or the 'We', is tainted with individualism and particularity and in itself no critical safeguard against a parochial society constituted by a privileged race or a class whose members mutually recognize each other but treat outsiders as nonpersons.[9] As will become evident in the course of this study, these claims are symptomatic of a failure to appreciate the universalizing and transformative ethical significance that recognition has for Hegel, and why he believes the concept of mutual recognition is the root of ethical life. The significance of recognition for Hegel's ethics as a whole may be stated thus: The threshold of the ethical is reached when the other comes to count. Part of what it means to say that the other counts is to be found in Hegel's concept of love, but also in his account of the reciprocal correspondence of rights and duties, a correspondence that is foreshadowed by the family, presupposed by abstract right and contract, but becomes explicit only at the level of the state.

In view of Wood's dismissive interpretation of Hegel's logic, I hasten to add that Hegel's ethics, particularly as set forth in the *Philosophy of Right*, is categorically organized. For Hegel, such categorical organization is crucial to understanding the *Philosophy of Right* as a philosophical science (*Wissenschaft*). He tells us that this "work, as a whole, like the construction of its parts, is

8. For the term 'mediated autonomy', see Andreas Wildt, *Autonomie und Anerkennung: Hegels Moralitätskritik im Lichte seiner Fichte-Rezeption*, Deutscher Idealismus Band 7 (Stuttgart: Klett-Cotta, 1982).

9. Wood, *HET*, 93.

based on the logical spirit. It is also chiefly from this point of view that I would wish this treatise to be understood and judged." [10] Hegel does not spell out exactly what he means by logical construction of the *Philosophy of Right*, and that is a topic that would require another study beyond the scope of this one. It is clear that the *Philosophy of Right* presupposes the prior derivation and deduction of the concept of right and freedom, [11] but it is not clear that or how those concepts are delivered by the logic. Nor is it clear how the general logical divisions and categories organize Hegel's *Philosophy of Right*. This does not mean that Hegel does not occasionally illumine ethical and social issues with incisive analyses that make use of the categories. [12] For those interested in the architectonics of Hegel's system and exploring correlations between the logic and *Philosophy of Right*, Reyburn's and Kolb's studies remain the best. [13]

I shall not attempt here to solve the problems inherent in Hegel's assertion of a correlation between the logical categories and the *Gestalten* of consciousness. [14] However, I do not agree with the recent study by Vittorio Hösle that argues that the categories of the logic are all mundane and consequently cannot support Hegel's account of intersubjectivity in the *Realphilosophie*. [15] Although the *Philosophy of Right* follows a categorical rather than an empirical order, this does not mean that experience and intersubjectivity are unimportant or superfluous. Hegel himself comments often on both the distinction between and the relation of categorical thought to experience; the following is typical.

> We merely wish to observe how the concept [*Begriff*] determines itself, and we force ourselves not to add anything of our own thoughts and opinions. What we obtain in this way is a series of thoughts and another series of existent shapes in which it may happen that the temporal sequence of their actual appearance is to some extent different from the conceptual sequence. Thus we cannot say, for example, that property existed before the family, although property is nevertheless dealt with first. One might accordingly ask at this point why we do not begin with the highest instance, that is, with the concretely true. The answer will be that we wish to see truth precisely in the form of a result. . . . What is actual . . .

10. Hegel, *Grundlinien der Philosophie des Rechts*, *Werke*, Theorie Werkausgabe (Frankfurt: Suhrkamp, 1970); *Elements of the Philosophy of Right*, trans. H. Nisbet, ed. Allen W. Wood (Cambridge: Cambridge University Press, 1991 [hereafter cited as *PR*]), preface, 10.

11. Ibid., §§3–4.

12. Ibid., §§61, 67, argue that the relation of use to property is the same as that of substance to accident, or force to its manifestation.

13. Hugh Reyburn, *The Ethical Theory of Hegel: A Study of the Philosophy of Right* (Oxford: Oxford University Press, 1921); Kolb, *Critique of Pure Modernity*.

14. For an inconclusive study, see Johannes Heinrichs, *Die Logik der Phänomenologie des Geistes* (Bonn: Bouvier Verlag, 1974).

15. Vittorio Hösle, *Hegels System*, 2 vols. (Hamburg: Meiner Verlag, 1987). For a critique of Hösle, see my "Discernment in the Realm of Shadows," *Owl of Minerva* 26, no. 2 (Spring 1995): 133–148.

is therefore from our point of view only the subsequent and further stage. . . . The course we follow is that whereby the abstract forms reveal themselves not as existing for themselves, but as untrue.[16]

This passage shows that the categorical order moves from primitive and simple categories to more complex and mediated categories, that is, from the categories of the logic of being to those of the logic of essence to those of the logic of the concept. However, this categorical ordering does not imply any specific existence claims; in the empirical sociohistorical order, the family exists prior to and as a condition of property. Further, if we consider the *Philosophy of Right* as a phenomenology of freedom, then the above passage makes it clear why Hegel's theory of property (*Eigentum*), set forth first in categorical order in abstract right, must be understood as a subordinate aspect of and abstraction from the family and from his philosophical anthropology, in which freedom and recognition are central.

While recognition is less prominent as a discrete theme in Hegel's later thought, it has not disappeared or become superfluous. Recognition is the existential genesis of the concept of spirit, and remains *aufgehoben* in spirit. Moreover, in Hegel's mature *Encyclopedia*, recognition is the phenomenal appearance of the concept (*Begriff*) of freedom.[17] This fact undermines any nominalist reading of Hegel that identifies spirit (*Geist*) with an empirical individual ego, or *ego cogito*. The phenomenological-empirical aspect of the *Begriff* of freedom is for Hegel an intersubjectivity and/or community. Recognition mediates the important transition from subjective to objective spirit, from subjectivity to intersubjectivity. Hegel's *Philosophy of Right* is a further elaboration of his concept of objective spirit, set forth in outline in his *Encyclopedia Philosophy of Spirit*.

I think there is at least an important analogy, if not positive correlation, between the threefold mediation constitutive of reciprocal recognition and the threefold mediation constitutive of the system as a whole.[18] Further, I will show that Hegel conceives the state by means of the logical category of organism, which is prior to the systematic distinction between nature and spirit. Hegel and Fichte believe that the concept of organism is not restricted to the natural sphere, that is, that there are spiritual organisms, and that communities are in some important respects best understood as spiritual organisms. Both Fichte and Hegel believe that organism is a concept that illumines civic and social relations and the concept of community. I shall argue that recognition is the ideal unity of the social organism that is expressed in and as the spirit of its laws. Recognition is an account of how communal spirit is for itself as a 'We'.

---

16. *PR*, §32 Zusatz.   17. *E*, §484.
18. Ibid., §187; see also the syllogism of recognition below in chap. 3, fn. 25.

Distortions of Recognition
in the French Reception of Hegel

If the concept of recognition has not received sufficient attention in English-speaking scholarship on Hegel, the opposite is true in French philosophy. In the French reception of Hegel between 1937 and 1960, given powerful impetus by Alexandre Kojève's lectures, the struggle for recognition and master/slave are a central topic and focus, and have continued to be central in French discussion.[19] Yet, important as Kojève's work was in mediating Hegel to the generation of 1937–1960, and although Kojève made the struggle for recognition central to his interpretation of Hegel, the irony is that Kojève's work obscures and distorts Hegel's concept of recognition. The distortion lies in Kojève's identification of recognition with master and slave. However, for Hegel, recognition is a general concept of intersubjectivity, wider than master and slave. For Hegel, master and slave are a determinate shape of recognition, in which the possibilities inherent in the concept are deficiently actualized. The deficiency resides in the attempt to compel and coerce recognition, which, if successful, ends in domination. Master and slave is an unequal recognition that fixes and institutionalizes violence, hierarchy, and domination. For this reason, Hegel considers mastery to be self-subverting. In contrast to Kojève, Hegel's master and slave is but an important first phase of unequal recognition that *must* and *can* be transcended. It is not the final, but merely a transitional, inherently unstable, configuration of intersubjectivity. Genuine recognition is fundamentally reciprocal and involves the mutual mediation of freedom. For this to occur, both parties must renounce coercion. Reciprocal recognition involves freedom and liberation. Hence it is a gross interpretive error to equate, as Kojève does, recognition with the struggle between master and slave. These distortions and obscurings continue in present-day discussions of Hegel, and represent the "standard interpretation," the contemporary "dogma" about Hegel. This standard interpretation must be overcome if Hegel's ethics of recognition is to be properly understood and appreciated.

Kojève arrives at his interpretation through a rejection of Hegel's speculative dialectic and reconciliation. As Judith Butler observes, "Kojève's refusal of Hegel's postulation of an ontological unity that conditions and resolves all experiences of difference between individuals and between individuals and the external world is the condition of his own theorizing."[20] Kojève reads the *Phenomenology*, no longer as an introduction to the system of philosophy, but as a philosophical anthropology. The perspective of human agency and therefore

---

19. Vincent Descombes, *Modern French Philosophy*, trans. L. Scott-Fox and J. M. Harding (Cambridge: Cambridge University Press, 1980), 158. Hereafter cited as *MFP*.
20. Judith Butler, *Subjects of Desire: Hegelian Reflections in Twentieth-Century France* (New York: Columbia University Press, 1987), 63. Hereafter cited as *SD*.

the struggle for recognition become central themes in his interpretation of Hegel. For Kojève, recognition is synonymous with the unequal recognition of master and slave. Kojève thinks the concept of recognition primarily on the basis of an ontology of negation and finitude. This point is crucial for appreciating the limitations of Kojève's understanding of recognition.

Kojève, like Sartre, affirms an absolute heterogeneity of principles that precludes the possibility of mediation.[21] Kojève appropriates and conceives Hegel's concept of recognition on the basis of this heterogeneity, this radical ontological opposition between being and nothingness. Any mediation and reciprocal recognition become impossible. This has practical implications. For Kojève and Sartre, the opposition of master and slave is final, whereas for Hegel, master/slave is the first mediation of the sheer opposition of the life and death conflict. Master/slave is a *Gestalt* of consciousness that ends sheer violence, on the one hand, while institutionalizing it in the form of coercion and unequal recognition, on the other. However, for Hegel, master and slave do not exhaust the possibilities inherent in the concept of either recognition or freedom. There are other modes of recognition in which opposition either does not arise or in which it can be transformed and transcended.

On his anti-Hegelian ontological assumptions, Kojève understands recognition simply in terms of opposition and struggle. Kojève believes the desire for recognition leads necessarily to struggle.

> Man's humanity "comes to light" only in risking his life to satisfy his human Desire—that is, his Desire directed towards another Desire. . . . In other words, all human, anthropogenetic Desire—the Desire that generates Self-consciousness, the human reality—is finally, a function of the desire for recognition. And the risk of life by which the human reality "comes to light" is a risk for the sake of such a Desire. Therefore to speak of the "origin" of Self-consciousness is necessarily to speak of a fight to the death for recognition.[22]

Kojève thus collapses Hegel's analyses of the life and death struggle (*Begierde*) and master and slave into the concept of recognition, without seeing that this is but one possible and contingent configuration and mode of recognition. He determines recognition as ontological conflict—absence of mediation and absence of reciprocity. To be sure, Kojève knows that Hegel discusses love as a possibility, but he brushes this off with the question-begging assurance that "in the *Phenomenology*, love and the desire for love have become Desire for

---

21. The heterogeneity is manifest in the title of Sartre's great work of this period (1943), *Being and Nothingness*, trans. Hazel Barnes (New York: Philosophical Library, 1956). For a critical discussion of Sartre and Hegel on this heterology, see Klaus Hartmann, *Sartre's Ontology: A Study of Sartre's Being and Nothingness in the Light of Hegel's Logic* (Evanston: Northwestern University Press, 1966).

22. Alexandre Kojève, *Introduction to the Reading of Hegel*, ed. Allan Bloom, trans. J. H. Nichols, Jr. (New York: Basic Books, 1969), 7. Hereafter cited as *IRH*.

recognition and fighting to the death for its satisfaction."[23] Later he asserts that love as a sentiment lacks formal universality and seriousness because love does not involve any risk of life. For Kojève—but not for Hegel—love is not a genuine form of recognition because it lacks risk and struggle.

Kojève's interpretation is misleading, because he grasps the concept of recognition, and Hegel's philosophy as a whole, at a subordinate level where opposition and conflict appear absolute and incapable of mediation. From Hegel's point of view, Kojève's position would be deficient and self-subverting. Vincent Descombes agrees; he charges that it is not Hegel's but rather Kojève's version of the dialectic that cannot tolerate difference and suppresses it.[24]

Kojève's interpretation not only distorts Hegel's position but also makes it appear vulnerable to rather obvious criticisms, particularly criticisms oriented on the other, otherness, and difference. Kojève's "Hegel" reduces the other to the same (Levinas). According to Butler, Kojève's suppression of difference finds expression in his conception of recognition: "Recognition conditions the 'recovery' of the self from alterity, and thus facilitates the project of autonomy. The more fully recovered this self, the more encompassing of all reality it proves to be, for 'recovery' is not retreat, but expansion, an enhancement of empathy, the positing and discovery of relations in which it has all along, if only tacitly, been enmeshed."[25] This language appears to reduce external relations to internal relations, mediation by other to self-mediation, as if the other were merely an implicit dimension of the self. No wonder recovery from alterity "facilitates" the project of autonomy. The other appears here to be merely a vehicle for the recovery of the self, an occasion for self-reflection and self-consciousness.[26] Kojève understands recognition quite differently from Hegel. For Hegel, the I becomes a We through affirmative self-knowledge in other conferred by reciprocal recognition. However, as Butler notes, for Kojève "recognition does not have the effect of assimilating the individual into a more inclusive community; following the tradition of classical liberalism, Kojève views recognition as a process in which individuals form communities, but these communities facilitate the development of individuality and not its transcendence."[27] In Kojève's reading, recognition does not overcome but reinforces the individualism that is the target of Hegel's critique.

The Kojèvean "Hegel" tames the other, the negative, and the difference by making them instrumental to the development of individual identity and unity.

---

23. Ibid., 243.
24. For a fuller treatment of this issue and Hegel's response to this misreading, see chapter 15 below.
25. Butler, *SD*, 87.
26. Later we shall see that for Hegel the other is indeed crucial for the mediation of freedom and for self-recognition. But this does not mean that the other is merely an instrument or means of self-reflexive self-recovery. Mutual recognition not only means a renunciation of coercion, it includes mutual release, or allowing the other to be.
27. Butler, *SD*, 77.

No wonder that, as Butler observes, students of Kojève came to repudiate "Hegel" for being all the things that Kojève argued that he never was, namely, the philosopher of the subject, metaphysics of closure, or presence that excludes difference and, according to Nietzschean critics, is anti-life.[28] If Kojève were the twentieth-century Hegel, the students who advanced the aforementioned criticisms of Kojève's "Hegel" were quite possibly reacting against the abstract identity inherent in Kojève's position. The irony is that such reactions against Kojève's "Hegel" in favor of difference and alterity draw closer to Hegel himself.[29]

Recognition as Counterdiscourse of Modernity: Habermas

Kojève identifies recognition with master and slave and with coercion. In contrast, Habermas and Axel Honneth see in Hegel's concept of recognition at least the possibility of reciprocity and reconciliation, which are important for the concept of a community of communicative freedom. As Honneth observes, Hegel interpreted love as a form of recognition, and he was right to discern in love the structural core of ethical life.[30] Where Kojève sees in recognition only the possibility of struggle or of master/slave relationships based on coercion, Habermas affirms the possibility of community based on communicative freedom and reciprocal interaction.

Habermas's critical theory is an eclectic, wide-ranging synthesis that makes use of Hegel's concept of recognition to articulate the intersubjective-communication aspect of the life-world (Husserl). Habermas's relation to Hegel is ambiguous, because he believes that Hegel is both a critic and a representative of the "philosophy of the subject." His essay "Labor and Interaction" contains a useful discussion of the concept of recognition in Hegel's early Jena manuscripts.[31] Habermas claims that the early Hegel has a communitarian conception of spirit that includes language and labor as subordinate dimensions. Habermas also lays the foundations for his criticism of Hegel, to wit, that Hegel presents two models of spirit (*Geist*), the intersubjective model and the idealist-monological, self-reflexive model, and that the latter tends to take priority over the former. In his more recent *Philosophical Discourse of Modernity*, Habermas interprets the two models of spirit in terms of a distinction be-

28. Ibid., 176.
29. Perhaps Foucault sensed this when he wrote, "We have to determine the extent to which our anti-Hegelianism is possibly one of his tricks directed against us, at the end of which he stands, motionless, waiting for us." Michel Foucault, "The Discourse on Language," in *Archeology of Knowledge*, trans. A. M. Smith (New York : Pantheon Books, 1972), 235.
30. Axel Honneth, *The Struggle for Recognition*, trans. Joel Anderson (Cambridge, Mass.: Polity Press, 1995), 107.
31. Jürgen Habermas, *Theory and Practice*, trans. J. Viertel (Boston: Beacon Press, 1974), 142–169.

tween the so-called early Hegel and the mature Hegel of the system. According to Habermas, the early Hegel's concept of recognition and intersubjective concept of spirit is overridden by and subordinate to the self-reflective monological subjectivity of absolute idealism.

Habermas believes that the concept of recognition of the early Hegel presents a *counterdiscourse against the philosophy of the subject* constitutive of modernity. But this divergent path is not the one that the mature Hegel chose, either in his philosophy of spirit or in his *Philosophy of Right*. Instead says Habermas, Hegel "could carry out his critique of subjectivity only within the framework of the philosophy of the subject."[32]

While distancing himself from the Hegel that he believes to be the culmination of metaphysics and the philosophy of the subject, Habermas remains heavily indebted to Hegel's concept of recognition. Habermas's exact position vis-à-vis Hegel is difficult to determine. On the one hand, given the historical collapse of the Hegelian school and the associated critique of metaphysics, Habermas appears to stand closer to left-Hegelian critics of Hegel. Perhaps this means he would agree with Hegel's recent critics, such as Emmanuel Levinas, who believe that the monological self-reflective subject subsumes intersubjectivity and that Hegel ultimately reduces the other to the same.[33] On the other hand, Habermas claims that Hegel's concept of recognition is one of the most important, yet suppressed, counterdiscourses of modernity. By identifying recognition as a counterdiscourse, Habermas means that the concept of recognition carries out a deconstructive move of delivering reason over to its other, yet without ending in sheer negation or annihilation.[34] This reading of recognition as a counterdiscourse to modernity depends on seeing it not simply as reciprocal exclusion of the other but rather as having positive ethical significance. I believe that Habermas is correct but fails to appreciate how fully Hegel developed the affirmative dimensions of recognition in his mature ethical theory.[35] Here I seek to develop the positive significance of recognition for Hegel's ethics.

A central theme running throughout Habermas's *Philosophical Discourse of Modernity* is the dispute between two divergent paradigms of reason, namely, inclusive reason and exclusive reason. In the latter, reason's self-coincidence is purchased at the price of necessary exclusion. Exclusive reason is subject-centered, Cartesian. Once reason is identified with the subject—be it a *cogito* or transcendental subject—it becomes subject-centered and excludes what is

32. Jürgen Habermas, *The Philosophical Discourse of Modernity*, trans. F. Lawrence (Cambridge, Mass.: MIT Press, 1987), 41; cf. p. 295. Hereafter cited as *PDM*.

33. Emmanuel Levinas, *Totality and Infinity*, trans. A. Lingis (Pittsburgh: Duquesne University Press, 1969). Following Husserl, Levinas argues that philosophy is ultimately an egology and that this implies that the other is reduced to the same.

34. Habermas, *PDM*, 310–311.

35. For a discussion of this issue, see John McCumber, *Poetic Interaction: Language, Freedom, Reason* (Chicago: University of Chicago Press, 1989).

other, be this 'other' the 'object,' the body, world, or another subject. For Habermas, the most recent representatives of exclusive reason are Friedrich Nietzsche and Michel Foucault. For them, the inclusive paradigm of reason that Habermas finds in the early Hegel and champions is a metaphysical fiction. For Foucault, inclusion is really disguised exclusion. Note that Foucault's thesis reflects the abstract concept of identity that is found in Kojève and that is a target of Hegel's critique.

Habermas favors the inclusive paradigm, which he believes Hegel's concept of recognition provides and supports. Inclusive reason interprets the boundaries drawn by exclusive reason not as exclusions but as dichotomies within reason. Inclusive reason exhibits a logic of reciprocal inclusion, holism and totality. Such a holism, Habermas believes, need not fall back into foundationalist metaphysics but rather provides resources for overcoming it. Habermas believes that such holism decenters and desublimates the subject-centered reason of idealism, the "philosophy of the subject." The concept of recognition provides an alternative to subject-centered reason. Habermas believes that participation in a free community escapes the subject-object paradigm, objectification, Foucauldian dividing practices, and the like. In a free community, participants in interaction and institutions are no longer originators who master others and situations but are members and products of traditions in which they stand and solidarity groups to which they belong.[36]

Honneth develops Habermas's interpretation in the direction of social psychology by distinguishing what he calls three positive forms of recognition: (1) primary relations such as love and friendship, (2) legal relations, and (3) a community of value and solidarity. The three forms of recognition in turn make possible affirmative self-relations. Love makes possible self-confidence, right makes possible self-respect, and social esteem develops self-esteem. There are three corresponding negations of recognition, or disrespect: (1) abuse and rape, (2) denial of rights and exclusion, and (3) denigration and insult.[37]

Unfortunately, in Honneth's and Habermas's interpretation, the early Hegel is sharply distinguished from the mature Hegel. Recognition is allegedly a topic of interest only for the "young Hegel" of the Jena period and ceases to be important in Hegel's subsequent intellectual development. Honneth repeats Habermas's line that in Hegel's mature thought the concept of recognition is displaced by a monological conception of self-reflective subjectivity. Hegel displaces intersubjective relationships by the relationship between a subject and its self-externalizations. This is an updated Spinozan version of the relation between substance and its accidents. For Honneth, "ethical life has become . . . a form of monologically self-developing Spirit and no longer constitutes a . . . form of intersubjectivity."[38] It is ironic that despite their apparent

36. Habermas, *PDM*, 299.
37. See Honneth, *Struggle for Recognition*, 129 ff.
38. Ibid., 61.

divergence from Kojève and the French reception of Hegel, both Honneth and Habermas end by repeating the French criticism of Hegel as a philosophy of the subject. However, neither Honneth nor Habermas supports his disparaging claim about the mature Hegel by a study of his philosophy of spirit or his *Philosophy of Right*.

Michael Theunissen: Hegel's Repression of Intersubjectivity

Michael Theunissen believes that while Hegel presents some concept of intersubjectivity in his *Philosophy of Right*, this intersubjectivity is repressed (*verdrängte*), not only in the book as a whole but also in the details of the argument.[39] Theunissen attributes the repression of intersubjectivity to Hegel's metaphysical commitments, to his alleged siding with the ancients against the moderns, and to his monological concept of the subject. Further, the repression of intersubjectivity means that intersubjectivity appears only as disfigured, serving at most as a critical principle, present in disfigurement.[40] Theunissen does not explain how intersubjectivity can be a critical principle if it is repressed and excluded from the book.

He does attempt to show that intersubjectivity is derivative from a presocial will, or a transcendental monological subject, and that objective *Geist*, while supposedly the consciousness of individuals, nevertheless comes to have self-consciousness and self-relation, thereby creating an asymmetry and a heteronomous relation between objective *Geist*, ethical substance, and independent individuals. This asymmetry finds expression in a pantheistic conception of the substance/accidents scheme: self-conscious, self-relating objective *Geist* is identified with absolute *Geist*, the ultimate subject, that is at the same time ethical substance. In this scheme individuals are reduced from independent free beings to mere accidents of substance. Theunissen thus argues that Hegel's concept of the social deprives individuals of their independence. The metaphysical conception of the relation displaces and/or undermines intersubjectivity. The pantheistic conception of objective *Geist* "removes all intersubjectivity from ethical life."[41] Again, "Hegel displaces every intersubjective relation into a relation of ethical substance to these persons and as a result the independence of the persons disappears."[42]

Theunissen justifies the above reading by citing the *Philosophy of Right*, §156: here Hegel lays out two alternatives for thinking of community, either begin with the independent individuals or with ethical substance. Hegel believes that the former leads to a conception of ethical life as a spiritless exter-

---

39. Michael Theunissen, "The Repressed Intersubjectivity in Hegel's Philosophy of Right," in *Hegel and Legal Theory* (London: Routledge, 1991). Honneth refers to and relies on Theunissen's essay.

40. Ibid., 37.   41. Ibid., 12.   42. Ibid.

nal aggregate. The latter alternative, Theunissen believes, leads to a pantheistic metaphysical conception of community. Hegel allegedly takes the latter alternative. Since Hegel starts with ethical substance, Theunissen reasons, he must ultimately side with the ancients over the moderns, and this means he lapses into metaphysics, thereby repressing intersubjectivity. This so-called repressed intersubjectivity is Theunissen's attempt to turn Hegel's criticism of Plato and Aristotle—that they do not acknowledge individual subjective freedom—against Hegel himself.

Further, Theunissen believes that intersubjectivity is excluded from the concept of the will sketched in the opening paragraphs of the *Philosophy of Right*. Theunissen thinks that Hegel understands the will individualistically from the very outset; consequently the concept of the will and of freedom are intersubjectively deficient. Although Hegel may attempt to ground intersubjectivity, he ends up undermining it. Hegel's alleged adoption of a monological conception of the will and subjectivity reveals that Hegel sides with the modern concept of subjectivity. Hegel's criticism of the formal and empty subject of modernity applies to his own position.[43] Note that in this analysis Theunissen reverses his previous charge that Hegel sides with the ancients against the moderns. He now criticizes Hegel for allegedly trying to ground intersubjectivity in monological, solipsist subjectivity, and for undermining dialogue and dialogical reciprocity.[44] Hegel's intersubjective alternative to modernity allegedly reduces to modernity's formal and individualistic concept of the subject.[45]

This reversal in Theunissen's portrait of Hegel reveals problems in his analysis. The first is that although Theunissen speaks of some sense of intersubjectivity in Hegel, he nowhere clarifies what this intersubjectivity means. Although his footnotes show that Theunissen is aware of German scholarship on the concept of recognition (*Anerkennung*) in Fichte and Hegel, he does not focus on this concept and its patterns as central to Hegel's conception of intersubjectivity. Instead, he considers recognition as bearing only on abstract right and property relations and presents piecemeal, abstract discussions of intersubjectivity that assimilate it to love, freedom, and dialectical unity. Theunissen openly acknowledges that his account of Hegel is not a serious attempt to characterize "the" intention of Hegel's *Philosophy of Right*, but only to present "what I like about it."[46] This approach overlooks that the *Philosophy of Right* presupposes the deduction of the concept of right from elsewhere,[47] namely, the account of recognition in Hegel's *Encyclopedia Philosophy of Spirit*. I will show that Hegel by no means restricts recognition to abstract right and property but clearly indicates that the concept of recognition is the general structure of ethical life, including not only all the virtues but also his account of institutions—family, civil society, and state. Theunissen does not take the concept of recognition se-

43. Ibid., 18.   44. Ibid., 37.   45. Ibid., 47.
46. Ibid., 4.   47. *PR*, §2.

riously enough to examine its place in Hegel's *Philosophy of Spirit*, in which Hegel's concept of *Geist* has its existential phenomenological genesis in mutual recognition and is the result of mutual recognition.[48] Nor does Theunissen think through the connection between recognition and the development of ethical freedom as affirmative self-recognition in other. If *Geist* is the result of mutual recognition, then *Geist* is not inherently a reification that necessarily represses intersubjectivity from ethical life.

Second, Theunissen misidentifies his critical issue as an either/or: Either the ancients or the moderns; which one does Hegel favor? In fact, Hegel's view is that neither position is adequate by itself. The ancients suppress subjective freedom; the moderns attempt to ground ethics and politics in individual subjective freedom. Hegel believes the point of view of modernity is inadequate because of its formalism and individualism, on the one hand, and because of the absence of normative content, or nihilism, on the other.

Hegel's project is not to pick and choose between these unsatisfactory alternatives but rather to mediate them and work out a third alternative.[49] This alternative requires that subjectivity be expanded to intersubjectivity and that freedom itself be intersubjectively mediated. This move requires more than the Kantian and Fichtean view that the other is a limit to freedom. The other not only summons the self to freedom, it also enlarges and enhances the self's own identity, raising the subject to a higher ethical level. The other is not a merely external check (*Anstoß*) that is discarded once its stimulus is over; the other also comes to count for something. The result of such self-recognition in other is *Geist,* which is not the original parochial self, any more than the result of a dialectical *Aufhebung* is abstract identity. The other opens up new possibilities; these new possibilities include not only a destructive life and death struggle but also a life enhancement, an enlarged mentality and community based on freedom and reciprocity. The institutions of ethical life, including family, civil society, and state, are not heteronomous impositions on or limitations of freedom but rather conditions of freedom's self-realization in the world. Without these, freedom would not be actual and would never achieve a determinate existence in the world. Hegel's concept of *Geist* cannot be reduced to either the abstract ethical substance of the ancients or the individualistic monological subjectivity of modernity but is an intersubjective alternative.

Theunissen's reading of Hegel is seriously flawed, not only because he inconsistently identifies Hegel's position but also because he conceives it in terms of alternatives that Hegel rejects or seeks to mediate. *If* Hegel sided with the ancients over the moderns and subordinated modern ethical life to ethical

48. For further analysis of the concept of *Geist*, see my *Recognition*.

49. See Manfred Riedel, *Zwischen Tradition und Revolution: Studien zu Hegels Rechtsphilosophie*, pts. 1 and 2. Stuttgart: Klett-Cotta, 1982. English translation: *Between Tradition and Revolution: The Hegelian Transformation of Political Philosophy*, trans. W. Wright (Cambridge: Cambridge University Press, 1984).

substance, and *if* Hegel sought to ground intersubjectivity in an ultimate, mono-logical, presocial subjectivity, then there would be grounds for thinking that he represses and excludes intersubjectivity from the *Philosophy of Right*. But I will show that Hegel does not do this and that Hegel's concept of spirit is a third alternative overlooked in Theunissen's analyses. In chapter 6 I will show that Hegel does not accept the radical either/or of ancients and moderns or the either/or of individuals versus the substantial ethical life. Rather for Hegel the modern concept of subjectivity is expanded into an intersubjective conception of spirit. This in turn makes it possible for Hegel to develop the concept of a mediated freedom and autonomy. This mediated autonomy becomes the basis for Hegel's retrieval of the institutions of classical ethical life as conditions of the realization of freedom. Thus our analysis will show that, far from being re-pressed, intersubjectivity and recognition are irrepressible.

Ludwig Siep's Studies of Hegel's Practical Philosophy

Ludwig Siep's recent work on Hegel exhibits some exemplary historical-philosophical studies that uncover the concept of recognition and clarify its importance for Hegel's thought. The current interest in recognition is almost entirely due to Siep's groundbreaking *Anerkennung als Prinzip der praktische Philosophie* (1978).[50] This book is a serious intellectual challenge to the domi-nant, Kojèvean reading of recognition. Siep begins with an investigation of Fichte's account of recognition as a transcendental condition of right in his *Grundlage des Naturrechts* (1796). Here is perhaps the first "deduction" of in-tersubjectivity as a condition of freedom, including right and ethics. Fichte introduced the concept of recognition as a concrete existential grounding of social contract theory. He saw that social contract presupposes antecedent so-cial practices that create trust and a necessary precontractual consensus that contracts are acceptable forms of achieving and expressing enforceable agree-ments. Simply put, social contract theory presupposes intersubjective recogni-tion. Siep examines Hegel's appropriation of Fichte's concept of recognition in his Jena period, which includes Hegel's earliest publications, his unpublished Jena manuscripts, and his *Phenomenology of Spirit* (1807). Siep notes that Hegel had already worked out a basic social theory in his *Early Theological Writings* (Frankfurt, 1795–1797) and interprets love as an intersubjective union

---

50. Ludwig Siep, *Anerkennung als Prinzip der praktische Philosophie: Untersuchungen zu Hegels Jenaer Philosophie des Geistes* (Freiburg: Alber Verlag, 1978). Hereafter cited as *APP*. For a review, see my "The Concept of Recognition in Hegel's Jena Philosophy," *Philosophy and So-cial Criticism* (Fall 1982): 101–113. Cf. Siep's influential earlier essay "Kampf um Anerkennung: Zu Hegels Auseinandersetzung mit Hobbes in den Jenaer Schriften," *Hegel-Studien* 9 (Bonn: Bouvier Verlag, 1974), 155–207; English translation in *Hegel's Dialectic of Desire and Recogni-tion*, ed. John O'Neill (Albany: SUNY Press, 1996), 273–288.

with and affirmation of the other. This gives Hegel's concept of recognition greater richness and complexity than Fichte's.

Siep distinguishes two levels (*Stufen*) of recognition: (1) recognition between individuals in face-to-face situations, including love, marriage, and family; and (2) recognition between individuals and institutions, or between the I and the We. Siep notes that in the Jena period Hegel regards social institutions as important loci of individual self-recognition in the other. When individuals are unable to find themselves reflected in their institutions, then alienation and decline result. It should be recalled that Hegel was first drawn to philosophy because of his concerns with contemporary alienation and that Hegel regarded Kant, Fichte, and Jacobi as espousing Enlightenment reflective philosophies of finitude that were both causes and products of alienation.

Within the first level of recognition, Siep distinguishes further two patterns, namely, love and struggle (*Kampf*). In love there is a form of recognition without opposition of wills, that is, a union of wills. Struggle, on the other hand, reflects a conflict and opposition of wills. Siep points out that the struggle for recognition is often misconceived as beginning with the life and death struggle. Rather he shows that the life and death struggle is itself precipitated by a desire for the other. "According to Hegel the process of recognition begins with the fact that the self is 'outside of itself,' that it is canceled as being-for-itself, and intuits itself only in the other. However this structure is not one of struggle, but of love. . . . The life and death struggle embodies not the origin of the process of recognition in desire, but only the initial attempt of self-consciousness to overcome the situation of being-othered."[51] These distinctions are important because they reveal that Hegel interpretations like Kojève's, which simply identify recognition with struggle or with master/slave, are inadequate and distort Hegel's actual position. The Kojèvean reading misses what Siep finds especially important about recognition, namely, its significance for understanding self-identity, practical philosophy, and ethics.

In his analysis of the second level of recognition, Siep focuses on the relation between individuals and institutions. The early Hegel develops recognition as a critical principle for assessing the legitimacy of social institutions. Individuals are supposed to find themselves and their interests reflected in their institutions, which in turn supports their willingness to identify with and make sacrifices for such institutions. This includes a structure of self-recognition in the other. Hegel finds in the concept of recognition a principle of organizing a system of institutions as a teleological process, proceeding from conditions of unfreedom through a series of mediations that develop potential freedom to its maximal realization. Thus recognition names not only a structure of intersubjectivity but also a teleological process in which freedom is progressively mediated and realized, beginning with the family and continuing through owner-

---

51. Siep, "Kampf um Anerkennung," 194.

ship, law, civil society, and state. This process proceeds in the direction of an increasing recognition of freedom and an increasing realization of freedom. The state is supposed to complete this process of freedom and recognition as its telos.[52] Siep believes recognition is important for Hegel's practical philosophy because it allows Hegel to renew the classical tradition of practical philosophy on a postmodern, postliberal, intersubjective-social basis. This reading supports Habermas's contention that recognition is an important counterdiscourse of modernity.

According to Siep, Hegel shows that freedom cannot be adequately understood within the individualistic framework of modern (liberal) natural law theory. Freedom is not reducible to a merely technical organization of a rational community, or to the mere securing of legal relations between individuals. Rather freedom is the substance of individuals and their self-realization. Making use of the concept of recognition, Hegel seeks to develop community and its determinate institutions from the concept of freedom itself, as the conditions of freedom's realization in the world. This is a friendly corrective to classical liberal individualism: individual freedoms, rights, and so on, are intersubjective-socially secured, and what secures them is being-recognized. In this way, Siep contends, Hegel attempts to reconcile the Aristotelian tradition with the principle of transcendental philosophy.[53]

In another important essay, "Der Freiheitsbegriff der praktischen Philosophie Hegels in Jena,"[54] Siep identifies four dimensions in Hegel's concept of freedom: *autonomy, union, self-overcoming,* and *Freigabe,* or *release.* These dimensions of freedom are important, not only in their distinctness, but in their interconnection. It is only when they are taken together that the richness and complexity of Hegel's mature account of recognition, freedom, and ethical life begin to come into focus. For Hegel, autonomy is not actual in isolation but only in community with others. That is, autonomy is intersubjectively mediated. Further, autonomy is an ethical conception, involving self-overcoming. The autonomous self must overcome its merely natural inclinations and egoism. What occasions this self-overcoming is the encounter with the other. When the other comes to count, the responsible self is constituted. Self-overcoming results in an ethical subjectivity. Finally, *Freigabe,* or the release of the other in its otherness, allowing it to be, makes explicit what has been implicit all along, namely, that freedom for Hegel is intersubjective. As we shall see, *Freigabe* is the consummation of reciprocal recognition, through which *Geist* is constituted as the I that is a We. *Freigabe* makes it clear that the 'We' Hegel is after is a community of freedom that does not absorb or reduce individuals to some abstract homogeneity but rather presupposes, requires, and accepts individuals

---

52. Siep, *APP,* 233.   53. Ibid., 190.
54. Ludwig Siep, *Praktische Philosophie im Deutschen Idealismus* (Frankfurt: Suhrkamp, 1992), 159–171. Hereafter cited as *PPDI.*

in their differences. *Freigabe* is the recognition of the otherness of the other, the difference of difference.

Siep enumerates and describes these important dimensions of Hegel's concept of freedom in an essay that is restricted to an examination of Hegel's early thought, prior to any of his published writings. I believe that these are not only dimensions and aspects of Hegel's concept of freedom, but also are dimensions of his concept of recognition. This claim does not violate Siep's intentions, because Siep himself has pointed out that freedom for Hegel is intersubjectively mediated and social. However, I shall extend these concepts beyond Siep's limited discussion. I shall seek to show that they are features, not only of Hegel's early concept of intersubjective-social freedom, but also of his concept of recognition and his mature conception of freedom. They illumine not only Hegel's early Jena writings, including the *Phenomenology of Spirit*, but also his mature philosophy of spirit set forth in his *Encyclopedia* and *Philosophy of Right*. In my opinion these themes of autonomy, union, self-overcoming, and release help to bring into focus the highly complex, positive ethical significance of recognition in Hegel's thought in an unparalleled way, and illumine Hegel's concepts of freedom, recognition, rights, and ethical life. In my estimation this nexus of elements is crucial for a correct understanding, not only of affirmative reciprocal *recognition*, but also of Hegel's *ethics*. That this is so will be the burden of the following investigation and analyses from chapter 4 on. The results are for the reader to judge.

Recognition and the Actuality of the Rational

Finally, a word about the famous *Doppelsatz* of the preface to Hegel's *Philosophy of Right*: The rational is actual and the actual is rational (*das, was vernunftig ist, ist wirklich, und das, was wirklich ist, ist vernunftig*). This formulates a central interpretive issue: Is Hegel's account of the Idea of the state meant as an account of ethical life as it ought to be? Or is he describing actual social conditions? The potentially conservative implications of this statement depend on truncating it and reducing it to its second half, whereby the actual is identified as rational. This not only truncates and thereby distorts Hegel's statement; it also seems to align Hegel's thought with the status quo, that is, political conservatism, an alignment from which subsequent Hegel interpretation has never quite recovered.[55]

Heinrich Heine, on hearing the *Doppelsatz* in Hegel's lecture, asked him what he meant by it, and reports that Hegel told him, "It may also be expressed

---

55. For an antidote to this view, see Jacques D'Hondt, *Hegel in His Time*, trans. J. Burbidge (Lewiston, N.Y.: Broadview Press, 1988).

thus: all that is rational must be (*Alles, was vernunftig ist, muß sein*)."[56] While Heine's comments have been known for some time, Heine was not always a reliable reporter. But now Heine's account has been independently confirmed by the recently available earlier lectures on the *Philosophy of Right* (1817, 1818, 1819). Far from being an expression of servile conservatism that equates reason with the present status quo, we now know that Hegel's remark originally occurred in the context of a discussion of constitutional history, in which the constitution of a people is regarded as an expression of their communal spirit. Hegel writes, "The *Volksgeist* is the substantial element: what is rational must happen."[57] To say that the rational must happen is not to assert that it has happened in any final sense. It does not authorize any triumphalist reading of the proposition as announcing a realized eschatology, an end of history, or the *parousia* of reason, pure presence. Hegel's proposition, far from being a conservative deification of the status quo, in fact points to his belief and hope that reason will triumph over the merely positive and traditional elements inherited from the past.

Hegel was aware that his statement was capable of being understood in a conservative way, as identifying the rational with the status quo. To correct the conservative interpretation, he subsequently made a distinction between actuality (*Wirklichkeit*) and existence (*Dasein*).[58] The actual, whatever else it may mean, is not everything that happens to exist; it implies a critique of the given and the merely traditional. The actual is not what happens to exist but what can withstand and has withstood rational criticisms and maintains itself in the face of opposition.

The *Doppelsatz* is given yet another twist in the 1819–1820 lectures. Hegel takes it from its original place in the discussion of constitutional history and places it in the preface to the lectures. After contending that philosophy is not an idle, otherworldly speculation, Hegel says,

> [Philosophy] knows that in the actual world what counts and can have validity is what is present in the [living] concept of a people. It would be folly to impose on a people arrangements and institutions towards which it has not progressed by itself. What the age possesses in its inner spirit clearly comes to pass and is necessary. A constitution is a matter of the orientation and organization of this inner spirit. Spirit is the foundation; there is no power in heaven or on earth capable of

56. Heinrich Heine, *Hegel in Berichten seiner Zeitgenossen*, ed. Günther Nicolin (Hamburg: Meiner, 1970), 235, cited by Shlomo Avineri, "The Discovery of Hegel's Early Lectures on the Philosophy of Right," *Owl of Minerva* 16, no. 2 (Spring 1985): 202.

57. Hegel, *VPR*17, §134.

58. Hegel, *E*, §6. For a criticism of this distinction, see Hans-Christian Lucas, "The Identification of *Vernunft* with *Wirklichkeit* in Hegel," *Owl of Minerva* 25, no. 1 (Fall 1993): 23–45. Lucas reformulates Paulus's critique of Hegel, contending that Hegel's distinction between two types of actualities reintroduces the problem of the ought-is distinction that Hegel criticized in Kant's and Fichte's conception of the ethical (*Sollenkritik*).

prevailing against the power of the spirit. This is obviously something different than reflection and representations that one can draw out of abstract thinking or out of the goodness of one's heart. *What is rational becomes actual, and the actual becomes rational.*[59]

Here the emphasis is on the rational as a historical-social process rather than on a static or fixed tradition. But what sort of process is it by which the rational becomes actual? My thesis, which the rest of this study will explore, is that this process in its real, as contrasted with its logical aspect, is a process of affirmative mutual recognition. Recognition is the intersubjective existential configuration, the actuality, in which the concept (*Begriff*) of freedom appears.[60]

Hegel's transposition of his remark from its original setting in the discussion of constitutions to the preface of the work underscores the importance he attached to understanding the development of spirit in history. Hegel began by looking at constitutional history and discerned in such history a process of rational criticism of merely positive social structures and constitutions. He looks beneath constitutional history because the constitutional arrangements and institutions of a people are reflections and expressions of its communal spirit, the spirit animating and embodied in its laws.

Looking more deeply into spirit, at its center Hegel believes is a rational freedom, which demands and struggles for recognition. The demand for recognition of freedom leads to criticism of coercion; coercion is inherently self-contradictory and self-subverting. It leads to social and political criticism of inequalities, including mastery and slavery, and on higher levels, criticisms of mere authoritarian positivity and tradition. Rational criticism and social criticism are inseparable, because rationality itself is socially mediated and actualized in social modes and practices, which are determinate shapes of recognition. Hegel believes that such rational and social freedom will ultimately prevail over what is merely positive, traditional, authoritarian, and coercive.

Further, since spirit itself comes to be in the process of recognition, this implies that the ways in which human beings recognize each other in family, in civil society, and in the state constitute the existential nexus and medium wherein the rational becomes actual. But what sort of recognition is it in which the rational becomes actual? Recall Hegel's famous analysis of master and slave in the *Phenomenology*. This might be regarded as a "realization" of the concept of recognition, particularly if one follows Kojève's reading. However, master/slave is not a form of recognition in which the rational becomes actual in Hegel's sense. Master and slave begins in the violent coercion of the life and death struggle and ends by institutionalizing coercion, hierarchy, and domination. Such coercive practices do not establish but rather undermine the con-

---

59. *VPR*19, 50–51. Italics mine.
60. *E*, §484.

cepts of right and ethics. Hegel observes that "slavery falls into the transitional phase between natural human existence and the truly ethical condition; it occurs in a world where a wrong is still [considered as] a right."[61]

In contrast to Kojève, Hegel believes that only affirmative and reciprocal recognition, in which the other is allowed to be and affirmed in his difference, embodies actual, that is, ethical, rationality. He explains this normative distinction between shapes of recognition based on coercion and those shapes based on freedom in an important passage from the *Philosophy of Right*:

> The point of view of the free will, with which right and the science of rights begin, is already beyond that false [*unwahren*] point of view whereby the human being exists as a natural being . . . and is therefore capable of enslavement. This earlier and false appearance [*Erscheinung*] is associated with a spirit that is only at the standpoint of its consciousness; the dialectic of the concept and of the as yet only immediate consciousness of freedom results in the struggle for recognition and the relation of master and slave. However, that the objective spirit, the content of right, should no longer be apprehended merely in its subjective concept, and consequently that the human being in and for itself is not destined for slavery, should no longer be conceived as something that merely ought to be, is an insight that comes only when we recognize that the Idea of freedom is truly actual only as the state.[62]

Hegel believes that reciprocal recognition not only is constitutive of love and family, but it is also the central structural feature of the idea of the state as an ethical community. As such it is equivalent to freedom and has the connotation of liberation from bondage and oppression. In his *Philosophy of History*, Hegel identifies freedom as the dominant theme and plot of world history. Thus to say that the rational must happen is to identify reciprocal recognition and liberation as the trajectory and telos of constitutional history.

The plotting of the actuality and actualization of reciprocal recognition in Hegel's thought is very complex. Without going into this complexity here, suffice it to say that Hegel seems to be more optimistic about reciprocal recognition at the interpersonal level, and the level of the corporations and ethical state, than at the international level of world history. In his insistence on the affirmativity and reciprocity of relationship, Hegel may legitimately be seen as an ally of dialogical philosophy, if not, together with Fichte, the co-originator of its principle.[63] Hegel extends the principle of reciprocal recognition beyond

61. Hegel, *PR*, §57 Zusatz.
62. Ibid., §57.
63. See Martin Buber, "The History of the Dialogical Principle," in *Between Man and Man*, trans. R. G. Smith and Maurice Friedman (New York: Macmillan, 1965), 209–224. Buber explicitly identifies Fichte and Jacobi as important predecessors. He also refers to Feuerbach, who formulated the concept of human nature in terms of 'I and Thou'. Buber does not mention Hegel. It is ironic that the specific theme that Buber singles out in this literature, the "essential reciprocity"

the dialogical situation into the political sphere. Reciprocal recognition is an immediate unity in the family, but it is also embodied in the concept of law that constitutes abstract right. Moreover, just as the other interrupts natural egoism and summons the self to responsibility, so also the state must both promote private interests and restrain their excess and degeneration into privatism and atomistic individualism. The state is supposed to uphold the affirmative ethical concern of the family for its members against the merely individualistic self-seeking of civil society and extend the affirmativity of reciprocal recognition throughout civic life. Nevertheless, these actualizations of reciprocal recognition do not mean that Hegel's thought is utterly opposed to Fichte, but rather a gloss on Fichte's *Sollen*. Hegel's "optimism" concerning the actuality of reciprocal recognition at the interpersonal level and national level is counterbalanced by his tragic view of the realization of freedom in history.

Plan and Overview

The story of recognition is a story about Fichte and Hegel. Fichte introduced the concept but did not make it the basis of either his ethics or his politics. Hegel appropriated and transformed the concept of recognition and regarded it as the fundamental intersubjective structure of ethical life. The story of recognition is in part an extended debate between Hegel and Fichte concerning its proper interpretation and significance. I shall return to the Fichte-Hegel discussion throughout the study. Although we shall see that Hegel criticizes Fichte, such criticism by no means implies repudiation. As Siep notes, Hegel worked out his overall *Rechtsphilosophie* in an extended debate with Fichte's *Grundlage des Naturrechts* (1796), "at first in harsh repulsion, but later in a scarcely noticed rapprochement."[64] Moreover, in his treatment of international law as an 'ought to be' (*Sollen*), Hegel makes it evident that in certain important respects his thought remains Fichtean. For this reason I shall begin my analysis in Part I with a rehearsal of the discussion of recognition from Fichte through Schelling and Hegel, noting the important differences between Hegel's formulation of recognition in the *Phenomenology of Spirit* and his later mature *Encyclopedia Philosophy of Spirit*. Both are important; the former for Hegel's critique of morality, the latter for Hegel's affirmative account of ethical life.

Hegel's most complete formulation of the concept of recognition occurs in his *Phenomenology of Spirit*. There Hegel sets forth the general dialectical

---

between man and man, is in fact Hegel's most important contribution. Also curious is the fact that while Buber refers to Fichte, he is silent about Fichte's concept of recognition and does not make use of it in his theory of encounters. Nevertheless, Buber articulates and defends reciprocity—which for Hegel is fundamental to the concept of recognition and relation—as basic to the interhuman in his classic *I and Thou*.

64. Siep, *PPDI*, 41. Manfred Riedel also stresses the rapprochement between Hegel and Fichte; see "Hegel's Critique of Natural Law," in his *Between Tradition and Revolution*, 76–104.

pattern and structure of the concept and shows that *Geist* originates in mutual reciprocal recognition. However, Hegel conceives this early work as a self-accomplishing skepticism, and so he develops the negative implications and aspects, not of recognition, but of nonrecognition, failure, and so on. The positive implications of the concept of recognition are more fully developed only in Hegel's *Philosophy of Spirit*, the earliest drafts of which are found in his early Jena manuscripts. Many of the ideas and formulations in his mature philosophy of spirit are repetitions and elaborations of his earlier unpublished writings. These early Jena materials, as well as Hegel's *Propadeutik*, are important background for understanding his constructive position, not only in the mature *Encyclopedia* but also in the *Philosophy of Right*. For this reason I shall "backtrack" in chapter 5 to an examination of the Jena manuscripts before taking up the *Philosophy of Right*.

By far the largest part of this study (Part II) is an examination of Hegel's *Philosophy of Right*. I begin by discussing the issue of the systematic unity of the book—the quarrel of the ancients and the moderns—which was raised by Theunissen, and offer some proposals concerning its interpretation and its unity. I shall follow Hegel's categorical order of presentation, starting with abstract right and continuing with crime, punishment, morality, and ethical life. At the same time, however, I shall uncover and bring to light the concept of recognition as crucial to the systematic unity of the book, which allows it to be read as a phenomenology of freedom. Viewed from this perspective, recognition illumines Hegel's discussion of contract, crime and punishment, morality, and poverty as well as his critique of the social contract theory of the state and his theory of the state as a social organism.

In addition to consulting the published version of the *Philosophy of Right*, I have made use of the newly discovered lectures on *Rechtsphilosophie* of 1817 (Wannemann), 1818 (Homeyer), and 1819–1820 (Henrich) as well as the four-volume critical edition of Hegel's lectures on *Rechtsphilosophie*, 1818–1831, edited by Karl-Heinz Ilting. There is no question that the published version of the *Philosophy of Right* is the most important. However, it is itself but a compendium outline for the use of Hegel's students and intended to be supplemented in Hegel's lectures. Thanks to Ilting we are now in a position to correct the *Zusätze* of the published version, which were themselves editorial creations of Eduard Gans and not always as reliable as the student notes from which they were compiled. The recently available earlier lectures also provide valuable formulations that flesh out and clarify Hegel's position, particularly on recognition, poverty, and his criticism of natural law and Fichte's *Grundlage des Naturrechts*. They make it possible to understand Hegel's thought in a more nuanced way than before.

In the concluding chapter, I return to critical issues in Hegel interpretation, above all Kojève's identification of recognition as a struggle. This theme has been developed further, but not always consistently, by Jean-Paul Sartre, Gilles

Deleuze, and Jacques Derrida. Since Kojève, master/slave has been a constant theme of French philosophy that has undergone several variations. One such variation belongs to Deleuze, who believes that Nietzsche's account of master/slave not only refutes Hegel's, it shows Hegel's master, as well as Hegel himself, to be servile. This charge is echoed by Derrida. I shall explore their relation to Hegel and some of the implications of reciprocal recognition for the question and possibility of ethics.

Part One

Preliminaries

Recognition, Right, and Ethics

2

Recognition in Fichte
and Schelling

Fichte

We begin with a paradox: Idealism asserts the primacy of the subject and the corollary primacy of freedom. The rule is, no subject, no object. For the object is transcendentally constituted by the subject.[1] Thus Fichte says, "All being, whether of the ego or the non-ego, is a determinate modification of consciousness; and without consciousness there is no being."[2] But Fichte also makes a claim that appears to contradict this axiom of idealism: It is impossible, he says, to begin with freedom, because the self depends on the recognition of the other for the consciousness of its freedom.

Fichte writes, "The question was, how may the subject find itself as an object?"[3] This question has a history. It reflects Kant's delineation of the problems of self-knowledge (paralogisms) and of the self-consciousness of freedom. According to the third analogy of the first *Critique*, freedom—the capacity for self-originated causality—is possible. But Kant leaves open the question whether there actually is such freedom, and whether there is a being that is able to generate spontaneously its own causality. As the condition of possible objects of experience, the transcendental subject cannot itself be an object of experience and thus cannot be an object of knowledge. Consequently, Kant

---

1. To be sure, constitution is one of the murkier concepts. Its range of possible meanings runs from metaphysical production and causality (metaphysical idealism) to clarification of sense or meaning.

2. Fichte, *Grundlage des Naturrechts nach Principien der Wissenschaftslehre* (1796), *FW* 3:2. Hereafter cited as *GNR*.

3. Ibid., 33.

affirms the possibility of freedom but only for practical rather than cognitive purposes. Thus the problem: The free self cannot know itself, that is, know that it is free.

According to Kant, freedom is theoretically unknowable, on the one hand, and yet a practically necessary assumption, on the other. In the second *Critique*, Kant asserts that the consciousness of freedom arises from and is mediated by the moral law. The moral law is the *ratio cognoscendi* of freedom, and freedom is the *ratio essendi* of the moral law. Thus freedom comes to explicit self-consciousness only through the moral law, which is the *ratio cognoscendi* of freedom.[4] The self-consciousness of freedom is not a given; rather freedom is something that must be discovered, and it is discovered through a consciousness of obligation, the unconditional command of the moral law. Ought implies freedom. This is the formal structure of autonomy. Kant's formulation is noncognitive, formal, and individualistic in that the moral self-consciousness does not require intersubjective mediation, but only the consciousness of the moral law.

Kant's so-called practical imperative, respect freedom, whether in yourself or in another, always as an end in itself, presupposes that the other has somehow already come to count. This intersubjective-social presupposition stands in tension with a certain methodological individualism in Kant's reflective procedure.[5] Husserl charged that Kant's transcendental a priori presupposes the concrete a priori of the intersubjective life-world.[6] To this I would add that Kant both overlooks and yet presupposes mutual recognition.

Consider the following principles that Kant lays down in his *Critique of Judgment*:

1) *Selbstdenken*, or Think for yourself.
2) *An der Stelle jedes anderen denken*, or Think in the place of every other (everyone else).
3) *Jederzeit mit sich selbst einstimmig denken*, or Always think consistently.[7]

4. Kant is not entirely consistent on this point; he also mentions a consciousness of spontaneity that counts as a nonmoral consciousness of freedom.

5. Kant's ethics is widely interpreted in English-speaking circles as a first-person reflective standpoint; this reflects the nominalism that pervades English-speaking culture. However, Burkhardt Tuschling and Ludwig Siep have correctly pointed out that this nominalist reading is highly misleading. Kant's practical philosophy is oriented on the concept of rational universality, in terms of which each individual is not an absolute originator a priori but a co-legislator in a rational community, the kingdom of ends. For a discussion of Tuschling, see chapter 9 below. For Siep's analysis, see *PPDI*, 7–11.

6. Edmund Husserl, *The Crisis of European Science and Transcendental Phenomenology*, trans. David Carr (Evanston: Northwestern University Press, 1970), §§28–34. For a discussion of the relation between Husserlian phenomenology and the phenomenological dimension of German Idealism, see Williams, *Recognition*, chaps. 1–6.

7. Immanuel Kant, *Kritik der Urteilskraft, Werke 5*, Akademie Textausgabe (Berlin: Walter de Gruyter, 1968), §40, 294–295; English translation: *Critique of Judgment*, trans. J. H. Bernard (New York: Hafner, 1961). The rule Think for yourself is identified by Kant as the fundamental motto of Enlightenment in his prize-winning essay, *What Is Enlightenment?*

These principles are important, because they clarify that Kant is not a nominalist or correctly identified with the solipsist tradition of Cartesian idealism, at least in his practical philosophy. Kant explains that the first principle is the maxim of prejudice-free thinking. It is Kant's formulation of the Enlightenment principle. Think for yourself (*Selbstdenken*) is the maxim of a reason that is never passive. For Kant, passivity is linked with heteronomy and with prejudice, the antithesis of an enlightened mentality. The second is the maxim of an enlarged or expanded mentality. The third is the maxim of consistent thought.

The maxim of an enlarged mentality involves some transcendence of one's own particular judgment and a reflection on it from a putatively universal standpoint. Kant asserts that the universal standpoint can be attained by imagining oneself in the other's position. The question is whether this "putting oneself in the place of every other" (*sich in den Standpunkt anderer versetzen*) is primarily a reflective act or whether it is a joint-reciprocal intersubjective action. It seems that what Kant has in mind by the universal perspective is not an encounter with an other that calls me into question, or an address of an I to a Thou, but rather a reflective act, a judgment in which there is an attempt to take a larger perspective than the merely self-interested and egoistic. Elsewhere Kant indicates that the principle of enlarged mentality is a principle of judgment, and judgment is a reflective principle.[8] For Kant, therefore, the enlarged mentality is universal; however, it is not explicitly intersubjective. Rather it is a reflective-imaginative attempt to put oneself in the place of another, a metacritical self-reflection that presupposes or implies intersubjectivity.

Kant's third principle is a combination of the first two. But it is not without ambiguity. Within a reflective program, consistency involves self-coincidence. But what does self-coincidence mean? Is self-coincidence to be understood in a narrow individualistic sense, or does it involve the coincidence of the particular self with a universal self or point of view? Interpreted in the most generous way, it would appear that for Kant consistent thinking is not the Cartesian enterprise of making sure that certain ideas do not contradict each other. Rather consistent thinking is an attempt to harmonize one's own thought with one's best estimate of the thought of others. Thus consistency for Kant is not an endless reiteration of one's own point of view, but includes a possible critique and reversal of one's view from the standpoint of the other, or from a universal perspective. However, Kant does not indicate what such a reversal might mean or what it might look like. Further, consistency in Kant's sense, although presupposing others, does not imply intersubjective acts such as empathy or sympathy or recognition; it remains primarily reflective.[9]

8. Kant indicates that the first is the maxim of enlightenment, or maxim of *Verstand*, the second is the maxim of judgment (*Urteilskraft*), and the third is the maxim of reason (*Vernunft*). See his *Introduction to Logic*, *Werke*, Akademie Textausgabe, 9:57.

9. Although Kant's ethical philosophy appears as a kind of methodological individualism and theory of pure reflection a priori, Kant is not simply a continuation of Cartesian individualism. This is clear from Kant's rules for successful thinking cited above. Kant's philosophy, particularly

Kant's three principles make clear that while his practical philosophy has a social dimension and intersubjective implications, it falls short of mutual recognition in Fichte's and Hegel's sense. This is by no means to contend that Kant's principles are false, but only to observe that they have a first-person, reflective character that is different from and yet presupposes intersubjective reciprocal acts of mutual recognition, or face-to-face encounters in Levinas's sense. Kant's third principle presupposes a situation in which there is intersubjective harmony, if not explicit agreement. But Kant has not given an account of how such harmony and/or agreement is constituted in the first place. Is this harmony something natural and given? Or must it be accomplished and constructed? If one takes the latter view, answers to such questions are what the concept of recognition and the struggle for recognition are supposed to provide.

Although respect for humanity and freedom is a cardinal principle of Kant's ethical thought, Kant's neglect of recognition is a covert factor in the often-reiterated charge of Kant's formalism in ethics. Kant's ethical theory presents an ideal case of respect for freedom and humanity. However, it abstracts from sociohistorical and practical questions concerning the formation of a free community under conditions where respect for freedom and humanity is lacking. Kant's reflective principles remain void of determinate content in part because they abstract from the life-world.

The post-Kantian development of German idealism is in part an attempt to overcome Kant's formal notion of autonomy, not by denying it, but by recontextualizing it in the intersubjectivity and historical conditions that it presupposes.[10] From this vantage point, Kant's concept of autonomy is an abstraction from a particular sort of intersubjective and communal relationship. Habermas puts the point in the following way:

> By presupposing autonomy—and that means the will's property of being a law unto itself—in practical philosophy in the same way as he does the unassailable and simple identity of consciousness in theoretical philosophy, Kant expels moral action from the very domain of morality itself. Kant assumes the limiting case of a pre-established coordination of the acting subjects. The prior synchronization of those engaged in action within the framework of unbroken intersubjectivity banishes the problem of morality from the domain of moral doctrine. . . . Uni-

---

his ethical theory, presupposes a sociohistorical context, even if it is not clear how the transcendental method and the sociohistorical reflections are supposed to fit together. See Yirmiahu Yovel, *Kant and the Philosophy of History* (Princeton: Princeton University Press, 1980). See also Lewis White Beck, introduction to the Torchbook edition of *Kant, Lectures on Ethics* (New York: Harper, 1963), xii. However, pointing out that Kant's transcendental theory has sociohistorical context is not equivalent to asserting that for Kant autonomy is social and intersubjective from the outset. Hegel takes that step, which is why recognition (*Anerkennung*) and mediated autonomy become important issues in his thought. See below, chapter 4.

10. As noted above, there is a tension in Kant's thought between the program of transcendental philosophy carried out in the three *Critiques* and Kant's own writings on history and culture. See footnote 9.

versality of moral law here not only means intersubjective obligation as such, but the abstract form of universal validity which is bound a priori to general agreement.[11]

In other words, Kant's concept of autonomy presupposes as well as points toward a particular form of intersubjective agreement, to wit, the community of ends in themselves. This passes over the question how such a community could be intersubjectively accomplished in the first place; it abstracts from actions and questions concerning the realization of freedom. Kant presents the concept of an autonomous subject, whose consciousness of freedom is problematic owing to the very abstraction from action and what Habermas terms "the problems of morality."

Fichte was among the first to react to the austere abstract formalism of Kant's position. There is a prior question concerning the autonomous subject. Fichte seeks to go "beneath" Kant's autonomous subject by posing the question concerning its genesis and development. In 1794 Fichte wrote,

> There are a few questions which philosophy must answer before it can become *Wissenschaft* and *Wissenschaftslehre*. . . . Among these questions are the following: . . . How does the human being come to assume and recognize that there are rational beings similar to it outside of it, since such beings are not at all immediately or directly given to or present in its pure self-consciousness? . . . The relation of rational beings to each other I term *Gesellschaft*. But the concept of *Gesellschaft* is not possible except on the presupposition that there actually exist rational beings outside of us. . . . How do we come to such a presupposition . . . ?[12]

Clearly Fichte is suggesting that Kant's autonomous subject is in fact not entirely self-standing, but is part of a larger complex account of intersubjectivity and community. This leads Fichte to propose an alternative explanation to the problem of how one knows that one is free. According to Fichte, the self cannot give itself the consciousness of freedom; rather the consciousness of freedom is intersubjectively mediated. If the question of freedom is, "how may the subject find itself as an object?"[13] Fichte's reply is that the subject requires an other subject to "objectify" it and thereby occasion its consciousness of freedom. The self cannot give itself this experience of "objectification" on which the consciousness of its freedom depends. This is a different sense of objectification than that of a theoretical or reflective act. It requires an objectification of the self by another subject, namely, recognition. Fichte's account of this in-

11. Jürgen Habermas, "Labor and Interaction: Remarks on Hegel's Jena *Philosophy of Mind*," in *Theory and Practice*, trans. J. Viertel (Boston: Beacon Press, 1974), 150.

12. J. G. Fichte, *Über die Bestimmung des Gelehrten* (1794), *Werke* 6, Hrsg. I. H. Fichte (Berlin: Walter de Gruyter, 1971), 302.

13. Fichte, *GNR*, 3:33. English translation: *The Science of Rights*, trans. A. E. Kroeger (1889). Reissued London: Routledge & Kegan Paul, 1970; hereafter cited as *SR*.

tersubjective mediation of freedom leads him to introduce the concepts of recognition (*Anerkennung*) and summons (*Aufforderung*) to freedom.

Fichte introduces the topic of *Anerkennung*, not in his early *Wissenschaftslehre of 1794*, but in his *Grundlage des Naturrechts* (1796).[14] He identifies *Anerkennung* as a transcendental condition of natural law, the underpinning of his theory of right and ethics. For Fichte, the consciousness of freedom is intersubjectively mediated. Fichte formulates the point in the following way: "The finite rational being cannot ascribe to itself a freedom efficacious in the external world without also ascribing such freedom to others, and without therefore assuming the existence of other finite rational beings besides itself."[15] A condition of ascribing freedom to oneself is that such freedom must also be ascribable to others. In other words, freedom is not purely private, but intersubjective and universal. However, Fichte does not rest his case with transcendental argument, which may only establish that the other is a transcendental condition of freedom. Fichte takes a further step; namely, the other is not merely a transcendental *condition*. The other *acts* on the self and influences it. Fichte's claim is that the self discovers itself as free not simply through reflection but through the summons (*Aufforderung*) of the other. The summons of the other and thus the other are conditions of the subject's consciousness of freedom.

How does the summons by the other lead to the discovery and self-consciousness of freedom? Fichte explains that the other is not an unmoved mover exerting causality on the self; rather the other's influence is ethical in the broadest sense. The other functions as a kind of ethical *Anstoß*, a summons (*Aufforderung*) to autonomous freedom. By summoning the self to autonomous responsibility, the other occasions the self's discovery of its freedom. The other summons the self to free activity; the summons can be accepted, declined, or ignored, and in each case, one comes to a consciousness of one's freedom that was previously not simply latent in oneself. Fichte mentions education as an example of what he means by the summons to freedom and responsibility. This links the problematics of freedom, recognition, ethics, and education (*Bildung*).

The summons implies recognition. The summons is not a physical-causal action or an *Anstoß*: "the rational being is not determined or necessitated to act by the summons . . . but merely seizes this summons as occasion to determine itself to act."[16] The summons is an expression of a freedom (the summoner) that limits itself to create space and possibility for another freedom (the one who is summoned) to be. Such self-limitation presupposes and exhibits a recognition of the other's freedom: "This outside being has addressed a summons to the subject to manifest free activity; hence it has restricted its freedom by a

---

14. *GNR*, §3, 30; *SR*, 48. For the *Wissenschaftslehre*, see *Fichtes Werke 1*, Hrsg. I. H. Fichte (Berlin: Walter de Gruyter, 1971). English translation: *Science of Knowledge*, trans. Peter Heath and John Lachs (New York: Appleton Century Crofts, 1970).

15. *GNR*, §3, 30; *SR*, 48.   16. *GNR*, 36; *SR*, 56.

conception of an end entertained by the subject, wherein the freedom of the subject . . . was presupposed."[17] In responding, the summoned comes to the consciousness of her freedom.

Note that this freedom or autonomy is a mediated one. Mediated autonomy means that *freedom has a divided ground*, partly in the subject and partly in the other: "The ground of the action of the subject lies immediately in the being outside of it, and in the subject itself. . . . Had that other being not acted and summoned the subject to activity, the subject would not have acted. Its action as such is conditioned by the action of that being outside of him."[18] The self, when summoned by the other, attains an original self-consciousness of its freedom that it cannot give to itself, or achieve through reflection, namely, freedom as response to and for the other. This new self-consciousness of freedom points to the other beyond the subject as the ground of its determination.[19] Fichte's concept of the summons involves an ethical decentering of the subject that parallels the ontological decentering of the subject through the *Anstoß*.[20]

Fichte's account of the *Aufforderung* makes it clear that the other precedes and conditions the self's consciousness of freedom. Consequently the other cannot be collapsed into the positing of the self. This means that transcendental philosophy can no longer have a unitary or monopolar ground or foundation in transcendental subjectivity or ego. Fichte accordingly changes his account somewhat in the *Wissenschaftslehre (1801)*. It remains true that no free being can become self-conscious without at the same time being conscious of other free beings. Intelligence is not to be understood solipsistically but rather as social.[21] Nevertheless, despite reciprocity with others, there is an asymmetry between the ego and the other. The former feels itself directly, while the latter is merely conceived or represented. Moreover, the other is not an object that is constructed or known in the transcendental sense. For this reason in his 1810 lectures on the *Tatsachen des Bewusstseins*, Fichte acknowledges that the other "contradicts all our previous presuppositions,"[22] that is, the transcendental approach.

If freedom has a divided ground, partly in the subject and partly in the other summoning the subject to freedom, this raises a question concerning the appropriate relation between the "inner" and "outer" grounds of freedom. Fichte

---

17. *GNR*, 43; *SR*, 66.   18. *GNR*, §4, 41; *SR*, 63.

19. "The subject therefore, just as it has posited itself, at the same time must posit something outside of itself as its determining ground." Fichte, *GNR*, 35.

20. Ethical is here taken in a broad sense: Fichte distinguishes the question of right from the question of ethics. For Fichte, the concept of intersubjectivity seems to be more important for right than for ethics. At least Fichte devotes more space to *Anerkennung* in the *Grundlage des Naturrechts* than in his *System der Sittenlehre*.

21. Fichte, *Werke*, 2:143.

22. Fichte, *Tatsachen des Bewusstseins* (1810), *Fichtes Werke*, Band 2 (Berlin: Walter de Gruyter, 1971), 601. Hereafter cited as *TB*.

believes that the appropriate relation between the divided grounds of freedom is not one of exclusion or opposition but reciprocity: "The relation of free beings towards each other is therefore the relation of reciprocal causality upon each other through intelligence and freedom."[23]

Although the summons of the other decenters the self and calls it to responsible freedom, the priority of the summons is not absolute, and the relation to the other does not remain asymmetrical. The response of the subject to the summons of the other leads to reciprocal recognition (*Anerkennung*). To put the point in different terms, only a decentered, responsible self is capable of entering into positive reciprocal relations with others, including reciprocal recognition. In Fichte's words, "The relation of free beings to each other is . . . a relation of mutual influence through intelligence and freedom. Neither can recognize the other unless both reciprocally recognize each other, and neither can treat the other as a free being unless both reciprocally so relate to each other."[24] Fichte claims that "the concept of individuality is a reciprocal concept [*Wechselbegriff*] that can be thought only in relation to another concept."[25] More determinately put, "The human being becomes human only among other humans. . . . The concept of the human is therefore not a concept of a particular, but of a species."[26]

Levinas criticizes German idealism, Fichte in particular, for an allegedly egological conception of ontology that reduces the other to the same. Levinas is convinced that idealism means that the self can know only the products of its own activity.[27] Against such a conception Levinas pits his phenomenological discovery of the Face. The Face of the other calls me into question and assigns to me a responsibility for the other that is prior to my own choosing. Thus the Face of the other summons me to ethical freedom and responsibility for the other. But long before Levinas, Fichte already ascribed ethical significance to the face of the other: "Everyone can say: Whoever you may be, because you bear a human face, you are still a member of this great community. No matter how countlessly many intermediaries may be involved in the transmission, I nevertheless have an effect on you, and you have an effect upon me. No one whose face bears the stamp of reason, no matter how crude, exists for me in vain."[28]

However, although the subject is decentered in Fichte's account of intersubjectivity, and although he clearly affirms intersubjective reciprocity, Fichte also

23. *GNR*, 3:44.   24. Ibid.   25. Ibid., 47.
26. Ibid., 39.
27. This criticism was first brought against transcendental idealism by F. H. Jacobi. See my "The Other: F. H. Jacobi and German Idealism," in *Hegel on the Modern World*, ed. Ardis Collins (Albany: SUNY Press, 1995). See also Jacobi, "Open Letter to Fichte," trans. Diana I. Behler, in *Philosophy of German Idealism*, ed. Ernst Behler, 119–142, *The German Library*, vol. 23 (New York: Continuum, 1987); see also Frederick C. Beiser, *The Fate of Reason* (Cambridge, Mass.: Harvard University Press, 1987).
28. Fichte, *Some Lectures Concerning the Scholar's Vocation*, 19.

tends to regard community as something restrictive and negative.[29] The decentering of the subject by the other has a predominantly negative connotation; Fichte conceives the other primarily as a restriction on freedom. In his early writings, Hegel believes that Fichte's concept of community is negative, heteronomous, and potentially tyrannical. Later Hegel achieved a little-noticed rapprochement with Fichte. The *Philosophy of Right* is in part a commentary and continuation of the "recognition strand" of Fichte's thought in opposition to its "coercion strand." Hegel thinks through the concept of recognition and develops its positive implications for social ontology and philosophy. But he also had some help from Schelling.

Schelling

In his early career Schelling was influenced by Fichte. However, he was also critical of Fichte's position as one-sided, tending to privilege subjectivity at the expense of nature. A genuinely objective idealism would be ontological in the sense that it must regard both nature and ego as expressions of the absolute. In Schelling's language, nature is also connected to the absolute. This means both ego and nature depend on the absolute and that the ego therefore has a real other. These convictions find expression in his treatment of recognition in the *System of Transcendental Idealism*.[30]

The question of the other is taken up by Schelling in his discussion of the distinction between nature and freedom and the parallel correlative distinction between the realm of nature and the realm of history and society as conscious constructions of freedom. The other plays a pivotal role in the transition from necessity to freedom. Schelling begins with Fichte's problem of the self-consciousness of freedom: Since the intelligence contains nothing save what it produces and since it cannot produce its own self-objectification, the self's consciousness of its freedom seems to be *impossible*. In other words, the idealist principle that everything *in* the subject exists *through* the subject is insufficient to account for the self's consciousness of its freedom. Hence Fichte's question, how does the self become conscious of its own freedom? Schelling acutely explains that the act whereby the self becomes conscious of its freedom must be both explicable and inexplicable by the subject. To the extent that the act is explicable by the subject, a quasi-transcendental account of some

---

29. This tension in Fichte's thought is further explored below in chapter 12. I will seek to isolate two strands of Fichte's thought in *GNR*, the "recognition argument for community strand" and the "coercion argument for community strand." In my view Hegel develops the former but rejects the oppressive aspects of the latter.

30. F. W. J. Schelling, *System des Transzendentalen Idealismus* (Hamburg: Meiner Verlag, 1962); English translation: *System of Transcendental Idealism* (1800), trans. Peter Heath (Charlottesville: University Press of Virginia, 1978). Hereafter cited as *STI*, with the English translation first and the German references second [G].

sort can be given. But to the extent that the act is inexplicable by the subject, this points beyond the subject to an independent other as its condition. This strange, explicable and yet inexplicable action constitutes the paradox of inter-subjectivity, and points to an even stranger divided or dual ground of freedom.

Schelling qualifies the latent solipsism of transcendental idealism when he maintains that the ground of free self-determination must lie partly "within" the subject and partly "outside" of the subject. Schelling's point in affirming that the ground of freedom is divided is that freedom is social and intersubjec-tive. Hence the ground of freedom cannot be identified with subjectivity alone; the grounds of freedom must be both "in" the subject and yet transcend the subject. Freedom and the consciousness of freedom must obviously be the sub-ject's own doing, yet the subject is incapable of making itself and its freedom into an object and so it cannot be autonomously self-conscious in the crucial sense. Something irreducibly other is required to make the subject available to itself and to arouse the subject to freedom and responsibility. For this reason self-consciousness and freedom require reciprocal interaction between self and other. Neither self nor other is, by itself, sufficient; consequently, the ground of freedom must be twofold, and yet correlative. This account of a "divided" ground and intersubjective realization of freedom is at the same time a "de-duction of the other." Denial of such a "twofold ground" of self-determination means acceptance of solipsism and incoherence (circularity), for the self would have to precede its own freedom, or will prior to willing.[31] The reference to the other obviates this circularity.

Yet the correlation of the internal and external grounds of freedom, or self and other, is not simply a positive empirical one. Schelling shares Fichte's ten-dency to conceive the other in terms of negation. The other is not-I, and I am not-other. Both the other and the self mutually condition each other, but such conditioning is negative. There is no direct presence of the other to the self, or vice versa. Thus "the most important question of this enquiry" arises, namely, "How then, by pure negation, can anything positive be posited in such a way that I am obliged to intuit what is not my activity, simply because it is not mine, as the activity of an intelligence outside me?"[32] What is the relation or connection between the 'internal' and 'external' grounds and conditions of freedom? The problem here is fundamental. It goes to the heart of the question concerning the other as a problem for first philosophy, which possibly "ex-plodes" the very concept of first philosophy. The heart of the problem is that once the grounds of freedom are divided into internal and external, how can they be correlated and connected? The difficulty is increased by the apparent facticity and contingency of the other, as well as the apparent facticity of the

31. *STI*, 162; G, 209.   32. *STI*, 166; G, 214.

summons of the other.[33] How can freedom, as transcendental and transphenomenal, stand in correlation with an apparently contingent other? Or, if the other is also transphenomenal freedom, then it is an absence, and access to it seems problematic or at best indirect. How then is any correlation possible with such an apparent absence? Schelling proposes three different approaches to this question.

The first is an appeal to preestablished harmony. This appeal is required by the following premises: the self can know only the products of its own activity, and all that is 'in' the self exists 'through' the self. In short, each self is conceived as a windowless monad (Leibniz). No self can act directly on an other, or apprehend the other as it conditions freedom; instead each self is conceived as completely self-contained and self-enclosed. The apparent coexistence of and correlation between the internal and the external grounds of freedom happens "as if one were determined by the other."[34] But since there is no interaction or mutual determination between the two, "such a relationship is conceivable only through a pre-established harmony."[35] This metaphysical solution to the problem threatens to undermine the very freedom that it is supposed to explain. If the harmony of the inner and outer conditions is *preestablished*, then there seems to be no room for contingency or freedom.[36] Schelling rejects such an interpretation when he insists that his entire discussion—including preestablished harmony—is directed not to a denial of freedom but to uncovering its conditions.

The second way Schelling tackles the problem of relating the internal and external grounds of freedom proceeds by appropriating and analyzing Fichte's concept of the summons (*Aufforderung*) of the other. Schelling believes that the summons is a mediating concept that removes the contradiction of the divided ground of freedom. But how does the summons resolve the contradiction? It must not be understood as a cause or stimulus to which the subject "automatically" responds. Schelling explains: "Only the condition for the possibility of willing must be generated in the self without its concurrence. And thus we see forthwith a complete removal of the contradiction, whereby the same act of intelligence had to be both explicable and inexplicable at once. The concept which mediates the contradiction is that of the summons, since by means of the summons the action is explained, *if it takes place*, without it *having to*

33. This strange combination of transcendence and facticity is a central problem in Sartre's account of the other as the subject of the Look. For a discussion of the problem in Sartre, see Michael Theunissen, *The Other: Studies in the Social Ontology of Husserl, Heidegger, Sartre and Buber*, trans. Christopher Macann (Cambridge, Mass.: MIT Press, 1984).

34. *STI*, 160; G, 207.   35. Ibid.

36. See Vittorio Hösle, "Zur Interpretation von Fichtes Theorie der Intersubjektivität," in *Fichtes Lehre von Rechtsverhältniss: Die Deduktion der §§ 1–4 der Grundlage des Naturrechts und ihre Stellung in der Rechtsphilosophie* (Frankfurt am Main: Vittorio Klostermann, 1992).

take place on that account."[37] The summons of the other does not create or cause freedom (as if that were intelligible) but rather provides the possibility of the self-consciousness of freedom. The self catches sight of itself as a possibility in the 'mirror' of an other. The summons creates conditions for a free response without, however, causing a 'free' response or making it necessary. Schelling characterizes the summons as a mediating concept that connects the 'internal' and the 'external' grounds of freedom, while preserving the contingency of both the other and the free response to it.

The summons is not a causal concept but an ethical one. Schelling contends that the summons is an obligation (*Sollen*). The summons does not create freedom but presents freedom to itself as a possibility. As such it does not predetermine or cause the realization of this possibility. The other summons the self to responsible freedom and provides a glimpse of such freedom as a possibility. The summons implies a self-recognition in an other, which in turn can be actualized only through reciprocal mutual recognition. However, a clarification is in order: Schelling's analysis is not an attempt to promote ethics as first philosophy. He warns his reader that "what we seek to establish here is not a moral philosophy of any kind, but rather a transcendental deduction of the thinkability and explicability of moral concepts in general."[38] Although the analysis of the *Aufforderung* is transcendental, the thing itself is immanent in moral experience and reflection.

Note that this analysis of the *Aufforderung* seems to contradict the appeal to preestablished harmony. For the latter is invoked on the presupposition that there is no direct interaction and no positive reciprocity between monadic selves. Self and other are conceived as self-enclosed and self-contained monads that relate to each other only negatively or as negations. But *Aufforderung* on the contrary requires a positive self-recognition in the other. Such positive self-recognition in turn implies both interaction and reciprocity. However, such reciprocal interaction is indirect; Schelling denies any immediate or direct awareness of the other.[39] Schelling's discussion vacillates between *Aufforderung*, which implies a positive relation to other and an affirmative self-knowledge in the other, and preestablished harmony, which presupposes windowless and relationless monads. The concept of the *Aufforderung* points to and requires a separation between selves that makes possible indirect interaction and reciprocity. Preestablished harmony is invoked, but it is only a negative, indirect sort.[40] It seems to amount to nothing more than a reiteration of the claim that as surely as there exists a single intelligence, as surely there are other intelligences with the same determinations and capacities. Individual and community

37. *STI*, 163; G, 210.   38. *STI*, 155; G, 200.
39. *STI*, 162–163; G, 210–211.
40. *STI*, 161, 165; G, 210, 215.

mutually require and condition each other, but this claim is known and verified only in the praxis of recognition.[41]

A third set of considerations on the relation between the internal and external ground of freedom runs as follows. Self-consciousness is not given but comes to be out of some prior or preconscious condition. Further, self-consciousness is determinate, whereas the prior condition from which it emerges is indeterminate. Thus the problem is, how to explain or account for the transition from indeterminacy to determinacy? As Schelling puts it: how, by pure negation, can anything positive (i.e., determinate) be posited? How to make the transition from the fact that an action is *not mine* to the other as the ground of the action? Schelling invokes a social conception of reason, freedom, and intelligence that stands in correlation with a common objective world.

His analysis deepens Fichte's conception of *Aufforderung*. Prior to *Aufforderung*, the consciousness of freedom is indeterminate; the summons of the other is the possibility of transition from indeterminacy to determinacy, the possibility of the consciousness of responsibility and freedom. But this determination by summons is a limited one.[42] As Fichte pointed out, the other's summons assumes freedom and intelligence in the one who is summoned, and this assumption is the new possibility that the latter grasps and to which she responds. Thus the determinacy constitutive of self-consciousness is possible only if there are others: "It is a condition of self-consciousness that I intuit in general actions of intelligences outside me."[43]

Schelling summarizes the point in the following way:

> These restrictions (determinations) are possible only through intelligences outside of me in such a fashion that, in the operations of these intelligences upon me, I discern nothing save the original bounds of my own individuality, and would have to intuit these even if in fact there were no other intelligences beyond myself. Although other intelligences are posited in me only through negations, I nevertheless must acknowledge them as existing independent of me. This will surprise no one who reflects that this relationship is a completely reciprocal one, and that no rational being can prove itself as such save by the recognition of others.[44]

Again it should be noted that in this text Schelling embraces both the conception of selves as self-contained windowless monads that relate to each other as

---

41. *STI*, 169; G, 218.

42. This is a possible source of Hegel's concept of determinate negation (*bestimmte Negation*), which is distinguished from abstract or simple negation. Determinate negation is limited, in that it both negates and preserves what is negated. Determinate negation finds expression in Hegel's concept of *Aufhebung*. See *Wissenschaft der Logik*, note on *Aufheben*.

43. *STI*, 166; G, 213–214.

44. *STI*, 169; G, 218. I have altered the English translation.

negations, and the concept of reciprocal interaction between selves in mutual recognition. According to the former, self and other are related via mutual negation; according to the latter, there is mutual recognition that yields positive self-knowledge mediated by an affirmative reciprocal relation to the other. This apparent paradox shows the dialectical structure of intersubjectivity and must be accepted; its acceptance is the basis on which Schelling builds his account of truth and the world.

According to Schelling, the problem of truth is not reducible to the correspondence theory, which focuses on the correspondence (or lack thereof) between idea and its object. In addition to the correspondence between idea and object, there is the question of the intersubjective agreement (*Übereinstimmung*) about such epistemological idea-object correspondences. It is such intersubjective agreement between such individual subject-object correspondences that grounds objective truth.[45] In short, the other is not only a condition of such a consensus-coherence view of truth but also a condition of the objective world. For Schelling, then, the very objectivity of the world depends on others. "It therefore follows self-evidently . . . that a rational being in isolation could not only not arrive at a consciousness of freedom, but would be equally unable to attain to consciousness of the objective world as such; and hence that intelligences outside the individual, and a never-ceasing interaction with them, alone make complete the whole of consciousness with all its determinations."[46] There are in Fichte some hints that the interpersonal other is the foundation of the belief that there is a reality outside of and independent of the individual.[47] Thus the very concepts of "reality" and "world" are dependent on and mediated by others. Schelling supports this view when he writes,

> The sole objectivity which the world can possess for the individual is the fact of its having been intuited by intelligences outside the self. . . . For the individual these other intelligences are, as it were, the eternal bearers of the universe, and together they constitute so many indestructible mirrors of the objective world. The world is independent from me, although it is posited only through the ego, because it resides objectively for me in the intuition of other intelligences, and this social world is the archetype whose correspondence with my representations alone constitutes the truth.[48]

Schelling's analysis remains rather formal and ontological. To be sure, he contends that transcendental ontological analysis is not a moral or existential philosophy but a probing of the conceivability of moral and interpersonal-

45. *STI*, 164; G, 212.
46. *STI*, 174; G, 224–225.
47. Cf. his comments that the other underlies the concept of the nonego (*Vocation of the Scholar*, 13, *Gelehrte*, 304). See also Joachim Widman, *Fichte* [Sammlung Göschen] (Berlin: Walter de Gruyter, 1982), 77–78, 101.
48. *STI*, 174; G, 224–225.

social concepts. Given this orientation, it comes as no surprise that Schelling tends to downplay *Aufforderung* as an *act* of an other, and treats it instead as an ontological limit principle of finitude. When that is done, the facticity of the *Aufforderung* and the other seems to be given up, and the other tends to be reduced to an ontological condition or structure.[49] Moreover, there is a tension between Schelling's appeal to preestablished harmony that tends to reduce freedom to necessity and his acknowledgment, however minimal, of indirect free reciprocal interaction between selves.

Any inconsistencies or other inadequacies in Schelling's account pale into insignificance in comparison with his acute exposition of freedom as essentially intersubjective and social. In making explicit Fichte's hints that freedom is intersubjective and consequently has a double grounding, Schelling implicitly undermines the twin concepts of windowless monads and preestablished harmony by exposing a fundamental dependence and relation between self and other. This relation is fundamental in that it is a condition of any judgment about the objectivity of the world. It is also fundamental in that it precedes and is a condition of transcendental epistemological inquiry. The other is thus opened up as an issue for first philosophy. For the self-other relation is by no means limited to anthropology; it appears on a variety of levels, from first philosophy to the intersubjective grounding and mediation of reason and truth to the social-political-anthropological.

Moreover, although Schelling warns his reader that he is not "doing ethics," it is evident that the fundamental relation of self and other has ethical implications. The other summons the self to responsible freedom, placing the self under obligation to respond in some way to this summons. In short, although Schelling claims to be doing nothing more than setting forth a system of practical philosophy according to the principles of transcendental idealism, the fundamental relation between self and other he uncovers in the course of his exposition is also an important formulation of the so-called dialogical principle.[50] The latter principle makes relation and reciprocity central concepts, and in such representative figures as Buber and Levinas, it is a central category in the most substantive ethical philosophy of the twentieth century. Although these figures are highly critical of German idealism, they nevertheless are indebted to its leading figures and continue important, if hitherto concealed, aspects of its practical philosophy.

49. *STI*, 166. In Schelling's defense, transcendental philosophy abstracts from particularity and contingency.
50. I take the term "dialogical principle" from Buber, *Between Man and Man*, 209–224.

3

Recognition in the
Phenomenology of Spirit

Schelling's account of recognition reflects a dialectic between a Leibnizian conception of selves as windowless, relationless monads and Fichte's concept of intersubjective *Aufforderung*, or summons to responsible freedom. The latter opens up the "monad" and reveals a doubled ground of freedom and a relational freedom. However paradoxical it may appear, this dialectic must be accepted. The doubled ground of freedom is most plausibly interpreted as both preserving and breaking down the sharp and rigid distinction between inner and outer and opening the windowless monad to the influence of the other. The breaking open of the putatively windowless monad is a process that begins with Fichte and Schelling and continues in Hegel. The important concept of a doubled ground of freedom makes central the issue of coordinating and ordering the dual grounds of freedom: each self, in its independence, depends on an other that it is not. In spite of its claims to freedom and independence, each seeks security and legitimation from an other whose recognition is contingent and not guaranteed. Schelling may not have appreciated fully the implications of his own novel formulation of the divided ground of freedom, but Hegel did. The double ground of freedom reemerges in Hegel's account of the doubling of self-consciousness, that is, that consciousness exists only as doubled and thus as social.[1]

In this chapter I summarize Hegel's concept of recognition in the *Phenomenology of Spirit*. In the next chapter I focus on the later, differently nuanced

---

1. For the concept of intersubjective doubling, see my *Recognition*, chap. 7; H.-G. Gadamer, *Hegel's Dialectic: Five Hermeneutical Studies*, trans. P. Christopher Smith (New Haven: Yale University Press, 1976), 54–74. See also Husserl's concept of intersubjective pairing, *Cartesian Meditations*, trans. Dorion Cairns (The Hague: Martinus Nijhoff, 1960), §51.

account in his *Encyclopedia*, wherein the phenomenology is part of the *Philosophy of Spirit*. These works have different agendas. The *Phenomenology* is an introduction to Hegel's system of philosophy. It is a self-accomplishing skepticism that traverses the shapes of consciousness (*Gestalten des Bewusstseins*) and demonstrates that they subvert themselves and self-destruct. Thus the emphasis is on restlessness, negativity, and self-subversion. Relation to other is portrayed primarily in negative terms. It is not the full process of reciprocal recognition but the failure to achieve such reciprocal recognition that receives emphasis. For this reason the figure of master/slave tends to dominate the *Phenomenology*'s account of intersubjectivity. The *Phenomenology* shows that the shapes of consciousness—including master/slave—subvert themselves, demolishing all alternatives save holism.[2] The *Encyclopedia*, on the other hand, expounds the mature Hegelian system, in which, although skepticism continues to play a critical role, it is subordinate to philosophical construction. This means that the affirmative aspects of the concept of reciprocal recognition previously downplayed or bracketed now receive emphasis and elaboration, particularly in Hegel's lectures. Hegel now comes to emphasize and focus on affirmativity in the relation to the other; the other is more than a negation or limit. This affirmativity is constitutive of morality and ethical life. The different agendas of the *Phenomenology* and the *Encyclopedia* mean that different nuances and patterns of the concept of recognition are developed in each account.

Unfortunately, the English translations of Hegel's works, particularly the older ones, are of limited usefulness in discerning these nuances and stand in the way of critical work. This is not surprising since most of the translations were made prior to recent studies of *Anerkennung*, and tend to convey a metaphysical tone far removed from intersubjectivity and ethics. This is unfortunate because Hegel considers intersubjective recognition to be genuinely speculative in his sense of speculation: "This relation is thoroughly speculative, and if one believes that speculation is something far removed and inconceivable, one needs only to consider the content of that relation in order to convince oneself of the groundlessness of such an opinion."[3]

The Intersubjective Doubling of Self-Consciousness

Hegel's critics tend to identify him with German idealism, which in turn is understood as an assertion of the primacy of subjectivity, the "philosophy of the subject." They tend to locate Hegel within the Cartesian-Kantian tradition of transcendental philosophy, which includes as its essential features individu-

2. See J. N. Findlay, *Hegel: A Re-Examination* (New York: Collier Macmillan, 1962), 54. For an extended argument along these lines, see Michael N. Forster, *Hegel and Skepticism* (Cambridge, Mass.: Harvard University Press, 1989).

3. Hegel, *E*, §436 Zusatz.

alism and freedom as autonomy. Such an interpretation of Hegel overlooks his transformation of the concept of subjectivity into intersubjectivity. Hegel appropriates from Fichte the concept of recognition, according to which freedom is intersubjectively mediated, and individuality is a reciprocal concept with community. At the very least, this implies that autonomy is mediated, and surely the notion of a mediated autonomy is not part of the standard picture of the "philosophy of the subject."[4] Autonomy as a feature of individuals is an abstraction from autonomy as an intersubjective-social accomplishment and institution.

Hegel appropriates Schelling's account of the divided or doubled ground of freedom and transforms it into an account of desire (*Begierde*). Hegel conceives the self not as a simple, stable, quiescent self-identity but as a complex, restless, self-repulsive, negative identity that, as desire for the other, is driven beyond itself, including its natural existence. The doubled ground of freedom implies a mediated autonomy, where the other is no longer merely external but mediates the self's relation to itself. In light of this conception of a mediated self-identity, Hegel reformulates Schelling's divided ground of freedom in terms of the now virtually canonical terminology of being-for-self and being-for-other. Owing to the divided ground of freedom and self-repulsing negative self-identity, the self is not initially present, much less transparent to itself; rather self-consciousness requires an other for its own self-mediation. Being-for-self and being-for-other have long since made their way into the intellectual framework and vocabulary of existential philosophy, the so-called existential turn of Husserlian phenomenology.[5]

Hegel never wrote an essay on or systematic account of the concept of recognition, but in the *Phenomenology of Spirit* he presented his most explicit analysis of the concept. In the chapter on self-consciousness, Hegel runs through the concept of recognition twice: first, from the perspective of the phenomenological We, the onlookers who observe ordinary consciousness; and second, from the standpoint of ordinary consciousness that undergoes the experience of struggling for recognition. In other words, Hegel distinguishes between the analysis of the *meaning* of the concept and its existential-phenomenological *portraiture*, that is, the way the concept appears to ordinary consciousness in action. This distinction is not merely one of perspective; it is a distinction between an ontological analysis of general structure(s) and patterns of intersubjectivity, on the one hand, and empirical analyses of their potentially endless contingent variations in determinate actualizations, on the other.[6] It is impor-

---

4. For the novel conception of a mediated autonomy (*vermittelte Autonomie*) in Hegel, see Wildt, *Autonomie und Anerkennung*, 173 ff.

5. See Kojève, *Introduction to the Reading of Hegel*; Sartre, *Being and Nothingness*. Hegel must be regarded an important source of existential thought, especially the French phase of existential phenomenology, even as much of this literature reacts against and seeks to distance itself from Hegel.

6. For a fuller account, see my *Recognition*, chaps. 7–8.

tant to note that some determinate instances of recognition do not embody all of its essential features and thus are deficient realizations of the concept. Master/ slave is one such "deficient realization" of the concept of recognition. Moreover, the full significance of the concept is often concealed from the participants in the struggle for recognition, owing to their immediacy and false consciousness. Hegel's ontological analysis serves a heuristic and hermeneutic function for his account of ordinary consciousness in its struggles for recognition.

Since the *Phenomenology* sets forth a genetic history of the shapes of consciousness, its starting point is logically and conceptually primitive. In focusing on the transition from consciousness to self-consciousness, Hegel brackets its social-institutional and political background and considers an interpersonal confrontation in the absence of any mediating institutions.[7] Each party operates with an immediate certainty: the naive presumption of being absolute, that is, exclusive of relation and qualification by the other. This presumption will be shown to be self-subverting.

There are three phases (*Stufen*) of recognition: immediacy, or abstract parochial universality; opposition between particulars; and emergent concrete, that is, mediated, universality. The first is the phase of initial confrontation with other under the conditions of abstract immediacy. It is well known that Hegel criticizes the identification of immediacy with truth. This criticism applies to self-knowledge as well. Immediate self-consciousness is for Hegel a false consciousness. It both discloses and conceals and thus systematically distorts its situation; it rejects the very thing it needs and on which it depends, namely, the other. It is essential, and the other inessential. Moreover, what it takes to be the truth turns out to be only a parochial part of the story and so is self-subverting. Since the parochial self, as self-repulsive negativity, is hidden from itself, it depends on the other for its own critical self-consciousness. That is why self-knowledge for Hegel takes the form of *self-recognition in other*. The road to interiority passes through the other. The self is for itself only by being for an other, and the self is for an other only by being for itself. The 'for itself' formulates not the beginning but the result and telos of the process of recognition.

Hegel precedes his analysis of recognition with a discussion of desire (*Begierde*). The analysis of desire as a lack and as a process of satisfaction through the negation/consumption of its object(s) is well known. However, what is often overlooked is that desire is also a preethical, prerational condition of individual consciousness that must be sublimated if recognition is to occur. Desire

---

7. Hegel does not claim that such conditions prevail generally in modern society. However, political philosophy employed the historical fiction of a "state of nature" to clarify central conceptions of the human condition and to explain the transition from presocial to social conditions. Hegel rejects the state of nature and the social contract speculations precisely because of their methodological individualism, which inevitably makes the social and communal appear derivative from the individual. Hegel's point is that humans are fundamentally social; hence individuality and the social are correlative concepts. I shall return to these issues below.

begins as a kind of natural solipsism that is naively self-centered and narcissistic; its self-centeredness is manifest in the fact that it regards its objects as non-essential, that is, as consumables to be used and consumed at will. The natural "solipsism" of desire is a condition that must be transformed and sublimated if the self is to become capable of enduring relationships with others. Hegel's account of the process of recognition is at the same time an account of the sublimation of desire. In this process desire is not eliminated but deepened: *"Self-consciousness attains its satisfaction only in another self-consciousness."*[8] In this sense it is correct to see that desire is fundamentally a desire for the other. The point to be underscored here is that the other, or the confrontation with the other, both shatters the natural solipsism of the self, and "pulls" it out of its natural solipsism. The analysis of recognition therefore is also and at the same time a story of *self-overcoming*, through which an enlarged ethical-social mentality (to use Hannah Arendt's term), or *Geist*, is attained.

Hegel begins his analysis of the concept of recognition thus:

> Self-consciousness is in and for itself through the fact that *it exists in and for itself for an other*. That is, it exists only as recognized. The concept of this its unity in its doubling, the infinity realizing itself in self-consciousness, is a many-sided intersection of and correlation between multiple meanings. Consequently these elements must on the one hand be precisely distinguished and kept separate, and, on the other hand, they must be taken and known in their *opposite* meaning, namely, in this very differentiation they are nevertheless *not different*. The double signification of the distinguished elements lies in the nature of self-consciousness to be infinite, or to be immediately the opposite of the determination in which it is posited. The exposition of this spiritual unity in its doubling will present the movement of recognition [*Anerkennen*].[9]

There are several points to be noted. First, Hegel treats the concept of recognition in a series of brief imaginative variations. In this conceptual play, the determinations of self and other are to be distinguished and kept separate, yet, in this separation, they are nevertheless taken as not different, or as united. The analysis must focus on the difference of self and other and, within this difference, on their identity and union. It is easy to err by focusing on difference to the exclusion of identity (as do Kojève and Sartre) and by focusing on identity to the exclusion of difference (as does Levinas in his criticism that Hegel reduces the other to the same). Both the difference of self and other as well as their identity within this differentiation must be faithfully attended to. But why is such attention to double meanings necessary?

8. Hegel, *Phänomenologie des Geistes*, Hoffmeister (Hamburg: Felix Meiner Verlag, 1952), 139; hereafter cited as *PhG*. Italics in original. English translation: *Phenomenology of Spirit*, trans. A. V. Miller (Oxford: Oxford University Press, 1977); hereafter cited as *PhS*.

9. *PhG*, 141. Translation taken from Williams, *Recognition*, 149.

The reason is that not only subjectivity, but intersubjectivity is in play: recognition is a relation that plays out between two self-conscious beings; it is a joint act of double and opposing significations. In drawing on Fichte's and especially Schelling's thesis that freedom has a divided ground, Hegel expresses the point simply: self-consciousness is "doubled."[10] Ludwig Siep explains:

> This doubling does not signify a totality laid out in various moments . . . such as occurred in the species process. Since both moments are here determined as self-consciousnesses, their relation to each other is layered in double-meanings. . . . Two self-consciousnesses do not relate to each other like mere things that have an effect on each other, or like forces that interact with each other. The reciprocal relation between two self-consciousnesses transcends these, because for each the other is a moment in its own self-relation. Both depend, not only on the relation of the one to the other, but on the self-relation and self-understanding of the other. Neither can alter itself without co-altering the other insofar as it stands in relation to it. A friend undergoes a change himself through a change in his friend. The relation is therefore not simply causal interaction (*Wechselwirkung*), but rather a double-signification. Recognition, as a double-signifying act of two self-consciousnesses, is a relation in which the relata relate to themselves through the relation to the other, and relate to the other through their own self-relation. Thus the self's relation to itself is made possible by the corresponding relation to the other.[11]

We do not move from an isolated individual *cogito* to the social. The paradoxical dialectic of intersubjectivity means that "each of the two contains the whole relation."[12] This is not evident at the outset of the process of recognition. But the process unfolds through a dialectic in which there is a sharp distinction between self and other, on the one hand, and there is a union of the two, on the other hand, since each is only through its other. Or, in the more dialectical language of the *Jena Realphilosophie*: "Each is . . . equal to, and the same as, the other, but only in opposition to the other."[13] The divided ground, or social me-

---

10. The German term is *Verdoppelung*. Miller and Baillie both translate it as "duplication." But duplication suggests that the other is a copy of the one, which implies that it is derivative from a first or primal ego. When 'my' ego is identified as primordial, the road is open to Cartesianism, or to the view that the other is an analogue, or analogical inference. Both tend to reduce the other to the same. However, for Hegel, the other is not a copy, or duplicate, but another member of the same species that exists as a plurality of individuals. This plurality is real. Hegel's claim is not that consciousness doubles but rather that the living species itself doubles, that is, is a one and a many. This doubling is a higher-level repetition and transformation of the interplay of forces described in the previous chapter: *PhG*, 142, 109; *PhS*, §184, §141. Hegel also makes this point in the *Philosophie des Geistes 1805/06*, translated as *Hegel and the Human Spirit*, by Leo Rauch (Detroit: Wayne State University Press, 1983), 105; hereafter cited as *HHS*. There the will is doubled, and this doubling constitutes the contrast between individual will (*Willkür*) and the universal will. Moreover, Hegel treats the relation between the wills as a relation of recognition. So despite the terminology of the will that suggests a faculty psychology, Hegel conceives the relation of wills as an intersubjective relation, that is, a relation of "two independent egos" (ibid).

11. *APP*, 137.   12. Ibid., 138.   13. *HHS*, 192.

diation, of freedom presents a series of antinomies and practical political problems that require resolution.

The process of recognition is influenced by the concept of self-identity as negatively dialectical and inherently antinomic and by the concept of recognition as inherent double signification. This means that whatever particular determination self-consciousness may have, it is also immediately the opposite determination. The self is what it is not, and is not what it is. However, this formulation has an affirmative intersubjective-relational sense for Hegel that is missing from Sartre. Hegel conceives the individual self in its desires not as a simple, stable, quiescent self-identity but as a complex, restless, self-repulsive, negative identity. This self-repulsing negativity means that the self is not initially present to itself, much less transparent to itself. The immediate self does not yet know what it is. What it is, is still implicit and must become explicit to it. It can become explicit to itself, that is, discover what it is, only through the mediation of an other. Self-consciousness requires an other to confirm and transform its own self-understanding. The self's presence to itself is mediated by an other that is likewise a self-repulsing negative identity. But this does not mean that the relation to the other is inherently or essentially negative. Rather only the other is capable of satisfying the desire for recognition, which is at the same time a desire for an other. "Self-consciousness attains its satisfaction only in another self-consciousness."[14] There is no reason to interpret this satisfaction necessarily in a narrow, self-directed sense, according to which the other might be deemed "inessential" or as not counting. There is reason to take such satisfaction in an ethical sense, in which the other would be essential; that is, the other would count. Believing at first that it has no need of the other, the self makes the discovery that it needs and depends on the very other that it originally deemed "unessential." This is more than a "decentering" of the subject. It is an inversion of the original standpoint that transforms the subject into a potential intersubjective-ethical partner.

The Double Significations
in the Concept of Recognition

As we have seen, the double significations of the concept of recognition are rooted in the self-repulsing subjectivity that is the opposite of itself, that is, at once itself and the opposite determination of itself. Recognition implies that subjectivity is intersubjectivity, and intersubjectivity introduces additional possibilities of double signification, which Hegel plays on in the course of his analysis. Double signification in turn creates possibilities for dramatic reversals in "self-understanding" on the various levels of recognition. Reversals in turn

14. *PhG*, 138.

mean that the "truth" of subjectivity may turn out to be the opposite of what originally seemed to be.[15]

As immediate, each self operates with the presumption of being absolute. According to Hegel, desire signifies a condition of natural egoism in which the self's satisfaction is the end to which everything else is regarded as merely instrumental and subordinate. Natural egoism is immediate, parochial, and abstract; it excludes the other, difference, and relation. For this reason, the confrontation with the other is experienced as an abrupt self-transcendence, that is, a plunge into a relation that "others" or alters the self. In Hegel's words: "Self-consciousness is confronted by an other self-consciousness. It has come out of itself. This has a double [equivocal] significance: first, it has lost itself, because it finds itself as an *other being*. Second, it has thereby canceled [*aufgehoben*] the other, because it does not look upon the other as essential, but rather sees only *itself* in *other*."[16]

This analysis of the encounter with the other recalls Fichte's *Anstoß* and *Aufforderung*. The presence of the other precipitates a crisis in abstract parochial self-identity. The "shock" or upsurge of the other is immediate and underivable. The encounter with an other calls into question the immediate natural solipsism or naive self-identity. The encounter with the other reveals that naive or parochial self-identity is exclusive. The self achieves its identity by excluding the other. The other constitutes a shock to this naive parochial identity, which works an immediate change. The self now finds itself as other, or as "othered." The presence of the other signifies a loss of the original naive certitude, and this may be experienced as a loss of self.

If one seeks to avert or shun the encounter with the other in order to recover or restore the exclusive *Fürsichsein*, the simple identity I = I, one merely persists in the narrow, parochial, and "thin self" of natural egoism and solipsism. Thus natural solipsism becomes *Eigensinn*, a self-seeking that seeks to preserve the abstract, simple, and exclusive self-identity. Moreover, there is a connection between abstract identity and the abstract immediacy of self-consciousness. Just as abstract identity excludes the particular, and proves itself to be a false infinite, so also immediate self-identity is constituted by excluding what is other. This exclusion implies a hierarchy: the excluded is not merely alien but of lesser importance and value, that is, inessential, while the self that excludes assumes a posture of superiority. This could take several forms, for example, an aggressive rejection and/or elimination of the other, or a flight from the other and retreat within oneself, as in Hegel's discussion of the beautiful soul. To persist in such exclusive parochial *Fürsichsein*, or simple identity, is to be

---

15. Ever since his early essay contrasting ancient and modern skepticism, Hegel incorporated reversal into his conception of dialectical, social reason. For a discussion, see my *Recognition*, chaps. 5–6.

16. *PhG*, 141. Translation is my own.

unable to recognize the other *as other*. Such is the peril of nominalism and abstract identity. As Hegel observes, the self does not regard the other as essential or substantial and so finds only *itself* in the other.

It should be noted that being-for-self, or *Fürsichsein*, has two distinct senses for Hegel:[17] an immediate or abstract sense, namely, the first-person "I," and a mediated or more concrete sense, namely, the first-person plural, or "We." Immediate *Fürsichsein* is abstract, formal, and empty.[18] Practically expressed in action it is egoism, or *Eigensinn*. For this reason, immediate being-for-self (*Fürsichsein*) is only a starting point for recognition, not its foundation. Recognition is a process of development from simple *immediate Fürsichsein* to intersubjectively mediated and qualified *Fürsichsein*, namely, from the I to the We. The We designates the self as mediated and enlarged through the mediation of the other; it is a mutual enrichment and expansion of the initial *Fürsichsein*. *Fürsichsein* in this second, enlarged, intersubjective sense is a result of being recognized by the other, and of experiencing relation to the other no longer as a bondage but as freedom, that is, being at home with oneself in the other. This *Fürsichsein* is no longer an abstract, but a mediated, differentiated identity in which both self and other are *aufgehoben*.

It is crucial to note that the *self-othering* or alteration of which Hegel speaks is occasioned by the *other*. This means that the other is a condition of self-othering, and for this very reason *the other cannot be collapsed into the self-othering or self-positing of the first*. The other is the "objective" condition of self-othering. Conversely, self-othering, or the self's "inner" diremption from itself, is the "subjective" condition of relation to other. *Self-othering and the other are correlative and should not be confused or identified*. The self's alteration (or self-loss) consists in its discovery that its putative universality is merely presumptive parochialism. The upsurge of the other is the self's discovery that it is not universal but rather is a particular opposed to another particular. This is a reversal of the initial naive, immediate self-understanding. The starting point was that the self is absolute, unqualified, and not a mere par-

---

17. Levinas fails to observe this distinction and so interprets Hegelian self-consciousness as a straightforward egological system of identity. In this interpretation the other can only be instrumental to self-coincidence and self-identity. (See Levinas, "Substitution," in *The Levinas Reader*, ed. Sean Hand [Oxford: Basil Blackwell, 1989], 89, 91, 103, 116.)

18. *Fürsichsein* denotes both a *Gestalt des Bewusstseins* and a logical category. See Hegel, *Wissenschaft der Logik, Werke*, TWA, 5:174, hereafter abbreviated as *WL*; English translation: *Hegel's Science of Logic*, trans. A. V. Miller (New York: Humanities Press, 1969), 157, hereafter abbreviated as *SL*. As a logical concept, being-for-itself (*Fürsichsein*) is similar to Leibniz's concept of a monad; it is the center of a network of relations. (*WL*, 5:174 ff.; *SL*, 157 ff. The monad concept goes back to atomism.) However, Leibniz's monad has "no windows"; all its apparent relations to and interaction with others are due to divinely preestablished harmony. In contrast, Hegel's being-for-self not only has windows, but the windows are open. Everything is related to and qualified by everything else. The self is *for itself* only by being-for-itself *for an other*. Each is for itself by not being the other, by excluding the other, and yet this apparently exclusive *Fürsichsein* depends on the very other it excludes!

ticular; but this posture self-destructs and the truth turns out to be the opposite of what it was originally taken to be: the "absolute self" is a particular!

This reversal leads to the second moment in the process of recognition, namely, opposition between particulars. The issue here is the cancellation or superseding of being-other. In Hegel's words: "It must cancel this its other-being [*Anderssein*]. This is the cancellation of the first equivocal meaning and is itself the creation of a second equivocal meaning. First, it must proceed to cancel the other as an independent being in order thereby to become certain of itself as an independent being. Second, when it cancels this other, it cancels it-self, for this other is itself." [19] Again there are two, irreducible yet mutually related and conditioning sublations, and both are ambiguous. First the other must be sublated. This sublation is ambiguous in that it presents the possibilities of the elimination of the other or depriving the other of his "otherness" or strangeness, that is, entering into relation and community with the other. Second it means that being-other must also be overcome. This is likewise ambiguous. The first possibility is that to negate the other is to negate oneself insofar as one depends on the other. The second is to negate or decenter oneself, that is, not to insist on one's own way or on one's rights. This apparent self-negation opens up the possibility of an affirmative relation to the other.

We have seen that the encounter with the other challenges the self in its presumed absolute independence and is at the same time a "fall" into particularity. The self is not in fact absolute or unrelated but a particular in relation to another particular. This "loss of self" must be overcome. Being-other, self-estrangement, or not-being-what-one-is, is intolerable, and must be canceled (*aufgehoben*). Being-other, the fall into particularity, must be canceled. This means that the condition of self-othering, namely, the opposing other, must be sublated. This *sublation of the other* presents two further possibilities.

One possibility is to cancel the other by eliminating her. However, Hegel shows that this option is self-defeating; for if the other is simply eliminated, this deprives the self of the possibility of the other's recognition, which the self needs and on which it depends. Thus to cancel the other is at the same time to cancel oneself. The principle is that what is done to the other is also done to the self, and vice versa.

The second possibility is to cancel the otherness or alien character of the other by entering into relation and mediation with the other. The opposition between self and other may be transcended and overcome in a way that transforms the relation between self and other. In this case the self negates itself, that is, its exclusive parochial identity. Since this identity is expressed primarily at the level of immediate desire, which regards the other as nonessential, this self-negation is not really negative. Rather what is negated here are the negative limitations of parochial self-identity that exclude the other or lead to

19. *PhG*, 141–142; *PhS*, 111.

its coercion and domination. In other words, the parochial self is negated, enlarged, and opened up to what is other. This recognition means that it renounces domination and ceases to dominate the other. This is the third moment or phase in the process of recognition. Hegel formulates this transformation in the language of dialectical doubling: "This equivocal sublation of its equivocal other-being is likewise an equivocal return into itself. First, through the sublation of the other-being it gets itself back, because it becomes once more self-same through the sublation of its other-being [*seines Andersseins*]. Second, it gives the other self-consciousness back to itself, for it was conscious of itself in the other; it cancels its being in the other [*sein Sein im Andern*], and lets the other go free." [20]

The starting point of the process of recognition is the apparent loss of self before the other, or conversely, an apparent loss of the other owing to the inability to see anything but oneself in the other. The second phase is the attempt to cancel the self-othering, which can take two forms: elimination and/or domination of the other, or finding some accommodation with the other. The former involves eliminating the other, or compelling the other to recognize. Either form of violence is self-subverting in Hegel's view. Hegel believes that the concept of recognition must take the second path. This means that the self may "return" to itself out of its "othered" state, but it can do so only if it abandons mastery and domination. The recognition that is needed cannot be coerced or controlled. Mutual-reciprocal recognition is possible only if coercion is renounced. The authentic "cancellation" of other-being means that the other is not eliminated but allowed to go free and affirmed. But if the other is allowed to go free, this means that it is affirmed, not simply in its identity, but also in its difference. Without the release and allowing of the other to be as *other, in its difference*, the 'We' would be merely an abstract, parochial identity. The release and affirmation of the other is constitutive of the determinately universal identity of the 'We'. The 'We' is not a return to abstract, parochial self-identity of the original self-certain I. It is a determinate universal that reflects both the common identity and individual differences. Releasement of the other is the condition for the other's release of the self and the self's "return to itself" from "being-other," both of which constitute the We qua determinate universal.

The self's return to itself out of self-othering is not simply a restoration of the original parochial and abstract self-identity. It is not a simple satisfaction of desire, a filling of the lack by consumption of the object. Rather the original absolute self-identity of desire is decentered and relativized by relation to other, while being enlarged and legitimated by the other's recognition. This return to self in freedom is intersubjectively mediated. The condition under which the self can pass through the other and the other's freedom and return to itself affirmatively is that coercion and mastery must be given up. The inter-

20. *PhG*, 142; *PhS*, 112.

subjectively mediated return to self is possible only if the self releases the other and allows the other to go free.[21] This mutual releasement, or "letting be," connotes not indifference but allowing the other to be and granting the other freedom. "Letting be" means to renounce domination, to renounce seizing on the other's possibilities and freedom. Renunciation of violence toward the other is a self-limitation and decentering of the ego, but at the same time it is a liberation of the self from its natural solipsism and immediate desire. Thus the "natural subject of desire" undergoes an ethical transformation. Return to self out of otherness is not a return to the status quo ante recognition but a development to a higher level, mediated by the acknowledgment of the other in its difference.

Note that the pattern of mutual recognition differs from the pattern of desire (*Begierde*). Instead of simple self-coincidence through seizing on, negating, and consuming the object (as in desire), recognition is a mediated self-coincidence made possible by and conditioned on allowing the other to be what it is, a letting the other go free. This is Hegel's version of *Gelassenheit*.[22] Not only must the other be allowed to be; the other's free, uncoerced recognition is crucial to the self. The recognition that is needed and really counts is one that is not at the disposal of the self. The self depends on and is bound up with an other that cannot be cognitively or emotionally mastered. The accomplishment of genuine mutual-reciprocal recognition requires the renunciation of mastery and domination. Thus the resulting enlarged self-identity results from a joint reciprocal action that is not completely under the control of the self. As we shall see later, this enlarged self-identity involves risk and courage.

The upshot of the process of recognition turns out to be the opposite of that originally intended. The putative "absolute self" is no longer absolute but is decentered, qualified by and dependent on the other. The other whose presence initially alienated the self, and which the self sought to eliminate, turns out to be that on which the self depends, and with whom the self must peaceably coexist. Conversely, the self that undergoes loss and alienation before the other cannot overcome this alienation by itself. Rather such alienation is overcome only in *mutual-reciprocal releasement*. Cancellation of self-othering (internal diremption and alienation) is correlative with and conditioned on letting the other go free. This is the meaning of Hegel's assertion that self-consciousness attains satisfaction only in and through another self-consciousness.

21. It is striking that Hegel uses the same verb (*entlassen*) to refer to reciprocal recognition that he uses to refer to the Idea releasing itself into nature (*E*, §244).

22. Hegel is no less appreciative of Meister Eckhart than is Heidegger. Hegel's concept of the universal as love that does not dominate its particular may not be far from Eckhart's vision, but translated into the form and language of holism. (*WL*, TWA 6:277). For a discussion, see Reiner Schürmann, *Meister Eckhart* [*Studies in Phenomenology and Existential Philosophy*] (Bloomington: Indiana University Press, 1978), 113, 190, 245. Schürmann writes, "It was this very concept of a totality at the beginning and at the end of releasement, unfolding itself without a why, that was to enchant Friedrich Hegel five centuries later" (p. 113).

This process and relation to the other cannot be one-sided. The attempt to constitute or to determine the relationship from one side is the essence of violence and violation. If the desire for recognition is to be fulfilled and find satisfaction, each side must count for the other, and mastery must be renounced. Freedom and recognition require each side do something; freedom is won, not by dominating, but by uniting with another freedom. As a fundamentally intersubjective *action*, recognition must be two-sided and reciprocal. In Hegel's words,

> This movement of self-consciousness in relation to another self-consciousness has been set forth as the doing of the one. But this action has the double significance of being just as much the doing of the one as the doing of the other. For this other is likewise independent, self-determining, and there is nothing in it except what originates through it. The first does not have a merely passive object before it as in the case of desire. Rather the other is an independent being existing for itself. Consequently the first may not use the other for its own ends, unless the other does *for itself* what the first does. The movement [of recognition] is therefore without qualification the doubled movement of both self-consciousnesses. Each sees the other do the same that it does. Each does itself what it requires of the other, and does what it does only insofar as the other does the same. A one-sided action would be useless, since what is supposed to happen can only come about through the joint action of both.[23]

Here the transcendental-logical analysis of the *concept* of recognition points beyond itself to the necessity of a reciprocal joint *action*. Demonstrating the necessity of such joint action is the limit of logical-conceptual analysis. The renunciation of violence toward the other requires a decentering of the ego; such decentering is not a purely intellectual act. However, if the process of recognition is a doubled movement, a joint mutual action, the self is both restricted owing to its releasement of the other and enriched owing to the contribution of the other to the resulting corporate identity. Neither self is by itself "the" universal We; both selves must contribute to and subordinate/sublate their private dimensions in their corporate identity. That corporate identity in turn must preserve individual difference; only then can it be determinately, and not merely abstractly, universal. Only under such conditions are reciprocal recognition and *affirmative* self-knowledge in the other possible. The universal We that emerges here is a mediated intersubjective universality. It is not an egologically construed transcendental unity of apperception, not a higher nominalism, but a posttranscendental, mediated determinate social universality.

Hegel's account of the joint reciprocal action of mutual recognition is cast in the formal scheme of a syllogism. We could call this the "syllogism of recognition." In Hegel's words,

23. *PhG*, 142; *PhS*, 112.

Each extreme exchanges its determinacy and makes a complete transition into its opposite. As consciousness it comes outside of itself. However in its self-transcendence it also abides in itself and it is conscious of its self-transcendence. It is for consciousness that it immediately is and is not another consciousness. Likewise this other is only for itself, when it cancels itself as [pure] being-for-itself and is for itself only in the [independent] being-for-itself of its other [*nur im Fürsichsein des andern für sich ist*]. Each is the mediating term for the other, through which each mediates itself with itself and coincides with itself. Each is for itself and for the other an immediate self-existing being, which at the same time is such only through this mediation. They recognize themselves as reciprocally acknowledging each other.[24]

This is the "syllogism of recognition"; each term is both extreme and mean. Each self must serve as mediator for the other, while receiving in turn mediation—that is, recognition—from the other. Only through such reciprocal action can the self "return" to itself out of its "othered" state, by gaining itself in the other's recognition. Yet this syllogism contains a paradox: Recognition is both needed and yet cannot be coerced. If it is coerced, the resulting recognition is phony and inauthentic, as Hegel's analysis of mastery shows. Affirmative self-recognition in the other cannot be coerced; it must be freely proffered by the other, who in turn must be allowed to be.

Hegel characterizes affirmative self-knowledge in other as being at home in an other (*bei sich im Anderen*). Being at home in an other is the existential phenomenological form and genesis of ethics, right, and the concept of *Geist*. The attainment of such concrete universality or spirit (*Geist*) means that being with other is no longer a limitation or restriction on freedom but rather an enhancement and concrete actualization of freedom. Conversely, freedom is intersubjective and social in its actualization; its actuality is not to be located in the *cogito* but in a relation in which being-for-other is equivalent to being-for-self, and vice versa.

Mastery and Slavery as a Determinate Shape of Recognition

The foregoing is an analysis of the general concept of recognition and its structure as set forth in Hegel's *Phenomenology*. It is an analysis made *für uns*, that is, a conceptual ontological analysis of possibility that brackets the experience of ordinary consciousness in the natural attitude.[25] Hegel is clear about the different standpoints from which recognition is considered, namely, the transcendental-logical and the phenomenological description of ordinary consciousness: "We will now consider this pure concept of recognizing, the dou-

24. *PhG*, 143; *PhS*, 112–113.
25. For a further discussion, see my *Recognition*, chaps. 5–8.

bling of self-consciousness in its unity, *as it appears for the self-consciousness.*
First we shall set forth the inequality of the two, or the middle as it steps out
into the extremes, and which, as extreme, stands in opposition, such that the
one is only recognized, and the other is only recognizing."[26] We are led from a
conceptual analysis of the concept of recognition to a phenomenological account of the life and death struggle and to master and slave. This latter is a determinate instance of recognition that is unequal: one party recognizes the other
but is not recognized in turn, and the other is recognized but does not recognize. For this reason master and slave represent a *deficient* realization of the
process of recognition.

Master/slave is preceded by and is the outcome of a life and death struggle.
The life and death struggle presupposes that the parties confront each other in
the absence of mediating social institutions. This is a methodological abstraction employed in discussions of the so-called state of nature (*Naturzustande*).
Hegel regards this abstraction as a fiction constructed for purposes of analysis.
But although Hegel mentions and discusses the state of nature, it is clear that
he does not join with the liberal thinkers such as Hobbes in making use of it to
explain the origin of society or the state from a prior presocial condition. As
far as Hegel is concerned, real individuals are social, living in communities,
for example, the family. Hegel is not concerned with the question of the origin
of the social-communal sphere or the state. Insofar as this invites speculations
concerning the transition from a presocial condition of isolated atomic individuals to the social condition, Hegel would reject the question as an invitation
to the fallacy of misplaced concreteness. He is not concerned with how the
state originated but with what the state is. He remarks that although the state
may originate in violence, this is not its justification. Hegel focuses on the latter question.

Granting that individuals are assumed to confront each other in the absence
of social mediating institutions, this implies that they are still immersed in
nature, that is, in uncivilized conditions. Thus the problem of recognition here
is to show that one is more than mere nature. What each seeks is not the recognition of the mere fact of his existence but the recognition of his freedom.
Freedom is the possibility of abstracting from every determinacy, including
life itself. Freedom thus can transcend mere natural existence; this possibility
of self-transcendence is concretely demonstrated by a willingness to risk one's
life. Moreover, freedom is mere possibility until it is asserted, and to assert it
is to run a risk. In the absence of social institutions, even common language,
the parties are absolutely uncertain of each other. The risks of freedom are
even greater, and yet each needs recognition from the other. Consequently under such conditions, each seeks to compel the other to recognize and acknowledge it.

26. *PhG*, 143; *PhS*, 112. Italics mine.

The relation is such that each tests both itself and the other through a life and death struggle. They must undergo this struggle, because they must elevate the private certainty each has of being-for-itself, to *truth in the other* and for itself. It is only in the risking of life that freedom is proved, i.e., that it is proved that the essence of self-consciousness does not consist in mere being, nor in the immediate way that it first appears, nor in the immersion in the expanse of life. Rather *freedom is proved by showing that there is nothing in consciousness which cannot be reduced by it to a vanishing moment,* by showing, in other words, that it is pure being-for-self.[27]

Thus the demand for recognition initiates a life and death struggle.

However, if the other is simply eliminated, his death is an abstract total negation that produces the opposite of what is desired. For what each seeks is not the death of the other so much as his recognition. If the other is killed, there is no possibility of recognition. Consequently some way has to be found to stop the struggle for recognition short of death. Abstract negation, or murder, is counterproductive as well as risky since going after the death of the other may bring about the opposite of what was intended. Prosecution of the struggle to the point of death would not show genuine transcendence of facticity; it would merely show that both despised life. However, the point is not to end life but to secure recognition and intersubjective legitimation of one's own certainty. This requires that abstract negation of murder and death be displaced in favor of a negation appropriate to the kind of being that consciousness is, namely, a determinate or limited negation. This is what happens in the constitution of master and slave.

Hegel depicts this determinate negation in the following way. One of the parties to the struggle begins to realize that life, which he was hitherto willing to risk for recognition, is just as "essential" or important to him as recognition. Death would mean the absolute end of all possibilities. This party fears death, and fearing death, prefers to survive, even if that means giving up his claim for recognition. He renounces his claim to and demand for recognition; better endure this determinate (partial) negation of recognition than face death, the absolute master. However, to survive, he must give up his claim to recognition and become an object for the master; that is, he becomes a slave. The other, who has "won" the struggle, becomes master. The master does not fear death and does not undergo a determinate negation. His victory is that he is recognized as master by the slave.

Note that master and slave, as miserable an institution as it is, nevertheless represents a relative ethical-cultural advance over the sheer slaughter that would take place if the desire for recognition had remained absolute and unqualified. Odd as it may seem, master and slave is a "positive" development in that coercion, struggle, and violence are restrained and stopped short of mur-

27. *PhG*, 144; *PhS*, 113–114. My emphasis.

der. Thus master/slave represents a cultural development away from sheer savagery and violence. However, while master/slave may represent a restraint on violence, it also institutionalizes violence. Violence is thus *aufgehoben*, preserved in the inequality of recognition: The master is recognized by the slave but does not reciprocally recognize the slave. The master is essential, substantial, while the slave is inessential, accidental. The fundamental inequality of the substance-accidents relationship is institutionalized in the intersubjective-social shape of domination and submission, lordship and bondage.

The master has no fear of death. Through successfully risking his life, the master proves that he transcends the natural world, and his own natural existence. Conversely, the slave prefers bare survival to death, which shows that he is in thrall to the fear of death, the absolute master. In negating and stifling his desire for recognition, the slave not only gives up his independence, he also complies with and carries out in himself the master's attempted negation and nullification of him. He sinks to the level of a mere commodity, not only for the master but also for himself. His very life and the means of sustaining it are subject to an other. He labors for an other. Thus the master relates immediately to the slave through the threat and fear of death, and to the world mediately through the slave.

This alters the master's relation to the world. The master relates to the world by interposing the slave between himself and the world. The prototypical world-relation in the *Phenomenology* is that of desire. But now the slave labors for the master, procuring and fashioning objects desired by the master, who is spared the labor necessary to satisfy his desire.

> What mere desire cannot do, namely, have done with the thing, the master succeeds in doing, and he achieves the enjoyment of the thing and gratification of his desire. Desire alone could not do this because of the independence of the thing. The master however, has interposed the slave between himself and things, and can appropriate to himself only the dependent aspect of things, and so is pure enjoyment. The independent aspect of things he leaves to the slave who works upon it.[28]

For Hegel, the relation of mastery and slavery is inherently unstable and contains the seeds of its own downfall. The master leads a life of pure enjoyment and satisfaction unsullied by laboring on things. He directly appropriates and enjoys things (that is, as worked over and preshaped by the slave). He becomes a passive consumer. And since the slave works not to satisfy his own desire but only that of the master, his labor is inessential.[29] What the slave does is actually the doing of the master. The master remains the absolute power before which the independent being of things is negated and reshaped.

28. *PhG*, 146; *PhS*, 115–116.
29. Note that Hegel uses the substance/accidents scheme to clarify and explain the master/slave relationship.

The master obtains the needed recognition under such conditions. The paradox of mastery is that it has "won" the recognition of a *slave*, whom it considers to be inessential and unimportant. What then is this recognition really worth? Owing to his fear of death, the slave accepts the status of a thing to survive. The slave has surrendered his claims to recognition and independent being-for-self (*Fürsichsein*) and exists as a commodity or property of the master. But this means that the recognition that the master receives from the slave is uncertain and deficient at best. Moreover, the master despises the slave as unessential and holds his recognition to be unreliable, unsubstantial, and worthless. And yet the master is dependent on such "worthless" recognition.

> The unessential consciousness [of the slave] is merely an object for the master; nevertheless it constitutes the truth of the master's self-certainty. But it is obvious that this object does not correspond to its concept. Rather the object in which the master has accomplished his mastery is quite different than an independent consciousness. What confronts the master now is not an independent, but a dependent consciousness. Therefore the master is not certain of the truth of his being-for-self, because his truth is found in an unessential consciousness and in an unessential action.[30]

The master's goal was to gain recognition, that is, independent confirmation and legitimation of his freedom. But in spite of his victory over the slave, the master remains uncertain of his own truth, precisely because the slave's recognition is coerced. The "truth" of mastery is the servile consciousness. Although the slave can and does "recognize" the master, his recognition, as slave, is deficient because it is coerced, and thus provides the master an unreliable, distorted recognition. Believing the slave, the master lapses into false consciousness. Not believing the slave, the master must remain suspicious and "on guard." Thus the "winner" loses.

The truth of the master is the slave. That is, the reduction of the slave to a mere commodity makes explicit what domination and mastery are. Moreover, having reduced the other to a slave, to something unessential, the master must now find the *truth* of his self-certainty in the slave. This is impossible. For the slave is no longer an *independent self-consciousness which alone can jointly elevate self-certainty to truth*. Truthful intersubjective communication requires that the recognition of the other must be authentic, that is, freely bestowed. It cannot be coerced or forced and remain genuine. Since the slave does only what the master wants, the master cannot receive from him a *genuinely independent recognition*. So the master can never be intersubjectively "certain" of his self-certainty: "Therefore the master is not certain of his being-for-self as the truth, because his truth is found in an unessential consciousness and unessential ac-

30. *PhG*, 147–148; *PhS*, 116–117.

tion."[31] Even the slave's confirmation of mastery is worthless because the slave is *for the master* unessential.

Since the slave is unessential, merely an extension of the master, recognition by the slave does not count even for the master. The slave is not genuinely other, it is only "the master's other." Mastery represents a vain attempt to coerce recognition, that is, reduce mediation by other to self-mediation. Mastery succeeds merely in reducing the other to a slave, only to discover that coerced recognition is both phony and worthless. Phony recognition is the truth of mastery. Thus we find a reversal: mastery, as sheer self-affirmation, turns out to be self-subverting and brings about the opposite of what it intended. Mastery ends in failure, a dead end that can only be maintained by force.

The Servile Consciousness

The analysis of servitude is probably the most famous passage in the *Phenomenology*. Hegel observes that servitude, as well as mastery, proves to be the opposite of what it at first seems to be. "Just as mastery showed that it is the opposite of what it intends to be, so servitude will, in its working out, become the opposite of what it immediately is."[32] Thus he highlights the reversal (*Umkehr*) of situation. At the outset the master is pure being-for-self (*Fürsichsein*) that suppresses being-for-other (*Füreinanderssein*), and conversely the slave is pure being-for-other (*Füreinanderssein*) that suppresses its being-for-self (*Fürsichsein*). What is merely for an other has surrendered any intrinsic being of its own.

Hegel considers the servile consciousness first in its subordination to mastery. The servile consciousness fears death, and surrenders its claim to recognition in order to survive. Anxiety over death is constitutive of the servile consciousness: "The servile consciousness does not have anxiety about this or that particular, or for a few isolated moments. Rather it is 'in *Angst*' about its entire existence. For it has felt the fear of death, *the absolute master*. It has fallen apart; it has trembled throughout its being and everything firm and fixed in it has been shaken."[33] Fear of the mundane master is the occasion for fear or anxiety (*Angst*) about death, the "absolute master." Death is a negativity that shakes and dissolves everything solid and substantial; the fear of death leads the servile consciousness to renounce the need for recognition. We have previously pointed out the terrible price of negating the desire for recognition. The

31. Master/slave can also be read as a demonstration of the futility of conceiving intersubjective praxis in terms of a metaphysical substance/accidents scheme (e.g., Spinoza), or in terms of the ontological primacy of the ego (Descartes, Husserl, Sartre).

32. *PhG*, 147–148; *PhS*, 117–118.

33. *PhG*, 148. Kojève has no trouble demonstrating that Hegel anticipates Heidegger's existential analysis of finitude and that in certain respects Hegel's analysis is superior in that it situates death anxiety in a socio-ontological matrix. On the ontological level Dasein is being toward death, but it is the master that brings this ontological possibility to light and plays it against the slave.

slave complies with and carries out on himself the master's attempted negation and nullification of him. The master could not make the slave a slave without the slave's own cooperation. Thus the slave sinks to the level of a mere commodity, not only for the master, but also for himself. This renunciation of being-for-self (*Fürsichsein*) goes hand in hand with the transformation of the slave into a dependent thing, a commodity laboring for the master. The servile transformation is a flight from sheer negativity into objectivity, but in a way that denies or flees from freedom. The flight of the slave from death reveals the slave is in thrall to its existence. Hegel gives a brilliant account of the genesis of the inauthentic servile consciousness first described by Fichte.[34]

However, the servile consciousness undergoes a transformation and reversal not unlike mastery. The world-transforming power of negation, or being-for-self (*Fürsichsein*), which is first intuited ultimately in death, externally and proximately in the master, is discovered to be the slave's own power. "Although the fear of the lord is the beginning of wisdom, it has not yet occurred to consciousness that it is *for itself* being-for-self. But through his labor the slave comes to himself, i.e., becomes conscious of what he really is [*Fürsichsein*]."[35] In an important move Hegel locates the inversion of the servile consciousness in labor. The possibility of liberation of the slave from his thralldom lies in the transformation of the world by his labor.

Under conditions of involuntary labor, the slave must learn to restrain his desire and postpone gratification. The master, not the slave, immediately appropriates, consumes, and enjoys the products of labor. The master leads a life of pleasure. But this leads to decadence: "In the moment which corresponds to desire in the master's consciousness, it seemed that the aspect of the unessential relation to the thing fell to the lot of the slave, since the thing retained its independence. Desire has reserved to itself the pure negating of the object and therein its unmixed self-feeling. This satisfaction of the master is for this reason a vanishing one, for it lacks the objective side [of things] and permanence. In contrast, labor is restrained desire, a delayed vanishing, or, labor shapes and forms."[36] The slave's labor is desire held in check, a delayed gratification. Through this delayed gratification, the slave negates his thralldom, transforms himself, and overcomes his servilty.

Although the slave lacks direct enjoyment of the products of his labor, he nevertheless comes to see that the shaping and producing of objects is the key

34. See his first introduction to the *Wissenschaftslehre* in *Science of Knowledge*, trans. Peter Heath and John Lachs (New York: Appleton Century Crofts, 1970), 3–78. There Fichte isolates a strange consciousness that thinks of itself as a mere thing. It is not yet conscious of its freedom, but depends on external things to give it self-identity and solidity. This deficient mode of self-consciousness has many philosophical progeny: it becomes Hegel's servile consciousness, Kierkegaard's aesthetic stage of existence, Nietzsche's ascetic ideal, Heidegger's inauthentic existence, and Sartre's bad faith.

35. *PhG*, 148; *PhS*, 117–118.

36. Ibid.

to objective permanence and independence. "It is precisely in laboring, where it initially seemed to find only an alien significance [namely, working for someone else] that the slave rediscovers his own mind and independent significance."[37] He becomes *for himself* being-for-self, and when this occurs, the slave has overcome his self-alienation [expressed in the primacy of being-for-other (*Füreinanderssein*)].

Note that in this account the slave "comes to himself" not through the mediation of intersubjective recognition but through labor. This raises the question whether Hegel is consistent. Does he really think that recognition is superfluous for self-identity? On the other hand, if recognitive self-identity is a joint two-sided action that presupposes, requires, and needs an other as a condition of its possibility, does the slave "come to himself" through labor only partially? In a useful study, Habermas shows that Hegel's Jena philosophy of *Geist* is shaped by three concrete categories—language, tools, and family, which correspond respectively to three patterns of dialectical relation: symbolic representation, labor, and interaction.[38] In the Jena *Realphilosophie* these diverse elements appear in a framework Hegel later abandoned. Subsequently he unified the elements of the philosophy of *Geist* under the concept of intersubjective interaction, thus depriving the concept of labor of its previously independent role.[39] Because the *Phenomenology* reflects Hegel's Jena period, labor appears to be an independent basis of being-for-self (*Fürsichsein*), which in turn suggests that recognition is superfluous for self-identity, or at least superfluous for the slave's identity. Habermas contends that this is not the case. He observes that Hegel had not yet brought his views on the nature of labor and intersubjectivity into coherence and unity,[40] but eventually subordinated labor to the concept of recognition.

Consequently, important as Hegel's analysis of master and slave is, it is possible to overestimate its significance. A prime example of overestimation is afforded by Kojève, for whom master and slave constitutes the central theme of Hegel's *Phenomenology*.[41] There are several problems with Kojève's interpretation: He passes over the fact that the *Phenomenology* is supposed to function

---

37. *PhG*, 149; *PhS*, 118.

38. Jürgen Habermas, "Arbeit und Interaktion: Bemerkungen zu Hegels Jena Philosophie des Geistes," cited in *Frühe politische Systeme*, Hrsg. G. Göhler (Frankfurt: Ullstein, 1974), 786 ff. English translation: "Labor and Interaction: Remarks on Hegel's Jena *Philosophy of Mind*, in *Theory and Practice*, trans. John Viertel (Boston: Beacon Press, 1974), 142–169.

39. Ibid., 807–812; English: 162–167.

40. This may be a false antithesis, since Hegel treats labor and economic relations—at least in the modern state—as involving complex forms of recognition. On the other hand, Harris contends that even in the Jena manuscripts, including the *System der Sittlichkeit* (1801), recognition is the medium of social existence, although it is not always as clearly phenomenologically displayed as it is in the *Phenomenology*. In the *Philosophie des Geistes 1803/04*, recognition is the general medium of political existence. See H. S. Harris, "The Concept of Recognition in Hegel's Jena Manuscripts," *Hegel-Studien 20* (Bonn: Bouvier Verlag, 1979), 234–235.

41. Kojève, *IRH*.

as the self-accomplishing skeptical introduction to Hegel's system and instead treats it as a philosophical anthropology, thereby truncating and abridging Hegel's intentions. As a result, Kojève collapses the distinction between the concept of recognition per se and master/slave as a particular determinate figure or instance of the concept of recognition. When this distinction is collapsed, the affirmative or positive dimensions of the concept of recognition, to wit, the very possibility of reciprocal recognition, are concealed and closed off. Contra Kojève, *master and slave do not exhaust the possibilities present in the concept of recognition.* Kojève misses or suppresses the reversal of the figure of the unhappy or servile consciousness alienated from itself, from world and from God, that occurs in Hegel's discussion of reason as an objective "in-the-world" dynamic structure. Hegel asserts that reason functions as the mediating link, the "between" of relationship, and consequently, since self-consciousness is reason, its previously negative relation to otherness changes into an affirmative one.[42] Further, Kojève overlooks the reciprocal recognition constitutive of the family, and of brother-sister relationships that Hegel describes in his discussion of Antigone's relationship with her brother.[43] Most important of all, Kojève overlooks or simply dismisses the affirmative reciprocal recognition that Hegel locates in forgiveness and the "reciprocal recognition that is the absolute spirit."[44] These passages in the *Phenomenology* bring out the affirmative reciprocal relation to other that is the telos of the concept of recognition.

Kojève's anthropological, master/slave interpretation of Hegel's *Phenomenology* tends to exaggerate the figure of the servile consciousness. It is true that for Hegel mastery is a dead end and that Hegel's genealogical history of self-consciousness continues through the figure of the slave. But it would be unwarranted to infer that the slave's coming to himself through labor makes mutual recognition superfluous for self-identity, or that self-identity is inherently ascetic, repressive, and exclusive, or that Hegel's system is an expression of the demand for and creation of meaning by the ascetic servile consciousness. For Hegel, the reason that mastery and slavery fail is that each is in its own way one-sided. Neither the immediacy and aestheticism of mastery nor the asceticism of the slave is acceptable. The point is to transcend the master/slave opposition, and this does not happen if meaning is oppressively imposed by masters on slaves, or if meaning is created through self-repression on the part of "self-liberating" slaves.[45] Recognition culminates, not in a logic of oppression or repression, but in a reciprocal relationship beyond such alternatives. In his *Early Theological Writings* Hegel put the point in this way: "To

---

42. *PhG*, 175–176; *PhS*, 139.
43. *PhG*, 325–326; *PhS*, 274–275.
44. *PhG*, 471; *PhS*, 408.
45. I shall deal with these issues more fully in the last chapter.

conceive is to dominate . . . but only in love one is at-one with the object, neither dominating it nor dominated by it."[46] However, in the *Phenomenology*, Hegel does not explicitly develop the alternative to master and slave. The figure of master and slave is repeated on higher levels, and remains oppositional. This is part of the project of showing that all shapes of consciousness subvert themselves. In his subsequent account of master and slave in the *Encyclopedia Philosophy of Spirit*, Hegel presents master and slave in light of the full dialectic of reciprocal recognition. He shows not only the opposition but also the transcendence of opposition and the move to mutual liberation and freedom.

46. Hegel, *Entwürfe über die Religion und Liebe* (1797–1798), TWA 1:242. Note that Hegel later changed his mind about *Begreifen*, as he discovered and developed his speculative dialectical conception of the *Begriff* that is like love in not dominating but rather allowing the other to be.

4

Recognition in the *Encyclopedia Philosophy of Spirit*

Introduction and Overview

The *Phenomenology of Spirit* (1807), as a self-accomplishing skepticism, proceeds by a process of skeptical self-subversion. Hegel shows that certain shapes of consciousness self-destruct and subvert themselves. He explores the negative dimensions of recognition—refusal, coercion, deception—although there are a few instances of affirmative reciprocal recognition. The *Encyclopedia*, by contrast, proceeds constructively. Here Hegel emphasizes the affirmative relationships based on reciprocal recognition. Reciprocal recognition has four main themes and elements that qualify and explicate reciprocity: autonomy, union with other, self-overcoming, and *Freilassen*, that is, an affirmation of the other in his singularity and difference.

The *Encyclopedia* account of the concept of recognition is at once abridged and yet more complex than the account in the *Phenomenology*. The philosophy of spirit presupposes the logic and the philosophy of nature, and is conceived as spirit's becoming conscious of itself, a "reversion" to self out of nature. The latter reversion is conceived as a gradual ethical-religious process wherein spirit liberates itself from nature and natural immediacy. Further, the outcome of master/slave is different from the *Phenomenology*. In the mature system, the possibility of a mutual recognition that transcends coercion and domination is clearly exhibited, and master and slave mutually and reciprocally achieve liberation together. From this perspective, the concept of reciprocal recognition is more completely developed in the *Encyclopedia* than in the *Phenomenology*. Moreover, the account of recognition merges with the account of freedom, such that mutual recognition is the medium of liberation from coercion and domination, and as such it results in a universal social consciousness, or We, that is central to objective *Geist* and ethical life (*Sittlichkeit*). The struggle for recognition that ended in master/slave has been consigned to a subordinate, transitory level of cultural history. Hegel holds that while slavery is part of human cultural history, it is not the foundation, much less the justification, of the state, nor does it necessarily belong to modern forms of recognition.

Further, Hegel's *Encyclopedia* discussion of recognition is not an account of the existential phenomenological genesis of spirit but is part of a larger philosophy of spirit that has been systematically differentiated into subjective, objective, and absolute. The account of recognition provides the transition from individual self-consciousness to universal self-consciousness, from subjective to objective spirit.[1] The pivotal significance of recognition leads Hegel to propose an important modification and interpretation of the basic principle of German idealism, the so-called self-identity of the ego, or I = I. This principle is easy to caricature and lends itself to a merely tautological interpretation of a solitary *ego cogito*. This appears to be subjective idealism, the view of consciousness as a notorious "prison" of subjectivity. However, such an interpretation reflects Hegel's own criticism of the idealist position as "subjective" idealism from Kant through Schelling. Hegel proposes something different.

Although the I = I is the principle of reason and freedom, its mere assertion is not tantamount to its actualization or actuality. Autonomy and rationality are not actual at the outset, but merely *an sich*, implicit or potential. They are results of a process that attains its true beginning only in its completion. Immediate self-consciousness, prior to its elaboration and development, is not yet fully aware of its own freedom. The immediate shape is one in which self-consciousness takes itself merely as an object or thing and as undifferentiated identity. This is the basis of Hegel's criticism, not only of Schelling (whose abstract identity Hegel criticizes as the night in which all cows are black), but also of Kant's formalism in ethics.[2] Hegel believes that since the abstract I = I of pure reason and abstract autonomy excludes difference, it is impossible for it to be normatively concrete and determinate; that is, it cannot generate or support any determinate duties.[3]

For Hegel, the other and the difference are crucial to determinacy and to normativity. This becomes clear in his exposition of the principle of idealism, or I = I, which has three *Stufen* of development; the second is not simply an extension of or derivative from the first:

1)   The first level represents the immediate particular self-consciousness in its simple self-identity, and in contradiction to this simple identity, its relation to

1. *E*, §417.

2. "To pit this single insight, that in the absolute everything is the same, against the full body of articulated cognition, . . . to palm off its absolute as night in which, as the saying goes, all cows are black—this is cognition naively reduced to vacuity" (*PhS*, 9).

3. This is clear from Hegel's early discussion of Kant in *Natural Law*, trans. T. M. Knox (Philadelphia: University of Pennsylvania Press, 1975), 76. Hereafter cited as *NL*.

an external object. Thus determined, self-consciousness is the certainty of itself and of its object, against which the object has the determination of being something only apparently independent, but in fact a nullity [*Nichtigen*]. This is the appetitive self-consciousness or *Begierde*.

2) In the second, the objective ego receives the determination of [being] *another ego*. Thus arises the relation of *one self-consciousness* to *another self-consciousness*, and between the two, the process of recognizing.[4] Here self-consciousness is no longer merely an individual self-consciousness; rather in self-consciousness the union of individuality and universality begins.

3) Further, the otherness [*Anderssein*] of the two selves standing over and against each other is sublated. These selves, while remaining independent, nevertheless become identical with each other. Thus emerges the third *Stufe*, the universal self-consciousness.[5]

In the first stage (*Stufe*) the I = I is abstract, expressing an identity that excludes difference and the other. Since Hegel regards the exclusion of difference as a primitive, immediate form of identity, he treats this identity here in the context of desire, or *Begierde*. Desire is an emptiness that attains satisfaction by consuming its object and demonstrating that its object is a nullity. When the object of desire is nullified, it shows itself to be merely instrumental to the satisfaction of desire, or self-coincidence.

Hegel wants to overcome the abstract, solipsistic principle of idealism together with its principle of empty, undifferentiated identity that vitiates it in both philosophy of nature (Schelling) and ethics (Kantian formalism). The central issue is the problem of the difference. The empty tautology of the I am I, or I = I, requires post-Cartesian, postidealist moves. We have already seen some of these, notably the doubling of self-consciousness, the *Aufforderung* (Fichte) and the divided ground of freedom (Schelling). For Hegel, the other is crucial to the consciousness of real difference, on which the possibility of self-consciousness, freedom, and reason depends. Hegel begins with the abstract self-identity, but only in order to transcend it. "In self-consciousness I am free; I do not relate to an other; I am at home with myself. The principle of truth and of freedom is that subject and object are identical (*gleich sind*)."[6] This assertion appears to situate Hegel within the Cartesian and Kantian transcendental tradition. However, Hegel differentiates himself from that position when he continues: "Here we have truth and freedom, but these are still merely *abstract*. . . . I am I, but *the difference* is completely lacking, I am only conscious of myself and know only of my own experience; the identity is too strong such

---

4. Italics in original.   5. *E*, §425 Zusatz.

6. Hegel, *Philosophy of Subjective Spirit*, ed. and trans. M. J. Petry, 3 vols. (Dordrecht: D. Reidel, 1979), 3:316. Volume 3 contains the Griesheim transcript of the 1825 lectures. This transcript has also been published by M. J. Petry as *G. W. F. Hegel: The Berlin Phenomenology* (Dordrecht: D. Reidel, 1981). This reference and all subsequent references are to the Griesheim manuscript in vol. 3 of the *Philosophy of Subjective Spirit*, hereafter cited as *PSS* 1825.

that the difference is missing, and for this reason self-consciousness is abstract rather than concrete identity."[7] This formulation recalls an earlier discussion in the *Philosophical Propadeutik*:

> What does the realization of self-consciousness mean? The concept of self-consciousness is the consciousness that relates to itself as pure ego; it is for itself. In this concept there is a difference between the ego as subject and the ego as object. But this is not a genuine difference because identity excludes other-being [*Anderssein*]. The pure self-consciousness lacks an objective realization, it lacks the shape of an other. Self-consciousness lacks *Dasein* (determinate existence); or, its concept has not yet been realized.[8]

The second level of development is an explicitly postidealist move, namely, recognition. The I is no longer simply self-identical, but is "othered." Prior to or apart from the other, self-identity remains abstract and immediate. The original I = I is a distinction without a difference, a merely empty and formal tautology. The self requires an other to objectify it in order to become conscious of its freedom. The other makes possible the separation of autonomous freedom from mere desire. In recognition, desire becomes sublimated to the ethical level. In this way the possibility of ethics and ethical life is bound up with the concept of recognition.

The other is *the difference* that differentiates the I = I. The interpersonal other first introduces serious difference into the ego. The other decenters self-consciousness and drives it beyond mere abstract identity or the I am I. When the self is "othered" and "differenced" by the other, this "shock of recognition" pushes the self beyond any merely subjective idealism, or solipsism. In the initial moment of recognition, I am not-I; the other is the condition of possibility of such self-othering. Hegel continues Schelling's thesis that the other is the mediator of objectivity and world to the self. Freedom and reason, as forms of the I = I, turn out to be intersubjective and social.

According to Hegel the distinction of individuality and universality arises in self-consciousness as a result of the doubling of consciousness and the process of recognition. The distinction between universal and particular, or at least the capacity to make it, is based on and/or a result of the distinction/difference between self and other. The universal therefore cannot be identified with the I = I as a particular ego, or even with a transcendental ego that remains solipsistic at its own level. The relevant universal is attained in a reciprocal, mediated union and relation between particular selves. For Hegel, the road to concrete, *differentiated* universality runs through the process of recognition. The other must be affirmed and allowed to be in his difference. Only on

---

7. *PSS* 1825, 316. Italics mine.

8. Hegel, *Texte zu Philosophischen Propadeutik, Werke*, Theorie Werkausgabe (Frankfurt: Suhrkamp, 1970), 4:83. Hereafter cited as *Propadeutik*.

this condition is the emergent 'We' a determinate universal. This means that the concrete or determinate universal is a fundamentally ethical and social conception and that the "universal consciousness" is not a transcendental ego but an intersubjective community.

That this universal is a social and ethical conception becomes explicit in the third *Stufe*. The second level introduced the other, the principle of difference, and the third level proceeds to a sublation of otherness (*Anderssein*). This sublation of otherness is not a return to abstract undifferentiated identity or the empty tautology of the I am I that excludes difference. Rather the sublation of otherness means the formation of an intersubjective or social totality: the I becomes a We. In an important move, Hegel asserts that the We requires an affirmative or positive self-knowledge in other. Such affirmative self-knowledge in other implies that the other is not simply a negation, nor is self-identity merely exclusive. The sublation of otherness means that isolated, atomic particularity is transcended; the limits of individuality are broken through and both a higher selfhood as well as an interpersonal-corporate union are achieved.

As mediated autonomy, freedom is not understood as radical isolation and difference but rather as a union with the other. Such an assertion of the identity between the independent selves raises the issue of fusion. But as will become clear, Hegel does not go the fusion route: His claim is rather that the subjects remain independent in their identity, and are identical in their independence. The truth of idealism as Hegel understands it includes a process of mutual recognition whereby an I becomes a We. Idealism therefore leads beyond "the subject" to a social universal or a community. Freedom and reason are not merely intersubjective-socially mediated but are themselves social.

Reciprocal Recognition

The account of recognition in the *Philosophy of Spirit* differs from the *Phenomenology*. Not that the two accounts are incompatible, but the fundamental conception is differently developed and nuanced. To be sure, the fundamental distinction between concept and its determinate appearance-instantiations is retained.[9] However, Hegel himself tends to blur this distinction somewhat because he discusses recognition as if master/slave were an integral aspect of it, rather than a contingent, deficient exemplification of its possibilities. On the

9. This distinction between concept and its *Wirklichkeit* is present in the mature system as a distinction between logic and *Realphilosophie*, a distinction that structures the *Lectures on the Philosophy of Religion* as well as the *Philosophy of Spirit* in the *Jena Realphilosophie 1805/06*. See Hegel, *Jenaer Systementwürfe III: Naturphilosophie und Philosophie des Geistes* [Philosophische Bibliotek 333] Hrsg. Rolf-Peter Horstmann (Hamburg: Felix Meiner, 1987). This is a selection of materials from the new critical edition of Hegel's *Werke*, Band 8. English translation of the *Philosophy of Spirit* only: *Hegel and the Human Spirit*, trans. Leo Rauch (Detroit: Wayne State University Press, 1983).

other hand, Hegel also clearly maintains that recognition does not necessarily involve conflict and opposition and that there can be recognition *ganz ohne Kampf*. Were that not so, love, and all the virtues, as well as marriage and the state (which is modeled after the determinate intersubjectivity of the family), would constitute oppressions. Moreover, in the *Encyclopedia* Hegel uses terminology that, while reminiscent of the Leibnizian monadological conception, nevertheless points beyond its external aggregation toward interpersonal/social relation and community. The ethical dimensions of recognition are developed, as are its social-psychological aspects. The realization of freedom through mutual recognition is emphasized, and the concept of freedom is developed both in negative (i.e., freedom from external influence) and positive dimensions (i.e., as being at home with self in other). The process of recognition ties these two dimensions together; recognition results in an ethical intersubjectivity that is fundamental for Hegel's theory of *Sittlichkeit* and theory of right.

The starting point once again is a confrontation, or zero mediation: "There is a self-consciousness for a self-consciousness, first of all immediately as an other for an other."[10] Hegel conceives such a confrontation between two selves understood as abstract or immediate identities. Their self-identities are abstract, immediate, and exclusive. Their encounter takes shape as a contradiction that drives the process of recognition.[11] Recognition is a process that seeks to remove or dissolve the contradictions of immediacy, abstract identity, and its parochialism. So long as the two selves confronting each other remain in immediacy, recognition is impossible. In Hegel's words,

> In this determination [of immediacy] there lies a tremendous contradiction. On the one hand, since the ego is universal, absolutely indeterminate and general, and uninterrupted by any limit, a feature [*Wesen*] common to all humans, the two selves here relating to each other constitute a *single* identity, a *single* light so to speak. On the other hand, despite such identity, they are and remain two [selves] opposed to each other in complete, unyielding inflexibility. As reflected into itself, each remains something absolutely different from and impenetrable by the other.[12]

The opposition of the two selves cannot take place without a common identity, but it is equally true that the common identity does not undermine or annul the opposition by annulling its individual relata. In other words, the individual selves remain independent in this identity. This paradox generates not a logical "solution" but a struggle (*Kampf*).

This struggle is first described in logical terms as a struggle to overcome, not the other per se, or otherness, but rather the *immediacy* of both selves. What does immediacy mean here? Immediacy denotes for Hegel not only the

---

10. *E*, §430.
11. Cf. *E*, §431. He identifies this level of conception with *Natürlichkeit*.
12. *E*, §430 Zusatz.

prereflective, but also *Natürlichkeit*, that is, a raw uncultivated particularity, a natural egoism and solipsism in which the self is directed toward its own needs and satisfactions. Hegel points out that the term "nature" has opposite meanings: It can mean what is raw, undeveloped, and uncultivated; however, it can also mean what is cultivated, what is developed, and what is rational.[13] Further, when used in reference to the human being, the natural is a subordinate aspect of the process of psychological-cultural development from nature to spirit, from the will in its particularity and arbitrariness, to a universal rational ethical-social will. In political terms nature is the *Naturzustande*, the so-called state of nature, which Hegel conceives similarly to Hobbes, as a condition of conflict. Hegel claims that the human being is in part a natural being; however, as immersed in its natural particularity, the human being is not yet conscious of its freedom, and has not transcended the merely natural level of its existence. Such a human being is not in conformity with its concept, it is not what it ought to be. It is immediate; it is *Begierde*, desire.

The contrast term to *Natürlichkeit* and immediacy is "mediation." When something is immediate, it is not open, but exists by itself, closed off from influence. It is impervious to and exclusive of otherness. However, when something is removed from its immediacy, that is, enters into mediation, it is deabsolutized, decentered, and made relative, that is, open to influence and modification.[14] In mediation it undergoes an influence from its other that changes, that is, negates and preserves, it.

Recognition likewise has a moment of immediacy, namely, the raw encounter between selves. The initial encounter exhibits an extreme tension and combination of absolute proximity to the other with complete uncertainty concerning the other. As Hegel observes, in spite of their underlying identity, "they are and remain two [selves] opposed to each other in complete, unyielding inflexibility. As reflected into itself, each remains something absolutely different from and impenetrable by the other."[15] This tension is intolerable. It

---

13. *VPR*17, §2. Hegel believes that this ambiguity vitiates the natural law tradition by confusing the rational natural law with the law of wild nature. He follows Rousseau, Kant, and Fichte in identifying freedom, not nature, as the principle of the modern state. In Hegel's concept of the ethical state, the state does not exist by nature; rather it is the totality of conditions that freedom requires in order to be actual in the world.

14. This may be illustrated from the opening category of Hegel's logic, namely, *Sein Nichts Werden*. As *aufgehoben* in *Werden*, *Sein* and *Nichts* cease to be what they are in abstraction from each other, namely, *Sein* and/or *Nichts*. Instead they are sublated to become *Entstehen* and *Vergehen*, or origination and perishing. Thus they are canceled on one level, but also transformed and preserved on another level. Their dynamism is the very process whereby they are related. Note that when *Sein* and *Nichts* are thus *aufgehoben*, they undergo influence from each other by virtue of coming into relation and mediation. On the higher level of transformation and sublation, *Sein* has become origination and *Nichts* has become perishing. They have been transformed, not because they have been removed from external influence, or because their openness to external influence has been terminated. Rather they have become transformed because they are open to influence from their opposite. Each has incorporated its other into itself, and the other now co-constitutes it.

15. *E*, §430 Zusatz.

is necessary to transcend immediacy, that is, the self as a raw particular, and enter into a process of mediation. "I cannot know myself in another insofar as the other is an immediate other existent for me. I therefore seek to cancel the immediacy of this other. Likewise, I cannot be recognized if I remain in immediacy, but only insofar as I cancel this immediacy in myself and through this give my freedom determinate objective existence."[16]

Hegel characterizes recognition as a process in which both self and other cancel their respective immediacies. He observes that immediate needs and natural necessities bring human beings together only in an external way. On the other hand, "Men must want to rediscover themselves in one another. However, this will [to recognition] cannot arise so long as they are confined to their immediacy and naturalness [*Natürlichkeit*], for it is precisely these that cut them off from one another and prevent them from being free in regard to one another. . . . Thus freedom has to be struggled for; merely to assert that one is free is not enough."[17] Each self seeks to give itself objective determinate existence (*sich Dasein geben*) "not in a [mere] external object, but a present object that is also a consciousness. The other's consciousness is the ground [*Boden*], the material, the space in which I realize myself."[18] Although this may appear to have "imperialistic" or aggressive overtones, such an interpretation is not necessary. The need to break out of abstract or immediate identity and achieve determinate existence (*Dasein*) drives self-consciousness beyond its mere parochial interests and subjective certainty in search of objective confirmation and legitimation in another's recognition.[19] This "need" is better characterized as a desire for the other. Although this desire may assume coercive forms, it is not necessarily or essentially a desire for mastery. Rather it is a desire for the other that supports and finds fulfillment in affirmative relations to others:

> It is necessary that the two selves standing over and against one another in their determinate being for others, posit and recognize what they implicitly are, or are according to their concept, namely they are not merely natural [things] but are rather free. Only in this way does genuine freedom come about, for since freedom consists in the identity of myself with the other, I am truly free only when the other is free and I recognize that the other is free. This freedom of the one in and through the other unites human beings in an inner way. In contrast, need and necessity bring people together only in an external manner.[20]

Freedom involves a mutual reciprocal union with the other, in which the other comes to count for something. "The other has to count within my existence [*Dasein*] as well."[21] When the other comes to count for me, then the threshold

---

16. *E*, §431. Hegel points out that immediacy includes the embodiment of self-consciousness, i.e., the body as a sign and instrument.

17. *E*, §431 Zusatz.   18. *PSS* 1825, 332.   19. Ibid., 318–332.
20. *E*, §431 Zusatz.   21. *PSS* 1825, 332.

of the ethical is crossed; recognition is the medium in which and through which ethical life is constituted.

Crossing the Threshold
of Ethical Life

Hegel's account of the relation between master and slave in the *Encyclopedia* differs from the *Phenomenology* account. In the latter master/slave represents a negation and sublation (*Aufhebung*) of the life and death struggle; specifically, it is a sublation of violence and death as abstract negation. The victory of the master over the slave and the slave's renunciation of his claim to recognition constitute a partial sublation of violence that ends it short of sheer slaughter. But while master/slave negates and ends violence as abstract negation, it also institutionalizes coercion in the form of unequal recognition, domination and oppression. For this reason, Hegel believes, the one-sided master/slave relationship is unstable and contains the seeds of its own reversal. Thus the master, although initially victorious and without any fear of death, subsequently becomes decadent and undergoes a decline. In the *Phenomenology*, Hegel's history of consciousness goes forward through the figure of the slave, because the slave learns to postpone gratification and to transform the world through labor. Through laboring the slave comes to realize his independence from the master, and that the master has come to be dependent on the slave. However, coming to oneself through laboring does not necessarily resolve the issue of the need of and desire for recognition. Moreover, a reversal of the master/slave relationship does not necessarily imply an end to or transcendence of domination; it might only produce a new pattern of domination.

In the *Encyclopedia*, master/slave is expounded as a relatively justified transitional stage from the state of nature (*Naturzustande*) to ethical life (*Sittlichkeit*). Hegel observes that the "justification" for slavery depends in part on taking the human being merely as a natural thing (*Ding*) and not recognizing freedom as essential. In such a transitional period or historical-social level, wrong is still (mis)taken for right.

> The struggle for recognition and subjection to a master constitute the phenomenal shape out of which the common life of human beings has arisen—the origin of the state. Coercion, which is the ground of this phenomenon, is not therefore the ground or basis of right. Rather coercion is a necessary and relatively justified moment in the transition from the condition of self-consciousness sunk in desire and particularity to the condition of the universal self-consciousness [ethical life]. Coercion is the external or phenomenal origin of the state, but not its substantial principle or basis.[22]

22. *E*, §433.

Viewed on its own historical level, coercion is relatively justified, for the state of nature is a state of violence wherein "might makes right." However, coercion is a negation that must itself be negated; coerced recognition ends in failure. Genuine reciprocal recognition requires that the other be allowed to be, and this implies that coercion, force, and violence must be renounced as the basis of human relationships. Freedom can be actual only in a community of reciprocal recognition, because only in such a community can being for others be reconciled with being for self (autonomy).

Let us consider the account of master/slave in the *Encyclopedia* more closely. Differences from the *Phenomenology* are immediately apparent. Hegel now maintains that both master and slave are in bondage, and that if they are to achieve liberation, they must do so jointly, together. This clarifies the point that mastery, that is, coercion, must be renounced. In the *Encyclopedia* account, the master too is unfree and remains in bondage. Hegel observes that in winning the struggle for recognition, the master remains in a condition of immediacy, that is, immersed in his natural particularity. Mastery's affirmation is thus a purely individual, egoistic self-affirmation and self-glorification. As far as Hegel is concerned such self-affirmation remains preethical; it does not leave behind the ethos of the Hobbesian state of nature. The master's freedom is a lawless, savage freedom, that is not yet "in conformity with its concept" as Hegel says. The master's self-affirmation is in fact a negative relation of domination toward the slave.[23] Caught in this unequal recognition, the master is not yet really free. The apparent winner of the struggle for recognition loses.

Hegel maintains that servile obedience is a beginning, but only a beginning, of freedom, because the slave is subjected, not to the genuine universal-rational will in and for itself, but to the merely particular contingent will of another subject, to wit, the master.[24] The problem in slavery is not its relativity to the other per se but the other to which it is relative. The "problem of slavery" is really a problem of the inherent arbitrary incoherence of mastery; its choice of domination and coercion is self-subverting. The slave, in being subject to the will of the master, is not obedient to an inclusive, universal will, but only to another particular will that remains immediate, particular, egocentric, and coercive.

In mastery and slavery, only the negative, exclusive aspect of freedom is initially manifest, namely, the negativity of self-seeking particularity. In contrast, Hegel believes that freedom becomes actual only when such negative self-seeking particularism is overcome, and when the servile consciousness liberates itself from the incoherent particularity of the master, by working off its own natural particularity. Only then is it possible to apprehend the rational in its universality.[25] The positive aspect of freedom manifest in affirmative re-

23. The two are inseparable, in spite of Deleuze's attempts to separate them. See the discussion of Deleuze's Nietzschean differential self-affirmation in chapter 15.

24. *E*, §435 Zusatz.   25. *E*, §435.

lation to other requires that the master's self-consciousness be transformed by concern for the slave as a human being. Specifically, it requires the recognition of a community of needs between master and slave and mutual concern for their satisfaction. The master must recognize the slave as another free human being, and no longer regard him merely as a thing. When the master recognizes that the slave is a human being, he also observes in the slave's laboring a postponement of gratification, a cancellation (*Aufhebung*) of immediacy, and realizes that this cancellation of immediacy is the truth for the master as well. The master must therefore subject his own arbitrary will to the law of the will that is in and for itself, namely, the universal will.

However, this does not mean that the master must work off his immediacy independently and in isolation from the slave. Nor does it mean that the master achieves liberation by copying and imitating the slave while remaining unrelated to him. Rather the master and the slave find liberation together and through each other.

> In this third stage, the mutually related self-conscious subjects, by setting aside their unequal particular individuality, have risen to the consciousness of their real universality, of the freedom belonging to all, and hence to the intuition of their specific identity with each other. The master confronted by his slave was not yet truly free, for he did not yet see himself in the slave. *Consequently it is only with the release and liberation [Freiwerden] of the slave that the master also becomes fully free. In this condition of universal freedom, in being reflected into myself, I am immediately reflected in the other person, and conversely, in relating myself to the other I am immediately related to myself.*[26]

Hegel here brings for the first time the discussion and problematic of master/slave within the full concept of reciprocal recognition. The final "moment" of the concept of recognition, namely, the moment of release, of allowing the other to be, becomes, in master/slave, the moment of mutual liberation. Liberation in turn designates a situation of mutual release, a release of the other that is made possible by setting aside unequal particularity, by abandoning self-aggrandizement. Note that in liberation there is also a union with the other, such that self-relation (being-for-self) and relation to other (being-for-other) are equivalent and reciprocal: in relating to the other I am also free myself.

The result of such reciprocal recognition is a universal consciousness, or We. Reciprocal recognition constitutes a universal self-consciousness that results from and reflects affirmative self-knowledge in other and therefore is explicitly an intersubjective-social universality. The crucial transformation from negative to affirmative relation to other in reciprocal recognition is sketched in a few terse but important lines:

26. *E*, §436 Zusatz. Italics mine.

The universal self-consciousness is *affirmative self-knowledge in another self.* In this relationship each self as a free individual retains its absolute independence on the one hand, but, on the other hand, by negating its immediacy or desire [*Begierde*], it no longer distinguishes itself from the other. Each is thus universal self-consciousness and objective; each has real universality in the shape of reciprocity. Each knows itself to be recognized in the other free person, and knows this insofar as it recognizes the other and knows him to be free.[27]

The universal self-consciousness resulting from reciprocal recognition here must not be confused with the putative universality of transcendental unity of apperception or transcendental ego. For Hegel, the latter is an abstraction from the former. The transcendental ego maintains only an asymmetrical ground-consequent relation to the phenomena that it constitutes, whereas the universal self-consciousness or spirit (*Geist*) is constituted by reciprocity between individuals and so stands in a relation of thoroughgoing reciprocity and community with them.

The universal consciousness or community in turn is the practical expression of the concept of reason as social.[28] Reason is the identity of the subjective and the object, that is, the breaking down of this very distinction. The universal consciousness constitutes a social reason because its dynamic structure of reciprocal recognition is to be both different from its other and nevertheless at the same time identical with it.[29] That reason is social and has a social structure for Hegel should come as no surprise, since he holds that reason is actual only in the life of a people, above all in their constitution and laws.

Four Dimensions of Recognition

Here I want to examine more closely the connection between freedom and recognition. Hegel's claim is that freedom becomes actual through the process of recognition and emerges as liberation in the final moment of mutual-reciprocal releasement. In an important essay, Ludwig Siep identifies four main features of Hegel's early concept of freedom: autonomy (*Autonomie*), union (*Vereinigung*), self-overcoming (*Selbstüberwindung*), and release (*Freigabe*).[30] Although Siep fails to connect these features of freedom explicitly with recognition, his analysis both presupposes and implies that freedom is intersubjectively mediated through recognition. I shall first examine these elements or moments of freedom and then note some of their connections with Hegel's concept of recognition, particularly as it is set forth in the *Encyclopedia*. Siep explains these general features of freedom as follows. *Autonomy* for Hegel as for Kant constitutes a break with nature and natural causation; it is the self-originating capacity of

---

27. *E*, §436. Italics mine.
28. *E*, §437.   29. *E*, §437 Zusatz.
30. See Siep, *PPDI*, 159–171.

the will that makes it independent of everything else. Autonomy is the independence of the will from coercion by external or heteronomous laws and from influences that do not or cannot originate from reason itself. External heteronomous influences in this sense can come from nature (inclinations, passions, goods such as happiness) and from human communities, for example, legal coercions and other forms of dependencies. Autonomy is understood negatively as freedom from external influence, and positively as independence, self-determination, and spontaneity. However, Siep observes that Hegel does not understand autonomy in the strict Kantian sense; for Hegel, autonomy can be realized only in and as a determinate way of coexisting in a community (*Zusammenleben*). In other words, for Hegel, autonomy is intersubjective and social from the beginning.

The second moment or feature of freedom appears to stand in tension with the first, namely, *union*, or *Vereinigung*, which can also be translated as "association."[31] Union does not mean fusion but relationship. The other ceases to be a hindrance or limit to freedom. In union with other the limits that divide and separate self and other—be it another, community, or nature—are both preserved and overcome. Freedom does not signify the isolation of one from the other, or ethical life from sensibility, but rather union and reconciliation with other. Love is a unifying power in the broadest sense. Love does not produce a fusion with or absorption of the other. As we shall see, love overcomes not otherness per se but enmity, conflict, and estrangement.

A question arises at this point. Does union contradict autonomy? Or is it rather the condition of autonomy? Kant and Jacobi believe the former. However, Hegel sides with Goethe and Herder in holding the latter view.[32] He criticizes Kant's and Jacobi's position on the grounds that it absolutizes finitude and difference: "The fundamental principle common to the philosophies of Kant, Fichte and Jacobi is, then, the absoluteness of finitude, and, resulting from it, the absolute antithesis of finitude and infinity, reality and ideality."[33] Consequently, for Kant and Jacobi, autonomy and union with other "stand opposed to each other in the connection of domination."[34] Union might imply domination if autonomy were conceived narrowly in abstract individualist terms. But this is precisely the point at issue as far as Hegel is concerned. For Hegel, individualism abstracts from a larger social whole. Union and autonomy are not mutually exclusive alternatives but are two basic features of a comprehensive intersubjective account of freedom.[35] Although an account of

31. Dieter Henrich traces the concept of *Vereinigung* to the influence of Hölderlin on Hegel. See his "Hegel und Hölderlin," in *Hegel im Kontext* (Frankfurt: Suhrkamp, 1967).

32. *PPDI*, 159. In an earlier essay, Siep observes that Goethe and Herder defended the conception of freedom as union, while Kant and Jacobi argued that the concept of freedom as autonomy is incompatible with the concept of union (pp. 116–117).

33. Hegel, *Faith and Knowledge*, trans. W. Cerf and H. S. Harris (Albany: SUNY Press, 1977), 62; see also pp. 56, 60. Hereafter cited as *FK*.

34. Ibid., 60.   35. *PPDI*, 118.

freedom can be given in individualist terms, such an account is either spiritless or methodological abstraction from a social whole.

The underlying issue can be reformulated as follows: autonomy and union would be contradictory on the assumption that they are absolute and actual in separation from each other. From such a perspective, autonomy seems to exclude union because entering into relation appears as a loss or at least a restriction on freedom. However, Hegel's view—following Fichte's and Schelling's thesis concerning the divided ground of freedom—is that entering into relation not only does not contradict or diminish freedom, rather relation is a condition of genuine freedom. In Hegel's words, "Since freedom consists in my identity with the other, I am truly free only when the other is also free and recognized as such by me. This freedom of the one in the other unites [*vereinigt*] human beings in an inner way."[36] Union therefore is a condition of genuine freedom as relational. Union involves affirmative relation to and self-knowledge in other. As will become evident, this has ethical implications.

The third feature of freedom is *self-overcoming* (*Selbstüberwindung*). Siep claims self-overcoming follows from union; that is, association and union with an other transform and enlarge the formerly narrow individualist self. Siep formulates this point thus: "The cancellation of the boundaries to others always appears as a kind of de-individualizing, a renunciation of the [attempt to] mark off and delimit one's own."[37] I would formulate the point in different, perhaps Sartrean language. The other cancels the boundaries of narrow individualism, deabsolutizes and relativizes the self. The "absolute" or self-centered self is another term for Hegel's *Begierde*, which names a self-seeking particularity that relates only to itself.[38] *Begierde* signifies a natural solipsism and provincial self-identity in which the self lives simply for its own satisfactions and pleasures. For this reason Hegel tells us that the satisfaction that *Begierde* seeks is generally destructive because it is purely a self-seeking (*selbstsüchtig*).[39] This basic posture, wherein the self is its sole end, is a source of mastery and domination. Hegel believes that immediacy is not only a natural solipsism, it is also a bondage, a restriction on freedom that must be overcome. Self-overcoming therefore is an ethical conception that expresses the *Aufhebung* of immediacy and natural solipsism. What is *lost* in mutual recognition is egoism and the desire for domination; what is gained through mutual recognition is substantive ethical freedom and community with other. Under conditions of reciprocal recognition, self-renunciation (of being-for-self) is transformed into an enlarged and enriched mentality that is at home with itself in its other.

Self-overcoming is not under the control of the self. The term "self-overcoming" designates a possible change in the self under the impact of the other.

---

36. *E*, §431 Zusatz.   37. *PPDI*, 160.   38. *PSS* 1825, 334.
39. Ibid., 326. Closely related to *Begierde* are *Eigensinn*, or obstinacy, and *Willkür*, or subjective arbitrary will.

The other decenters the self and provides the occasion for it to overcome its narrow, parochial individualism. The decentered ethical self in turn renounces domination and allows the other to be. This is what occurs in reciprocal recognition wherein each party acts as mediator and as extreme. Through such a reciprocal triple mediation the universal-social consciousness or 'We' is constituted: "In this condition of universal freedom, when I am reflected into myself I am immediately reflected in the other, and conversely, when I relate to the other I am immediately related to myself."[40]

As an illustration of self-overcoming, let us consider how Hegel shows that immediacy and "naturalness" (*Natürlichkeit*) inhibit or prevent entry into relationship and mediation. In his account of the initial encounter Hegel writes that "the two self-conscious subjects relating to one another, have an immediate existence as physically and naturally determined. Consequently they exist as mere things [*Dinge*] subjected to an alien power and dominion. In this crude way they come at each other."[41] But these selves are also *potentially* free, ethical subjects, who, as immediate, do not yet correspond with their own free human nature. In Hegel's view, such absolute self-seeking is overcome through the process of recognition. In recognition the other pulls the self out of its natural solipsistic egoistic individualism. "In order to overcome the contradiction, it is necessary that the two selves who are facing off, posit each other in their concrete determinate existence, in their being for other, and recognize each other for what they implicitly (*an sich*) are, and act in accordance with their concept [*Begriff*]. For they are not merely natural entities, but free beings. Only through such recognition does genuine freedom come to be."[42] Authentic freedom is not radically individual, nor does it isolate the self from relation. Rather genuine freedom is *bei sich in anderen zu sein*, to be at home with self in other. Hegel contends that

> I am genuinely free only when the other is also free, and recognized as such by me. This freedom of the one in the other unites human beings in an internal way, whereas in contrast, need and necessity bring them together only externally and contingently. Human beings must want to find themselves in others. But this cannot occur so long as they remain confined to their immediacy, their naturalness, for it is precisely these that exclude them from each other and hinder them from being free for each other.[43]

---

40. *E*, §436 Zusatz.   41. *E*, §431 Zusatz.   42. Ibid.

43. Ibid. I translate *Natürlichkeit* as "naturalness." The terminology is elusive, but the basic point is not. Naturalness is identified with *Begierde*, which regards only itself, i.e., a kind of narcissistic solipsism. Naturalness or the egoistic self-seeking self must be overcome, in order for union with others and an enlarged mentality to be achieved. Hegel is not far from Kant and Rousseau on this point. It should not be forgotten that Hegel was an avid yet critical reader of Rousseau. Rousseau's position is outlined by N. J. H. Dent: "When Rousseau stresses the need to transform each individual into part of a greater whole, it is in order that people shall overcome their preoccupation with narrow, self-absorbed private concerns that set them in conflict and com-

Mutual recognition is a reciprocal working off of immediacy and "natural egoism."

The fourth feature of freedom is *Freigabe*. Negatively, this means the renunciation of attempts to dominate and control the other. Positively, *Freigabe* signifies allowing the other to be, being open to the other, and affirming the other as she determines herself to be. In short, it means to accept and respect the other as an end in herself such that controlling, dominating, and manipulating behaviors are inappropriate. *Freigabe* makes explicit what had been implicit all along in Siep's analysis, namely, that for Hegel freedom is not simply individual but fundamentally intersubjective and social. *Freigabe* corresponds to the final moment of recognition in the *Phenomenology* account, namely release, allowing the other to go free. *Freigabe* is the consummation of reciprocal recognition, through which *Geist* is constituted as the I that is a We. *Freigabe* makes it clear that the 'We' Hegel is after is a community of freedom that does not absorb or reduce individuals to some homogeneity but rather presupposes, requires, and accepts individuals in their differences. *Freigabe* is the recognition of the otherness of the other, the difference of difference. This "letting be" does not have the sense of alienation or indifference. For *Freigabe* must be taken as the ethical condition of union with other; in this union with other, freedom becomes actual. Actual freedom is *bei sich im anderen zu sein*, to be at home with self in an other or others.

Siep believes that *Freigabe* stands in tension to self-overcoming. However, not only does he fail to make a plausible case for this claim, the claim itself seems doubtful. *Freigabe*, far from being opposed or in tension with self-overcoming, is rather its "external" manifestation and expression. Being open to the other and allowing her to be can occur only if the egocentrism, the inflamed self-love that underlies attempts to control and dominate others, is overcome. When the other is recognized as counting or having a claim on one's freedom, narrowly individual, egoistic selfhood is overcome. *Freigabe* expresses and makes manifest such self-overcoming.

Moreover, both self-overcoming and *Freigabe* qualify and reveal the nature of the union of the selves. Unification with other is no fusion with other in some undifferentiated universality as Levinas has charged.[44] Rather union is a rela-

---

petition with others. For so long as this remains their conception of personal interest, no proper social association can be established, let alone endure, on stable and just terms. People must come not just to see, but to feel that the good of others and their own are intimately bound together. . . . If they achieve this state of mind, they will no longer see themselves as wholly set apart from or in conflict with others; they will, to a degree, have taken on the good and need of others as part of their own enlarged sense of personal good." *Rousseau Dictionary* (Oxford: B. H. Blackwell, 1992), 85.

44. See Emmanuel Levinas, *Ethics and Infinity*, trans. Richard Cohen (Pittsburgh: Duquesne University Press, 1985), 66; see also Levinas, *Time and the Other*, trans. Richard Cohen (Pittsburgh: Duquesne University Press, 1987), 84–87. Like Levinas, Hegel opposes such romantic fusion: "In love the separate does still remain, but as something united and no longer as something

tion in which the selves not only remain free, but release each other from control, manipulation, and coercion. *Freigabe* is a condition of union, and union in Hegel's nondominating, nontotalizing sense is a result of mutual-reciprocal *Freigabe*. In other words, union in Hegel's sense, far from suppressing or canceling otherness, is rather its manifestation. Emmanuel Levinas, a critic of Hegel, nevertheless makes Hegel's point: "It should be observed that the act whereby the I withdraws and thus distances itself from the Thou or 'lets it be' in Heidegger's terms, is the same act which renders a union with it possible. In effect, there is no union worthy of the name except in the presence of this sort of otherness: union, *Verbundenheit*, is a manifestation of otherness."[45]

The concept of *Freigabe* is closely tied to Hegel's concepts of union and love: "In this simple beholding of itself in other, being-other is not posited as such: it is a distinction that in pure thought is immediately no difference—a recognition of love in which both lovers are by their very nature not opposed to each other."[46] The crucial point is that love's absence of opposition does not mean fusion or absorption of the other but rather an overcoming of enmity and conflict.

For Hegel, absolute autonomy leaves no room for the other; it contradicts and undermines the possibility of relation. When it nevertheless comes into relation, absolute autonomy manifests itself in postures of coercion and domination. Such autonomy must be relativized. On the other hand, being in a relation that includes self-overcoming and *Freigabe* is no contradiction to autonomy. Rather such relation to other is the condition of the development of autonomous freedom, that is, mediated autonomy. These ideas are forcefully expressed in Hegel's 1825 lectures:

> If we speak about justice, ethical life, and love, we know that since we recognize others, that we recognize their complete personal independence. I do not suffer loss in recognizing others; rather I count myself as free. We know that because others have rights, I also have rights, or that my rights are essentially the same as others', i.e., that I am a free person and this is essentially identical with the fact that others are persons with rights. In benevolence and in love, my personality is not destroyed. But in the case of Master/slave, we do not yet have to do with such reciprocal relations. Instead there is the determination that I am a free and at the same time an immediate particular self-consciousness, such that my freedom has not yet been distinguished from the immediate particularity of my self-consciousness. Consequently I cannot give up anything of my particularity without at the same time renouncing my freedom and independence. [However] in social-legal relations I know that if I respect the property of another, I do not

separate." *Early Theological Writings*, trans. T. M. Knox (Chicago: University of Chicago Press, 1948), 305.

45. Emmanuel Levinas, "Martin Buber and the Theory of Knowledge," in *The Levinas Reader*, ed. Sean Hand (Oxford: B. H. Blackwell, 1989), 66.

46. *PhG*, 536.

suffer injury or loss. If I renounce claims to the property of others, I realize that respect for justice in general implies justice in my own case. But in the case of Master/slave, self-consciousness remains at the level of mere immediate individuality. It has not yet abstracted from its own particularity; mere desire [*Begierde*] predominates, and insofar as self-consciousness simply is its own interests and desire, it experiences the property of others as a limitation on its freedom.[47]

In this important text Hegel explains that prior to recognition, freedom is not distinguished from immediate particularity; in other words, the self in its immediacy is naturally egoistic and solipsist. If freedom is not yet distinguished from immediate particularity, then to give up any aspect of that particularity appears to be tantamount to giving up freedom and independence. Such a concept of freedom is narrow, parochial, and inadequate.

In the process of recognition, immediate, parochial selfhood is overcome. The individual self no longer considers itself to be the center of the universe, but recognizes others not merely as limits to its freedom, but as coequal and worthy of respect. We shall examine this "enlarged mentality," or universal self-consciousness, shortly. Suffice it to note here that the contrast between universal and particular now emerges in self-consciousness itself, and this implies a decentering of the self. That is, at the level of ethical life, the self no longer identifies itself simply as the universal, but rather as a particular instance of the universal and as subordinate to the whole. Thus the self recognizes itself as one particular among others, with reciprocal obligations of mutual respect and recognition toward others.

Does the preceding analysis mean that Hegel thinks recognition is possible without a life and death struggle? That it might be possible to bypass both the life and death struggle and master and slave? That a phase of conflict is not a necessary but a contingent feature of recognition? Hegel's answer to these questions depends on a prior question, whether we are speaking of the process of recognition at the level of individuals or at the level of objective spirit, that is, a people. This distinction between subjective and objective spirit Hegel did not make until 1817, when he first formulated it in his *Encyclopedia*. It may have been such questions as whether struggle is a universal feature of recognition that led him to distinguish subjective and objective spirit. Given this distinction, what is necessary for human spirit in general, that is, at the collective social-cultural world-historical level, may not be necessary for every individual. Hegel makes this point in his discussion of madness.

This interpretation of madness as a necessarily occurring form or stage in the development of the soul is naturally not to be understood as if we were asserting that every spirit, every soul, must go through this stage of extreme derangement. Such an assertion would be as absurd as to assume that because in the *Philoso-*

47. *PSS* 1825, 332.

phy of Right crime is considered as a necessary manifestation of the human will, therefore to commit crime is an inevitable necessity for every individual. Crime and insanity are extremes which the human spirit in general has to overcome in the course of its development. However crime and insanity do not appear as extremes in every individual, but only in the form of limitations, errors, follies and offenses that are not criminal in nature.[48]

Hegel's answer to our question would be that struggle (*Kampf*) is a universal and necessary feature of recognition at the level of human spirit in general, that is, at the world-historical level. However, the extreme situation of struggle to the death is not necessary for every individual. At the individual level of subjective spirit, development through extreme conflict is, fortunately, an avoidable contingency. Thus Hegel holds that there can be individual cases of recognition in which there is no life and death struggle and in which master and slave are bypassed. Life and death struggle and master/slave appear to be universal and necessary stages only at the world-historical level of the human spirit.

The foregoing interpretation is confirmed by Hegel's mature system. In the *Philosophy of Spirit* and the *Philosophy of Right*, recognition is the general form of objective spirit and ethical life. However, ethical life includes family, civil society, and state, and it is impossible to make generalizations about the necessity of conflict that apply to all three as forms of recognition. The family is ethical life in its immediacy and intimacy. Conflict in Hegel's sense of a struggle for recognition either does not arise or is already overcome on this level. Moreover, the relations of recognition between family members are not reducible to the abstract, formal recognition of contract. Of the three levels of ethical life, civil society is a sphere of difference, of competition and conflict. The patterns of struggle and master and slave remain important on this level. But it is the task of the state as an ethical institution to rectify and overcome certain inequalities generated in civil society. The most that can be said is that for Hegel some forms and levels of recognition involve conflict and some do not.

In the mature *Philosophy of Spirit*, Hegel expounds master/slave as a relatively justified transitional stage, not of individual development, but of historical-cultural development from the so-called state of nature (*Naturzustande*) to the condition of ethical life. Master/slave is a figure or *Gestalt* of consciousness that both presupposes and constitutes a certain level of sociocultural development. Hegel observes that the "justification" for slavery depends in part on taking the human being merely as a natural thing (*Ding*) and not recognizing that freedom is its very "nature."[49] It is clear that Hegel thinks master/

---

48. *E*, §408 Zusatz. I have altered the Wallace translation.
49. *E*, §431 Zusatz; *PR*, §57. This is a categorical critique of slavery; namely, it misconceives the human being as a mere thing that can be used as a means, rather than recognizing that human beings are free. Once freedom is acknowledged, and/or comes to be 'for itself', then slavery is seen as fundamentally incompatible with it.

slave is a constitutive feature of spirit's historical and cultural development. But this does not mean that it is necessary, constitutive, or an essential feature of interpersonal recognition per se. In the *Encyclopedia* Hegel writes, "In order to avoid misunderstandings . . . we must note that the struggle for recognition pushed to its most extreme form can occur only in the state of nature, where men exist only as single separate individuals. But it is absent from civil society and the state, because the result of that struggle, namely being-recognized [*Anerkanntsein*], already exists."[50] Hegel makes a similar point in his 1825 lectures: "in a civilized situation, particularly in the case of the family, civil society and the state, I recognize and am recognized by everyone *without any struggle* [*ganz ohne Kampf*]."[51] Hegel observes that although the state may have originated in violence, violence and might are not its justification.[52] Exactly the opposite is true: the state, as the totality of the conditions of freedom, is an ethical bulwark against struggle and violence.

Universal Self-Consciousness as Affirmative Self-Recognition in Other

The term 'universal self-consciousness' can be somewhat misleading, because considered from the standpoint of individuals, the term 'universal' suggests an inflation or expansion of an individual self-consciousness. In becoming universal, the self "absorbs" or "overreaches" its other. But this is obviously one-sided and incompatible with a free relationship or free community. No individual I is simply or immediately identical with the universal 'We', but can only regard itself as an instance of the universal, or a member of the We. However, the universal consciousness of which Hegel speaks is a union, not in the sense of abstract undifferentiated identity or of fusion, but a union of individuals in reciprocal mediation, and for which reciprocity is crucial. Thus this universal is not an abstract ego, or I am I, but a determinate social totality that does not suppress but rather justifies its constituent individuals. Reciprocal recognition forms a union, a 'We' in which individual selves not only preserve their freedom and independence, but their freedom and independence are conditions of that very union. In Hegel's words, "Each self is a free individuality that has absolute independence, but, by virtue of the negation of its immediacy or desire [*Begierde*], no longer distinguishes itself from the other. Each is thus universal self-consciousness and objective; each has its real universality as reciprocity, so that it knows itself to be recognized in the other's freedom, and knows this insofar as it recognizes the other and knows him to be free."[53] On

50. *E*, §432 Zusatz.   51. *PSS* 1825, 336.
52. *E*, §§432 Zusatz, 433.
53. *E*, §436.

the one hand, each is independent, and as independent it is 'other than' the other. On the other hand, each sublates its immediacy, and so no longer distinguishes or separates itself from its other, but is united with its other. From this perspective, the We is a whole that is greater than the sum of its parts, and prior to each of its parts. The point is that the We is not negative but affirmative: "The universal self-consciousness is the *affirmative knowledge* of itself in another self."[54] This is the thesis on which Hegel's idea of ethical life rests.

Hegel characterizes affirmative self-knowledge in the other or self-recognition in other as the way in which the self achieves determinate objective existence, or *Dasein*. Through reciprocal recognition self-consciousness attains *Dasein*, or determinate existence. Note that this determinacy presupposes that the other is different from the self; if it were not different, there could be no real difference in self-consciousness and the latter would remain abstract, empty, a merely formal I = I, or an inwardized 'beautiful soul'. The requisite determinacy of *Dasein* is not only intersubjectively mediated, it is also intersubjectively embodied and expressed. Thus the realization of self-consciousness means not merely articulating or acting on a subjective certainty but also receiving intersubjective confirmation of that certainty. How do I know that I have 'realized myself' in the other? Clearly this is not a 'knowledge' that I can give to myself; a one-sided action here would be useless. Genuine recognition cannot be coerced. If I am to know myself in an other, the other must act, must confirm or legitimate my identity and worth; in short, the other must reciprocally recognize me.

Consequently, my *Dasein*, or determinate existence, must be *recognized* if it is to be 'for' me at all. The realization of self-consciousness in an other's recognition means that it attains existence, presence, visibility, and influence in an other: "More closely considered, this duty of recognition involves that as free, I give myself a determinate existence [*Dasein*], not in an external object [*Objekt*] but in a present object [*Gegenstand*] that is a consciousness. The consciousness of the other is the soil, the matter, the space, in which I realize myself."[55]

Two points should be noted here. (1) Giving oneself determinate existence or embodiment in another is not something that can be done directly, or one-sidedly, for that would involve coercion. Such a relation would undermine or cancel freedom. Recognition is inherently reciprocal, for only reciprocity sustains the freedom and independence of each in the relation. (2) Giving oneself determinate existence in an other is practical activity, or practical reason translating itself into existence. Practical activity is an extension of freedom into the world that includes the forms of ownership, of gaining recognition from others, not merely recognition of one's ownership, but of oneself as a member of ethical life itself. This realization of freedom, its attaining determinate existence in property, in others, and in the world, is the origin of Hegel's theory of objective spirit. Respect, honor, and property are all determinate forms of intersubjective recognition and practical rationality.

Hegel shifts his metaphor from the other as the soil, or space, in which I realize myself, to the metaphor of reflexion or mirroring. He speaks of a "universal reappearance of self-consciousness [*Dies allgemeine Wiederscheinen des Selbstbewusstseins*]."[56] This formulation was first used in the 1817 Heidelberg *Encyclopedia*,[57] and continues through the 1825–1826 lectures to the final 1830 version. Despite the persistence of this language, the text presents a puzzle. What does 'reappearance' (*Wiederscheinen*) mean? My thesis is that it means a mirroring by other, a mutual intersubjective affirmation, that constitutes *positive* self-knowledge in other.[58] The universal self-consciousness results from

56. Ibid.

57. G. W. F. Hegel, *Enzyklopädie der philosophischen Wissenschaften im Grundrisse* (Heidelberg, 1817), reprinted in *Sämtliche Werke*, Band 6, Jubliäumsausgabe in zwanzig Bänden, hrsg. H. Glockner (Stuttgart: Frommann-Holzboog, 1968), §358. English translation: *Encyclopedia of the Philosophical Sciences in Outline*, trans. Stephen A. Taubeneck, *The German Library*, vol. 24, ed. E. Behler (New York: Continuum 1990). Hereafter cited as *HE*.

58. However, there is a textual difficulty that besets any interpretation of this strange passage. In the German text cited above, Hegel uses the term '*Wiederscheinen*'. The problem is that there is no such German word as *Wiederscheinen*. In view of the continuity of Hegel's usage one would have thought that meticulous German scholarship would have sorted out this conundrum by now. But apparently it has not. Instead, Hegel's German editors present two possibilities of rendering this word. The first is to construe it as an archaic form of *Widerscheinen*, or reflection. This is the rendering of the most recent edition by Pöggeler and Nikolin (*Enzyklopädie* (1830), hrsg. Nikolin und Pöggeler [Hamburg: Felix Meiner Verlag, 1969]). The other possibility is to render it as "*Wiedererscheinen*," or reappearance, as does the Suhrkamp edition, and as I have translated it above. This is the rendering given by Taubeneck and Wallace, who (respectively) translated the 1817 and 1830 editions of the *Encyclopedia*.

In favor of Pöggeler's construal of Hegel's meaning as reflection (*Widerschein*), the rest of the sentence speaks about the *Begriff* that knows itself in its objectivity as self-identical subjectivity. Such self-identity is reflective. However, the term 'reflection' makes it appear as if the identity in question is a reflective act that expresses the unity of a reflective self-consciousness. If this were the case, then Hegel's universal consciousness would turn out to be indistinguishable from the abstract, formal, and empty I am I. And Hegel here would be denying the very point on which he insisted previously, namely, that the I am I lacks difference, while the universal consciousness is differentiated by the other. Since reflection of the I am I believes it can attain the universal at a single stroke, intersubjective mediation would be superfluous.

I believe, therefore, that the context of the passage points to the latter term, 'reappearance' (*Wiedererscheinen*) and not to 'reflexion' (*Widerscheinen*). Recall Hegel's previous claim that the self gives itself determinate existence (*Dasein*) in the recognition of the other. He now maintains that this determinate existence (*Dasein*) is a reappearance of the subject in the other subject, that is, an acknowledgment and/or confirmation of the self by the other. Reappearance is another term for recognition. The selves exist as reciprocally recognized and recognizing.

In support of this reading it should be noted that *Wiedererscheinen* is conceptually linked to the doubling of consciousness, that to give oneself *Dasein* in an other is to be reflected in an other, i.e., to find one's impact or influence reflected by the other, and vice versa. While the reappearance of self in the other's recognition may also be construed as a mirroring or 'reflection' of the self by its other, this 'reflection' or mirroring should not be construed as a merely interior mental act of reflection whereby the self divides itself into knower and known. While reflection (*Widerscheinen*) may be involved in the reappearance of self-consciousness in other, the term 'reflection' is not essentially social, but can be construed precisely in terms of the solipsism and individualism that Hegel criticizes and rejects. In contrast, Hegel intends an intersubjective doubling wherein we find ourselves reflected in others and vice versa. This intersubjective sense of reflection breaks down the traditional spatial metaphors of 'inner' and 'outer' on which the epistemological debates of

positive recognition and articulates that joint reciprocity and mutuality. Further, Hegel claims that such universal consciousness, in which both self and other reappear in a union of reciprocal recognition, is "the substance of every essential spirituality [*wesentlichen Geistigkeit*], including family, fatherland, justice, as well as of all virtues—love, friendship, bravery, honor and fame."[59]

This is a sweeping claim with sweeping implications. These include (1) mutual recognition is the existential phenomenological genesis of Hegel's concept of objective spirit; (2) since Hegel identifies this universally reappearing consciousness with reason (*Vernunft*), reason is socially constituted;[60] and (3) recognition is at the heart of the virtues. Conversely, the virtues are inherently intersubjective and social. The virtues, even so-called duties to oneself, are virtues of communal human existence.

The Social Constitution and Mediation of Reason

It is a most important claim that Hegel struggles to articulate in this account of universal consciousness, the reappearance of self-consciousness in other. The claim is that reason and freedom are social, socially mediated and constituted. He tells us that the intersubjectively mediated universal consciousness is both subject and object. In calling it object, he does not mean that it is *an* object, but rather that it is objective, present in the other as well as the self. The self that negates its immediacy and enters into relation with other does not disappear; rather it reappears transformed on a higher level in its union with other. The self is both subject in that it recognizes the other and objective in that it is recognized and legitimated by the other. The relation of reciprocal recognition, far from canceling or undermining the self's independence, confirms and preserves it. Thus the self both sustains and is sustained in relation.

The reappearance or mirroring of the rational self by another rational self, Hegel tells us, is the concept (*Begriff*) that knows itself in its *objectivity* as a *subjectivity identical with itself*. If this *Begriff*, or concept, is understood sim-

---

modern philosophy turn. Hegel's point is that the universality of reason and its *Begriffe* depends on and is constituted by the reciprocity of mutual recognition.

Edith Düsing supports this interpretation. She observes that *Wiederscheinen* echoes Leibniz's monadology according to which each monad reflects the universe from its particular point of view. She interprets *Widerscheinen* as an intersubjective, rather than monosubjectival, reflection, a self-recognition in an other. "In this instance of the special relation of reflection in other, the *relata* are not merely ontological or logical determinations whose significations contain or imply relations to others, as is implicit in the universal '*Scheinen im anderen*'. Rather, the *relata* here are concrete existing self-conscious individuals in which each, in its self-representation has essentially a relation to another ego as a necessary moment of its self-consciousness." Düsing, "Genesis des Selbstbewusstseins durch Anerkennung und Liebe: Untersuchungen zu Hegels Theorie der konkreten Subjektivität," in *Hegels Theorie des subjektiven Geistes*, ed. Lothar Eley (Stuttgart: Frommann-Holzboog, 1990), 263.

59. *PSS* 1825–1826, 344.

60. *E*, §§437–439.

ply as subjectivity, the result would be a subject-centered reason. *Geist* would then be understood as an alternative term for transcendental subjectivity.[61] However, the subjectivity of the *Begriff*, as a universal subjectivity, is also an intersubjectivity. This important nuance is what Hegel's term *Geist* is intended to capture. *Geist* is Hegel's correction—he would say completion—of the concept of subjectivity and the corresponding philosophy of the subject. *Geist* has its actuality not merely in a subject but in the life of a people.

Further, he explicitly identifies *Geist*, or the universal self-consciousness, with *reason*. Since reason is intersubjectively reciprocally mediated, it is not a merely subjective certainty, but a certainty that is both subjective and objective. Mutual recognition is the basic shape assumed by reason's practical activity. Consequently, reason presses beyond and transcends any merely subjective posture or certainty.

> The formal rationality of drives and inclinations consists in the general drive *not* to exist as [merely] subjective, but to become actual through the activity of the subject itself wherein it suspends its subjectivity. . . . The immanent reflection of spirit is to transcend its particularity as well as its natural immediacy, and to give its content rationality and objectivity, in which it exists as necessary relations, rights and duties. This objectivation demonstrates their content, as well as their relation to each other, to be true and genuine. Plato had a firm grasp of this point when he showed that what justice is in and for itself—which he correctly understood in its entirety to be included under the right of spirit—can be exhibited only in the objective configuration [*Gestalt*] of justice, namely the construction of the state as ethical life.[62]

61. See my "Hegel's Concept of *Geist*," in *Hegel's Philosophy of Spirit*, ed. Peter G. Stillman (Albany: SUNY Press, 1986), 1–20; "Hegel and Transcendental Philosophy," *Journal of Philosophy* 82, no. 11 (November 1985): 595–606; and *Recognition*, chaps. 1–7.

62. *E*, §474.

5

Recognition and Right in the Jena Manuscripts

Hegel observes that the *Philosophy of Right* is part of his system of philosophy and that as such it presupposes the derivation/deduction of its concept. "The concept of right, so far as its coming into being is concerned, falls outside of the science of right; its deduction is presupposed and assumed as given."[1] The deduction of the concept of right is given, not only as Allen Wood claims in the *Encyclopedia*, §§485–487, but much more significantly and explicitly in an *affirmative self-knowledge in other* mediated by reciprocal recognition that is constitutive of the universal-social self-consciousness in *Encyclopedia*, §436. "This universal reappearance of self-consciousness, the concept that knows itself in its objectivity to be identical with itself in its subjectivity and thus is universal, is the [ethical] substance of every essential spirituality, the family, fatherland, *right*, as well as all the virtues—love, friendship, bravery, honor and reputation."[2] This reappearance of self-consciousness in an other's recognition means that recognition is the existential-phenomenological source and genesis of both the concept of ethics, including the virtues, and the concept of right in the broadest sense. This broad view of right is what Hegel has in mind in his *Philosophy of Right*: "When we speak here of right, we mean not merely civil right, which is what is usually understood by this term, but also morality, ethics and world history."[3]

According to Hegel, the deduction of right occurs in the philosophy of spirit.

---

1. *PR*, §2.
2. *PSS* 1825–1826, 332. Also found in *G. W. F. Hegel: The Berlin Phenomenology*, ed. and trans. M. J. Petry (Boston: D. Reidel, 1981), §436, 92. My italics.
3. *PR*, §33 Zusatz.

But behind the mature philosophy of spirit lies Hegel's earlier unpublished Jena manuscripts, beginning with the *System of Ethical Life* and the two Jena *Philosophies of Spirit*.[4] These early manuscripts contain accounts of the struggle for recognition and of what was to become Hegel's mature constructive concept of objective spirit. Even more important, they show Hegel's appropriation and transformation of Fichte's concept of recognition. Specifically, they show that for Hegel the concept of recognition is central for understanding not only the important concept of right but also the even more fundamental concept of ethical life (*Sittlichkeit*). As far as the deduction of right is concerned, the *Philosophy of Spirit 1805–1806* is the most important, because there Hegel achieves a certain rapprochement with Fichte and links the concept of right to the concept of recognition. As we shall see, right now receives an existential-phenomenological grounding: right is mediated by and is a relation of mutual recognition. Being recognized is the origin and foundation of right. Not only does this claim bring Hegel closer to Fichte than he had been in the earlier *Difference* and *Natural Law* essays, it also lays the foundation for Hegel's mature theory of objective spirit.

Accordingly we shall turn our attention first to the *Jena Realphilosophie 1805–1806*, where the connection between recognition and right is established. This involves a critique of the natural law tradition. Hegel agrees with Rousseau, Kant, and Fichte against classical natural law theory that right does not exist by nature, but is based on and an expression of freedom.

> The expression 'natural law', which has hitherto been common in the philosophical doctrine of right, is ambiguous as to whether the law is, as it were, already implanted directly by nature, or whether it exists because of the nature of things, i.e., because of the concept [*Begriff*]. The former used to be the customary meaning, so that . . . a 'condition of nature' was poetically created, in which the law of nature should dominate; whereas the condition of society and the state required a limitation of freedom and a sacrifice of natural rights. In fact however, right and all its determinations are based on free personality alone, a self-determination which is the opposite of the determination of nature. A natural condition is therefore a condition of violence and injustice, of which nothing truer may be said than that one ought to leave it. Society, by contrast, is the only condition in which right has actuality. What is to be limited and sacrificed are precisely the arbitrariness and violence of the state of nature.[5]

Hegel also criticizes the individualism of modern thinkers, both from the standpoint of the classical Aristotelian doctrine that the community as a whole is

---

4. These have been translated: *The System of Ethical Life (1802) and First Philosophy of Spirit* (1803), trans. H. S. Harris (Albany: SUNY Press, 1979); the *Jena Philosophie des Geistes 1805/06*, in Hegel, *Jenaer Systementwürfe III,* Hrsg. Rolf-Peter Horstmann (Hamburg: Felix Meiner Verlag, 1987), has been translated as *Hegel and the Human Spirit*, trans. Leo Rauch (Detroit: Wayne State University Press, 1983). Hereafter cited as *Philosophie des Geistes 1805/06* and *HHS*, respectively.

5. *HE*, §415. For a discussion, see Riedel, *Between Tradition and Revolution*, 35 ff.

prior to its parts and from the standpoint of recognition. In this way he seeks to retrieve the classical normative conceptions of right, not on the basis of natural law or modern individualistic liberalism, but on the basis of intersubjective recognition. The concept referred to in the above note has its existential phenomenological correlate not in modern subjectivity, which Hegel sees as culminating in Enlightenment eudaimonism and individualism, but in mutual recognition. Enlightenment eudaimonism tends toward a naturalistic egoism that reinforces individualism, and it is precisely this modern 'natural law' (Hobbes's account of the state of nature) that must be overcome. Consequently, for Hegel, it is not modern subjectivity but rather recognition that effects and mediates the transition from the so-called state of nature egoism to ethical life.

The importance of recognition for the concept of right leads Hegel to propose replacing the ambiguous concept of 'natural law' with the concept of objective spirit. Hegel develops his critique of both classical and modern natural law theories further in the following passage.

> The sphere of right is not the soil of nature—certainly not of external nature, but also not of subjective human nature, insofar as human will, when determined by nature, remains in the sphere of natural needs and instincts. On the contrary, the sphere of right is the sphere of spirit [*Geist*], the sphere of freedom. . . . The term 'natural right' or 'natural law' [*Naturrecht*] ought to be abandoned and replaced by the term 'philosophical doctrine of right' or (as will emerge) 'doctrine of objective spirit'. The expression 'nature' [*Natur*] contains the ambiguity that by it we understand (1) the essence [*Wesen*] and concept [*Begriff*] of something, (2) unconscious, immediate nature as such. So by 'natural law' has been understood the supposed legal order valid by virtue of immediate nature; with this is connected the fiction of a 'state of nature' [*Naturzustand*] in which authentic right or law supposedly exists. This state of nature is opposed to the state of society, and in particular the political state. There has been a prevalent misconception in this regard, as if society were not something implicitly and explicitly in conformity with the essence of spirit, and necessary for it, but rather a kind of artificial evil and misfortune, and as if genuine freedom were limited in it. On the contrary, a 'state of nature' would be one in which there were no such thing as right or wrong because spirit would not yet have attained to the thought of its freedom. It is only with the consciousness of freedom that right and wrong begin. Moreover since the human being exists essentially as self-consciousness with the concept of good and evil, the state of nature is a state of unfreedom and wrong which must be superseded, for freedom and its actuality lie beyond it.[6]

For Hegel the so-called state of nature is a fiction in a certain sense; it is not meant as an actual historical transition from a presocial individualism to a social condition. Hegel denies that there is such a transition, since human beings

---

6. *VPR*17, §2. I have altered the English translation slightly.

are social beings. If it is not an actual historical period, the 'state of nature' is a heuristic methodological fiction for sorting out the emergence of social rationality and the replacement of custom and tradition by the rule of law.[7] In this connection Hegel is close, but not too close, to Hobbes's view of the 'natural condition' as conflict and war.[8] For Hegel, the 'state of nature' is a fictional projection prior to the development of the consciousness of freedom, and prior to the development of distinction between right and wrong. It is a condition in which the consciousness of freedom and the recognition of freedom in right have not yet emerged.

According to Hegel we must not identify freedom with the state of nature, for that is to commit the fallacy of misplaced concreteness. On the contrary, freedom is actual only when the state of nature has been transcended. Traditional conceptions of natural law obscure the crucial point that autonomous freedom entails a break with nature. They forget that the very notions of right and wrong, justice and injustice arise only together with the concept and consciousness of freedom, such that "right without freedom is meaningless."[9] They pass over and conceal the very thing that needs to be investigated, namely, how right is freedom's own intersubjective self-manifestation. As we shall see, Hegel's thesis is that recognition is the pivot of this transition from nature to freedom, from nature to spirit. Through recognition consciousness is 'elevated' from mere particularity and singularity to socioethical universality.

Recognition in the 1805 Jena *Philosophy of Spirit*

Hegel distinguishes two levels of recognition. The first is the immediate level of interpersonal or intersubjective relations, the "face to face" that is constitutive of love and the family. The family is for Hegel the highest level of 'natural ethical life'. The second level concerns the relation between families in the absence of any law or larger social institutions. It deals with the question of regulating relations between families and focuses on possessions and exchange of possessions. Here it is a question of constituting a larger, transfamily 'universal consciousness' that is a common will binding on both parties. This second level involves possible conflict between families and the overcoming of such conflict. Hegel considers conflict between families and/or clans as a prelegal condition roughly equivalent to the 'state of nature', or possibly

---

7. See Hegel's *Doppelsatz*, the rational becomes actual, discussed above in chapter 1. The state of nature is not a "mere fiction." Hegel believes that the international scene with its conflicts between nation-states is 'the state of nature,' i.e., there is no genuine international law. International agreements and treaties are backed by force or the threat of force, which in turn implies the absence of law.

8. See Siep, "Kampf um Anerkennung"; English translation in *Hegel's Dialectic of Desire and Recognition*, 273–288.

9. *VPR3*, 100.

as the beginning of a transition from it. The concept of right points to the over-coming and surpassing of such conflict. It assumes a transcendence of the state of nature; specifically, it involves the constitution through mutual recognition of an enlarged mentality that transcends the family. The origin of right is co-extensive with this universal consciousness and is the origin of the state.

The family is a determinate intersubjectivity of a special sort. Hegel agrees with Schelling that intersubjectivity does not mean immediate or direct access to the other. There is an ontological separation of subjects that precludes any direct knowledge or presence of the other and makes each member uncertain of the other. However, Hegel does not leave it at that. He believes that it is pos-sible to qualify the ontological separation and that love is a form of mutual recognition that overcomes or suspends the negative dimensions of ontological separation. "To be sure, they approach one another with uncertainty and timid-ity, yet with trust, for each knows itself immediately in the other, and the move-ment is merely the inversion whereby each realizes that the other knows itself likewise in its other. . . . [I]t is the condition of not being satisfied in oneself, but rather having one's essence in another—because one knows oneself in the other, negating oneself as being-for-oneself, as different." [10]

Against this background, Hegel regards the family as a natural institution, a 'natural' determinate intersubjectivity. Although the family exists prior to the construction of law, this does not mean that the family is preethical. On the contrary, even at the level of natural ethical life, for Hegel the family is also an *ethical* institution; as such it is the highest form or level of 'natural *Sittlich-keit'*. The family is the point of transition from lawless *natürliche Recht*, where as Hegel wryly observes, wrong still counts as right, to *Naturrecht*, that is, where nature begins to be sublated into spirit and universal ethical freedom is developed.

For example, in the *System der Sittlichkeit* Hegel discusses the patriarchal family; it is clear that for Hegel even this type of family is an ethical institu-tion. Hegel observes that while the patriarchal husband is the master and man-ager, he is not a property owner vis-à-vis other members of the family. [11] More-over, although marriage appears to be a contract, in fact it is 'a contract to have no contract'. This typically Hegelian locution makes the concept of contract self-destruct and reveals it to be inappropriate for conceiving not only this de-terminate intersubjectivity but also the state. [12] Contract is an appropriate cate-gory or concept for exchanging possessions that are external, but it is not ap-propriate for treating or thinking about persons. While it is possible for a person to become property as in slavery, Hegel laconically observes that such a relationship is not a marriage. [13] In the *Philosophy of Spirit 1803/04*, Hegel points out that marriage is the sublation of physical desire and passion into

---

10. Hegel, *Philosophie des Geistes 1805/06*, 193; *HHS*, 107.
11. *System of Ethical Life*, trans. H. S. Harris, 127.
12. Ibid., 128.   13. Ibid.

love, an ethical conception: "The woman comes to be a being on her own account for the man. She ceases to be [simply] an object of his desire; desire becomes something ideal, a conscious intuiting. . . . Desire thus frees itself from its connection with enjoyment, it comes to be an immediate union of both, . . . it becomes love; and the enjoyment is this intuiting of oneself in the being of the other consciousness. This connection becomes in the same way the being of both, . . . it becomes marriage." [14]

If the family is an ethical institution, what makes it ethical? In what does its ethical character consist for Hegel? Ethics here means that the other has come to count, both as an object of desire and as an end in herself. In light of this, the self undergoes a further transformation (*Aufhebung*). The transformation involves "not being satisfied in oneself, but in having one's essence in another— because one knows oneself in the other, negating oneself as being-for-self, as different." [15] Marriage is a determinate intersubjectivity in which each partner knows itself in the other. Second, this determinate intersubjectivity requires that each renounces its drive toward independence for the sake of the desired union with other. This self-renunciation is not asceticism, because the self at the same time returns to itself in and through the other's recognition. The narrow egoistic self is renounced and transformed in the acquisition of a larger self-identity in which the well-being of another is inextricably bound up with one's own. Both selves are what they are only within this relationship of determinate intersubjectivity. For this reason Hegel characterizes marriage "as love, this being-recognized without opposition of the will." [16] Union with other means overcoming not only the contractual standpoint of atomic individuals standing in isolation but also the opposition of subjective wills. In the union of a marriage the two are as one; their individual will is to have a common life and will.

Nevertheless, the family is love in its immediacy. This means that its universal consciousness, or 'We', may nevertheless be parochial and limited. The family is an exclusive universality that takes up a hostile attitude toward outsiders. The Jena manuscripts are full of examples of such hostility, namely, struggles and conflicts between families over possessions and honor. This provides an important clue about what Hegel means by natural ethical life, which involves struggles between families and clans; at the level of natural ethical life there is not yet any institution transcendent to the family or clan, with their parochial identities and loyalties. In the *System of Ethical Life 1802* Hegel observes that mastery and slavery belong to this natural ethical life because it manifests the way that outsiders are regarded and treated at this level.[17] Mastery and slavery are natural because there are not yet mediating social institutions such as the concepts of law or justice. Thus on this level of natural ethi-

---

14. *Philosophy of Spirit 1803/04*, trans. H. S. Harris, in *System of Ethical Life*, 231–232.
15. *Philosophie des Geistes 1805/06*, 193; *HHS*, 107.
16. Ibid., 200; *HHS*, 114.
17. P. 125.

cal life, justice is highly problematic and usually takes the form of revenge. But in the absence of mediating institutions such as law and impartial judges, revenge may only continue the cycle of violence, and 'justice' may degenerate into feuds between clans.

While the earlier Jena manuscripts explore the natural *Sittlichkeit*, the *Philosophy of Spirit 1805/06* shows that natural *Sittlichkeit* as a state of nature that must be transcended. The overcoming of natural particularity, egoism, and desire, which is reflected in the family as the highest institution of natural ethical life, must be extended to the level of relations between families and clans. Family parochialism must be overcome. The explicit focus of this *Aufhebung* is the institution of ownership. Ownership at this level is a question of family possessions. Hegel's example is taking possession of a piece of land. To take possession is to exclude a third party, and in this sense possession is negative: "Through his labor he has designated it as his, giving to the sign his own content as existent: a negative and exclusive significance. Another party is thereby excluded from something which he is." [18]

The issue now becomes the recognition of this exclusion of others from possession. "Taking possession is the empirical act of seizure, and this is to be justified through recognition. It is not justified merely by the fact that it has occurred." [19] From this it is evident that Hegel appropriates Fichte's argument concerning the dependence of ownership on recognition in the *Grundlage des Naturrechts*: "The . . . right of ownership, that is, the right of exclusive possession, is . . . completed and conditioned by mutual recognition and does not exist without it. All ownership is based upon the union of many wills into one will. Through this mutual recognition . . . possession changes into ownership." [20] Hegel's version of this runs thus: "Property is thus an immediate having, mediated through being-recognized." [21]

Specifically, the other who is excluded by ownership must recognize that what is mine (ours) belongs to someone other than him. This means he must recognize not only the fact of taking possession, but the possession as an embodiment and extension of another's freedom. In respecting another's freedom, he must acknowledge the right of the other to exclude him from the other's possession. The mere fact of possession (*Besitz*) becomes property (*Eigentum*) only through reciprocal recognition. Ownership is mediated by reciprocal recognition. Ownership is a right to exclude others that does not become objective or actual until it is recognized by others. This is one factor, but by no means the only factor, that may lead to a struggle for recognition. [22]

18. *Philosophie des Geistes 1805/06*, 196; *HHS*, 110.
19. *Philosophie des Geistes 1805/06*, 198; *HHS*, 112.
20. *GNR*, 129; *SR*, 182.
21. *Philosophie des Geistes 1805/06*, 208; cf. *HHS*, 123.
22. Kojève and Strauss interpret the struggle as simply a struggle over goods in conditions of scarcity. But for Hegel it is family parochialism that is another even more important factor in the struggle. In the *Phenomenology* of 1807, the struggle is necessary to prove freedom's transcen-

Recognition as the Origin
and Relation of Right

In the state of nature the concepts of ethical freedom and right have not yet emerged. The concept of relation has not yet become definite as an ethical issue. Relations are thus functions of might, force, and coercion. The problem is to cancel merely natural relations of desire, inclination, and force and replace them with relationships of rational freedom. "Their only relation, however, lies in overcoming their present relation: to leave the state of nature. In these circumstances they have no rights and no duties towards each other, but acquire rights and duties only leaving behind these circumstances."[23] The concept of right presupposes that intersubjective recognition has transcended the level of the state of nature.

Kant formulated the idea of right in the following way: "right is the sum total of those conditions within which the will of one person can be reconciled with the will of another in accordance with a universal law of freedom."[24] Right, autonomy, and freedom signify a break with nature and natural ethical life. The reconciliation of wills is not one that exists by nature, but must come about through freedom. Kant does not articulate or spell out this reconciliation in an explicit, intersubjective form. Rather, Kant's analysis presupposes that the reconciliation has already somehow occurred. According to Kant, "external and right equality . . . is that relationship among citizens whereby no one can put anyone else under a legal obligation without submitting simultaneously to a law which requires that he can himself be put under the same kind of obligation by the other person."[25] This extremely important assertion clearly implies a relation of reciprocity lying at the basis of right; however, Kant fails to show how this reciprocity might be constituted or created. He thus passes over the practical-existential problems of achieving right and morality. Kant presupposes the very thing that must be shown, namely, that and how right can be constituted and constructed as an interhuman relationship.

Hegel's proposal is that the transition from the natural condition where right does not yet exist to the civilized condition where right signifies the reconciliation of wills that confers right and imposes duty is mediated by and originates in mutual recognition. According to Hegel, "Right is the relation of persons in their comportment towards others. Right is the universal element of their free being—the determination and limitation of their empty freedom."[26] Hegel's

---

dence of nature, by placing life itself at risk. Hegel's model for this is not Hobbes's but the duel (*Zweikampf*), which in turn reflects even as it sublates conceptions of family and personal honor. See Siep, "Kampf um Anerkennung."

23. *Philosophie des Geistes 1805/06*, 197; *HHS*, 110–111.

24. Kant, *Metaphysics of Morals*, trans. H. B. Nisbet, in *Political Writings*, ed. H. Reiss (Cambridge: Cambridge University Press, 1970), 133.

25. Kant, *Perpetual Peace*, in *Political Writings*, 99n.

26. Hegel, *Philosophie des Geistes 1805/06*, 197; *HHS*, 111.

formulation of right as the universal element of freedom clearly reflects Kant's general conception of right. But he conceives right more broadly than Kant when he claims that right is any determinate existence of freedom. However, this does not deny but rather presupposes recognition, because right is not actual or objective until it is recognized. Right is a determinate intersubjectivity that is not a mere postulate or hypothesis that must be constructed and displayed.

> I need not concoct this relation or limitation for myself or produce it; rather the object itself is this producing of right in general, namely the relation of recognition. In recognition the self ceases to be this individual; it exists by right in recognition, and this means it exists no longer immersed in its immediate [natural] existence. The one who is recognized is recognized as immediately counting as such in his being. But this being is itself generated from the concept [*Begriff*]; it is being-recognized.[27]

Hegel shows here that the concept of right is a determination, not of the individual subjective will, but of the *universal* will. This universal will is not merely a formal conception, but one that arises out of and expresses the *doubled* relation of reciprocal recognition. In such reciprocal recognition, the human being ceases to be a mere individual and becomes recognized as an end in himself. He does not cease to be an individual, but his individuality and freedom count as an 'in itself'. Being-recognized (*Anerkanntsein*) means that the individual now exists as a 'universal individual', that is, an intersubjectively reciprocally recognized member of the 'We'. As a member of the 'We', he exists *by right* in recognition. *Recognition is the right to have rights.*

The right that is conferred by such recognition is not something particular, valid only in one case, but something universal. It may be claimed by one only if it may be claimed by others. Right implies a duty of others toward someone (e.g., to recognize their exclusion from his possession), on the condition that he recognizes and accepts the same duty on his part toward others. However, this universality is not abstract or formal but a reciprocal determinate, intersubjectively mediated universality. For this reason recognition constitutes Hegel's alternative or friendly amendment to Kant. Recognition means that the state of nature, in which there are no rights, but only force and coercion, has been transcended and sublated. "The human being is necessarily recognized and necessarily gives recognition. This necessity is his own, and not merely that of our thinking. . . . As recognizing, the human being is itself the movement of recognition, and *this movement is what sublates the natural state: they are recognition.*"[28] This recognition and validation of freedom by another freedom involves an exchange of abstract 'empty' freedom and/or wild lawless freedom for substantial-rational freedom, or ethical necessity. For Hegel,

---

27. Ibid.
28. *Philosophie des Geistes 1805/06*, 197; *HHS*, 111. My italics.

a 'state of nature' would be one in which there were no such thing as right or wrong because spirit would not yet have attained to the thought of its freedom. It is only with the consciousness of freedom that right and wrong begin. Moreover since the human being exists essentially as self-consciousness with the concept of good and evil, the state of nature is a state of unfreedom and wrong, which must be superseded, for freedom and its actuality lie beyond it.[29]

This ethical substance and necessity constitutes the *Anerkanntsein*, being-recognized, or recognized status. The ethically necessary demands recognition of freedom, and its reception in consciousness signifies that substantive freedom has acquired recognized status.

Hegel identifies the concept (*Begriff*) of freedom and the correlative substantial concept of freedom and right with the social universal consciousness or general will. "This knowing will is now universal. It is the state of being-recognized [*das Anerkanntsein*]; juxtaposed to itself in the form of universality, it is being, actuality in general. . . . The will of the individual is the universal will—and the universal is the individual. It is the totality of ethical life [*Sittlichkeit*] in general, immediate, yet as right." [30] In his concept of *Anerkanntsein*, being-recognized, Hegel synthesizes Rousseau's general will, Kant's concept of right, and Fichte's concept of recognition.

What should this actualized recognition, or patterns of spirit's recognition, be called? Hegel uses the term *Anerkanntsein*, or being-recognized. This denotes recognition no longer as a mere ought, or a single interpersonal action, but as an enduring pattern or structure. *Anerkanntsein* is a forerunner of what Hegel would later call objective spirit. He eventually settled on the term 'objective spirit' after 1817, but he never abandoned the term *Anerkanntsein*. Instead he continued to use it to designate the phenomenological aspect of the concept of freedom. "Freedom, which has grown into the shape of an actual world, receives the form of necessity, whose substantial connections constitute the system of freedom's conditions, and whose phenomenal connections constitute freedom's power, its being-recognized [*Anerkanntsein*], its validity in consciousness." [31]

Mutual recognition, or *Anerkanntsein*, is for Hegel the phenomenal aspect of practical reason; *Anerkanntsein* is the concept (*Begriff*) of freedom in its existential, practical aspect. The *Begriff* presupposes that self-consciousness has attained the contrast between universal and particular, and in light of that contrast, the *Begriff* cannot consistently be whittled down to the level of the merely particular. This is the defect and the structural inconsistency in nominalist individualism. For Hegel the 'subjectivity' of the *Begriff* is intersubjectivity, and reason (*Vernunft*) is inherently social, actual in the life of a people.

29. *VPR*17, §2. I have altered the English translation slightly.
30. *Philosophie des Geistes 1805/06*, 203–204; *HHS*, 118.
31. *E*, §484.

Anerkanntsein involves an affirmative self-knowledge in other. This affirmative self-recognition in other constitutes the universal social consciousness, which grounds and structures the concept of right. Right is both subjective and objective, and both conditions must be met if right is to be actual. Subjectively regarded, right is the determinate existence of freedom, the presence of freedom in something, be it my body, my possessions, or my self-esteem. Objectively right is the recognition of those presencings of freedom. Recognition intersubjectively reflects and confirms the right of freedom's presencing in the world. Thus right is intersubjectively mediated and grounded; it is at once both personal and interpersonal-social. The explication of the concept of right involves a social ontology of freedom, which Hegel elaborates initially as *Anerkanntsein*, then as objective spirit.

Being-Recognized, Right and Wrong

Once being-recognized is achieved as an enduring social condition, rational-ethical freedom has started to become actual. Right does not exist by nature; rather it is intersubjectively constituted.[32] However, once right is constituted, so is the possibility of wrong. Wrong is a negation of right, the assertion of difference against the established *Anerkanntsein*. We shall consider Hegel's theory of crime and punishment later. However, in the interest of a brief clarification of *Anerkanntsein*, it may be useful to consider Hegel's analysis of something short of crime, namely, insult. Hegel observes that "there is crime only insofar as I am recognized as an individual, and my will is taken as universal counting in itself. Prior to recognition there is no insult, no injury."[33]

Hegel's account of insult is scattered over several passages and divisions of the *Philosophy of Spirit 1805/06*. The general line of analysis is clear, but the illustrative details and examples vary. Hegel reenacts the struggle for recognition, but at a higher level, namely, on the basis of established right. This dispute is not simply about possession or property, but is a higher-level struggle for affirmative recognition or honor. "The excluded party spoils the other's possession, by introducing his excluded 'being-for-self' [*Fürsichsein*] into it, i.e, his sense of 'mine'. He ruins something in it, annihilating it as desire . . . but rather positing his own self in another, in the knowing of the other. The activity does not concern the negative aspect, the thing, but rather the self-knowledge of the other."[34] In Sartre's terms, the presence of the other means that I am no longer master of the situation. The other spoils my enjoyment of my possession; his mere presence is a disturbance. At the heart of this disturbance is the problem of one totality imposing itself on another.

---

32. The reader must keep in mind that Hegel is interested in the idea of right and the idea of the state, i.e., what these mean. He is not commenting on the origin of any particular state.

33. *Philosophie des Geistes 1805/06*, 210; *HHS*, 125.

34. *Philosophie des Geistes 1805/06*, 201; *HHS*, 115.

The one who is excluded is angered by his exclusion. His exclusion from the other's possession is also an exclusion from the other's knowledge, that is, he does not count for the other. "He becomes aware that he has done something altogether different from what he intended. His intention was the pure relating of his being to itself."[35] But instead of getting himself back from the other, he is frozen out, given the cold shoulder. 'It's mine'. "Thus angered, the two parties stand opposed to each other, the one as insulter, the other as the insulted."[36]

Precisely where one might expect a discussion of overt violence, struggle (*Kampf*), and so on, Hegel takes a different turn and proceeds to an analysis of insult and verbal injury. This analysis is important because it makes explicit a linguistic dimension of recognition. Since language is a universal medium, and since Hegel has argued that the truth of sense-certainty's particular 'this' is the enduring universal 'This', it comes as no surprise that Hegel asserts that verbal injury, or insult, is a 'universal crime'. It is a linguistic and symbolic violence that negates the other while appearing to preserve the outward appearance of nonviolence. "In verbal injury I do not say about someone that he has done this or that evil to me, but rather that he *is* this evil. The verbal injury places the other in the universal, as canceled and negated (*als ein Aufgehobenes*). . . . The word of abuse (*Schimpfwort*) transforms the victim's totality into a nullity."[37]

Unlike an overt act of violence like a physical assault that may break the other's leg or his arm, insult verbally cancels the other as a *totality*. "The one works underhandedly, while the other is openly injurious. Open murder . . . is generally the least underhanded, yet is the greatest injury. However, underhandedness consists in relating to another person as though he were nonexistent, while yet retaining the form of inwardness, so that my deed does not come to light and cannot be grasped for what it truly is, but remains cunningly reflected into itself."[38]

Hegel observes that "the honor of one who is robbed or murdered is not aggrieved, for he is recognized in himself. In other words, his being-recognized (*Anerkanntsein*) exists—not as in the state of nature where honor was attacked through injury to possessions. . . . The verbal injury injures one's honor, but not absolutely, for the injured party is not without rights."[39] But these qualifications should not obscure an important point, namely, that verbal injury is a concealed or symbolic nullification of the other. This strikes directly at the other's status as a totality and therefore strikes at the general status of recognition, or *Anerkanntsein*. The one who is nullified as a totality is clearly not genuinely recognized. Since mutual recognition is the origin of right, verbal injury calls a person's rights into question. To be sure, verbal injury does not take the person's life; he exists, but without affirmative recognition; that is, he is with-

35. Ibid.   36. Ibid.
37. *Philosophie des Geistes 1805/06*, 214; *HHS*, 130.
38. *Philosophie des Geistes 1805/06*, 215; *HHS*, 130.
39. *Philosophie des Geistes 1805/06*, 216; *HHS*, 132.

out honor. This is dangerous, for, as Hegel writes, "considered in himself, the one who is without honor is also without rights."[40]

Elsewhere, Hegel furnishes us with a humorous account of an insult and verbal injury, and portrays it as an instance of abstract thinking. In his essay "Who Thinks Abstractly?" Hegel depicts a marketplace encounter between a seller and an unfortunate shopper, who has just discovered that the seller's eggs are spoiled:

> "Old woman, your eggs are rotten!" says the maid to the market woman. "What?" she replies. "My eggs are rotten? You may be rotten! You say that about my eggs? You? Did not lice eat your father on the highways? Didn't your mother run away with the French?" "We know well where she got that scarf and her hats: if it were not for those officers, many wouldn't be decked out like that these days. . . ." [Hegel comments:] In brief, she thinks abstractly and subsumes the other woman—scarf, hat, shirt, etc., as well as her fingers and other parts of her, and her father and whole family too—solely under the 'crime' that she has found the eggs rotten. Everything about her is colored through and through by these rotten eggs, while those officers of which the market woman spoke—if, as one may seriously doubt, there is anything to that—may have got to see very different things.[41]

The maid's not so tactful remark about the rotten eggs is taken by the market woman as an insult, an affront to her honor, a challenge to her integrity. But the maid's remark requires considerable hermeneutical filtering to become an insult; it is only a potential insult. It pales by comparison with the market woman's response. Hers is an unambiguous, powerful, and well-developed verbal injury that does not stop with a riposte against a tactless remark. She launches an all-out frontal assault against the maid's honor and proceeds to nullify the maid in her entirety. She regards the young woman solely from the perspective of the latter's unwelcome remark about the rotten eggs. From this limited, partial perspective, she deprecatingly revalues all other dimensions, aspects, and relationships of the maid. Her displacement of the predicate 'rotten' from the eggs to the young woman herself transforms the latter's totality as a human being into a mere nullity. And this nullification does not stop with the young woman; it is extended to her entire family as well. All of them are, on this day at least, nullified, and banished from the market woman's universe.

The Intersubjective Concept of the Will

We turn our attention now to Hegel's account of the will and freedom in the *Jena Realphilosophie*. This earlier formulation allows us to see that Hegel's

40. Ibid.
41. G. W. F. Hegel, "Who Thinks Abstractly?" in *Hegel: Texts and Commentary*, trans. and ed. Walter Kaufmann (Notre Dame: University of Notre Dame Press, 1977), 117–118.

view of freedom and the will is intersubjective and social and that the initial account of the will in the mature *Philosophy of Right* is set forth by means of an abstraction, or methodological individualism. We shall turn to the account of the will in the *Philosophy of Right* in the next chapter.

The *Jena Philosophy of Spirit* is structured in terms of a distinction between the *concept* of *Geist* and *Geist's actuality*. This distinction reflects the distinction between subjective and objective spirit that was discussed in the previous chapter. The concept of *Geist* in turn is divided into intelligence and will. However, this apparently familiar distinction should not be interpreted as a faculty psychology philosophy of mind. Such a conception is burdened with Cartesian faculty psychology and other presuppositions that Hegel rejects. He has no intention of offering a faculty psychology: "Spirit is in general thought and the human being is distinguished from the animal by thought. But one should not imagine that the human being *thinks* on the one hand, and *wills* on the other, as though he has thought in one bag and will in another. This would be a vacuous account. The distinction between thought and will is only a distinction between theoretical and practical attitudes. These are not distinct *faculties*; rather the will is a particular mode of thinking, namely, *thinking translating itself into existence, thinking as the drive to give oneself determinate existence [Dasein]*." [42] Thus reason is practical activity.

Hegel identifies will as practical activity, namely, the activity of rational thought translating itself into existence. Mutual recognition is the basic shape assumed by reason's practical activity. To assert that reason is practical means that it presses beyond and transcends any merely subjective posture or certainty: "The formal rationality of drives and inclinations consists in the general drive *not* to exist as [merely] subjective, but to become actual through the activity of the subject itself wherein it suspends its subjectivity." [43]

Also important is Hegel's claim, advanced above, that thinking is the drive to give oneself determinate existence (*sich Dasein geben*). We have seen this terminology before, in Hegel's mature account of recognition. [44] The self gives itself determinate existence in another's recognition. This concept of the self giving itself determinate and objective existence is more general than a philosophy of the will, although the latter is an important aspect and specific working out of the former. As we will see, the will, or reason in its practical activity, can give itself existence *in things* by taking possession, and give itself existence *in an other*, namely, through mutual recognition.

The question of right is bound up with both presencings of the will, but the concept of right as such, including the right of ownership, remains founded in recognition. The recognition that confers right is the recognition that expresses the general will. Hegel understands the will as intersubjective and social.

---

42. *PR*, §4 Zusatz. Italics mine.
43. *E*, §474.   44. Chap. 4.

Specifically, he develops the contrast between the universal and the particular will as having intersubjective implications. In the *Jena Realphilosophie*, Hegel treats the will in terms of a relation of reciprocal recognition. The will itself undergoes a doubling not unlike the doubling of self-consciousness.[45] The doubling of the will involves both a contrast between universal and particular and a correlative intersubjective doubling of two independent egos.[46] There is an important correlation between both 'doublings'. The attainment of the contrast between universal and particular is a 'subjective' condition of affirmative relation with others, and relation to other is the 'objective' condition of the contrast between universal and particular that introduces difference and pushes the universal beyond abstract identity. This connection/correlation is at the heart of Hegel's distinction between subjective *Geist* and objective *Geist* and his critical interpretation of the general will.[47]

Let us examine the subjective aspect first, while keeping in mind that this examination is an abstraction from the concrete correlation. The central point is that prior to the contrast between universal and particular, self-consciousness is immediate. But immediate self-identity is abstractly universal. Abstract universality is parochial because as 'pure identity' or universality it excludes its other, namely, the particular. The parochial self excludes the other because it has not yet abstracted from its own particularity and naively equates the latter with the universal. This is the reason why Hegel portrays an initial encounter as negative, mutual repulsion. However, once the distinction between universal and particular is attained, the self's identity cannot be simply equated with the universal without suppressing the critical moment, namely, a decentering of the self. The appropriate relation between universal and particular involves a We that decenters the self. For Hegel, mature self-identity is internally complex, and at the heart of this internal complexity is an ability to abstract from one's own particularity and take a larger view of things. This abstraction from particularity and taking a larger view implies an openness to other, and to mediation.

The 'internal' doubling of the will into universal and particular is correlative to an intersubjective doubling. The I = I ceases to be an ego and instead formulates an intersubjectivity. The important point is not to collapse the intersubjective doubling of consciousness into the intrasubjective doubling of the will. In a marginal note to the *Jena Realphilosophie* Hegel writes, "First union of intelligence and will; i.e., there are two independent egos for one another. . . . These two egos . . . are opposed to one another insofar as one is internally what the other is externally. First the equivalence of the extremes is overcome and in its place has come the I, being-for-self. This is the first knowledge an indepen-

45. *Philosophie des Geistes 1805/06*, 191; *HHS*, 105.
46. Ibid.
47. See below chaps. 6 and 12.

dent I has of an independent I. And because both are egos, knowledge, there is *for them* this equality of both in their opposition."[48] How important is this note? One assessment is offered by Hegel's translator. Leo Rauch maintains that "Hegel elucidates the clash between intelligence and will as though the two were independent egos. Obviously we ought to read this as a metaphor."[49]

I am not so sure. Rauch overlooks the doubling of the will and misses the important parallel with the doubling of self-consciousness in the *Phenomenology* account of recognition. The two accounts are very similar, which suggests that intersubjectivity is more than a metaphor. Further, if the intersubjectivity here is metaphorical, what is the metaphor about? If intelligence and will were merely opposing faculties within a single subject, their synthesis would reside, as it were, in the subject, and the result would be a monosubjectival conception of the will. This would be a reversion to the abstract individualism that Hegel is seeking to overcome. Moreover, Rauch himself subsequently grants more than metaphorical significance to the contrast between intelligence and will when he writes that "the synthesis is provided by *recognition*. By considering recognition we transfer our attention from the individual/psychological plane to that of the interpersonal and social."[50] In this Rauch is surely correct, whatever may be the proper reading of the marginal note. Hegel's concept of the will, like his concept of freedom, is inherently intersubjective and social. The basic pattern of self-recognition in other is present in Hegel's concepts of recognition, will, and freedom.

Although Hegel stresses the abstract tautology of the ego = ego as a conceptual formula for the will, he also points out that the will, so conceived, remains abstract because it lacks difference. Since it lacks difference, it does not constitute a world for itself. In order to overcome this abstract identity, "the will must achieve a form in which it is different from itself."[51] This is a difference that points to the concept of recognition as the phenomenological transition from subjective to objective spirit. The latter, as a concrete unity of the will, is a unity that is "attained in the independence of both extremes."[52] This concrete unity of the will, embodied in determinate existence (*Dasein*), constitutes both right and duty, that is, a system of ethical life.

48. *Philosophie des Geistes 1805/06*, 191 f.; translation, 105. Italics in original.
49. Rauch, *HHS*, 25.
50. Ibid., 29. Italics mine.
51. *VPR*18, Ilting, 220.   52. Ibid.

Part Two

Recognition in the *Philosophy of Right*

6

Systematic Issues in the
Philosophy of Right

Right, like the concept of spirit, has its existential genesis in the process of recognition. Right without freedom is meaningless. Right is recognition of freedom, not simply as or by a particular subjective will, but by the general will. That is why the validity and legitimacy of right are fundamentally a matter of the 'We', that is, of objective spirit. Objective spirit signifies in part the securing of freedom and right through and by means of recognition, that is, an *Anerkanntsein*, or being-recognized. Objective spirit is the ensemble of the conditions and institutions necessary for freedom to be actual in the world.

In what follows we shall focus on the *Philosophy of Right* as an elaboration and extension of the concept of objective spirit whose phenomenological genesis in intersubjective recognition already has been explored. Our initial interest will be to understand the structure of the *Philosophy of Right*—its fundamental divisions of abstract right, morality, and ethical life—and to clarify what right is. Right is properly appreciated only when its rational-universal grounding in intersubjective recognition is understood. If there were no recognition, there would be no right, but only the subjective certainty of freedom. In such a circumstance, right would not be actual but merely a claim or an idea. Everything else that is said about right or rights is an articulation of recognition in its various determinate modes and *Gestalten*.

This is not to deny that the *Philosophy of Right* is part of a categorical philosophy, a philosophy whose concept of the concrete or determinate universal is one of its major contributions. Hugh Reyburn, whose *Ethical Theory of Hegel* first appeared more than seventy years ago and which remains a valuable study, correctly notes that the basic divisions of the *Philosophy of Right*—abstract right, morality, and ethical life—correspond respectively to the logic of being, the logic of essence, and the logic of the concept.[1] Klaus Hartmann is likewise correct in his observation that the *Philosophy of Right* is categorically ordered.[2]

The categorical aspect of Hegel's philosophy can perhaps best be appreciated when we note that contemporary philosophy, and not only liberal political theory, is dominated by nominalism. This means that they are more or less confined to individualism and cannot offer a plausible account of social institutions. For Hartmann, the main interest of Hegel's thought lies in its theory of categories. Whatever else may be said about Hegel's reconstructed theory of universals, its supreme merit, as far as ethics and social and political philosophy are concerned, is that the concrete universal explicates affirmative intersubjective relations and makes possible an account of social institutions that is a third alternative to abstract atomic individualism and collectivist communitarianism. However, the aim of this study is not to develop at length the connections between the logic and the *Philosophy of Right*; Reyburn and Hartmann have already done that. The aim of this study remains focused on the concept of recognition. But the two aims are not antithetical. For Hegel, the concept of recognition is the practical aspect and realization of the concept (*Begriff*) of freedom. It is the 'existential-phenomenological aspect' of the concept of freedom. Although the categorical order is distinct from the phenomenological order, there is no inherent conflict between the two.

Recognition in the Argument of the *Philosophy of Right*

Karl-Heinz Ilting has written a helpful structural analysis of the *Philosophy of Right*.[3] Beneath the presentations of abstract right, morality, and ethical life, there is a systematic issue, namely, the relation, mediation, and/or reconciliation between modern views of individual subjectivity and freedom, on the one hand, and the objective collectivism of classical political philosophy, namely, Plato and Aristotle, the founders of the natural law tradition, on the other. Hegel's project is in part to mediate between Kant and Aristotle. In his analysis of Hegel's proposed mediation between the ancients and the moderns, Ilting believes that the *Philosophy of Right* contains two separate and distinct systems of political philosophy, modern individualism and classical collec-

---

1. Reyburn, *The Ethical Theory of Hegel*. I can accept Reyburn's analysis only with the qualification that for Hegel the state is a singular universal, i.e., an individual among other individual states. At the international level there is no We, only a quasi-Hobbesian state of nature. However, the state is not the ultimate or final point of view; for Hegel, the state is subordinate to world history and absolute spirit. See below chap. 14.

2. Klaus Hartmann, "Towards a Systematic Reading of Hegel's *Philosophy of Right*." However, the "yield" of such an analysis, while important at the ontological-categorical level, is also thin. For another categorical approach to Hegel, see Kolb, *The Critique of Pure Modernity*.

3. Karl-Heinz Ilting, "The Structure of Hegel's *Philosophy of Right*," in *Hegel's Political Philosophy*, ed. Z. A. Pelczynski (Cambridge: Cambridge University Press, 1971), 90–110.

tivism. Ilting seeks to mitigate this apparently stark contrast and opposition by arguing that for Hegel the first two parts, abstract right and morality, are abstractions from the third, ethical life. Thus in parts 1 and 2, Ilting believes that Hegel adopts a *methodological* individualism. The term abstract right is a signal that "Hegel makes use of the same method as all his predecessors since Hobbes. He abstracts from all conditions of social life which are created by human activity itself. The background of his arguments . . . is the fiction of a state of nature without any form of established society. . . . In order to make clear to the reader that this methodological fiction underlies the whole section, Hegel has given the heading 'abstract right' to the first part of the *Philosophy of Right*."[4]

Modern moral and political philosophy rests on individualist conceptions and assumptions. Missing from the political discourse of modernity is an adequate understanding of and vocabulary for expressing social and political institutions. To overcome the individualistic basis and bias of modern moral philosophy and to arrive at a theory of the state as an ethical-political community, Hegel finds it necessary to go beyond modern thought by retrieving the thought tradition originated by Plato and Aristotle. Ilting maintains that "the *Philosophy of Right* . . . contains two different systems of practical philosophy. This means that any interpretation of the framework of Hegel's theory of the modern state has to answer the question how the legal and moral theory of the first two parts is related to the theory of communities and social institutions of the third part."[5] How is the modern nominalist concept of subjectivity of the first two parts related to the intersubjective theory of ethical life and social institutions of the third part?

Ilting answers his own question with the following proposal, which is at the same time a proposal concerning the unity of the work, how the two halves of it are supposed to go together: "The answer is that the juristic and moral theory is meant to be understood as a methodological fiction; man abstractly conceived as an autonomous person and as a moral subject, lives in reality, in a situation of manifold social interrelations. Insofar as . . . individualistic rational law and . . . individual morality presuppose these interrelations which are not created by the free decisions of individuals, Hegel maintains that juristic and ethical theory achieve their true meaning and validity only in the context of the theory of institutions and communities."[6] Ilting's proposal that Hegel sets forth abstract right and morality in terms of a "methodological individualism" is a useful clarification. Without it we would have the problem of explaining

---

4. Ilting, "The Structure of Hegel's *Philosophy of Right*," 91. See also Ludwig Siep, "Intersubjektivität, Recht und Staat in Hegels *Grundlinien der Philosophie des Rechts*," in *Hegels Philosophie des Rechts: Die Theorie der Rechtsformen und ihre Logik*, Hrsg. D. Henrich and R.-P. Horstmann (Stuttgart: Klett-Cotta, 1982), 255–277; Manfred Riedel, "Hegel's Criticism of Natural Law [Theory]," in *Between Tradition and Revolution*, 76–106.

5. Ibid., 99.   6. Ibid.

how Hegel conjures social institutions of ethical life, such as family, civil society, and state, out of some version of the Cartesian *cogito*, or monological subjectivity. Ilting's distinction helps to avoid that confusion.[7] Nevertheless, he exaggerates the differences between the first two parts (abstract right and morality) and the third (ethical life).

In its general outline, Ilting's proposal is correct. His proposal that a methodological individualism undergirds the first two parts of the work is a helpful clarification of a certain abstruseness in the exposition of abstract right. But this is only helpful as a first approximation, for Ilting's "methodological individualism" obscures rather than clarifies the concept of subjectivity present in the work as a whole. Ilting makes it appear as if Hegel employs a conception of the Cartesian *cogito* or abstract subjectivity in parts 1 and 2, only to discover its formalism and vacuity, and then is compelled to abandon the *cogito* in favor of an objective heteronomous concept of right and collectivism in part 3, which is ultimately borrowed from Plato and Aristotle. On these assumptions Ilting would be correct to speak of *two different systems* of practical philosophy within Hegel's *Philosophy of Right*. Then the problem would be how to reconcile the abstract individualism of part 1 with the equally abstract collectivism of part 2. To this problem there is no solution, other than a forced choice between classical objective collectivism and modern individualist subjectivity. Confronted with these options, Ilting maintains that for Hegel the classical collectivism ultimately takes priority over modern subjectivity. Ilting's proposed "solution" merely restates the problem to which he has called attention.

If Hegel employs a methodological individualism in parts 1 and 2, what is the concept of subjectivity from which this individualism is an abstraction? Ilting gives us no account of this "concrete" subjectivity, nor does he mention, much less offer, a treatment of the concept of recognition. Given this omission, it is not surprising that Ilting thinks that Hegel ultimately sides with Plato. However, Ilting neglects and passes over the important transition from subjective spirit to objective spirit, which, in the mature post-*Phenomenology* system, the concept of recognition accomplishes and mediates. This transition is important, not only for objective spirit, but also for Hegel's project of mediating Kant and Plato/Aristotle.

My thesis is that the concept of recognition is crucial to Hegel's project of mediating modern individualist subjective freedom (Kant) and classical ethical

7. On the other hand, Seyla Benhabib does not. Failing to note the methodological abstraction underlying the first part of the *Philosophy of Right*, she believes like Michael Theunissen that Hegel's account of the will is solipsistic and fails to do justice to otherness. Hence she has the apparent problem of reconciling the individualism of abstract right and morality with the theory of social institutions in ethical life. See her otherwise valuable study, *Critique, Norm and Utopia: A Study of the Foundation of Critical Theory* (New York: Columbia University Press, 1986), 90–95. Allen Wood touches on this systematic problem only in passing as a tension between Hegel's reflective and substantive principle; see *HET*, 243–247.

substance (Plato, Aristotle). Hegel shows that mutual recognition transforms subjectivity into an intersubjectivity that is compatible with the classical thesis that the whole is greater than and prior to its parts, and has as its telos a thoroughgoing reciprocal recognition that culminates in a nonparochial universal-social consciousness. This in turn makes possible a critical appropriation and transformation of the structures of classical ethical substance into social institutions necessary for freedom. To be sure, not all the classical social structures of the polis survive this translation owing to the critical principle that subjective freedom demands recognition. For example, the institution of slavery is not compatible with the universal principle of subjective freedom that demands reciprocal recognition and political equality. Moreover, new institutions are demanded by subjective freedom, namely, the institutions of ownership, contract, and civil society. The problem is to provide an ethical critique and restraint on these institutions, by qualifying and delimiting the individualism to which they give rein. Hegel does this by placing these institutions in a larger social-ethical framework, which is made up of enduring institutions, namely, the family and the state. These institutions are not simply given by nature; they are institutions of ethical freedom.

Ilting forgets that Hegel reaches his position through a *critique* of both classical and modern political philosophy. Hegel views these as abstract collectivism and abstract individualism, respectively. However, Hegel's task is not to pick one side of the ancient/modern, or collectivist/individualist debate while suppressing the other, but rather to work out a third alternative that acknowledges the truth while overcoming the defects of both abstract individualism and abstract collectivism. In support of this interpretation, Manfred Riedel makes an important historical observation:

> At the end of the Jena period Hegel's criticism of modern natural law theories from the standpoint of classical politics undergoes a transformation when he also criticizes classical politics from the standpoint of [modern] natural law theory. . . . On the one hand Hegel interprets Rousseau's theory of the general will, originating in the wills of individuals by recollecting the Aristotelian thought that the whole is prior to its parts, from which it follows that for individual wills the general will is primary and the essential. On the other hand . . . Hegel contrasts the separateness of the absolute knowledge of individuality as the higher principle of modern times to the immediate unity of universal and individual in ancient polis morality.[8]

However, in spite of his incisive comments, Riedel fails to appreciate the importance of recognition and intersubjectivity in Hegel's critique of both ancients and moderns and in his third alternative.

Hegel agrees with Rousseau against Plato and Aristotle that freedom is the

---

8. Riedel, "Hegel's Criticism of Natural Law," 96–97.

principle of state. "The right of the subject's particularity to find satisfaction, or . . . the right of subjective freedom, is the pivotal and focal point in the difference between antiquity and the modern age."[9] Subjectivity and subjective freedom are fundamental for modernity, but subversive for classical political philosophy. Hegel points out in reference to Plato that "this subjective particularity, excluded from the organization of the whole and not reconciled within it, consequently shows itself . . . as a hostile element, as a corruption of the social order."[10] Hegel believes that modernity requires the recognition and inclusion of subjective freedom. This means that for Hegel, contrary to Plato, the good is the *good will* (Kant), and as such, the good is not actual apart from the agency of subjective freedom: "the universal does not attain validity or fulfillment without the interest, knowledge and volition of the particular."[11] Apart from freedom, the good would remain abstract.

On the other hand, Hegel is also critical of modern, that is, Cartesian-Kantian, understandings of subjectivity. "The great progress of our time is that subjectivity is recognized as an absolute moment. Subjectivity is essential. But everything depends on how subjectivity is understood."[12] Modernity tends to understand its principle of subjectivity nominalistically as an abstract individualism. Hegel does not believe that such a view is simply false. It is, however, only a part of the truth about subjectivity. Hegel accepts to a certain extent (i.e., methodological individualism) this partial truth and its way of speaking when he asserts a concept of right that is broader than Kant's: "Right is any determinate existence in which the free will is present."[13] But it is one thing for the will to be present in some determinate existence, whether property or another, and quite another for the will to be *recognized* as present. I am not free until I realize that freedom is what I am; but even this self-consciousness is still deficient, at best a subjective certainty. My freedom remains a subjective certainty and not yet a right in the full sense, until it is recognized and acknowledged by others. Both of these conditions—the presence of freedom in something (consciousness, body, property) and the intersubjective *recognition* of that presence—must be satisfied if right is to be actual, that is, objective as well as merely subjective. This dual condition makes it evident that the individualist concept of subjectivity, while not false, is insufficient for a proper understanding of right. Individualism does not reach the level of recognition or of objective spirit, which it nevertheless presupposes.

Moreover, Hegel believes that the Cartesian *cogito*, or nominalist individual subjectivity, is formal and empty, and so incapable of providing a foundation

9. *PR*, §124.   10. Ibid., §206.   11. Ibid., §260.

12. Hegel, *Vorlesungen über die Philosophie der Religion, Werke*, Theoriewerkausgabe (Frankfurt: Suhrkamp, 1970), 17:190. Hereafter cited as *VPR*. English translation: *Lectures on the Philosophy of Religion*, vol. 3, ed. and trans. Peter C. Hodgson et al. (Berkeley: University of California Press, 1985), 166.

13. *PR*, §29.

for normative culture. Specifically, the individual by himself is insufficient to ground or establish the concept of right. Right is grounded in the intersubjective general will, not the individual will. However, Hegel's alternative to modernity's individualism is not simply to introduce dogmatically classical collectivism or to graft its objective theory of right heteronomously onto an individualistically conceived subject. Rather he criticizes and decenters the concept of 'the subject'. Hegel's thesis is that the modern individualist concept of subjectivity must be completed in an intersubjectively constituted general will. That is, the general will constituted in mutual recognition is a condition and presupposition of subjective freedom. The concept of freedom has its telos, its full deployment in the concept of community. Hegel writes, "This right of *subjectivity . . . has the structure [Gestalt] of recognition.*" [14]

Both Hegel and Fichte seek to ground right in mutual recognition. Simply stated, right is the relation of persons to each other, as they recognize (or fail to recognize) each other. The genesis of right therefore coincides with the recognition of the other as other. Right is present whenever the other is recognized as counting, as carrying weight against one's freedom, and vice versa. Both right and ethics are conceived as interhuman modes of existence. In mutual recognition, nominalist individualism is transcended in principle; for mutual recognition establishes a nonheteronomous, concrete universal subject or general will that is constituted when individuals overcome their isolation and abstraction. The structure of reciprocal recognition implies that a right can be asserted only on the condition that it may be asserted or claimed by all. Reciprocity further implies a correlation between rights and duties. A's right corresponds to a duty on B's part, and vice versa. The intersubjective origin of the concept of right opens the way to further substantive normative considerations. In this way Hegel seeks a critical retrieval of the classical concept of substantive freedom within his social phenomenology of right. The classical concept of justice is not a bloodless abstraction floating above history but captures and expresses an insight grounded concretely in mutual recognition.

This does not mean that right is thus reduced to a merely arbitrary or optional interpersonal transaction. Such a confusion arises when subjectivity is construed nominalistically. Then right tends to be interpreted as a contract; that is, a commercial contract between individuals is taken to be the paradigm case of right. Hegel complains that this view of right as a contract has confused property relations with ethical and political relations, to the detriment of the latter. [15] We shall see that although contract is a determinate shape of recognition, it is also abstract and intersubjectively deficient. For this reason contract fails to express what right is. Hegel believes that the result of recognition is spirit, the I that is a We. Spirit is a determinate objective social world, an ob-

14. *VPR*, 3:181. My italics.
15. *PR*, §75.

jective rational structure, or ethical substance. Consequently, for Hegel, right cannot be fully present at the level of the abstraction of individual subjectivity, but only at the level of recognition and spirit. "The concept of right is not something that one has at one's fingertip or gets at first look, or that each one conjures up out of his own brains. . . . The basis of right is freedom; right without freedom would be meaningless. . . . This determinate existence [of freedom] is not something accidental, but determined by the concept itself, and only thus is it appropriate and legitimate." [16] Right follows not from the particular consciousness or will but from the general will or spirit. Mutual recognition is the phenomenal aspect of practical reason; it is the *Begriff* or self-consciousness of freedom on its existential and practical side. The general will, as a normative conception, unfolds itself into the shape of a free and just community and expresses the animating spirit of that community. The *Begriff* of freedom, as a determinate universal, includes the contrast between a social universal and particular, which is the logical possibility of judgments of right and wrong. In light of that contrast, the *Begriff* cannot consistently be whittled down to the level of the merely particular. This is the defect and the structural inconsistency in nominalist individualism.

Hegel believes that both the ancients and the moderns have important insights, but they express their insights in a one-sided way. Hegel's alternative is the concept of a free and just community constituted by reciprocal recognition. Such a community is not a given, or a natural community, but a community of spirit realized, if at all, through freedom. Both modernity with its concept of subjective freedom and the classical polis with its concept of social structures articulate important insights and dimensions of a community of freedom. But neither by itself is sufficient as an account of that community as such. For Hegel, the individualist subjectivity of modernity is insufficient to ground normative culture, because such subjectivity makes difference absolute. [17] The collectives of classical thought provide structures and content but are ultimately authoritarian and leave no place for subjective freedom. The defect of each is to be made good by the other: modern subjectivity receives content in certain classical structures in which the whole takes priority over the parts. Conversely, classical holist structures achieve critical realization only through subjective freedom, provided that such is "expanded" through recognition to intersubjectivity. The concept of right for Hegel finds expression in a free and just community:

> In the life of a people the concept of the realization of self-conscious reason has its full reality. In this living totality we intuit the independence of the other in complete union with him. . . . Here there is nothing that would not be reciprocal.

16. *VPR*, 3:100–101.
17. G. W. F. Hegel, *The Difference between Fichte's and Schelling's System of Philosophy*, trans. H. S. Harris and W. Cerf (Albany: SUNY Press, 1977), 81.

... In the universal spirit therefore each has self-certainty, i.e., each is certain of finding nothing other than himself in existing reality. Each is as certain of the others as he is of himself. I intuit that all the others are for themselves the same independent being that I am. I intuit in the others the same free union with other, so that just as this unity exists through me, it exists through the others as well. I regard them as myself, and myself as them. In a free people therefore reason is realized in truth.[18]

The concept of *Geist* is both a social reason and a community of ethical life.

Hegel's Method of Abstraction

The *Philosophy of Right* is an exposition of reason in its practical activity. This practical activity is expressed in traditional terms as an activity of the will, which drives toward self-realization. The account of the will that Hegel sketches here is very difficult and compressed. The will is reason in practical activity; it is not a particular topic of faculty psychology, or a topic of freedom versus determinism couched within the abstract categories of mind-body dualism. "Those who regard thinking as a particular distinct faculty, divorced from the will as an equally distinct faculty, who in addition even consider that thinking is prejudicial to the will—especially the good will—show from the very outset that they are totally ignorant of the nature of the will."[19]

Since the will is reason in practical activity, Hegel considers the will in a series of steps that proceed from abstract to concrete, from the will-in-itself to the will-for-itself. This progression is from simple, not yet conscious shapes, to more complex self-conscious shapes of the will. Hegel explains this gradual, stepwise procedure as follows:

But in order that this progression from something abstract to a concrete which contains it as a possibility, may not be regarded as an isolated and therefore doubtful phenomenon, we can remind ourselves that in the *Philosophy of Right* a similar progression must take place. In this science [*Wissenschaft*] we begin with something abstract, namely the concept of the will; we then go on to the actualization of the as yet abstract will in an external existent, i.e., to the sphere of [abstract] formal right. From there we go on to the will that is reflected into itself out of external existence, i.e., to the sphere of morality. Thirdly and lastly we come to the will that unites within itself these two abstract moments and is therefore the concrete ethical will.[20]

The abstract is contained within the concrete as a possibility. But ethical life is the concrete totality, the actual reality in which abstract right and morality are embedded and grounded, even though it comes "after" these in Hegel's order of exposition.

18. *PhG*, 257–258.   19. *PR*, §5.   20. *E*, §408 Zusatz.

In comparison with the concretely actual, the abstract is merely a possibility. The *Philosophy of Right* begins with a methodological abstraction or methodological individualism, in which the will is considered as a concept that suspends itself qua 'mere' concept and presses on toward self-realization in the world of things and in others. Abstract right is abstract not simply because it abstracts from the social but also because it considers the presence of freedom only in things (*Sachen*) and possessions. This presencing of freedom in things constitutes the meaning of the legal person for Hegel. The concept of the legal person is the first shape of the will; it is highly abstract, formal, and "impersonal." But note that the presencing of freedom in things, even if all that is meant is the presencing of individual freedom in its possessions, cannot be formulated as right apart from some sort of recognition of that presencing. Recognition transforms possession into ownership. As we shall see, in respecting property one is really respecting the right of presencing of another's (as well as one's own) freedom in a thing, or possession. This recognition generates a normative ethical-legal imperative: "Be a person and respect others as persons."[21]

Similarly morality is also abstract in that it considers the presencing of freedom in consciousness, in subjectivity. Morality represents a higher level of the presencing of freedom than does abstract right. In abstract right, freedom has determinate existence and presence in a thing. Moreover, its presencing is immediate, that is, as "mine." But such presencing of freedom, that is, its immediate existence in property, is not adequate to freedom. Awareness of this deficiency points to a higher level of freedom's presencing, namely, in subjectivity itself. I am no longer free merely in reference to this particular thing; rather I am free in my reflection and thought. Hegel treats morality as a self-reflexion of the will. This is the second shape of the will in subjectivity itself.

In morality the locus wherein freedom presences and embodies itself is subjectivity itself. So everything in this presencing of freedom now turns on the right of subjective intention and insight. It is easy to construe this right of subjectivity as sheer individualism. But such a "subjective" interpretation of subjectivity is for Hegel a misinterpretation, as his long polemic against the identification of truth with subjectivity makes evident.[22] On the contrary, for Hegel, "this right of subjectivity has the *Gestalt* of recognition."[23] That is, the right of free subjectivity presupposes intersubjectivity. Recognition is crucial to the right of freedom to be actual and present in the world. However, moral reflection abstracts from and tacitly presupposes this intersubjective sense of right. Moral reflection focuses on the presencing of freedom in subjectivity in the abstract, that is, in abstraction from its intersubjective *Gestalt*. Following Kant, morality is a matter of individual reflection, which is why Hegel regards morality not only as abstract but also as a potential sickness, a brooding over possi-

21. *PR*, §36.   22. Ibid., §140.   23. *VPR*, 3:181.

bilities. He agrees, however, that the right of insight and intention is such that it cannot be consistently claimed for oneself without at the same time being claimed on behalf of others. In this way morality is pushed beyond mere consideration of possibilities to the intersubjective substantive ethical level. Moreover, through mutual recognition the right of reflection and conscience becomes objective, that is, becomes established as right. Morality, when thought through, negates its own abstraction and becomes ethical life.

Consequently, Hegel believes that abstract right and morality are both abstractions that attain their truth only in ethical life, which is the unity of subjectivity and the general concept of rational freedom, or will. "The unyielding atom of the person, of subjectivity, must have yielded, and given up its exclusiveness and made itself commensurate with the good. Thus the person has attained its concept, no longer to be merely as the abstractum [abstract inwardness] of the good, but rather to exist in concrete actual freedom."[24] Such is the dynamism and telos of freedom: not to be merely subjective, but to be objective in the form of a social world of ethical life. Freedom is actual not simply in individuals, but in the community that secures, justifies, and grounds individual freedom. The state is the realization of the totality of the conditions of freedom.

But note that Hegel's concept of ethical life is not an abrupt turning away from subjectivity toward an abstract objective collectivism. Hegel reaches the concept of ethical life in part by decentering the individualist concept of subjectivity and enlarging it toward intersubjectivity. This makes possible a critical, nonheteronomous appropriation of the classical insight into the insufficiency of individuals and the necessity of community in order to meet their needs. The whole constituted by mutual recognition is prior to the parts, and the parts depend on the whole. Hegel's conviction is that there is no necessary or inherent conflict between freedom and community; rather community is crucial for the safeguarding and full development of freedom. However, unlike the classical polis, critical ethical life must recognize the right of its constituent individuals. "The principle of modern states has enormous strength and depth because it allows the principle of subjectivity to attain the fulfillment in the self-sufficient extreme of personal particularity, while at the same time bringing it back to substantial unity and so preserving this unity in the principle of subjectivity itself."[25]

As far as the structure of the *Philosophy of Right* itself is concerned, ethical life (part 3) must be understood to be the concrete carrier of the abstract right of part 1 and morality of part 2. Even though the latter come first in the order of exposition, they have their actuality and truth only within the larger whole of ethical life, which has its own development from family through civil society and state. Hegel puts the point quite clearly in the following discussion.

24. Ibid., 182.   25. *PR*, §260.

In the sphere of ethical life [*Sittlichkeit*] itself we again start from an immediate, from the natural undeveloped shape possessed by the ethical spirit in the family. Then we come to the splitting up of ethical substance in civil society. Finally, in the state, we attain the unity and truth of the previous one-sided forms of ethical spirit. However, the course followed by our exposition does not in the least mean that we want to make ethical life later in time than right or morality, or that we would want to explain the family and civil society to be antecedent to the state in the actual world. On the contrary, we know very well that ethical life is the foundation of right and morality, and that the well-ordered distinctions of family and civil society already presuppose the existence of the state.[26]

The Concept of the Will

For Hegel, the will is reason in practical activity. But just for this reason the will has an internal complexity. Two dimensions of this complexity are familiar; but the third, the speculative unity, seems to the understanding to be a nest of contradictions and so 'impossible'. Hegel's language concerning the will reflects Kant's terminology. Kant discussed the will in terms of a distinction between *Wille* and *Willkür*. This distinction in turn reflects a political metaphor and distinction between legislative and executive functions. For Kant, *Wille* is identical with practical reason. It 'gives' or legislates a law. The moral law is thus a product of freedom in this legislative sense. But the will, or practical reason, is formal in that it commands simply by virtue of its form and not by virtue of any specific content. That is why Fichte could reformulate Kant's categorical imperative as simply 'Be consistent' or 'Do not contradict yourself'. However, while the *Wille* imposes or legislates certain commands, it does not act. *Wille* commands not as an agent but only as a principle.[27]

But who or what does *Wille* command? Kant's answer is that *Wille* commands a subservient, agential power, which he calls *Willkür*. This is usually rendered as subjective will or subjective freedom. It is negative in the sense of being independent of nature. *Willkür* signifies a break with nature and natural mechanism. It has needs and requires incentives. Since it is negative, it needs to supplement its negativity or emptiness with a positive content and freedom. But its content must be given, and it depends on such givenness. The content of *Willkür* appears to be contingent, and it may be arbitrary. Ideally, however, it is supposed to derive its content from its concept, that is, the *Wille*, or practical reason. When *Willkür* conforms to *Wille*, then it is as it ought to be. For Kant, the *Wille* legislates but does not act, while *Willkür* acts but does not legislate.

---

26. *E*, §408 Zusatz.

27. See Lewis White Beck, *A Commentary on Kant's Critique of Practical Reason* (Chicago: University of Chicago Press, 1960). For a more recent qualification of and dissent from some aspects of Beck's reading of the *Wille/Willkür* distinction, see Henry Allison, *Kant's Theory of Freedom* (Cambridge: Cambridge University Press, 1990), 129–136.

The question is, what are the ontological implications of this distinction? Kant maintains that *Wille* and *Willkür* designate not two different wills but rather one will with two different kinds of freedom: the freedom to project possibilities, legislate universal unconditional commands, and the freedom of action. But if for Kant there are not two wills, there nevertheless is a disproportion between ought and is, and so a noncoincidence of *Wille* and *Willkür*. This is a Platonic element in Kant's conception.

Hegel takes up the distinction between *Wille* and *Willkür* as part of the complex structure of the will but, like Aristotle, rejects any dualistic interpretation. He believes that Kant's and Fichte's analyses remain caught in dualism, or noncoincidence between transcendental and empirical, between substantive and reflective freedom.[28] In turning to Hegel's analysis, I must add the qualification that the following exposition is not intended as a comprehensive treatment of Hegel's philosophy of the will, but only as an analysis of the relevant sections of the *Philosophy of Right*. In addition the methodological abstraction and methodological individualism of the first parts of the *Philosophy of Right* should be kept in mind, for this influences both what is said and what is not said about the will.

The will, like the concept of right, is initially considered abstractly, that is, from the perspective of a methodological individualism. The social and mundane context of the will is bracketed, as is the distinction 'subjective/objective'. Hegel's discussion is oriented on the distinction between theoretical and practical reason: "The distinction between thought and will is simply that between the theoretical and practical attitudes. But they are not two separate faculties; on the contrary, the will is a particular way of thinking—thinking translating itself into existence [*Dasein*], thinking as the drive to give itself determinate existence."[29] The practical orientation of the will "immediately sets up a separation"[30] from the world. That is, autonomy is a break with nature and merely natural processes and activity. "Insofar as I am practical or active . . . I determine myself, and to determine myself means precisely to posit a difference."[31]

Hegel's analysis of willing thus begins with the moment of difference, or separation, the negative dimension of autonomy. The will, he tells us, includes an element of pure indeterminacy, or the I's reflection into itself (I = I), in which every limitation, every determinacy, and every content can be dissolved. This first element in the will's complex structure is "absolute abstraction or univer-

---

28. See Hegel, *Faith and Knowledge*. In this essay Hegel criticizes the reflective philosophies of finitude as part of the Enlightenment, which he characterizes as a hubbub of vanity without a firm core (p. 56). Those coming in for such censure are Kant, Jacobi, and Fichte, who, Hegel believes, have exhausted the possibilities of the position.

29. *PR*, §4 Zusatz. It should be noted that for Hegel even the theoretical attitude, insofar as it is a self-determining autonomous activity, presupposes and embodies the will: "It is equally impossible to adopt a theoretical attitude or to think without will, for in thinking we are necessarily active."

30. Ibid.   31. Ibid.

sality, the pure thinking of oneself."[32] The pure identity of self-reflection, the gathering of the self into unity, is also a negation of all determinacy. The will is the power of negation, the power of abstracting from every determination—whether given, or posited by the will.[33] Hegel also describes this power as a flight from every content as a limitation. The flight from determinacy manifests negative freedom. Since it is a flight from everything determinate, this freedom cannot have any positive expression. It is empty, a freedom of the void. It can come to expression only in destruction, or in reaction. Those who are familiar with Hegel's discussion of the transition from pure being to nothingness in the opening category of the logic will be able to appreciate more fully Hegel's connection of pure willing of the I = I (or abstract identity) with the negative freedom of the void. Pure being turns out to be indistinguishable from nothing.[34] This analysis lies behind Hegel's critique of Kant's *Wille* as formal and empty and his critique of Rousseau's general will, which came to negative expression in the terror following the French Revolution.

However, this capacity for abstraction and freeing from determinacy is for Hegel not necessarily nihilistic, nor is negative freedom inherently evil. Negation presupposes something that it negates or flees. It also underlies and makes possible a break from determination by the past and opens new possibilities, such as occurs in forgiveness and reconciliation. In the event of a violation or injury, the injured party is tempted to insist on his rights. While it is not wrong to do so, such a posture, if it becomes fixed, would make reconciliation impossible. Reconciliation requires a giving up of the legal-penal standpoint, where the question of right is central and constitutive. In not standing on or insisting on his rights in the face of violation, the 'beautiful soul' makes forgiveness and reconciliation possible.[35] Note that in this case, the abstraction from the determinacy of violation and violated right is not a flight from determinacy per se but a *voluntary* renunciation of right. In not insisting on rights, in giving up the demands and claims of abstract legal personhood, Hegel believes that the wounds of the spirit can be healed and that reconciliation is possible.

Nevertheless, the pure will of abstract freedom, despite its putative universality, remains deficiently universal. "For since it is an abstraction from all determinacy, it is itself not without determinacy; and the fact that it is abstract and one-sided constitutes its determinacy, deficiency and finitude."[36] Conse-

---

32. *PR*, §5.

33. This is another version of the negative, dissolving power of the analytical understanding.

34. This is why the first category of thought turns out not to be being, but becoming. Since the determination of being is to have no determination, being is indistinguishable from nothing. Being is thinkable only as transition, as becoming. Hence being turns out to be an abstraction from becoming and an abstract possibility in becoming. See Hegel, *SL*, 82–105.

35. See Hegel's important analysis of the beautiful soul and reconciliation in *ETW*, 234 ff.

36. *PR*, §6. This argument draws on and parallels Hegel's analysis of pure being in the logic. Pure being is without any determinate feature or characteristic. Its 'determination' is to have no determinations.

quently, although it is a dimension of the will and freedom, negative freedom does not exhaust freedom, nor can it be regarded as genuinely free. It is not a satisfactory concept of freedom because it remains bound up with and tied to what it negates or abstracts from. Hegel brings out the deficiency of this freedom with the following example: "But a human being who flees from an enemy and negates him, is not free before him, or free in his presence. Thus abstract freedom is conditioned by what it negates. It is not non-negating [*unnegierend*]; it is only conditioned."[37] Negative freedom is not free from what it negates. Negative freedom can only flee or shun relation; *it is not free to be in relation.* For relation implies limit and determinacy, which in turn cancel indeterminate freedom and indeterminacy. This negative moment of freedom is related to the phenomenon of resentment.

The second moment of freedom is the moment of determinacy. Hegel conceives this as a negation of the first moment, which itself is negative. The first negation says no, it is flight from; it is the will of the void. But to be actual, a will must will *something*. "For a will that remains in indeterminacy is no will at all."[38] Again, "A will which . . . wills only the abstract universal, wills *nothing* and is therefore not a will at all."[39] In willing *something*, the will ceases its brooding over possibilities and gives itself presence and embodiment in what it wills. The will gives itself determinate existence (*Dasein*) in something.

In order to will something, there must be a resolution or decision that displaces the moment of abstract possibility and indeterminacy. Resolution thus involves an element of closure that cancels and sets aside abstract possibilities. But Hegel observes that resolution and decision (*beschliessen*) can also be expressed in German as *sich entschliessen*, which means the opposite of closure, namely, to unclose oneself.[40] In other words, closing off an otherwise interminable reflection on abstract possibilities is the negative side of an opening toward something. The second element of the will is thus a closing and ceasing of consideration of possibilities and a simultaneous opening of the self in which it enters into determinacy and exposes itself to contingency and risk. "Only by making resolutions can the human being enter actuality, however painful the process may be; for inertia would rather not emerge from that inward brooding in which it reserves a universal possibility for itself. But possibility is not yet actuality."[41]

It is important to note that although this second moment of freedom is a negation of the first moment of indeterminacy, it too remains a *negative*, deficient concept of freedom. Willing something is the second form of the *finitude* of the will. Like the first, it presupposes an opposition between the subjective and objective elements. Where the first moment of the will could not be determinate, and was a flight from determinacy into indeterminacy, the second moment of

37. *VPR*, 3:113.   38. Ibid., 116.   39. *PR*, §6.
40. Ibid., §12.   41. Ibid., §13 Zusatz.

the will is excessive in its affirmativity. In willing *something*, the will immerses itself in its object and becomes entangled with it. "In this opposition [of objective and subjective] the will is not at home with itself; rather it is entangled with its object, and its finitude consists in the fact that it is not [yet] subjective."[42] According to Hegel, "one can call that will 'objective' that is completely immersed in its object, that stands in childlike innocence without subjective freedom, or like the slave, does not yet know itself to be free and consequently is a will without a will of its own [*ein willenloser Wille*]."[43] In identifying itself with its object, the will "loses itself" as freedom or is not yet aware of its freedom; immersion in its object is an entanglement that corresponds to naïveté, loss of perspective, and so on. It is a will without a will of its own.

Thus far Hegel has been expounding and elaborating a somewhat existential and romanticized version of Kant's and Fichte's concept of the will. In this view of the will, its finitude is not only stressed but also rendered absolute.[44] The finitude of the will consists in the noncoincidence of substantive and reflective elements. The poles of this duality can neither be identified nor separated, and this constitutive instability is manifest in both moments of the will, namely, its indeterminacy and its determinacy. In other words, *Wille* and *Willkür* are in unresolved contradiction or tension, which is the fundamental defect of the position. There is an unstable oscillation between (1) freedom as negation, absolute indeterminacy that cannot come to positive expression but, since it is conditioned by its opposite, can only destroy; and (2) positive freedom, which wills something but loses or immerses itself in its positive determination, resulting in a loss of critical perspective. The presupposition common to both elements is that being-free and being in relation are mutually exclusive. Thus the other and relation to the other are experienced as negations and alienations. This makes ethics problematic.

The third, speculative position that Hegel favors is to conceive the will as an activity in which both indeterminacy and determinacy are united. This union signifies the infinity or universality of the will. The infinity of the will consists in its being at home with itself in its other. The will remains free in its determination. Hegel formulates his position initially in somewhat ponderous language:

> Every self-consciousness knows itself as universal, as the possibility of abstracting from everything determinate, and as particular, with a determinate object, content and end. But these two moments are only abstractions; what is concrete and true (and everything true is concrete) is the universality which has the particular as its opposite, but this particular, through its reflection into itself, has been reconciled with the universal.[45]

42. Ibid., §26.   43. Ibid., Zusatz.
44. See Hegel, *Faith and Knowledge*. Kant, Jacobi, and Fichte are characterized as philosophies of absolutized finitude. See pp. 58–66.
45. *PR*, §7.

However, Hegel explains this synthesis of negative and affirmative freedom in direct personal terms: "When I know myself to be free, I know that, on the one hand, I am undetermined, and on the other that I am only free in the positive sense because I will something."[46] In willing something I nevertheless remain free, not merely in the abstract, but *in the determinacy*. "The actual will wills something, but in its determination it knows that it is not tied down, but is at home with itself in its determination."[47]

For Hegel, willing something puts an end to the broodings of reflection. However, freedom is not lost but is retained in determinacy, that is, in relation. The will remains free in its determinations precisely because they are its own. There is no contradiction between freedom and determinacy, between absolute and relative. Being in relation to other does not prevent the return of the will to itself in its determinacy, or in its other. Rather, relation can facilitate these. Hegel conceives the will as a totality of negative and affirmative freedoms. To be at home with self in an other is a holist conception of the will as a totality: "Thus freedom lies neither in indeterminacy nor in determinacy, but in both at once. . . . Freedom is to will something determinate, yet to be with oneself [*bei sich*] in this determination and to return once more to the universal."[48]

This holist concept of the will as being at home in a determination makes possible a transition to another level, namely, the level of interhuman relations. The principle that there is no inherent conflict between freedom and determinacy now becomes there is no inherent conflict between freedom and relation. Recall the starting point of the analysis of the concept of recognition: the encounter with the other appears initially to be a loss of self. But as the process of recognition is worked out, it becomes apparent that entering into relation is not a loss of self. This is true above all in the case of mutual recognition, which is a prime, even paradigmatic, case of speculative freedom.

> In this state of universal freedom, in being reflected into myself, I am immediately reflected into the other person, and conversely, in relating myself to the other I am immediately related to myself. . . . The nature of this relationship is thoroughly speculative. When it is supposed that the speculative is something remote and inconceivable, we have only to consider the content of this relationship to convince ourselves of the baselessness of this view. . . . This unity . . . forms the substance of ethical life, namely of the family, of sexual love, of patriotism, of love towards God, of bravery too when this is a risking of one's life in a universal cause, and lastly also of honor.[49]

In mutual recognition, the self gets itself back, as it were, in the recognition of the other. As a member of the reciprocally constituted universal will, each re-

46. *VPR*, 3:119.   47. Ibid.
48. PR, §7; see also VPR, 3:119–120.
49. *E*, §436 Zusatz. My italics.

mains free in relation; in its other, in its determinacy, it coincides with itself. This third moment in which freedom is a coincidence of opposites is one "the understanding refuses to enter into, because the concept is precisely what the understanding always describes as incomprehensible."[50] The understanding finds this incomprehensible because it operates with abstract pure identity that excludes the difference, the other, and so on, and conceives the other, relation, and community as negations or hindrances to freedom.

Hegel believes that only speculative thought can comprehend something as elementary and basic as positive self-recognition in other. Genuine freedom means to be in a restriction, yet without restriction; it is to be limited (*Schranke*), yet without limits (*Schrankenlos*).[51] This structure of freedom, to be in a restriction yet without restriction, is the will as an intersubjective totality or spirit. Hegel's claim is not merely that there is no conflict between authentic freedom and community, but that freedom, to be actual, requires community. Hegel illustrates his speculative conception of freedom with reference to the familiar intersubjective phenomena of love and friendship: "We already possess this freedom in the form of feeling [*Empfindung*], for example in friendship and love. Here we are not one-sidedly within ourselves, but willingly limit ourselves with reference to an other, even while knowing ourselves in this limitation as ourselves. In this determinacy, the human being should not feel determined; on the contrary, he attains his self-awareness only by regarding the other as other."[52]

Hegel's early writings on love remain important articulations of what he is driving at, even though these formulations have not yet fully attained the later speculative form. Hegel comments that to conceive is to dominate (*Begreifen ist beherrschen*), but "in love alone one is united with the object, neither dominating it nor dominated by it."[53] I want to emphasize this middle alternative—neither dominating nor dominated—in Hegel's speculative conception of the will.

Recall that abstract negative freedom is unable to be determinate; it remains essentially tied to and dependent on what it negates. "Thus abstract freedom is conditioned by what it negates. It is not non-negating [*unnegierend*]; it is only conditioned."[54] On the other hand, in affirmative freedom, or willing *something,* the will itself tends to be negated, and becomes entangled and bound up with its object. In contrast to these, genuine freedom negates neither the other nor itself; it is *non-negating.* Thus it is free to be with and 'in' its other without loss of self or becoming 'entangled' or 'ensnared' by its object. This idea of freedom as non-negating (*unnegierend*) is important; moreover, it should be

50. *PR*, §7.   51. *VPR*, 3:120.
52. PR, §7; see also *VPR*, 3:119–120.
53. Hegel, *Werke*, TWA 1:242.
54. *VPR*, 3:113.

familiar to us now in view of our previous analysis of the concept of reciprocal recognition. Non-negation corresponds to the final phase of mutual recognition, namely, union with (*Vereinigung*) and release (*Freigabe*) of the other, allowing the other to be, wherein the self returns to itself out of and through the other. Non-negation and release of the other are constitutive of the universal-social consciousness. This universal has an ethical dimension. It is nondominating, yet determinate, which means that in it differences are allowed to be, and its universality consists in the reciprocal recognition and affirmative relation of the individual differences.

This release of the other, allowing it to be, is also constitutive of Hegel's conception of love. We have already seen that in his *Early Theological Writings* Hegel characterized love as a mean between dominating and being dominated. This means that "the beloved is not opposed to us; he is one with our being. We see only ourselves in him, and yet he is not we. This is a miracle that we are unable to comprehend."[55] Or again: "In love the separate one remains, but no longer as separate; rather he is united [with us]. Life senses life."[56] For Hegel, love embodies an orientation beyond conflict and beyond the active-passive, dominating-subservient postures. This opens up a new possibility, namely, that entering into relation is not a limitation or loss of self but rather a mutual enhancement and increase. Love is the core of Hegel's concept of ethical life, and the key to Hegel's concept of community, not as a limitation or tyranny but as an enhancement of human life.

Lest one be tempted to believe that these are merely youthful expressions, it is important to note that Hegel retains his conception of love as nonreductive union with the other in his *Science of Logic*. There he makes clear the logical basis of the transcendence of opposition. Negative freedom is incapable of anything other than exclusive, negative relation because it remains stuck in the logical antithesis of universal *versus* particular. But the universal that *excludes* the particular shows itself to be an abstract and parochial universal, as Hegel's analysis of the false infinite shows. However, in Hegel's conception of the concrete or mediated universal, particularity is no longer opposed to the universal, but is co-constitutive of the universal. It is an other that is allowed to be, and this allowing to be is what the concrete universal is. Consequently, the concrete universal itself is portrayed by Hegel as love: "As it has been called free power, the universal can also be called free love and boundless blessedness (*schrankenlose Seligkeit*). For in relating to its other [the difference, the particular] it is only relating to itself. In its difference it has returned to itself."[57] The concrete universal is a community of universal and particular; it represents Hegel's attempt to conceive community as a distinct level of being that is irre-

55. Ibid., 244.   56. Ibid., 246.
57. Hegel, *Logik, Werke*, TWA 6:277.

ducible to a merely abstract collective identity or to the mere difference of an external aggregate of particulars.[58]

From 'In-Itself' to 'For-Itself': The Development of the Will

The *concept* of the will does not exhaust the will's reality, or determinate actualization. Hegel employs his favorite locutions for denoting the stages of development of the will: the 'in-itself' (*an sich*) and 'for-itself' (*für sich*). The 'in-itself' designates the will in its concept, that is, apart from or prior to its unfolding and development. In this sense, the 'in-itself' is equivalent to 'for us', that is, those who are considering the will in its concept. Hegel writes, "Thus the will is free only in itself or for us, or it is in general the will in its concept."[59] However, the 'in-itself' also designates the will in a condition of immediacy, or natural will, prior to the process of recognition and mediation. The will is not actual or actually free until it is *for-itself* [*für sich*] not at the beginning but at the end of the process. Prior to being for-itself, its freedom is merely potential, or existing only for philosophical reflection, but not yet actual. "Only when the will has itself for its object is it *for-itself* [*für sich*] what is in-itself [*an sich*]."[60]

In itself, the will is not yet actual, not yet free; it is only a potential freedom. Hegel observes that the understanding (*Verstand*) takes this 'in-itself-ness' (being-in-itself) of the will as not only actual, but "as absolute and perennial,"[61] and so attains only an abstract conception of freedom. This conception is abstract because the relationship of freedom to what is willed is mistaken as an application of freedom to a given material, "an application which does not belong to the essence of freedom itself."[62] The determinacy of the will is thus dismissed as external, falling outside of the will 'in-itself' or the will's (abstract) essence and thus without interest. But for Hegel the will's determinacy is immanent self-determination. Moreover, nothing is accomplished without interest; if the will cannot find itself in what it wills, it remains shut up in itself, that is, alienated.

Rationalist misconceptions aside, Hegel observes that the will in-itself is immediate, and, as immediate, natural: "The will which is free only in itself is the immediate or natural will."[63] But to be immersed in nature is to be actually unfree, or not yet to have developed the autonomy that breaks with nature and becomes self-determining. As a merely natural will, it exists only in immediate forms, namely, "drives, desires and inclinations by which the will finds itself naturally determined."[64] To be sure, being in such a situation or condition

58. See below, chap. 12.   59. *PR*, §10.   60. Ibid.
61. Ibid.   62. Ibid.   63. Ibid., §11.
64. Ibid.

contradicts the very concept of the will and freedom: "As spirit, man is a free being who is able not to let himself be determined by natural drives. When he exists in an immediate, uncultivated condition, he is therefore in a situation in which he ought not to be, and from which he must liberate himself."[65] Elsewhere Hegel explains the general pattern and progression of the will's self-development from potential to actual freedom.

> At first will appears in the form of immediacy. It has not yet posited itself as intelligence freely and objectively determining itself, but only *finds* itself as such objective determination. As such it is . . . practical feeling, has a single content and is itself an immediately individual, subjective will, which . . . feels itself objectively determined, but still lacks a content that is liberated from the form of subjectivity, a content that is truly objective, universal in and for itself. For this reason the will is, to begin with, only implicitly free, or free according to its concept. But it belongs to the idea of freedom that the will should make its concept, freedom itself, into its own aim and content. When it does this, it becomes objective spirit. It constructs for itself a world of its freedom and thus gives to its content a self-subsistent existence. But the will achieves this aim only by ridding itself of its abstract individuality, by developing its initially only implicit universality into a content that is universal in and for itself.[66]

This path of the will's development is not a call for delivery from bondage to the drives, passions, desires, as if these were inherently evil, or to be morally condemned or repressed. We do well to take notice that Hegel, whom Kierkegaard caricatured as a speculative thinker who forgot what it means to exist, wrote the following Pascalian sentence: "Nothing great has been or can be accomplished without passion."[67] According to Hegel, the passions, drives, and desires are not to be condemned because they are intrinsic determinations of the will or practical reason, even though their form is not yet rational.[68] For Hegel, passion signifies that a human being has limited himself by placing the entire living interest of his spirit, talent, character, and happiness in a single content. In passion, the will wills something. This is at once its strength and its limitation.

It is by passion that human freedom attains presence in the world. For this reason passions are not to be extirpated, destroyed, or repressed. Their content, but not their form, is rational. The passions must be educated and cultivated toward universality, and when this occurs they take on the shapes and forms of social rationality. The will in its self-realization constructs a realm of objective

65. Ibid., §18 Zusatz.   66. *E*, §469 Zusatz.
67. Ibid., §474. Hegel adds that "it is only a dead, hypocritical morality that inveighs against the form of passion as such."
68. "This content, along with the determinations developed within it, does indeed originate in the will's rationality, and it is thus rational in itself, but expressed in so immediate a form, it does not yet have the form of rationality." *PR*, §11.

spirit, including family, civil society, and state. In broad outline, this is how Hegel understands and portrays a development whereby the rational becomes actual.

> The formal rationality of drive and inclination consists in their general impulse not to be merely subjective, but to suspend the subjectivity of the subject and become realized through its own activity. . . . It is the immanent reflexion of spirit itself to go beyond its particularity and its natural immediacy and to give their content rationality and objectivity, in which they exist as necessary relations, namely as rights and duties. It is this objectification that makes manifest their intellectual substance, their mutual connections, and their truth.
>
> Plato was right therefore to include the spirit's nature in totality under the concept of its right, or justice; he was also right to show that what justice truly is in and for itself, can be exhibited only in the objective shape of justice, namely in the construction of the state as ethical life.
>
> The answer to the question, what are the good, rational inclinations and what is their proper relation, resolves itself into an exposition of the relations spirit itself produces when it develops as objective spirit. In this development the content of free self-determination loses its contingency and arbitrariness [*Willkür*]. The discussion of the true content and ethical substance of drives, inclinations and passions is therefore essentially a theory of legal, moral and ethical duties.[69]

The actuality of freedom is thus not to be found exclusively or even primarily in the individual *cogito*; the will and freedom are actual in their full, integrally developed sense only in a free, rational community whose articulated, interdependent existence is the supreme objective realization of freedom and right. As Stephen Houlgate puts it, "The . . . state is immanent in the very idea of the free will. . . . [I]t is only when the state is present that human freedom is rendered objective and universal."[70] It is in this sense of an articulated universal, or organic totality, that we are to understand Hegel's declaration that right is the determinate existence of freedom. The totality of the conditions required for freedom, including right, to become actual is the state. This will become clearer in our subsequent analysis in chapters 12 and 13.

69. *E*, §474.
70. Stephen Houlgate, *Freedom, Truth and History: An Introduction to Hegel's Philosophy* (London: Routledge, 1991), 123.

7

Persons, Property, and Contract

My intention is not to provide a commentary on the *Philosophy of Right* as a whole. Hugh Reyburn, Shlomo Avineri, Allen Wood, and Fred Dallmayr have already done that.[1] Instead my project is more modest. I want to examine the *Philosophy of Right* as a phenomenology of intersubjective freedom. My specific concern is to focus on and track the concept of recognition and its implications through Hegel's analyses of abstract right, morality, and ethical life. Since freedom is intersubjectively mediated, recognition is not only important for understanding the concept of freedom, it is also the origin and foundation of the concept of right. Objectively, right designates not only the determinate objective shapes of existence and social institutions that freedom creates for itself; right also denotes the intersubjective recognition of freedom in those determinate shapes and institutions. The *Philosophy of Right* is an extended account of diverse mutual recognitions that are embodied in social institutions such as property, contract, morality, family, and state. Since freedom is intersubjectively mediated through mutual recognition, the phenomenology of will and freedom in the *Philosophy of Right* is necessarily a social phenomenology.

Avineri has observed that "the three moments of ethical life can also be projected as three alternative modes of inter-human relationship. Hegel's argument would be that men can relate to each other in either one of the three following modes: particular altruism—the family; universal egoism—civil society; universal altruism—the state."[2] However, Avineri does not develop this fruitful

---

1. Reyburn, *The Ethical Theory of Hegel*; Shlomo Avineri, *Hegel's Theory of the Modern State* (Cambridge: Cambridge University Press, 1972), hereafter cited as *HTMS*; Wood, *HET*; Dallmayr, *G. W. F. Hegel: Modernity and Politics* (Newbury Park, Calif.: Sage, 1993).
2. Avineri, *HTMS*, 33–34.

suggestion, nor does he focus on the concept of recognition. But it is clear that he regards recognition and the interhuman as important dimensions of Hegel's *Philosophy of Right*.

Our concern is to understand how recognition as the general form or shape of right plays out *in the details* of Hegel's ethics. We turn our attention to the beginning of Hegel's *Philosophy of Right*, that is, abstract right, which includes his analyses of property, contract, and punishment. As we do so, we confront again an interpretive problem previously touched on, namely, the 'abstraction' of abstract right. The question is whether abstraction means that Hegel sets forth an individualist interpretation of property and contract. For if Hegel's analyses are in fact individualist, this may mean that Hegel brackets or omits the very thing we are interested in focusing on, namely, recognition and intersubjectivity. Such bracketing, if total, would suggest that recognition plays little or no role in Hegel's actual analysis of social institutions. Consequently, in what follows we address first the interpretive issue concerning abstract right and then proceed to examine Hegel's determinate analyses of taking possession, ownership, and contract.

Abstract Right and Person

Hegel begins abstract right with an analysis of the person or personality in the legal sense. It is important to realize that this is an abstraction and that as such it presupposes institutions and concepts that will be set forth later in the *Philosophy of Right*. Although he treats property before the family in the *Philosophy of Right*, the institution of property does not exist before the family, and in fact presupposes the family.[3] Commenting on the distinction between his categorical order of presentation and the actual existential order, Hegel observes that "this course followed by our exposition does not in the least mean that we would make ethical life later in time than right and morality, or would explain the family and civil society to be antecedent to the state in the actual world. On the contrary, we are well aware that ethical life is the foundation of right and morality."[4] Abstract right, although discussed first, presupposes the ethical life presented later in the *Philosophy of Right*. Hegel observes that legal personality and its correlate ownership have their historical origins in the institutions of agriculture and family. "The proper beginning and original foundation of states has rightly been equated with the introduction of agriculture and of marriage. For the former principle brings with it the cultivation of the soil and in consequence exclusive, private property. . . . [T]he marriage bond is in

---

3. *PR*, §32: "What we obtain . . . is a series of thoughts and another series of existent shapes, in which it may happen that the temporal sequence of their actual appearance is to some extent different from their conceptual sequence. Thus we cannot say, for example, that property existed before the family, although property is nevertheless dealt with first."

4. E, §408 Zusatz.

turn extended to become a lasting and inherently universal union, while need becomes care for the family and possession becomes family property."[5]

The abstraction in abstract right and the abstract concept of person in particular reflect the ability of the will to tear itself loose from every determinacy and become indeterminate. Abstract personality is a formal-ontological concept that results from a series of intellectual and sociopolitical negations or abstractions. As such it is not only an intellectual but also a historical accomplishment:

> Personality begins only at that point where the subject has not merely a consciousness of itself as concrete and in some way determined, but a consciousness of itself as a completely abstract 'I' in which all concrete limitation and validity are negated and invalidated. In the personality therefore, there is knowledge of the self as an object . . . raised by thought to simple infinity and hence purely identical with itself. Insofar as they have not yet arrived at this pure thought and knowledge of themselves, individuals and peoples do not yet have a personality.[6]

The abstraction requisite to the formation of abstract personality is not a single act or event; rather it results from a long sociohistorical process of education in the broad sense (*Bildung*). For Hegel, the concept of right is mediated by recognition, but conversely, what is recognized is in part the way in which human beings think of themselves. It is bound up with their level of cultural and intellectual attainment, that is, their *Bildung*, or education. It is through education that the abstraction of personality in a formal legal sense is achieved. "It is part of education, of thinking as consciousness of the individual in the form of universality, that I am apprehended as a universal person, in respect to which all humans are identical. A human being counts simply because he is human, and not because he is a Jew, Catholic, Protestant, German, Italian, etc."[7] The person of abstract right is a person in an abstract universal sense, purged of the determinate contingencies of birth, race, religion, gender, and so on.

The person of abstract right is a formal-universal person. When human beings think of themselves in this way, the result is a formal individualization that all share.[8] That is, the abstract universal person in whom all are identical or equal is simply the formal generic element constitutive of individuality. According to Hegel, personality is something both sublime (in its universal or infinite indeterminate dimension) and yet wholly ordinary (as a mere common element and something finite and determinate). When human beings think of themselves as individuals, this individuality (which all share) is at the same time negative and exclusive. The same negativity that allows me to differentiate my humanity from contingencies of birth, race, gender, and religion also radically

---

5. *PR*, §203.   6. Ibid., §35.   7. Ibid., §209.
8. This abstract identity anticipates the phenomenon of leveling, of a mass of atomized units. It is important to realize that Hegel seeks to overcome the leveling inherent in abstract right and civil society in his account of ethical life, at the level of family and state.

individualizes me and opens up my private sphere. Thus the very abstraction that uncovers the abstract universal legal person also individuates that person as a private person. This paradoxical combination of abstract universality and private, atomistic individualism constitutes the concept of the legal person. The formal-universal legal person is constituted as a private domain.

A historical reference may clarify matters somewhat. Hegel believes the concept of a person as a paradoxical combination of abstract universality and private particularity is the somewhat dubious achievement of Roman culture.[9] The centralization of political life in the emperor had its corollary in the expulsion of citizens from the public into the private sphere, that is, the reduction of citizens to mere atoms, or private persons. In the Roman interpretation, personality is construed not in social terms, as having a public presence, but simply as abstract inwardness. This interpretation leads to privatism, which conceives right not as public but merely as private right. Private right signifies that the person counts only in the reality that it gives to itself, that is, property. "We have found that the Romans proceed from the principle of abstract inwardness which is realized as personality in private law [*Privatrecht*]. Private law means that the person as such counts, in the reality that it gives itself, namely in property. . . . [T]he organism of the state here dissolves into the atoms of private persons."[10] But such atomistic private individualism means that mutual recognition, and with it public life, disappeared from the Roman state. The concentration of public power in the emperor and the alienation of the many were the result. All that is recognized under such conditions is property ownership in which human beings relate to themselves as abstract owners.

The abstract person is formal, individual, and private. Hegel brings out this formal individualism by noting that in the abstract person, the immediate will is a negative, exclusive will, a will that excludes others.[11] Thus we can express more fully the abstraction in abstract personality in the following way: the will relates positively only to itself, and relates negatively to what is other by excluding it. In Hegel's words, "The particularity therein is that I relate simply to myself, and regard everything other as a nullity [*Nichtiges*]."[12]

The last sentence appears to be radically individualist, and emphasizes the private dimension almost to the point of solipsism. By abstracting itself from the contingencies of birth, race, gender, and religion, has the abstract person also divested itself of intersubjectivity? of all relation to others? of the need for recognition? As noted above, Hegel believes that the Roman empire closely ap-

---

9. "These two moments constitutive of Roman culture, political universality for itself and the abstract freedom of the individual, are first of all comprehended in the form of inwardness itself." *Vorlesungen über die Philosophie der Geschichte*, Theorie Werkausgabe (Frankfurt: Suhrkamp, 1970), 12:340. Hereafter cited as *VPG*. Roman "culture" is for Hegel also a symbol for what Hegel opposed in his own.

10. Ibid., TWA 12:384.

11. Cf. *VPR*18, §17, 223.

12. *VPR*18, §17, 223. See also *VPR*17, §12.

proximated several of these conditions, where human beings were reduced from citizens to mere abstract persons, property owners, and relations. He is far from recommending such a form of life. Nevertheless, the question is whether Hegel's account of the abstract person in the *Philosophy of Right* means that Hegel adopts the very privatism and individualism that he attacks elsewhere? Ludwig Siep poses the issue thus: How are we to understand the fact that Hegel, one of the severest critics of individualism, begins his *Philosophy of Right* with a theory of private right, and appears to argue his case for property right in an individualist manner similar to John Locke?[13] Can we conclude from this that the *Philosophy of Right* begins from an individualist principle?[14] If so, does this show that Hegel is not a critic but rather an example of liberal ethical theory?[15]

Hegel confounds this individualist interpretation and shows it to be one-sided when he introduces the *Rechtsgebot*, or imperative of right: "Personality in general includes the capacity for right and constitutes the concept and the abstract foundation of abstract formal right. Therefore the imperative of right is: Be a person and respect others as persons."[16] It is true that the imperative of abstract right has a negative sense of prohibition, of not infringing on freedom, rather than a sense of a positive duty toward others. The point of this prohibition is to delimit a realm of permissions open to abstract persons. The imperative to respect human beings as persons means everything is permitted that does not infringe on freedom, that is, the right of possession. However, this is scarcely a solipsistic imperative. Moreover, earlier formulations of this imperative remove any doubt that it is at least formally intersubjective. Consider the following from Hegel's *Propadeutik*: "Right is the relation of human beings insofar as they are abstract persons. That action is contrary to right that does not respect the human being as person, or which infringes upon his freedom. This relationship is, according to its basic determination, negative in that it does not require that something positive be granted to the other, but only that he be allowed to be as person."[17] Again, from the 1818 lectures: "Respect human beings as persons. . . . Right means that [the] others must recognize this [freedom]."[18]

Ilting rightly points out that this imperative is without any apparent justification in abstract right because it contradicts the radical individualism that such right expresses. However, Ilting believes that abstract right is radically individ-

13. Siep, "Intersubjektivität, Recht und Staat in Hegels *Grundlinien der Philosophie des Rechts*."

14. See Peter Landau, "Hegels Begrundung des Vertragrechts." In Manfred Riedel (Hrsg.), *Materialien zu Hegels Rechtsphilosophie*, Bd. 2 (Frankfurt: Suhrkamp, 1975); see also Benhabib, *Critique, Norm and Utopia*.

15. See Ilting, "The Structure of Hegel's Philosophy of Right."

16. *PR*, §36.

17. *Propadeutik*, TWA 4:59.

18. *VPR*18, §19.

ualistic to the point of excluding or suppressing even the possibility of recognition and intersubjectivity. He then has the problem as to whether any plausible sense can be made of a purely individual right. Again, a historical reference may clarify the issue. In his discussion of Roman *Privatrecht*, Hegel claims that a purely private right is no right at all precisely because it excludes the moment of recognition: "This *Privatrecht* is therefore equally a non-existence and non-recognition of the person; consequently, this situation of right amounts to the utter absence of right [*vollendete Rechtslosigkeit*]. This contradiction is the misery of the Roman world." [19] At the heart of Ilting's interpretation seems to be a partial, one-sided understanding of what Hegel means by right. Ilting seems to ascribe to Hegel the very atomized individualism and nonrecognition of persons that Hegel criticizes in Roman *Privatrecht*.

It must be conceded that the intersubjectivity of abstract right is obscure. There seem to be three possibilities. (1) There is no mutual recognition at all in abstract right, but at most mutual exclusion of private persons; Hegel thus begins with abstract individualism and has the problem of moving from such practical solipsism to intersubjectivity. [20] (2) There is no mutual recognition in abstract right, but in his discussion of abstract right Hegel presupposes and borrows from the intersubjectivity of ethical life. [21] (3) There is mutual recognition in abstract right, but it is formal, limited, and impersonal, and as such, not yet the intersubjectivity of morality, much less ethical life. I believe that the third is the most plausible interpretation. My thesis is that for Hegel right is grounded in mutual recognition. [22] Any situation in which the possibility of recognition is excluded in principle is therefore a situation of *Rechtslosigkeit*, the denial of right. Hence alternatives 1 and 2 seem to exclude the very possibility of right, and so undermine the concept of abstract right. In addition, the second possibility amounts to a corruption of the distinction between abstract right and ethical life. Both fly in the face of §36, the imperative of abstract right, namely, to respect persons. That imperative implies some intersubjectivity, however formal, abstract, and minimal.

In support of the third alternative is Hegel's own procedure in the *Philosophy of Right*. The determinations of the will—at once conditions and shapes of

19. *VPG*, TWA 12:387.
20. This is Ilting's position as I understand it. It is also held by Benhabib and Theunissen.
21. This seems to be the view taken by Kenneth Westphal when he writes, "Hegel's discussion of 'abstract right' concerns the basic principles of property rights. It is abstract in three ways. First, *actions and principles are (initially) abstracted from interpersonal relations*; second they are abstracted from moral reflection; third they are abstracted from legal and political institutions. These abstractions are sequentially shed as Hegel's analysis develops." "The Context and Structure of Hegel's *Philosophy of Right*," in *The Cambridge Companion to Hegel* (Cambridge: Cambridge University Press, 1993), 247. Italics mine. It is not clear what Westphal means by abstracting actions from interpersonal relations. For Hegel, recognition is both an action and a relation. Any principle abstracted from the action and process of recognition would also be intersubjective. If it were not it would either distort or suspend the very intersubjectivity at issue.
22. *E*, §436.

freedom—form a conceptual logical order and an order of empirical shapes (*Gestaltungen*) such as family and civil society. The task is to work out a correspondence between the two, despite the fact that the conceptual ordering is different from the empirical-experiential ordering. Hegel writes, "This procedure implies that since we develop the concept, we start with the abstract concept. Similarly we start with abstract shapes (*Gestaltungen*) that are only formal and that cannot exist by themselves. Since we start with what is abstract, this abstraction is still shapeless, and as such it requires a ground, something from which it can be distinguished. Actuality demands concreteness, and the abstractions are only abstract totalities that cannot exist independently by themselves."[23] The abstract right of property presupposes social institutions of intersubjective freedom that are conceptually "later" in Hegel's analysis. The private property of abstract right is an abstraction from the determinate intersubjectivity of the family.[24] However, this does not mean that abstract right and property dispense with intersubjectivity as such, precisely because abstract right is a right of persons in relation to each other. Kenneth Westphal correctly notes that "Hegel aimed to show that possession and other rights of property exist only on the basis of mutually recognizing the principles that constitute those rights. . . . While mutual recognition may be implicit in simple possession, it is quite explicit in contractual relations."[25]

For Hegel, there are two facets of the concept of right. The first is the presencing of freedom in the world, in things, in the body, and so on. As Hegel puts it, "Right is any existence [*Dasein*] in general which is the existence of the free will."[26] The presencing of freedom in a thing means that it is mine and that others are excluded from the thing. Moreover, the presencing of freedom is an assertion of right. However, this language about the existence of freedom is somewhat misleading, because "abstract right is initially a mere possibility. . . . Consequently a determination of a right gives me a warrant, but it is not absolutely necessary that I should pursue my rights, because this is only one aspect of the whole relationship."[27] Right designates a series of possible permissions, which articulate the fundamental principle of noninfringement of freedom. But it is not necessary to assert or pursue right in every conceivable sense. That is, rights need not be asserted; they may be waived. To be sure, if a right is asserted, then freedom seeks presence, and it should be respected. However, the assertion of right is not necessary, and the presencing of freedom in ownership, while important, does not exhaust the concept of right.

The second facet of right is the recognition by others of freedom's presencing in the world, that is, in ownership. That is, others must recognize "mine"

---

23. *VPR*, 3:168; *PR*, §32.

24. "Thus we cannot say, for example, that property existed before the family, although property is dealt with first." *PR*, §32 Zusatz.

25. Westphal, "Context and Structure of Hegel's *Philosophy of Right*," 247–248.

26. *PR*, §29.   27. Ibid., §37.

and my right to exclude them from my things. This recognition is an imperative; but this imperative can be disregarded or violated. Right is not actual until it is both exercised and recognized. Right is always exercised and asserted by individuals. But it is not fully actual unless it is recognized by others. Both facets are crucial; neither by itself is adequate to the notion of right. In short, *abstract right has the fundamental structure of recognition itself: namely, a joint, complex, two-sided action.*

For this reason I do not believe, as Ilting does, that Hegel contradicts himself in the *Philosophy of Right* when he presents an individualist account of property and contract, alongside the concept of recognition. His presentation is not inconsistent with but exemplifies the basic pattern of recognition itself. Rights can be exercised and asserted only by individuals, but they are not fully actual until recognized and respected by others. Moreover, Hegel's presentation in the *Philosophy of Right* focuses on distinct aspects or moments of abstract right, namely, the presencing of freedom in things. This presencing has undeniable individualist dimensions. At the level of abstract right, it is individuals who assert property claims and rights. But this mode of analysis simply reflects a methodological individualism. It does not rule out but rather presupposes recognition. This point is clear from the following statement: "In property as a determinate shape of existence, the person exists for another, and to be sure only for other persons. This real determinacy, considered first of all as a positive relation, is mutual recognition: the consciousness of having one's personality in identity with other free persons. The concept of recognition, qualified as ownership, has its reality in contract."[28] This is the same position that Hegel elaborates two years later in the published version: "Contract presupposes that the contracting parties recognize each other as persons and owners of property; and *since it is a relationship of objective spirit, the moment of recognition is already contained and presupposed within it.*"[29]

The Intersubjectivity of Ownership

For Hegel, property, that is, ownership, is rational. This apparently strange assertion derives from Hegel's concept of the will and person, in which reason is practical. The rationality of property refers to the power of reason to be practical. For Hegel, practical rationality is the drive to suspend and go beyond mere subjectivity and to achieve an objective existence and presence in the world. Taking possession is one expression of this practical drive; seeking recognition is another. Possession is a determinate form of practical reason's and freedom's presencing in the world. "The rational aspect of property is to

28. *VPR*18, §37, 231.
29. *PR*, §71. Italics mine.

be found not in the satisfaction of needs, but in the superseding of the mere subjectivity of personality. Not until he has property does the person exist as reason."[30] Conversely: "He who has no property or who is denied property, has suffered an absolute injustice."[31] Deprivation of property will become an important issue in Hegel's subsequent analysis of poverty.

Hegel distinguishes between possession and ownership (property). Possession signifies that the person has placed his will in a thing, and thereby embodied himself in something external and mundane. Ownership is the reciprocal recognition of possession as property. More abstractly put, ownership is a recognized expression of the person's freedom, activity, and presence in the world, in things. Conversely, those who are denied property and ownership have not only suffered injustice, they are thrown into a struggle for recognition.[32]

Hegel observes that the concept of a thing is ambiguous, having opposing meanings.[33] The first meaning is substantial, as when we say, That's the *thing*! or The thing, not the person, matters. The second meaning is opposed to the first, when we contrast and distinguish persons and *things*. In this contrast, the thing means the opposite of what is substantial; it is something accidental, external, and subordinate to the person. Taking his cue from the latter accidental, external meaning of the thing, Hegel develops his theory of property. This externality underlies the account of ownership and contract.

When a person places his will in a thing, the thing thereby becomes his, and acquires from the person its substantial end, determination, and soul.[34] His will thus becomes objective in the thing, and the thing takes on the character of being private property, of being 'mine'.[35] "A possession means that I have something in my external power, even if that something is natural. Possession hangs together with my needs, drives and special interests. I possess something because I need to have it. . . . The human being has this in common with animals."[36] Further, "possession becomes property insofar as the I who possesses it is a free will that *wills* to possess it. Thus in property my will has become objective to me. In property my will has determinate existence, and this determinate existence of the will must be respected. Mere possession is not to be respected, but my free will, that has placed the predicate 'mine' in a thing, constitutes possession as property. With this assertion right begins, for right is freedom as such."[37]

However, although right begins with the assertion that a thing is 'mine', this is not yet the full sense of the right of ownership. "Taking possession is the empirical act of seizure, and this is to be justified through recognition. It is

30. *PR*, §41.   31. *VPR*, 3:215.
32. Avineri, *HTMS*, 89: "Property is thus to Hegel a moment in man's struggle for recognition."
33. *PR*, §42.   34. *PR*, §44.   35. *PR*, §46.
36. *VPR*, 4:186. Note that need is the sublimation of desire (*Begierde*).
37. Ibid.

not justified merely by virtue of its having occurred."[38] Recognition justifies possession as property by introducing reason, that is, practical-intersubjective rationality, into possession. In this way the sheer contingencies of taking possession are overcome, and possession becomes property, that is, ownership. Property and ownership are concrete universals; that is, in the recognition of my property, the property of everyone is recognized in principle, and so secured.

Ownership implies an intersubjective and rational mediation; the right of freedom to presence itself in its possessions becomes actual in mutual recognition. The actualization of this right of property presupposes and involves an intersubjective doubling, namely, that the thing I have taken possession of and made mine, *is mine*; that is, it must be recognized as mine by others. Here having is more than taking because it is mediated through an other, and as such is universal, that is, property. Intersubjective doubling, mediated by reciprocal recognition, makes possible the concept of (universal) law, even though the concept of law has not yet been made explicit. This intersubjective concept of legal property is evident in several of Hegel's formulations concerning ownership: "Possession becomes property, or legal [*rechtlich*] insofar as others recognize that the thing that I have made my own, is mine. Conversely, I recognize the possessions of the others as their property."[39] "All that I have, I have . . . in being-recognized [*Anerkanntsein*]."[40] "Property attains determinate existence when the person becomes a person for others, that is, when he is recognized."[41]

This view of the intersubjective mediation of property by no means disappears from Hegel's mature philosophy. Possession becomes property only through intersubjective recognition and its doubling.

> In property the person coincides with itself. But the thing is something abstract and external, and the ego is likewise abstract and external. The concrete return of the ego to itself in externality means that I, the *infinite* relation of myself to myself, am as person the repulsion of myself from myself, and have the determinate existence of my personality in the *being of other persons*, i.e., in my relation to them and in being recognized [*Anerkanntsein*] mutually by them.[42]

Through recognition the contingent fact of possession of a particular thing by a particular individual becomes universal. Possession is always particular, while property, as recognized possession, has universal and social significance. As Avineri puts it, "*property pertains to the person as recognized by others*, it can never be an intrinsic quality of the individual prior to his recognition by others. While possession relates to the individual, property relates to soci-

38. Hegel, *Philosophie des Geistes 1805/06*, 198; *HHS*, 112.
39. *Propadeutik*, TWA 4:237.
40. *Philosophie des Geistes 1805/06*, 208; *HHS*, 123.
41. *VPR*18, §37. Hegel follows Fichte; see chap. 4, fn. 20. See also *GNR*, 129; *SR*, 182.
42. *E*, §490. Italics in original.

ety. . . . [P]roperty is a social attribute."[43] Although we have not yet taken up contract, it is clear that contract will codify or institutionalize ownership as a relation of mutual recognition. And since mutual recognition is the intersubjective form of practical rationality, it also anchors the possibility of law or lawfulness.

At the same time, it must be pointed out that property, as 'mine', is also private. That is, the private sphere itself is an intersubjective achievement, and an inherently social concept. The privacy of property reflects the subjective individual will that has appropriated the thing. As the abstract individual excludes others, so his subjective will or freedom presencing in the thing appropriates it and renders it private and exclusive. Hegel believes that the appropriation of things is an expression of freedom and that freedom implies idealism—one of the rare occasions in which he uses this term without criticizing it.

> To appropriate something means basically only to manifest the supremacy of my will in relation to the thing [*Sache*], and to demonstrate that the latter does not have being in and for itself and is not an end in itself. This manifestation occurs through my conferring upon the thing an end other than that which it immediately possessed. I give the living creature, as my property, a soul other than that which it previously had. I give it my soul. The free will is consequently that idealism which does not consider things as they are, to be in and for themselves, whereas realism declares them to be absolute. . . . Even the animal has gone beyond this realist philosophy, for it consumes things and thereby proves that they are not absolutely self-sufficient.[44]

It is worth noting that Hegel draws on the categories of substance and accidents to conceive the relation of thing to person. The thing is like an accident, since in relation to its owner it is not an absolute end in itself, but is subordinate to his will. Hegel notes that "the relation of use to property is the same as that of substance to accident, of inner to outer, or force to its manifestation."[45] Thus the owner may use the thing, that is, subordinate it to his will. Further, the owner has whole use of the thing. If I have a stick, I may make use of all of it and not merely the part touching my hand. Through use of the thing, it is my need that "finds satisfaction and the thing, as negative in itself, exists only for my need and serves it. Use is the realization of my need through the alteration, destruction or consumption of the thing, whose selfless nature is thereby revealed."[46]

Appropriation of the thing, making the thing mine, also makes it private. But this privacy of property is far from solipsism. Solipsism would of course be involved if all that I do is merely *think* about taking possession of a thing. "My inner idea and will that something should be mine is not enough to constitute property, which is the existence of personality. On the contrary, this re-

---

43. Avineri, *HTMS*, 88. Italics in original.
44. *PR*, §44 Zusatz.   45. Ibid., §61; cf. §67.   46. Ibid., §59.

quires that I should take possession of it."[47] However, "the existence [*Dasein*] which my will thereby attains [in actual taking possession] includes its ability to be recognized by others."[48] Hegel notes that "as soon as one takes possession of something, one imbues it with one's will and excludes others."[49]

This exclusion of others constitutes the private sphere. The exclusion of others from 'my' property must be recognized by others. The exclusion of others constitutive of the private sphere does not cancel or undermine intersubjectivity but rather is itself intersubjectively achieved and accomplished. The concepts of property and ownership are universals that are constituted in and through mutual recognition. "The security of my possession becomes the security of the possessions of all; in my property, all have their property."[50] However, this intersubjectivity is, as Hegel notes, not yet a set of positive duties toward others. Right is not yet ethics. The imperatives of abstract right are not duties but permissions, and the permissions are qualified by the fundamental prohibition: do not infringe freedom. The supreme imperative of right, Be a person and respect others as persons! has the meaning, Leave other(s) alone! Let them be and allow them to pursue their private interests.

Clearly there is some intersubjectivity here, but of a minimalist sort. What is recognized is not the other per se but the other qua potential owner, or ownership. This is a formal mutual recognition that remains external: the person is not recognized as a totality or as a full human being but only as the abstract formal ontological capacity of freedom, of being able to be embodied in things. Yet it would be obtuse to deny that such recognition has potential ethical significance and ramifications. For example, property is not for Hegel a 'pure' economic concept but an ethical one. It is grounded in his concept of embodied, indigent freedom, and as such belongs to his philosophical anthropology.

Embodiment, or Taking Possession of Oneself

Hegel's discussion of property occurs as part of his philosophy of spirit (and its extension in the *Philosophy of Right*) and constitutes part of a complex philosophical anthropology. In other words, property is for Hegel a subcategory of philosophical anthropology, namely, a qualification of the concept of recognition. Property is not a simple given that Hegel's analysis presupposes and from which it proceeds; it is a result of taking possession (*Besitzergreifung*), and taking possession is something that human beings do.

However, before I can take possession of things, I must be able to take possession of myself and be in control of myself. But what could this mean? The language of taking possession implies that the one who takes possession is distinct, different and separate from that which is possessed. In other words, there

---

47. *PR*, §51.   48. Ibid.   49. *VPR*17, §17.
50. *Jena Realphilosophie 1803/04*, cited by Avineri, *HTMS*, 88n.

is a gap between the self and the thing to be possessed. It is the act of 'taking' that closes the gap between self and thing, and possession designates the closing of this gap. To be sure, on the grounds of Descartes's theoretical position of mind-body dualism, there might be a gap between mind and body that somehow would need to be suppressed or closed. But Hegel is no Cartesian here. He does say that "as person I possess my life and my body, like other things, only insofar as my will is present in them."[51] But Hegel denies that it is literally necessary to 'take possession' of one's body. "Here is the place to speak about property that I have 'immediately,' and that I do not have first to take possession of. As external I am immediately in [self] possession; I am living, I am [an] organic body, and this is the real possibility of all further determinate existence."[52] Thus embodiment is not a property relation but rather the condition of the taking possession that occurs in property relations.

Hegel views embodiment as the primal form of self-possession and self-expression, as well as the primal form of human vulnerability. The language of taking possession refers to education and training as the means whereby the body is disciplined: "Insofar as the body is supposed to become the organ of spirit, I must take possession of it, exercise it, and must learn to see and hear."[53] Again: "The training (*Ausbildung*) of my organic body in various skills, like the education of my spirit, is likewise a more or less complete penetration and taking possession thereof."[54] Such discipline and self-mastery are necessary, not because of any putative mind-body dualism, but because the human being starts out as a merely natural being, and a natural being for Hegel is one whose existence does not yet correspond to its concept: it is not yet what it is supposed to be. "Insofar as the body is immediate existence, it is not commensurate with the spirit; before it can be spirit's willing organ and soul-inspired instrument, it must first be taken possession of by the spirit."[55] That is where care, discipline, and training and above all education come in. This constitutes a difference between human beings and animals: "I have these limbs and my life only insofar as I so will it; the animal cannot mutilate or destroy itself, but the human being can."[56]

Embodiment, although constitutive of the sphere of privacy, also opens the self to external existence and to others. This opening toward others constitutes vulnerability. In his examination of the vulnerability of the person, Hegel discusses critically the views of Fichte and Rehberg. He finds in Rehberg the following, more or less Cartesian position: "In brief they make this distinction: that if one gives a man one-hundred lashes, one beats only his body, and not his spirit. Consequently his soul remains free. Similarly, slavery is nothing false, for freedom and servitude have their seat only in spirit."[57]

---

51. *PR*, §47.
52. *VPR*, 4:195. Hegel is not far from Gabriel Marcel's concept of an embodied subject.
53. Ibid.   54. *PR*, §52.   55. Ibid., §48.
56. Ibid., §47.   57. *VPR*4, 196.

These views amount to a failure to appreciate embodiment as opening the person to vulnerability, to the possibility of injury and violation.

It is only because I am a free being living in a body that this living body [*diess lebendige Dasein*] may not be misused as a beast of burden. Insofar as I am alive, my soul and my body are not separated. My body is the determinate existence of my freedom and I sense everything through it. It is only a sophistical and thought-less understanding [*Verstand*] that can make a distinction whereby the thing in itself—the soul—is not touched or violated if the body is mishandled and the existence of the person is subjected to the power of another. I can withdraw from my outward existence into myself, and can make my situation external to me; I can separate myself from my feelings, and can be free even if in chains. But all of this is due to *my will*. For others, *I am in my body*. I am free for the other only insofar as I am free in my existence [*Dasein*]. But violence done to my body by others is violence done to me.[58]

In opposition to Rehberg's Cartesianism, Hegel claims there is no real distinc-tion between spirit and its body. When others violate my body, they violate me.

Taking possession of oneself is a fruitful concept. It is related to the dimen-sion of freedom that we earlier characterized as self-overcoming. According to Hegel, to overcome one's natural drives and inclinations is to take possession of oneself, to transcend and sublate the level of mere natural existence.

The human being in his immediate existence, is a natural entity that does not yet conform to its concept. It is only through the training [*Ausbildung*] of his own body and spirit that essentially occurs through his self-consciousness compre-hending itself as free, that the human being takes possession of himself and be-comes his own property as distinct from that of other[s]. Conversely, taking pos-session of oneself also consists in translating into actuality what one is in terms of one's concept (as a possibility, capacity or predisposition). In this way, what one is according to one's concept [potential] is posited for the first time as one's own doing, and thus as objective.[59]

The idea of taking possession of oneself, of self-overcoming and self-formation, allows Hegel to explore the human significance of slavery.[60] Taking possession of oneself implies a distinction "between what the human being is in itself or in principle, and what it has become through its process of forma-tion. The human being is free in principle, but this freedom must be formed and developed so that the human being can be free in fact. For only then does the human being exist as it is supposed to, and thus is worthy of being free."[61]

58. Ibid. My italics. For a slightly different rendering of this text, see *PR*, §48.
59. *PR*, §57.
60. Hegel writes, "Through the process of self-formation the human being first becomes his own property. This topic belongs here, because it touches a point of view from which slavery can proceed, although this point of view is long behind us." *VPR*3, 225.
61. Ibid., 226.

Only then has the human being taken possession of itself, not only in the sense of disciplining the body, but also in the sense of asserting control over one's life. The necessity of taking possession of oneself in this larger global sense implies that one's freedom, conscience, and personality in the ethicoreligious sense are not and cannot be alienable like external possessions. On the contrary, Hegel claims that these rights and powers are inalienable:

> The right to such inalienable things is imprescriptible, for the act whereby I take possession of my personality and substantial nature [*Wesen*], and make myself a responsible being with moral and religious values and capable of holding rights, removes these determinations from that very externality which alone made them capable of becoming possessions of someone else. . . . This return on my part into myself, whereby I make myself existent as Idea, as a moral and legal person, supersedes the previous relationship and the wrong which I and the other have done to my concept and reason in treating . . . self-consciousness as something external, and in allowing it to be so treated.[62]

If we consider the human being from the perspective what it is 'in-itself' (*an sich*), that is, that it is free in principle, then we must judge that slavery is a gross injustice. The slave is prevented from taking possession of himself; he belongs instead to someone else. As an institution, slavery belongs to the transitional period between the state of nature and the genuinely ethical condition. "The alleged justification of slavery . . . as well as the justification of the master's status as simple lordship in general, and all historical views on the right of slavery and lordship, depend on regarding the human being simply as a natural being [*Naturwesen*] whose existence is not in conformity with its concept."[63] From this perspective, then, the one who is a 'natural' slave, or slave 'by nature', has not yet taken possession of himself. And for someone not yet self-possessed or self-determining, the condition of slavery is not an absolute injustice. Hegel approaches such alleged justification of slavery with historical perspective and acknowledges a certain relativity when he writes, "Slavery falls within a period when injustice is still regarded as justice, and where justice has not yet become fully appreciated or absolutely realized. Under such conditions, injustice counts; here it is relative to, even necessary for its epoch."[64]

On the other hand, although the human being is a natural being, this does not deny his freedom and responsibility for what he has become. Thus, if a particular human being is a slave, servitude, says Hegel, is due in some measure to his will. For since the human being is free in principle, or implicitly, "he does not have to be a slave; he can always take his own life."[65] However, on a more relative, less absolute level, Hegel claims that the human being cannot freely alienate its freedom or personality, and if it is forced by circum-

62. *PR*, §66.   63. Ibid., §57.   64. *VPR*3, 227.
65. Ibid., 226.

stances to become a slave, this is an impossible, unjust situation. "I cannot make myself a slave, for this possession that I grant to another ceases as soon as I so will. Even if I am born a slave and am fed and brought up by my master, and even if my parents and ancestors were all slaves, I am free the moment I so will it, the moment I come to the consciousness of my freedom."[66]

The Intersubjectivity of Contract

We have previously noted that property and ownership are intersubjectively mediated. This means that "property attains determinate existence when the person becomes a person for others, that is, when he is recognized."[67] "In property as a determinate shape of existence, the person exists for another, and to be sure only for other persons. This real determinacy, considered first of all as a positive relation, is mutual recognition: the consciousness of having one's personality in identity with other free persons. The concept of recognition, qualified as ownership, has its reality in contract."[68] The intersubjectivity of ownership is now the focus of our inquiry.

We have seen that property is an embodiment of the will. But the will that is thus placed in things has not yet been differentiated into universal or particular.[69] However, in the intersubjective relation of persons to each other vis-à-vis their possessions, the will shows itself to be a particular will in opposition/exclusion to other particular wills. This raises the possibility of a collision of property claims, and some versions of the life and death struggle in the *Jena Realphilosophie* seem to be about property. However, the *Philosophy of Right* in general and abstract right in particular presuppose that the initial struggles for recognition are over, and that some rightful *Anerkanntsein* exists. Consequently, the transition from property to contract brings to light the differentiation between universal and particular will, or *Willkür*. The 'for others' dimension of property reveals that my will is a particular will that happens to be embodied in a particular thing and thus excludes others from that thing. In an exchange of property, the subjective arbitrary will (*Willkür*) must suspend itself as mere particular and posit itself as identical with another will, thus creating a common will. Out of a mutual giving and receiving, a common will arises. This common will is an intersubjective convergence of subjective arbitrary wills about an external matter (*Sache*). In this way a new, determinate intersubjectivity emerges, namely, contract. In exchanging, transferring, or alienating property, persons are obviously relating to each other, albeit in an abstract 'impersonal' manner. Contract is a new form of taking possession, namely, the rightful, legal acquisition of a thing.

Contract makes explicit the intersubjective doubling that was implicitly present in property. In contract an embodied will exists for and in relation to

---

66. *VPR*17, §29.   67. *VPR*18, §37.   68. Ibid.
69. *VPR*17, §32.

another. "As determinate being, *Dasein* is essentially being for other. . . . But the determinate being of the will can only be determinate . . . for the will of another person. . . . Contract presupposes that the contracting parties recognize each other as persons and owners of property. Since it is a relationship of objective spirit, the moment of recognition is already contained and presupposed within it."[70] As a determinate form of mutual recognition, contract posits a convergence or agreement between two wills. This agreement implies doubling, and the doubling implies both identity and difference. The agreement implies that the two wills relinquish their differences; however, each of them remains a will distinctive for itself and is not simply identical with the other. There is no fusion or shared identity, but only an external relation of wills because "a contract requires two acts of consent."[71] Mutual consent is an intersubjective mediation that results in an exchange. "This is a mediation of the will to give up a property and the will to accept such a property (of someone else). The context of this mediation is one of [intersubjective] identity, *in that the one will comes to a decision only insofar as the other will is present.*"[72]

However, despite the mutual recognition inherent in contract, we do well to recall that this intersubjectivity is of a minimalist sort. What is recognized here is not the other as a total human being, but only the other qua owner, or legal person. This is a formal mutual recognition[73] in which there is a convergence of wills that nevertheless remains external, and falls short of an enduring common will or an intersubjective union. This convergence is about an external matter, not about the contracting parties themselves personally; consequently, the contracting parties remain external to each other. From the later vantage point of love and family, the intersubjectivity of ownership is deficient, impersonal, abstract, and formal.

In view of this deficiency, Hegel observes several important limitations on the intersubjectivity of contract. These have the effect of relativizing the concept of contract by delimiting its conditions of validity and applicability. Like Kant's transcendental deduction of the categories, the very moves that secure the validity of the concept of contract also confine and restrict its application to a discrete, limited sphere of existence. There is in contract a convergence of separate wills; however, this convergence is 'about' or resides in the value of an external thing (*Sache*). Contracts are properly about particular, external things, for these alone are capable of being both possessed and alienated. Only such things can be 'owned' in the strict sense of the term.

There must be at least two contracting parties who relate to each other im-

---

70. *PR*, §71.

71. Ibid., §76 Zusatz. Italics mine.

72. Ibid., §74. Italics mine.

73. David Kolb has rightly noted that according to Hegel, one basic problem of modernity is that recognition tends to become formal and impersonal. See Kolb, *The Critique of Pure Modernity*, 23–28, 74 ff. Hegel seeks to overcome this abstract formal universality at both the conceptual and the social levels.

mediately as self-sufficient persons. Contract implies reciprocity and coequality between the parties who make the contract. Each party voluntarily enters into the agreement. The contract proceeds from and is the joint product of mutual arbitrary wills (*Willkür*). As such, it is subject to the contingency of needs and interests and the possibility of joint revocation or dissolution. Further, although both parties voluntarily enter into an agreement, contract remains a limited, partial commitment, for "they nevertheless should and want to remain *independent*."[74] In spite of their mutual agreement and commitment, both parties retain their independence and self-sufficiency, and the contract remains subordinate in principle to their contingent agreement. Thus the unity of the contract does not undermine or transform, but rather presupposes the autonomous self-sufficiency and independence of the contracting persons. In contract individuals remain autonomous, private, and independent and thus retain their freedom and power to revoke or dissolve the contract. The contract is derivative from and an expression of their common but nevertheless private and external self-interests.

Second, although contract expresses and reflects an intersubjective agreement, "the identical will which comes into existence through the contract is only a will posited by the contracting parties, hence only a common will."[75] Although contract is reciprocally and jointly mediated, the mediated will of contract is not the universal will in itself (*an sich*) to which individuals should subordinate themselves, but only a common will. The common will is, to be sure, binding on the parties, but only relatively, not absolutely. It is an extension of their private interests and arbitrary wills, and hence external. It is not something to which these must be inherently subordinate. Hence the common will of contract remains subject to contingency. "The contract is only a [partial] exception to the personal, natural arbitrary will; it is only a [partial] exception within contingency in general."[76]

Moreover, the unity expressed by the common will remains dependent on external conditions such as need, interest, and willingness. It presupposes that those conditions obtain; as such it remains open to and subject to arbitrariness and contingency. "For this reason not every human relationship can be subsumed under the contractual category,"[77] and the attempt to do so results in a view of life and the state as an extension of property relations and corresponding possessive individualism. This is a conceptual blunder, a category mistake that is by no means innocuous. Hegel complains that "the intrusion of this relationship, and of relationships concerning private property in general, into political relationships has created the greatest confusion in constitutional law, particularly in recent times."[78] To view and conceive all human relationships

74. *VPR*3, 266. Italics mine.
75. *PR*, §75.   76. *VPR*17, §38.
77. Dallmayr, *G. W. F. Hegel*, 110.
78. *PR*, §75.

and institutions through the contract metaphor is to subordinate everything to private self-interest and property relations and to regard the state as an instrument for the preservation and defense of private property. We shall examine this contract metaphor further in subsequent chapters.

The discussion of contract thus far has assumed a convergence, if not agreement, of individual subjective wills in the common will of contract. But since the common will of contract is only a contingent convergence of subjective arbitrary wills, there is always the possibility that someone will fail to abide by the contract, or that someone will break the contract. A breach of contract involves a separation of my will from the common will to which I have pledged myself. Breaking the contract signifies that I have withdrawn my arbitrary will from the common will, rendering it nugatory and leaving the other "holding the bag." The breach of contract constitutes the transition to wrong (*Unrecht*) and transgression.

8

Crime and Punishment

The *Anerkanntsein* of contract involves the mutual recognition between individuals and thus incorporates a sense of legitimate and justified individuality in the rational forms of ownership. At the conclusion of our analysis of contract we saw the emergence of a separation and conflict between the subjective arbitrary will of individuals and the common will, or *Anerkanntsein*. This separation constitutes wrong. Wrong thus presupposes the establishment and existence of some mutually recognized common will that finds expression in contract, or the general situation of *Anerkanntsein*, that is, recognized status, custom, or lawfulness. Wrong arises when an individual breaks, violates, or usurps these arrangements. Wrong consists in the violation of *Anerkanntsein*. The presumptive universality of right no longer commands honor and respect. It is undermined when people regard it as a mere particular, as of no binding importance on individuals, or merely as a means to a private end.

On the interpersonal level wrong means that the other is either not yet or no longer regarded as counting as an end in itself, but rather is regarded and treated as a nullity. Wrong is the absolute self-assertion of one individual against another, as well as against the universal *Anerkanntsein*. Wrong signifies a violation of the other, as well as the rational structures inherent in recognition, namely, lawfulness, equality, and justice. Wrong appears as the self-aggrandizement of the individual. Thus the principle of abstract right—abstract possessive individualism—when pushed to its extreme self-assertion, undermines abstract right and becomes the 'principle of wrong'. The individual regards everyone else as a nullity, while regarding contract, the universal custom, or law (*Anerkanntsein*), either as a mere particular that he may set aside—at least in his own case—or as of no importance, thus placing himself above the universal or in violation of it.

In what follows we shall explore Hegel's account of wrong (*Unrecht*), coercion, and punishment. In the *Philosophy of Right* Hegel identifies three kinds of wrong, ranging from naive collisions of rights to fraud and deception, which preserve the appearance of right while undermining right itself, to coercions and transgressions that openly violate and reject right. In naive or nonmalicious wrongs, the offender has no intention of infringing right itself; he admits that whatever is right should be done. He errs in a particular situation; for example, two persons may lay claim to ownership of the same thing, each believing that right is on his side. Here we have a collision of ownership claims that requires adjudication but does not involve wrongdoing per se. Both parties agree that universal right should be realized, even though it may be temporarily thwarted.

In fraud the situation is otherwise: here the universal right (*Anerkanntsein*) is reduced to a mere semblance. The perpetrator of fraud tacitly withdraws from intersubjective agreements and treats right as a means to his own private end. He thereby reduces the outward manifestation of right to a mere semblance while concealing his private interest. The particular person who is deceived is 'shown respect' in the sense that he is offered the semblance of right as part of the deception. Deception and fraud thus depend on right even as they seek to undermine it in a particular case, and are thus parasitic on right. Finally, the third form of wrong is transgression or crime. Transgression dispenses with deception; it attacks both the universal right in itself and the particular right of an individual; it leaves the victim with neither the substance nor even the semblance of right. Since fraud obtains the assent of the victim, and makes the victim cooperate in his undoing, fraud does not need to coerce or resort to violence. However, transgression attacks the person in his totality and coerces him directly.

Both fraud and transgression are assaults on right that are culpable and so punishable. Consequently, Hegel's theory of punishment belongs in this context. My concern is not a full account of these topics for their own sake, but to discern the significance and importance of the concept of recognition in Hegel's treatment. I shall begin with Hegel's earlier writings and then consider his mature formulations in the *Philosophy of Right* and the lecture manuscripts.

Wrong and Fraud

The Jena *Philosophie des Geistes 1805/06* follows and continues the practice of the earlier Jena manuscripts in treating its topics first in terms of a static conceptual analysis and second in terms of a dynamic analysis of action, in which individual difference is asserted, the original concepts are negated, put to the test of opposition. Fraud and transgression are determinate manifestations of this individual assertion that negates the universal-general will, while punishment is the negation of this negation that reinstates or upholds the general will.

Up until now the analysis of contract presumed a harmony between the individual's subjective arbitrary will and the common will of contract. Contract expresses a common will that is a contingent convergence of two or more private subjective wills who recognize each other as abstract private persons. Mutual recognition implies a formal ontological equality of each individual or private person. The common will of contract, a determinate form or shape of recognition, expresses a mutual but external and contingent interest. It arises out of intersubjective recognition that introduces practical rationality into mere possession. Possession, when mutually recognized, becomes property. Mutual recognition thus confers the right of ownership.[1]

Inherent in such intersubjective doubling and recognition is the possibility of lawfulness and objective spirit. *Anerkanntsein* is both universal and particular. For example, in the recognition of my possessions as mine, that is, as my property, everyone's property ownership is also recognized in principle. Consequently, knowing oneself to be recognized while recognizing others results in a reciprocally constituted universal-social consciousness and situation: "This knowing will is now universal. It is the state of being-recognized [*Anerkanntsein*]. Juxtaposed to itself in the form of universality . . . the will of the individual is the universal will, and the universal is the individual. It is the totality of ethical life in general; immediate, yet as Right."[2]

Wrong presupposes that some social order (*Anerkanntsein*), however minimal, has been established and exists. "There is crime only insofar as I am recognized; the individual will appears as the negative of the universal will. There is crime only insofar as I am recognized as an individual, and my will is taken as universal, counting in itself. Prior to recognition, there is no insult, no injury."[3] Indeed, prior to recognition there is no right; that is, right has not yet been constituted or established, and if right has not been established, there is no wrong. Deception, trespass, crime, and so on, presuppose mutual recognition, that is, *Anerkanntsein*. Prior to the establishment of *Anerkanntsein* or right, there is no trespass or crime.

Against such a background, Hegel discusses a breach of contract. Since contract is a determinate form of mutual recognition, the existence of contract implies that recognition is actual in some sense, however minimal. A breach of contract means the assertion of difference.[4] In breaking the contract, I break with and contradict the common will. However, in breaking the common will, I also contradict myself, for I am this common will; that is, this common will

---

1. The German term 'Eigentum' can mean both property and ownership. The latter brings out the intersubjective mediation inherent in the German concept, whereas property may not.
2. Hegel, *Philosophie des Geistes 1805/06; HHS*, 118.
3. *Philosophie des Geistes 1805/06*, 210; *HHS*, 125.
4. *Philosophie des Geistes 1805/06*, 210; *HHS*, 125.

is also my will; I have consented to it. Moreover, when I break a contract I do not act merely as an atomic individual, I violate my contract partner by denying my agreement and my implicit equality with him. My action declares that I am different from him, and this difference amounts to an inequality. I declare that the common will we have mutually recognized and constituted is no longer binding on me. Thereby I not only contradict myself, I assert an absolute difference. As an individual I claim to be above the common will of contract, above the existence I share with the other party. I thus contradict myself as part of the general *Anerkanntsein*.

Hegel observes that "my will exists only as recognized. In going back on my word, I not only contradict myself, but also the fact that my will is recognized. My word cannot be relied upon, i.e., my will is merely mine, mere opinion."[5] In contract as a determinate form of recognition, each party is bound by the terms and stipulations of the contract. This binding unity articulates what is necessary if a contract is to be actual and have any validity. My will must also be your will, and vice versa. The common will is jointly and reciprocally established. As such it is greater than and so objective for any one individual. It is no longer simply my will or simply your will, but 'our will'.

However, when I go back on my word, I show that my word is 'only' *my* word. My word, as 'only mine', is not to be trusted. I have not actually committed myself to the mutually established stipulation of contract. I have only appeared to do so. If my word is 'only mine', then it is something merely subjective, changeable, and revocable like opinion. But an individual whose word is not to be trusted, whose word is only his, is like the skeptic who retreats into subjectivity and phenomenalism of mere seeming.[6] He never becomes a We. This is a condition of moral skepticism that is far from ethically neutral.

Implicit in these remarks is an important insight into right and wrong. Wrong clarifies the substantial nature of right. It shows that right is more than a contract; it is more than an artificial, posited universal that is subject in principle to revocation by the arbitrary subjective will of individuals. Rather right is the basic requirement and fundamental condition of a community of freedom. In contrast, wrong is a semblance of right, a seeming that is inherently null and vacuous, and as such parasitic on right. As the semblance of right, wrong must be unmasked, its nullity must be brought to light. That is what punishment does, thereby restoring right as a power over wrong. Only thus does right achieve actuality and objectivity. Hegel develops this interpretation further in his mature philosophy.

---

5. *Philosophie des Geistes 1805/06*, 210–211; *HHS*, 126. Hegel plays on the word *Meinung*. What is mere opinion has no objectivity; it is merely 'mine'.

6. See my *Recognition*, chap. 5. See also my article, "Hegel and Skepticism," *Owl of Minerva* 24, no. 1 (Fall 1992): 71–82.

Wrong, Semblance, and the Logic of Essence

Hegel conceives right and wrong in terms of the logic of essence.[7] Right is what is essential; that is, right is a condition of any community of freedom at all. Wrong is the contrary of essence, or what is nonessential. Although contrary to right, wrong masquerades as right, as the essential, and thus opens up an inverted world in which genuine right—the condition of community—is held to be nonessential. Punishment is the inversion (*Aufhebung*) of this inverted world of wrong, wherein right is established as valid and actual.

> The principle of rightness, the universal will, receives its essential determinate character through the particular will, and so stands in relation to something inessential. This is the relation of essence to its appearance. . . . In wrong however, appearance proceeds to become mere semblance or show. A semblance is a determinate existence inappropriate to the essence, namely an empty detachment and positing of the essence. . . . Semblance is therefore the untruth that disappears because it seeks to exist for itself, and in this disappearance, essence has shown itself as essence, as the power and authority over the semblance. The essence has negated that which negated it, and is thereby confirmed. Wrong is a semblance of this kind, and through its disappearance, right acquires the determination of something fixed and valid.[8]

There are several reasons why Hegel's reference to the logic of essence is significant. We have found that right originates in reciprocal recognition; specifically, right is the universal consciousness and universal will that are constituted by mutual recognition. *Anerkanntsein* denotes not only the accomplishment of a universal social consciousness (*Geist*, or spirit) but also enduring institutions such as right, property, and contracts. *Anerkanntsein* and right require categories of essence, because essence denotes what is permanent and enduring in things.[9]

Further, since *Anerkanntsein* involves universality and relation, it requires categories that are explicitly rather than implicitly *universal* (as are the categories of the logic of being) and *relational*. The categories of essence are self-relational, but only insofar as they are related to what is other.[10] The logic of essence is a logic of relation and mediation, but imperfectly and incompletely realized.[11] Hence at this level there is opposition and conflict. The essential is asymmetrically related to its other, the inessential; conversely the inessential, as semblance, depends on the essential. Hegel believes that wrong is the inessential semblance of right that posits itself as self-sufficient, as no longer

---

7. *PR*, §82; cf. *E*, §131.   8. *PR*, §82 Zusatz.   9. *E*, §112 Zusatz.
10. Ibid.
11. Cf. Kolb, *Critique of Pure Modernity*, 69–72.

subject to right. This is the reason why Hegel claims that semblance is the untruth that disappears because it seeks to exist simply for itself.

In punishing wrong and making it disappear, essence shows itself as essence, namely, as the power and authority over semblance. Wrong negates right, and attempts to set itself up as independent and self-sufficient; but right is the essence that negates that which negated it, and is thereby confirmed. Consequently, through the disappearance of wrong, right acquires the determination of something enduring and valid; it is actual as a negation of a negation. Right becomes actual only in overcoming wrong and canceling it. The actuality of right thus means not only that right is recognized in its other (wrong) but sustains itself in its otherness and contradiction; that is, it endures in spite of opposition.

This apparently abstract logical pattern Hegel finds exhibited in the various levels of wrong. This does not mean that he simply imposes on his particular discussions of deception and punishment some alien speculative categorical structure. Rather Hegel's penetrating intuitions and descriptions of deception and transgression are often illumined and sharpened by his conceptual-logical grasp, and conversely, his speculative dialectical conception serves an important hermeneutical function. Semblance is for Hegel both a logical subcategory of essence (*Wesen*) and a complex mode of interpersonal relation.

Hegel observes that we must create a semblance in order to deceive another person. But when I deceive someone, then right and *Anerkanntsein* have become for me mere semblance. That is, the universal will, the principle of right, is reduced to a mere semblance and treated as a contingent particular. It is not something that is effectively obligatory for me. Rather I seek to make *use* of right (the general will) for my own private purposes. I seek to create for someone else the appearance of respecting right while reducing it from its real effective universality to a mere semblance. I contrive to put on a show of duty, but not the real thing. Consequently, "when I deceive someone, he believes that I do him no wrong. For to him [my action] is right. From this perspective [of the deceived] right appears to be still recognized as valid. I create the illusion that he should receive his right and that I mean him no wrong."[12] However, "the right that is thus offered him is a mere semblance, not the real thing. This constitutes the deception."[13] Hegel characterizes this situation as vileness, or "underhandedness," which "consists in relating to another person as non-existent."[14]

Under such circumstances, therefore, a contract is reduced from actual reciprocal recognition to a wholly external community of wills. But an external community is no community at all. Hegel observes that while no penalty attaches to unintentional wrong, in the case of deception, penalties are appropriately introduced because now right itself is infringed.

---

12. *VPR*4, 269.   13. *PR*, §87.
14. *Philosophie des Geistes 1805/06*, 214; *HHS*, 130.

Transgression as Coercion

Deception was an indirect attack on *Anerkanntsein* that undermines right while seeming to uphold it. Transgression is a direct attack without any subterfuge on right itself. In the deception there is still some recognition of right, however deficient. But in transgression even this minimal recognition of right is absent or rejected.

We have found that for Hegel "right is the relation of the person in its comportment towards others."[15] Recognition is the 'right to have rights'. In reciprocal recognition, individuals cease to relate to each other as raw particulars and, restraining their particular subjective wills and desires, relate to each other through "the universal element of their freedom," or through their universal will that wills freedom itself. Law, as an expression of the intersubjectively constituted general will, demands "that every individual be respected and treated by others as a free being, for only thus does the free will find itself as its subject and contents in another [human being]."[16] So the basic imperative of abstract right is, "Be a person and respect others as persons."[17] This is to identify coercion as the basic wrong. An act is right if it does not restrict or infringe on the freedom of others, and wrong if it violates the freedom of another and/or treats the other as a mere thing to be used. For this reason Hegel considers slavery to be an outrage against the very concept of a human being.[18] Coercion is incompatible with freedom.

But this is only the beginning and not the end of Hegel's analysis of coercion. Although in general coercion is a violation of right, sometimes coercion is necessary, and if necessary, then justified. Our question is, How is coercion of freedom—which is strictly speaking impossible— nevertheless possible? How is coercion, which is in itself illegitimate, nevertheless legitimate? How can something that is wrong nevertheless be right? Part of the answer will be that Hegel distinguishes crime and punishment. Transgression (crime) is an unjustified coercion because it infringes on and violates the right of freedom to existence in the world. Punishment is a second coercion directed against the first; it is a coercion of coercion. As such, punishment is a justified coercion. It is evident that here the concept of coercion is doubled: the first coercion is a negation that infringes on right. Punishment, as the second coercion, negates the first. Punishment is thus a negation of a negation. This recalls the doubling in Hegel's analysis of encounter and recognition and the negation of opposition in the constitution of the 'We'. I want to examine how Hegel's account of punishment renders determinate the general pattern and structure of the concept of recognition.

15. *Philosophie des Geistes 1805/06*, 197; *HHS*, 111.
16. Hegel, *Nurnberg Propadeutik*, cited in I. Primoratz, *Justifying Legal Punishment* (Atlantic Highlands, N.J.: Humanities Press, 1989), 68.
17. *PR*, §36.   18. Ibid., §2.

The Impossible Possibility
of Coercion

Hegel's philosophy of spirit (and its extension in the *Philosophy of Right*) presents an elaborate system that includes elements of a complex philosophical anthropology. We have found that the will has two important dimensions, an infinite universal inner aspect, which includes the capacity to negate and abstract from determinations, and an external finite and determinate aspect, the will that wills something, namely, its embodiment, its possessions, honor and esteem. Considered from the perspective of the latter dimension of the will, coercion is possible. But considered from the former universal dimension, Hegel believes that, strictly speaking, coercion is impossible. If coercion nevertheless occurs, it occurs because the subject allows itself to be coerced. Vulnerability and susceptibility to coercion are permanent possibilities of the determinate existence of the will and an embodied freedom. Nevertheless, the goal of freedom is to be at home with self in other, and this has the connotation of liberation from coercion.

According to Hegel *Anerkanntsein* is both a right and the general form and medium in which rights exist. It is the right of recognition that secures particular determinate rights. There are at least three determinate forms or patterns of giving oneself determinate existence, each of which corresponds to a right: embodiment, ownership, and intersubjective recognition, or *Anerkanntsein*. Embodiment is not a property relation but rather a condition of taking possession. Before I can take possession of things, I must have a right to live; further I must be able to take possession of myself, and be in control of myself. Hegel views embodiment as the primal form of self-possession and self-expression. "Insofar as the body is immediate existence, it is not commensurate with the spirit; before it can be spirit's willing organ and soul-inspired instrument, it must first be taken possession of by the spirit." [19] "I have these limbs and my life only insofar as I so will it; the animal cannot mutilate or destroy itself, but the human being can." [20] Thus taking possession of oneself is a basic right and condition of freedom: "I am free for the other only insofar as I am free in my existence. . . . Violence done to my body by others is violence done to me." [21]

Just as I have a right to my body and my life, I also have a right to give my will determinate existence in things; that is, I have a right to possession. The right to possession is crucial; a denial of it leads to impoverishment and poverty, and to loss of real freedom and recognition. Possession requires recognition to become legitimate and actual. Possession, when recognized by others, is transformed into property: "The concept of property requires that a person should place his will in a thing, and the next stage is precisely the realization of this concept. My inner act of will which says that something is mine must also be-

19. Ibid., §48.   20. Ibid., §47.   21. Ibid., §48.

come recognizable by others."[22] Thus the institution of property depends on the intersubjective recognition and confirmation of possession. In other words, property ownership is an intersubjective-social conception and right.[23]

With this sketch of property as an intersubjectively recognized determinate existence of the will in things, we can now appreciate how Hegel conceives the possibility of coercion. "Coercion is possible because as a person I must give myself external realization, in which I place my will, and in this thing I find myself reflected. But since the will is thus objective, in such objectivity it is also open to attack and injury; it can be posited under necessity and this includes the possibility of coercion."[24] In his 1824–1825 lectures Hegel asks, "How is it possible that I, as free, can be compelled?" His answer is that "I will to hold, to possess something, and this something can come under the power of another. . . . [T]hus does coercion occur."[25] Again, from the 1817 lectures: "Considered abstractly in itself, my will is independent. However, because it has determinate existence in a thing, it is present therein, but other elements are present as well, because the thing is something external. Consequently I can be prevented from the use of my property, and from the exercise of my rights. If I wish to regain these, I can be compelled to do or allow something else. . . . On account of the determinate existence and externality of my will, coercion can gain a foothold and exert an influence on me."[26]

In spite of this apparent foothold of coercion on the external presencing of freedom, Hegel believes all that this shows is that human beings can be externally dominated. But while domination is possible, Hegel believes that coercion of the will or freedom itself is impossible. For despite external domination, the human being remains inwardly, that is, ontologically (*an sich*), free. Hegel distinguishes between domination and coercion thus: "As a living being, the human being can certainly be dominated (*bezwungen*)—i.e., his physical side and external attributes may be brought under the power of others. But the free will in and for itself cannot be coerced (*gezwungen*) except insofar as it fails to withdraw itself from the external dimension in which it is arrested. . . . The only one who can be coerced is the one who *allows* himself to be coerced."[27] Hegel illustrates this point in reference to slavery: "If we hold firmly to the view that the human being in and for itself is free, we thereby condemn slav-

---

22. Ibid., §51.

23. Avineri also stresses this point. However, for Hegel to say that property is social means that the will's extension of itself and presence in property is recognized. What is intersubjectively and socially recognized is the right to exclude others from one's property. Consequently property is a socially recognized and mediated possession. But this social *recognition* of property does not imply a social nature of property in Marx's sense, for that implies the abolition of what Hegel is asserting, namely, private property and its recognition. Hegel himself is also concerned with the social problem of poverty. We shall return to this issue in chapter 11.

24. *VPR*3, 291.   25. *VPR*4, 271.   26. *VPR*17, §40.

27. *PR*, §91.

ery. But if someone is a slave, his own will is responsible, just as the responsibility lies with the will of a people if that people is subjugated. Thus the wrong of slavery is the fault not only of those who enslave or subjugate people, but [also] of the slaves and subjugated themselves."[28]

Note that these analyses presuppose and render determinate patterns of reciprocal recognition: (1) the principle of subjectivity: that is, nothing happens in the subject except what happens through the subject's freedom and consent; and (2) the principle of reciprocity and coequality. However, in this case reciprocity is negative; namely, the one who is coerced allows himself to be coerced. This is a variation on the general pattern of intersubjective doubling; namely, each does to himself what the other does. Strange as it may seem, the doubling of consciousness and the reciprocity of intersubjectivity mean that coercion is a joint, cooperative intersubjective affair. Coercion, if carried out by only one side, would fail. If coercion is to succeed, the coerced must at some level allow himself to be coerced. What makes coercion so terrible is the vulnerability of embodied subjectivity to being coerced.

The embodied finitude of being in a situation opens the human being to the possibility of being coerced. However, by virtue of his negative, abstract freedom, the human being can abstract from and transcend his facticity and situation. In spite of coercion, the human being is able to escape or at least mitigate coercion by abstracting from and withdrawing his claim and right to property. He is free to avoid coercion by withdrawing his right to recognition (as does the slave in the *Phenomenology*) and ultimately his right to life itself. Choosing death is the ultimate manifestation of human freedom's transcendence of nature and situation. The choice of death, terrible as it is, is the ultimate possibility of escaping coercion.

Not that Hegel advocates such extreme measures, for although the choice of death means that avoidance of coercion is always possible in principle, this does not make coercion itself right. Rather coercion is wrong because it infringes on freedom. Moreover, it is inherently self-contradictory. This is not evident if it is considered simply as a single act of an isolated abstract individual. But the first-person perspective is itself an abstraction that utterly misses what coercion is, because it ignores its inherently intersubjective dimension. *Inter*subjectively regarded, coercion is "the expression of a will which cancels the expression or existence of a will."[29] *Intra*subjectively regarded, "coercion by its very nature turns back upon itself."[30] Coercion is thus doubly paradoxical: it is a free action that seeks to injure and violate another freedom. Coercion is a strange action because it negates its own presuppositions, namely, rightful freedom, *Anerkanntsein*, and law. When this negation of right and law becomes overt and explicit, the result is transgression or crime.

28. Ibid., §57 Zusatz.   29. Ibid., §92.   30. *VPR*19, 87.

Banquo's Ghost

Let us assume that a transgression has occurred. In response to transgression, the law strikes back and exacts retribution. But what does this mean? It is significant that Hegel formulates his earliest views on punishment in the context of tragedy. In his *Early Theological Writings*, Hegel presents the following "Banquo's ghost" theory of punishment as retribution.

> The illusion of trespass, its belief that it destroys the other's life and is enlarged thereby, is dissipated by the fact that the disembodied spirit of the injured life comes on the scene against the trespass, just as Banquo who came as a friend to Macbeth was not blotted out when he was murdered, but immediately thereafter took his seat, not as a guest at the feast, but as an evil spirit. The trespasser intended to have done with another's life, but he has only destroyed his own, for life is not different from life, since life dwells in the single Godhead. In his arrogance he has destroyed indeed, but only the friendliness of life; he has perverted life into an enemy. It is the deed itself which has created a law whose domination now comes on the scene; this law is the unification in the concept, of the equality between the injured, apparently alien life, and the trespasser's own forfeited life. It is now for the first time that the injured life appears as a hostile power against the trespasser and maltreats him as he has maltreated the other. Hence punishment . . . is the equal reaction of the trespasser's own deed, of a power which he himself has armed, of an enemy made an enemy by himself.[31]

This early text contains in germ much of Hegel's mature theory of punishment.[32] Macbeth's murder of Banquo is not only a violation of Banquo's life, it also destroys the harmony and primordial equality of life, its friendliness. Macbeth's murder of Banquo perverts life itself into an enemy. Macbeth's murder creates a law that now boomerangs against Macbeth. The concept of law signifies an equality between Banquo's injured life and Macbeth's life: "Life is not different from life." On the basis of such equality, the law effects a negative reciprocity or retribution: Macbeth must forfeit the same right he has violated.

---

31. Hegel, *ETW*, 229–230. For one of the best accounts of Hegel's theory of punishment, see Igor Primoratz, *Banquo's Geist: Hegels Theorie der Strafe*, Hegel-Studien Beiheft 29 (Bonn: Bouvier Verlag, 1986).

32. Hegel returns to the Banquo's ghost metaphor in his theory of action set forth in the *Philosophy of History* (1830). There we are told that the actions of human beings in history may produce an effect entirely different from what they themselves intend and accomplish, and from what they immediately recognize and desire. These implications and consequences of an action that transcend the subjective conscious intentions of the agent react on the individual. A crime or transgression therefore recoils on the perpetrator and destroys him, thereby annulling the original action itself and restoring justice. (Hegel, *Lectures on the Philosophy of World History*, trans. H. B. Nisbet [Cambridge: Cambridge University Press, 1975], 75.) This recoil of the original deed on itself is the germ of Hegel's concept of the cunning of reason. This concept, logically expressed, is that the particular turns against and violates the universal. In so doing, it violates itself in principle, and the universal, active in its own right, does to the particular what it has done, thereby annulling the deed and reestablishing justice, *Anerkanntsein*, which is the correspondence of particulars with their universal, the I with the We, that transgression presupposes. *PR*, §82.

A life for a life. Finally, there is a power symbolized and personified by Banquo's ghost, that is stirred up, armed, and made hostile by Macbeth's action. This hostile power—Banquo's ghost—carries out the retribution, that is, forfeiture of right, authorized by the law of equality. This hostile power maltreats, that is, coerces, Macbeth, as Macbeth had previously maltreated Banquo.

Note that this earliest formulation of the theory of punishment occurs in the context of a complex tragic vision. Hegel's earliest views on punishment originate in his peculiar vision of tragic guilt and reconciliation. It is no accident that Hegel illustrates his view of punishment by reference to Shakespeare's great tragedy, *Macbeth*. The underlying tragic themes are important aspects of Hegel's account. Macbeth, in slaying Banquo, acts in false consciousness, what Hegel terms the 'illusion of trespass'. Macbeth's illusion is that he will gain his end through murdering Banquo. At a deeper level, Macbeth's illusion is the positivist dream of pure, externally related facts, events, and persons and an "emotive theory" of ethics. Macbeth intends, not only to get away with murder, but to profit from it. His false consciousness or illusion conceals from Macbeth the fundamental harmony, reciprocity, and coequality of life.

But then a dramatic reversal occurs, the moment of discovery or recognition as Aristotle describes it. Macbeth's false consciousness is shattered. He intended to have done with another, but he succeeds only in perverting life itself into an enemy and destroying his own life. The original harmony and benign reciprocity of life undergo a violation and turn negative. Consequently, this dramatic reversal constitutes a tragic recognition on Macbeth's part.[33] Despite his murder of Banquo, Macbeth has not really finished him off. Banquo reappears as a ghost, a hostile power that Macbeth's transgression has armed and made an enemy. This tragic self-recognition in other makes Macbeth's guilt manifest. Macbeth's illusions are stripped away: he has not gained anything; instead he has forfeited his own right to life and life itself.

According to the Banquo's ghost metaphor, punishment is a self-inflicted coercion. The coercer ultimately coerces himself. What is done to the other is also done to oneself. The coercion Macbeth inflicts on Banquo boomerangs on Macbeth, as life reasserts itself against injury. From the perspective of the one being punished, that is, Macbeth, it is clear that he is being coerced, whether this coercion is exerted by life, Macbeth's conscience, Banquo's ghost, or the law itself. Whatever the agency of punishment may be, this coercion is justified in Hegel's view. In murdering Banquo, Macbeth violates the fundamental human equality that he shares with Banquo and creates a terrible inequality and injustice. Macbeth seeks to invert the world order. But in a dramatic reversal of this inverted world of transgression, the law strikes back and dominates Macbeth; it coerces and maltreats him as he has maltreated Banquo. The

33. Aristotle identifies this moment of reversal as the moment of discovery or recognition. Not only Hegel's theory of punishment, but also his theory of recognition is closely connected with his appreciation of Greek tragedy.

nullification of life inherent in Macbeth's murderous action is turned against Macbeth himself.

However, it is crucial to note that this coercion and maltreatment are different from Macbeth's coercion of Banquo. For their purpose is not to create inequality but to eliminate it. In other words, the purpose of the second coercion is to reestablish the original equality and reciprocity. The metaphor of Banquo's ghost articulates a retributive view of justice: a life for a life. As he has done to Banquo, so shall it be done to him. Macbeth gets what he deserves.

The Mature Theory: Punishment as the Second Coercion

When we move from Hegel's early discussion of punishment in the context of tragedy to his mature political philosophy, a different set of considerations come into play. The system of right is freedom made actual. The question is, What place can coercion have in a philosophy that supposedly articulates the conditions and determinations of freedom? How can punishment, as coercion, be justified? It can be justified only if punishment is not itself evil, but the realization of freedom and right. But how can punishment, as a coercion, fail to be evil? How can coercion, which is a negation of freedom, nevertheless actualize freedom?

Hegel follows Kant in distinguishing between a *first* coercion, or *transgression*, and a *second* coercion, or *punishment*. According to Kant,

> everything that is contrary to right is a hindrance to freedom based on universal laws, while coercion is a hindrance or resistance to freedom. Consequently if a certain use to which freedom is put is itself a hindrance to freedom . . . (i.e., if it is contrary to right), any coercion which is used against it will be a hindrance to a hindrance of freedom, and will thus be consistent with freedom according to universal laws—that is, will be right. It thus follows . . . that right entails the authority to apply coercion to anyone who infringes it.[34]

Transgression, or primary coercion, is contrary and injurious to freedom and right. Transgression therefore is a negation; it negates the socially constituted order of right and freedom. But it is a negation that presupposes what it negates, and is inherently self-nullifying in a sense we shall shortly explain. Consequently, transgression is a coercion, and the coercion of freedom is for Hegel the primal, fundamental wrong and injustice.

Punishment is not a coercion in this primary sense. Instead punishment is a coercion directed *against coercion*, a *second* coercion that cancels the *first*.

34. Immanuel Kant, *Metaphysics of Morals*, in Kant, *Political Writings*, trans. H. B. Nisbet (Cambridge: Cambridge University Press, 1991), 134. Both Fichte and Hegel follow Kant in their treatment of punishment as a coercion directed against coercion.

Punishment therefore is not an evil that is contrary to right but the realization of right, that is, the way in which right, the universal *Anerkanntsein* in which all, including the offender, have a stake, is maintained in spite of transgression. In Hegel's words, "Coercion by its very nature turns back upon itself. Punishment makes his own will count against the transgressor himself."[35] Again, "Since coercion destroys itself in its concept, it has its real expression in the fact that *coercion is canceled [aufgehoben] by coercion*. Coercion is therefore not only conditionally but necessarily *right*, namely as a second coercion which cancels the first."[36] The second coercion is not coercion for coercion's sake, or for some private gain at another's expense; the second coercion is relative to the first; it is a reaction to and a cancellation of the original violation of freedom. The second coercion is justified because it defends freedom against coercion and thereby maintains and upholds both freedom and right.

In Hegel's view, punishment is not externally or contingently related to the transgression; it is the second half of a joint reciprocal action that begins with transgression and ends with the reversal of transgression.[37] This reflects the structure of reciprocal recognition. What one does to another, one also does to oneself. Hegel proposes that transgression and punishment are not two separate, externally related actions but correlative aspects of an organic whole.[38] Punishment, as a second coercion, is intrinsically connected with the transgression: "The second coercion is conditioned by the first. The second is necessary if the first has been posited. Necessity connects the two that appear otherwise as independent."[39]

Transgression, as the first coercion, reveals and divides the whole. Recall that for Hegel, prior to recognition, there is no violation of right. Transgression simultaneously reveals and threatens the original order, harmony, and reciprocity of the whole, the *Anerkanntsein*. Prior to transgression, recognition, the *Anerkanntsein*, is immediate, it is taken for granted, passed over and ignored. The act of transgression reveals what is at stake. For transgression seeks to cancel explicitly the universal and substantial element of the *Anerkanntsein*, namely, the intersubjective rational will. Thus transgression digs deeper into the very being of right and brings to light the universal-social rational will "whose being is rooted in something more profound than the accidental agreement of particular wills."[40] This social-universal will is necessary if there is to be any community of freedom at all.

35. *VPR*19, 87.

36. *PR*, §93. Italics mine.

37. "Punishment is merely a manifestation of the crime, i.e., it is one half which is necessarily presupposed by the other." *PR*, §101 Zusatz.

38. "The trespass . . . reveals the whole, but as divided, and the hostile parts can coalesce into the whole. Justice is satisfied, since the trespasser has sensed as injured in himself the same life that he has injured." *ETW*, 232.

39. *VPR*3, 294.

40. Reyburn, *The Ethical Theory of Hegel*, 144.

By threatening to divide the whole, the transgressor seeks to make himself an exception to the general concept of right. He negates the universal *Anerkanntsein* and places his own private end above the common good. He acts as if freedom were not something social and universal, but merely particular. He acts as if everyone else is either a nullity or exists as instrumental to his own private end and purpose.

If allowed to stand, transgression would undermine recognition, because it treats others as nullities; on the universal level of law, transgression would nullify right itself. The transgressor's attack on right creates the possibility of the disappearance of right itself. "Transgression injures the generally recognized existence of freedom, namely, the validity of the laws. Whoever commits a transgression says in effect 'These laws are invalid, and I thumb my nose at the generally recognized consensus.' . . . Thus we can understand how transgression is dangerous, because people say that if the transgression is allowed to stand, then no one is secure any longer."[41] Punishment is the response to the potential destruction of recognition and right—the foundations and conditions of community—signified by transgression. Punishment negates the negation inherent in transgression and allows the elements of right—the proper relation of free persons to each other—to coalesce once again. However, punishment is not coercion for its own sake but a *second* coercion that is justified only to the extent that it reverses and nullifies the first.

Recognition and the Second Coercion

The fact that Hegel justifies punishment as the *second* coercion shows that he conceives transgression and punishment through the doubling inherent not only in the concept (*Begriff*) but also in reciprocal recognition. That is, punishment is an essentially reciprocal action. It is the original action of coercion reciprocated and/or inverted. However, there are two ways in which this reciprocation can occur, two forms it can assume, namely, revenge and retribution. According to Hegel, revenge involves a particular subjective will in immediate opposition to and retaliation against another subjective will. But in this form, we are not yet speaking of justice. Revenge is a "tit-for-tat" reciprocity. The retaliation, as subjective, does not aim at justice and right, which are universal, but at "getting even" with the offender, paying him back in kind. Consequently "revenge, as the positive action of a particular will, becomes a new infringement or injury; because of this contradiction, it becomes part of an infinite progression and is inherited from generation to generation."[42] So revenge, as subjective, does not reconcile or end the cycle of coercive violence but perpetuates it.[43]

The second form of reciprocation is retribution, which Hegel conceives as

41. *VPR*19, 176–177.   42. *PR*, §102.

43. Hegel observes that punishment typically takes the form of revenge in social conditions where there are neither laws nor magistrates. He further notes that among uncivilized peoples re-

an infringement of an infringement, a coercion that cancels a coercion. Here the end is universal reciprocity and equality; its operative idea is justice as fairness. Hegel's *concept* of retribution supports and articulates justice, because it implies an identity between transgression and punishment. In other words, punishment, as the cancellation of the transgression, is not external to the transgression, nor does it supervene on the transgression 'from without'. Rather punishment is inherent in transgression. In Hegel's words, "This determination of the concept . . . is precisely that necessary connection which means that crime, as the will which is null and void in itself, accordingly contains within itself its own nullification. This nullification appears in the form of punishment. It is this inner *identity*, which for the understanding, is reflected in determinate external existence as *equality*."[44] In a note Hegel adds,

> When the criminal meets with retribution, this has the appearance of an alien determination which does not belong to him. Yet as we have seen, the punishment is merely the manifestation of the crime, i.e., it is one half which is necessarily presupposed by the other. What is at first sight objectionable about retribution is that it looks like something immoral, like revenge, and may be interpreted as a personal matter. Yet it is not the personal element, but the concept itself which carries out retribution. . . . [I]t signifies merely the Gestalt of transgression turned around against itself.[45]

In his discussion of retribution, Hegel invokes the image of the sleeping *Eumenides*, who are aroused from their slumber by the crime.[46] The image of the aroused Furies seems to point toward vengeance and revenge. But this is misleading as far as Hegel is concerned, for his point is exactly the opposite. In the Hotho manuscript (1822) that the *Philosophy of Right* only partially cites, Hegel emphasizes the protective rather than the vengeful function of the Eumenides: "Right is the well-disposed Eumenides that are for the protection of the transgressor, and only execute what lies in the necessity of the thing itself. Therefore no subjective individual caprice may be brought to bear upon the transgressor."[47] Whether Hegel is correct in his interpretation of the Eumenides does not concern us; his point is that retribution *protects* the offender from vengeance and revenge. How is this so?

The concept of retribution implies that "nothing happens in the punishment

---

venge is undying, e.g., the vendetta, and can be suppressed only by superior force that prevents revenge or makes it impossible to carry it out.

44. *PR*, §101.   45. Ibid., §101 Zusatz.   46. Ibid.

47. *VPR*, 3:670. Eduard Gans, not Hegel, compiled the Zusätze for the *Philosophy of Right* by editing materials drawn from the lecture notes of Hotho (1822) and Griesheim (1824) and inserting them in the text. Nisbet warns that these materials should be treated with caution, not because they are based on students' notes, but rather because "Gans's extracts are highly selective, combining material from two distinct lecture series and consisting in paraphrase rather than verbatim quotation" (*PR*, xxxvi). This text referring to the Eumenides illustrates the problem. Gans's Zusatz not merely confuses, but inverts Hegel's meaning. For this reason it is necessary to make use of Ilting's 4-volume *Hegel: Rechtsphilosophie* (Stuttgart: Frommann-Holzboog, 1974), which contains some of the materials from which Gans composed his Zusätze.

except what already lies in the transgression."[48] Here retribution coincides with justice and fairness. Just punishment must add nothing to the transgression. Retribution demands and asserts an *equality* between the crime and punishment and between offender and victim. This equality means that the criterion of punishment must be derived from the offender's own action. Punishment is thus distinguished from the emotions of revenge and from the external ends of society with which it is often confused, namely, protection of society, deterrence, and reform of the offender. These considerations deny the humanity of the offender by treating him as a means to some external end, or as an animal to be threatened.

The fundamental question of punishment is whether punishment is just.[49] Hegel asks, "To what extent is threat compatible with right? The threat presupposes that human beings are not free, and seeks to coerce them through the image of an evil. But right and justice must have their seat in freedom and the will, and not in that lack of freedom at which the threat is directed. To justify punishment in this way is like raising one's cane at a dog; it means treating the human being like a dog instead of respecting his honor and freedom."[50] Hegel believes that retribution is just because retributive punishment is simply the reversal of the offense;[51] that is, it demands that the principle of the transgression be applied to the offender. Such punishment is not revenge but justice, because the offender is punished by being subjected to his own principle. Such a punishment is fair, for he cannot consistently both assert and deny his own principle. And he has no plausible cause for complaint if, as equality and reciprocity demand, his own principle is applied to him.

The equality between crime and punishment is the reason why punishment is capable of annulling the transgression. For punishment is simply a reciprocal negation of the original negation (transgression). Crime and punishment are not utterly external events that occur in complete isolation but opposite sides of the same coin. Such pure equality allows punishment to cancel or suspend the transgression, and restore right. For this reason Hegel regards punishment as a form of reconciliation, not only between offender and victim, but also of the offender with himself. In contrast, revenge, which is carried out by particular against particular, merely seeks to 'get even'. In 'getting even' it perpetuates the original negation and inequality, and so perpetuates the cycle of coercion and violence.

In conceiving transgression as coercion, and punishment as a justified second coercion, Hegel brings these concepts into the general framework of intersubjective recognition. By conceiving punishment as the second coercion,

---

48. *VPR4* (1824/25), 282.
49. *PR*, §99.   50. Ibid., §99 Zusatz.
51. "The essence of punishment, its concept, is this transition, the inversion of the injured universal recognition [*Anerkanntsein*]. It is revenge, but as justice. That is to say, the recognition which is in itself and was injured is to be restored." *Philosophie des Geistes 1805/06*, 215–216; *HHS*, 131.

Hegel reflects the intersubjective doubling of self-consciousness, as well as the coequality of the parties in the dialectic of reciprocal recognition. This dialectic is expressed in the principle that what one does to the other one does to one-self. This principle has moral as well as legal significance. In the 1819–1820 lectures we read: "Expressed in a general moral form, Whatever you will, that should the people do to you because that is what you do to them."[52] This recip-rocal inversion of punishment is why transgression, coercion, and so on, are self-contradictory, self-subverting actions. Kant emphasizes the contradiction in immoral maxims that are brought out by the categorical imperative. A maxim is immoral if, when universalized, it is self-contradictory. Hegel places this in an intersubjective context; transgression is not merely self-contradictory, it is also self-subverting: what one does to another one also does to oneself. Crime and transgression are parasitic on right and mutual recognition.

> The injured party is recognized in himself; everything proceeds in the element of recognition, of Right. *Dolus*, the crime, has this significance: that the one doing the injury has previously recognized the one he injures, that the criminal (usually the thief) knew what he did, not [necessarily] in its determinate scope, but in its general determinacy. That he knew it to be prohibited, and knew that in this act he does injury to a person, such as is recognized in himself; that he [the criminal] lives in the element of recognition; [and] that whatever exists derives its meaning in such recognition.[53]

The Nullity of Transgression

If an action is self-contradictory and self-subverting, then it is neither right nor plausible. "When an infringement of right as right occurs, it does have a positive existence. But this existence is *in itself* null and void."[54] The nullity of the transgression consists in its being an act of freedom that attacks and can-cels another freedom, and so places the general will, the *Anerkanntsein*, in contradiction to itself. Transgression and wrong are phenomena that contra-dict the general will. But this contradiction is, as we have seen, a mere sem-blance or show.

> In wrong . . . appearance proceeds to become mere semblance or show. A sem-blance is a determinate existence inappropriate to the essence, namely an empty detachment and positing of the essence. . . . Semblance is therefore the untruth that disappears because it seeks to exist for itself, and in this disappearance, essence has shown itself as essence, as the power and authority over the sem-blance. The essence has negated that which negated it, and is thereby confirmed. Wrong is a semblance of this kind, and through its disappearance, right acquires the determination of something fixed and valid.[55]

52. *VPR*19, 88.
53. *Philosophie des Geistes 1805/06*, 215–216; *HHS*, 131.
54. *PR*, §97.   55. Ibid., §82 Zusatz.

For Hegel, the function of punishment is to bring to light and make manifest the inner, self-contradictory nullity of coercion and to reveal coercion as mere show or semblance. Thereby right and freedom are made actual: "Whereas right previously had only an immediate being, it now becomes actual as it returns out of its negation; for the actual is effectual, sustaining itself in its otherness, while what is merely immediate remains susceptible to negation."[56] Punishment is necessary, because failure to punish transgression would allow the transgression to stand and thereby become part of the accepted social order (*Anerkanntsein*). If transgression were allowed to stand, that would be equivalent to recognizing wrong as right, injustice as justice. It would legitimate transgression, thereby subverting the social order of freedom. This would allow the irrational to become actual, which is itself irrational. Such is Hegel's 'objective' justification of punishment.[57]

Turning to the 'subjective' justification of punishment, Hegel explains the self-subverting nullity of transgression for the transgressor in the following way: "Since the agent is a rational being, there is a universal rational dimension in his action. If you rob someone else, you rob yourself. If you kill anyone, you kill all, including yourself. Your action contains a law that you have propounded."[58] For Hegel, every action has an implicit general dimension that can be expressed and formulated as general rule or principle. To act is to presume some possible intersubjective validity for one's action.

However, coercion and transgression overtly deny the possibility of intersubjective validity even as they covertly imply it. As actions of rational agents, coercion and transgression have a universal aspect and dimension; they propound an intersubjective rule or law. Thus Hegel would say to a transgressor: "By acting upon this law, you have recognized it as valid in and for itself. The agent therefore may be subsumed under the very mode of action that he himself has propounded. Thereby the equality which he has infringed may be restored."[59] The criminal who robs others proclaims by his action the principle that property may be stolen; his action implies his consent to this principle, which makes it not only possible but fair, to apply his principle to the criminal himself. He has already consented to it, and thus to punish him by subsuming him under his own principle is fair and just.

---

56. Ibid.
57. It is a separate question whether punishment should be light or severe. Hegel believes this is an empirical question whose answer depends in part on the degree of historical-cultural development and in part on the self-confidence and assurance of the social consensus. See *PR*, §218 plus Zusatz.
58. Hegel, *Nurnberger Propadeutik*, TWA Sk 4:244. It is quite possible that Hegel here is thinking of Kant's discussion of right and punishment in the *Metaphysics of Morals*: "But what kind and what degree of punishment does public justice take as its principle and norm? None other than the principle of equality, . . . the principle of not inclining to one side more than the other. Thus any undeserved evil which you do to someone else among the people is an evil done to yourself. If you slander him, you slander yourself; if you rob him you rob yourself; if you strike him you strike yourself, and if you kill him you kill yourself." Kant, *Political Writings*, 155.
59. Hegel, *Propadeutik*, 4:244.

To be sure, the content of the transgressor's principle is no doubt irrational. But Hegel claims that the form of the principle—as chosen and acted on by the criminal as a rational agent—is rational. The transgressor propounds a law that ironically only he recognizes, because only he, not the others, has acted on it. Although the content of his law may, as an infringement on freedom, be irrational and unjust, it is no injustice to subsume him under his own law. "The injustice, that he has committed, is, when carried out against him, justice, because through this second action, that he himself recognizes as valid, the original equality is restored."[60] This is a crucial point because Hegel insists that in punishment the state must do nothing that is not just.[61] But it is no injustice to the transgressor to subsume him under the very principle that he propounds and recognizes in his transgression.

It is not possible to overestimate the importance of this point. Against pragmatic and utilitarian theories that view punishment as a protection of society, as a deterrent, or as rehabilitation, Hegel insists that justice requires that the criterion of punishment derive from the criminal himself and not from elsewhere. No doubt there may be such elements as deterrence, education, and reform in punishment, but these are not its fundamental measure or criteria. The basic question in punishment is whether the punishment is fair and just. Hegel's view is that retributive punishment alone meets this requirement. "To punish an offender because he has offended is to punish him because he deserves it; for to relate to another in accordance with his deserts is to take the way he treats others as the criterion of the way he is to be treated. To treat another according to his deserts, is to relate to him as a responsible and free being."[62]

Hegel's theory of punishment presents a striking and provocative combination of the seemingly offensive concept of retribution with a profound respect for freedom, dignity, and justice. Punishment is not only the right of the state to uphold and legitimate the law but also the right of the transgressor, not so much to be punished, but to be recognized as a human being. Hegel mitigates the severe concept of retribution, the *lex talionis*, by locating it within the concept of recognition and respect for humanity. Recognition is an interhuman relation that is inherently mutual and reciprocal. Applied to punishment, recognition qualifies retribution. So understood as a form of reciprocal recognition, retribution is not the mindless external "tit-for-tat" reciprocity of the *lex talionis* but an enduring reciprocity that acknowledges the human being as an end in itself: "Recognition does not have [conditional] reciprocity as its ground. I do not recognize [you] because you have recognized me (and vice-versa). Rather the ground of this mutual recognition lies in the nature of the thing itself. I recognize the will of the other simply because he is to be recognized as counting in and for himself."[63]

60. Ibid.   61. *VPR*17, §46.
62. Primoratz, *Justifying Legal Punishment*, 79.
63. *Propadeutik*, TWA Sk 4:237.

If the human being is an end in itself, this requires a distinction between the sinner and his sin, the criminal and his trespass. Hegel observes that "the sinner is more than a sin existent, a trespass possessed of personality; he is a human being, trespass and fate are in him. But he can return to himself again, and if he does so, then trespass and fate are under him."[64] Hegel makes this same point in another early essay, "Who Thinks Abstractly?" He criticizes the abstract thinking that shapes public perception of a murderer as little more than an existent crime.

> A murderer is led to the place of execution. For the common populace *he is nothing but a murderer*. Ladies perhaps remark that he is a strong, handsome, interesting man. *What? A murderer handsome?* How can one think so wickedly and call a murderer handsome? . . . This is the corruption of morals that is prevalent in the upper classes, a priest may add, knowing the bottom of things and human hearts.

Hegel comments on this scene:

> *This is abstract thinking: to see nothing in a murderer except the abstract fact that he is a murderer, and to annul all other human essence in him with this simple quality.*

Such abstract thinking is superficial and shallow. Hegel contrasts it with another point of view that remembers the criminal is more than a crime existent:

> In a quite different manner I once heard a common old woman who worked in a hospital kill the abstraction of the murderer and bring him to life for honor. The severed head that had been placed on the scaffold, and the sun was shining. How beautifully she said, the sun of God's grace shines on Binder's head!—you are not worthy of having the sun shine on you, one says to a rascal with whom one is angry. This woman saw that the murderer's head was struck by the sunshine and thus was still worthy of it. She raised it from the punishment of the scaffold into the sunny grace of God, and instead of accomplishing the reconciliation with violets and sentimental vanity, saw him accepted in grace in the higher sun.[65]

Like the old woman, Hegel's contextualizing and situating the theory of retribution within his principle of recognition corrects the abstraction of the criminal and honors him as a free and responsible human being. This is no sentimental humanism that shies away from punishment, especially capital punishment. "The punishment that [retribution] entails is seen as embodying the criminal's own right, [and] the criminal is honored as a rational being. He is denied this honor if the concept and criterion of his punishment are not derived from his

---

64. *ETW*, 238.
65. Hegel, "Who Thinks Abstractly?" in *Hegel: Texts and Commentary*, trans. and ed. Walter Kaufmann (Notre Dame: University of Notre Dame Press, 1977), 117–118. Italics mine.

own act, and he is also denied it if he is regarded simply as a harmful animal which must be rendered harmless, or punished with a view to deterring or reforming him."[66]

Hegel's retributivism thus grants the state power to retaliate against crime and transgression but qualifies this potentially terrifying retaliation by the principle of recognition. This requires that in punishment the state may do no wrong. The state offends against justice if its principle of punishment is not taken from the transgression itself. A just punishment should contain nothing more than the original transgression; that is, justice requires that the criterion of punishment be taken from and add nothing to the criminal's own transgression. However, "transgression is in itself null. Punishment is only the manifestation of this nullity. Nothing comes out in the punishment except what was already present in the transgression."[67]

Is Punishment Necessary?

Allen Wood presents two criticisms of Hegel's account of punishment: (1) that he cannot make satisfactory sense of Hegel's thesis that transgression is a nullity, a thesis that is "shrouded in obscure metaphors";[68] and (2) that Hegel's theory that the transgressor forfeits in himself the right he violates in another, answers only the question by what right the state punishes the transgressor, and not the separate question, whether punishment must actually be inflicted. In other words, granting that punishment does no injustice, we might still ask whether there is any good reason for the state to punish.

Concerning the first criticism, it is no secret that Wood disdains to enter into Hegel's 'discredited' conceptual and philosophical universe, and prefers to carry on a discussion that makes connections between "issues that still interest moral philosophers" and selected discrete themes present in Hegel's texts.[69] Moreover, although Wood is aware of the concept of recognition, he treats it as merely one more discrete theme among others. Although he refers to recognition, Wood does not attempt to think through Hegel's concept of punishment as a determinate shape of intersubjective recognition.

Wood's posing of the question contains an antinomy: on the one hand, Wood acknowledges that the very concept of punishment appears retributive, while, on the other hand, he denies that this constitutes a justification of the practice. This seems to assume that justification is a wholly external matter. Further, Wood construes punishment as an autonomous social practice that stands in need of justification. This too assumes that justification must be ex-

---

66. *PR*, §100.   67. *VPR*4 (1824), 282.
68. Wood, *HET*, 109; for Wood's admission of inability to make Hegel's claim that crime is implicitly null intelligible, p. 117.
69. A. W. Wood, Reply, Symposium on Wood, *Bulletin of the Hegel Society of Great Britain*, no. 25 (Spring/Summer 1992): 34.

ternal to the practice, an exercise in *raisonnieren* that is at best contingent and at worst sounds like mere rationalization.

In contrast, for Hegel the justification of punishment, that is, its criterion, must ultimately reside in the very act of coercion and transgression. The task of justification consists in an uncovering and articulation of this immanent rationality, the immanent identity wherein transgression includes and carries with it its own punishment. Hegel's whole position is that punishment must contain nothing except what is inherent in the primary coercion or transgression. If punishment is not already contained in or implicit in the transgression, if the transgression does not contain its own principle that, by reciprocity, can become the criterion of punishment, then there is no acceptable justification. Moreover, Wood's language of analytical-discursive argument shuns the collisions, paradoxes, ironies, and self-subversions that are the lifeblood of Hegel's speculative thought. Even so, some of the latter creeps into Wood's exposition, and allows him to make better sense of the nullity of transgression than he gives himself credit for.

The nullity of transgression does not mean that it does not exist but rather that it is self-contradictory and thus self-subverting. The self-contradiction is to be found on two levels. The first is the intrapersonal: the will is in contradiction to itself (i.e., the *Willkür*, or arbitrary freedom, contradicts the universal rational freedom, or the *Wille an sich*). Hegel says, "The criminal has set up [and consented to] a universal law: it is right to violate freedom."[70] The second level is the interpersonal: the transgressor, acting on this principle, cancels the freedom of his victim and thereby cancels in principle his own. For Hegel, transgression is implicitly or *an sich* null because "it is the expression of a will that cancels the expression or existence of [another] will."[71] To coerce is to violate another's freedom, and the violation of another's freedom implies and sets up a law, recognized by the transgressor but no one else, that right may be violated. This law, which is manifestly unjust, is, when applied reciprocally to the transgressor, justice, because it is his very own law.

Wood seems to understand this very well when he writes, "by invading another's sphere of freedom I declare by my action that I no longer recognize that right as inviolable. . . . In effect my crime is an act of consent to someone else's invasion of my own sphere of freedom to the same extent that I have invaded sphere of my victim. . . . Hence my renunciation of right applies—ironically—only to me."[72] Of course, irony is a good Hegelian 'turn' of thought. Is it intelligible? It seems so, for Wood suggests that this ironical analysis of punishment clarifies Hegel's claim that transgression is a nullity: "The criminal's

---

70. *VPR*17, 70.
71. *PR*, §92. Cf. §93: force or coercion are null because they immediately destroy themselves in their concept.
72. *HET*, 114.

claim to punishment enables us to interpret Hegel's insistence on the nullity of the criminal will in the sense of its self-destructiveness. My criminal act is self-destructive in the sense that the right it actually revokes is not my victim's, but only my own."[73] Here Wood makes the important point that Hegel's retributive account of punishment upholds the universal *Anerkanntsein* that includes the rights of the victim; retributive punishment revokes only the forfeited right of the transgressor. It would appear that Wood's own analysis of the ironic justice of punishment refutes his charge that Hegel's meaning is unintelligible and shrouded in obscure metaphors.

The foregoing analysis also takes care of the second issue Wood raises, that Hegel justifies the right of the state to punish but not the necessity of its actually doing so. Wood overlooks the fact that Hegel treats retributive punishment as a determinate shape of reciprocal recognition and misses Hegel's point that failure to punish coercion and transgression amounts to positing them as right.[74] This is to uphold injustice as justice. Even more relevant to this issue is our analysis of transgression and punishment as determinate, negative modes of recognition. Recall that recognition must be a two-sided reciprocal action; a one-sided action is useless because what is to be brought about can only occur as the mutual reciprocal action of each. For Hegel, transgression and punishment, as determinate modes of recognition, are two sides of the same coin, two halves of the same whole or action. Transgression is the first half. It is not something positive in and for itself, but a negation and violation of right. And right, it should be noted, is simply the relation of persons to each other, how they recognize each other. Recognition is the right to have rights. Transgression infringes not only a particular right but also the right to have rights, that is, recognition itself. That is why the criminal act is self-destructive as Wood notes.

For these reasons transgression must in turn be negated; if it is not negated, then transgression itself is upheld as right. Punishment, as the second negation of negation, or coercion against coercion, upholds and maintains the relations constitutive of right. Hegel finds the justification of punishment—whatever rationality it may possess—to be immanent in the transgression, because he conceives punishment as a determinate inverse form of intersubjective recognition. The subjective justification of punishment resides in the fact that by his deed the offender has already consented to the principle by which he is punished.[75]

---

73. Ibid., 115.   74. *PR*, §218.

75. Ibid., §100 Zusatz. Beccaria, a social contract theorist, holds that, in general, legitimacy derives from contract and consent and that human beings must, in principle, give their consent to being punished. Beccaria locates this consent in the social contract itself. Beccaria questioned capital punishment, on the ground that it could not be presumed that the social contract includes the consent of individuals to allow themselves to be killed, and that we ought rather to assume the contrary. Hegel denies that the state is a social contract but agrees with Beccaria that human beings should give their consent to being punished. However, Hegel locates this consent, not in a social contract, but in the criminal's act itself: "The criminal gives this consent by his very act." Ibid.

I find myself in agreement with Stephen Houlgate when he writes that for Hegel "punishment is not just a social practice for protecting rights to which there may be better alternatives, but can be seen to follow necessarily from the very concept of right and its violation."[76] However, I would put this point even more strongly: punishment is not only necessary to avoid positing wrong as right, but necessary in the sense of being the other side, the self-correcting half of the original transgression. Punishment is already contained in the transgression as its own inversion. The act of punishment makes manifest the nullity of coercion, and shows that right is not a merely ideal 'ought to be', but has actuality and endurance in mutual recognition and in the institutions of right.

Nevertheless, although punishment is necessary, it is necessary only from the standpoint of right and justice. Of course, this is the standpoint from which Hegel carries out his analysis in abstract right. He is focusing on the essence and justification of punishment, its immanent rationality. Later in his discussion of the administration of justice, Hegel takes up Wood's question concerning punishment considered as a social practice. He observes that "whereas it would be impossible for a society to leave a crime unpunished—since the crime would then be posited as right—the fact that society is sure of itself means that crime, in comparison, is always of a purely individual character, an unstable and isolated phenomenon. The very stability of society gives crime the status of something merely subjective."[77] On the other hand, "if society is inwardly unstable, punishments must be made to set an example, for punishment is itself a counter-example to the example of crime."[78] These remarks are made from the perspective of the administration of justice, not abstract right. They reflect Hegel's sensitivity to changing historical and cultural circumstances that have bearing on the severity, but not the justification or necessity of punishment.

The standpoint of right, while important, is by no means the only possible standpoint from which to view punishment. Within this standpoint, justice requires that the offender be punished; that is, punishment is necessary. However, there is a higher standpoint, the standpoint of mercy, clemency, and pardon. Hegel affirms that "the right of pardon is one of the highest acknowledgments of the majesty of spirit."[79] He also notes that "pardon is the remission of punishment, but is not a cancellation of right. On the contrary, right continues to apply, and the pardoned individual still remains a criminal. The pardon does not state that he has not committed a crime."[80] If pardon does not cancel right, it nevertheless sets aside the standpoint of right in favor of a larger, higher

76. Houlgate, "Hegel's Ethical Thought," in Symposium on Wood, *Bulletin of the Hegel Society of Great Britain*, no. 25 (Spring/Summer 1992), 12.

77. *PR*, §218 Zusatz.   78. Ibid.   79. *PR*, §282.

80. Ibid., §282 Zusatz.

standpoint. From this higher standpoint of mercy and pardon, punishment need not be automatic or necessary. Hegel observes that pardon may have a religious basis, in that "what has been done can be undone in spirit by spirit itself."[81] Something like this is what Hegel admired in the old woman who killed the abstraction of the criminal by bringing him to life for honor through her recognition.[82]

81. Ibid.   82. See fn. 65 above.

9

Morality

We have seen that transgression challenges and threatens to undermine right, which is a necessary condition of community. The consciousness of right, having maintained itself throughout its struggle, its trial with transgression, is no longer immediate. It is now self-conscious, or, as Hegel prefers to say, *for-itself*. This is the transition from abstract right to morality. The moral standpoint involves the explicit self-consciousness of freedom, or freedom *for-itself*.

Abstract right focuses on the presencing of freedom in things, in possessions and ownership. Morality is the presencing of freedom, not in things, but in subjectivity itself. In abstract right, the right of personality was simply the right of ownership, and involved a somewhat deficient intersubjectivity of persons as owners and exchangers of property. But in morality the focus is on the presence of freedom to itself, and freedom is present to itself as subjectivity. Morality therefore involves self-reflexivity and self-relation. But this subjective self-relation must be recognized in order to become actual as right.

In spite of the section title "Morality," Hegel does not present a moral doctrine so much as an account of what morality is, its strengths and limitations and its decline into hypocrisy and evil. In other words, Hegel's concern is not with the determinate moral themes but with an account of morality as a point of view.[1] Hegel's discussion of morality is not practical in the sense of being action-guiding, but rather is a hermeneutical analysis of the moral point of view. Although Hegel follows Kant's account of morality, and praises Kant for giving it the most complete philosophical articulation, he is also critical of it. Hegel believes that morality may be a spiritual illness,[2] a form of conscious-

1. In the *PhG* Hegel explicitly identifies morality as the Moral View of the World (*Die moralische Weltanschauung*).
2. *E*, §408 Zusatz.

ness symptomatic of cultural alienation and disruption. "What comes first is the ethical substance, the substantive life of a people, of a family; and it is only later, when ethical life declines, that the subject turns back into itself and seeks its point of support in morality. It seeks what is good in *itself* rather than seeking it in ethical life and actuality."[3]

The moral point of view receives special emphasis in modernity, owing to the modern recognition of the right of subjectivity and subjective freedom. The acknowledgment of this right of subjectivity is, according to Hegel, the distinguishing characteristic of modernity: "The right of the subject's particularity to find satisfaction, or—to put it differently—the right of subjective freedom, is the pivotal and focal point in the difference between antiquity and the modern age."[4] The right of subjectivity includes and implies the right of self-determination, of insight, of intention, and of conscience. Hegel's analysis of conscience reflects and brings together German Protestantism and Enlightenment culture; it draws on his analysis of Kant, Fichte, and Jacobi. Hegel is keenly aware of the ambiguities of moral conscience, and how conscience can degenerate into hypocrisy, moral subjectivism, skepticism, and ironic nihilism.

Against the moral vision of the world that tends toward a superficial, optimistic rationalism, Hegel pits a profound awareness of the tragic view of life. He believes that morality cannot fulfill its own teleological orientation toward universal good will on its abstract formal individualist premises, for the latter frustrate positive relation to and self-knowledge in other. Consequently the substantive basis of morality must be found in ethical life, and the moral point of view is a deficient form of, or abstract moment in, ethical life. Its universal consciousness is formal, and falls short of being a social consciousness mediated by mutual recognition. Morality presupposes the mutual recognition constitutive of ethical life.

In what follows we examine first the moral subject, then the intersubjectivity of morality in reference to moral action. Although morality is a higher, more developed form than abstract right, its intersubjectivity remains abstract and deficient. Finally we examine Hegel's treatment of conscience, his critique of Kant, and the intersubjective presuppositions of Kant's theory of morality. I shall follow the outline of the published version of Hegel's *Philosophy of Right*, while drawing on the transcripts of his lectures.

The Moral Subject and the Difference

In morality we are concerned with the right of freedom's presencing in subjectivity. This involves reflection, for in morality the will is no longer implicit or in-itself, but also for-itself: "This reflection of the will into itself and its

3. *VPR*17, §69. My italics. Cf. *PR*, §138 Zusatz.
4. *PR*, §124.

identity for itself . . . determine the person as *subject*."[5] Moral subjectivity involves a contrast between universal will (*Wille*) and particular will (*Willkür*) that establishes what is ethically necessary. In abstract right, the focus was on ownership as the right of freedom to external embodiment. Such external embodiment of the subjective will is contingent. The appropriation of things, the making of contracts, and transgression are all pervaded by contingency and are subject to felt need, caprice, and circumstances: "The first recognition of personality is contingent, for the subjective will has not yet posited itself as identical with the universal will. . . . Only through the subjective will does right attain actuality, and in this way right is contingent."[6] Thus legal personality remains pervaded by contingency and need.

In contrast with the contingency of abstract right, morality imposes a demand, what 'ought to be', or what is ethically necessary. The 'ought' implies a higher ground for freedom than external contingency, namely, the universal will *in itself* (*Wille an sich*). However, the universal rational will is not already actual in itself, but requires actualization through the subjective will. (*Willkür*): "Only in the will as subjective can freedom, or the will which has being in itself, be actual."[7] When the subjective will corresponds to or is identical with the rational will in itself, then it will have liberated itself from the one-sidedness of its 'mere subjectivity'. Then "the subjective will determines itself as correspondingly objective and hence as truly concrete."[8]

However, in morality this actualization has not yet occurred, and does not occur; morality is constituted by difference, including the difference between ought and is. Consequently, the moral point of view assumes the *Gestalt* of the right of the subjective will (*Willkür*), but this will is not yet fully united with or correspondent to the universal rational will. It merely intends or struggles to achieve such a union. The subjective will, in its noncoincidence with and distinction from the universal rational will, "is therefore abstract, circumscribed and formal."[9] Nevertheless, the right of the subjective will means that "the will can recognize something or be something only in so far as that something is its own, and insofar as the will is present to itself in it as subjectivity."[10] This subjective presencing includes the right of self-determination, of insight, of intention. These are what must be recognized and conferred as rights. As a moral subject, I can be rightfully held accountable for doing something only to the extent that I am aware of it and intend it.

The identification and isolation of the moral subject constitute the moral point of view. Such isolation of the subject from the unintended consequences of its actions is also important for determining responsibility and blame. Isolation of the moral subject means that I am responsible for my action only if I had

5. Ibid., §105.   6. *VPR*17, §49.   7. *PR*, §106.
8. Ibid.   9. Ibid., §107.   10. Ibid.

certain knowledge, premeditation, and intentions, and these are present in the outcome. By contrast, in abstract right, such 'subjective' phenomena, inwardness, and so on, are not important or even taken into account. All that counts is that a contract be observed. Although the objective dimension of actions remains undoubtedly important for the moral point of view, *subjective* phenomena such as knowledge, intention, and motive have become equally if not more important and essential.

> In recent times especially it has become customary to enquire about the motives of actions. Hitherto the question used to be simply 'Is this man honest [*rechtschaffen*]? Does he do his duty?' Nowadays we seek to look into people's hearts, and thereby presuppose a gulf [*Bruch*] between the objective realm of actions and the inner, subjective realm of motives. *Above all, this separation, this break, between the inner and the outer is what one calls morality.* The moral point of view propounds the basic thesis that everything depends not so much on what has been done, but on the intention behind the deed.[11]

Hegel regards the moral point of view as a potential spiritual illness, because it is constituted by a break or rupture between the inner and the outer.[12] Morality asserts and demands recognition of the right of subjectivity and subjective freedom. This demand for recognition of subjective freedom creates or points to a break or rupture between the inner and the outer. Instead of finding himself in his culture and its institutions, the moral subject is thrown back on himself, on his own insight and conscience. For this reason Hegel believes morality "is thus the point of view of *difference*."[13] The difference here includes several important dimensions. First, subjectivity as a term, stands in contrast with objectivity. Subjectivity is, in comparison with the objective, difference. Second, from the moral point of view, subjectivity is always individual, and as individual, differs from others. The assignment of moral responsibility and accountability depends on singling out and recognizing the moral subject in its singularity and assigning guilt in proportion to responsibility. Third, the moral point of view as a whole is constituted by the noncoincidence, or difference, between the universal rational will in itself (*Wille*) and the subjective particular will (*Willkür*). The moral point of view is constituted by the *Sollen*, the ought. Fourth, the moral point of view is constituted by a gap or break, between the inner 'subjective' intentions and 'outer' public deeds and their consequences. Recall that the isolation of the moral subject is carried out in order *not* to assign total responsibility for a deed with all its consequences, but only a partial

---

11. *VPR3*, 374–375; cf. *PR*, §121 Zusatz. My italics.

12. See Hegel's account of madness in *E*, §§406–408. See also Daniel Berthold-Bond, *Hegel's Theory of Madness* (Albany: SUNY Press, 1995). Bond does not explore Hegel's identification of morality as a kind of madness.

13. *PR*, §108.

responsibility commensurate with subjective premeditation (*Vorsatz*) and in-tention (*Absicht*). In these diverse ways, the difference and the rupture between inner and outer underlie Hegel's whole presentation of morality and the moral point of view.

The Intersubjectivity of Moral Action

Moral action is a distinctive type of action. We have already found that for Hegel action suspends mere subjectivity and translates the subjective into the objective. The will is thus one with itself in its externality; that is, my posses-sions are *mine*. In morality this suspension of mere subjectivity and translation into externality constitutive of action are now *for the will* itself, that is, become explicit for the moral consciousness.[14] "The content [of my action] is deter-mined for me as mine in such a way that, in this identity [of self in its other-ness] it contains my subjectivity for me not only as my inner end, but also in-sofar as this end has achieved external objectivity."[15] This means that "my act should be recognized only insofar as it was inwardly determined by me as my purpose and intention. Only what was already present in my subjective will do I recognize as mine in that will's [external] expression, and I expect to re-encounter my subjective consciousness in it."[16]

What makes moral action distinctive are the following features. (1) The moral subject must recognize the external consequences of its action as its own; these externals are 'mine' and I am responsible for them only insofar as the external situation manifests and corresponds to my subjective purpose and intention. (2) In such action my subjective will is supposed to correspond to the requirement of the universal rational will; hence the subjective will's rela-tion to the universal rational will is obligation; this implies the possibility of a noncoincidence between my subjective will and its obligation. (3) Given the universal as obligation, moral action is not simply self-regarding, but has an essential relation to others. Moral action differs from abstract right in that it entails some positive relation to others. For Hegel, there is a systematic con-nection between the embodiment of the subjective will in property, the univer-sal rational will, and the positive relation to others. This connection will be-come clearer as we consider the difference between the intersubjectivities of right and morality.

We saw that the fundamental imperative of abstract right is, "Be a person and respect others as persons." This imperative does not imply any positive duty toward others, but only the duty of allowing others to be; that is, it is a duty of permission. Everything is permitted that does not infringe on freedom as embodiment and ownership. Thus this imperative implies only a formal inter-subjectivity of abstract legal persons, whose interests converge only in the ex-

---

14. Ibid., §§105, 110.   15. Ibid., §110.   16. Ibid., §110 Zusatz.

ternality of property and ownership and find articulation in contracts concerning the sale and exchange of property. We have found that "contract presupposes that the contracting parties recognize each other as persons and owners of property" and that as "a relationship of objective spirit, the moment of recognition is already included within it." [17] The mutual recognition of ownership is deficient because it is abstract and involves only the external convergence of interests in property. It is as if the persons who make contracts exist only 'in their property', but not for themselves. Thus this abstract deficient intersubjectivity is a negative one. However, a negative intersubjectivity is hardly a 'real' intersubjectivity at all. It can exist only as a moment in a larger whole, and so presupposes certain minimal social institutions like the family. "In right I exclude others, and they exclude me. Thus I relate always negatively to others. But in the moral will such atomism disappears." [18]

We have seen the gradual disappearance of the negative exclusive intersubjectivity and atomism of abstract right in our analysis of crime and transgression. Crime reveals that right is not something merely external, subjective, or contingent, but a necessary condition of human community. As a necessary condition, right cannot be merely subjective, but must be objective and universal. When consciousness attains this level, it has reached the moral point of view. In the consciousness of freedom constitutive of morality, the interest in right and the other lies deeper than and the convergence of wills goes beyond mere optionality, permission, and contingency.

I depend on the other to recognize my freedom, as the other depends on me. The externalization of freedom is not confined to embodiment in possessions and property; the determinate existence and externalization of freedom consists equally if not more crucially in the other's recognition. Through this relation to other "I acquire my subjectivity as an object [Gegenstande]. In this way my subjectivity becomes external to me as an other subjectivity, an other will." [19] Hegel speaks of recognition as a *duty*: "More closely considered this duty of recognition [diese Pflicht des Anerkennens] implies that as free I give myself a determinate existence [Dasein], not in an external object [Objekt] but in someone who is a present consciousness standing over against me. The consciousness of the other is the ground, the material, the space, in which I realize myself." [20]

Note that this duty is inherently reciprocal, doubled, and has a universal telos. If I have a duty to seek realization in the other's recognition, this is because this duty corresponds to a right of freedom to recognition and respect. Further, my 'duty' to realize myself in another is a duty that can be fulfilled only if I am prepared to recognize the other's freedom as having a right and therefore a claim to my recognition, and if I am willing to actually recognize the other. In his *Propadeutik*, Hegel put the point in this way: "Recognition does not have

17. Ibid., §75.   18. *VPR*3, 347.   19. Ibid., 346.
20. *PSS* 1825, 332.

[conditional] reciprocity as its ground. I do not recognize [you] because you have recognized me (and vice versa). Rather the ground of this mutual recognition lies in the nature of the thing itself. I recognize the will of the other simply because he is to be recognized as counting in and for himself."[21]

Thus the subject of this duty, and the duty of recognition itself, cannot be conceived as a bare particular or atomic individual; the duty can be realized only reciprocally and jointly. Reciprocal recognition imposes a central requirement or obligation that I may pursue my freedom only if I am prepared to allow and extend to others the same right. The recognition of my freedom is inseparable from my recognizing the freedom of others. "The external subjectivity which is thus identical with me is the will of others . . . and the will of others is the existence which I give to my end. . . . The implementation of my end therefore has this identity of my will and the will of others within it—has a positive reference to the will of others."[22] The atomic individual of abstract right is thus *aufgehoben*: "Morality is not concerned with bare immediate particularity, but with what we call the moral subject. . . . The will exists as recognized insofar as it counts in and for another will."[23] Through such recognition the individual will is no longer an atomic particular but doubled and universalized, in the sense that it has made freedom, including the freedom of others, its own end. The self sees that the accomplishment of its purposes and ends requires identity with and the agreement and cooperation of others.[24] What is recognized, confirmed, and legitimated is freedom itself as the universal end and good.

The moral point of view implies duties toward others in the positive sense noted above. The first duty of morality is to will and do what is right. This means that since morality is in a certain sense the explicit consciousness of right, "the first moral duty is . . . to be rightful [*rechtlich zu sein*], and consequently, insofar as one is rightful, moral ends can enter in or supervene. Authentic right action as such is that right be done for the sake of right."[25] While the moral point of view is distinct from abstract right, it deepens and extends the concept of right. The imperative of right enjoins us to respect persons and not to infringe on the freedom of ownership. But morality enjoins us to do right for its own sake because in so doing we uphold the conditions of universal freedom. Further, the moral point of view acknowledges the right of subjective freedom to find recognition in its actions and to be held accountable for such actions only to the extent that its intentions are manifest in its actions and their consequences.

The strengths and the limitations of morality flow from this. Although morality involves a positive relation to others and posits universal freedom and/or the good will as its general, all-inclusive end, this point of view nevertheless remains individualistic in focus and orientation. The moral point of view is the

21. Hegel, *Propadeutik*, TWA Sk 4:237.
22. *PR*, §112.   23. *VPR* 1817, §50.   24. *VPR*4, 307.
25. *VPR* 1817, §62.

standpoint of difference, and consequently it is committed to individualist premises that hinder and threaten to undermine the positive relation to others: "we must bear in mind the point of view from which right and welfare are being examined here—namely as formal right and the particular welfare of the individual. The so-called common weal or welfare of the state, i.e., the right of the actual concrete spirit, is an altogether different sphere."[26] The positive relation to others constitutive of the morality finds fulfillment in ethical life: "The ought which is present in morality, is fulfilled only in the ethical sphere."[27] The moral point of view presupposes and finds fulfillment in ethical life.

Purpose and Intention, Responsibility and Welfare

Action suspends the mere subjectivity of the will and translates it into objectivity. This externalization includes a universal demand for a positive relation to the will of others. Everything turns on how this transition from subjectivity into objectivity is to be understood. When the right of subjectivity is not acknowledged or passed over, action, or the transition from subjective intention to objective expression, appears more or less automatic. The subjective purpose and intention of the agent do not enter the picture. Assessment of a deed turns mainly on the question whether it has occurred or not. Hegel believes this view is not only constitutive of classical philosophy, it is part of the naive immersion in traditional social roles constitutive of the natural attitude.

In the moral point of view, however, the right of subjectivity is acknowledged. This implies a gap, a distinction, between what is subjectively intended and what objectively happens. In this view, the subject is a free *moral subject*, who is to be held responsible not for all possible consequences of his action, but only for his subjective aim and intention. Accordingly "it is . . . the right of the will to recognize as its *action*, and to accept *responsibility* for, only those aspects of its deed which it knew to be presupposed within its end, and which were presupposed within its *purpose*. I can be made accountable for a deed only if *my will was responsible* for it—the right of knowledge."[28] This break (*Bruch*) or distinction between subjective intention and the external unfolding of the action in all its consequences is central to the moral point of view and shows it to be constituted by difference.

But what if the difference and the isolation of purposing subjectivity are not acknowledged? Then the individual must assume complete responsibility for his action, including its unknown dimensions and unforeseeable consequences.

---

26. *PR*, §126. Hegel adds: "One of the commonest errors of abstraction is to insist on private rights and private welfare as valid in and for themselves in opposition to the universality of the state."

27. Ibid., §108 Zusatz.   28. Ibid., §117.

Hegel shows such unrestricted accountability for action in reference to Greek tragedy. He observes that "according to the ancients, there is no innocent suffering; everyone who suffers is guilty." [29] Hegel refers to Sophocles' *Oedipus*: "Oedipus took responsibility for his deed, despite the fact that he did not know that it was his own father whom he slew. Nevertheless he assumed responsibility for the deed in its entirety." [30]

Elsewhere Hegel elaborates further on the tragedy of Oedipus.

> But we see in the tragic portrayals of the ancients, how Oedipus regarded himself as guilty of murder of his own father and took full responsibility for the deed. The heroic element lies in the fact that the human being burdens himself with everything that lies before him. That the innocent suffer is always a terrible spectacle. When the guilty suffers, that is his own affair, for he gets what he deserves. But in Oedipus' case we have tragedy. Oedipus, the great knower, the one who solved the riddle of the sphinx, here, where knowing whom one confronts mattered crucially, *did not know*.[31]

The irony of this tragedy is not simply that Oedipus did not intend to kill his father; rather it is that he did not know or recognize his father when he confronted him. The tragic background of action is presented as the dimming of the cognitive powers of the moral subject who proves, in tragic retrospect, to have been in false consciousness: the great knower did *not* know. But in spite of his ignorance, Oedipus is nevertheless responsible and bears a tragic guilt.

However, according to the moral point of view, the difference between subjective intention and objective deed is crucial: in order to be held responsible for something I must have willed it. Consequently, from the moral point of view, Oedipus should not be held responsible for the murder of his father, since he did not *intend* to kill him. However, Hegel is not interested in extolling the superiority of the moral point of view against tragedy; on the contrary, his sympathies lie with tragedy against the often superficial clarity of the moralizing consciousness. In this connection we should keep in mind his sarcastic comment that human intelligence "is not confined to the shape it assumes in Wolff's psychology—namely that of clear representations." [32]

Hegel's Critique of the Moral Point of View

Hegel regarded Kant as the culminating figure of the Enlightenment. Although he accepted the broad outlines of Enlightenment critical rationalism, Hegel believed that the Enlightenment was chiefly negative and critical, and

---

29. *VPR4*, 321.   30. Ibid.
31. *VPR19*, 94. My italics.
32. *PR*, §132.

"in its positive aspect, was a hubbub of vanity without a firm core. It obtained a core in its negative procedure by grasping its own negativity."[33] Autonomy involves a break with nature and natural determination. Autonomy is the critical principle of the Enlightenment, namely, the assertion of the rights of individual subjectivity in thought, ethics, and politics against nature and tradition. In Hegel's words,

> The one self-certifying certainty . . . is that there exists a thinking subject, a reason affected with finitude; and the whole of philosophy consists in determining the universe with respect to this finite reason. Kant's so-called critique of the cognitive faculties, Fichte's doctrine that consciousness cannot be transcended nor become transcendent, Jacobi's refusal to undertake nothing impossible for reason, all amount to nothing but the absolute restriction of reason to the form of finitude, an injunction never to forget the absoluteness of the subject in every rational cognition. . . . So these philosophies have to be recognized as nothing but the culture of reflection raised to a system.[34]

Individual autonomy is the negative, critical principle of morality, its principle of difference. However, Hegel believes that the individual is insufficient to provide or ground any ethical, political, or cognitive norms, beyond the pragmatic norms of utility and expediency: "What is here called reason consists in calculating the worth of each and every thing with respect to this singularity."[35]

Previously we examined Hegel's account of the abstracting negativity of the will, its ability to free itself from and dissolve all determinations. The negative moment of autonomy consists in the will breaking with immediacy, the given, and so on, and rising to its abstract indeterminacy. However, "abstract reflection fixes this moment in its difference from and opposition to the universal."[36] But this critical posture, fixed in reflection as the principle of difference, proves itself unable to be concretely positive or normative. As Hegel points out, to will is to will *something*, and to will something is to be committed to something determinate.

According to Kant the only thing that can be called good without qualification is the good will. The will is good not because of its consequences, or success in realizing its ends, but good simply in its willing, that is, in the principles on which it bases itself in its actions. Hence the goodness of the will in Kant's sense must be a priori. Further, the will does not have to wait for ends to be given to it from elsewhere; as practical reason, it can determine its own ends. Its supreme self-legislated principle is the categorical imperative, which is supposed to provide criteria for determining which ends, which principles, and thus which actions, have moral worth, that is, which are *duties*. The categorical imperative has two major forms: (1) the universality principle: act so that the

---

33. *FK*, 56.   34. Ibid., 64.   35. Ibid., 61.
36. *PR*, §124.

maxim of your action can at the same time be willed as a universal law; (2) the practical imperative: act so that you respect humanity, whether in yourself or in another, always as an end in itself and never merely as a means.[37] The common theme in all forms of the categorical imperative is the unconditionally good will, which "is a will whose maxim, when made a universal law, can never conflict with itself."[38]

Hegel advances several criticisms of Kant in the *Philosophy of Right*. First, Kant's attempt to determine duty wholly a priori is unable to develop immanently a positive account of particular duties, and so remains empty and formal. Second, morality as an abstract a priori presupposes a concrete a priori, namely, the realm of concrete ethical life, or the life-world. Third, the problem of a conflict or collision of duties. Contrary to Kant, who believes that the good will can never conflict with itself, Hegel shows and emphasizes that the good will can indeed come into conflict with itself, with tragic results. For Hegel, freedom has a tragic depth and may have tragic realization.

Hegel takes Kant at his word that the good is to be understood as a universal-rational good will. The subjective will, or *Willkür*, has worth and dignity only insofar as its insight and intention conform to the universal will in itself. This conformity is not a given; it is a task that must be accomplished. "The good is the truth of the particular will, but the will is only what it commits itself to; it is not by nature good, but can become what it is only by its own efforts. On the other hand, the good itself, without the subjective will, is only an abstraction, devoid of that reality which it is destined to achieve only through the subjective will."[39] Here we see the importance of action for Hegel. Apart from action the substantive good will in itself would remain an abstraction devoid of actuality. Conversely, apart from the substantive good or substantive freedom, the subjective arbitrary will (*Willkür*) is void of content; that is, it would be nihilistic. This insistence on the mutual mediation of substantive and subjective freedom through action implies a criticism of Kant, for whom, says Hegel, "the good is eternal rest, it has no activity, it is not yet determined as substance, whereas it must be actual, must realize itself; as the idea of the good, it is still without movement. This good is accordingly given in Kantian philosophy as an 'ought to be', but 'ought' as such implies something incomplete."[40]

Since the good will is abstract and incomplete, "the good is initially determined only as *universal abstract essentiality*, i.e., as *duty*. In view of this determination, *duty* should be done *for the sake of duty*."[41] But what is duty?

---

37. There is a third form of the principle, but Kant never formulates it as an imperative; so it is a consequence or result of the imperative, namely, the idea of a community of rational beings as ends in themselves that legislate universally for all. Each rational being is both a member and subject to the law he legislates. See Kant, *Foundations of the Metaphysics of Morals*, trans. Lewis White Beck (New York: Library of Liberal Arts, 1959), 39–55.

38. Ibid., 55.   39. *PR*, §131.   40. *VPR*17, §65.

41. *PR*, §133. Italics in original.

When the question, What is truth? is put to logic, and answered by logic, it affords to Kant 'the ludicrous spectacle of one man milking a he-goat and another holding a sieve beneath.' The question: What is right and duty?, put to and answered by pure practical reason is in the same position. . . . For practical reason is the complete abstraction from all content of the will [*Wille*]; to introduce content is to establish a heteronomy of choice [*Willkür*]. But what is precisely of interest is to know precisely what right and duty are. We ask for the content of the moral law. . . . But the essence of pure will and pure practical reason is to be abstracted from all content. Thus it is a self-contradiction to seek in this absolute practical reason a moral justification which would have to have a content, since the essence of this reason is to have none.[42]

Hegel believes that the most that can be said on the formal premises of Kantian morality is that duty consists in doing right, promoting welfare—including one's own, but only insofar as it is consistent with the welfare of all. This is at once the sublime majesty of Kantian *Moralität* and its weakness. For, as Hegel goes on to observe,

The 'welfare of all' is an empty word. For are not both the dead and future generations are naturally to reckoned among the 'all'? Or does it simply refer to those who are contemporary [*Mitlebenden*]? How can I advance the welfare of the Chinese? The Bible is more rational when it commands, Love your neighbor as yourself, that is, love the human beings with whom you are in relation or with whom you come to be in relation. 'All' is merely empty bombast.[43] The universal formal aspect of good 'cannot be fulfilled as an abstraction; it must first acquire the further determination of particularity.'[44]

Determinacy and particularity are problems for any ethical theory that insists on duty as universal rational self-determination a priori and rejects inclinations as unworthy determining bases of the will. The requisite determinacy is not included within the concept or determination of duty itself. Hegel complains that "in Kant's philosophy there is not the least sign of worry about the contradiction between empty universality and living particularity."[45] Given that duty for Kant must be determined a priori, "all that is left for duty itself . . . is abstract universality, whose determination is identity without content or the abstractly positive, i.e., the indeterminate."[46] If one remains at the abstract moral point of view, one finds that morality gets reduced to the "empty rhetoric of duty for duty's sake. From this point of view no immanent theory of duties is possible."[47]

And there is more: duty is abstractly determined as mere "absence of contradiction, as formal correspondence with itself, which is no different from the

42. Hegel, *NL*, 76. Hegel cites Kant's *Critique of Pure Reason*, A58.
43. *VPR*4, 338.   44. *PR*, §134.   45. *FK*, 153.
46. *PR*, §135.   47. Ibid.

specification of abstract indeterminacy."[48] If a duty is to be willed merely for duty's sake and not because of its content, duty is conceived as a formal identity which necessarily excludes every content and determination. However, if determinate content is excluded from the concept of duty, then not even absence of contradiction remains as a test of the validity of the content of a duty or an action. For "a contradiction must be a contradiction with *something*, that is, with a content which is already fundamentally present as an established principle."[49]

In spite of such criticisms, Hegel does not believe that the moral point of view is false; rather it is incomplete, and as such it presupposes and requires the concept of ethical life: "to cling to a merely moral point of view without going on to the concept of ethical life, reduces this gain to an empty formalism and . . . rhetoric of duty for duty's sake."[50] Hegel believes that ethical life (*Sittlichkeit*) mediates and completes the abstract formality of the moral point of view. What is involved in the concept of ethical life? Kant's practical imperative, respect humanity whether in yourself or in another always as an end in itself and never merely as a means, clearly assumes the existence of others. This comes out especially in Kant's concept of the realm of ends, where each is a member as a legislator and yet is subject to the laws that are universally legislated. Thus Kantian morality presupposes and implies intersubjectivity. Burkhard Tuschling rightly observes,

> It is absurd to suppose a 'monological' or 'solipsistic' ethics even to be possible on Kantian principles. On the contrary, to be free, to be a moral agent, necessarily involves citizenship in the empire of all rational beings, the realm of ends or the city of God. It is on this condition alone that for Kant a 'deduction' of categorical imperatives is possible at all. Thus Kantian practical philosophy does not merely have a social dimension, it is intrinsically social by its constitutive rationalistic concepts of the human being as a free agent and person.[51]

Although Kant implies and presupposes some sort of intersubjectivity, he never works out an account comparable to Fichte's and Hegel's concept of recognition. Respect for freedom in Kant's sense presupposes and implies some sense of intersubjectivity. But respect for freedom both falls short of and presupposes mutual recognition in Hegel's sense. Recognition is a condition of respect, part of the concrete life-world a priori presupposed by morality. Mutual recognition is constitutive of ethical life. Mutual recognition and ethical life are necessary to complete and fulfill the positive program of Kantian *Moralität*.

If we are speaking of ethical life, then we are speaking of families and people

48. Ibid.   49. Ibid.   50. Ibid.
51. Burkhard Tuschling, "*Rationis societas*: Remarks on Kant and Hegel," in *Kant's Philosophy of Religion Reconsidered*, ed. Philip J. Rossi and Michael Wren (Bloomington: Indiana University Press, 1991), 185.

whose lives and property must be secured. That is why, in Hegel's view, crime against life and property generates substantive, as contrasted with merely formal, contradictions. But given that for Kant duty is to be determined merely as absence of contradiction or formal correspondence with self, there is no criterion for deciding whether this or that content is a duty.

> On the contrary, it is possible to justify any wrong or immoral mode of action by this means. Kant's further form—the capacity of an action to be envisaged as a universal maxim—does yield a more concrete representation of the situation . . . but it does not in itself contain any principle apart from formal identity and that absence of contradiction already referred to.—The fact that no property is present is in itself no more contradictory than is the nonexistence of this or that individual people, family, etc., or the complete absence of human life. *But if it is already established that property and human life should exist and be respected, then it is a contradiction to commit theft or murder.*[52]

Thus Hegel implies that the content required to generate a substantial, as contrasted with a merely formal, contradiction, cannot be generated by the abstract formal individualism or formal reflection of morality. Rather such substantial content is presupposed by the moral point of view. It belongs to the life-world, and the mutual recognition that constitutes *Anerkanntsein* of an ethical community. Judgments of right and wrong presuppose that an *Anerkanntsein* has already been constituted, and provides the normative basis for judgments, as well as for possible generation of contradictions. Hegel accepts the role Kant assigns to contradiction in determining moral right, but he believes that the genuine contradictions of morality are not merely formal and reflective, but are substantive, and present in ethical life itself.

For this reason Hegel spends a lot of time discussing tragedy in his analysis of moral action. In contrast to Kant's bland assurance that the good will can never come into contradiction with itself, Hegel repeatedly is drawn to tragic conflicts precisely because they are conflicts between justified ethical powers and rights. He observes, "This is the authentic tragic interest, that there are ethical powers whose representatives are agents which in their action infringe upon another ethical relationship. These are responsible for their suffering, since they injure a substantial ethical relationship. . . . What comes thus into collision here are ethical powers themselves. . . . What each asserts injures the other."[53] Hegel goes on to illustrate his point by references to Oedipus, Orestes, and Antigone. He writes that "Antigone is the highest drama of the ancient or the modern period. She buried her brother, but by so doing violated the law of the state according to which her brother should not have received burial, since he had fought against his own country and perished as a traitor. Thus Creon

52. *PR*, §135. Italics mine.
53. *VPR*4, 321.

was justified in punishing her with death, for Antigone infringed the right of the state, and took seriously only her ethical relation to her brother."[54] On Hegel's reading, the tragedy of *Antigone* consists in the irreconcilable conflict of legitimate and otherwise justified ethical powers, namely, the family and the state. Hegel sees, in a way that Kant does not, the tragic dimension of freedom and ethical action. His tragic sense of life makes him critical of the often superficial rationalism of the moral vision.

The Decline and Fall of Conscience

If Kant is important for Hegel's account of morality, it is Jacobi who is important for his account of conscience. Both Kant and Jacobi belong to the moral point of view with its absolutized finitude, and subjectivity as the difference principle. "Within this common ground however, these philosophies form antitheses among themselves, exhausting the totality of possible forms of this principle. The Kantian philosophy establishes the objective side of this whole [subjective] sphere: the absolute concept, existing strictly for itself as practical reason is the highest objectivity within the finite realm. . . . Jacobi's philosophy is the subjective side. It transposes the antithesis and the identity, postulated as absolute, into the subjectivity of feeling, into infinite longing and incurable grief."[55] Again, "In Kant's philosophy finitude and subjectivity have an objective form, the form of the concept. Jacobi's philosophy, on the contrary, makes subjectivity entirely subjective, it turns it into individuality. This subjective core of the subjective thus regains an inner life so that it seems to be capable of the beauty of feeling."[56] In assigning Kant to the objective side, Hegel has in mind the importance for Kant of the moral law. The moral law is the *ratio cognoscendi* of freedom, that is, the occasion for the discovery of freedom. Hence for Kant the law and reason assume priority over individual subjectivity and freedom.

For Jacobi, it is the opposite: he shows his Protestant background when he declares that "the law is made for man and not man for the law."[57] In this declaration Jacobi asserts and upholds the right of individual conscience. It is not that the individual is above the law so much as that law requires interpretation and application to a particular situation. Moreover, not only does conscience interpret and apply the law, conscience may also set it aside as in a pardon.[58] It is in pardoning that the majesty of conscience is exhibited. Hegel agrees with certain features of conscience as noted by Jacobi. Conscience as "pure certainty of itself alone, relativizes and nullifies all determinate aspects of right, duty and existence."[59]

54. Ibid., 322.   55. *FK*, 62.   56. Ibid., 97.
57. Ibid., 143.
58. Ibid., 144n. Jacobi is thinking of Kant's discussion of the sovereign prerogative of mercy and pardon.
59. *PR*, §138.

Conscience for Hegel involves "the right of the subjective will," which is "that whatever it is to recognize as valid should be perceived by it as good."[60] However, as Hegel notes, this right of conscience is ambiguous, involving two distinct possibilities, namely, *genuine* conscience and *formal* conscience. According to Hegel, "The right to recognize nothing that I do not perceive as rational is the highest right of the subject, but by virtue of its subjective determination, it is at the same time formal; on the other hand the right of the rational—as objective—over the subject remains firmly established."[61] Genuine or authentic conscience asserts the right of intersubjective-social rationality over the private subject. In Hegel's words, "Genuine conscience is the disposition to will that which is good in and for itself,"[62] or what is intrinsically and substantially good.

Conscience determines universal modes of action that are valid in and of themselves and thus valid for all. As universal and objective, true conscience is subject to judgments of its truth and falsity. Consequently, "If I have genuinely acted in accord with my conscience, this is nothing subjective, but is a universal objective duty. Conscience is this pure subjectivity; my genuine conscience is universal conscience."[63] Thus far Hegel agrees with Kant against Jacobi. The good, as universal rational will, is objective; it has fixed principles, determinations, and duties that are objective in and for themselves and so universal. However, Hegel breaks with Kant when he goes on to observe, "But the objective system of these principles and duties . . . are present only when the point of ethical life has been reached."[64] The moral point of view, as formal and individualistic, does not include genuine conscience, which is both intersubjective and determinately rational.

Considered from the moral point of view, moral conscience lacks intersubjectivity and intersubjective mediation and so lacks content; it is merely individual. Hegel distinguishes between formal conscience and 'genuine conscience'. "Here within the formal point of view of morality, conscience lacks this objective content, and is thus for itself the infinite formal certainty of itself, which is for this very reason the certainty of this subject."[65] Again, "The point of view of morality, which is distinguished in this treatise from that of ethical life, includes only the formal conscience; the true conscience has been mentioned only in order to indicate its different character, and to prevent the possible misunderstanding that we are here discussing the genuine conscience rather than the formal conscience which is in fact our exclusive concern. Genuine conscience is included in the ethical disposition which will be considered only in the following section [of ethical life]."[66] Genuine conscience is determinately intersubjective. It is astonishing that in light of this important distinc-

60. Ibid., §132.   61. Ibid.   62. Ibid., §137.
63. *VPR*17, §66.   64. Ibid.   65. *PR*, §137.
66. Ibid.

tion, Hegel offers no explicit account of intersubjective 'genuine conscience' in his account of ethical life. Perhaps the closest approximation to what he means by it is to be found in his discussion of patriotism.[67]

In contrast, formal conscience—especially in Jacobi's account—is radically individualistic and atomistic; it dissolves what is inherently rational and objective, and retreats into the empty form of particular subjectivity itself. Since it lacks substantial content, formal conscience lacks substantive universality and objectivity. Lacking such objective substance, all that is left for conscience to be is merely formal and private self-certainty, that is, the self-certainty of a particular individual. Under such conditions the very idea of appealing to conscience proves to be the very opposite of what is supposed to be: "its appeal solely *to itself* is directly opposed to what it seeks to be—that is, the rule for a rational and universal mode of action which is valid in and for itself."[68] In this way conscience, which is supposed to be and provide a universal way of acting, in fact acts as a private particular. Formal conscience thus declines into *hypocrisy*.

But there is worse to come. Conscience is morally ambiguous in that it can be either good or evil: "Conscience as formal subjectivity, consists simply in the possibility of turning at any moment to evil; for both morality and evil have their common root in that self-certainty which has being for itself and which decides for itself."[69] Hegel observes that human beings are capable of taking as their principle either the universal will in and for itself or the arbitrariness of their own private particularity. "When the subject has attained this level and yet holds fast to the particular, it has transcended all specific duties. But where it still, after disposing of everything, makes itself, in its particularity, its end, then it is absolute evil, and hypocrisy."[70] When the particular private self and its interests take priority over the universal, the result is evil. When private interest masquerades as public interest, the action is not in conformity with genuine conscience. For "evil is represented for others as good, and the evildoer pretends in all external respects to be good, conscientious, etc."[71] This dissemblance is hypocrisy.

The dissemblance of hypocrisy is the homage that vice pays to virtue, that formal conscience pays to genuine conscience. "For to describe evil as hypocrisy implies that certain actions are in and for themselves misdemeanors, vices and crimes, and that the perpetrator is necessarily aware of them . . . insofar as he acknowledges the principles and outward acts of . . . rectitude even within the pretence in whose interest he misuses them."[72] However, when the 'subjective turn' or 'retreat into subjectivity' continues, the difference constitutive of moral subjectivity deepens, and dissolves all ethical content. The emptiness of the merely subjective individual standpoint becomes increasingly explicit.

67. See chaps. 11–13.   68. *PR*, §137.   69. Ibid., §139.
70. *VPR*17, §67.   71. *PR*, §140.   72. Ibid.

The result is the disappearance of the possibility of objective moral standards, and with that goes the possibility of even dissembling. The moral point of view subverts itself and becomes moral skepticism. "Subjective opinion is at last expressly acknowledged as the criterion of right and duty when it is alleged that the ethical nature of an action is determined by the conviction which holds something to be right."[73] Such a retreat into subjectivism and moral skepticism undermines even the possibility of hypocrisy: "if a good heart, good intentions and subjective conviction are said to be the factors which confer value on actions, there is no longer any hypocrisy or evil at all."[74]

If there is no longer any hypocrisy or evil, because all norms and standards have been nullified by subjectivity, Hegel observes that this would have disastrous consequences for punishment. If all that we have are subjective opinions instead of social reason and truth, then crime and punishment become wholly arbitrary: "It may be remarked that, as far as the mode of action of other people in relation to my own action is concerned, it follows on this principle of justification on grounds of subjective conviction that, if their faith and conviction regard my actions as *crimes*, they are *quite right* to do so."[75] Right here means nothing more than subjective feeling or opinion.

If right is made to depend on feelings and passions, any idea, any action, any thing may be criminalized. But such criminalization is wholly arbitrary and contingent, and what gets identified as criminal is nothing more than a positivistic extrinsic determination. If I am regarded as a criminal simply on these grounds, "I am not only denied all credit in advance, but am on the contrary simply reduced from a position of freedom and honor to a situation of unfreedom and dishonor."[76] Consequently, social praxis becomes driven by sheer power interests and considerations, and mutual human recognition becomes corrupted and undermined. There is no longer any place for honor, rational freedom, or justice: "In the justice to which I am subjected . . . I merely experience someone else's subjective conviction, and, when it is implemented, I consider myself acted upon merely by an external force."[77]

The final stage in the retreat into subjectivity is irony, which Hegel traces to Fichte. In his *Aesthetics* lectures, Hegel discusses irony as Schlegel's bowdlerizing of Fichte's doctrine of the absolute ego: "every content is negated in it, since everything is submerged in this abstract freedom and unity, while . . . every content which is to have value for the ego is only posited and recognized by the ego itself. Whatever is, is only by the instrumentality of the ego, and

---

73. Ibid.   74. Ibid.   75. Ibid., 180.
76. Ibid.
77. Ibid. Nietzsche also calls attention to the external and amoral character of punishment when he writes "the man whose lot it was to be punished considered his punishment as a misfortune. He no more felt a moral pang than if some terrible unforeseen disaster had occurred, if a rock had fallen and crushed him." Friedrich Nietzsche, *The Birth of Tragedy and Genealogy of Morals*, trans. F. Golffing (New York: Doubleday Anchor, 1956), 215.

what exists by my instrumentality I can equally well annihilate again."[78] The irony of formal subjectivity empties everything of intrinsic worth and value and regards everything as relative to the ego. Consequently,

> nothing is treated in and for itself as valuable in itself, but only as produced by . . . the ego. . . . [I]n that case the ego can remain lord and master of everything, and in no sphere of morals, law, things human and divine, profane and sacred, is there anything that would not first have to be laid down by the ego, and that therefore could not equally well be destroyed by it. Consequently, everything genuinely and independently real becomes only a show, not true or genuine on its own account or through itself, but a mere appearance due to the ego in whose power and caprice and at whose free disposal it remains. To admit or cancel it depends wholly on the pleasure of the ego, already absolute in itself simply as ego.[79]

The ironic nullification of everything also finds expression in Hegel's epigram concerning the small-minded valet: "No man is a hero to his own valet; not however because the man is not a hero, but because the valet is a valet."[80] The 'moral valet' is a rich metaphor for moralism, for servile consciousness, for a psychologizing nominalist interpretation of history, for instrumental reason (*Verstand*), and a *ressentiment*-laden, rancorous mentality. The 'valet' refuses to recognize a hero as a hero. The valet both envies and fears greatness. Hegel observes that every human action presents a universal aspect and a particular aspect.[81] The valet mentality overlooks the universal world-historical significance of the hero and focuses instead on the hero merely as a particular individual. He regards the results (e.g., fame) of the hero's actions as his actual end and reduces the deeds of the hero as mere means to that end, declaring that the hero "acted solely out of lust for fame, lust for conquest and the like."[82] Such a judgment is vile not only because it fails to appreciate greatness but also because it manifests an envy that is negative. Rancor deprecates the action and person of the hero. By pulling the hero off his pedestal, the rancorous individual seeks to establish his equality to the hero and to force the hero or others to recognize him as the equal of or even superior to the hero.

Hegel also locates the beautiful soul within Fichtean irony, and its implied assertion of subjectivity's lordship over everything else. The beautiful soul, explored by Jacobi in several novels, is a wholly inwardized character whose form is subjective emptiness and who is conscious of itself as an absolute power ca-

78. Hegel, *Aesthetics: Lectures on Fine Art*, trans. T. M. Knox (Oxford: Clarendon Press, 1975), 1:64.

79. Ibid., 64–65.

80. *PhS*, 404; *PhG*, 468. I have cited the *PhG* because it is the earliest and clearest of Hegel's three discussions. The other two are in *PR*, §124, and *Philosophy of History*, trans. H. B. Nisbet (Cambridge: Cambridge University Press, 1980), 87. Hereafter cited as *PH*.

81. *PhS*, 404; *PhG*, 468.   82. *PH*, 87.

pable of nullifying all objective content. Such a self believes that its noble sentiments and fine feelings are equivalent to actions. But in fact the beautiful soul is fearful of and cuts itself off from action, the world, and others. "This can be termed the absolute hypochondria of spirit, that regards only itself and annuls all ties, friendly relationships and wherein the subject hates objective relations and duties because it is afraid of losing itself in them."[83] The end-station of the 'turn to the subject' is the hypocritical 'beautiful soul' that is turned in upon itself and incapable of mutual recognition and friendship. For such an individual, hell is other people, to use Sartre's famous phrase. However, as far as Hegel is concerned, the reality is exactly the opposite: hell is to be eternally bound to and incapable of escaping from oneself.

> In the poets who can tell what is eternal and what is finite and damned, we find Hell and damnation expressly identified as being bound forever to one's subjective deed, being alone with what is most peculiarly one's own. It is a deathless consideration of this possession. Think of Dante among the earlier poets, or of Goethe's Orestes who surrenders to Hell for a period while still alive. In Jacobi we can observe this very same torment of eternal self-contemplation in the heroes Allwill and Woldemar, but they do not even contemplate themselves in a deed, they contemplate themselves in the even greater boredom and impotence of their empty being.[84]

Transition to Ethical Life

Both abstract right and morality cannot exist independently by themselves. They are not independent phenomena but elements and moments within a larger social whole. Right focuses on the presencing of freedom in things; morality focuses on the presencing of freedom in subjectivity itself. They are true, but one-sided and partial, realizations of freedom. But just for this reason they are incomplete by themselves, and reveal themselves to be abstractions. "The sphere of right and that of morality cannot exist independently [*für sich*]; they must have the ethical as their support and foundation."[85] As we have seen, Hegel believes the immanent teleology of morality—the telos of the universal good and welfare—cannot be realized within the confines of morality's restrictive individualist premises. To pursue that enterprise ends in moral skepticism and empty nihilistic irony. Morality finds its fulfillment and completion only in ethical life.

Moreover, although both right and morality presuppose and depend on mu-

---

83. *VPR*17, §67.
84. *FK*, 146–147. Jacobi's relevant novels are *Allwills Briefsammlung* and *Woldemar*.
85. *PR*, §141 Zusatz.

tual recognition, this recognition remains formal and abstract. It is structured by reciprocity and equality, but equality is for Hegel an external relation. Recognition in the concrete determinate sense transcends the abstract individualism constitutive of the standpoints of right and morality. Its moments of autonomy, union, self-overcoming, and release are explicit only in and as constitutive of ethical life.

10

Ethical Life
and the Family

We take up again the systematic problem of the unity of Hegel's *Philosophy of Right*. The first two parts—abstract right and morality—are set forth in abstraction from the theory of ethical life comprising part 3. This abstraction implies a methodological individualism. My thesis is that the concept of recognition transforms the apparently individual subject of part 1 into an ethical intersubjectivity; the latter is a presupposition and condition of the methodological individualism. The threshold of the ethical is reached when the other comes to count. In the process of recognition, the I becomes a We. The We is a whole or totality that is nonheteronomous because its unity is qualified by *Freigabe*, that is, releasement and affirmation of difference and otherness. This whole, while a creation of its members, is from another perspective an enduring union that is prior to its parts. This transformation of subjectivity into ethical intersubjectivity is an important aspect of Hegel's proposed mediation between the ancients and the moderns.

The other 'counts' on at least two levels of recognition. First, the other counts as a particular—the interpersonal level that corresponds to the family, and which has been developed in twentieth-century dialogical philosophy from Buber through Levinas. For Hegel, love, marriage, and family are the shapes and institutions in which we first experience the nonheteronomous priority of the whole over the part. Second, the other counts as a 'universal other', as a social institution, that is, as civil society and state, including constitution and laws.

In Hegel's analysis, civil society arises out of the disintegration of immediate family unity, in which the parts assert their priority over and independence from the whole. Civil society is ethical life in disintegration, a disintegration that must be overcome on the higher level of the state. This complex second

level of recognition constitutive of objective spirit involves Hegel's retrieval
and critical transformation of certain social and political structures of Greek
ethical life, as bulwarks against the excesses of civil society. Although classical
practical philosophy lacks an adequate appreciation of individual subjective
freedom, it nevertheless contains important, indispensable insights into social
life and community. For example, Plato's famous account of the necessity of
honor and justice even among a society of thieves shows that justice is an immanent condition of any functioning, much less successfully functioning, community.[1] Justice in Plato's sense is not a contingent, much less optional, condition, subject to a human convention or contract. Rather justice is an ontological
condition of freedom and community, without which neither freedom nor community would be possible. This insight into ethical substance is one important
aspect of what Hegel means by objective spirit; it is a classical insight that Hegel
believes can be retrieved on modern grounds of freedom by means of his concept of mutual recognition and derivative concept of spirit. The price of this retrieval is that the classical institutions such as family and, more important, the
state must no longer be regarded as simple givens, that is, as 'natural' institutions, but as conditions necessary for freedom's self-actualization. This means
that their legitimacy depends on human beings finding themselves in such institutions. Such a condition of self-recognition in other Hegel calls 'being at home'.

In what follows, we consider first Hegel's concept of *ethical substance*. Ethical substance is one of two modalities of freedom, namely, its rational modality. It designates the determinations and conditions of freedom, and as such includes institutions such as family, civil society, and state. It also includes an
account of the reciprocal correlations between rights and duties, as well as elements of traditional doctrines of virtues and habits. In designating these as ethical substance, Hegel means that these institutions and structures have objective
validity and weight. Not that they are heteronomous structures imposed on us,
but that they are necessary conditions of freedom and human welfare, to which
we voluntarily subordinate ourselves while at the same time realizing our trans-
individual corporate identities in them.

The second modality of freedom Hegel calls *ethical freedom*, or subjective
freedom, including subjective arbitrary will (*Willkür*). Apart from subjective
freedom, the universal structures and institutions of ethical substance would
remain merely abstract and potential. For Hegel, "the universal does not attain
validity or fulfillment without the interest, knowledge and volition of the particular."[2] We have already examined subjective freedom in abstract right and

---

1. Plato, *Republic* 351d, trans. G. M. Grube (Indianapolis: Hackett, 1992). For a discussion of
Hegel's criticism of and relation to Plato, see Michael B. Foster, *The Political Philosophies of
Plato and Hegel* (Oxford: Clarendon Press, 1935; New York: Garland, 1984). Foster's discussion
of subjectivity and social theory in Hegel passes over his concept of recognition and intersubjectivity.

2. *PR*, §260.

morality. Apart from ethical substance, subjective freedom is a merely formal capacity, which finds expression in arbitrariness, inwardness, reflection, and the empty beautiful soul. It culminates in the vanity and nihilism of ironic individualism, the hypochondria of spirit. But when subjective freedom comes to appreciate substantive freedom as its own condition, then such decadent forms are put aside and transcended.

Hegel brings these two modalities of freedom together in the following proposal: subjective freedom requires ethical substance for its content and ends; conversely, ethical substance requires subjective freedom for its realization. When the human being acts merely out of subjective arbitrary freedom, the result is evil. But when the human being acts in accordance with ethical substance, the latter comes to intersubjective realization and the result is human flourishing in ethical life: "individuals do not live as private persons merely for their particular interests without at the same time directing their will to a universal end and acting in conscious awareness of this end. The principle of modern states has enormous strength and depth because it allows the principle of subjectivity to attain fulfillment in the self-sufficient extreme of personal particularity, while at the same time bringing it back to substantial unity and so *preserving this unity in the principle of subjectivity itself.*"[3]

Next, we will consider Hegel's concept of marriage and family. For Hegel, the family is extremely important because he locates here the cultural-historical emergence of the human as such, that is, the beginnings of the transition from nature to spirit. The family is both a natural community and an ethical community. It is a determinate form of intersubjective recognition in which the other counts simply because she or he is. The family also institutionalizes the transition from nature to spirit in the procreation and rearing of children to the ethical level which prepares them to enter the world as independent individuals.

Ethical Substance, Rights, and Duties

We have previously seen that conscience has for Hegel a certain majesty, in that it relativizes the abstract principles of morality by interpreting them and applying them to determinate situations. For Hegel, as for Aristotle, there are no absolute ethical principles universally applicable to all situations. This does not imply ethical skepticism; rather it implies an appreciation of the limits of abstract formal rationalism. Moreover, Hegel appreciates, as Kant does not, that ethical duties that appear justified in 'pure reflection' can nevertheless come into conflict in actuality. We have seen that Hegel was attracted by Sophocles' *Antigone* because of its vivid dramatization of a conflict, not between right and wrong, but between the right of the family and the right of the state.

---

3. Ibid. My italics.

Such awareness of potential conflict of rights and duties leads Hegel to conscience as the ultimate ethical tribunal. Conscience may resolve the conflict of duties and determine within itself what is good in a specific situation and content. Conscience is the power whereby the abstract good of principles and obligations attains realization and actuality.[4] Hegel believes that conscience presupposes and draws on the negative dimension of freedom, namely, its power to dissolve and tear itself away from every determinacy and every given. This means that conscience exhibits the power to relativize and volatilize all the substantial determinations of freedom. In Hegel's words: "If we look more closely at this process of evaporation and observe how all determinations are absorbed into this simple concept and must issue again forth from it, we can see that this process depends primarily on the fact that everything which we recognize as right or duty can be shown by thought to be null and void, limited, and in no way absolute."[5] When conscience evaporates all substantive content, it appeals only to itself. But in appealing only to itself and seeking only its own certainties, conscience becomes evil.[6]

Thus subjective conscience has the power to relativize everything, including itself. However, at the end of this process of relativization stands empty formal conscience, which in irony and ironic gestures stands above and dissolves every substantial determination into a play of differences. This takes the modern principle of subjectivity too far; by dissolving every determination, it runs the risk of ending in nihilism or merely aesthetic play. Hegel observes that romantic irony has given rise to the excesses of the artistic genius, whose ironical individuality destroys what is excellent, great, and noble. Such an individual is unable to take anything seriously, including others: "he who has reached this standpoint of divine genius looks down from his high rank on all other men, for they are pronounced dull and limited, inasmuch as law, ethical life, etc., still count for them as solid, essential and obligatory."[7]

Hegel's alternative to the dissolution of the ethical by formal conscience, irony, and aestheticism is the formation of genuine conscience in ethical life. Hegel thus retrieves the original etymological sense of conscience as intersubjective, that is, *con-scientia, mit-wissen.* Unfortunately, Hegel does not present an explicit account of genuine conscience. It must be reconstructed from his discussion of ethical substance and patriotism. Here we confine ourselves to an examination of ethical substance. Although Hegel is sympathetic to Greek *Sittlichkeit,* he breaks with its natural law theory. But neither does he simply embrace modernity's concept of autonomy.

We have seen that for Hegel autonomous morality and moral reflection are constituted by a break with nature, and a break between the inner and the outer. In mutual recognition this gap is partially overcome, not by subordinating the

4. Ibid., §138.   5. Ibid.
6. Ibid., §§137–140; *E*, §396 Zusatz.
7. Hegel, *Aesthetics*, 66.

ethical to the natural, but by constituting the ethical as a second nature wherein the subject is at home with himself in another.[8]

> Here, on the other hand, at the standpoint of ethical life, the will is present as the will of spirit and has a substantial content to which it conforms. Education is the art of making human beings ethical: it considers them as natural beings and shows them how they can be reborn, and how their original nature can be transformed into a second, spiritual nature so that this spirituality becomes habitual to them. In habit the opposition between the natural will and the subjective will disappears.[9]

Ethical habits heal the gap between nature and spirit that autonomy opens up. In a note Hegel comments that habits are at once subjective and objective. The consciousness of habit is not simply subjective as in morality's reflection, but has objective existence "outside of me—my unity outside of me—the unity of individuals."[10]

Genuine conscience has its intersubjective/social matrix and nexus in ethical life. Individuals by themselves are insufficient to ground meaning, ethics, and culture, but they may find meaning and purpose in mutually recognizing each other and by becoming part of a larger social whole. In working for the common good of the whole, freedom ceases to be mere subjective play and acquires a substantive transcending end: "it is in ethical being that self-consciousness has its motivating end and a foundation which has being in and for itself."[11] Genuine conscience thus has its normative aspect in a social-communal universality. Morality is a deficient, abstract, and formal expression of this social universality.

Genuine conscience is not a mere play of difference, but is rather serious, not so much about itself (moralism) as about the whole of which it is part and its membership and participation in the whole. "Genuine earnestness enters only by means of a substantial interest, something of intrinsic worth like truth, ethical life, etc.—by means of a content that counts as such for me as essential, so that I only become essential in my own eyes insofar as I have immersed myself in such a content and have brought myself into conformity with it. . . . When the ego . . . dissolves everything out of its own caprice . . . such earnestness can find no place, since validity is ascribed only to the formalism of the ego."[12]

Hegel believes that conscience is both negative and positive. As negative, it may dissolve and volatilize all ethical content, resulting in a morbid beautiful soul, a possible hypochondria of spirit, a risk of nihilism, or a self-seeking that is evil.[13] However, conscience can also be positive. When we act, we develop and re-create anew through our action the substantial content of freedom and

---

8. *PR*, §151; *E*, §410 Zusatz.
9. *PR*, §151 Zusatz.
10. Ibid., §151 Anmerkung.
11. Ibid., §142.
12. Hegel, *Aesthetics*, 65.
13. *PR*, §§137–140; *E*, §396 Zusatz.

ethical life. That which had been relativized and volatilized through reflection and irony now returns in and as the conditions and exigencies of social practice and action. Instead of remaining confined to the inner self-contemplation of the morbid 'beautiful soul,' [14] in action we break out of such inwardness; we rediscover the necessity of and regenerate the universal determinations and conditions of freedom constitutive of ethical life. The substantive ethical content that had been volatilized is recovered and reconstructed. In Hegel's words: "Conversely, just as subjectivity evaporates every content into itself, it may also in turn explicate this content out of itself. Everything which arises in the ethical realm is produced by this activity of spirit." [15]

To appreciate this claim, we must recall that for Hegel action, although always particular, also has a universal aspect or dimension. This universal aspect of action is not the abstract universality of formal conscience but a social, reciprocally mediated, determinate universality. Although conscience has the power to dissolve and relativize everything, if conscience actually succeeds in dissolving everything, including the distinction between good and evil, then it becomes evil. However, no action is ever wholly private or unrelated to anyone else, as Macbeth learns when, after murdering Banquo, Banquo's ghost appears on the scene. The universal dimension of action includes its reciprocal effects and potential rationality: "When I will what is rational, I act not as a particular individual, but in accordance with the concepts of ethics in general: in an ethical act, I vindicate not myself, but the thing. But a person who does something perverse gives the greatest prominence to his particularity. The rational is the high road which everyone follows and where no one stands out from the rest." [16] Genuine conscience involves social participation in and action on behalf of a communal end. Such action suspends mere self-reflexive subjectivity and requires taking the other seriously. This in turn requires universal objective determinations. "But if I proceed to act and look for principles, I reach out for determinations, and there is then a requirement that these should be deduced from the concept of the free will. Thus while it is right to evaporate right or duty into subjectivity, it is on the other hand wrong if this abstract foundation is not in turn explicated." [17]

When the abstract substantial foundation is thus immanently reexplicated and reconstructed through freedom, determinations of freedom arise in the course of its explication which are not merely subjective, but have a content that is necessary and objective. "These distinctions give the ethical a fixed content which is necessary for itself, and whose existence is exalted above subjective opinions and preferences: they are the *laws and institutions* which have being in and for themselves." [18] In genuine conscience an important reversal

---

14. Hegel observes that Fichtean philosophy with its infinite striving and yearning gives rise to a morbid beautiful soul. However "a truly beautiful soul acts and is actual." *Aesthetics*, 67.

15. Ibid.   16. *PR*, §15.   17. Ibid., §138.

18. Ibid., §144. Italics mine. This is a Platonic-Aristotelian element in ethical life (*Sittlichkeit*).

occurs; instead of being relative to freedom, the substantive content that freedom requires is at the same time that to which freedom must be subject as an ethical power or as a duty. As the substantial content of freedom is explicated and developed in its various determinations, I realize that in seeking my own welfare, I am obliged to do so only insofar as it is consistent with the welfare of others. I act not simply as a particular individual: in an ethical act, I vindicate not myself, or my particularity, but the thing itself, namely, the ethical substance, the conditions whereby freedom can become actual in the world.

Hegel's explication of substantial freedom yields a series of social institutions such as family, civil society, and state. These institutions are not mere subjective opinions, but are rather necessary ends in themselves that are conditions and determinations of rational freedom. These 'determinations' of freedom, although relative to human subjectivity, are not reducible to merely subjective preferences or whims. "The objective sphere of ethics . . . is substance made concrete by subjectivity. . . . It therefore posits distinctions within itself which are thus determined by the concept. These distinctions give the ethical a fixed content which is necessary in and for itself, and whose existence is exalted above subjective opinions and preferences; they are laws and institutions which have being in and for themselves." [19] The family and state, for example, are not optional; [20] they are social institutions necessary to freedom. These objective institutions of ethical substance Hegel terms 'ethical powers' (*sittliche Mächte*), whose ethical necessity is manifest concretely in their asymmetrical relation to individuals as substance to accidents: "Freedom, or the objective ethical sphere, forms a circle, a totality of spiritual necessity of immanently explicated determinations whose moments are the *ethical powers* [*die sittliche Mächte*] that rule the life of individuals and have in individuals their accidents, their representation, phenomenal shape [*Gestalt*] and actuality." [21] The objectivity of these substantial ethical powers is such that "the individuals relate to them as accidents. Whether the individual exists or not is a matter of indifference to these objective powers, for they are the enduring elements, the power through which the ethical life of individuals is ordered. [They are] the absolutely essential aspect of individuals, who, apart from these essential powers, would be nothing but the empty form of subjectivity." [22] Hegel observes that peoples have regarded these ethical powers as gods, as something sacred. He even invokes the language of Aristotle's unmoved mover: "the ethical character knows that the end which moves it is the universal which, though itself unmoved, has developed through its determinations into actual rationality." [23]

19. Ibid.
20. It is important to recall the distinction between subjective and objective spirit. The family, state, and civil society are institutions necessary at the level of objective spirit. However, this does not mean that it is necessary that every individual marry or form a family. *E*, §408 Zusatz.
21. *VPR3*, 484; *PR*, §145.
22. *VPR3*, 485.
23. *PR*, §152; cf. §§142, 258.

Although the ethical powers are objective and superior to individuals, nevertheless they "are not something alien to the subject. On the contrary, the subject bears spiritual witness to them as to its own essence in which it feels itself and lives."[24] In becoming conscious of ethical substance, or substantive freedom, ethical subjectivity finds itself at home. "This being of spirit is therefore not like being in nature, where spirit is in an other. Rather these eternal, uncoercible powers are nothing alien to the subject; the subject has in them its self-feeling, its most proper being and thus lives therein in its proper element."[25]

Hegel's analysis of right, morality, and ethical life suggests that ethical substance is pursued through several modes of realization. The earlier modes are deficiently subjective. For example, abstract right does not present an appropriate form of subjectivity, because in it the abstract legal person is recognized only in its external embodiment in ownership and remains unaffected by the ownership relation. Similarly moral subjectivity remains at the level of abstract individualism; when it asserts the reflective moral standpoint absolutely, such assertion can only relativize, volatilize, and negate ethical substance. Ethical life embodies what abstract right and morality have not yet attained, namely, spirit.[26] The subjectivity of spirit is an intersubjectivity: "The ethical substance, as containing self-consciousness which has being for itself and is united with its concept, is the actual spirit of a family and a people."[27]

Hegel's concept of immanent social duties is nothing more than the development of those intersubjective relations and institutions that are necessary for freedom. If duty were regarded as a restriction on freedom, this would presuppose that freedom is abstract, indeterminate, and merely individual. As we have seen, for Hegel morality is a deficient form of freedom that we need to be liberated from, and what liberates us is a social cause or duty. "The individual finds his liberation in duty."[28] Duty, he tells us, liberates us from our merely natural drives and from the subjective broodings of morality. Hegel's difference from morality is clearly evident in his contention that duty liberates us from "that indeterminate subjectivity which does not attain determinate existence or action, but remains within itself and has no actuality."[29] Elsewhere Hegel explains that substantive duty is a liberation from the spiritual sickness of endless reflection. "For the human being reflected into himself eternally thinks things over and over; he broods in impotence and sickness of spirit. Duty liberates us from this disease and brooding. For in duty the human being acts in a universal manner and surrenders his particularity. The sickness of reflection is to be a mere particular [and nothing more]. This is the disease of morality; it is in part depression and in part self-complacency, in which one is nevertheless not actual and out of harmony with what is objective."[30]

In ethical life the distinction between "ought" and "is" is replaced by a recip-

24. Ibid., §147.   25. *VPR*3, 486.   26. Ibid., 4, 406; *PR*, §151.
27. *PR*, §156.   28. Ibid., §149.   29. Ibid.
30. *VPR*3, 491.

rocal correspondence between right and duty. We observed this correspondence earlier in abstract right; there it meant that a right on my part corresponds to a duty on the part of someone else. However, the idea of this correspondence is borrowed from ethical life. Ethical life embodies the reciprocal correlation between rights and duties such that these coincide in each member. In Hegel's words, "In this identity of the particular will with the universal will, duty and right coincide. In ethical life a human being has rights insofar as he has duties, and duties insofar as he has rights."[31]

Recall Hegel's fundamental point that rights are acquired through recognition as the right to rights: when I am recognized my possessions become my property and my right to ownership is secured. The rights that I acquire through recognition imply duties on the part of others, namely, to acknowledge and respect these rights both in general and in particular cases. But it is not only others who have to recognize me and my rights; I am secure in my recognition and possessions as an owner only if I recognize that others have the same right. Thus the right in question is mine, but it is never merely mine. Right is universal, a function of the universal will, and as such a duty. In this reciprocity between and coincidence of rights and duties we find the general pattern of mutual recognition. Ethical life is the accomplishment and realization of mutual recognition. In ethical life, what is my right is also my duty: the recognition I receive from the community as a right, I also owe to the community as a duty. In ethical life, every right corresponds to a duty on the part of someone else who honors that right and fulfills his duty toward it, and vice versa. Thus the correlation of rights and duties specifies further mutual recognition.

This point becomes clearer when we consider the limiting case of the slave. According to Hegel, the slave is not recognized, and thus has no rights. "Human beings, insofar as they have no rights [i.e., are not recognized], recognize no duties. The slave can have no duties."[32] The recognition accorded the slave is the unequal form of recognition and implies the fundamental inequality of master and slave. This means that in the master's domination of the slave, there is no ethical life in Hegel's sense, or at best a deficient one. "If all rights were on one side [i.e., mastery] and all duties on the other [i.e., slavery], the whole would disintegrate."[33] Master and slave represent the extreme, limiting position of an unequal totality: absolute freedom for the master, and for the slave, fear of death, renunciation of freedom, and reduction to a commodity.

But in ethical life, we are no longer dealing with such extreme inequalities. Logically we have moved from the categories of being (right) through the categories of essence (morality) to the categories of the concept. The concept, as a dialectical unity of opposites, underlies the presentation of ethical life. We have previously seen that mutual recognition, the two I's that become a We, is

31. *PR*, §155. I have altered the translation.
32. Ibid.; *VPR4*, 502.
33. *PR*, §155.

the phenomenal form of the concept. Both identity and difference are equally constitutive of the We. The coincidence of rights and duties is part of the identity of the 'We' of mutual reciprocal recognition. "The identity [of rights and duties] is the foundation we have to hold fast to here."[34] This correlation between rights and duties is foundational for ethical life. Hegel chooses to begin his portrayal of ethical life with the institution of the family, which is ethical life in its immediacy. Thus the correlation between rights and duties is at first only implicit.

Love

Hegel begins his discussion of marriage with love. This seems to be an obvious place to begin. However, as Dieter Henrich has pointed out, the concept of love is an important technical one, because it is the origin of Hegel's concepts of recognition and spirit, and ultimately the system itself: "Once Hegel adopted the concept of love as the basic principle of his thinking, the system came forth without interruption. The theme 'love' was replaced by the richer structure of life—for apparent reasons—and later by the still richer concept of spirit (*Geist*)."[35] The concept of love for Hegel is both a speculative ontological principle and an account of intersubjectivity. His speculative dialectical ontology and his phenomenological account of recognition are not two entirely different and separate analyses but two sides of the same coin. Henrich observes that Hegel was influenced by Hölderlin's *Vereinigungsphilosophie*, in which love is the principle of union and synthesis. Love reconciles and overcomes oppositions and separations. However, Hölderlin's philosophy of union has monist and mystical tendencies. We have already identified the element of union (*Vereinigung*) in Hegel's concept of freedom and recognition, which reflects the early influence of Hölderlin. In view of the fact that Hegel makes use of the concept of substance/accident in setting forth his account of ethical substance—a scheme that is notoriously associated with Spinoza—the question is whether Hegel follows Hölderlin in conceiving love monistically. If he does, then the other might be a mere accident that would disappear in love's union, or be reduced to the same.

Although Hegel agrees with Hölderlin that love involves union, he does not agree that this union is to be conceived as an abstract substantial monism. Here he parts with Hölderlin and conceives the union in dialectical and relational-interpersonal terms. Henrich observes that there are important differences between Hegel and Hölderlin concerning how love and above all union are to be understood: "Hegel must constantly conceive all structures which Hölderlin understood as deriving from original Being, as modes of relation which coalesce. The event of coalescence itself, and not a ground out of which coales-

34. Ibid.
35. Henrich, "Hölderlin und Hegel," 27.

cence derives, is for Hegel the true absolute, the 'all in all'. We will see that for this reason Hegel was convinced that the absolute must be conceived as *Geist* and not as *Being*."[36] Hegel does not aspire to substance metaphysics, or to a mystical unification of all in the One. Instead Hegel's holism is relational: "This is Hegel's distinctive idea, that the *relata* in opposition must, to be sure, derive from a whole. However this whole does not precede its *relata* as Being, or as intellectual intuition. Rather the whole is only the developed and explicit concept of the *relata* themselves."[37] This holistic conception is crucial to Hegel's mediation of Kant and Aristotle.

Hegel's early formulations of love's unity are not entirely free from ambiguity, as shown in the following: "love completely destroys objectivity and thereby annuls and transcends reflection, deprives man's opposite of all foreign character."[38] This looks like love's overcoming all oppositions also eliminates objectivity, and with it, eliminates the other on which it supposedly depends. However, this is not what Hegel means. Love's 'destruction of objectivity' is not the elimination of the other but the suspension of objectification, domination, and enmity that imply distance, separation, and alienation between self and other. Love renounces coercion and domination, for the sake of its object.

Consequently, when he says that love "destroys" objectivity, Hegel means that it deprives the other of its *foreign* or *alien* character. But this does not mean elimination of the other as such. Rather it means that "in love the separate does still remain, but as something united and no longer as something separate; life senses life."[39] Hegel seeks to express an intimate intersubjective unity that, far from excluding, *requires* the ontological separation and difference of subjects as its conditions. For this reason Hegel believes interpersonal union must be conceived in dialectical terms as a union that depends on differentiation and opposition. "The nature of this relationship is thoroughly speculative; and when it is supposed that the speculative is something remote and inconceivable, one has only to consider the content of this [interpersonal] relationship to convince oneself of the baselessness of this opinion. The speculative, or the rational and the true, consists in the unity of the concept [*Begriff*]. . . . This unity is manifestly present in the standpoint in question. It forms the substance of ethical life, of the family, of love, of patriotism, of love towards God, of bravery . . . and of honour."[40]

Transforming the Dialectics of Recognition

In the initial dialectic of recognition, the confrontation with the other is experienced as a loss of self. Hegel identifies the first moment of recognition as

36. Ibid., 28. My emphasis.
37. Ibid., 36.
38. *ETW*, 305. Fragment on Love.
39. Ibid.   40. *E*, §436 Zusatz.

a loss of self before the other. If the two parties cannot or do not give up their absolute, exclusive independence, they can never get beyond this immediate confrontation, and the result is either a struggle to the death or the unequal recognition of master and slave that institutionalizes inequality and domination. A similar negative opposition is present in abstract right; ownership is recognition by others of the right to exclude them from property. Each agrees to be excluded from the other's property on condition that the other will reciprocate. In this way the right of ownership is bestowed through reciprocal mutual exclusions. In both cases the aim is establishing or maintaining independence.

However, in the case of love, both the initial moment of loss of self before the other and the pursuit of exclusive independent individuality in ownership undergo dramatic reversal and qualification. "This reversal . . . rests in the fact that *each gives up its independence. . . .* [I]t is the condition of *not being satisfied in oneself*, but rather having one's essence in another—because one knows oneself in the other, and negates oneself as being-for-oneself, as different. This self-negation is one's being for another, into which one's immediate being is transformed."[41] In love the very independent selfhood that was previously defended to the death is now found to be insufficient, unsatisfying. Consequently it must be *aufgehoben*.

The individual self of legal personality is a 'thin' self; it is the self merely as a potential or actual owner, and not the self in its totality. But in marriage, "the person gives himself [or herself] up as an entirety."[42] Again, "In marriage, each partner is mutually in the consciousness of the other, so each is mutually consciousness in the other as his/her *whole singularity*, and the spouses give themselves a wholly communal existence."[43] In the *Philosophy of Right* Hegel observes that marriage is a substantial relationship involving "life in its totality, namely as the actuality of the species and its process."[44]

This reference to the species does not mean that Hegel conceives marriage simply as a natural-biological relationship, or one in which such natural drives and inclinations are primary. On the contrary, desire, nature, and biology are here sublated and transformed into an ethical and spiritual relationship. In his early *Jena Philosophy of Spirit* (1803/04), in reference to the patriarchal family, Hegel explicates one aspect of the ethical transformation in the following passage: "the woman comes to be a being on her own account for the man. She ceases to be [simply] an object of his desire."[45] The sexual union is transformed into an ethical-spiritual union in which desire, nature, and biology are necessary but subordinate elements. "Marriage is essentially an ethical relationship."[46] "The ethical aspect of marriage consists in the consciousness of

41. *Philosophie des Geistes 1805/06*, 193; *HHS*, 107. Italics mine.
42. *System of Ethical Life (1802/03) and First Philosophy of Spirit (1803)*, trans. H. S. Harris (Albany: SUNY Press, 1979), 128.
43. *Philosophie des Geistes 1803/04*, 232. My italics.
44. *PR*, §161.
45. *Philosophie des Geistes 1803/04*; *HHS*, 231.
46. *PR*, §161 Zusatz.

this union as a substantial end, and hence in love, trust and the sharing of the whole of individual existence. When this disposition is present, the natural drive is reduced to the modality of a moment of nature which is destined to be extinguished in its satisfaction, while the ethical union asserts its rights as the substantial element as . . . indissoluble in itself and exalted above the contingency of passions and arbitrariness."[47]

Marriage is a determinate intersubjectivity. It originates in the free consent of the concerned parties. This is a free "consent to constitute a single person and to give up their natural and individual personalities within this union. In this respect, their union is a self-limitation, but since they attain their substantial self-consciousness within it, it is in fact their liberation."[48] This is the ethical core of what Hegel means by ethical life and objective *Geist*. The marital union is, when viewed from the standpoint of self-sufficient individualism, a self-limitation. However, this self-limitation is only apparent. Viewed from the standpoint of the marriage union itself, the self-limitation is *aufgehoben* into a liberation of and mutual participation in substantial ethical freedom. Individuality is not suppressed but enhanced and enlarged within the determinate intersubjectivity of marriage. The break with nature constitutive of self-sufficient autonomous morality is healed, not by nature, but by an ethical freedom that sublates nature and transforms it in spiritual union. "This bond, as involving the totality of someone's consciousness, is just for this reason sacred."[49]

Love thus transforms the dialectic of recognition. In the first moment of confrontation, being for other appears as a loss of self. Being-for-self and being-for-other seem to be mutually exclusive, and each self clings to his independent separate existence. But in the case of love, this independence is no longer felt to be sufficient or satisfying, but insufficient and dissatisfying. Consequently it is negated and renounced. However, this negation is not a loss but a gain that transforms and enlarges the selfhood of the lovers. Thus love overcomes the mutual exclusion between selves by removing the opposition between being-for-other and being-for-self.[50] When this opposition is removed, then giving to the other does not make one poorer. Being in relation is no longer a loss of self but rather a mutual gain and ethical enhancement and enrichment. Unlike the economic sphere, in the realm of spirit the more one gives, the more one has in union with the other. Hegel once expressed this point by citing Shakespeare: "The lover who takes is not thereby made richer than the other; he is enriched indeed, but only so much as the other is. So too the giver does not make himself poorer; by giving to the other he has at the same time and to the same extent enhanced his own treasure (compare Juliet in *Romeo and Juliet* [ii.1.175–177]: 'My bounty is as boundless as the sea, my love is as deep; the more I give to thee, the more I have')."[51]

---

47. Ibid., §163.   48. Ibid., §162.
49. *Philosophy of Spirit 1803/04*, 232.
50. Hegel reached this conclusion in his Jena *Philosophie des Geistes 1803/04*, 231.
51. *ETW*, 307.

The early conception of love as dialectical union with another finds clear expression in Hegel's mature *Philosophy of Right*. Here the speculative dialectical elements and the phenomenological intersubjective elements of Hegel's concept of love continue to exist side by side. One important text for Hegel's concept of love in the *Philosophy of Right* is an addition to *PR*, §158, which I cite, not from Gans's *Zusatz*, but from Hotho's transcript of the 1822 lectures:

> Love means in general a consciousness of my unity with another, so that I am no longer isolated for myself, but have my independence [*Fürsichsein*] only in the unity of my self-consciousness with that of another. Thus I gain my self-consciousness only when I surrender my independence and self-knowledge through knowing myself in union with another, and the other in union with me.
>
> The actuality of spirit [*Geist*] consists only in this unity. Love therefore is only for itself through the suspension of its being-other [*Andersseins*]. Love is the infinite negation of itself that is also infinite affirmation in identity with the other existing negation.[52]

In the above passages it appears that love requires the renunciation of independence. This is only part of Hegel's view, and if mistaken for the whole, it would lead to Hölderlin's monist interpretation of love as abstract union that suppresses otherness and individuality. But Hegel's point is that in love I both *renounce* my abstract independence and *gain* my concrete, genuine independence *in union with other*. For Hegel, love's union not only cancels the abstract formal independence of individual subjective freedom; more important, love achieves and consists in genuine substantive independence: namely, it offers a more satisfying freedom in relationship with another. Substantive independence is intersubjective and achieved through reciprocal recognition. Here being in relation to the other does not cancel my genuine independence and freedom; rather independence and freedom are realized together in union with the other.

Hegel covers this same topic somewhat more explicitly and with different nuances in his 1824/25 lectures (Griesheim transcript).

> Love has this significance, that I feel myself needy and incomplete. I am independent, and this independence is precisely that which, when I am in love, I find to be deficient. In love I don't want to be this independent person by myself. In love I negate my independence. This is the first moment [of love].
>
> The second moment [of love] is that I maintain and preserve myself in this negation, because I gain myself in another person. In her I have the intuition, the consciousness, that I count for something, in her I have worth and validity. But it is not only I who counts, she also counts for me. This means that each person has in the other the consciousness of the other and of the self, this unity. Goethe says quite correctly that one is conscious of oneself only in others.
>
> Love is the most tremendous contradiction that the understanding cannot dis-

52. *VPR3*, 507–508.

solve. There is nothing harder or more intractable than the punctiliousness of the self-consciousness. This is negated and yet I have it as affirmative. The negation is a unity of two self-consciousnesses that remain utterly different, each for itself. And yet this infinite intractability melts and is rendered gentle in union. Love is not the suppression or non-existence of this contradiction, but its resolution. Reason, the concept, is the conceptual resolution of this contradiction which the understanding fails to grasp.[53]

In the above passage there are two moments of love: (1) the very independent selfhood that I have struggled to attain I now find insufficient and incomplete; and (2) I find myself in another person and gain recognition in this other person who in turn gains recognition in me. The self finds its abstract relationless independence to be lacking and unsatisfying. Genuine satisfaction requires intersubjective union, or mutual recognition.

But the self and its personality are not simply negated, much less alienated, given away, or handed over to the other. Hegel has already declared this to be impossible. Recall that he claims that one's freedom, personality, ethical life as a whole, and religion are inalienable and imprescriptible, because "the act whereby I take possession of my personality and substantial essence and make myself a responsible being with moral and religious values and capable of having rights, removes these determinations from that very externality which alone makes them capable of becoming the possessions of someone else."[54] The point is that love's self-surrender is not a self-alienation in the foregoing sense. In love, as in mutual recognition in general, the self's relation to itself and even its self-surrender are immanently mediated by the self's relation to the other. Consequently, the independence that is negated in the first moment of love is enriched, enlarged, and reappropriated in the second moment: Although relation involves self-negation, the self is not simply negated but enhanced, because it gains itself back in union with another person, that is, in the other's recognition. Hegel makes this point thus: "In a relationship based on love, the individual is conscious of himself through the consciousness of another. He renounces his own self, and in this mutual renunciation [gegenseitige Entäusserung] each gains not only the other self but also his own self in return because it is united with the other."[55] In this case, being in relation to other confers a worth and value on the self that it cannot simply bestow on itself. It is not by myself but in and for the other that I realize I count for something. This fact of 'counting' I both need and yet cannot bestow autonomously on myself. This honoring can only be interpersonally bestowed; for my honor, I depend on the other. This is the 'tremendous contradiction' that the understanding cannot dissolve or understand.

Love is not just a determinate realization of mutual recognition; it is the in-

53. VPR4, 420.   54. PR, §66.

55. Philosophie der Geschichte, Werke, TWA Sk 12:60; translation: Lectures on the Philosophy of World History, 100.

version and fulfillment of the earlier forms and patterns. The independent self that was earlier defended to the death is now found to be insufficient and is voluntarily pledged to the other. But such self-surrender is not a real loss, because all that is being surrendered is the abstractly independent legal personality as ownership, and the empty independence that is incapable of anything more than irony or ironical pseudorelationships. In love one gains a higher, substantial self. Love founds a relationship that involves a liberation from abstract, isolated selfhood and the creation of genuine substantial independence as a determinate intersubjectivity or a corporate person. Thus substantial independence, in contrast with the empty independence of irony, is paradoxically found in union with other.

Marriage as an Ethical Relationship

Hegel presents his concept of marriage as an alternative to three other views. This manner of presentation allows him to highlight and set off his position from the others. In natural law theory of the seventeenth and eighteenth centuries, marriage was treated as a relation that is partly legal and partly ethical. We have already examined Hegel's observation that there is an ambiguity in the term 'nature' in natural law theory: it can mean what is raw, primitive, uncultivated, what is 'merely natural' or 'by nature', or it can have the opposite significance, meaning what is cultivated, rational, and ethical. In natural law theory, marriage was considered primarily in its natural-physical aspect, subordinate to biology, sex, and reproduction, while its ethical dimension, Hegel believes, was slighted or neglected. Thus marriage was regarded as a principle governing or legitimating a sexual relationship and its possible offspring. This view is still prevalent as a general definition governing anthropological inquiries into the subject.

Hegel presents two criticisms of the 'naturalistic view' of marriage. The first is that this approach to marriage has blocked the way for further exploration of other aspects and dimensions of marriage, namely, the ethical and spiritual dimensions. Hegel claims that in marriage the sexual relationship or natural union of the species "is transformed into an ethical-spiritual union, into self-conscious love."[56] Second, the naturalistic view "fails to account for the exclusive, enduring shape of marriage as monogamy. When marriage is considered merely in its natural-physical aspect, monogamy does not 'follow'."[57] That is, if marriage were simply a way of socially legitimating sexuality and procreation, monogamy would be merely one possible form that such legitimation may take alongside other forms. But Hegel suggests that marriage is fundamentally monogamous because he believes that monogamy, as the exclusive ethical union of two people, is the most stable and enduring ethical shape

56. *PR*, §161.   57. *VPR*4, 425.

of marriage. It is the most stable and enduring form because only in monogamy do the marriage partners achieve full mutual recognition and freedom.[58] We shall return to this point later.

The second view considers marriage simply as a civil contract. Hegel finds this view articulated by Kant, and refers to Kant's remark that "the contract of marriage [is one in which] man and woman will the reciprocal enjoyment of one another's sexual attributes."[59] Kant continues his analysis of the marriage contract thus:

> The natural use that one sex makes of the sexual organs of the other is an enjoyment for which one party surrenders itself to the other. In this act persons make themselves into things, which conflicts with their human rights in regard to their own person. The sole condition under which this is possible is that, in one person's being acquired by the other (as a thing), the latter in reciprocal fashion acquires the former; for in this way each regains himself and re-establishes his personality. . . . But to acquire one of the limbs of the person is to acquire his entire person.[60]

Hegel comments that "Kant presents marriage in a shameful, ugly manner."[61] Kant's view of marriage as a contract treats the persons and their relationship as mere things (*Sachen*), "and the contract is merely a contract for reciprocal use."[62] This view is not only crude and barbaric, it also makes the commercial contract, which is about the convergence of private wills in external things or property exchanges, the norm for interpersonal relations in general and marriage in particular.

The third view is that marriage is simply the feeling of love. Love is the main thing, and if it is not already present in a relationship, it cannot be rendered present by the formal marriage ceremony. While this view is not entirely misguided, love in the form of feeling is open to contingency and transience. But a merely temporary liaison or affair is not a marriage. Hegel refers to the notoriety created by Schlegel's *Lucinde* that emphasized the subjective dimension of marriage to the exclusion of the objective. "Friedrich von Schlegel in his *Lucinde* and a follower of his . . . have argued that the marriage ceremony is superfluous and a formality which could be dispensed with on the ground that love is the substantial element and that its value may even be diminished by this celebration. These writers represent the physical surrender as necessary in order to prove the freedom and intensity of love—an argument not unknown to seducers."[63] Hegel believes that such contingent and temporary

---

58. In *VPR*17, §76, Hegel maintains that monogamy is the rational form of marriage.

59. Kant, *Metaphysik der Sitten*, §24, Rechtslehre, GS 6:278, 277–278 (English translation: *Metaphysical Elements of Justice*, trans. J. Ladd [Indianapolis: Bobbs-Merrill, 1965], cited in *PR*, 413).

60. Kant, *Metaphysik der Sitten*, §25, cited in *VPR*17, §79.

61. *VPR*17, §79.   62. *VPR*4, 425.   63. *PR*, §164 Zusatz.

shapes are not appropriate for ethical relations: "Marriage should therefore be defined more precisely as rightfully ethical love, so that the transient, capricious and purely subjective aspects of love are excluded from it."[64]

Hegel agrees with the first view that marriage is a natural sexual relationship. But it is more; in marriage "the union of the natural sexes . . . is transformed into a spiritual-ethical union."[65] "The way in which this natural relationship is raised and transformed into the ethical is that the species is rationality . . . and that this love . . . is the essential element and goal. The drive and passion vanish in satisfaction, turning into this relationship itself; and the rational, purified through this sublation of the natural, . . . emerges as conjugal love. . . . This makes family life something rational and ethical. Now the aim of sexual union is that this love, this rationality, should take on concrete existence in the partners' life. . . . The merely natural relationship becomes immediately an ethical one."[66] Both the natural sexual union and the ethical disposition and union are necessary dimensions of marriage. However, they do not have equal importance or weight; the ethical should relativize and take priority over, but by no means suppress, the natural:

> The ethical aspect of marriage consists in the consciousness of this union as a substantial end, and hence in love, trust and the sharing of the whole undivided existence. When this disposition and actuality are present, the natural drive is reduced to the modality of a moment of nature which is destined to be extinguished in its satisfaction, while the spiritual bond asserts its rights as the substantial element and thereby stands out as indissoluble in itself and exalted above the contingency of passions and particular transient whims and caprice.[67]

Marriage has a different mode of temporalization from the affair. Where the affair is a temporary liaison that is pervaded by contingency because the parties try to retain the abstract independence they had apart from relationship, in marriage two people seek to become one person and forge "a union for the duration of life."[68]

Since the *telos* of marriage is the formation of an enduring ethical union, Hegel believes that marriage is indissoluble in principle. However, since marriage embodies love in the form of feeling, "it is not absolute but unstable and has within it the possibility of its dissolution."[69] While marriage as such aims in principle to be an enduring ethical union, particular marriages may break up. Such dissolutions occur when the relation ceases to be vital, or when there is withdrawal from the shared unity; for example, adultery, willful desertion, and temperamental incompatibility all can be grounds for dissolution. Such dissolution reflects the will of someone who wishes to be separated. On the other

---

64. Ibid., §161 Zusatz.   65. Ibid., §161.
66. *VPR*17, §76. I have altered the order of the passage.
67. *PR*, §163.   68. *VPR*17, §76.   69. *PR*, §163 Zusatz.

hand, Hegel observes that the above grounds for divorce do not make divorce itself necessary, much less automatic: "marriage in itself is not dissolved by adultery, willful desertion, incompatibility, bad economic management—but only if both parties consider these to be grounds [for divorce] and want the dissolution."[70] This qualification underscores Hegel's concept of marriage as a primarily ethical relation and union, rather than a merely natural or merely legal-contractual union.

Marriage as
a Contract to Transcend Contract

In his treatment of contract, Hegel seeks to clarify the conditions and limitations of the contractual point of view. His reason for undertaking such a clarification is "in order *not* to apply this relation to every instance in which two wills are present or in agreement. For in the state and in marriage two wills are also present, yet nothing could be more false than to consider the state and marriage as a contract."[71] He believes that to apply the contractual model of relation universally and indiscriminately to the state and marriage results in distortion. "The intrusion of this relationship, and of relationships concerning private property in general, into political relationships has created the greatest confusion in constitutional law and in actuality."[72] What follows is an examination of some of Hegel's efforts to sort out this confusion.

We have found that a contract is an expression of an agreement between two wills concerning the exchange of property. Thus contract includes the moment of mutual recognition. However, the two arbitrary wills converge only in respect to the exchange or transfer of property. In this exchange "both persons remain, and want to remain independent as owners. Such independence is the decisive element in contract. Both persons act in such a way as to retain their independence."[73] Thus while contract necessarily includes the moment of mutual recognition, the intersubjectivity of contract is deficient because it is limited to the exchange of external goods and things. Other possible relations that the owners might have to each other remain out of consideration; the contractual point of view abstracts from these. There is no ethical tie or obligation between owners per se; there is only a legally enforceable contract. There are no commitments that compromise or qualify the basic recognition of ownership, namely, the recognition of one's independence and right to exclude others from one's property.

Hegel contrasts ethical relations as necessary and enduring with contractual relations, which are contingent and transitory. Contractual relations are characterized by the following features: "Since the contracting parties relate to each

---

70. *Philosophie des Geistes 1805/06*, 220; *HHS*, 136.
71. *VPR3*, 265.   72. *PR*, §75.   73. *VPR3*, 266.

other as immediate, self-sufficient persons, it follows that a) the contract is the product of the arbitrary will [*Willkür*], b) the identical will that comes into existence through the contract is only a will posited by the contracting parties, hence only a common will, not a will that is universal in and for itself, c) the object of the contract is a particular external thing [*Sache*]."[74] In contrast, the "ethical relation involves the rational will, and the rational will is not posited by the arbitrary will, but exists in and for itself. . . . [It is] through the concept of the will that I possess ethical substance. *This is a completely different universality than that of a contract.* In contract the will is merely a common will, and the identity is merely a semblance because it can be dissolved."[75] But the 'common will' of marriage aims at an ethical, enduring union that is permanent in principle.

The mutual recognitions constitutive of contract and marriage differ dramatically. In contract the common will or 'we' is 'about' property; this common will is a merely superficial, external convergence. This is why in contract, the two selves expressly retain their independence and self-sufficiency. In *VPR*17, Hegel shows that the mutual recognition constitutive of marriage and family is different from that constitutive of ownership.

> The rights that are founded on the family are different from the rights we dealt with in the case of property; their foundation is quite distinct and of another kind. Here we are dealing with substantive freedom and the foundation is a universal will, whereas the will on which property rests is quite different from substantive freedom. Personality, which is at the basis of ownership or property, is dissolved in family. The family is founded on an identity of will. . . . The disposition [*Gesinnung*] is here an essential moment. . . . *This consciousness, or ethical life, has the shape of love, of the self-consciousness that one has not in oneself, but in another, in which one has one's own self-consciousness in such a way that this knowledge of the identity [of self and other] is the essential point.*[76]

Ownership is a form of mutual recognition that recognizes legal personality. But this 'legal person' is dissolved in a marriage. The marriage partners form a new union, a new corporate or legal person, and their property is no longer exclusive, but is now held in common. From the standpoint of ethical life and marriage, contract is a deficient form of intersubjectivity because it passes over or lacks altogether the central intersubjective disposition, namely, self-recognition in other and the will to make this an enduring union, an end in itself.

Hegel observes that in the case of marriage, the intersubjective disposition is important, indeed crucial. "In abstract right [subjective] disposition [*Gesinnung*] is superfluous; it makes no difference what my disposition is when I act;

---

74. *PR*, §75.
75. *VPR*3, 268. Italics mine.
76. *VPR*17, §73. My italics. I have modified the English translation.

whereas in marriage disposition itself is an absolute moment."[77] In contracts and property exchanges, what counts are the terms of the contract and their observance, not the subjective disposition. The subjective disposition is irrelevant. The contracting parties may not even know or care about each other as human beings. All that counts is the observation of the contract, which is enforceable by some binding authority. Thus in the reciprocal recognition constitutive of contract, owners remain unrelated in spite of their relations.

However, in the case of a marriage, what counts is the subjective disposition toward union and the emotional ties that lie deeper than the external contingencies of contract. This subjective disposition cannot be created by contract or legally enforced. For this reason disposition is not irrelevant but central. If marriage partners were to seek legal enforcement of their marriage contract against each other, that marriage would already be breaking up. Further, as Hegel has noted, "marriage in itself is not dissolved by adultery, willful desertion, incompatibility, bad economic management—but only if both parties consider these to be grounds [for divorce] and want the dissolution."[78] Whether a married couple regard adultery, desertion, incompatibility, and bad economic management as grounds for divorce and so want a dissolution depends on their intersubjective disposition, which provides the crucial framework within which such 'breaches of contract' are interpreted. This will and disposition to form a union can remain in spite of infidelity and other 'breaches of contract'.

In marriage, the two partners agree to form a union, a single person, and this union "involves life in its totality."[79] The two selves "consent to constitute a single person, and to give up their natural and individual personalities within this union."[80] Thus while marriage shares with contract a starting point in the arbitrary will of individuals, "the precise nature of marriage is to begin from the point of view of contract—i.e., that of an individual personality as a self-sufficient unit—in order to transcend it."[81] Hegel believes that marriage is a situation different from contract, for marriage is not about a convergence of wills in an external thing (*Sache*), but in each other, the We. For this reason the marriage relation concerns "the whole of my personality. I do not retain my [abstract independent] personality, I give it up. Thus I give up precisely that which is the condition of contract."[82]

Embodied Intersubjectivity and Gender Roles

Hegel conceives love and marriage as determinate realizations of mutual recognition. The enduring ethical union elevated above the contingencies of

77. Ibid., §79.
78. *Philosophie des Geistes 1805/06*, 220; *HHS*, 136.
79. *PR*, §161.   80. Ibid., §162.   81. Ibid., §163.
82. *VPR3*, 513–514.

passion and caprice is an accomplishment and realization of mutual-reciprocal recognition. Thus marriage is an important counterexample to Hegel's famous discussion of master and slave in his *Phenomenology*. Both are shapes, or *Gestalten*, of recognition. The analysis of master and slave develops recognition in the shape of inequality and domination. The analysis of marriage is of interest because it develops recognition in the shape of love, which renounces domination and inequality. Although Hegel never developed his concept of marriage as explicitly as master and slave, what he has written shows that he really did believe that there is an alternative to domination and inequality and that mutual-reciprocal recognition is possible.

Consequently it is disappointing to discover that when he turns to the analysis of marriage and family, Hegel presents a traditional view in which gender identification and role are anything but equal. To be sure, it is unfair to judge Hegel by contemporary standards, particularly since by the standards of his own time, Hegel was by no means a reactionary. Moreover, we recall that Hegel asserts that philosophy is its own time comprehended in thought and that it is "foolish to imagine that philosophy can transcend its contemporary world."[83]

Nevertheless, there is a tension in Hegel's thought. On the one hand, the concept of mutual-reciprocal recognition implies coequality. Coequality implies that marriage is, ethically speaking, essentially monogamy. On the other hand, Hegel's concept of marriage and family exhibits a fundamental inequality between men and women in that women are restricted to the family sphere and seem excluded from public life. Consider the following statement:

> Man . . . has his actual substantial life in the state, in learning, etc., and otherwise in work and struggle with the external world and with himself, so that it is only through his division that he fights his way to self-sufficient unity with himself. In the family, he has a peaceful intuition of this unity, an emotional subjective ethical life. Woman however has her substantial vocation in the family, and her ethical disposition consists in piety. In one of the most sublime presentations of piety— the *Antigone* of Sophocles—this quality is therefore declared to be primarily the law of woman . . . as the law of the ancient gods . . . an eternal law of which no one knows whence it came.[84]

In this passage there is no question that Hegel identifies the substantive life of men with the public realm of the state and the substantive life of women with the private sphere of home and family.

This sorting out of gender roles is mitigated in part by Hegel's reference to Antigone. The reference to Antigone implies not simply that "woman's place is in the home" but also that the family is a legitimate institution of ethical life, equiprimordial with the institution of the state. In short, male and female are

83. *PR*, 21.   84. Ibid., §166.

separate but equal. Hegel is fascinated by Sophocles' play because in it the institutions of the family and the state, which are otherwise justified, come into tragic conflict in the persona of Creon and Antigone. The reference to Antigone indicates a separate but equal view of male and female gender roles. However, in a student note Hegel is reported to have said:

> Women may be well educated, but they are not made for the higher sciences, for philosophy . . . which requires a universal element. Women may have insights, tastes, and delicacy, but they do not possess the ideal. The difference between men and women is the difference between animal and plant; the animal is closer to man, the plant to woman, for the latter is a more peaceful process of unfolding whose principle is the more indeterminate unity of feeling.[85]

This comment appears to undercut any interpretation along the lines of separate but equal. Women are separate but plainly unequal. Hegel thinks women are incapable of grasping the ideal and rational, and to this extent are intellectually inferior. This inferiority makes them unsuited for public life; however, it stands in tension if not contradiction with Hegel's lavish praise for Antigone, who made the personal political in the profoundest sense: "the heavenly Antigone, the most magnificent figure ever to have appeared on earth."[86] Antigone is an exception to woman's traditional role precisely because she challenges the leadership of the polis, reveals its parochial male dominance, and asserts the right of individual conscience against its parochial male universality.

It is not surprising that some conclude that Hegel has nothing to offer feminists. They contend that the inequality of women is not perceived by Hegel as a problem because he accepts the traditional view of women as naturally determined for and confined to the family; that is, the inequality of women is grounded in nature and biology. Heidi M. Ravven, an otherwise sympathetic commentator, charges Hegel with an inconsistent rejection of Aristotle's arguments about the natural inferiority of slaves while accepting similar claims concerning the natural inferiority of women.[87]

Further, Patricia Jagentowicz Mills believes that "the family is the sphere of 'merely natural existence,' 'mere particularity,' and as such its supreme value is essentially inactive *biological existence* or *animal life*."[88] Mills's formulations make it appear as if the family were a purely natural, biological entity that cannot yet be self-conscious because it has not undergone the struggle for recognition. This is biological reductionism with a vengeance, which misreads

85. Ibid., §166 Zusatz.
86. Hegel, *Geschichte der Philosophie*, TWA Sk 18:509.
87. Heidi M. Ravven, "Has Hegel Anything to Say to Feminists?" *Owl of Minerva* 19, no. 2 (Spring 1988): 159.
88. Patricia Jagentowicz Mills, "Hegel's Antigone," *Owl of Minerva* 17, no. 2 (Spring 1986): 131. My emphasis.

Hegel's concepts of nature, recognition, family, and *Sittlichkeit*. Hegel's point is that since the family is a form of mutual recognition, the other is a member (*Mitglied*), and no longer a mere object to be consumed, used, or exploited as in the case of *Begierde*. The family marks the transition from the natural to the ethical and constitutes the first institution of ethical life (*Sittlichkeit*). As we have seen, the transition from nature to ethical life begins when the woman ceases to be merely an object of male desire and comes to count in her own right. However, the traditional view of marriage that Hegel articulates does not, by contemporary standards, allow women to count enough.

Mills's reading of Hegel's conception of marriage is untenable, because Hegel criticizes naturalistic reductionism, especially in reference to marriage and family in his *Philosophy of Right*.[89] We have already noted that Hegel criticizes earlier interpretations of marriage for reducing it to a merely physical or natural relation. For Hegel, marriage is not primarily a natural-biological relationship, although it includes nature and sexuality; rather "marriage is essentially an ethical relationship."[90] Hegel observes,

> The ethical [*sittliche*] aspect of marriage consists in the consciousness of this union as a substantial end, and hence in love, trust and the sharing of the whole of individual existence. When this disposition and actuality are present, the natural drive is reduced to the modality of a moment of nature which is destined to be extinguished in its very satisfaction, while the substantial bond asserts its rights as the substantial factor and thereby stands out as indissoluble in principle and exalted above the contingency of the passions and caprice.[91]

Hegel does not simply hold that women are naturally inferior to men, nor does he understand 'rationality' so narrowly as to identify it exclusively as a male trait. Alan Wood has correctly pointed out that Hegel believes that men and women think differently, that "men are better at grasping abstract ethical principles, but women are more perceptive about particular ethical relationships, better at responding emotionally to them. The woman 'orders things according to her feelings and thus governs [the family] in a genuine sense, deriving what should happen from her individuality.'"[92] Hegel has something in common with contemporary views concerning women's distinctive moral capacities and viewpoints, for example, Carol Gilligan and Sarah Ruddick.[93] Hegel holds that men and women have different but complementary capacities. The family is a concrete form of rationality, in which "the rational purified through the sublation of the natural . . . emerges as conjugal love. . . . In

89. *PR*, §§161, 163, 164.
90. Ibid., Zusatz.   91. Ibid., §163.
92. Wood, *HET*, 245. Wood cites *VPR3*, 530–531.
93. Carol Gilligan, *In a Different Voice* (Cambridge, Mass.: Harvard University Press, 1982); Sarah Ruddick, *Maternal Thinking* (Boston: Beacon Press, 1989).

self-consciousness the species is rationality knowing itself as universal; the sexes know universality, and this immediate knowing, this feeling is love. This makes the family something rational and ethical."[94] The rationality of the family is a species of rationality to which both male and female make important contributions and have complementary roles to play.

This interpretation is supported further by Hegel's ethical defense of monogamous marriage. The focus of our concern here is not whether Hegel succeeds in his defense of monogamy but rather on the way Hegel goes about constructing his defense. This defense supports the contention that he does not reduce marriage to biology, sex, or nature as Mills believes but conceives marriage as an ethical relation grounded in mutual recognition. According to Hegel, marriage must be monogamous because it involves the mutual surrender of the entire personality to the other, and such complete mutual surrender presupposes coequality. Recall that the principle of marriage is love, and love is a form of reciprocal recognition. Reciprocal recognition implies mutual coequality. Without such coequality, at least in principle, marriage would be a one-sided relation of inequality and/or domination.

Hegel believes this is what happens in polygamy. "Marriage is essentially monogamous, because this relation of inwardness can occur only among two persons of different sexes, and every other number distorts it. . . . It is not nature, but freedom that constitutes the ground of marriage. . . . Since in marriage the immediate personality is given up in favor of the [mutual-reciprocal] union, this union is not possible in polygamy because in this case the two or more wives or husbands of a spouse cannot appear to each other in unity, and cannot be mutually honored. If the husband has several wives, the wife does not attain to her rights, and the marriage does not become a genuinely ethical relationship, but remains at the natural standpoint."[95]

Hegel's critique of polygamy is an ethical one with which we are already familiar. We have seen that marriage requires the renunciation of immediate independent personality and/or natural egoism for the sake of the intersubjective union. Here Hegel extends this point. His claim is that polygamy remains on a preethical level; it does not break with nature and natural determinations, but is an extension of natural inequality. Consequently Hegel believes that cultures that practice polygamy do not adequately recognize the right of freedom and personality, and thus perpetuate in an external way the inequalities of master and slave: "wherever there is polygamy women are enslaved."[96] That is why in such cultures "the wife does not attain her rights." Once the infinite

---

94. *VPR*17, §76.   95. Ibid., §80.

96. *VPR*18, §83. Hegel adds that "wherever women dominate, there is no ethical life." Is this because it is women rather than men who do the dominating? Or is it rather the generic point that domination of others is incompatible with the freedom of ethical life? Surely it must be the latter generic point.

worth of freedom and personhood are recognized, the concept of mutual recognition rules out such inequality. Hegel does not flatly deny the possibility of some sort of ethical union in polygamous marriage, but insists that this is a different sort of ethical unity than monogamy precisely because of its inherent inequalities and what he takes to be less than total mutual commitment and surrender in it. Whatever else may be going on in polygamy, such marriages are not ones in which two become one person.

We have previously pointed out Hegel's conservative tendencies that confine women's role to the family, and which imply a de facto inferiority. It is therefore striking that Hegel argues against polygamy precisely on the grounds that it confers inferior status on women: "If the husband has many wives, the woman does not get her rights, and marriage is no longer an ethical relationship, but remains on the level of mere nature. In India women are [believed to be] capable of producing children only from their twelfth to their twentieth year. But precisely this inequality of the sexes in producing children is a proof that merely producing children cannot be the exclusive or essential purpose of marriage. The subjective disposition is an essential moment of marriage, that depends on the voluntary approval and commitment of *both*."[97] However one may evaluate these considerations, it is apparent that Hegel's case against polygamy is an ethical one: polygamy violates the mutual equality of sexes implied by mutual recognition. Moreover, if the subjective disposition of the will is an essential moment of marriage, this involves the recognition of woman as a bearer of subjective will and freedom that must be acknowledged and respected, particularly in procreation.

Hegel believes that the recognition of subjective freedom is the historical accomplishment of Christian culture, and he applies this general principle to women in his 1824/25 lectures on the *Philosophy of Right*. There he claims that from an ethical perspective, monogamy is the genuine, authentic conception of marriage. The union of marriage is a reciprocally constituted one, and

in this union the intention of the one must be likewise the intention of the other, otherwise a misrelation occurs. In polygamy the husband counts more than the wife; she surrenders herself entirely to him, but not he to her, and consequently she does not receive the entire undivided total personality of her husband. From a purely natural perspective of marriage, this would not make any difference. However, since genuine marriage is spiritual and ethical, everything depends on the spiritual union. From the ethical perspective both partners are equal, as a spiritual 'We', as an immediate exclusive singularity. In this union they are related such that one has its entire self-consciousness in the other, and intuits this union with the other with its self-consciousness.[98]

97. *VPR*17, §80. My italics.
98. *VPR*4, §167, 446.

Moreover, in view of Ravven's charge that Hegel has an ahistorical conception of woman that he carries over largely intact from Greek *Sittlichkeit*,[99] it is interesting to note that he defends monogamous marriage as something historically and culturally constituted.

> Women come into their rights only in monogamy. Monogamy belongs to Christianity, because it includes the principle that the individual is entirely independent of distinctions in sex, gender, from natural differences, and that what counts is the particular character. *The woman is just as much spirit (Geist) as the man.* In Christianity there is talk about the subject as God's end. This implies that the soul, spiritual individuality intrinsically (*an und für sich*) have infinite value and worth. This same infinite value and worth is granted to the woman in monogamy. This constitutes the authentically religious element in marriage.[100]

Christian thought acknowledges individuality as having intrinsic worth. The acknowledgment of individual freedom as such is independent of contingent distinctions of sex, gender, natural differences, and so on. All of the latter, while important, must be subordinate to ethical considerations, and made instrumentalities and conditions of freedom. The ethical justification of marriage is monogamy, because only in monogamy does woman receive equal recognition and therefore equal right. If woman is just as much spirit as is man, this implies an acknowledgment, in principle, of women as subjects of individual freedom. It is ironic and unfortunate that Hegel failed to see that his ethical argument against polygamy applies to his own assertions concerning the unequal status of women in marriage in the *Philosophy of Right*.[101]

To be sure, Hegel's claim that woman is just as much *Geist* as is man is made in the context of his discussion of marriage. It does not directly address the question whether woman is capable of having a public vocation and development outside of the home, which Hegel denies, or at least does not support, with at least one notable exception, namely, Antigone. However, the text cited above is surely relevant to the issue. If woman is also *Geist*, then there is no reason in principle why she may not have a public vocation, even if Hegel seems to confine her ethical substantiality to the family in the *Philosophy of Right*.

Nevertheless, feminist criticism that Hegel's *Philosophy of Right* does not fully recognize women as human beings is, on Hegel's terms, legitimate. In his determinate analyses of family and gender, Hegel is inconsistent with his own

---

99. Ravven, "Has Hegel Anything to Say to Feminists?" 160.

100. *PR*, 1824/25, 447. Italics mine. Cf. *E*, §147 Zusatz.

101. Hegel is often attacked for confining women to the family and for consigning the family to the private realm, thereby removing it from political and ethical considerations. The fact that Hegel criticizes polygamy on ethical and political grounds confounds this line of attack. But his overlooking the inequality of women in his own discussion of family—itself a determinate form of reciprocal recognition—highlights Hegel's own inconsistency.

ontological conceptions of recognition and of objective spirit. However, such criticism appeals to the same ethical and intersubjective considerations concerning freedom as does Hegel himself in his ethical defense of monogamy. This criticism cites Hegel against Hegel; that is, it is an *immanent* criticism that is particularly instructive. Although it is devastating to Hegel's traditional conception of marriage, such criticism nevertheless confirms his fundamental position. The feminist demand for recognition is Hegelian in spirit, and this fact both reveals Hegel's inconsistency and makes evident the antisexist significance of Hegel's ontology of recognition. I shall return to these issues in the final chapter.

11

Civil Society, Poverty, and the Corporations

Hegel's term 'civil society' refers to the modern recognition of subjective freedom, specifically, the right of subjective freedom to find embodiment in the world in labor and property. This embodiment is not merely another interesting shape that freedom may assume; it is crucial to the satisfaction of the needs of that embodied freedom. The system of needs, including labor, property, and recognition, is an important, original aspect of Hegel's philosophical anthropology. Civil society is the sphere of individual freedom and is the concrete bearer and locus of abstract right.[1] The inclusion of civil society within Hegel's social and political philosophy is unique among his contemporaries, and it shows that Hegel accepts in part the capitalist economic system. However, Hegel's acceptance is qualified by the fact that he regards civil society as the external state, the state based on need (*Notstaat*), or the state as the understanding conceives it (*Verstandesstaat*). In light of this qualification, it is important not to confuse or identify the external state with the state as such, the state in the ethical and political sense. The external state makes the free pursuit of individual self-interest its fundamental principle and regards everything else as subservient and instrumental to private self-interest.

Shlomo Avineri has rightly pointed out that while Hegel may accept Adam Smith's model of the free market guided by an invisible hand, he does not accept the optimistic implications of this model.[2] Rather, like Marx, Hegel is sensitive to the dark side of capitalism, that is, its structural contradictions and its

1. *PR*, §§209ff.; cf. Riedel, *Between Tradition and Revolution*, 183.
2. Avineri, *HTMS*, 148.

tendencies toward monopoly and excess production and producing extremes of wealth and poverty.

Although for Hegel the term 'civil society' includes the external state, it designates something more: it also includes institutions that are supposed to be concerned for the welfare of individuals within the whole. Thus it is important to distinguish *within* civil society, between the *external state*, on the one hand, and *public authority* (*Polizei*) and the ethical *corporation*, on the other.[3] The latter institutions do not 'fit' the 'market model' of civil society, but are intended to mitigate its excesses and correct its defects. In such institutions, Hegel claims that civil society functions as a 'second family' that is supposed to be concerned with the welfare of individuals.

The ethical institution of the corporation has received relatively little attention; its implications for Hegel's argument have not been sufficiently considered or explored. This neglect has led Avineri, among others, to conclude that Hegel has no solution to the problem of poverty, which in Avineri's view remains one of the few unresolved problems in Hegel's thought.[4] In what follows I hope to mitigate Avineri's interpretation somewhat by examining how Hegel's concept of the corporation is supposed to provide some 'solution' to the problem of capitalist overproduction and the attendant problem of poverty.

Hegel's term 'corporation' does not have the contemporary sense of a purely business organization whose objective is profit. Rather it is a voluntary cooperative society, comprising both manufacturers and worker-tradesmen; it bears a resemblance to the medieval guild, organized around trade, professional interests, and grounds. Perhaps the term 'cooperative' rather than 'corporation' better captures what Hegel has in mind. For Hegel, the corporation is a mediating institution: "The mediating link is ethical, like the state. On the one hand it is concerned for the interest of the individuals in their particularity, but on the other hand, it has in common with the state, that the particular interest be intended and pursued as a universal end. This is the great organic member, with which we will become better acquainted in the constitution."[5] The corporation mediates between civil society's ethos of universal egoism and exploitation and the ethical state in which all are citizens. The corporation provides its members with a determinate form of recognition, namely, honor.

But before we can address the question of the corporation and honor as a potential solution to the problem of poverty, we must first address some preliminary issues. The first is civil society, which Hegel characterizes as ethical

3. Hegel observes that the term 'police' (*Polizei*) is derived from the Greek term *polis*. This gives it a much wider significance than law enforcement or crime prevention. Rather the police function is much broader, including many forms of public authority aiming at the general welfare and regulation of industry, environmental concerns, etc. In *PR*, §236 Zusatz, Hegel says "the police should provide for street-lighting, bridge-building, the pricing of daily necessities and public health." For this reason Hegel's *Polizei* is better translated as 'public authority' than as 'police'.

4. Wood does not fundamentally challenge Avineri's reading. See *HET*, 250.

5. *PR*, §251; *VPR4*, 620.

life in its disintegration. Second, we must consider labor and production, especially as Hegel portrays them under the conditions of modern civil society. Third, we shall examine the image of civil society as a machine and as a wild beast that requires taming. These reflect two interpretations of the external state or market system: an optimistic one in which the market is self-regulating and self-correcting and a pessimistic one in which unemployment and poverty are structural accompaniments of the inequalities produced and allowed by the market system. Hegel discerns the 'dark side' of the market, which is one reason why poverty becomes an issue in his thought. Next we shall consider the complex problem posed by poverty, not merely for civil society but for the poor themselves. Finally we shall consider the corporation as a second family, especially as it permits the problem of poverty to be analyzed in large part as a problem of recognition.

Civil Society as the Sphere of Disintegration and Difference

Hegel's logical method is to proceed from concepts that are abstract, simple, and immediate to concepts that are mediated and concrete. We saw this method at work in the consideration of abstract right, where ownership, the right of embodied freedom to presence in the world, is taken up in abstraction from and prior to the family. This method of abstraction is based in part on Hegel's logic and in part on his often-stated desire to see the truth—the whole— emerge as a mediated result.[6] While this method may have been intellectually satisfying to Hegel, it creates certain problems for his interpreters, particularly for those who seek to understand the *Philosophy of Right* as a phenomenology of intersubjectivity, a social phenomenology of social institutions. Above all it is crucial to avoid the fallacy of misplaced concreteness, of mistaking an abstraction for the whole. Hegel seeks to counter such a fallacy, but his efforts have not prevented some interpreters from falling into this trap. The categorical order is not necessarily the existential historical-temporal order. Hegel warns us that although property is treated before the family, it nevertheless does not in fact exist prior to the family, and that the family is its presupposition and condition.[7] Hegel writes, "This course followed by our exposition does not in the least mean that we would . . . explain the family and civil society to be antecedent to the state in the actual world. On the contrary, we are well aware that ethical life is the foundation of right and morality, as also that the family and civil society presuppose the existence of the state."[8]

Thus when Hegel maintains that civil society is the dissolution of ethical life, this is meant primarily in a logical sense, not in a chronological sense. It is true that particular families dissolve when their children are reared to indepen-

---

6. *PR*, §32.   7. Ibid.   8. *E*, §408 Zusatz.

dent adults and the parents die. But the dissolution of which Hegel intends to speak is a dissolution of a certain kind of unity, namely, immediate ethical unity represented by the family, and its replacement with another kind of unity, constituted by subjective freedom. In its initial stages, the unity of civil society is a disunity in which ethical life is 'lost in its extremes' of universality and particularity. That is, the immediate unity of ethical life is replaced in civil society with reflective separation and difference. However, civil society and family are not temporally successive phases but coexist in an unstable, uneasy relationship.

Hegel tells us that civil society, as the external relation of the extremes of individuality and universality, is the stage of *difference*: "The moments which are bound together in the unity of the family, as the ethical Idea which is still in its concept, must be released from the concept to attain self-sufficient reality. This is the stage of difference."[9] This difference has several important senses. First, it reflects the assertion of subjective freedom or self-sufficient particularity. This is a modern development. It was not recognized by classical political philosophy. Hegel believes that Plato could not

> come to terms with the principle of self-sufficient particularity, which had suddenly overtaken Greek ethical life in his time, except by setting up his purely substantial state in opposition to it and completely excluding it from his state, from its very beginnings in private property and the family to its subsequent development as the arbitrary will of individuals and their choice of social position. This deficiency explains why the great substantial truth of his *Republic* is imperfectly understood, and why it is usually regarded as the dream of abstract thought, as what is indeed often called an ideal.[10]

Plato's substantial social theory passed over or ignored the right of subjective freedom; consequently it overlooked or excluded the difference. In contrast, modernity asserts the right of individual subjectivity and subjective freedom. This right means that particular self-interest and particular subjective freedom are not unessential but an absolute moment of the social, such that "the universal does not attain fulfillment or validity without the interest, knowledge and volition of the particular."[11] The right of self-sufficient particularity means more than consent; it means that nothing must come to pass without individual subjective freedom and self-interest.

Second, difference is the principle of reflection. This means that everything that was previously immediate and traditional must become posited, that is, mediated through reflection. This indicates that the logical categories of essence correspond to and/or underlie Hegel's discussion of the external state. If everything must be posited, this means that all particular traditions must be translated into the form of universality: "To posit something as universal—i.e., to

9. *PR*, §§181–182.   10. Ibid., §185.   11. Ibid., §260.

bring it to consciousness as universal, is to think. . . . Only when it becomes law does what is right take on both the form of its universality and its true determinacy." [12] Thought exposes the contingency and arbitrariness of all merely traditional or natural arrangements and institutions. In being posited, everything is brought into the universal medium of reflection, that is, recognition.

> In civil society everything is reflected into other. What I am, I am not for myself but have my reality through another. I am not only naturally dependent on others [e.g., family], I also depend on their representation [*Vorstellung,* or *Anerkennung*] of me. . . . If the individual attains his end in civil society, it belongs to this end that he be recognized, and this being recognized [*Anerkanntsein*] is an essential moment of his reality.[13]

Everything is thereby found to stand in relation to everything else. Reflection purifies traditional conceptions and forms of recognition: "It is part of education, of thinking as consciousness of the individual in the form of universality that I am apprehended as a universal person in which all are identical. *A human being counts as such because he is a human being*, and not because he is a Jew, Catholic, Protestant, German, Italian, etc." [14]

The universality posited by reflection is a formal and abstract universality. This universality abstracts from difference and concrete particularity. It conceives not the actual person who happens to be German and Jewish, but only the universal person, the human being as such. This universal person, while important, remains abstract and formal. From the standpoint of the external state, the 'universal person' is a legal and a private person, free to pursue his own private self-interest without making the welfare of others his end. This universal person is an abstraction. This fact shows something important about civil society; namely, it is a series of incomplete mediations. Practically considered, these incomplete mediations amount to a complex set of ethical and social-political problems. Civil society as external state is not an ethical institution but ethically problematic.

Hegel gives perhaps the clearest introduction to the concept of civil society as the external state in his earliest lectures on the *Philosophy of Right* (*VPR*17); these are less analytically segmented than the published version.

> The more precise concrete determination of the universality in civil society is that the subsistence and welfare of individuals is conditioned by and interdependent with the subsistence and welfare of all other individuals. This communal system provides individuals with the framework of their existence and with security both externally and in regard to right. Civil society is in the first place the *external state* or the *state as the understanding takes it* [*Verstandesstaat*], because the universal as such is not an end in and for itself, but merely a means for the existence

12. Ibid., §211.   13. *VPR*19, 204.   14. *PR*, §209.

and preservation of individuals. This is the state based on need [*Notstaat*], because its main purpose is to secure the needs of individuals.[15]

Here burghers are *bourgeois*, not *citoyens*.[16] Individuals have their own welfare as their purpose, they are persons governed by right and the moment of right emerges in a universal form. But the individual's subsistence and welfare are conditioned by the welfare and preservation of all. Individuals care only for themselves, have only themselves as their purpose, but they cannot care for themselves without at the same time caring for all and without all caring for them. In pursing their own self-interest they at the same time work for the others.

Here everything, including all acquisition of property, depends on contract. Every product is the product of many others; every individual product that satisfies my needs, presupposes this chain of production. . . . This is the sphere of mediation; the individual's purpose also has universality as one of its aspects. *But we do not yet have life within the universal for the universal.* Rather the end is the subsistence and right of the individual. . . . The purpose of acquiring rights is to satisfy one's needs; the purpose of the state based on need is to secure and protect property. . . . *The state based on need is not an ethical state. . . . Consequently the universality that counts here is only abstract universality, a universality that is only a means. This is the state as the understanding envisages it* [*der Verstandesstaat*].[17]

The external state is the state based on need. Its end is to serve private self-interest; any connection of individuals with the universal is mediated by their self-interest. Consequently the universal here is not regarded as an end in itself; the universal is only a means to meeting needs and self-interest.

The unity of the external state is just this reciprocal self-interest taken as a system of universal relativity and exploitation: "The fact that I have to fit in with other people brings the form of universality into play at this point. I acquire my means of satisfaction from others and must accordingly accept their opinions. But at the same time I am compelled to produce means whereby others can be satisfied. Thus the one plays into the hands of the other and is connected with it. To this extent everything particular takes on a social character."[18] Thus "private persons, despite their self-seeking, find it necessary to have recourse to others. This is accordingly the root which links self-seeking with the universal."[19] Note that the other here is not affirmed for his own sake, but only because it is in someone's private self-interest to do so. In contrast, Hegel's corporation and ethical state will seek to correct the formal, abstract, and incomplete mediations of civil society, in which everything, even the universal, is a means to be exploited. Hegel's concept of corporation is an attempt

15. *VPR*17, §89. I have followed the English translation but have made slight alterations.
16. The distinction is between the person in his economic role (*bourgeois*) and his public role as citizen (*citoyen*). See *VPR*17, §72; see also English translation, p. 137n.
17. *VPR*17, §89. My italics.
18. *PR*, §192 Zusatz.   19. Ibid., §201 Zusatz.

to treat difference ethically by situating the 'universal person' within an inter-subjective, social-historical context in which life is 'within the universal and for the universal'.

In civil society, that is, the external state or the state based on need, human beings come together only under compulsion of necessity and are only su-perficially united in difference. Hegel observes that while the intersubjective mediation of freedom of one by another unites human beings immanently, "in contrast, need and want bring human beings together only externally." [20] That is, what unites people in civil society is simply the principle of individual self-interest. Civil society is universal egoism and reciprocal exploitation. This means that in the external state, persons are related to each other only in an ex-ternal and contingent manner. This strange relationship combines both free-dom ('free enterprise') and necessity (*Not*). In *VPR*19, Hegel put it this way:

> With civil society the principle of self-interest is posited. Each is his own end. Consequently these differences are at the same time identical. . . . The relation of individuals to each other is not a relation of freedom but of necessity. They are related to each other against their knowledge and their will. . . . As a particular, I have my own end and needs and am concerned only for myself. But I am not utterly isolated; I can satisfy my needs only in relation to others, who remain im-penetrable to me. This relation to other is a relation of necessity. I have to com-ply and conform, because I cannot satisfy my needs without the help of others. Thus I exist in dependence on others. This is the sphere of dependence and need. . . . Since I can satisfy my needs only through the will/cooperation of others, I am thus for the others; I must be what they want, and I must conform myself to their ideas. Thus I must in general depart from my idiosyncrasies and posit my-self in conformity and correspondence to them. I must give myself the form of universality, to make myself something [useful] for the others. [21]

Civil society tears individuals away from their natural families and compels them to become self-sufficient, but they can achieve economic self-sufficiency only by being useful. Unlike the family where individuals count for something immediately by virtue of who they are (father, daughter, etc.), in civil society individuals can expect to count and have their needs met only if they are useful to the system. Civil society is organized around the principles of mutual ex-ploitation and utility: the universal is what is useful. Everything, including hu-man beings, is valued because it is useful.

Self-sufficiency in civil society is far from genuine independence; it is rather a mode of relation that signifies a dependency: Civil society is the sphere of ar-bitrariness and contingency, "the sphere of need, since every individual is de-pendent on others." [22] Hegel observes, "If one calls this freedom, this is only partially correct; for it is freedom, but only the freedom of particularity. On the

20. *E*, §431 Zusatz.   21. *VPR*19, 147–148.   22. Ibid., 149.

other hand, we fail to understand that this freedom is at the same time the highest dependence. Necessity and freedom are here in battle against each other, and one always veers round into the other. Freedom becomes necessity and necessity becomes freedom. Particular self interest is a content, but not a [proper] content of freedom. This is not true freedom."[23]

Thus civil society, as the realm of difference in which particular and universal are divided into extremes, presents an *imperfect* or *inadequate mediation*. That is, difference, asserted without qualification, means that civil society is not a genuine society with an immanent cohesion of its own but an atomistic, externally related aggregate that is *geistlos*.[24] For this reason civil society tends to subvert itself: "Particularity in itself . . . indulging itself in all directions as it satisfies its needs, contingent arbitrariness and subjective caprice, destroys itself and its substantial concept in the act of enjoyment. . . . [C]ivil society affords a spectacle of extravagance and misery as well as of the physical and ethical corruption common to both."[25]

The imperfect mediation constitutive of civil society reflects the imperfect mediations of the categories of essence (*Wesenslogik*). Although universal and particular have fallen apart in civil society, they are nevertheless reciprocally bound up with each other and are reciprocally conditioned, although these connections and conditions are not always evident.[26] At the existential level of recognition, imperfect mediation means that persons remain unrelated in spite of their relation. Consequently in civil society recognition takes on a formal character.[27] In civil society people recognize each other, not as whole human beings, but only in their abstract formal capacities as owners of property, or as abstract laborers necessary for the mutual satisfaction of needs. The recognition found in the external state is thus humanly and intersubjectively deficient. This deficiency provides an important hint concerning the ethical function of the corporation; namely, it exists to counteract the merely formal instrumental and reductive types of recognition inherent in the external state and to provide a more substantive and ethical interpersonal recognition.

Need and Labor, Town and Country

We have seen that for Hegel ownership and property are part of a larger philosophical anthropology. In this context, need is a lack, a felt contradiction that spurs one to action: "all activity is founded on some need."[28] Property and ownership are institutions that are either direct or indirect means of satisfying needs. This fact is highly significant, for it means that for Hegel property is not an independent reality but relative to a larger human context. Ownership is

---

23. Ibid., 150. I have altered the order slightly.
24. *PR*, §156 Zusatz.   25. Ibid., §185.   26. Ibid., §184 Zusatz.
27. See Kolb, *Critique of Pure Modernity*, 27–28.
28. *VPR*17, §99.

necessary to secure freedom's right to be present in the world; labor and ownership are the presence of an embodied, indigent freedom in the world.

In abstract right, ownership or presencing of freedom is located 'within' individuals in the sense of abstract legal persons. However, we must recall that abstract right is a methodological individualism. In ethical life, Hegel removes the brackets of this abstract, methodological individualism and restores the intersubjective context and social-historical background. In reference to agrarian economy, Hegel maintains that the actual unit of ownership is not the individual but the family: "Abstract property contains the arbitrary moment of the particular need of the single individual; this is here transformed, along with the self-seeking of desire, into care and acquisition for a communal purpose, i.e., into an ethical quality. The introduction of permanent property appears in conjunction with the institution of marriage."[29] It is clear from this historical observation that Hegel is thinking of property not as a consumable item but as an enduring possession and resource; as such the institution of enduring property presupposes the institution of the family, wherein the property passes from one generation to another. Property thus loses the significance of being appropriated exclusively to a single individual—'mine'—and becomes instead a family resource. The recognition of ownership, which in abstract right was located in the abstract legal person, the singular universal, shifts to the recognition of the family and its resources.

Property is a resource held in common for meeting needs of the family, especially its children, even if it is managed for the family by the husband, father, and/or head of the household.

> The proper beginning and original foundation of states has rightly been equated with the introduction of agriculture and marriage. For the former principle brings with it the cultivation of the soil, and in consequence private property, and it reduces the nomadic life of savages . . . to the tranquillity of civil law and the secure satisfaction of needs. This is accompanied by the restriction of sexual love to marriage, and the marriage bond is in turn extended to become a lasting . . . union, while need becomes care for the family and possession becomes family property. Security, consolidation, lasting satisfaction of needs, etc.,—qualities by which these institutions primarily recommend themselves—are nothing but forms of universality and shapes assumed by rationality, the absolute and ultimate end.[30]

Hegel observes that the family is an institution essential to agriculture, and it is in the family unit that Hegel locates self-sufficiency. The farm family is self-subsistent and does not depend on the work and needs of everyone else.[31] Agriculture constitutes one of the divisions of labor and one of the estates that Hegel identifies in civil society. Unlike nomads, farmers are tied to the soil and

29. *PR*, §170.   30. Ibid., §203.   31. *VPR*17, §103.

to place. Those who farm regard themselves as dependent on nature, and their livelihood is not so much dependent on their own efforts as rather nature's gift. They take possession of the land and through their cultivation lay claims to ownership. Through such cultivation-ownership they enter into an enduring relationship with the land, from which they receive their subsistence as a gift. Owing to their dependence on nature, Hegel regards this class as the substantial class, whose mental orientation is characterized by an innocence and naïveté arising from a direct relation to nature and its bounty. Hegel believes that "this first estate will always retain the patriarchal way of life and the substantial disposition associated with it. . . . In this estate, the main role is played by nature, and human industry is subordinate to it." [32]

However, as we have seen, the rise of modern civil society dissolves the substantial unity of ethical life. This alters the agrarian way of life for masses of people. The relation of people to the world, their modes of ownership and possession, and their work all undergo transformation. "Civil society tears the individual away from family, alienates the members of the family from one another and recognizes them as self-sufficient individuals. Furthermore it substitutes its own soil for external inorganic nature and paternal soil from which the individual gained his livelihood, and subjects the existence of the whole family itself to dependence on civil society and to contingency." [33] Civil society alters the modes of acquisition and transfer of property: "The original, i.e., immediate, modes of acquisition and titles are in fact abandoned in civil society. . . . Property is accordingly based on contract and on those formalities that make it capable of proof and valid before the law." [34]

The relation of human beings to their world and to their resources undergoes a fundamental change, which affects the family. In the family, children have a claim on parental love and resources simply because they are, simply because they exist. However, in civil society this natural unity and communal property dissolve. Torn from the family, the existence and welfare of each individual depends on his own work and effort. These changes can be readily seen in Hegel's description of the rising bourgeoisie, or classes of trade and industry.

The class of trade and industry, or "town class," is different from the traditional agricultural class. In the town, one must earn one's livelihood by one's own efforts and labor; one must become self-sufficient. This class is described by Hegel as reflective, rather than substantial, because its aim is profit, which is abstract, rather than direct gratification. [35] This class has a much different orientation toward the world and nature. It regards nature as a natural resource, a raw material that must be exploited and transformed by labor. For such transformation to occur, labor becomes important, and mediation with others is

32. *PR*, §203 Zusatz.   33. Ibid., §238.   34. Ibid., §217.
35. *VPR*17, §104.

necessary. Further, the products produced by this class are not necessarily those that serve the immediate needs of the producer; the aim is to produce, not goods, but a profit from which one can supply one's own needs. This class does not regard its livelihood as a gift of nature, but as due to itself and its own activity.[36] "In this class of trade and industry, the individual has to rely on himself, and this feeling of selfhood is intimately connected with the demand for a condition in which right is upheld. The sense of freedom and order has therefore arisen mainly in towns. The first estate, on the other hand, owes little to its own efforts; what it gains is an alien gift, a gift of nature. This feeling of dependence is fundamental to it."[37] In contrast, the second estate or class seeks not to be thus dependent on nature,[38] but turns to labor and manufacture as sources of wealth. Even the farmer is drawn into the business ethos; farming is no longer self-subsistent, but becomes drawn into the interdependent web of civil society. Farm production is increased in order to make a profit from its surplus production in order to buy other needed products and services.[39]

It is in laboring that some of the most important changes occur. For in the external state, laboring no longer is connected with immediate satisfaction of need; rather it becomes abstract, specialized, and more productive. The abstract nature of labor means that it is no longer a particular action to acquire or produce something for immediate satisfaction. Rather, Hegel notes, labor becomes a "universal routine."[40] Labor is no longer the satisfaction of need, but a *means* to satisfy needs: "man no longer works up what he uses himself, or he no longer uses what he has worked up himself; that becomes only the *possibility* of his satisfaction instead of the actual satisfaction of his needs. His labor becomes a formally abstract universal. . . . [H]e limits himself to labor for one of his needs and exchanges it for whatever is necessary for his other needs. . . . The satisfaction of needs is a universal dependence of everyone upon one another."[41] Thus we have a paradox: as human beings become more self-reliant and specialized, at the same time they become increasingly dependent on others. This in turn exposes them to contingency. Their individual labor provides them only the *possibility* of satisfaction rather than satisfaction itself.

Labor itself undergoes change; it becomes more specialized: the division of labor increases, and specialization means that the production process is broken up into abstract, formal segments and movements. It becomes more and more machinelike.

In the machine man supersedes just this formal activity of his own and lets it do all the work for him. But this deceit that he practices against nature . . . takes its

36. *PR*, §204.   37. Ibid., Zusatz.   38. *VPR*17, §104.
39. Ibid.
40. *Philosophy of Spirit 1803/04, Hegel's System of Ethical Life and First Philosophy of Spirit*, 246.
41. *Philosophy of Spirit 1803/04*, 247. My italics.

revenge upon him; what he gains from nature and the more he subdues it, the lower he sinks himself. . . . The laboring that remains to man becomes itself more machinelike. . . . [T]he more machinelike labor becomes, the less it is worth, and the more one must work in that mode.[42]

The more specialized and machinelike laboring becomes, the more dependent it becomes on other 'parts of the machine' to be productive and to satisfy its needs. Hegel speaks about the machine state and workers as cogs in a machine, whose minds are "impoverished to the last extreme of dullness."[43] Note the type of recognition that this suggests: laborers, as cogs in the machine, are only externally related and intellectually humanly impoverished.

While modern labor is abstract, specialized, and machinelike, it is also more efficient and productive. But paradoxically, the more productive labor is, and the more goods it produces, the less value labor itself has: "In the same ratio that the number produced rises, the value of the labor falls."[44] This implies that excess production will create serious social and ethical problems. The inverse relationship between the productivity and value of labor leads Hegel to make a further observation about the external state: "Need and labor, elevated into this universality, form on their own account a monstrous system of community and mutual interdependence . . . *a life of the dead body*, that moves itself within itself, one which ebbs and flows in its motion blindly, like the elements, and which requires continual strict dominance and taming like a wild beast."[45] In the external 'machine' state, recognition is formal and mechanical. Individuals become alienated from it, owing to its destruction of traditional institutions and modes of production and exchange and to its cycles of prosperity and recession. Although civil society is an expression of economic freedom, it also wreaks havoc on human beings; Hegel portrays it as moving blindly like a wild beast that needs to be tamed.

Antinomies in Civil Society

Hegel is not an optimist concerning the traditional (Adam Smith) concept of capitalism or its real-world possibilities. To be sure, he accepts the general model of civil society whereby self-seeking pursuit of private interest can produce some contributions toward the general social welfare. He even reformulates Smith's concept of the invisible hand as a form of the cunning of reason. He sometimes makes it sound as if the market system is meeting all the needs it is supposed to: "This necessity which is inherent in the interlinked dependence of each on all now appears to each individual in the form of universal

42. Ibid.
43. Ibid., 248. For the machine state and cogs in machine image, see *Das älteste Systemprogramm des deutschen Idealismus*," cited by Avineri, *HTMS*, 11.
44. *Philosophy of Spirit 1803/04*, 248.
45. Ibid., 249. My italics.

and permanent resources in which, through his education and skill, he has an opportunity to share; he is thereby assured of his livelihood."[46]

Nevertheless, his characterization of civil society as a wild beast that requires strict dominance and constant taming[47] shows that Hegel is far from optimistic about the harmonious implications of the basic model.[48] The crux of the matter is this: for Hegel, civil society as traditionally conceived provides for the mere *possibility* for individuals to achieve economic freedom and satisfaction. "In the system of needs, the livelihood and welfare of each individual are a *possibility* whose actualization is conditioned by the individual's own arbitrary will and particular nature, as well as by the objective system of needs."[49] Whether individuals do in fact find freedom and satisfaction depends on a variety of other factors, including their own education, ability, and effort, and whether others allow them such freedom and satisfaction. This leaves open the possibility that the needs of some will not be met. From the perspective of the external state, this failure is socially acceptable. All that the external state needs to do is extend to all the *possibility* and *opportunity* of satisfaction of their needs. Whether needs are in fact satisfied is a separate question.

However, this answer is insufficient for Hegel. He believes that individuals have a right against civil society to freedom and welfare. After all, civil society has uprooted individuals from family and traditional agrarian independence and self-sufficiency and compelled them to adopt abstract labor in which they become dependent on and useful to its market system. Consequently Hegel believes that the possibilities and opportunities civil society affords them should not remain mere abstract possibilities. That would be tantamount to their needs never being met, and this would be a denial of their rights.

Previously in abstract right we saw that possession becomes property through intersubjective recognition. Ownership presupposes recognition. In civil society, matters are reversed: in the external state, ownership, resources, assets, and capital are *conditions* of the recognition afforded by civil society; that is, they become conditions of participation in the opportunities and possibilities presented by civil society. This raises the stakes and reveals the dark side of modern civil society.

46. *PR*, §199.

47. *Philosophy of Spirit 1803/04*, 249.

48. "Hegel's acceptance of Smith's 'hidden hand' does not entail following the optimistic and harmonistic implications of the model. . . . Hegel accepts Smith's view that behind the senseless and conflicting clash of egoistic interests in civil society a higher purpose can be discerned; but he does not agree with the hidden assumption which implies that everyone in society is thus being well taken care of." Avineri, *HTMS*, 148. For a view of Hegel as more optimistic and more of a complacent capitalist, see Bernard Cullen, *Hegel's Social and Political Thought* (New York: St. Martin's Press, 1979). Cullen believes that in the *Philosophy of Right*, Hegel attempts to set forth a harmonious political system that overcomes conflicts between individual and community, private interests and communal responsibilities (p. xii). See also p. 77. However, Cullen also acknowledges that Hegel's analysis of poverty constitutes an important exception within his overall analysis and tendency (ibid., 77 f., 85 ff.).

49. *PR*, §230. Cf. *VPR*19, 191. My italics.

Hegel believes that the external state produces inequalities of wealth and poverty: "civil society affords the spectacle of extravagance and misery as well as the physical and ethical corruption common to both."[50] Hegel observes that the possibility of participating and sharing in the resources made available by civil society "is *conditional* upon one's own immediate basic assets (i.e., capital) on the one hand, and upon one's skill on the other."[51] Thus the issue of property and ownership reappears, albeit in a different form. The possibility of participating in the opportunities made available by the external state is dependent not so much on land as on economic resources, assets, and capital. Such resources and assets become conditions of freedom's presence in the world.

In his discussion of ethical life, Hegel formulates a dialectical, self-reflexive proposition concerning rights. "The absolute right is the right to have rights."[52] This memorable sentence prompts a question: What is this absolute right and how is it secured? My proposal is that the absolute right is the right of recognition. Ever since the Jena manuscripts, Hegel grounds the concept of right in the intersubjective recognition of freedom. Freedom is the subjective basis and possibility of right, but freedom's right to presence in the world, in subjectivity, or in institutions is not objective until it is recognized. Recognition thus assumes paramount political significance.

However, in civil society, immediate ethical life including recognition, the right to have rights, disintegrates. Here the externality of relations affects everything, including recognition. What is recognized here is ownership and abstract labor. Consequently, property, resources, assets, and so on, become here both conditions and manifestations of bourgeois, economic freedom. This means that *in the external state, the "right to property is a right to right."*[53] In civil society, the 'right to right' is a right to property, assets, capital. At the same time we could with equal justice say that the right to work, to labor, is a right to right, for laboring is at once the production of and participation in the opportunities and resources that civil society makes available.[54] Consequently a person without such property, assets, or work is in trouble. Without recognition, rights, or resources, such a person would be excluded from civil society.

Does civil society generate others whom it excludes? This question must be answered in the affirmative. It is well known that civil society generates inequalities. Hegel believes that some inequalities are inevitable and defensible. But there are limits: "For while human beings are certainly equal, they are equal only as persons, that is, in relation to the source of their possessions. Ac-

50. *PR*, §185.
51. Ibid., §200. Italics in original.
52. *VPR*19, 127.
53. Hegel, *System of Ethical Life*, 118. My italics.
54. *PR*, §196: "The process of formation gives the means their value and appropriateness, so that man, as a consumer, is chiefly concerned with human products, and it is human effort that he consumes." Cf. §§197–198.

cordingly, everyone ought to have property. . . . In this context it is false to maintain that justice requires everyone's property to be equal; for it requires only that everyone should have property." [55]

The problem of inequalities reveals the limitations of civil society. Hegel believes that civil society, precisely because of its ethos of universal self-seeking and exploitation, generates a contrast between wealth and poverty and creates a group of people whose needs are not met. This is no accident because in civil society "each individual is his own end, and all else means nothing to him." [56] For this reason, civil society requires a public authority to see to it that the general welfare and individual needs are actually met. This responsibility falls to the police, or public authority, and the corporation. Civil society must oversee individual rights and welfare and make sure that the rights of freedom and satisfaction of needs are met as far as possible.

A question arises concerning the relation between the public authority's concern for the general welfare and welfare of individuals and the self-sufficient, self-seeking ethos of the external state. As a first approximation to an answer, Hegel believes both interests—individual freedom and public welfare—must be satisfied.

> Two main views are prevalent on this subject. One maintains that the public authority [police] should have oversight over everything, and the other maintains that the police should have no say in such matters since everyone will be guided in his actions by the needs of others. The individual must certainly have a right to earn his living in this way or that; but on the other hand, the public also has a right to expect that necessary tasks will be performed in the proper manner. Both viewpoints must be satisfied, and the freedom of trade should not be such as to prejudice the general good. [57]

Hegel believes that although public authority is not popular, it is nevertheless necessary.

> On the whole people are not well disposed towards public authority, but however unpopular it may be, it is all the more necessary. The system of needs continues to be strongly marked by contingency, which must be counteracted by means of something universal. . . . All citizens make their own welfare their sole end and rely on the universal connection [between their needs and those of others]. *But the universal must have itself for its purpose*, must become determinately existent as a universal. But each individual posits his own interest as the sole end and lets it stand opposed to the interest of another class; the *public authority then has to act as a moderating factor* and seek to maintain the equilibrium between all. [58]

Hegel agrees that public authority should not control everything because that would be equivalent to a police state. On the other hand, he believes that the

55. Ibid., §49 Zusatz.   56. Ibid., §182 Zusatz.   57. Ibid., §236 Zusatz.
58. *VPR*17, §117. My italics.

external state cannot remain external to everyone, and certainly not external to those whom it injures and deprives. In its role as the universal family, civil society must assume responsibility for the general welfare, including the welfare of those who are harmed by its own ethos and activity.[59]

Poverty:
Freedom and Recognition in Peril

Hegel does not maintain that poverty originates historically in modern civil society; his comments clearly show that the problem of poverty is older and wider than modern civil society. Nevertheless, if civil society does not create poverty for the first time, it exacerbates the problem for two related reasons. First, the external state, in tearing individuals away from the family and traditional modes of acquisition, does so in order that individual subjective freedom may be allowed to develop without restriction. Civil society, particularly in its town or city version, encourages self-sufficient individualism and the pursuit of private interests. Thus it spawns and legitimates an atomistic principle that abandons all individuals to contingency. "The atomistic principle—that each individual fends merely for himself and does not concern himself with a common social good—such an atomistic principle abandons the individual to contingency."[60] The atomistic principle thus legitimates and encourages the pursuit of self-interest at the expense of the common welfare and good. Those who succeed in promoting and furthering their private interests see themselves as reaping the rewards to which they are entitled, and have no reason to be concerned about the disadvantaged and the less fortunate: "The reflective standpoint of our time, this atomistic spirit, the spirit that places its honor in individual private interest and not in what is social and communal, is harmful."[61]

The second reason civil society exacerbates the problem of poverty has to do with the efficiencies and tremendous increases in quantity of production brought about by the division of labor and with abstract labor that allows itself to be replaced by a machine.[62] Hegel observes that "work becomes abstract, uniform and thus easier, since there is only one skill the individual learns, only one routine he practices, and so can acquire more efficiency at this single operation. . . . This is why factory workers become deadened and tied to their factory and dependent on it, since with this single aptitude they cannot earn a living anywhere else."[63] The other side of this terrible human cost is a tremen-

---

59. *PR*, §§238–239.　　　60. *VPR*17, §121.　　　61. Ibid.

62. Ibid., §101. "The preparation of specific means calls for a particular aptitude and familiarity, and individuals must confine themselves to only one of these. This gives rise to a division of labor, as a result of which labor becomes less concrete in character, becomes abstract, homogeneous and easier, so that a far greater quantity of products can be prepared in the same time. In the final stage of abstractness, the homogeneity of labor makes it mechanical, and it becomes possible to install machines instead of people."

63. Ibid. Hegel does hold out the hope that as automation increases, the mechanical displacement of human labor will be consummated, thus liberating human beings from abstract labor and restoring human freedom.

dous increase in efficiency of production of goods. This efficiency not only increases the quantity of goods, it also allows manufactured goods to undersell similar goods produced by traditional methods, thus putting artisans out of work. Fewer, less skilled laborers can produce goods in greater quantity and at a lower price.

However, the efficiency and increase of production creates a new problem, namely, surplus production. From one perspective, this surplus is what everyone wants; it represents additional profit and the ability to satisfy additional needs. But from another standpoint, the surplus is a problem, because it represents an excess of what can be consumed in a given domestic market. When a surplus of goods is produced, workers are laid off, creating unemployment, and pressures build for overseas colonial adventures to create external markets to accept the surplus production. This situation Hegel describes as the spectacle of extravagance and misery, and the attendant physical and ethical corruption that civil society exhibits.[64]

Hegel believes that the emergence of poverty is an inevitable accompaniment of civil society: "The origin of poverty is generally a consequence of civil society, and poverty in its totality arises necessarily out of civil society."[65] When wealth accumulates in one sector of society, poverty, need, and misery are created in another sector. As Avineri has pointed out, civil society is essentially a zero sum equation in which poverty in one sphere is the price that society pays for wealth in another.[66]

Poverty arises, not as an aberration of civil society, but when it functions as it is supposed to. On the one hand, "this inequality of wealth is absolutely necessary. . . . The urge to increase wealth is nothing but the necessity for carrying to infinity the specific individual thing which possession is."[67] On the other hand, "this inequality produces a relation of master and slave. The individual who is tremendously wealthy becomes a might. . . . [G]reat wealth . . . is bound up with the deepest poverty."[68] The inequalities of wealth and poverty produce a potentially antagonistic social situation and threaten a return to the life and death struggle that precedes master and slave. The external state tears apart families and ethical life and increases the contingencies and insecurities to which families and individuals are subject.

Since civil society tears individuals away from family and makes individuals dependent on it and subject to its contingencies, Hegel believes that civil society has responsibilities for and obligations to individuals: "The individual becomes a son of civil society, which has as many claims upon him as he has rights in relation to it."[69] Again, "Civil society . . . is the immense power which draws people to itself and requires them to work for it, to owe everything to it, and do everything by its means. Thus if a human being is to be a member of civil society, *he has rights and claims in relation to it*, just as he had in relation

---

64. *PR*, §185.   65. *VPR*19, 193.   66. Avineri, *HTMS*, 148.
67. Hegel, *System of Ethical Life*, 170.
68. Ibid.   69. *PR*, §239.

to his family. *Civil society must protect its members and defend their rights,* just as the individual owes a duty to the rights of society." [70]

In civil society ownership is the 'right to rights', including the right to recognition. However, the poor are deprived of property and the possibility of acquiring property in civil society. [71] This deprivation leads to others, including nonrecognition and marginalization.

> Not only arbitrariness, however, but also contingent physical factors and circumstances based on external conditions [§200] may reduce individuals to poverty. In this condition they are left with the needs of civil society, and yet—since civil society has at the same time taken from them the natural means of acquisition [§217] and also dissolves the bond of the family . . . [§181] they are more or less deprived of all the advantages of civil society, such as the ability to acquire skills and education . . . as well as the administration of justice, health care and often even the consolation of religion. [72]

Such deprivation not only threatens the possibility of their membership and inclusion in civil society, it also threatens to undermine their right to life. For life itself has needs, and property resources are among the most basic way of meeting life's needs; to be deprived of the resources to meet these needs is to be deprived of one's ultimate right to life itself, as Hegel observes.

> Individuals have to rely for their capital on the general resources. Their skill or work is not the only condition for them to be able to draw on these resources, for this requires skill, health and a certain capital. Now that states have recently entered the field of business and commerce, it has been said that this is no affair of the state, and, even if individuals are ruined, only raises the level of the whole. [However,] all people have the right to live, and not only must this right be protected, not only do they have this negative right, they also have a positive right. The aim of civil society is the actualization of freedom. The fact that human beings have the right to live means that they [must] have this right positively fulfilled. The reality of freedom should be essential. The life and subsistence of individuals are accordingly a universal concern. [73]

Hegel contends that since persons have a right to life, the rest of their rights should not remain mere possibilities, but at least some of them must be actual, that is, realized. The most basic of these rights are the right of ownership and the right to work, to be self-supporting. Denial of these rights undermines freedom's ability to be present in the world. Civil society summons up the figure of master and slave and renews the struggle for recognition.

Hegel's vision of civil society is tragic, because the very conditions neces-

---

70. Ibid., Zusatz. My italics.
71. *PR*, §217: Hegel observes that in civil society traditional immediate modes of acquisition of property—such as cultivation of a field generating an ownership claim—are abandoned and replaced by contract.
72. Ibid., §241.   73. *VPR17*, §118.

sary for the liberation and exercise of individual subjective freedom are at the same time conditions that generate conflict, economic insecurity, unemployment, and poverty. The ethos of civil society is that individuals must be self-supporting; their moral worth and claims to recognition flow from their labor and membership in a trade or corporation. But as we have seen, civil society, when it functions the way it is supposed to, generates unemployment and poverty that deprive some people of the very resources and opportunities they need to be self-supporting. To maintain its legitimacy, civil society must assume responsibility for its inevitable, if unintended, consequences. Hegel believes that "the whole community must therefore make provision for the poor, in regard both to what they lack and to the disposition of unemployment and malevolence that may result from their situation and the feeling of the injustice they have suffered."[74]

However, if the external state intervenes through its public authority to assure welfare for the poor, it seems to contradict its own ethos. Hegel formulates the basic contradiction of the external state in the following terms. To maintain the unemployed poor through the direct subsidy or welfare is to claim that "the livelihood of the needy would be ensured without the mediation of work; this would be contrary to the principle of civil society and the feeling of self-sufficiency and honor among its individual members."[75] Direct subsidies could lead to contempt and scorn for the ethos of self-sufficiency. When this happens the result is a penurious rabble. But putting people to work is no solution either: "their livelihood might be mediated by work (i.e., by the opportunity to work) which would increase the volume of production; but it is precisely in overproduction and the lack of a proportionate number of consumers who are themselves productive that constitutes the problem, and this is merely exacerbated by the two expedients in question. This shows that despite an excess of wealth, civil society is not wealthy enough . . . to prevent an excess of poverty and the formation of a rabble."[76] Subjective freedom, when it is not modified, mitigated, or subordinate to any higher intersubjective ethical principle, comes to realization in tragic conflict and is a tragic freedom.

Hegel's Portrait of Poverty

Hegel presents an important portrait of what has been called the "culture of poverty." In this portraiture he shows sensitivity for the plight of the poor and draws not only on his earlier analysis of mastery and servitude as unequal recognition, but also on his depiction of the servile consciousness as alienated from itself. In civil society, the poor are deprived of work and property and the resources to meet their needs. Since in civil society recognition is bound up with work and property, the poor are in effect denied recognition, and suffer

---

74. Ibid. I have altered the English translation.
75. *PR*, §245.   76. Ibid.

scorn and rejection. The denial of recognition and exclusion from civil society while living in the midst of it constitute a kind of spiritual death. The poor are pushed to the margins; they become invisible. Poverty deprives the poor of the resources and opportunities for significant participation in civil society as the following text from the 1817 lectures makes clear.

> In states where the poor are left to fend for themselves their situation may become miserable in the extreme. . . . It is not possible for them to obtain their right through formal justice—merely appearing in court—owing to the costs involved in the formal process of justice. They are at a great disadvantage in religion and justice, and also in medicine, because it is only from the goodness of their hearts that physicians attend them.[77]

From his 1819 lectures Hegel continues in a similar vein.

> The emergence of poverty is in general a consequence of civil society, and on the whole it arises necessarily out of it. . . . Poverty is a condition in civil society which is unhappy and forsaken on all sides. . . . The poor are for the most part deprived of the consolation of religion; they cannot visit church often, because they have no suitable clothing or must work on Sundays. Further they must participate in a worship which is chiefly designed for an educated audience. In contrast, Christ said that the gospel is preached for the poor. . . . Equally the administration of justice is often made very difficult for them. Their medical care is usually very bad. Even if they receive treatment for actual illnesses, they lack the means necessary for the preservation and care of their health.[78]

These similar remarks about the poor come from two different lecture series and from two different sets of student notes. Their similarity in spite of these differences supports the inference that Hegel indeed held these views, which go beyond the published official version of the *Philosophy of Right*.

Bad and challenging as these conditions of poverty are, they do not necessarily constitute what Hegel characterizes as the rabble, or *rabble mentality*. "Poverty in itself does not reduce people to a rabble; a rabble is created only by the disposition connected with poverty, that involves an inner rebellion against the rich, against society, the government, etc. Also bound up with poverty is the fact that those who are dependent on contingency tend to become frivolous, wanton and averse to work."[79] The latter indignation and rebellion, coupled with lack of responsibility toward society and toward oneself, is the rabble mentality. Hegel expands his analysis of the rabble mentality in his 1819 lectures.

77. *VPR*17, §118.
78. *VPR*19, 194–195. Cf. the English translation in *Hegel: Elements of the Philosophy of Right* (Cambridge: Cambridge University Press, 1991), 453.
79. *PR*, §244 Zusatz. In *PR*, §195, Hegel shows that cynicism has its social location in the extremes of wealth and poverty.

Poverty is not only indigence in externals, it is also joined to moral degradation. . . . The poor are subject to yet another cleavage [*Zweispalt*], namely a
cleavage of heart and mind [*Gemut*] between them and civil society. *The poor
man feels himself excluded and shunned, scorned, by everyone. This exclusion
necessarily gives rise to an inner indignation.* He is conscious of himself as infinite and free, and so there arises the demand that his determinate external existence should correspond to this consciousness [i.e., that the exclusion should be
overcome]. In civil society it is not a merely natural need and distress against
which the poor man must struggle [*kämpfen*]. The poor man is opposed not only
by nature, by mere being, but also by my will. The poor man feels as if he were
related to an arbitrary will, to human contingency, and in the last analysis what
makes him indignant is that he is put into this state of division through sheer arbitrariness. *Self-consciousness appears to be driven to the extreme point where it
no longer has any rights, and where freedom no longer has any determinate existence. In this situation, where the existence of freedom becomes something wholly
contingent, inner indignation is necessary. Because the individual's freedom has
no determinate existence, the recognition of universal freedom disappears.*[80]

The external state generates an other who is deprived of means and resources
requisite for inclusion and membership. Without property and resources, the
poor are not recognizable within the framework of the external state. Thus the
'universality' and 'universal categories' and forms of recognition of the external state turn out to be parochial and exclusive. The putative claim of universal
freedom and corresponding universal recognition turns out to be a cruel sham.
Deprived of resources and the recognition that attaches to such, the poor have
no determinate being or status in civil society. The recognition of universal
freedom disappears, or turns out to be freedom for a few, and the general *Anerkanntsein* is thereby undermined.

To be sure, the external state is supposed to provide opportunities to all in
principle, but the disappearance of the possibility of property and the opportunity to work from the situation of the poor means that their freedom no longer
can have any determinate existence in the world. Freedom that can have no determinate existence or embodiment in property and resources is freedom that
is denied. At the end of the spiritual cleavage that civil society produces between
rich and poor stands the disappearance of recognition and a return to the unequal, asymmetrical recognition of master and slave, domination and servitude.

However, when the situation of poverty becomes the occasion for the formation of the rabble and the rabble mentality, then even the asymmetrical mas-
ter/slave form of recognition—which, in comparison with the life and death
struggle for recognition, presents a certain structure and stability—falls apart.
Given some hope for recognition and improvement in their situation, the poor
may accept their poverty peaceably. But when this hope vanishes, the rabble

---

80. *VPR*19, 194–195. Italics mine.

mentality will not be so accepting of the situation. It is more likely that they will engage in struggles for recognition that undermine or call into question the legitimacy of civil society.

Hegel observes that "envy and hatred arise in the poor and are directed against those who have."[81] For although poverty is at one level inevitable given the structure and workings of civil society, this very structure is not a natural necessity but rather depends on human will, convention, and contrivance. When this point is understood, then poverty is experienced as due to faceless human arbitrariness and malevolence. Hegel tells us that "the poor man is opposed not only by nature, by mere being, but also by my will. The poor man feels as if he were related to an arbitrary will, to human contingency, and in the last analysis what makes him indignant is that he is put into this state of division through sheer arbitrariness."[82] Thus the wrong and injustice of poverty are not simply bad luck or bad breaks; they are ethical and political: "No one can assert a right against nature, but within the conditions of civil society hardship at once assumes the form of a wrong inflicted on this or that class."[83]

It would not be surprising that the poor do not recognize the legitimacy of the laws and rules of civil society. On the one hand, the poor do not have rights in civil society because recognition is a condition of having rights, and they are not recognized by that society. On the other hand, since the poor are not recognized by civil society, neither do they recognize the society that excludes them. Since the poor do not recognize its legitimacy or have any stake in it, they do not accept or have duties to civil society. They see themselves as victims of economic and social injustice and owe nothing to the system that exploits and deprives them. Thus they threaten the general *Anerkanntsein* and the social stability of the whole.

Taken to its extreme, poverty is a life-threatening situation. In view of this Hegel believes that the 'right of distress' or 'right of emergency' (*Notrecht*) can be invoked by the poor. "Earlier we considered the right of distress [*Notrecht*], which refers to a momentary transient need. *But in poverty need and distress lose their transitoriness and momentary character, i.e., they become permanent and structural.* In the emergence of poverty the power of particularity comes into opposition to the realm of freedom."[84] Hegel explains:

> Life, as the totality of ends, has a right in opposition to abstract right. If for example, life can be preserved by stealing a loaf, this certainly constitutes an infringement of someone's property, but it would be wrong to regard such an action as a common theft. If someone whose life is in danger were not allowed to take measures to save himself, he would be destined to forfeit all his rights; and since he would be deprived of life, his entire freedom would be negated. . . . But the only thing necessary is to live *now*; the future is not absolute, and it remains exposed to contingency.[85]

81. Ibid., 196.   82. Ibid., 194–195.   83. *PR*, §244 Zusatz.
84. Ibid. My italics.   85. *PR*, §127 Zusatz.

In *VPR*17, Hegel gives the *Notrecht* increased urgency: "Where life is endangered, it claims a right of distress. The danger of infinite injury is the danger of a complete loss of right. In the face of this loss of right, *right as such disappears.* . . . In relation to the absolute claim to freedom and to life itself on the part of each human being, the particularity of other's rights disappears."[86]

Poverty raises the issue of a *permanent* right of need or distress that, in Hegel's view, overrides the right to property, which is the 'right to right' within the external state. Here is a truly tragic collision of rights and a revolutionary situation. The poor man has a justified sense of anger and frustration over his situation. "He is conscious of himself as an infinite free being, and thus arises the demand that his external existence correspond to this consciousness."[87]

Hegel suggests that poverty is a crime inflicted by civil society itself on its poor, namely, the wrong of exclusion. The extremes of wealth and poverty constitute a collision between civil society's principle of universal recognition and its nonrecognition and exclusion of the poor. Poverty resembles crime in being an infinite negative judgment. But who does the dividing and excluding? Hegel has referred to the poor as naive and innocent. This suggests that he regards the criminal or transgressor in this case as civil society itself. Civil society is the one who excludes and refuses to recognize those whom it forces to be self-sufficient while depriving them of the opportunities and/or conditions necessary to be self-sufficient. John McCumber is correct in finding in Hegel's thought an indictment of the state.[88] This assertion requires only the qualification that the state Hegel indicts is not the ethical state per se but, as dominated by civil society, the external state.

Recognition, Honor, and the Corporation

The preceding analysis of civil society focused on the external state, or system of needs. We recall that, for Hegel, needs bring human beings together only in an external way. In civil society mutual recognition is external. What is recognized here is ownership. But self-sufficient particularity is interested primarily in itself, and regards everything else as nothing. Self-sufficient particularity believes that it needs no recognition, or only a minimal formal abstract recognition like ownership. The external state is an aggregate of mutual exploitation and instrumentality. Difference and externality, taken to their conclusion, end up denying and defying human interdependence. Thus the external state ends up subverting itself by necessarily generating an other, in this case the poor, whom it excludes, and who, when they fall into the rabble mentality, regard civil society as illegitimate.

86. *VPR*17, §63. I have altered the English translation slightly. My italics.
87. *VPR*19, 195.
88. John McCumber, "Contradiction and Resolution in the State: Hegel's Covert View," *Clio* 15, no. 4 (1986): 379–390.

This analysis of the external state points to the need of mediation and mediating institutions, even within civil society. It is important to have an ethical dimension within civil society itself that challenges the sheer externality and exploitation that are its ethos. Hegel observes that modernity, in seeking political equality, overlooks the need for mediating structures and institutions.

> In modern times people have been concerned to consider the state, to determine how it should be organized and governed. They have so to speak, sought to build the upper floors, but have neglected or demolished the foundations of *marriage* and the *corporation*. But an organization cannot hang in the air. The ethical must exist not only in the form of universality of the state, but also essentially in the form of particularity.[89]

Civil society's ethos of atomistic individualism is the problem beneath the economic problems of overproduction and unemployment. Hegel's proposal is to place ethical constraints on such individualism and on its unrestricted labor and production. For it is not production but surplus production that creates poverty and unemployment and the conditions for the rabble mentality. Hegel believes that a mediating institution like the corporation is needed because the ethical must exist not only in the universal form of the state but also in the form of particularity, that is, within civil society itself. For this reason civil society is for Hegel more than a pure economic market 'mechanism'. It must also include mediating ethical institutions, namely, the family and the corporation: "the sanctity of marriage and the honor attaching to membership in a corporation are the two moments around which the disorganization of civil society revolves."[90] That is, "if marriage is [easily] susceptible to divorce, and the second ethical totality—the corporation—is lacking, then the state is disorganized."[91]

A major part of the social disorganization of which Hegel speaks is the atomism that accepts the extremes of wealth and poverty and the creation of the rabble and rabble mentality. "The atomistic principle—that each individual fends merely for himself and does not concern himself with the common social good . . . abandons the individual to contingency."[92] The atomistic principle thus legitimates and encourages the pursuit of self-interest at the expense of the common welfare and good. Some historical examples may clarify the point. Hegel refers to England, which was in his day one of the most advanced industrial nations. In spite of its wealth, England also had some of the worst poverty and some of the most alienated rabble. How can this apparent incongruity be understood? Hegel believes that England was dominated by the atomistic spirit of self-sufficient individualism and that this spirit brought about the

---

89. *VPR4*, 628. My italics.
90. *PR*, §255.
91. *VPR3*, 714–715. This is another case in which Gans's Zusatz distorts Hegel's meaning, as found in Hotho's lecture transcript from which the Zusatz was constructed.
92. *VPR17*, §121.

downfall of the corporations and the decline of social cohesion and esprit de corps. He writes, "In England there is also the most monstrous poverty and rabble mentality [*Pöbelhaftigkeit*], and a good deal of this cancer is due to the dissolution of the *corporations*." [93]

In addition, Hegel attributes the decline of Germany to the dissolution and demise of the corporations brought about by the atomistic spirit. "Through this spirit Germany disintegrated into atoms and . . . went into decline." [94] Hegel regards this atomistic spirit and principle as "the spirit of barbarism." [95] He contrasts it with a picture of the Hanseatic league and the Swabian league as representing the "high tide of civil life": "In the towns all the trades were . . . also corporations, and we had the *esprit de corps* of the guilds. This was the high tide of civil life; enjoyment lay in what was communal, and people did not amuse themselves for themselves but in the community. Now this spirit is undermined, so that people . . . take pride in themselves alone." [96]

These remarks suggest that for Hegel there is a connection between poverty, the formation of a rabble and rabble mentality, and the spirit of atomism that brought about the decline of corporations and communal life. I should like to explore this connection in reverse, as it were, by examining a suggestion by Stephen Houlgate that Hegel's concept of the corporation is an important part of Hegel's response to, even solution of, the problem of poverty. [97] Houlgate has two claims: (1) that the corporation is a mediating institution that effects an ethical transformation of the self-sufficient, self-seeking mentality of the external state, and (2) that the corporation has an important socioeconomic regulative function that can restrain excess production (which for Hegel is the genesis of the problem of poverty). My concern here is primarily with the first claim, because it is of most direct relevance to recognition.

It should be noted that Houlgate's is a minority view. Avineri states what is currently the majority view; he believes that Hegel sees the inevitability of poverty and the creation of a rabble but fails to propose any solution to these problems. [98] The most recent study by Allen Wood comes to a similar conclusion. [99] But Avineri does not consider Hegel's concept of the corporation or the recognition it affords as these bear on this issue. Avineri ignores Hegel's own suggestions along these lines. [100] Wood rejects Houlgate's proposal on historical and practical grounds. [101] But Wood fails to address the underlying issue

93. *VPR*3, 711. My italics.
94. *VPR*17, §121.   95. Ibid.   96. Ibid.
97. Houlgate, *Freedom, Truth and History*, 104–119.
98. Avineri, *HTMS*, 153–154.
99. Wood, *HET*, 250.   100. *PR*, §253.
101. See the symposium on Wood's *Hegel's Ethical Thought*, *Bulletin of the Hegel Society of Great Britain*, no. 25 (Spring/Summer 1992): 1–50; see esp. pp. 46–48. Wood claims that the corporations are no solution. But he discusses the corporations only in a historically anachronistic sense, rather than seeing them as mediating institutions. He agrees with Cullen in pointing out the problems with Hegel's own particular view of the corporation but passes over the larger systematic ethical point about the necessity for mediating institutions. Wood and Cullen may be right about

raised by poverty, which is the need for a mediating social and ethical structure. The corporation as Hegel envisages it may or may not fulfill this mediating role, but the most important part of Hegel's argument is his diagnosis of the need for a mediating institution to overcome the atomistic disintegration and self-subversion of the external state.

What follows is a reconstruction of Hegel's thought that focuses on two types of mutual recognition, namely, the external recognition of civil society and mutual recognition or honor, which is conferred by one's estate or corporation. Hegel contends that the recognition accorded by civil society is itself external and formal. This sort of recognition constitutes the atomistic ethos of civil society, that is, universal egoism and exploitation. Such egoism and exploitative attitudes and behaviors are factors that lead to overproduction. In contrast, the honor of one's estate or corporation is not simply external and formal. Honor goes deeper than that, affecting the individual in a socioethical sense. Honor might produce a different social self-identity and help to curtail exploitative behavior. For these reasons Hegel believes the corporation to be capable of providing an antidote to and a possible amelioration of the rabble mentality, if not the causes of poverty itself. Recall that for Hegel "poverty in itself does not reduce people to a rabble; a rabble is created only by the disposition connected with poverty, that involves an inner rebellion against the rich, against society, the government, etc." [102] Honor in one's estate speaks to this issue of the disposition connected with poverty.

To begin, civil society should not stand by idly as the poor slide into poverty. The danger is that a vociferous rabble might be created that neither is recognized by nor recognizes the general *Anerkanntsein*, and that questions its legitimacy. Hegel believes that civil society should "prevent a rabble from emerging." [103] The atomistic ethos of self-seeking exploitative particularity must be overcome in order for poverty to be acknowledged as a problem. After all, this atomistic spirit is itself an abstraction from and a suspension of the intersubjective and social. The atomistic spirit views self-interest as the highest interest; nothing else matters. Consequently, such an ethos is also blind to and fails to recognize the poor as the victims and casualties of its own success. This atomistic ethos fails to appreciate that "a human being cannot be an absolutely private person." [104] It sees no need for mediating ethical institutions like corporations. The atomistic 'suspension of the other' needs to be suspended.

Second, we recall that, according to Hegel's analysis, the problem of pov-

---

the specifics of Hegel's views concerning corporations—although I am not persuaded that Hegel's views need be interpreted so narrowly. But even if we grant their criticisms, the systematic problem is not addressed by such criticisms, and Hegel is correct about the need for a mediating institution of some sort, i.e., for the ethical to be present within the realm of particularity that civil society is. Neither Wood nor Cullen addresses that issue, thereby allowing to stand the alternatives that Hegel seeks rightly to avoid.

102. *PR*, §244 Zusatz.   103. Ibid., §240 Zusatz.   104. *VPR*19, 206.

erty is a result of excess production. That is why he argues that putting the poor to work merely exacerbates the problem. Third, Hegel explicitly links the atomistic ethos of civil society with overproduction. He believes there is a connection between being without the honor of an estate (corporation) and the tendencies toward overproduction that generate the dangerous inequalities, including the poverty, of the external state: "If the individual is not a member of a legally recognized corporation . . . he is without the honor of belonging to an estate. His isolation reduces him to the selfish aspect of his trade, and his livelihood and satisfaction lack stability. He will accordingly try to gain recognition through the external manifestations of success in his trade, and these are without limit."[105] Deprived of the honor that corporations provide, individuals are deprived of any larger social significance beside themselves. The atomistic spirit of self-sufficient individualism neither fulfills nor does away with the fundamental need for recognition; it merely perverts that need into the external manifestations of conspicuous production and excessive consumption. This reduces the individual to the selfish aspect of his trade, which lacks stability. This prompts him to gain recognition through external manifestations of success, and these are without limit. This removal of limits and constraints leads to unrestricted economic activity, which leads to excess production, and that in turn generates the antinomy of extravagance and misery.[106] Without the restraint that corporate honor may provide, the self-seeking individual creates or exacerbates the disparity between wealth and poverty in civil society. It is this very disparity that constitutes "the ruin of civil society."[107]

For Hegel, the corporation is necessary to counter the reduction of individuals to the merely self-seeking dimensions of their profession. We have already seen that the corporation is supposed to be a mediating social and economic institution, which looks after its members' interests and educates and admits members according to their skills and in appropriate numbers. For example, in *VPR*17 Hegel gives some hints that the corporations can control and restrict the number of workers in a given trade or field. He refers to the emergence of the guilds as preventing "excessive competition."[108] Further, the corporation looks after and protects its members against contingencies, including the contingency of unemployment; that is, it provides a kind of insurance. Most important for our purposes is the fact that the corporation is a mode of recognition. The corporation also provides an important sort of recognition to its members, namely, the honor of an estate.

Honor is a form of recognition different from that afforded by the external state. Honor is directed to the human being as a totality, which is more than an owner, producer, taxpayer, or consumer. For Hegel, the corporation is a second family through which individuals receive education, admission, recognition,

---

105. *PR*, §253.   106. Ibid., §§243, 185.   107. *VPR*19, 196.
108. *VPR*17, §104.

and honor.[109] The term 'honor' may sound quaint and innocent to us today. Hegel is fully aware that honor can be problematic; in fact some of his versions of the struggle for recognition are battles over family honor that cover not only family members but also family property.[110]

Nevertheless, Hegel takes honor seriously, and so should we. Specifically, honor is a particular shape and instance of mutual-reciprocal recognition. Hegel points out that the modern concept of honor differs from the ancient concept. Ancient honor was immediate: one was immediately honored for the sake of his wealth, deeds, and general manner. However, in civil society one is honored not immediately but mediately; one is honored not for who or what one is but for what one does. "Honor is a concept that differs in the modern world from that in the ancient. That the individual attains his purpose in civil society includes and requires that he be recognized, and this being-recognized [*Anerkanntsein*] is an essential element of his reality. What someone is and is supposed to be in civil society is not a matter for immediate determination. . . . Honor . . . comes from mediation."[111]

In honor individual singularity is recognized as universal. Honor regards and 'saves' the particularity of the subject by discerning in it something of universal importance and worth and by acknowledging the contributions of the individual to the community as a whole.[112] Hegel claims that it is through the honor of one's estate that the abstract legal person becomes *somebody*, that is, achieves a determinate social status and function. Being-recognized (*Anerkanntsein*) as a member of a corporation means that "the member . . . has no need to demonstrate his competence, . . . the fact that he is *somebody*. . . . In this way, it is also recognized that he belongs to a whole which is itself a member of society in general, and that he has an interest in, and endeavors to promote the less selfish end of this whole. Thus he has *his honor in his estate*."[113] In this way the individual takes on a corporate, shared identity; he counts as something and "gains recognition both in his own eyes and the eyes of others."[114]

Recognition in the determinate mode of honor is the medium wherein the individual is raised to universality.

> Honor is now a reflex of education [*Bildung*], that I am recognized and that in the particular relations of individuals to each other this recognition is expressed. *In this I treat the individual in all his particularity not as a mere particular, but as a universal.* This is the peculiarly modern element of honor. . . . The basis of this relationship is the higher element that I relate myself to particulars as a uni-

---

109. *PR*, §252.
110. See the Jena *Philosophy of Spirit 1803/04*: "The injuring of any one of his single aspects is therefore infinite, it is an absolute offense, an offense against his integrity, an offense to his honor; and the collision about any single point is a struggle for the whole" (p. 236).
111. *VPR*19, 204–205.   112. Ibid., 241.   113. *PR*, §253.
114. *VPR*17, §107.

versal. . . . In abstract right the individual is only an abstract person; in civil society on the contrary the individual is somebody who belongs to a particular association.[115]

In civil society, recognition and honor—being treated as a universal-individual worthy of respect—come to one (if at all) primarily insofar as one is a member of a corporation. The individual by himself is empty, formal, indeterminate, lacking substance or purpose. He must be *something* [*etwas*], and becomes something by entering a vocation, trade, field, occupation, or corporation. Then he attains ethical substance, a consciousness of rectitude as a member of a corporation.[116] In participating in its *esprit de corps*, the individual is a "useful moment for the universal";[117] that is, he now has a cause larger than himself, namely, the welfare of the cooperative, and through it, the welfare of the state as a whole.

In Hegel's view, being without honor of an estate is what produces the rabble mentality.[118] Hegel writes, "On the side of poverty there lies a rabble mentality, the non-recognition of right."[119] It is no small matter to be excluded from the universal modes of recognition in civil society. It is to be isolated and without the honor and support of others. Honor is an important element in being something, being somebody. Hence to be deprived of honor is to have a deficient self-identity. But beyond nonrecognition and marginalization, the poor must also contend with derision, scorn, and rejection, all of which involve moral degradation. Moral degradation in turn is evident in the shamelessness exhibited by the rabble themselves.[120]

Note that being without honor is not just a problem for the poor; it is a problem for everyone in the external state, including the affluent. Hegel observes that being without honor and shameless is not limited to the poor and that wealth can also lead to a rabble mentality. The rich person believes that he can buy anything, that everything is for sale as a commodity. He knows himself to be the power of the particularity of self-consciousness, the absolute power over the slave: "However . . . the master knows himself as master over another's freedom. . . . Here we have bad conscience, not only as inner, but as a reality that is recognized."[121] Further, the master does not consider himself as belonging to an estate or corporation in Hegel's sense, for he is above these. He sees nothing to be gained from such membership, but only losses and unprofitable compromises.

Moreover, there is a connection between the deficient external recognition constitutive of the atomistic external state and the belief that civil society should provide only the *possibility* or opportunity to satisfy needs and not the *actual-*

---

115. *VPR*19, 205. My italics.
116. *PR*, §207.   117. *VPR*17, §107.   118. *PR*, §244.
119. *VPR*19, 196.   120. Ibid., 194.   121. Ibid., 196.

ity of such satisfaction. So long as civil society needs to provide only the possibility of satisfaction, unemployment and poverty will not be perceived as social problems to which all have contributed and for which all are responsible. Instead the poor will be regarded as not having worked hard enough, or as not being smart enough to have taken advantage of the possibilities that are allegedly extended to them. That is, civil society will remain trapped within the complacency of its atomistic, deficient, and external recognition.

Hegel believes that the corporations can restrain and transform the ethos of self-seeking particularity into the pursuit of universal-social-ethical ends. The corporation as a mediating institution constitutes the ethical moment within civil society itself.

> *The interest of particularity is not supposed to be self-seeking; rather the interest of particularity is supposed to be a secured interest, something that is universally valid and an objective end in itself.* What concerns the securing of subsistence such that it is not abandoned to contingency, seems to be the concern of the public authority. But as we have seen, the public authorities are concerned only with the universal as such. Insofar as it is particularity itself that must be looked after, this requires a particular interest, knowledge and insight. Only those who live in such particular communities can undertake to be concerned for them. Only those who are familiar with, know and desire this particular [community] are the ones who are properly concerned with such particularity in its entire scope and compass. *Thus in the corporation's concern for particularity the ethical element returns in civil society. Those who are interested in and concerned with particularity are no longer concerned with themselves as individuals. Here arises the concept of a cooperative [Genossenschaft] Korporation, and this is the second level [Stufe] of ethical life.* The family is the first level [Stufe] [of ethical life] in substantial form. *The corporation is likewise an ethical society, but one that is unlike the family in that it no longer has nature and natural relations for its basis. The members of a cooperative exist in and through it. On the one hand they are active for themselves, and on the other hand they promote and further in their end and intention a universal, namely the cooperative itself.*[122]

The corporation supplements public authority (*Polizei*). Like the family, the corporation is concerned about its individual members. The members of a cooperative have a mutual stake in its existence and in helping each other. On the one hand, they are active for their own ends, and on the other, they promote and further ends that are universal-social, namely, the cooperative itself.

In this way corporations not only represent the ethical moment of civil society, they also can work to restrain private self-seeking that exacerbates the generation of extremes of wealth and poverty. By honoring individuals and giving them a larger common end to work for, they can curb and redirect at least some of the forces leading to overproduction and poverty. In this way the corpora-

---

122. Ibid., 201–202; cf. *PR*, §255. My italics.

tions can ameliorate and prevent not unemployment and poverty per se but the formation of a rabble.

In the case of the poor, Hegel believes the corporation has an important role to play. Hegel writes that "within the corporation, the help which poverty receives loses its contingent and unjustly humiliating character, and wealth, in fulfilling the duty it owes the association, loses the ability to provoke arrogance in its possessor and envy in others; rectitude also receives the true recognition and honor which are due it."[123] The corporation may assist unemployed and poor members in an economic way, by transfer of means from rich to poor, that is, act as insurance. Further, the corporation may prevent the hopelessness that nonrecognition and exclusion from civil society entail and that leads to the rabble mentality.

Membership in a corporation also might affect the 'rabble mentality' of the wealthy. This mentality acts and thinks that everything is for sale and seeks recognition through conspicuous consumption. If such a mentality were to become a member of a corporation in Hegel's sense, it would learn that

> a human being cannot be an absolutely private person. He becomes something substantial and essential only if he has a universal end. If individuals are reduced to living as particulars, they must necessarily strive to become recognized in their special activity by others. First they decline into pleasure seeking, and then they must put on an external show. This leads to luxury and excess in the trade which is a necessary consequence of the fact that they lack an ethical engagement with something universal.
>
> But in the corporation the individual has his true consciousness and here he has a genuine noble opportunity to acquire honor. In the corporation the corruption of wealth is set aside. . . . In the corporation wealth is no longer an end in itself. He has duties in this circle. . . . Here he becomes something through the way he applies his wealth for the sake of his cooperative association.[124]

The corporation presents the affluent individual with an ethical task, something for him and his wealth to do, that is more than self-seeking and self-glorification through conspicuous consumption. Now he works for a universal-ethical end, the good of the cooperative. This in turn brings the welfare of others into view and reveals their unemployment and poverty to be intolerable wrongs and not simply unfortunate but inevitable byproducts of the allegedly neutral market system. Honor in one's estate transforms atomistic self-seeking. The member of the corporation will seek his own good (end) only insofar as it is consistent with the good and welfare of others, that is, at least other members of his corporation. This could mean a self-imposed restraint of affluence and transformation of self-seeking consumption into concern for the common good. Thus corporations could restrict their production and consumption to appro-

123. *PR*, §253.   124. *VPR*19, 206–207.

priate rather than the excessive levels that generate extravagance and misery.

Note that the corporations are not yet the state; they are private voluntary organizations, and as such are self-limiting and self-regulating. In this sense the corporations are limiting and controlling factors present or immanent in civil society itself. They do not represent an external intervention in the 'pure economic system'. Rather corporations represent a turn toward ethical considerations that originates in the contradictions inherent in civil society itself, namely, its self-subverting atomism and its tendency to generate extremes of wealth and poverty.[125]

Hegel's argument for the corporation targets and aims at correcting civil society's ethos of self-seeking, self-sufficient individualism. However, it must be conceded that Hegel's discussion of corporations, and of the relation of state to civil society, owing to its linear categorical structure, does not clarify the interaction between these institutions.[126] His method mitigates against the

---

125. David Kolb passes over these problems when he writes, "It may be true that viewed from outside with an eye to totality and harmony, the state 'should' be there to contain the excesses of civil society and its harmful effects on human identity. But these are not problems from within civil society. They are simply effects. It is not easy to show that civil society fails by its own standards in any way that demands a transition to the state. Civil society succeeds: it allows the sway of particular interests, it generates wealth, it protects freedom. To ask more is to place external demands upon it" (*Critique of Pure Modernity*, 112). Note that Kolb identifies civil society in a minimalist sense as a market economy and administration of justice that enforces contracts, and so on. He believes that civil society is self-sufficient and succeeds on its own terms. However, in reaching this judgment he does not engage Hegel's point that civil society, understood simply as a market economy, merely holds out the *possibility* of satisfaction of needs, not the actual satisfaction of needs. Nor does he take up Hegel's analysis of poverty and the rabble mentality. Kolb's understanding of civil society is much narrower and appears to be more complacent than Hegel's.

126. Klaus Hartmann and David Kolb make this criticism. Kolb notes, "In his concern that civil society cannot be taken as an adequate theory of the social whole, Hegel has neglected to describe the more complex social totality he proposes. We get an economic discussion of civil society and a political discussion of the state, but not enough to see how state and civil society are to interact. The logical sequence does underlie the crucial moves" (*Critique of Pure Modernity*, 111). Hartmann points out that a categorical theory such as Hegel's involves a critique of nominalism—the atomistic individual ethos of civil society. He further notes that categorical theory such as Hegel's provides reasons for distinguishing between civil society and state, because the two are ontologically distinct as diremption and as affirmative unity. Hartmann fails to deal with the corporation as an affirmative ethical moment of unity arising within civil society itself. However, he offers the following criticism of Hegel's method: owing to the categorical linearity of his social theory, Hegel does not address in detail the interactions between corporations and civil society, or between state and civil society. He adds, "Our point is not that Hegel fails to discuss welfare, private and public poor relief, etc. He does this in the section on civil society within the context of his discussion of the state based on need, disregarding the political state as coming later in his linear scheme. What has to remain an open question in Hegel is whether the societal functions mentioned would, after his concrete exposition of the state, be left in the hands of society." (Hartmann, "Towards a Systematic Reading of Hegel's *Philosophy of Right*," 132–133.) Hartmann acknowledges that Hegel discusses interaction between civil society and state, but only in the context of his treatment of war and international relations, not in the context of interactions between economics and politics.

development of more specific and determinate proposals. Moreover, it is not clear how the corporation might have an impact on other factors, economic and extraeconomic, for example, the efficiency of industrial production itself that may be a contributing factor to overproduction, or the problems of over-population in a world of finite and diminishing resources. But while these problems undoubtedly complicate matters, they do not necessarily invalidate the general thrust of Hegel's proposal concerning the need for mediating ethical institutions. On the contrary, they make them all the more important and urgent.

Civil society's modes of production are for the most part human arrangements. Thus mediation is already in play in civil society, but it is incomplete partial mediation. That is why civil society is ethical life in disintegration. Such disintegration is evident in the problem of poverty, which is an unavoidable, ethical issue: "No one can assert a right against nature, but within the condition of society hardship immediately assumes the form of a wrong inflicted on this or that class." [127] Civil society's advocates of "pure economics," of letting "the market" solve the problem of poverty, are not only incoherent—for there is no pure economics "outside" of society and human choices—but also unethical because there is no market solution to this problem. The market economy, functioning as it is supposed to, generates the problem, that is, the disintegration.

This incomplete disintegrating mediation points to a need for a further corrective mediation, in which the negations produced by civil society are themselves negated. As Hartmann puts it, "There is no getting around Hegel's distinction between [civil] society and state and his claim that [civil] society be included in the state . . . otherwise [civil] society would sit in judgment over matters of universal relevance and deliver them up to particular interest groups and their conflicts, compromises or dictates." [128] This negation of the negations of civil society is not an afterthought external to civil society. Rather it is demanded by civil society's incomplete mediation, which requires to be thought through in order to overcome its intellectual as well as socioeconomic disintegration. When that is done, Hegel believes we are led to the idea of an affirmative, inclusive totality, namely, the ethical state. However, the demand for such inclusive wholeness and integration begins in the family and corporations, which make explicit Hegel's insistence that the economic system not merely hold out the abstract possibility of satisfying needs but actually recognize and meet the needs of its members. Just as recognition begins in a desire for the other that is sublated into love, so also the system of needs is more than mere

---

127. *PR*, §244.
128. Hartmann, "Towards a Systematic Reading of Hegel's *Philosophy of Right*," 135.

economics; it too has a sublation that begins in the corporation and is completed in the inclusive ethical state.[129]

Granting that corporations, or mediating institutions, in Hegel's sense are needed, the question is whether Hegel thinks that such institutions already exist? Or is his discourse about corporations a proposal about something that ought to be? This recalls the question of the *Doppelsatz* that the rational must become actual and the actual must become rational. Hegel believes that mediating institutions, or corporations, are needed to prevent capitalist civil society from subverting itself by generating the extremes of wealth and poverty and creating a rabble. The need that corporations fulfill is ethical, social, and logical. Logically some mediating institution is needed to restore ethical order from the disintegration and chaos in civil society. Viewed in this respect, that the corporation exist, or be actual, is both a rational and an ethical demand.

Do such ethical institutions exist? I believe that there are some approximations to what Hegel is driving at, from churches and religious institutions to cooperatives, labor unions, environmental coalitions, and professional associations. Have such institutions prevented the emergence of poverty and the rabble? Hardly. But at least some of them probably have mitigated poverty and its effects, and prevented these from being even worse than they are. Hegel has made a proposal about a kind of institution and its appropriate function that 'ought to be' if it does not yet exist, and this 'ought to be' is not an empty utopian projection but something inherently rational. Pressing this demand then is not to acquiesce in the status quo but to advance a critique of the status quo, and such criticism is part of the process whereby the rational becomes actual.[130] The critical insight is that civil society is not wholly autonomous; rather its activities are carried out within a larger environment and social framework, and for the sake of human welfare.

Hegel's corporations are important not only to keep recognition alive, or to keep a human face on the economic misery that seems to be an otherwise

---

129. If Hegel's suggestions fail to convince, consider the alternatives. The alternatives are the disintegrated ethical life of civil society, namely, its unrestricted individualist self-seeking, or collectivist social planning that externally dictates what and how much will be produced. The former allows self-seeking freedom complete sway, which exacerbates the problem of overproduction and produces too much, including an alienated rabble. On the other hand, the collectivist model imposes external constraints on the market, which suppresses freedom. In contrast, Hegel seeks a mediating institution, a system of mutual recognition that makes connections between one's own good and the welfare of others and thereby enlarges one's mentality and restrains the egoistic self-seeking that demands unrestricted production and consumption. The corporation connects the welfare of others and one's own, and places both in ethical perspective. And that in itself is important. The corporation is the ethical moment within civil society that prepares the move to the more inclusive ethical state and other possible arrangements that tame the wild beast of global capitalism.

130. See Herbert Marcuse, *One Dimensional Man* (Boston: Beacon Press, 1964). Marcuse worries that civil society might be capable of containing and suppressing all intellectual and political criticism. Marcuse's fears have proven to be unfounded.

tragic destiny of modern civil society;[131] they are needed as an important first institutional-organizational step to prevent human beings from being reduced to mere commodities in national and international capitalism and to ensure that the promise of the 'satisfaction of human needs' becomes something more than a mere possibility or empty ideological rhetoric. Hegel's thought in this respect remains Fichtean.

131. Hegel's recognition of the problem of poverty is not "completely against the grain of the integrative and mediating nature of his whole social philosophy" as Avineri would have it. For Hegel recognizes an important tragic dimension in human freedom and existence. Poverty may be a symptom or expression of tragic finitude. Even if this is true, recognition of the tragic is no grounds for resignation to its inevitability, particularly since civil society is not a natural given but a matter of human freedom and arrangements. Hegel's proposal about the importance of honor in one's corporation is important because it places the problems of excess production and the attendant poverty within an intersubjective ethical framework.

12

Recognition and
the Social Contract Theory
of the State

Recognition provides the phenomenological framework (*Zusammenhang*) for the *concept* of freedom, within which and through which the concept of freedom is realized.[1] Recognition is the existential-intersubjective actualization of the concept (*Begriff*) of freedom, that is, its phenomenological dimension. The concept of freedom undergoes a doubling and a double movement, and mutual recognition is the telos and culmination of this double movement,[2] in which the divided or doubled grounds of freedom are reciprocally fulfilled and actualized. Recognition corresponds to the logical transition to objectivity, which is why it is the phenomenological introduction of objective spirit in Hegel's mature philosophy of spirit. On the historical-cultural level, Hegel's proposed mediation of the ancients and the moderns is effected by his concept of the state as an ethical construct. This takes the form of a mediation of a specific doubling in the concept of freedom, namely, ethical substance and subjective freedom.

We have seen that the *Philosophy of Right* begins with abstract right and freedom and moves in categorical order toward increasing determinacy and more complete actualizations of freedom in ethical life. Ethical life (*Sittlichkeit*) includes three institutions, the family, civil society, and the state. In the family, mutual recognition is expressed in love, and the family union takes the form of immediate feeling. However, love and feeling, as immediate, are intimate, pre-reflective forms of recognition. They are not forms of recognition appropriate

---

1. *E*, §484.
2. Manfred Riedel has called attention to the double movement of the concept, *Between Tradition and Revolution* (97), as has Jean Hyppolite, *Genesis and Structure of Hegel's Phenomenology of Spirit*, trans. S. Cherniak and J. Heckman (Evanston: Northwestern University Press, 1974), 115.

to either civil society or the state, which require more explicitly rational forms of mediation and mutual recognition, for example, law.[3] Consequently, in Hegel's account of ethical life, the immediate unity of the family dissolves and is replaced by the atomized individuality of civil society.

In civil society, individual subjective freedom is released and allowed to develop. If the family is an immediate unity and/or identity, civil society represents difference, competition, and conflict. The unity of civil society is an unstable, perpetually shifting unity of mutual exploitation for the sake of difference, that is, private interests. Liberal theories of the state that end here confuse the state with civil society and make it subservient and instrumental to property and individual subjective freedom. But for Hegel the state must not be confused with civil society. In our examination of the corporations, we saw that they constitute an ethical moment or element within civil society that moderates its exploitative ethos. The state takes such humanizing mutual recognition a step further by raising it to the universal level; that is, the state recognizes its members as citizens. The state is the realization of freedom, and freedom has the shape of self-recognition in other. The state is supposed to mediate the structures of difference constitutive of civil society and to bring difference back to the unity of a community with a sense of joint membership and shared identity similar to the family. In this community ethical substance and subjective freedom are mutually implicating, such that each is actualized through and by means of the other.

Recognition is not merely one topic among others in Hegel's theory of ethical life. Rather mutual recognition, being at home with self in an other, pursuing common causes and ends cooperatively with others—all these are elements and aspects of what the state is supposed to be. The state is a complex form of mutual recognition that extends the sense of joint membership, participation, and shared self-identity, so important in the family, throughout the larger social body, transforming it from an external aggregate into a vital community, a living organism. This becomes evident in Hegel's account of patriotism.

It is not my concern to provide a commentary on Hegel's account of the state, or his theory of government, for such would require a separate monograph. Instead I want first to examine his social ontology of the state from the perspective of recognition. I believe that the concept of recognition opens up and illumines that social ontology. Hegel presents an alternative to the abstract atomic individualism of modern liberalism and to abstract collectivism, whether of classical political philosophy (Plato) or of modern communitarianism. It is well known that Hegel is critical of atomic individualism of modern liberalism, but

---

3. "When what is right in itself is posited in its objective existence, i.e., determined by thought for consciousness and known as what is right and valid—it becomes law. . . . Only when it becomes law does what is right take on both the form of its universality and its true determinacy." *PR*, §211.

this does not mean that he conceives the unity of the state at the expense of its constituent individuals. Mutual recognition is an important critical dimension in Hegel's alternative.

Second, I want to focus on a systematic problem in Hegel's account, for which I believe the concept of recognition provides some clarification, as well as a central mediating role. There are various ways in which the systematic issue can be formulated and approached. It is a question of understanding the relation between substantive freedom, or the will in itself, and subjective freedom, or the arbitrary will (*Willkür*). It is also a question of an intersubjectively mediated autonomy. In the *Jena Realphilosophie* Hegel portrays the relation between the rational *Wille an sich*—his substantive principle of freedom—and the subjective arbitrary will (*Willkür*) as a relation of recognition.[4] This conception continues in his mature thought. With the theory of the state, Hegel introduces the concept of ethical substance, or substantial freedom. Substantial freedom completes and grounds his earlier account of conscience by providing conscience with a substantive normative content that is potentially intersubjective and social. At the same time, Hegel appropriates and transforms the modern concept of subjective freedom by means of the concept of recognition. Modern subjectivity is an abstraction from the intersubjectivity of mutual recognition. Mutual recognition serves as the critical principle for retrieval, on the basis of freedom, of the substantial ethical insights of classical political theory, to wit, the whole is greater than and prior to the parts. Substantive freedom refers to and includes ethical powers, duties, rights, and institutions (family and state, laws and customs) that unify individuals and govern their lives. For Hegel, the substantive principle, or *Wille an sich*, is intersubjectively constituted in mutual recognition; moreover, it is social and itself capable of action.[5]

Willkür is for Hegel the principle of subjective arbitrary choice. Taken by itself in abstraction, it is formal and empty. Subjective freedom (*Willkür*), the difference principle, receives its content from substantive freedom (*Wille an sich*), and the correspondence of the two is not external heteronomy but a mediated autonomy. Subjective freedom is supposed to derive its ethical foundation and justification from the rational *Wille an sich*. However, the starting point of Hegel's analysis of *Willkür* is its *noncoincidence* with *Wille an sich*. This noncoincidence constitutes the state of nature, or preethical condition. From this perspective, the ethical task is to deabsolutize, or to use Rousseau's term, denaturalize, the arbitrary will, and bring it into conformity with its concept, that is, the rational will in itself. Such 'denaturing' is for Hegel a self-overcoming,

---

4. *Philosophie des Geistes 1805/06*, 191 ff.; *HHS*, 105.

5. In the *Philosophie des Geistes 1805/06*, Hegel asserts that in punishing crime, the universal will is active (p. 215; *HHS*, 131). This assertion of activity on the part of the universal rational will represents a break with Kant's distinction between *Wille* and *Willkür*, and a transformation of Kant's transcendental empirical doublet into a social and historical conception of spirit. However, it does not imply any reification of the universal or general will.

or *Aufhebung*. In contemporary parlance, self-overcoming includes a decentering of natural egoism.[6] For Hegel, recognition accomplishes this ethical transformation. When the other begins to count, and is taken seriously both as a limit on subjective freedom and a liberation from arbitrary subjective freedom, the threshold of the ethical is reached, an expanded mentality arises, and ethical life in the authentic sense begins.

From another perspective, the systematic problem is the question concerning the interpretation of recognition and its relation to social contract theory. From a strict Kantian perspective, autonomy cannot be mediated; it is a priori and ahistorical. This makes such autonomy vulnerable to Hegel's charge of formalism. For Hegel, the autonomous individual is insufficient to ground a concept of community and/or ethical norms. The concept of recognition developed by Fichte and Hegel is intended to address this issue and to develop a mediated autonomy. Recognition is an implicit critique of a priori formal autonomy; beneath the a priori autonomy of transcendental philosophy is the life-world a priori of intersubjective struggles for recognition. However, the issue between Hegel and Fichte narrows to the question of the unity that mutual recognition affords. What is the result of mutual-reciprocal recognition? Can mutual recognition between individuals result in something more than a commercial contract that derives from antecedent independent individual wills? Can mutual recognition result in a substantial unity to which individual wills can and must be nonheteronomously subordinate?

Hegel observes that "concerning ethical life there are only two possible viewpoints. Either one starts with the substantiality as foundation, or one proceeds atomistically and moves upward from individuality. However the latter standpoint excludes spirit because it leads only to an aggregate and not to spirit. But spirit is not something individual; rather it is the unity of individual and universal."[7] This formulation captures Hegel's criticism of Rousseau and Fichte. Hegel believes that both start from the fundamental Cartesian standpoint of the *cogito*, that is, with the self-sufficient individual, and then attempt to proceed from the *cogito* to the intersubjective-social level of the state. However, Hegel believes that they only reach the concept of the state as a social contract between autonomous individuals who remain independent. Consequently they tend to conceive the state as civil society, rather than as spirit. This claim raises questions concerning Hegel's interpretation and assessments of Rousseau and Fichte, as well as his appropriation and interpretation of the concept of recognition.

Fichte introduces the concept of mutual recognition as a condition of the concept of right. Fichte starts out as a social contract theorist. But he sees that conventions such as contracts presuppose prior attitudes, orientations, and in-

6. This decentering of subjectivity establishes fundamental continuity between Rousseau, Fichte, Hegel, and Levinas.

7. *PR*, §156 Zusatz.

terhuman relationships. The concept of mutual recognition between individuals is for Fichte the condition of possibility of Rousseau's social contract.[8] This suggests that Fichte understands the concept of recognition as leading to and supporting the social contract view of the state.

Hegel accepts the concept of recognition but rejects the social contract concept of the state. Hence the issue is whether the concept of reciprocal recognition leads necessarily to a social contract view of the state. Conversely, to use Hegel's expression, when I becomes a We, does the We signify anything more than a common will of a contract, an externally related aggregate? If it does not, then Hegel's critique of Rousseau and Fichte would be in bad faith. If it does, then the 'We' is more than an aggregate. But what is this something more? The short answer is that it is objective spirit (*Geist*).

My thesis is that Hegel's account of recognition stakes out a third alternative to the classical collective social structures and to modern, that is, Cartesian-Kantian, conceptions of subjectivity and freedom. The 'We' that originates in mutual-reciprocal recognition is not an external aggregate, or a mere common will of contract, nor is it a preestablished harmony that excludes individual subjective freedom. The 'We' is a union of individuals that sublates and enlarges their self-identity and that depends on and requires the preservation of their individual freedom. Mutual recognition is the ideal unity of the state. This 'idealism' is an objective idealism, more or less synonymous with actuality.[9] Recognition unites Hegel's principle of substantive freedom with subjective freedom. Hegel sides with the moderns against classical theories by accepting the principle of subjectivity and by adopting Rousseau's thesis that the principle of the state is freedom.

However, modernity interprets subjective freedom as a theory of atomistic self-sufficient individualism. My thesis is that while modernity tends to interpret subjective freedom individualistically, Hegel, by thinking through the issue of the other, decenters subjectivity, on the one hand, and, on the other, transforms subjectivity into ethical intersubjectivity. The full concept of freedom and subjectivity is for Hegel found in mutual recognition and its resulting objective spirit. Expanded and decentered subjectivity is not merely open to ethical substance or substantial freedom, but finds itself in such substance, that is, recognizes itself in that larger whole. Consequently substantial freedom is not heteronomy but comprises the conditions and institutions necessary for freedom to be actual.

---

8. George J. Seidel, *Fichte's Wissenschaftslehre of 1794* (West Lafayette, Ind.: Purdue University Press, 1993), 4–5. See also Alexis Philonenko, *La liberté humaine dans la philosophie de Fichte* (Paris: Vrin, 1966); See also George Armstrong Kelly, *Idealism, Politics and History: Sources of Hegelian Thought* (Cambridge: At the University Press, 1969).

9. This point will be developed in subsequent chapters.

At this point a question arises, namely, if Hegel believes that the relation between the individual and the social whole is a self-recognition in other, does this imply that the social whole is itself a subject in some sense? How can the individual be intersubjectively related to the social whole or ethical substance, without claiming that the social whole itself is a subject? How is the I related to the We? Is the We a super-subject? I believe the answer to this question must be negative. Hegel does not reify objective *Geist*; nevertheless, he thinks that the relation between individuals and the institutions of ethical life is properly conceived as a self-recognition in other. Nicolai Hartmann has spoken clearly and trenchantly to this issue.

> What is "objective *Geist*"? One thinks here first of all of objectivity, which is a characteristic of all mental intentional life. All consciousness has its object, and the content of the object points to an objective world. This is not what objective *Geist* means. Such intentionality is characteristic of subjective *Geist*, for the latter is a consciousness. *The objective Geist is not a consciousness. There is to be sure a consciousness of objective Geist, and every human consciousness includes such. But Geist itself is not this consciousness.* It has another mode of being, namely an objective mode. Nevertheless objective *Geist* is far from being something hidden, mysterious or mystical, nor does it designate a particular psychological attitude. On the contrary it is something well known, an element of life in which we all stand, outside of which we have no existence, the spiritual air, as it were, in which we breathe. It is the sphere in which we are situated and nurtured by birth, education and historical influence. It is an all pervasive reality that we know in culture, customs, language, thought forms, prejudices, dominant values—all as supra-individual and nevertheless real powers, in the face of which the individual stands virtually powerless and defenseless, because his own being no less than all the others is permeated, carried along and shaped by these.[10]

For Hegel, reciprocal recognition and objective spirit are constitutive of the 'higher or ideal self' of a culture; they are the rational that must become actual, that is, the critical principles by which the legitimacy of any empirical sociopolitical situation is measured and ascertained. Far from being the nemesis of freedom, ethical substance is the totality of conditions that freedom requires. Freedom first becomes actual in the world as objective spirit, in which subjective freedom and ethical substance are reciprocally mediated. This actualization is not automatic, much less something that occurs by nature. On the contrary, the universal structures and institutions of objective spirit do not attain validity or realization without or apart from the interest, knowledge, and volition of individuals.[11]

10. Nicolai Hartmann, *Philosophie des deutschen Idealismus*, Zweite Auflage (Berlin: Walter de Gruyter, 1960), 497. Italics mine.
11. See footnote 23 below.

Overview of the State as a Unity of Reciprocal Recognitions

Hegel makes it clear that he is concerned with the idea of the state, not with any particular empirical state, or with the question of the origin of the state. Hegel's question is not how the state comes to be, or whether it originated in violence or in a contract, but rather what the state is. The state, Hegel tells us, is the actuality of the substantial will, which he describes in Aristotelian language as an absolute unmoved end in itself in which freedom comes to have its highest right.[12] As Hegel takes up the question of the state, he confronts the problem of the distinctive mediation of universal and particular, or substantive ethical freedom and subjective freedom constitutive of the state. The idea or concept of the state consists in a synthesis of universal ethical substance with subjective individual freedom in the shape of objective spirit. This synthesis is best understood in contrast to civil society.

For Hegel, civil society is the realm of difference; universal and particular are in disintegration, and individuals stand in exploitative relationships to each other and to the market. Everything becomes subservient to property and exchange value. There is no universal recognition except a purely formal and utilitarian sort; such formal recognition is capable of coexisting with the extremes of extravagance and poverty. That is why the figure of master and slave haunts civil society as its nemesis.

In contrast, for Hegel the state is an ethical institution: "The relationship of the state to the individual is of a quite different kind. Since the state is objective spirit, it is only through being a member of the state that the individual himself has objectivity, truth and ethical life. Union as such is the true content and end, and the destiny of individuals is to lead a universal life."[13] The state is a mediation of universal and particular, of individuals and the social, which are no longer in opposition and mutual exclusion as in civil society. Hegel's task is to clarify this mediation and union. He believes that social contract theory misconstrues it and confuses the ethical state with civil society. On the other hand, the classical state did not release subjective freedom and particularity but rather suppressed it. Hegel seeks a third alternative to these views. The state must embody and combine both ethical substance and modern subjective freedom. His proposal to reconcile the ancients and the moderns is that ethical substance provides the content and telos of subjective freedom, while subjective freedom is the means whereby ethical substance is actualized and realized.[14]

Now for some clarifications. By ethical substance Hegel means the ethical powers that govern the lives of individuals, that is, duties, virtues, laws, and institutions that have being in and for themselves. Consequently these ethical

12. *PR*, §258.   13. Ibid.   14. *PR*, §260.

powers are exalted above subjective opinions and preferences.[15] Hegel characterizes such ethical powers as the ethically necessary or as ethical substance, and employs language reminiscent of Aristotle's unmoved mover. However, such theological-metaphysical language does not mean that the state is not socially constituted and constructed. The state, as the most highly articulated and universal form of ethical life, is a social rationality that transcends and grounds the earlier forms of abstract right, morality, and civil society.

> Ethical life is what right and morality have not yet reached, namely spirit. For in right, particularity is not yet that of the concept [*Begriff*], but only the natural will. Similarly, from the point of view of morality, self-consciousness is not yet spiritual consciousness. . . . [T]hat is, the subject which determines itself in accordance with good as opposed to evil still has the form of the arbitrary will [*Willkür*]. In contrast, at the standpoint of ethical life, the will is present as the will of spirit, and has a corresponding substantial content.[16]

At the level of ethical life, the bad infinity of abstract identity and merely individual reflective morality are left behind.[17] The bad infinity of *Moralität*'s reflection is itself negated by reciprocal recognition and membership in the community. Freedom is no longer simply negative, the principle of difference, but, owing to mutual recognition, becomes affirmative, reflected in the positive relations to others constitutive of community.[18]

These affirmative and positive relations to others Hegel terms rights and duties. Duties are a liberation from the negative empty freedom of *Moralität*: "in duty the human being liberates himself from natural drives, from dependence, from oppression. . . . For the self-reflected individual eternally counsels with himself, broods within himself, and is without self-feeling and soundness of spirit. Duty liberates one from this brooding and sickness."[19] "That is, the self-willfulness and [formal] conscience of the individual who would exist simply for himself and oppose ethical substance, have disappeared. The ethical character knows that the end that moves it is the universal, which though itself unmoved, has developed through its determinations into actual rationality, and it recognizes that its own dignity and the whole continued existence of its particular ends are based upon and actualized within this universal."[20] Substantial freedom gives arbitrary and subjective freedom something to do and to be, that is, an ethical telos.

The state, as a union of ethical substance (necessity) with subjectivity (freedom), has an objective validity that transcends the level of private individual interests. In this objective validity individuals themselves come to count as ob-

15. Ibid., §§144–145.   16. Ibid., §151.
17. *WL*, TWA Sk 5:268–269.
18. *PR*, §112.   19. *VPR3*, 490–491.   20. *PR*, §152.

jective for the first time. "The authority of the state, for Hegel, is rooted in the fact that the state is immanent in the very idea of free will. The state must be recognized and respected as having the highest claim to right, because it is only when the state is present that human freedom is rendered objective and universal by becoming law for all."[21] The objective validity of individuals is achieved only within the ethical state. This objective validity alone constitutes the real refutation of slavery, that is, the inequalities generated by and constitutive of civil society.[22] Note that individual freedom is not lost or "swallowed up" in this union or in its objective substantial basis. As Hegel characterizes this substantial basis, its basic feature is recognition and the preservation of individual rights. "The essence of the modern state is that the universal should be linked with the complete freedom of particularity and the well-being of individuals, and hence the interest of family and civil society must become focused on the state; but the universality of the end cannot make further progress without the personal knowledge and volition of the particular individuals who must retain their rights."[23]

Individuals who are manipulated and exploited at the level of civil society come to recognize the ethical state as their common need. Conversely the state must recognize and protect its constituent individuals and members.

> The state is the actuality of concrete freedom. But concrete freedom requires that personal individuality [*Einzelheit*] and its particular interests should reach their full development and gain recognition of their right for its own sake (in the system of the family and civil society) as they pass over of their own accord into the interest of the universal, and knowingly and willingly recognize this universal interest as their own substantial spirit and actively pursue it as their ultimate end. Thus *the universal does not attain validity or fulfillment without the interest, knowledge and will of the particular.* Moreover, individuals do not live as private persons merely for their private individual interests without at the same time directing their will to a universal end and acting consciously for this end.[24]

Note that the state or universal is not something wholly or self-sufficiently actual in itself or apart from particulars. The universal does not have validity or actuality apart from the interest, knowledge, and will of the particulars. Particulars embody and express the universal, rendering it actual and determinate. Although the universal has priority over its constituent individuals, this does not mean that the universal exists a priori or apart from its individuals. Moreover, the very process whereby the universal is rendered actual and determinate also lifts individuals above their private interests and directs them toward the universal end and good. This process is an ethical one, and includes mutual

21. Houlgate, *Freedom, Truth and History*, 123.
22. *PR*, §57.   23. Ibid., §260 Zusatz.
24. Ibid., §260. My italics. I have altered the translation.

recognition: "The whole, the state, achieves inner stability only when what is universal, what is implicit [*an sich*], is recognized as universal."[25]

But what if the state is not so recognized? Hegel believes that just as individuals have a right to be recognized by others and by the state, so also they owe the state a duty of recognition in return. The ethical state has a right of recognition as well. Failure to recognize the state is a violation of and refusal to participate in the universal *Anerkanntsein* constitutive of the state. Against the latter refusal, Hegel asserts that "the right of the state is that its idea be recognized and realized. The individual has the right to enter the state voluntarily and to exist in it. But if he does not voluntarily participate in the state, he places himself in the state of nature [*Naturzustand*] in which his right is not recognized, and the process whereby his individual right may become recognized must come about in a natural way, namely through violence and the struggle for recognition. But in this situation of violence, the divine right is on the side of the founder of the state."[26]

Not only the I but also the We, the state, has a right to be recognized. The I is legitimate only insofar as it is co-constitutive of the We. To place oneself 'outside' of the state is to deny the intersubjective recognition constitutive of both individuals and the state. It is to act as if only one's own individuality counts. This can only have the status of a transgression. To deny the We is to place oneself in violation of the *Anerkanntsein*, and this is to place oneself in contradiction, not only to others, but to oneself as a member of the whole. Against such transgressive individualism Hegel defends the objective necessity and validity of the state, which he believes is something greater than a social contract. "In opposition to the principle of the individual will, we should remember the fundamental concept according to which the objective will is rational in itself, i.e., in its concept, whether or not it is recognized by individuals and willed by them at their discretion."[27] The state is not a contingent but a necessary and fundamental need of human beings because it is the condition of intersubjective-social freedom. As such the state has a right to be recognized by individuals; the state is the mutual-reciprocal recognition of its members taken collectively. However, its validity does not depend on the recognition of individuals taken distributively, nor is it at their individual option and discretion.

> For ethical substantiality is no longer merely the property of this or that individual, but is in and for itself stamped upon him in all his aspects down to the tiniest detail on its own account in a universal, necessary way. . . . [I]t does not matter in the least whether individuals as individuals want law and justice to count or not; law and justice count in and by themselves. Even if they did not want them to, law and justice would nevertheless count. Of course it does interest the universal and public authority that all individuals should comply with justice, but separate

25. *VPR*17, §121.   26. Ibid., §124.   27. *PR*, §258.

individuals do not arouse this interest on the ground that law and morals first attain their validity through the consent of this or that individual; law and morals do not require this individualized consent and determination. Punishment validates them if they are transgressed.[28]

Patriotism

In the *Aesthetics* Hegel mentions two alternatives concerning the relation of individuals to the state (*Sittlichkeit*). "In the genuine state, laws, customs, rights, etc., are valid by constituting the universal and rational characteristics of freedom, and moreover by being present in this their universality, are no longer conditioned by accidental whims and particular personal idiosyncrasies."[29] This objective rationality is objective spirit. Hegel believes that individuals are part of this objective, existing rationality, "but no longer are they with their heart and character the sole mode of existence of the ethical powers."[30] He continues: "This adherence [*Anschliessen*] to the objective rationality of the state does not depend on subjective caprice [*Willkür*]. This adherence may be either a) mere subjection, subjection pure and simple, because rights, laws and institutions, by being mighty and valid, have the power of coercion, or b) it can arise from the free recognition [*Anerkennung*] and insight [*Einsicht*] into the rationality of what exists, so that the subject finds himself again in the objective world."[31] In this case, heteronomous subjections are avoided, because the recognition and insight into the rationality of the actual is a self-recognition in other. Here is a text in which Hegel shows how the rational becomes actual in the form of self-recognition in other. As we will see shortly, this self-recognition in other is constitutive of patriotism.

Hegel expresses union with the state in terms of a relation of recognition between universal will and particular will that establishes both rights and duties: "Duty and right coincide in this identity of the universal and the particular will, and in the ethical sphere the human being has rights insofar as he has duties, and duties insofar as he has rights."[32] That is, duties and rights correspond to moments or dimensions of mutual recognition. Duty is the recognition of ethical substance of the other (i.e., an individual or an institution), and right is the concrete actualization and/or recognized existence of ethical substance in an individual or institution.[33]

Such self-recognition in other is at the same time an appropriation of ethical substance by the individual. We could say that the ethical substance *is* the I that has, through reciprocal recognition, become the We of ethical life, laws, and institutions. Such appropriation does not mean that the ethical substance

---

28. Hegel, *Aesthetik*, TWA Sk 13:240–241.
29. Ibid., 239; English translation: *Aesthetics*, 1:182.
30. Ibid., 240; English translation: 182.
31. Ibid.   32. *PR*, §155.   33. Ibid., §261.

depends on or is ratified by the individual's consent. Rather it constitutes who and what the individual properly and authentically is, the individual's 'higher' or 'true self': "There is something immanent in human nature through which the state exists; the state is one's own nature become actual in an objective manner."[34] Thus Hegel reformulates Plato's analogy between the individual soul and the structures of the state, but in terms of self-recognition in other.

Patriotism is an important aspect and dimension of the self-recognition in other that is constitutive of the state and Hegel's account of genuine conscience. What is patriotism? It is the moment of trust inherent in the mutual recognition between individual and state in which the former's rights are recognized and in which the individual's interests pass over of their own accord into the interest of the universal as their substantial spirit.

> The individuality of each as such must reside in the universal. The universal must be accomplished in such a way that the individual, in accomplishing the universal, is also working for himself. The particularity of the individual will must be preserved in the universal will. Here we have the real union of universality and particularity.[35]

> What matters most is that the law of reason and the law of particular freedom should pervade each other, and that my particular end should become identical with the universal; otherwise the state must hang in the air. It is the self-awareness of individuals which constitutes the actuality of the state, and its stability consists in the identity of the two aspects in question.[36]

Hegel thus identifies patriotism as the moment of union (*Vereinigung*) between individual and universal, which is not something transient or necessarily extraordinary, but "which in the normal conditions and circumstances of life, habitually knows that the community is the substantial basis and end. It is this same consciousness, tried and tested in all circumstances of ordinary life, which underlies the willingness to make extraordinary efforts."[37] Consequently patriotism is the central political disposition. "This disposition is in general one of trust, or the consciousness that my substantial and particular interest is preserved and contained in the interest and end of another (in this case the state), and in the latter's relation to me as an individual. As a result, this *other is immediately not other for me, and in my consciousness of this, I am free.*"[38]

---

34. *VPR*19, 212.   35. *VPR*17, §132.   36. *PR*, §265.
37. Ibid., §268. Hegel adds an important qualification on patriotism: "just as human beings often prefer to be guided by magnanimity rather than by right, so also do they readily convince themselves that they possess this extraordinary patriotism in order to exempt themselves from the genuine disposition, or excuse their lack of it."
38. Ibid. Italics mine. Patriotism is Hegel's account of genuine, as contrasted with formal, conscience. For a useful discussion of the issues and problems here, see Ludwig Siep, "The *Aufhebung* of Morality in Ethical Life," in *Hegel's Philosophy of Action*, ed. L. Stepelevich and D. Lamb (Atlantic Highlands, N.J.: Humanities Press, 1983), 137–156; see pp. 149 ff. Siep notes the ambiguity

Patriotism is a unity and identification of individual interest with the universal public interest. It is a form of mutual recognition that suspends and transcends the opposition and contrast between universal and particular. These concepts of universal and particular are usually understood to be a fundamental contrast and opposition, in which each is other for the other. This external, hard-and-fast opposition between universal and particular is constitutive of the utilitarian reciprocities between individuals in civil society. But mutual recognition brings about trust, a unity in which the other is no longer other, or not-other. In trust, the other, be it state or citizen, does not cease to *be*, but it ceases to be *alien*. "The state is here not an Other. I have trust in someone when I know that my interests and my welfare are also his end, and that our ends are identical."[39] Consequently mutual recognition constitutive of the state includes a

> trust that the state will continue to exist and that particular interests can be fulfilled within it alone; but habit blinds us to the basis of our entire existence. It does not occur to someone who walks the streets in safety at night that this might be otherwise, for this habit of living in safety has become second nature, and we scarcely stop to think that it is solely the effect of particular institutions. Representational thinking often imagines that the state is held together by force; but what holds it together is simply the basic sense of order which everyone possesses.[40]

The trust between individual and state involves a unity that transcends the unity constitutive of contract, as well as civil society or the external state. From the latter point of view, the state is regarded as instrumental and subservient to private property interests. Difference and otherness take priority. At the level of civil society people do not trust each other; that is why contracts are necessary. But in patriotism such distrustful individuality, difference, and otherness are transcended in a higher form of self-recognition in and union with other. In patriotism the other ceases to be other, and there is an identification of the individual with the whole in which the individual's private interests, property, and life itself are secured. Yet such securing does not return us to atomic individualism, because the patriotic individual is willing to subordinate and sacrifice his interests, property, and life itself for the sake and defense of the whole. Hegel believes that the state cannot be adequately conceived as a social contract, because it would be absurd for an individual to sacrifice himself for the sake of a mere vehicle or tool of individual self-interest.

---

of morality for Hegel: there is the supreme irony that the summit of morality is the dissolution of all determinate obligation and, conversely, that subjectivity, in thus wishing to be free of all determinations, undermines freedom itself, which depends on determinations and oppositions. (p. 145f.). More important, Siep claims that in the *Aufhebung* of morality in ethical life, Hegel does not subordinate modern subjective freedom to a heteronomous preexisting objective ethical substance, and calls attention to the fact that ethical life itself is subject to a four-stage development. Hegel identifies the third stage of development with civil society, as the sphere in which morality reigns (pp. 146 ff.). This observation is consistent with Hegel's treatment of the corporation as the ethical moment of civil society and poverty as the problem to which the corporation must respond.

39. *VPR4*, §268, 642.   40. *PR*, §268 Zusatz.

Social Contract Theory

According to Hegel, Rousseau rightly identified freedom as the principle of the state. In asserting that freedom is the principle of the state, Rousseau breaks with traditional natural law views and propounds an anthropological conception of the state. As Rousseau develops this position in detail, he believes that it requires that the state be founded on an explicit voluntary human convention, a social contract. Rousseau substitutes a contract between equals, a work of human making and art, for what traditional thought ascribed to nature or to 'man's natural sociability'.[41] Although Hegel is critical of Rousseau, he does not flatly reject Rousseau's social contract; rather in his *History of Philosophy Lectures* he gives a qualified approval to it. Hegel accepts the *problem* to which the social contract metaphor is addressed, namely, finding "a mode of association which will defend and protect with the whole common force the person and property of each associate, and in which each individual, while uniting himself with all, may still obey himself alone, and remain as free as before."[42] Hegel continues: Rousseau's "solution is the social contract. In this association [*Verbindung*] each is present voluntarily. *These principles, abstractly stated, we must find correct*. However, ambiguity quickly arises."[43] For Hegel, therefore, Rousseau's formulations are correct in the abstract, or in principle, but nevertheless ambiguous.

The ambiguity lies in a theoretical failure in conceiving the various aspects of freedom, that is, ethical substance and subjective freedom. The problem is the relation between the general will and the subjective arbitrary will. Hegel believes that Rousseau and Fichte consider the general will not as rational in and for itself but only as a common element arising from antecedent independent individual wills and expressed in a contract. In the *Philosophy of Right*, Hegel puts the point in the following way.

> It was the achievement of Rousseau to put forward the will as the principle of the state. . . . But Rousseau considered the will only in the determinate form of the individual will (as Fichte did subsequently also) and regarded the universal will not as the will's rationality in and for itself, but only as the common element consciously and deliberately arising from individuals. The union of individuals in the state thus becomes a contract, which is accordingly based on their arbitrary will and opinions, and on their express consent given at their own option. The further consequences which follow from this and relate merely to the understanding, destroy the divine element that has being in and for itself and also its authority and majesty.[44]

41. Louis Althusser, *Politics and History: Montesquieu, Rousseau, Marx* (London: Verso, 1982).
42. Hegel cites *Social Contract*, chap. 6, p. 191, in his *History of Philosophy Lectures*, TWA Sk 20:307.
43. Hegel, *Geschichte der Philosophie, Werke*, TWA Sk 20:307. My italics.
44. *PR*, §258.

This text raises several points. First we must note that Hegel links Rousseau and Fichte. Hegel's discussion of Rousseau is not developed in detail comparable to his discussions of Kant and Fichte. Hegel's relatively superficial reading of Rousseau is probably due to the fact that Kant and especially Fichte were in Hegel's time the leading representatives and exponents of Rousseau's social contract theory in Germany, and it is these figures, rather than Rousseau, to whom Hegel responds.[45] Second, the chief issue for Hegel is the relation and mode of union between the universal rational will (*Wille an sich*) and the arbitrary subjective individual (*Willkür*). Hegel claims that neither Rousseau nor Fichte has an adequate conception of this union, and thus they produce distortions of the general will that are by no means innocuous, but obscure the nature of the state and reduce it to the level of a mere commercial contract, a system held together by force and/or the threat of coercion.

Hegel accepts Rousseau's general principle that freedom is the basis of the state. He also accepts Fichte's account of the intersubjective mediation of freedom in recognition as the underlying precondition of the act of association that is supposed to issue in a social contract. But Hegel rejects both the social contract theory of the state and Fichte's belief that the concept of recognition necessarily leads to a social contract. My thesis is that Hegel thinks through and completes Rousseau's idea that freedom is the foundation of the state, by grounding the concept of the state not in a social contract but in mutual recognition. To be sure, for Hegel contract is a determinate form and instance of recognition, but not all recognition is a contract. For this reason Hegel finds it imperative to distinguish the mutual recognition and union that constitute the state from the external recognition and atomistic individualism inherent in contractual relations. Hegel's distinction of these two leads him to develop the concept of recognition differently, perhaps more fully than Fichte.

Hegel and Rousseau

Hegel interprets Rousseau's social contract theory as embodying a confusion that permits the reduction of the state to the level and status of a civil contract. This reductionism must be resisted: "The nature of the state has . . . little to do with the relationship of contract. . . . The intrusion of this relationship, and relationships concerning private property in general, into political relationships has created the greatest confusion in constitutional law and in actuality."[46] Is this criticism based on an accurate understanding of Rousseau's social contract? It is difficult to answer this question because there is little or no

45. In particular, Hegel explores and criticizes Fichte's *Grundlage des Naturrechts* (1796) and *System der Sittenlehre* (1798) in his early *Difference* essay and his essay on *Natural Law*. We shall examine this discussion below.

46. *PR*, §75.

consensus concerning what Rousseau meant by the social contract. In other words, Hegel was right in noting the ambiguities in Rousseau's formulation.

One recent study interprets Rousseau in a way that confirms Hegel's reading.[47] Asher Horowitz interprets the social contract on the model of a commercial contract, namely, an exchange of property between equals. The marketplace model of contract implies an instrumentalization of the other as a means to the self's private end and the external reciprocity that applies formally between two agents in the marketplace. "Each may serve as instrument for the other on the same terms as the other serves as instrument for him. The general will transposes into the public sphere the same logic embodied in the morality of the relation of instrumental reciprocity."[48] Further, the general will and the community are not party to the social contract but rather are created by the contract.[49] This clearly makes the general will dependent on antecedent independent individuals, as Horowitz observes: "the general will cannot exist except on the basis of particular wills."[50]

Whether Horowitz is correct about Rousseau is not my concern. However, such nominalist interpretation of the general will as an aggregate of individuals is the target of Hegel's criticism. "The misunderstanding of the general will begins when freedom is understood as contingent arbitrary will of each individual. On the contrary, freedom must be taken in the sense of the rational will, the will in and for itself. *The general will is not to be regarded as a collection of expressed individual wills, in which the latter remain absolute.*"[51] Hegel is concerned that on Rousseau's account of the contract, the individual will 'after' the union remains free in the same sense as before; that is, it is not affected or transformed by the union, and so remains absolute. Rousseau remains caught in an opposition between particular and universal, namely, an abstract atomic individualism, on the one hand, and an equally abstract concept of the general will as an abstract universal, on the other. In Hegel's view Rousseau treats the universal nominalistically; that is, a universal that remains opposed to particulars is itself another particular.

Given what he takes to be the theoretical deficiency in Rousseau's conception of the general will as an aggregate or collection, Hegel believes that Rousseau's version of social contract establishes not a state but merely a civil society, or the external state. The mode of union is contingent, and the union of wills articulated in the contract reflects only the exchange of property, goods, and services. Consequently it has no being or value in itself but is instrumental and subservient to private individual interests. These interests remain untransformed and absolute. On such a view, the state exists to protect and serve pri-

47. Asher Horowitz, *Rousseau, Nature and History* (Toronto: University of Toronto Press, 1987).

48. Ibid., 182.   49. Ibid., 186.   50. Ibid., 188.

51. Hegel, *Geschichte der Philosophie, Werke*, TWA Sk 20:307. My italics.

vate property interests. The social contract, in other words, institutes not a social but an instrumental rationality. In such a scheme, the conception of the general will may at most provide for limits on inequality and unequal distribution of property.[52] Further, in the union of wills articulated by the contract, the common will of contract is revocable in principle. Such revocability, transferred to the political sphere, means that each party to the social contract remains free to secede from the state, a position that Fichte defended in his early writings.

Horowitz points out that this is not the whole story as far as Rousseau is concerned. Given that the social contract establishes only a civil society, it is necessary to take a further step in order to form a genuine state. Thus Rousseau introduces the concept of the legislator, whom he describes as "capable, so to speak, of changing human nature, of transforming each individual, who is by himself a complete and solitary whole, into part of a greater whole from which he . . . receives his life and being; of altering man's constitution for the purpose of strengthening it; and of substituting a partial and moral existence for the physical and independent existence nature has conferred on us all. He must, in a word, take away from man his own resources and give him instead new ones alien to him, and incapable of being made use of without the help of other men."[53] According to Horowitz, the legislator stands for a higher form of rationality than the merely instrumental. This means that the legislator must somehow transform natural egoism and individualistic self-preoccupation into concern for others, seeing one's own good as inextricably bound up with the common good.[54] The legislator must transform civil society from a mere aggregate of isolated, externally related individuals into a community.

However, the introduction of the legislator makes apparent the inadequacy of the social contract model of the state, and more important, it points to recognition as a fundamental presupposition and condition of the social contract. It is striking that recent attempts to reformulate and clarify Rousseau's position on social contract wind up drawing on the concept of recognition as a presupposition and condition of the social contract. For example, N. J. H. Dent denies that the social contract is to be interpreted literally as a commercial contract. It is rather a metaphor for the act of voluntary association whereby one becomes a member of a community or group. When Dent defends the contract in this way, he shows that the contract assumes and expresses a prior recognition of the other as ethically significant: "The very willingness to observe the terms of a mutual promise—which no power or law can enforce—expresses a willingness to honor and respect those to whom one has promised. And this shows at least a minimal willingness to acknowledge the human significance

52. Horowitz, *Rousseau, Nature and History*.

53. Jean-Jacques Rousseau, *Social Contract*, trans. and intro. G. H. D. Cole (London: Everyman's Library, 1975), bk. 2, chap. 7, p. 214.

54. See also Dent, *A Rousseau Dictionary*, 144–146; see also pp. 68, 120–125.

of the other person, and to incorporate this as material to one's own concerns."[55] On Dent's reading, the social contract presupposes mutual recognition. Not surprisingly Dent goes on to formulate the social contract in Hegel's own words: namely, a contract to transcend the standpoint of contract.[56]

This move to recognition as the presupposition and condition of the contract would have pleased Fichte, for it prepares the way for his own proposal concerning recognition as the foundation of right. However, the concept of the legislator does not really help Rousseau, since what the legislator must do is effect an ethical-moral change in humanity. The legislator must transform the natural solipsism and self-seeking egoism of human beings into regard and concern for others, such that human beings come to see their own well-being and the well-being of others as inextricably linked. As far as Hegel is concerned, the account of the legislator is but an external projection of an intersubjective ethical transformation of human beings, which may involve a hero figure as Hegel observes in his *Jena Realphilosophie*, but need not.[57] However, the idea of an ethical transformation of human beings brings us to the heart of Hegel's objection to Rousseau's social contract theory and clarifies the deficiency in Rousseau's concept of freedom.

Earlier we examined Hegel's analysis of contract as the articulation and expression of a common will. This analysis of contract sought to articulate its conditions of possibility—the reciprocal formation of a common will—while at the same time restricting the application of contract to a certain sphere, namely, the exchange of goods, property, and services. This restriction means that as far as Hegel is concerned, there is a crucial distinction between the common will of contract and the general will. Both can result from mutual-reciprocal recognition, and both can reflect a certain 'We', that is, a certain kind of intersubjective unity. In the formation of the common will of contract, there is an external convergence of individual wills concerning alienable matters, that is, possessions, services, and so on. Consequently the common will expresses an external union that is not intersubjective in any interesting or profound sense, nor is it about the persons themselves, but about something external to them. The contract is conditional, subject to revocation by and/or enforcement against its constituent individuals.

However, the common will, even though it involves recognition of the private will, does not necessarily involve any *self-negation* of the private individual will, nor does it involve transformation of the self's relation to others; specifically, it need not involve any *positive ethical relation* to other. Rather in contract each person gets what he wants through a relation to an other that is merely instrumental and external. In this sense the individual subjective will (*Willkür*) remains untransformed. There is no self-negation or self-overcoming of nat-

55. Dent, *Rousseau Dictionary*, 68.
56. Ibid. Dent paraphrases *PR*, §163.
57. Cf. *Philosophie des Geistes 1805/06*, 234–235; *HHS*, 154–155.

ural egoism and solipsism. The other does not yet have any ethical depth or weight; for this reason the common will is not necessarily an ethical conception, nor is any ethical dimension or commitment necessary in its formation.

In contrast, for Hegel the general will has a necessary ethical dimension. He develops and clarifies this ethical dimension through analogies with love, marriage, and family. The point is not romantic sentimentalism concerning the family. We have seen in our discussion of marriage that the very independent selfhood that is the chief end of abstract right, property, and contract must be surrendered in order to constitute a marriage union. The "natural and individual personalities" are given up in the union, the corporate self that they participate in together. "In this respect, their union is a self-limitation, but since they attain their substantial self-consciousness within this union, it is in fact their liberation."[58] Similarly, the universal consciousness constitutive of the state must include self-negation and self-transformation by other into an enlarged mentality, in which natural egoism is replaced by a sense of membership and participation.

Although the common will of contract may involve mutual recognition, this is a reciprocity without the mutual mediation that includes self-transcendence and self-overcoming, and for this reason is insufficient and merely external. Without self-negation and self-overcoming through positive relation to the other, the individual selves remain absolute, and their natural solipsism is not interrupted, much less overcome. *Reciprocal recognition without self-overcoming and without union and identification with the other is deficient, external, and formal.* Individual subjective will (*Willkür*) is not necessarily decentered, transformed, and sublimated (*aufgehoben*) to the ethical level. The universal will in itself appears not as something vital in which the individuals have a stake, but remains merely instrumental, optional, and contingent. Hence Hegel believes that the social contract theory of Rousseau is seriously deficient.

Hegel believes with Rousseau that the principle of the state is freedom. But the atomic individualism inherent in Rousseau's concept of freedom must be overcome. Freedom is both individual and intersubjective. Hegel thinks the concept of freedom by means of the concept of recognition. The goal of mutual recognition is reciprocity, and reciprocity implies a coincidence and equivalence between being for other and being for self. In reciprocal recognition, in which each serves as mediator for the other, the difference between being for self and being for other vanishes. This 'vanishing' does not mean that the other disappears but rather that the self and its other enter into a positive relationship in which both are modified and redefined in terms of each other. Here is a union with other in which freedom is secured, liberated, and enhanced. This union with other is the core of Hegel's concepts of patriotism and state.

58. *PR*, §162.

Hegel's Criticism of Fichte

In his Jena period Hegel developed his *Rechtsphilosophie* in a long debate with Fichte's *Grundlage des Naturrechts* (1796). Hegel's attitude toward Fichte is marked by an early sharp disagreement and repulsion in the *Differenzschrift* and the essay on *Natural Law*, but this sharp rejection is followed by a later, not widely perceived or appreciated rapprochement in the Jena *Philosophy of Spirit 1805/06*.[59] Hegel's mature *Philosophy of Right* continues the critique of the natural law tradition started by Hobbes and deepened by Rousseau, Kant, and Fichte. With Rousseau, Kant, and Fichte, Hegel believes that freedom, not nature, is the principle of right. But Hegel believes that, like Rousseau, Fichte takes freedom to be not the universal rational will but freedom in the form of the isolated individual.

> Kant had begun to found right upon freedom. Fichte in his *Naturrecht* also makes freedom the principle of right. Like Rousseau, this is freedom in the form of an individual. It is a great beginning. But . . . they had to accept certain presuppositions: that there are a plurality of individuals; that the whole exposition of the state has for its chief determination that the freedom of individuals must be restricted by and in universal freedom. The individuals remain here always impenetrable and negatively related to each other. The prison house, the bondage, become ever more oppressive, instead of the state being conceived as the realization of freedom.[60]

Hegel criticizes Fichte's underlying individualism and dualism between transcendental and empirical subjectivity. Hegel believes that the concept of recognition requires a break with transcendental idealism that Fichte, in his early years at least, was unable to make.[61]

In spite of Hegel's polemics against Fichte, I believe that his *Philosophy of Right* is a further development of one of two important but contradictory strands in Fichte's *Grundlage des Naturrechts* (1796), against the other, opposing strand. The first strand may be identified as the 'recognition argument for community'. In this strand, community is conceived as a condition of freedom and liberation. We have already examined Fichte's concept of recognition. The other summons the self to freedom and responsibility; the concept of the summons in turn implies the concept of mutual recognition. "The human being becomes human only among other humans. . . . The concept of the human being therefore is not at all a concept of an individual—for such is inconceivable—

59. See Siep, *PPDI*, 41; see also Manfred Riedel, "Hegels Kritik des Naturrechts," in *Zwischen Tradition und Revolution; Between Tradition and Revolution*, 76–106.

60. Hegel, *Geschichte der Philosophie, Werke*, TWA 20:413; see also p. 503.

61. See Ludwig Siep, *Hegels Fichtekritik und die Wissenschaftslehre von 1804* (Freiburg: Karl Alber Verlag, 1970).

but rather the concept of a species." [62] Moreover, for Fichte recognition essentially involves reciprocity: "The relation of free beings to one another is therefore a relation of reciprocal interaction through intelligence and freedom. No free being can recognize another unless both reciprocally recognize each other, and neither can treat the other as a free being unless both mutually do so." [63] In this strand reciprocal recognition grounds and structures a community of mutual liberation (*Freilassen*) and freedom. Fichte expresses this in terms of a circle: "The possibility of reciprocal liberation [*Freilassen*] is conditioned by the whole future experience; but the possibility of future experience is conditioned by reciprocal liberation." [64] However, the community of freedom constituted through reciprocal recognition remains hypothetical, and thus contingent.

The second strand of Fichte's position I call the 'security-coercion argument for community'. Here community is conceived as a condition or means of restraint and/or punishment. In this strand Fichte is concerned not with liberation (*Freilassen*) but with security (*Sicherheit*). He develops a quasi-mechanical concept of community as a condition of surveillance necessary to detect, deter, and punish any violation of law and order. Fichte maintains that a law of coercion (*Zwangsrecht*) is possible only in a community. This community remains an external coercive agency, a third party, in relation to individuals. Fichte's emphasis here is on security rather than freedom and liberation (*Freilassen*). This external party or community is necessary for security, because only a community can grant each individual as much power as right to compel any unlawful will to contradict itself. [65]

In distinguishing these two strands in Fichte's thought, I am not contending that freedom and security are inherently incompatible. Fichte is quite right—and Hegel certainly follows him here—in finding freedom and security to be important dimensions and aspects of community. However, the way that Fichte develops his argument involves a method of abstraction that often treats connected themes in isolation from each other. [66] This creates the appearance that they are mutually exclusive and that there are at least two different senses of community in play. Even Fichte's development of the organism model of community may not overcome the problem, because his subsequent comments on police surveillance show the extent to which he was prepared to subordinate and even sacrifice the interest of freedom to the interest of security. In what follows I shall focus on Hegel's criticism of this negative strand of Fichte's thought, that is, the coercion argument for community. In the next chapter I shall focus on a positive rapprochement between Hegel and Fichte, that is, Hegel's development of Fichte's concept of social organism.

62. Fichte, *Grundlage des Naturrechts, Werke* 3:39. Hereafter cited as *GNR*. English translation: *The Science of Rights*, trans. A. E. Kroeger (1889), reissued (London: Routledge & Kegan Paul, 1970); hereafter cited as *SR*.

63. *GNR*, 44.   64. Ibid., 100; *SR*, 147.   65. *GNR*, 148; *SR*, 201.
66. *GNR*, 112; *SR*, 160.

Although Fichte first introduces and lays out the concept of mutual recognition as the foundation and condition of the concept of right, he does not make reciprocal recognition the principle or criterion of his account of rights and ethics.[67] Mutual recognition plays no affirmative, constitutive, or substantive role; it is pushed to the margins of these accounts, rendered problematic by Fichte's separation of transcendental from empirical subjectivity and by his treatment of the problem of (mis)trust.

Fichte retains the transcendental and empirical doublet. Any rational being has a dual aspect: he is rational, free in a formal sense, and at the same time he is a modifiable matter, something that can be treated as a *Sache* (thing). The transcendental-empirical distinction is carried through in Fichte's analysis of two different communities, the *legal community* of rights in his *Grundlage des Naturrechts* and the *moral community* of ends in his *System of Ethics*.[68] The difference between these two communities rests on the difference between the imperatives of right and morality, which Fichte discusses in his introduction to the *Grundlage des Naturrechts*. The object of right is a community between *free* beings. It is necessary that every free being should assume that other free beings exist. But it is not necessary that all free beings should coexist together; such peaceful coexistence is the concern of right. The concept of such a community and its realization are altogether arbitrary and contingent (*willkürliches*).[69] That is, a community of right is hypothetical. Here Fichte follows Rousseau and social contract theory in conceiving community as contingent and derivative from the antecedent wills of independent individuals. The whole is not prior to but derivative from its parts.

As Fichte sorts out the distinction between the community of rights and the moral community, it becomes apparent that right deals with something like an empirical intersubjectivity, and morality with something like a transcendental intersubjectivity. Fichte conceives the concept of right as involving a voluntary restriction of external freedom to make possible the freedom of others in the same sense. The concept of right is hypothetical; it does not demand that a community be established but only that *if* such a community be established, it must be established on the basis of the concept of rights. Morality differs from right in that moral commands are unconditional, not hypothetical. There may be a moral injunction to respect the concept of right, but this belongs to morality and not to right. The derivation of right from morality is incomprehensible, Fichte claims, since morality commands unconditionally and universally, whereas right is a matter of permission that may or may not be exercised. In the *Grundlage des Naturrechts* Fichte portrays human beings as bound only by their arbitrary resolution to live in community with others. But they do not have to do

---

67. See Siep, *APP*.

68. Fichte, *System der Sittenlehre, Werke* 4; hereafter *SdS* (English translation: *Science of Ethics*, trans. A. E. Kroeger [London: Kegan Paul, 1897]).

69. *GNR*, 9; *SR*, 19.

so. If someone is not willing to restrict his freedom, that is, his arbitrary will, then he is not bound to live by rights. However, he has excluded himself from human society.

For Fichte, rights are permissions that leave one at liberty to assert them or not—as one pleases. Duties are unconditional commands. Fichte extends the subjective arbitrary freedom inherent in the concept of permission to the issue of membership in the state as a community of rights. Fichte treats the state as a voluntary organization, and this reflects his acceptance of social contract theory. One enters a state by a free decision and resolve; moreover, one might opt not to enter or join. The individual is free to decide whether or not he will live in a state; the state is thus optional. However, as soon as one has decided to enter a state, Fichte contends one has also freely embraced its laws. In a revealing comment, Fichte observes that the laws of a state include self-imposed restrictions within which the citizen must be kept by force.[70] Why must citizens be coerced to abide by their voluntary, self-imposed restrictions?

The foregoing question highlights a puzzle in Fichte's *Grundlage des Naturrechts*: right, which is supposed to be grounded in freedom and recognition, requires coercion in order to be upheld. Recognition, which is supposed to be the ground and basis of right, plays no role in the actual maintenance and enforcement of right.[71] Instead Fichte sanctions and approves of compulsion, thereby marginalizing recognition in his account of right. Why? Siep helpfully points out that in paragraphs 1–7 of *Grundlage des Naturrechts* Fichte proceeds on the assumption that human beings behave rationally, that is, reciprocally recognize each other. This reflects the first strand of Fichte's thought, the recognition argument for community and freedom.

However in paragraph 8, Fichte raises the twin issues of egoism and mistrust, which require a third party, or a coercive community. This is the starting point of the second strand of Fichte's thought. The issue is in part the problem of an evil will that may come to expression in transgression. Fichte poses the question of an evil will against the background of a community based on mutual recognition. A transgression of the mutual recognition already present and expressed in law shows that the transgressor does not regard the rule of law as inviolable and that his prior apparent respect for law was based on other, perhaps merely tactical grounds.[72] This break with the law and its underlying mutual recognition creates a new situation. Fichte observes that the rational be-

---

70. *GNR*, 14–15; *SR*, 25. Fichte believes that the use of force and coercion is justified because the citizen, by his free decision to enter the state, has consented, in principle, to its laws and to punishment for the violations of its laws. He treats the state as a voluntary organization, but what is voluntary is only the decision to enter. This decision, viewed from the 'other side', is taken as an acceptance of coercion.

71. See Siep, *APP*.

72. *GNR*, 97. See Siep, *PPDI*, 58.

ings that he originally described as reciprocally recognizing each other are in fact uncertain whether they can depend on their rights being secured against the attacks of others.[73] The others might change their minds concerning the mutually recognized agreement to subject themselves to law, and the moment one supposes such a change, then confidence and security break down.

For Fichte, mutual confidence and trust are the conditions of possibility of legal relations (*Rechtsverhältnisse*). Consequently, if mutual fidelity and confidence between persons have been lost, mutual security and legal relations between them likewise become impossible.[74] However, while trust and confidence—in short, the good will—cannot be compelled, behavior and conduct that accord with them can be compelled. Fichte observes that "each wills and has the right to will that the other party's acts shall always be such as would result if he had a good will. Whether this good will really is the incentive of those acts or not, is a matter of indifference. Each has claim only to the *legality* of the other, not to his *morality*."[75]

Several points deserve notice. First, Fichte's general procedure in *Grundlage des Naturrechts* is to develop his position by formulating antinomies. Consequently in pointing out an antinomy in his thought, one is never sure whether this is a criticism or rather an illustration of Fichte's point. To be clear, I intend the following explication of a particular antinomy concerning recognition as a criticism.[76] The antinomy is this: On the one hand, Fichte argues that reciprocal recognition is supposed to remove the uncertainty, mistrust, and loss of confidence that make coercion necessary; on the other hand, he argues that recognition does not and cannot remove the mistrust because it leaves the security of both parties open to chance and contingency.[77] This is insufficient for Fichte; security requires a quasi-mechanical necessity from which no exception is possible.[78] He believes such an ironclad guarantee of security can be provided only by the community of coercion, not the community of recognition.

Second, when Fichte asserts that mutual confidence and trust have been lost, he undermines the concept of recognition and turns it into something wholly external. As if mutual trust and confidence did not presuppose or involve mutual recognition! Fichte here betrays how superficial and external his concept of recognition is. Consider the following text.

> The free being by its mere presence in the sensible world, compels every other free being to recognize it as a person. . . . In this way there arises a communal

73. *GNR*, 137; *SR*, 189.   74. *GNR*, 139; *SR*, 192.   75. Ibid.

76. The antinomy occurs in the context of Fichte's discussion of punishment and legal coercion (*Zwangsrecht*). In §13, Fichte introduces the principle of coercion; in general his view is like Kant's and Hegel's, namely, that coercion is justified not as an end itself, but only as a response to a prior illegitimate coercion.

77. *GNR*, 137; *SR*, 189.

78. *GNR*, 137–138; *SR*, 189–190.

knowledge [*gemeinschaftliche Erkenntniss*] and nothing more. *Each internally
recognizes the other, but they remain isolated as before.*[79]

That is, *after* a joint action of mutual recognition—in which there is supposed
to be an 'internal' mediation of the self to itself by the other—each person remains as isolated as she was *before* that act. It is as if the mutual mediation of
freedom in reciprocal recognition has no impact and makes no difference to
self-identity, or the self in relation to itself. Fichte does not indicate any changes,
transformations, or sublations that recognition may effect in the recognizing
selves, no breaking down of barriers, no breaking through limits, no ethical
Aufhebung. Yet it was precisely such intersubjective mediation and transformation of freedom and self-identity that mutual recognition was supposed to
provide and thereby take care of such issues as mutual trust and confidence. In
Fichte's account of recognition, there is no intersubjective-social universal, no
We or community of selves. Community does not arise or result immanently
out of the mutual mediation of freedoms. Rather community remains external,
and if it is external, then it must be a forcible union. This contradicts Fichte's
earlier point that recognition involves the intersubjective mediation of freedom. If the persons who recognize each other remain as isolated after recognition as before, then any intersubjective 'mediation' of freedom is merely formal, empty, and superficial. If that is so, recognition not only cannot mediate
the self's freedom to the self, it cannot ground the social contract either.

The potential negation inherent in otherness, which becomes explicit in
transgression, remains for Fichte an external negation. External negations leave
the subjects unaffected. This helps to clarify the difference between Fichte and
Hegel on recognition. For Fichte, negation and relation remain external. Hence
negation appears in the *Grundlage des Naturrechts* as a loss of trust and confidence. Since Fichte believes that the loss of faith and confidence cannot be restored, he abandons recognition and instead turns to coercion as the means of
maintaining social order and security.

In contrast, Hegel incorporates negation into his concept of recognition and
freedom; it becomes the initial moment, the first *Stufe*, or level. Negation manifests itself in the refusal of recognition, or nonrecognition. For Hegel, the acknowledgment of an evil will leads to various versions of the struggle for recognition that culminates in the figure of master and slave. Hegel's account of
the struggle for recognition is, in comparison with Fichte's, genuinely internal
and immanent, because self-identity is at stake and life is at risk. Negation for
Hegel therefore becomes the self-reflexive motive force of the dialectics of recognition. However, master/slave is only the first level of unequal recognition,
which carries within it the possibilities of its own subversion. The path beyond
negation is for Hegel a negation of negation that, by removing inequality, hier-

79. *GNR*, 85–86; *SR*, 126. My italics.

archy, and domination, not only restores freedom but also elevates it to the ethical level and gives it actuality and staying power in the world.

Third, to counter the loss of trust, Fichte embraces coercive mechanisms of punishment to enforce conduct and action in conformity to law. He thereby reveals the irrelevance of recognition to his system of rights. Mutual recognition, which was supposed to be the foundation of right, is displaced by coercion. Fichte introduces coercion as a permanent feature of the quasi-mechanical community of coercion. To be sure, this occurs in Fichte's discussion of punishment. Punishment is a quasi-mechanical contrivance that is supposed to make the lawless will annihilate or cancel itself. This bears certain similarities to Hegel's own conception of retributive punishment. Fichte shows that punishment is supposed to be a contrivance that coerces coercion. By threatening to bring about the opposite of what the potential transgressor intends, the threat of punishment keeps the lawless will within limits. Fichte himself draws the conclusion that the mechanism of punishment, rendered universal and certain, would make ethics and the good will superfluous as far as right is concerned: "The good will would be rendered superfluous for the external realization of right, since the bad will would be forced by its very badness to effect the same end."[80] The good will has become superfluous, at least as far as right is concerned. Ethics and politics thus become separated. Hegel complains that Fichte considers community not as an end in itself but merely as a condition of law and justice.[81]

From this consideration of community as a means and condition of justice, it is but a short step to Fichte's subsequent elaboration on the supervisory, policing function of public authority that carries the coercion strand of his thought to its extreme conclusion. Fichte haplessly confirms Foucault's thesis concerning the militaristic model of the modern state and its disciplinary apparatus.[82] Fichte is explicit about surveillance of the population that makes persons become visible and gives a sinister twist to the concept of recognition.

> The chief principle of a well-regulated police is necessarily the following: that each citizen shall be recognized as this or that person at all times and places when it may be necessary. No one must remain unknown to the police (public authority). This can be attained only in the following manner: each one must always

80. *GNR*, 142; *SR*, 195. Elsewhere he explains the point thus: "to the extent that the state is related to the evil will, to the extent that it is a compulsory power, then its final aim is undoubtedly to make itself superfluous, i.e., to make all compulsion unnecessary. This is an aim which can be achieved even if good will and the confidence in it do not become universal. For if everyone knows on the basis of long experience that every act of injustice will surely bring misfortune and that every crime will surely be discovered and punished, then one may expect that from prudence alone they will not exert themselves in vain, that they will not willfully and knowingly bring harm upon themselves." Fichte, *Lectures on the Vocation of the Scholar*, 157n.

81. G. W. F. Hegel, *Natural Law*, trans. T. M. Knox (Philadelphia: University of Pennsylvania Press, 1975), 83ff. Hereafter cited as *NL*.

82. Michel Foucault, *Discipline and Punish*, trans. Alan Sheridan (New York: Vintage, 1979).

carry a pass with him, signed by his immediate government official, in which his person is accurately described. There must be no exceptions to this rule.[83]

Fichte embraces surveillance as a deterrent to crime:

> The source of all evil in our states as presently constituted is disorder. . . . In a state such as we have described, each citizen has a definite position, and the police know pretty well where each citizen is, and what he does at every hour of the day. . . . By means of his pass each citizen can be identified at a glance. Crime is something very unusual in such a state.[84]

Although Hegel does not deny the importance of public security, public authority, or punishing crime, he parts company sharply with Fichte over the aforementioned surveillance measures.

> Fichte's state is centered on the police, to whom it seeks to accord a particularly wide scope, but it is also a state based on need. According to Fichte, no persons can go out without having their identity papers on them, and he deems this very important to prevent crimes. But such a state becomes a world of galley slaves, where each is supposed to keep his fellow under constant supervision.[85]

This world of galley slaves is precisely what Hegel wants to avoid in his conception of ethical life. While Hegel reluctantly sanctions some supervision by public authority, he is clear about its meaning and purpose: "This police supervision must go no further than is necessary. . . . *The purpose of what is hidden is that public life should be free.*"[86]

Hegel's criticism of the security and coercion strand of Fichte's thought is part of a larger critique: Fichte introduces the proper speculative principle of freedom, but then proceeds inconsistently in a way that undermines this principle. In the *Difference* essay, he points out the basic dualisms in Fichte's system: the ego and the nonego have no positive character, relation, or mediation but merely the negative character of being other.[87] Because otherness is seen primarily as negative by Fichte, freedom is also understood as negative; it is not the suspension of opposition but rather fixed in opposition to its other, the *Anstoß*, and so on. Because the nonego is understood only negatively as being other than ego, freedom is likewise fixed and understood in primarily negative terms.[88] On Fichte's premises, "What union is possible, though, once absolute opposites are presupposed? Strictly speaking, none at all, obviously."[89] Given such premises, community can only be a limit to freedom. On the other hand, since

---

83. *GNR*, 295; *SR*, 378.
84. *GNR*, 302; *SR*, 386.
85. *VPR*17, 212.   86. Ibid. My italics.
87. *Difference* essay, 128.
88. Ibid., 133.   89. Ibid., 126.

Fichte sets for himself the task of uniting opposites, what sort of union is possible when, as Fichte contends, individuals remain external to each other in their relationships? Hegel believes that on Fichte's assumptions any "union is forcible. The one subjugates the other. The one rules, the other is subservient."[90] Thus ego and nonego are supposed to be related reciprocally, but in fact they never constitute a whole or community; instead, the one dominates and the other is dominated and goes into servitude.[91] Since he conceives the state in terms of such fundamental oppositions, it is no surprise that Fichte finds the problem of mistrust insoluble, and sanctions coercion.

Hegel believes that Fichte's account of mutual recognition subverts itself because individuals remain external to each other in spite of their relationship. Thus community is either impossible or not genuine, exhibiting a system of forcible unions that both conceal and sanction domination and oppression. Once separation has been made basic, there is no longer any possibility of mutual relation and connection. "Rather, every connection is one of dominating and being dominated."[92] In his essay *Natural Law*, Hegel continues this line of criticism. Specifically, Hegel diagnoses Fichte's declaration that once mutual trust and confidence are lost they cannot be restored, as a popular expression for and symptom of the fundamental dualism and disunity at the heart of his system.[93] This dualism makes ethics for Fichte both necessary and yet superfluous. On Fichte's assumptions only a formal and external union is possible; moreover, relation as such is identified as essentially compulsion.

> In this way the external character of oneness is utterly fixed and posited as something absolute and inherently necessary; and thereby the inner life, the rebuilding of lost confidence and trust, the union of universal and individual freedom, and ethical life itself, are made impossible. . . . It really is an attempt at a consistent system that would have no need of the religion and ethics that are foreign to it.[94]

Here Hegel diagnoses the fundamental contradiction in Fichte's account: The recognition argument is supposed to lead to ethical life and community; but the coercion argument renders irrelevant or impossible the rebuilding of lost confidence and trust. The coercion argument undermines the ethical life that the recognition argument is supposed to generate.

It should not be forgotten that Hegel is criticizing and rejecting only one strand of Fichte's thought (the security and coercion argument for community) while tacitly affirming and developing the other strand (the recognition argument for community and freedom). Unless this point is kept in mind, Hegel appears to be unfair to Fichte, and his agreement with Fichte's community of recognition is concealed. In his earliest writings he takes Fichte to task for con-

90. Ibid., 115.   91. Ibid., 138.   92. Ibid., 144.
93. *Hegel, NL*, 84. My italics.
94. Ibid., 85.

ceiving community as forcible and as requiring the self-limitation of freedom. "In community with others, however, freedom must be surrendered in order to make possible the freedom of all rational beings living in community. . . . So freedom must suspend itself in order to be freedom."[95] In making this charge, Hegel fails to mention Fichte's declaration that the subjection of individual freedom to community is not a subjection to the arbitrary will of an individual but to a universal rational will, which is the principle (*Begriff*) of right and freedom. Fichte observes,

> Hence far from losing my rights by such subjection, I rather first obtain them through it, since only by this subjection [to universal rational will] have I fulfilled the condition under which alone the human being attains rights. Although I am subject, I am subject only to my own will. . . . All that has been taken from me is the concern to carry out my legal claims by my own physical might.[96]

Later Fichte adds, "It is clear that the individual who enters such an agreement receives his freedom although he renounces it, and receives it *because* he renounces it. Through these concepts all contradictions are dissolved and through their realization the rule of right is also achieved."[97] Note that Fichte here does not think of community as inherently a tyranny. Rather his point is exactly the opposite, that a community of mutual recognition, in which arbitrary lawless freedom is renounced and exchanged for recognized, civil, lawful freedom, is the condition under which genuine freedom and right are realized.

Fichte's concept of community is not exhausted by, much less fully developed in, the *Grundlage des Naturrechts*. There is another community, or at least another analysis of community, namely, a moral community or community of ends. We have seen that recognition proves ultimately to be superfluous in the community of rights and that recognition is displaced in favor of coercive mechanisms that seek to ensure at least an external compliance with right. But what about the ethical community? Doesn't this community have to be founded on mutual respect and recognition?

Apparently not. Fichte conceives the moral community of rational beings as independent, self-contained monads or entelechies. The ego, as a monad, depends on the summons of the other to awaken it to the consciousness of its freedom. But once the consciousness of freedom is aroused, the self develops independently by itself. Nothing in the ego happens except through the ego. Thus, although Fichte appeals to the summons of the other as the condition of the consciousness of freedom, and although the summons of the other in the *Naturrecht* leads to the concept of mutual recognition, in his *Sittenlehre* Fichte does not carry out the analysis of the relation between self and other by a further description and account of recognition but falls back on the doctrine of

---

95. Ibid.   96. *GNR*, 104; *SR*, 152.
97. *GNR*, 109–110; *SR*, 159.

preestablished harmony.[98] My influence on the other, as well as his influence on me, is predestined for each of us. This appeal to preestablished harmony allows Fichte to reduce all apparently external relations of the ego-monad to internal relations within the monad. This appeal to preestablished harmony renders mutual recognition superfluous.

Fichte's appeal to preestablished harmony is problematic for several reasons. It is an abstract theoretical metaphysical doctrine rather than a clarification of the relations between persons. Moreover, it is by no means clear that it is compatible with the transcendental freedom that Fichte seeks to defend. For if there is preestablished harmony between subjects, this establishment must be prior to freedom in the transcendental sense. This not only excludes freedom, it also excludes and conceals the intersubjective phenomena to which Fichte has previously called attention, namely, the summons and mutual recognition.

Consequently, by failing to develop intersubjective mutual recognition as the foundation of right and ethics and in falling back on metaphysical and political coercion, Fichte manages to produce not one but two inadequate concepts of community. It is not that these communities are inadequate for Fichte's purposes, but rather inadequate in the sense that in neither case is mutual recognition essential. Rather, mutual recognition, which was supposed to be the medium of access to one's freedom, to the other, and to be the foundation of rights, turns out to be superfluous. Intersubjective interaction is reduced either to compulsion and coercion as in the legal community of rights or to preestablished harmony as in the ethical community. Further, by appealing to preestablished harmony to ground and secure relations between the transcendental community of monads, Fichte excludes most of the interesting moral problems from morality, for example, the struggle for recognition, and the question how an ideal harmonious community could be realized in the first place. On the other hand, if a nontemporal preharmonized community of monads does not have to be realized because it is already in existence, this fact would be an unexplained mystery within a philosophy of infinite striving.[99]

The results of our inquiry are negative. It cannot be maintained that the concept of recognition is essentially tied to or necessarily bound up with social contract theory such that the latter is the only possible political expression and articulation of recognition. Nor can it be maintained that Fichte consistently developed the concept of recognition in such a way as to justify social contract theory as its necessary result. Fichte introduces the concept of recognition, only to abandon it subsequently in his appeal to coercion and to preestablished harmony. Despite a promising beginning, Fichte develops no consistent social theory on the basis of mutual recognition.

98. Fichte, *System der Sittenlehre, Werke* 4:226f.
99. Cf. Fichte's comment: "My thesis is the following: all free actions are predestined by reason from eternity, i.e., are outside of all time, and every free individual is, in reference to perception, posited in harmony with these actions." *SdS, Werke* 4:228.

In comparison with Fichte, Hegel takes the concept of recognition more seriously, thinks it through, and makes Fichte's recognition argument for community and liberation central to his theory of consciousness, *Bildung*, and social-political theory. Mutual recognition is the origin of the concept of spirit, the universal-social consciousness, the I that is We. Spirit is more than a mere common will of contract. In the latter, autonomy remains untransformed and absolute; there is no self-overcoming, and only a partial, impersonal union with other. However, the reciprocal recognition constitutive of the general will as Hegel understands it must overcome natural solipsism, egoism, and instrumentalism; otherwise we never get beyond civil society. The 'We' at the level of the state requires further clarification.

13

The State
as a Social Organism

When Hegel introduces his concept of spirit in the *Phenomenology of Spirit*, it is conceived as an I that in and through reciprocal recognition becomes a We. Reciprocal recognition means a dialectical union between being-for-self and being-for-other. Individuals gain a larger identity and unity in the We as a whole. In the *Philosophy of Right* Hegel inveighs against concepts that distort the intersubjective-social concept of spirit and ethical life. Included in Hegel's criticism is the concept of the state as a social contract. The commercial contract model implies a standpoint of abstract individualism that construes the state as a voluntary association arising from and dependent on the subjective will of individuals. In conceiving the state, the point is not to deny the contractual model altogether but to transform and transcend its individualist standpoint. For example, Hegel contends that although marriage begins in a contract between individuals understood as self-sufficient units, it is a contract to transcend, transform, and supersede the standpoint of contract. Marriage and family therefore are the first concrete universal 'We' in Hegel's account of ethical life, and the concept of state is intended to recapture on a higher level the ethical community and sense of membership inherent in family.

But the state is not a family. Hegel observes that "the state is not a family; it is a unity not of blood, but of spirit."[1] When the family model is taken literally and extended to the state, the result historically has been patriarchy. Patriarchy is an inherently unequal system of recognition that excludes and/or dominates others. For this reason it has legitimated treating others as subordinates and slaves, and even children as property. For Hegel, patriarchy subverts not only

1. *VPR*18, §114.

marriage and family relations, it subverts ethical life.[2] The We that arises through reciprocal recognition is, at the level of the state, not a family, yet it is supposed to extend the ethical concern and ethical unity of the family throughout the social body. What then is the 'We' at the level of the state? How is the We of reciprocal recognition to be understood? What does it mean to transcend and supersede the standpoint of contract?

Hegel's answer is that the We, at the level of the state, is best understood as a social organism.

> The state is an organism, i.e., the development of the Idea in its differences. These different aspects are accordingly the various powers with their corresponding tasks and functions, through which the universal continually produces itself in a necessary way and thereby preserves itself, because it is the presupposition of its own production. This organism is the political constitution; it proceeds perpetually from the state, just as it is the means by which the state preserves itself. If the two diverge and the different aspects break free, the unity which the constitution produces is no longer established. . . . It is in the nature of an organism that all its parts must perish if they do not achieve identity and if one of them seeks independence. Predicates, principles and the like get us nowhere in assessing the state, which must be apprehended as an organism.[3]

Note that Hegel conceives the state as an organism primarily at the level of its constitution and laws. He locates the organic aspect of the state in its constitution: "This organism is the political constitution."[4] In adopting the model of organism, Hegel follows the organic conception of Montesquieu's *Spirit of the Laws*: "Montesquieu stated the true historical view, the genuinely philosophical viewpoint, that legislation in general and its particular determinations should not be considered in isolation and in the abstract, but rather as a dependent moment within one totality, in the context of all other determinations which constitute the character of a nation and age; within this context they gain their genuine significance, and hence also their justification."[5] However, he criticizes and transforms Montesquieu's naturalistic and feudal concept of organic unity. The constitution does not arise from natural biological factors, but from the free spirit of a people. He replaces Montesquieu's naturalistic conception of organic unity with the concept of freedom, that is, spiritual organism. If the state is the realization of freedom, this freedom is not a merely natural given but

---

2. Consider Hegel's polemics against the Roman empire as an obnoxious form of patriarchy: *PR*, §§180, 357. Hegel portrays the Roman realm as follows: "The dissolution of the whole ends in universal misfortune and the demise of ethical life, in which the individualities of nations perish in the unity of a pantheon and all individuals sink to the level of private persons with an equal status and with formal rights, who are accordingly held together only by an abstract and arbitrary will of monstrous proportions" (*PR*, §357).

3. *PR*, §269 Zusatz.   4. Ibid., §269.   5. Ibid., §3.

rather "only a result and product of the consciousness of the deepest principle of spirit and of the universality and expansion of this consciousness."[6]

Thus Hegel is thinking not of a comparison between the state and an animal but of the state in terms of the logical categories of organism and teleology. Organism is for Hegel part of the general ontological conception of being developed in his logic. The concept of organism is for Hegel a determinate specification and teleological development of the category of life and vitality. As a logical concept, it is prior to the systematic distinction between Nature and Spirit. Hence it should come as no surprise that Hegel conceives organism not only as a concept of life but also as a concept of spirit.

Organism is a concept of something that produces itself and becomes what it already potentially is: "The living being reproduces itself; it is only a play with itself, for it produces only what already is."[7] In other words, organism is the presupposition of its own production; it is self-grounding. Moreover, as Hegel develops it, his concept of organism has nothing to do with racist or totalitarian theories of the state; on the contrary, Hegel's theory of organism contains a critique of totalitarianism as abstract monism, that is, a universal relation without *relata*, and equally a critique of abstract individualism, namely, atomism or individuals without relation.

But how does the concept of organism help us understand the We? Isn't organism an abstract metaphysical conception that conceals the We's origination in mutual recognition? Isn't the logical concept of organism antiphenomenological and anti-intersubjective? One writer claims that Hegel's concept of recognition and theory of intersubjectivity is only gratuitously present in the *Realphilosophie*, because there is no logical foundation for intersubjectivity and the categories of the logic do not support, justify, or clarify intersubjectivity.[8] Hence the appeal to the logical category of life and organism as the conceptual vehicle for thinking and clarifying the We, the state, and its political constitution must be misguided.

I shall try to show that Hegel makes some intersubjective sense out of the concept of the We as an organism and that he offers an expanded social phenomenology in the process. Put succinctly, mutual recognition constitutes the ideal unity and actuality of the state and its constitution. Mutual recognition does not remain simply a dialogue between I and Thou; it takes on the shape of an organic unity that is a third alternative to nominalism and pluralism, on the one hand, and monism and totalitarianism, on the other. Only if it takes on this shape can nominalism be avoided and will it be possible to understand how the We— the social identity—can be present in all its members without totalitarianism.

---

6. *E*, §539.   7. *VPR*17, §69.

8. See Hösle, *Hegels System*. For criticism of Hösle, see my "Discernment in the Realm of Shadows."

We have seen that mutual recognition is the phenomenal shape and system of the concept as it appears in and constitutes objective spirit.[9] This turn from subjective to objective spirit has its grounding in the logical transition to objectivity, which Hegel discusses under the rubrics of mechanism and teleology. In an important sense that Hegel's critics overlook or fail to appreciate, mutual recognition and organism are crucial to the central Hegelian concepts of objective spirit and objective idealism, and indeed, the very notion of objectivity itself.

But the development of an organic conception of community really begins with Fichte. Fichte is the one who first introduced the concept of organism as suitable for conceiving the civic relation. Moreover, his discussion anticipates some of the basic divisions of Hegel's *Philosophy of Right* and introduces points that Hegel will clarify or formulate in greater detail. However, Fichte did not explicitly connect organism to the concept of recognition, or make either concept central in his account of the state. In this respect Fichte remains a transitional figure between Kant and Hegel. After examining Fichte's concept of organism, we shall examine Hegel's criticism and further development of it and then pose some critical issues concerning the inclusivity and/or exclusivity of the organic theory of the state.

Fichte on Social Contract and Organism

We have seen that Fichte follows Rousseau in conceiving the state as a social contract and that Hegel criticizes the nominalism and individualism underlying the conception of the social contract. However, Fichte's treatment of social contract is quite complex, involving not one but several contracts, or levels of contract. As he works through the levels of contract, the social contract is subtly transformed from a commercial contract into an organic conception of the state. Fichte's careful analysis of this transformation is a suggestive account of what it may mean, in Hegelian parlance, to transcend and transform the standpoint of contract (*ihn aufzuheben*).[10]

Fichte's account of the social contract (*Staatsbürgervertrag*) is complex. Fichte distinguishes three sorts of contracts, the property contract (*Eigentumsvertrag*), the protection or security contract (*Schutzvertrag*), and the union contract (*Vereinigungsvertrag*). In Fichte's discussion, the concept of contract is deepened, expanded, and transformed. Fichte's analysis shows a gradual transition from the property contract artificially constructed by antecedent, independent individuals who remain external to each other to a union contract that involves an organic model of the state.

Fichte observes that the *property contract* is basically an agreement to ab-

---

9. *E*, §484.   10. *PR*, §163.

stain from interference in others' right to property. This is similar to Hegel's concept of abstract right as a set of permissions. The *security contract* goes beyond the property contract because it calls for a positive performance or contribution of the individual to the whole: "The security contract is like all contracts, conditional. Each promises to protect the other(s), on the condition that the other(s) will likewise protect him. The contract and the right grounded upon it, are null and void (*hinfällt*) if one party to the contract fails to fulfill it." [11] This contract remains conditional in the sense that individuals are free to enter it, and failure of an individual to fulfill it renders it null and void for that individual. Since the others cannot count on his support, neither can he count on their support or protection.

From the security contract, Fichte believes, the union contract itself arises or follows. For in protecting each other distributively, each individual implicitly pledges to protect and defend everybody collectively, that is, to defend the whole framework of settling issues reciprocally and by contract. The security contract forges a common will that is not simply a contingency in the sense of being at the option of each individual. On the contrary, it requires a contribution from each party to the whole and for the sake of the whole. The whole then is a common will that stands above and binds the private wills of the individuals.

> He gives his will to protect, without a doubt, the whole. In this way he becomes a part of the whole, and flows together with it. Henceforth through unforeseeable contingency, he may be either the one protecting or the one protected. In this way, through the contract of individuals with individuals, the whole has arisen, and through the fact that all individuals contract with all individuals, i.e., as a whole, the whole is completed. We call this contract, that secures and protects the first two . . . the *union contract*. Through the union contract the individual becomes a part of an organized whole, and fuses [*zusammenschmilzen*] with the whole. [12]

This fusion with the whole refers to the positive contributions of individuals to the maintenance and support of the whole. The whole is created and maintained out of these performances/contributions of individuals. These contributions are not simply self-limitations, but are positive duties and actions. To protect each other is at the same time, considered at the universal level, to work for and to protect the whole. Thus while the security contract is conditional in that if you fail to protect me this would nullify my contractual obligation to protect you, this contract is more than just a contract between two people. It is also a contract that has a universal dimension, a contract with the whole and between the whole and its individuals: "By undertaking to protect all the possessions of each citizen it recognizes his title to those possessions; and thus the property contract—which at first appeared to be concluded only between all

11. Fichte, *GNR*, 198; *SR*, 219.
12. *GNR*, 204; *SR*, 227.

considered as single individuals—is confirmed by the actual totality [*reelle Ganze*] of the state."[13] This move is not unlike Hegel's grounding of abstract right in the general will and ethical life.

However, for Fichte the agreement between individual and state remains contingent, and it is entered into conditionally by the state as well as the individual; the state extends recognition and protection to the individual on the condition that the individual fulfill his obligations and duties toward the state. The state contracts with the individual to secure and protect him and his property "only on condition of his furnishing his contribution, and hence the contract is canceled when he does not furnish it. Each one, therefore, guarantees with all his property that he will contribute [to the whole] and he loses his [socially guaranteed] right to his property if he does not make his contribution."[14] Fichte explains the exchanges inherent in contract: there is an exchange between individuals on the individual level, and on another level, an exchange between the individual and the whole.

> The two parties of the contract are: the individual and the state as a whole. The contract is conditioned by the free formal will of both parties to enter into an agreement. The material will, about which the parties must agree, is, on the one side, directed to the specific determinate property of the individual; on the other side, it is directed to the individual's relinquishment of any claim to all other property, and to his determinate contribution to the securing power. Through the contract the citizen obtains from the whole a secured property, and the whole obtains from the citizen his renunciation of all claims to the legal possession of the property of all its other citizens, and a definite contribution to the securing power of the state.[15]

Consequently, although the social contract as Fichte understands it is contingent in that one is either in it or not, once made or agreed to, it is self-guaranteeing because it contains an immanent necessity:

> This contract guarantees itself; it has in itself the sufficient reason that it will be kept, just as everything organized [*Organisirte*] has its sufficient reason in itself. Either this contract does not exist for a person at all, or if it does, it completely binds him. Whoever does not fulfill the contract, is not a member, and whoever is a member necessarily fulfills it completely. Whoever is not in the contract is in general not in any legal relation or relation of right, and is rightfully entirely excluded from the reciprocity with other beings of his equal in the sensible world.[16]

When he sums up and elucidates the union contract, Fichte proposes the organic model of the state.

---

13. *GNR*, 205; *SR*, 229.   14. *GNR*, 206; *SR*, 230.   15. *GNR*, 207; *SR*, 231.
16. *GNR*, 207; *SR*, 231.

The most fitting image [*Bild*] to elucidate this concept is that of an organized natural product, which has often been used in modern times to describe the different branches of official public authority/power as a unity, but not, as far as I know, to throw light on the entire civil relation. In the product of nature, every part can be what it is only in this organic connection/combination, and outside of this combination [*Verbindung*] would simply not be. Indeed, outside of all organic systematic connection absolutely nothing would be, because without the reciprocal action of organic forces preserving each other mutually in equilibrium, there would be no enduring or sustaining structure at all, but only an unthinkable eternal war between being and not-being. Similarly, the human being attains a definite place [*Stand*] in the order of things, a point of rest in nature, only in union with the state. And each attains and preserves this determinate position towards others and towards nature, only through the fact that he is in this determinate association. . . . Through the union of all organic powers, a nature constitutes itself. Through the union of subjective wills [*Willkür*] humanity constitutes itself.[17]

Fichte employs the concept of organism to elucidate "the entire civil relation" as an interdependent network of reciprocities. The concept of organism counters the conception of isolated abstract individuals that are actual apart from relation. These independent individuals, when conceived as and through the concept of organism, are embedded in a framework that shapes and conditions them and is co-constitutive of what they are. Second, it should be noted that organism is here an ontological conception that is irreducible to a set of perceptions or a merely formal conceptual structure, and cannot be adequately appreciated or understood within the traditional frameworks of rationalism and empiricism.[18] Ontologically considered, the organism is a dynamic totality: "without the reciprocal action of organic forces preserving each other in equilibrium there would be no enduring sustaining structure at all, but only an unthinkable war between being and non-being." This point was not lost on Hegel, who developed it further in his logic, where becoming is not only the first concrete category that mediates and relates being and nothing, but is their organic unity.

Third, Fichte uses the concept of organism to begin, if not complete, mediation between two ideas that stand in tension with each other, namely, the right of secession and the union contract. Previously Fichte maintained not only the legitimacy of revolution but also the right of the individual to secede from the contract/state. For the early Fichte, the right of secession is apparently absolute, a position that is not compatible with his support for majority rule. For majority rule implies a subjection, in some sense, of a minority.[19] But Fichte

17. Fichte, *GNR*, 208; *SR*, 232.
18. Josiah Royce observes that the whole is not reducible to a concept (rationalism) or a percept (empiricism). See Royce, *The Problem of Christianity* (Chicago: University of Chicago Press, 1968), chap. 11.
19. Klaus Hartmann, *Politische Philosophie* (Freiburg: Karl Alber Verlag, 1981), 170.

changes his position in his *Grundlage des Naturrechts*. Secession drops out of the picture, because Fichte is concerned with integration and totality, and eventually rejects the social contract concept for reasons similar to Hegel.[20] In the context of developing the concept of right as grounded in mutual recognition, he deepens the contract notion to include the security and union contracts. The concept of social organism is an outgrowth of this shift of position. Fichte maintains that the concept of the individual is reciprocal with the concept of the species, such that the human being becomes human only among others. The concept of organism fleshes out and renders determinate this position: "In the organic body, each part maintains and upholds the whole, and in maintaining the whole, it maintains itself. So also is the citizen related to the state."[21]

It is of interest that Fichte formulates the concept of community as an organism when he attempts to show that the concept of right is grounded in mutual recognition. This is sufficient to suggest that for Fichte, mutual recognition points in the direction of, and quite possibly requires, the conception of the organism as its most complete articulation. However, Fichte does not himself draw this conclusion, and both his concept of recognition and his concept of organism remain, in comparison with Hegel, underdeveloped. As we have seen, his conception of society as coercive is incompatible with his concept of mutual recognition; or to put it differently, under what Fichte characterizes as conditions in which trust is lacking, mutual recognition is either impossible or replaced by coercive measures. Similarly, although he insightfully identifies organism as an image of the union contract, he continues to treat the state as a mechanism (at least in the *Grundlage des Naturrechts*).

Hegel on Organism

Everyone "knows" that Hegel asserts that the truth is the whole and that the concept of the whole as a concrete, differentiated universal is one of the central concepts of Hegel's philosophy. Less well known is that Hegel, the putative philosopher of totality—whole and parts—subjects the category of whole and part to an extended criticism that shows it to be inadequate for conceiving life and intersubjectivity. To be sure, whole and part is one way of thinking identity and difference, and it is a central category and vocabulary within which Hegel is usually discussed, even by sympathetic interpreters. Nevertheless, whole and part as a category remains deficient and defective because it fails to do justice to life and vitality, namely, the living universal that continually produces itself and is the presupposition of its own production. When life, intersubjectivity, and community are thought of via the conceptual media of whole and part, the result is a distortion and obscuring of the former.

20. Ibid., 171n. Fichte expressly rejected the social contract idea in his *Staatslehre* of 1813.
21. Fichte, *GNR*, 208–209; *SR*, 232.

In what follows I am going to examine Hegel's discussion of the category of organism in his *Encyclopedia*, the mature form of his system, the *Science of Logic*, and his *Aesthetics*. Lest this seem a detour away from recognition, intersubjectivity, ethics, and the state, I should point out that Hegel's categories are not empty external forms, a procrustean bed foisted on intersubjectivity and ethical life, but rather have 'subjectivity' built into them. This is why we will see Hegel referring to social and political situations to illustrate a speculative logical point in his criticism of whole and part. The logical categories take on determinacy in the *Realphilosophie*, and conversely, contrary to what some have claimed,[22] the *Realphilosophie*, including the *Philosophy of Right*, really are illumined by Hegel's Logic.

Further, we have pointed out that for Hegel recognition (*Anerkanntsein*) is the phenomenological form of the concept (*Begriff*) of freedom.[23] Hegel advances this claim at the beginning of his exposition of the concept of objective spirit. I want to elaborate further on the significance of this claim. Recognition is the pivot on which turn the important moves from subjective spirit to objective spirit, and from so-called subjective idealism to objective idealism. Mutual recognition is an aspect of the constitution of objectivity, which is itself a special categorical move and topic in Hegel's Logic. At the logical level the move is from the subjective concept to the objective concept, which is at the same time the move from necessity to freedom.[24] In this transition, the objectivity that initially appears as an alien externality loses the significance of being something alien and opposed to the subject. The object—or other—which is not at the disposal of the subject, nevertheless is constituted out of the same ground as the subject, namely, freedom. In mutual recognition this constitution of objectivity—at the same time a constitution of social rationality—comes to be for the recognizing parties themselves. In mutual recognition, two dimensions of freedom, being-for-other and being-for-self, are brought into reciprocity and union; this reciprocal union is equivalent to liberation and reconciliation.[25]

Reciprocal recognition is objective idealism in that when the threshold of the ethical is crossed, the other comes to be not-other. In the process of mutual recognition, the other is no longer alien or a threat but an objective condition and mediator of freedom, a member of the 'We'. Conversely, the 'We' is not an abstract universal but a concrete, intersubjectively mediated universal-social consciousness, or spirit.[26] In the 'We' the transition from subjective to objective idealism is effected. This is Hegel's version of a point made by Schelling in his discussion of recognition, namely, that the other is the mediator of objectivity and that the objectivity of the world rests and depends on the other. Recogni-

22. Wood, *HET*.   23. *E*, §484.   24. Ibid., §§193–194.
25. Cf. Emil Angehrn, *Freiheit und System bei Hegel* (Berlin: Walter de Gruyter, 1977), 76–79.
26. *E*, §436.

tion involves a finding of self in other, or self-recognition in other in which the original self-certainty is transformed, confirmed, and legitimated. It is against this background that Hegel's oft-reiterated declaration that reason is actual only in the life of a people is to be understood. Further, Hegel's declaration that the rational is actual refers to the degree to which mutual-reciprocal recognition pervades and constitutes the life of a people and finds expression in its constitutional structures.

I shall begin by examining Hegel's discussion of whole/part in his *Encyclopedia*, then turn to his fuller discussion of mechanism and teleology in the *Science of Logic* and his most explicit discussion of organism in his *Lectures on Aesthetics*. None of these is a full treatment of organism per se, but each discussion is valuable and complements the others. The only discussions of this material in English are found in F. H. Bradley and Bernard Bosanquet, but both are derivative from Hegel without breaking any new ground or advancing the conceptual analysis, and lack Hegel's social criticism.[27] Thus Hegel's discussion of the state as an organism, although incomplete and fragmentary, remains among the most important and relatively adequate treatments of the topic.

Before examining the texts, I want to point out the correlations between civil society and state, on the one hand, and the logical categorical discussions of mechanism, chemism, and teleology, on the other. Strange as it may seem to the contemporary reader, Hegel's discussion of mechanism and organism is the logical basis and correlate of his important distinction between civil society and the state.

> If the state is confused with civil society, and its determination is equated with the security and protection of property and personal freedom, the interest of individuals as such becomes the ultimate end for which they are united; it also follows that membership in the state is an optional matter. But the relationship of the state to the individual is of a quite different kind. Since the state is objective spirit, it is only through being a member of the state that the individual himself has objectivity, truth and ethical life. Union as such is itself the true content and end, and the vocation [*Bestimmung*] of individuals is to lead a universal life; their further particular satisfaction, activity and mode of conduct have this substantiality and universal validity as their point of departure and result.[28]

---

27. W. H. Walsh, in reviewing the British Hegelians Bradley and Bosanquet, comments that Bradley's treatment of Hegel's ethics in "My Station and Its Duties" is "at best only a partial introduction to that subject: there are many features of Hegel's thought . . . which Bradley passes over in silence." About Bosanquet, Walsh comments that he is closer to Hegel than the others: "Bosanquet had none of the sparkle of Bradley and little of the penetration of Hegel. But he had a better grasp of the structure of the moral life than most of those who have written on moral philosophy since his time." Walsh, *Hegelian Ethics* (London: Macmillan, 1969), 74–76.

28. *PR*, §258. I have altered the English translation because *Bestimmung* is in this case better translated as "vocation" than "destiny." Cf. Fichte's *Bestimmung des Menschen*, which is translated appropriately as the *Vocation of Man*.

In this passage Hegel employs, without explicitly mentioning it, two quite different concepts of totality, namely, mechanism, which is the conceptual scheme of the external state, and organism, which is the conceptual scheme of the ethical state. Traditional whole/part language is inadequate to the ethical state, and carries with it important social and political implications. Mechanism signifies an externally related aggregate, not a genuine community. For Hegel, the concept of community finds most complete logical expression in organism. I shall now flesh out this distinction, pointing out Hegel's references to intersubjectivity, relation, and ethical life as we proceed.

The *Encyclopedia* Treatment of Mechanism and Organism

In §135, Hegel treats whole/part under the category of relationship.[29] For Hegel, the whole/part relationship is one of opposition. It shares this oppositional, incomplete mediation with all the categories of essence. The content is the whole and it consists of its opposite, namely, the parts. The parts are diverse from one another as well as from the whole. Thus, on the one hand, they possess independent being. On the other hand, they are only parts in their identical relation to each other, or insofar as they are taken together as making up the whole. Consequently Hegel observes that this 'togetherness' or ensemble is the *opposite* and *negation* of the part. His critical analysis of the category of whole and part anticipates a criticism that is frequently raised against him, namely, that ethical life and/or objective spirit constitute a unity that swallows up or absorbs individuals and individual differences. But it is the critics, not Hegel, who think in terms of the problematic category of whole and part. As will become clear, Hegel's point here is that the category of whole and part is inadequate to conceive ethical life and ethical relationship. The problem is not with the general idea of relationship, for Hegel appreciates and defends the relatedness of things: "Essential relationship is the determinate and universal manner in which all things appear. *Everything that exists stands in relationship, and this relationship is the authentic nature of every existence.* Consequently what exists does not do so abstractly, on its own account, but only within an other. But in this other it relates to itself and *relationship is the unity of self-relation and relation to others.*"[30] These comments about relationship explicate the structure of spirit as the I that is a We. The We is relationship, namely, the unity

29. "Correlation" is also a possible translation as Wallace does, because it suggests that the *relata* are related reciprocally, not just unilaterally or asymmetrically. But the new translation by Geraets, Harris, and Suchting is preferable to Wallace's and I have followed it here (*G. W. F. Hegel: The Encyclopedia Logic*, trans. T. F. Geraets, W. A. Suchting, and H. S. Harris [Indianapolis: Hackett, 1991]).

30. *E*, §135.

of self-relation and relation to others. In the We, to relate to the other is also to relate to oneself, and vice versa.

But now an ambiguity arises. Hegel observes that if we think of spirit or relationship simply as a whole of parts, we distort what spirit is. The reason is that

> the whole-part relation itself is deficient, 'untrue' inasmuch as its concept and reality do not correspond. The concept of the whole is to contain its parts; but if the whole is taken and made to be what its concept implies, i.e., a whole *in contrast* to its parts, then it is divided, then it ceases to be a whole. There are things that correspond to this whole-part relationship, but, just for that reason, they are only inferior and untrue existences. In this connection we should recollect the general point that when we speak of something's being untrue in a philosophical discussion this should not be understood to mean that the sort of thing spoken of does not exist. A bad state or a sick body may exist all the same, but they are 'untrue' because their concept and their reality do not correspond to one another.[31]

Whole/part is a category of essence, and involves an incomplete mediation. Whole and part signifies a division in which either the whole or the part is treated as essential, which implies the other is nonessential. But this apparent nonessentiality is false; it is the distortion that occurs when we attempt to think *Geist* through the category of whole and part. The priority of the whole over the parts implies that the parts are nonessential. This is the "totalitarian" view that Hegel rejects.

Hegel points out that whole/part language is the language of the analytical understanding (*Verstand*). This language is not simply false or mistaken, it is partially correct. It is suited for thinking of machines and mechanisms— wholes that are indifferent to their parts. However, it is inadequate to ethical life. It is misleading if one tries to think ethical life as a whole/part relation. Hegel observes,

> The relationship of whole and parts, being relationship in its immediacy, is one that recommends itself to reflective understanding. Hence the understanding is frequently content with it where deeper relationships are involved. For instance, the members and organs of a living body should not be considered merely as parts of it, for they are what they are only in their unity and are not indifferent to that unity at all. The members and organs become mere 'parts' only under the hands of the anatomist; but for that reason he is dealing with corpses rather than with living bodies. This is not to say that this kind of dissection should not happen at all, but only that *the external and mechanical relationship of whole and parts does not suffice for the cognition of organic life in its truth*. The same applies in a much higher degree when the whole-part relationship is applied to spirit and the configurations of the spiritual world.[32]

31. Ibid.
32. Ibid. Harris translation slightly modified. Italics mine.

In his criticism of whole/parts, Hegel develops further on the conceptual level Fichte's image of the organism. The subtle but important point Hegel is driving at is that the whole/part relation and the corresponding relation of mechanism—which we shall examine more closely below—are inadequate to conceive or portray recognition and its result, namely, the We, or spirit (*Geist*). He observes that in whole and parts, one or the other contrasting term is ultimately declared to be inessential.[33] When this happens, the result is either monism or pluralism. Neither of these options is adequate conceptually to the difference-in-identity that is the We, and for this reason whole/part is not able to articulate the pervasive and animating unity of organism, much less the We.

Mechanism and Chemism in the *Science of Logic*

Hegel's discussion of mechanism, chemism, and teleology has not received wide attention, and some of the attention it has received has been focused primarily on Hegel's critique of Newtonian science. Such a narrow focus is not wrong; however, it glosses over the fact that Hegel's Logic is a general ontology, prior to the systematic distinction between nature and spirit. Our concern here is not with the relevance of Hegel's treatment to scientific or philosophy of nature questions but rather with the social and intersubjective implications of the general ontology. What interests us are Hegel's own references to spirit and intersubjective relations to illustrate and exemplify the 'abstract' ontological analysis. Accordingly, any attempt to view Hegel's logical categories as restricted to natural mundane entities[34] must be resisted, since it fails to note

---

33. Ibid., §136. Mechanism is the preferred category of the understanding as Hegel indicates, and for this reason it is easy to interpret even organism reductively as mechanism. This is what occurs in Fichte, Hegel believes. Such an interpretation is thoughtless: "The relationship of whole and parts is the immediate and thoughtless relationship and overturning of self-identity into diversity. We pass from the whole to the parts and from the parts to the whole, forgetting in each the contrast and opposition to the other, because we take each of them by itself—now the whole, now the parts—as an independent existence. Or, since the parts are supposed to exist (*bestehen*) in the whole, and the whole is supposed to consist in its parts, it follows that, in one case, the whole is what endures, and in the other case, it is the parts that endure, and in each case the other (i.e., the opposite) is deemed unessential" (ibid.).

34. See Hösle, *Hegels System*. This issue surfaces in George Lucas, Jr., one of the more perceptive recent commentators, who approaches mechanism, chemism, and teleology entirely from the scientific side, ignoring the intersubjective and social dimension. See George Lucas, Jr., *The Rehabilitation of Whitehead: An Analytical and Historical Assessment of Process Philosophy* (Albany: SUNY Press, 1989), 93–108. To be sure, Lucas expresses perplexity concerning what is to count as an example of mechanism and organism in Hegel's sense. However in his earlier book, *Two Views of Freedom in Process Thought* (Missoula, Mont.: Scholars Press, 1979), Lucas rightly notes, "Organisms are defined by Hegel so as to apply in the realm of nature to describe biological entities (including human beings), as well as in realm of *Geist* to characterize political and cultural entities" (p. 92). My question concerning Lucas's formulations here is whether the term 'entity' is appropriate for intersubjective and social phenomena. From Fichte on, the critique of entity and substantialist language and conceptual schemes is central to German Idealism and its distinction

that the Logic is a general ontology and that Hegel himself significantly refers to social and spiritual relations and institutions in his exposition. These too are organisms in Hegel's ontological sense.

Mechanism according to Hegel signifies a paradoxical, contradictory whole/part relation. The contradiction of mechanism is that parts of the whole remain external to each other and external to the whole *in spite of their relations.* "In its superficial form this is what the mechanical relationship consists in: that the parts, as independent, stand over and against each other and against the whole."[35] According to mechanism, the different moments of the *Begriff* are "complete and self-subsistent objects that relate to each other only as independent, self-subsistent beings, and remain external to each other in every combination [*Verbindung*]. This is what constitutes the character of mechanism: whatever relation may obtain between the things combined, this relation is an alien, extrinsic one, that does not concern their nature at all. Even if it is accompanied by a semblance of unity, it remains nothing more than external *composition, mixture, aggregation*, etc."[36] This general point can be further developed and specified in a psychological sense, an intersubjective sense, and a social-political sense.

Hegel observes that the category of mechanism does not apply only to machines; there is '*spiritual* mechanism' as well. The core idea of mechanism is that things remain external in spite of their relation. What then is spiritual mechanism? Hegel explains: "The things related in spirit may remain external to one another and to spirit itself. The result is a mechanical style of thinking, a mechanical memory, habit, a mechanical way of acting, which signify that the peculiar penetration of spirit is lacking in what spirit apprehends or does."[37] This might be construed as an account of what happens in habitual behavior, in which we train ourselves to do certain things more or less automatically and without reflection. Moreover, Hegel observes that "laws, ethics, rational conceptions in general, are in the spiritual sphere such communicable entities which penetrate individuals in an unconscious manner and exert their influence upon them."[38] However, there is another, deeper point that Hegel is making, namely, in spiritual mechanism "there is lacking . . . the freedom of individuality, and because this freedom is not manifest in it, such action appears as a merely external one."[39] Mechanism of spirit can also be manifest as apathy, heteronomy, or a dysfunction such as madness.[40]

---

between the 'law of nature' and natural law in the ethical sense. His formulations of this position in traditional metaphysical language runs the risk of regressing into the kind of metaphysics that is the target of Hegel's (and Fichte's) criticisms.

35. *E*, §136. I have altered Harris's translation slightly.
36. *WL*, TWA Sk 6:409–410; *SL*, 711.
37. Ibid.
38. *WL*, TWA Sk 6:416; *SL*, 716.
39. Ibid., 6:409–410; *SL*, 711.
40. See Berthold-Bond, *Hegel's Theory of Madness*, chap. 3.

Second, mechanism also has an intersubjective or interpersonal sense. In their identity and relation, the *relata* remain external to one another. Mechanism is a manifest contradiction between the mutual indifference of the things related and the identity of their determinateness—the contradiction of externality in spite of identity. The unity of mechanism is a merely negative one; in this unity the objects repel one another, and such mutual repulsion is the mechanical process. These general remarks encompass Sartre's theory of intersubjectivity, at least in *Being and Nothingness*. It is well known that for Sartre the other is experienced as an alienation, the original "Fall" of the *cogito* into the world, the petrifying Look before whom one experiences shame and objectification. Sartre's theory of intersubjectivity never gets beyond what Hegel would characterize as mechanism, that is, this strange paradoxical relation in which selves remain external to each other in spite of their relation.[41]

Sartre's position recalls the Leibnizian monads, which, because self-sufficient and self-contained, are cut off from each other and exercise no influence on each other. Despite their relation they remain independent and external to each other. Hegel observes that just for this reason the concept of the monad is a deficient one.[42] If monads are self-contained, self-sufficient totalities, then they cannot influence or affect each other. Since they are already complete, they have no need of the other, and the other can be only be regarded as negative or as a negation of their internal completeness. Further, such a mechanistic view can make no sense of reciprocal relatedness. For reciprocity means that the monads are not merely self-constituting but also in important respects coconstituting, and that co-constitution is essential to self-constitution. The implication of mechanism is that *authentic mediated self-determination* is absent. This is why any appeal to preestablished harmony to account for ethical community is self-subverting; it implies a mechanistic conception of monads and their relations.

At the social-political level, Hegel believes that a mechanist understanding of the general will lies behind the concept of the state as a social contract. This is the point of attack of his critique of Rousseau and Fichte: "It was the achievement of Rousseau to put forward the will as the principle of the state. . . . But Rousseau considered the will only in the determinate form of the individual will (as Fichte also subsequently did), and regarded the universal will not as the will's rationality in and for itself, but only as the common element arising out of the individual will as a conscious will. The union of individuals within the state becomes a contract, which is accordingly based upon their arbitrary will and opinions, and on their express consent."[43] Why is social contract dependent on mechanism? Contract presupposes the standpoint of abstract atomic individualism. As Hans Jonas has observed, in the mechanistic view of things,

41. For a further discussion, see chap. 15.
42. *SL*, 714; *WL*, 6:413.   43. *PR*, §258.

"the finished product, the complete animal-machine, is the *sum of the component parts, and the most elementary of such parts, the simplest units of matter, are the ultimate and the only true subjects of individuality*."[44] Hegel rejects this view because it makes social relation and social unity something contingent and derivative from individuality: "The general will must not be regarded as put together or assembled out of explicit individual wills such that these remain absolute."[45] Mechanism is the individualist conception of the social, which, lacking any immanent bonds or relations, must be held together by external forces, for example, force itself, by self-interest, illusion, or by a deliberately constructed contract. Such unities merely paper over the externality and contingencies of relations between absolute individual units.

Such abstract relationless individualism is transcended on the level of what Hegel calls chemism: "The chemical object is distinguished from the mechanical by the fact that the latter is a totality indifferent to determinateness, and consequently the relation to other and the kind and manner of this relation belong to its nature."[46] The mechanical object is a pure self-contained monad that has no need of relation and remains the same whether in relation or apart from relation. In contrast, the chemical object stands in relation to its other by its nature, and so relationship enters into and co-constitutes its nature.[47] For this reason, "a chemical object is not comprehensible from itself alone, and the being of one is the being of the other."[48] Only on such conditions is something like a living totality possible. Again, our concern is not with Hegel's extended analysis of chemism or its relation to and significance for chemistry as a natural science. I merely wish to point out and underscore that with chemism we have a logical foundation for and/or reconstruction of intersubjective and social phenomena. Hegel himself observes in his discussion of chemism that "the expression must not be understood here as though this relation only exhibited itself in that form of elemental nature to which the name chemism so-called is strictly applied. . . . In the animate world, the sex relation comes under this schema, and it also constitutes the formal basis for the spiritual relations of love, friendship and the like."[49]

Of course, with chemism we are still only on the level of external relations.

44. Hans Jonas, "Spinoza and the Theory of Organism," in *Philosophical Essays: From Ancient Creed to Technological Man* (Chicago: University of Chicago Press, 1974), 215.

45. Hegel, *Geschichte der Philosophie*, TWA Sk 20:307.

46. *SL*, 727.

47. The distinction between mechanism, chemism, and teleology in the *Science of Logic* recapitulates the threefold distinction of the logic into logic of being, logic of essence, and logic of the concept.

48. *WL*, TWA Sk 6:430; *SL*, 728.

49. Ibid., 6:429; *SL*, 727. The latter count as 'good chemistry'. I am unaware of any German equivalent for this English expression; nevertheless, Hegel's analysis suggests that it is more than a mere metaphor.

All that has changed is the concept of the individual, from one in which relation is wholly external (corresponding to the absence of freedom or immanent self-determination) to one in which relation is co-constitutive of individuality and for this reason not utterly alien. This corresponds to the situation depicted by Hegel in his account of master and slave. At least here the individuals are conceived as standing in relation and as having need of each other, and as free to act in accordance with their need, or in contradiction to their need, for recognition.

There is a further development in teleology and organism. "Teleology is especially contrasted with mechanism, in which the determinateness posited in the object, being external, is essentially one in which no self-determination is manifested."[50] Teleology is thus associated with immanent self-determination or freedom, in contrast with mechanism or necessity (external determination).[51] In this regard, teleology is a third alternative to mechanism and chemism, and is their truth.[52] Teleology is superior to mechanism and chemism as modes of objectivity in that (1) it grasps everything in relation and (2) the end maintains itself in relation: "the end does not merely keep outside the mechanical process; rather it maintains itself in it and is its determination."[53] Teleology thus issues in organism and not in the asymmetrical relation of whole and parts.

What is the difference? It consists in the fact that in organism there is a reciprocal relationship instead of an asymmetrical relation between the whole and the parts. This means that whole and parts are reciprocally coproducing, and not related as substance to accidents. Hans Jonas observes that

> the concept of organism evolves organically, without a break, from the general ontology of individual existence. Of every such existence it is true to say that as a modal determination it represents just one phase in the eternal unfolding of infinite substance and is thus never a terminal product in which the creative activity would come to rest. *While a machine certainly is such a terminal product, the modal wholes, continuing their conative life in shift of their own parts and in interchange with the larger whole, are productive as much as produced, or as much 'natura naturans' as 'natura naturata'.*[54]

In the organism, both 'whole' and 'parts' are both produced and productive. They are simultaneously end and means, or, in other words, the organism is the

---

50. *SL*, 734.
51. Hegel observes that the opposition between mechanism and teleology is an instance of the more general opposition between freedom and necessity, and refers appreciatively to Kant's discussion of the third antinomy: "One of Kant's great services to philosophy consists in the distinction he has made between relative or external, and internal purposiveness; in the latter he has opened up the concept of life, the Idea, and by so doing he has done positively for philosophy what the *Critique of Reason* did but imperfectly, equivocally and negatively, namely, raised it above the determinations of reflection and the relative world of metaphysics." *SL*, 737.
52. *SL*, 739.   53. Ibid., 747.
54. Jonas, "Spinoza and the Theory of Organism," 215–216. My italics.

Aufhebung of the very distinction between end and means. Organism is likewise the transformation and preservation of the distinction between being-for-self and being-for-other.

This sublation/*Aufhebung* of distinctions of reflection by the organism is the focus of Hegel's interest in the concepts of teleology and organism. This is evident from his characterization of the general structure of teleological activity.

> It can therefore be said of the teleological activity that in it the end is the beginning, the consequent the ground, the effect the cause, that it is a becoming of what has become, that in it only what already exists comes into existence, and so forth. This means that all the determinations of relationship belonging to the sphere of reflection or of immediate being have lost their distinction, and what was enunciated as an other, such as end, consequent, effect, etc., no longer has in the end relation the determination of being-other, but on the contrary is posited as identical with the simple Concept.[55]

Strange as it may seem, this analysis sheds important light on the logic of mutual recognition and the We that is supposed to issue from it. In reciprocal recognition, two individuals mutually act as mediators to and for each other. As a result of their reciprocal cointendings, a new larger unity, a common will, a shared experience, a We, is constituted. Thus far, Hegel, Fichte, and Rousseau are agreed. However, this We, this common will, might be merely derivative from the individual subjective will (*Willkür*); if so, the latter remains absolute. This would imply that the standpoint of mechanism is not yet transcended.

Where Hegel diverges from Kant, Rousseau, and Fichte becomes clear in his account of marriage. Marriage transcends the individualist standpoint of contract because each individual subordinates his/her private subjective will to the corporate will or the relationship. The private subjective will is thus *Aufgehoben*, canceled, elevated, enlarged, and transformed. Having thus introduced one of Hegel's most famous terms, *aufheben*, it is well to pause to consider his explanation of it carefully, for it leads from mechanism to organism. *Aufheben* is closely related to Hegel's concept of negation; it is a determinate negation. A determinate negation is not an absolute or total negation—which Hegel calls abstract negation—but a partial negation. A partial negation means that something is canceled, namely, immediacy, while at the same time it is mediated, and by being mediated, it enters into union with its opposite. Thus it is both transformed and preserved on a higher level.

> *Aufheben* and what has been *aufgehoben* (the ideal) is one of the most important concepts of philosophy, a fundamental determination that recurs on all levels, and whose meaning must be carefully determined and distinguished from nothing and negation. What sublates itself does not reduce itself thereby to nothing. Nothing is

---

55. *SL*, 748.

immediate; in contrast, what is sublated [*aufgehobenes*] is something mediated. It is a non-being [of something] but as a result that has come forth from a being. It retains the determinacy of that from which it has come forth. . . . Something is sublated [*aufgehoben*] only insofar as it enters into union with its opposite.[56]

This analysis is not only pertinent to logic, it is also relevant to the ethical transformation of the I into an ethical We as each person comes to count for something in the other. One level of self-understanding—the raw natural egoism—is negated, restricted, and in this apparent restriction there is a gain and ethical transformation, an enlarged mentality. The 'We' is therefore not a simple product of two individuals that remain independent in spite of their relation but the common end and union that is the true 'beginning', that is, the foundation of the relationship, or the relationship itself. Thus two individuals enter into union with each other and create an ethical totality, a corporate person, a whole, that is more than the sum of its parts. In the 'We', being-other is transcended, but this does not return us to the abstract undifferentiated universal that suppresses all distinctions. The We is a social-spiritual organism that is constituted by both identity and difference.

For Hegel, the state is an extension and wider articulation of this basic idea of spiritual-ethical organism. The state is the moment of return to unity out of the competitive individualism of civil society. The state restores fluidity and vitality to the otherwise antagonistic units of civil society. In civil society, being for other and being for self are different and exclusive; one is for others chiefly as a means of furthering one's own private interests. But the sublation of the disunity between being for other and being for self is evident in and constitutive of Hegel's analysis of patriotism or loyalty: "This disposition is in general trust, . . . the consciousness that my substantial interest and my particular interest are preserved and included in the end of an other, in this case, the state, and in the state's relation to me as an individual. As a result, this other immediately ceases to be an other for me, and in my consciousness of this, I am free."[57]

The question is, what does the last sentence mean when it says that the other ceases to be an other? Stephen Houlgate passes over the crucial concepts of organism and determinate negation when he presents the following Spinozist reading of this passage. In his view, Hegel's analysis of recognition leads

> to the point at which the moment of otherness falls away in an even more radical way than is the case in the love between two individuals, and the self and its other become perfectly identified. One would expect this because, if recognition truly involves self-recognition in absolute otherness, then there must come a point at which the self recognizes an identity between itself and the other to such an extent that it loses any sense of itself as something over and against or other than

56. Hegel, *WL*, TWA Sk 5:113–114.
57. *PR*, §268.

the other, and so loses any sense that the other is actually other than what the self now understands itself to be.[58]

Houlgate is right in pointing to the overcoming of opposition between self and other. The vitality and animation of an organism is a constant surmounting of such oppositions among its parts. But Houlgate—and many other contemporary interpreters—are wrong in moving from the surmounting of opposition to the further, unwarranted conclusion that if opposition is surmounted, then otherness vanishes and the other must cease to be.[59] This is fanaticism, the wish to have the whole in every particular in such a way that the particular itself is destroyed or suppressed.[60]

Houlgate's interpretation may appear warranted if we try to think recognition in the traditional substantialist concepts of substance and accidents. Then we may be led to a monist and Spinozist interpretation such as Houlgate's. However, Hegel criticizes Spinoza for defrauding the other of its importance: "The so-called atheism of Spinoza is merely an exaggeration of the fact that he defrauds the principle of difference or finitude of its due."[61] Hegel's alternative is to think of mutual recognition in terms of life and organism. Here the other does not cease to be. Instead the self comes to have a new enlarged mentality in identification with the other, be this a marriage or a patriotic identification with the state. Hegel does not portray this in mystical terms as a loss of self or loss of otherness but rather as the attaining of a new consciousness of freedom in relation with an other. When the other ceases to be other for me, in my consciousness of this, I am free. As Hegel puts it in the *Phenomenology*, "in this simple self-intuition in other, other-being as such is not posited. It is a distinction . . . without a difference, a recognition of love in which the two lovers are by their very nature not opposed to each other."[62] Thus love, understood in terms of ethical organism, is a unity that liberates rather than suppresses its members. How this is possible will become clearer when we examine Hegel's discussion of organism in his *Aesthetics*.

Organism in the *Aesthetics*

In Hegel's *Aesthetics* is to be found perhaps the most accessible of his discussions of organism, which supplement and elucidate the position sketched in his published writings considered above. It occurs in his discussion of natural beauty, in which he analyzes the Idea as a living, vital process. This section reprises the discussion of objectivity in the logic. Hegel begins by discussing

58. Stephen Houlgate, "Hegel and Fichte: Recognition, Otherness, and Absolute Knowing," *Owl of Minerva* 26, no. 1 (Fall 1994): 8–9. For my reply to Houlgate, see "Discernment in the Realm of Shadows."

59. See William Desmond, *Desire, Dialectic and Otherness* (New Haven: Yale University Press, 1987); and *Beyond Hegel and Dialectic* (Albany: SUNY Press, 1992).

60. *PR*, §§5 Zusatz, 270 Zusatz. See below, pp. 327–329.

61. *E*, §151 Zusatz.   62. *PhG*, 536.

physical-mechanical bodies, such as metals. A metal is a manifold of chemical and physical qualities, but every tiny part of it possesses them in the same way. Hence such a body lacks articulation. The different parts are only an abstract multiplicity, and their unity is only the insignificant one of the uniformity of the same qualities.[63]

Next Hegel discusses higher-order natural objects that 'set free' the distinctions inherent in the *Begriff* and allow them to pass into objectivity, so that each is for itself outside of other, and being for the other is othered for itself. Hegel refers to the solar system as an example of this "letting difference go free." The sun, comets, moon, and planets appear as independent heavenly bodies each by itself. But they are what they are only through their determinate place (position) within a system of totality. Their specific type of movement as well as their physical attributes allow derivation only from their relation and condition within the system. This systematic connection constitutes their inner unity, which relates the particular existences to each other and holds them together. The position of the planets in the solar system is determined not as absolute in and for itself but only in relation to the rest of the system and totality. The point Hegel is driving at here is not astronomy but rather a critique of simple location and misplaced concreteness, in which individuals are what they are apart and in isolation.[64] On the contrary, position and embodiment within a context shape and condition individuals such that the latter cannot understand themselves or be understood apart from their context or situation.

While the solar system is a system of articulated differences, the differences remain somewhat external. The solar system exhibits only a partial realization or articulation of the concept as an organic system. However, there are higher forms of this systematic unity, whose logical structure Hegel expounds as follows:

> The true existence of the concept requires that the real differences, i.e., the reality of independent differences, and the equally independent objectified unity as such, are taken back into unity. Consequently, such a totality of natural differences on the one hand explicate the *Begriff* as a real externality in its determinations. But on the other hand, every part of the whole in its self-contained independence is posited as sublated.[65]

This simultaneous release of real differences, on the one hand, and return of differences into unity, on the other, is constitutive of the organic life process, which Hegel terms Idea.[66] This means that organism, as the embodiment of the Idea, is a living contradiction.

63. Hegel, *Aesthetics* 1:116.
64. Hegel anticipates Whitehead's important fallacy of misplaced concreteness, which continues many of the themes present in Hegel's critique of mechanism.
65. *Aesthetik*, 13:160; *Aesthetics*, 118.
66. This assertion places considerable distance between Hegel and what is normally understood by Platonism. It is an Aristotelian reading of the Platonic Idea.

For the ideal unity is not only not the perceived [*sinnliche*] separateness in which every particular member has an independent existence and separate particularity of its own; on the contrary, it is [also] the direct opposite of such external reality. To say that opposites are to be identical is precisely contradiction itself. Yet whoever claims that nothing exists which carries in itself a contradiction in the form of an identity of opposites is at the same time requiring that nothing living shall exist. For the power of life, and still more the power of spirit, consists in positing contradiction in itself, enduring it, and overcoming it. This positing and resolving of the contradiction between the ideal unity and real separateness of the members constitutes the constant process of life, and life is only by being this process.[67]

Note that Hegel characterizes the unity of the organism as ideal and as Idea. This is an important nuance, especially in view of the tendency toward literalism that leads to a monist interpretation that distorts and undermines the concept of organism. What holds the parts of an organism together in their differentiation is not another part, or superentity, or universal substance. Rather it is their own immanent animating principle. This animating spirit pervades all its members. Hegel characterizes this ideal unity as follows: "This ideality, in which the differences are turned back to a subjective unity, is allowed to emerge in them as their universal animating soul. In this case they are no longer *parts* that hang together in an aggregate, but rather *members*. This means that they no longer exist isolated and only for themselves. Rather *they have genuine existence only in their ideal unity*. Only in such an organic articulation does the ideal unity of the concept—which is their bearer and immanent soul—dwell in the members."[68]

What sort of ideality is this animating unity? Hegel terms it "the idealism of life [*Lebendigkeit*]. Philosophy is by no means the only example of idealism. Nature, as life, already does in fact what idealist philosophy brings to completion in its own spiritual field."[69] Hegel analyzes the process of the living organism in which differences are posited as real and objective and are brought back into the ideal unity, or the animating force of the organism. The animating force of the organism is already objective, that is, *in the organism*, prior to philosophical reflection coming on the scene. The organism is not a sheer unity that suppresses differences; its unity is ideal, and an ideal unity requires, depends on, and operates within and throughout the different members. "The life process comprehends and includes a doubled activity: on the one hand it constantly brings the real differences of all members and the determinations of the organism to sensible existence, and on the other hand, when they want to isolate themselves in independent particularity and to fix themselves in hard

67. *Aesthetik*, 13:162; *Aesthetics*, 120.
68. *Aesthetik*, 13:160; *Aesthetics*, 118.
69. *Aesthetik*, 13:163; *Aesthetics*, 120.

and fast differences, the life process makes valid in them their universal ideality [unity], which is their animating source. This is the idealism of life."[70]

The idealism of life is not a merely subjective condition or requirement of human epistemology. It has nothing to do with transcendental idealism as a theory that grounds reflective judgment. Rather Hegel explicitly opposes objective idealism to transcendental or subjective idealism. "This ideality is not merely in or for our reflection. Rather it is objectively present in the living subject [organism] itself. For this reason we may call its objective determinate existence [*Dasein*] an *objective idealism*."[71] This is the clearest and most forceful statement of what Hegel means by objective idealism that I know of. Objective idealism in Hegel's sense has been not incorrectly called "realism."[72] Hegel expands on the underlying conception in his discussion of teleology in the Logic.

> The end relation is not for that reason a reflective judging that considers external objects only according to a unity, as though an intelligence had given this unity for the convenience of our cognitive faculty; on the contrary it is the absolute truth that judges objectively and determines external objectivity absolutely. Thus the end relation (teleological relation to end) is more than judgment; it is the syllogism of the self-subsistent free notion that unites itself with itself through objectivity.[73]

Objective idealism signals a break with Kant and transcendental grounding of reflective judgment. Judgment implies division, dichotomy, analysis, and a propositional form of truth. Expressed in this form, idealism is subjective, 'on one side'. Judgment is appropriate to mechanical whole/part relation or mechanism per se but not to understanding living organisms. To do justice to the complexity of the latter, reflective judgment and its propositions must be replaced with the syllogism and its threefold mediation, in which the extremes are mediated by the universal or middle term that unites them. In this conception, the universal is the 'between' that animates the whole and not something located simply on the side of the subject. That is, the universal is a living organism.

Hegel proceeds to expound objective idealism in a way that is highly suggestive and illuminating for his concept of objective spirit. I shall reproduce extensively his exposition and then comment on it.

> Through this unity of doubled activity all members of the organism are constantly preserved and constantly taken back into the ideality of their animation [*Belebung*]. The members manifest this ideality [of their differences] in that their

---

70. *Aesthetik*, 13:162–163; *Aesthetics*, 120.
71. *Aesthetik*, 13:166; *Aesthetics*, 123.
72. See Kenneth Westphal, *Hegel's Epistemological Realism* (Dordrecht: Kluwer, 1989).
73. *SL*, 739.

animating unity is not something indifferent to them, but on the contrary is their very substance in which and through which alone they can preserve their particular individuality. This fact constitutes the essential difference between a *part* of a *whole* and a *member* of an organism. The special parts of a house, for example—the stones, the windows—remain the same whether they together form a house or not. Their community with the others is indifferent to them, and the *Begriff* remains in them a mere external form, that does not live in the real parts in order to raise these to the ideality of a subjective unity. In contrast, the members of an organism likewise have an external reality, but the concept is so much the indwelling essence [*Wesen*] of the organism, that it is not imprinted on them as a form uniting them only externally; on the contrary, *it is their only possible mode of enduring and surviving. For this reason, the members of the organism do not have a reality possessed by stones of a building, or the planets, moon and comets in the planetary system; rather, in spite of all their reality, they have an existence posited as ideal within the organism. For example, the hand, when severed from the body loses its independent existence. It does not remain the same as it was in the organism; rather its mobility, movement, structure, color, etc., are changed.* It begins to decay and its entire existence dissolves. It has a sustained, enduring existence only as a member of the organism, and has reality only as continuously brought back into the ideal unity. Herein consists the higher mode of reality within the living organism. *The real and the positive are constantly negated and posited as ideal, while this ideality is at the same time the preservation and sustaining element of the real differences.*[74]

This passage captures and articulates the important distinction between mechanism (whole/parts) and organism and its members. There is a difference between being a member of an organism and being a part within a whole. In the latter case, the unity of the whole is indifferent to the parts, which remain more or less what they are whether in isolation or as parts. But in the case of the organism, the organism is both the producer and the product of its members. Hence they are not indifferent to the unity of the organism, because in an important sense they are that unity, for the unity is their very life. The members of an organism therefore are truly independent only in their ideal actuality in the organism. If they are removed from their organic relationships, they lose their independence and subsistence. Organism is the inverse of mechanism in this respect.

Hegel cites Aristotle's example of the hand to make the point that the hand sustains an enduring independent mode of existence only as a member of the organism. It is only within this ideal union of the organism that the hand is sustained as a hand and functions as a hand. Severed from this objective ideal union to which it contributes and which sustains it, the hand does not entirely cease to be, but it loses its independence and ceases to be a hand. Further, any organism exhibits this objective idealism as its ideal sustaining unity; yet precisely be-

---

74. *Aesthetik*, 13:163–164; *Aesthetics*, 121. My italics.

cause this unity is ideal, it is not itself a part alongside the others. It is an ideal vital unity produced by its members that in turn shapes and produces them.

This distinction between mechanism and organism illumines Hegel's distinction between civil society and state. Civil society as the external state resembles mechanism and adopts mechanical metaphors for its own self-understanding. Its individualistic ethos tends toward a quasi-mechanical conception of its members in which community with others is a matter of indifference and in which they remain unrelated in spite of relation. However, although people in civil society may think of themselves as an externally related aggregate, in fact they are interdependent for the satisfaction of their needs. But this interdependence is rarely acknowledged, and when it is acknowledged, it is regarded as an exception to the rule rather than as the rule governing a social organism. Hegel not only acknowledges but also points out the ethical dimension of such interdependence in his view of the corporation and the state. There is no point denying that relation makes no difference to individuals, communities, and institutions, particularly if, as Hegel believes, they are not only related but organically related such that their only possible mode of enduring and surviving lies in their successful interrelation and dependence. The ethical institutions of corporation and state therefore are not superfluous or optional but necessary in order to complete in a rational ethical-political sense the system of needs and mediations begun in civil society. Without them civil society tends to be conceived merely as an impersonal machine, a system of alienation or spiritual desert.

My thesis is that mutual recognition, the *Anerkanntsein*, is for Hegel the distinctive form that the ideal unity or actuality of the organism takes in human society. As such it is a higher, more developed form and instance of what Hegel terms 'objective idealism'. Mutual recognition constitutes the universal consciousness, the We, the *Anerkanntsein*, or spirit, that is the unity of community present in all its members. Since mutual recognition is central to objective idealism on this level, it is for Hegel tantamount to objective spirit (*objektiver Geist*).

Recognition, the *Anerkanntsein*, unites subjective freedom with substantive freedom. The latter principle is not heteronomous vis-à-vis subjectivity, for in willing substantive freedom subjective freedom wills its own basis. Conversely, subjective freedom is not a merely empty form, but the vehicle for the realization of substantive freedom. Both are necessary dimensions of community as a social organism. This means that both ethical substance and subjective freedom are, in Hans Jonas's terms, "productive as much as produced, or as much 'natura naturans' as 'natura naturata'."[75] The reciprocity within organism between producing and product, cause and effect, means that for Hegel both substantive freedom and subjective freedom (autonomy) are intersubjectively socially mediated. Further, the reciprocity constitutive of the self-producing or-

75. Jonas, "Spinoza and the Theory of Organism," 215–216.

ganism means that ethical substance, while asymmetrical vis-à-vis subjective freedom in that it does not depend for its legitimacy on the recognition of any particular individual, is nevertheless an *Anerkanntsein*, a sociohistorical product. That is why, when Hegel asserts that "this substantial unity is an absolute and unmoved end in itself," a phrase reminiscent of Aristotle's unmoved mover, he completes his thought thus: "in it, freedom enters into its highest right."[76]

Objective Idealism and Organism in the State

Hegel develops a conception of the state as a social organism. Organism embodies an objective idealism: its animating principle is the self-constituting unity, coalescence, and coincidence of its members. This vital principle is the organism itself and is not a mere subjective maxim of reflective judgment, that is, a mere 'as if'. It is objective as the vital force of an organism whether or not that organism and its principle are cognized by an external knower. Thus organism is and requires an objective idealism or realism. The question is, how does this objective idealism apply to the state as an organism? My thesis is that for Hegel mutual recognition is the medium of the objective idealism of the state. The ideality of the state as a social organism resides in the mutual recognition of its members and in its institutionalizations in rights, duties, laws, and above all, separation of constitutional powers. The 'objective idealism' of the community in its laws and institutions is what Hegel means by *Anerkanntsein*, or objective spirit. Although he does not seem aware of or refer to Hegel's concept of recognition, Bernard Bosanquet nevertheless sensed the connection between recognition and the ethical conception of social organism when he wrote,

> The relation of each to the other is a special form of 'recognition'. That is to say, the mind of each has a definite and positive attitude towards that of the other, which is based on, or rather, so far as it goes, simply *is*, the relation of their 'positions' to each other. *Thus social positions or vocations actually have their being in the medium of recognition.* They are attitudes of minds towards one another, through which their several distinct characteristics are instrumental to a common good.[77]

Although Bosanquet does not know, much less appreciate, Hegel's concept of recognition as an account of intersubjectivity, it is interesting that when Bosanquet defends objective idealism and spirit, he often falls back on interpersonal examples: "Recognition is a matter of logic working on and through experience, and not a matter of choice or fancy. If my mind has no attitude to yours, there is no interdependence and I cannot be a party to securing your rights. . . . If my mind *has* an attitude to yours, then there is certainly a recognition between us."[78]

76. *PR*, §258.
77. Bosanquet, *The Philosophical Theory of the State*, 196. Italics mine.
78. Ibid., 197.

Hegel makes explicit use of the concept of the organism to his theory of the state in three topics or areas: (1) the systematic connection between rights and duties, above all, the question of the right of the state itself to recognition; this also raises the question concerning the rights and status of those who are not recognized by the state and those who do not recognize the state. This raises the further issue of toleration toward those who do not recognize duties toward the state, which in turn raises the issue of religious pluralism within Hegel's state; (2) the constitution, where Hegel both follows and transforms Montesquieu's theses concerning the connection between the fundamental disposition or virtue and the type of constitutional arrangements to which it corresponds; and (3) sovereignty, including peace and war. We shall examine the second first, since it involves the fundamental conception of the state as an organic totality, and then examine the first set of topics. The issues of sovereignty, war, and peace will be the subject of the following chapter.

Recognition and the Spirit of the Laws

For Hegel, the state is to be taken not in a narrow juridical or political sense but as the determinate existence of all the determinations and conditions [*Bestimmungen*] of freedom.[79] This determinate existence is, at the most general level, a social organism in which the unity of the whole pervades all its members as their social unity, their culture and sense of nationality.

> The spiritual individual, the nation, insofar as it is internally differentiated so as to form an organic whole, is what we call the state. . . . In this context, the word state is used in a more comprehensive sense, just as we use the word realm to describe spiritual phenomena. A nation should therefore be regarded as a spiritual individual, . . . what we have previously called the spirit of the nation, i.e., its self-consciousness in relation to its own truth and being and what it recognizes as truth in the absolute sense. In short, those spiritual powers that live within the nation and rule over it. The universal which emerges and becomes conscious within the state, the form to which everything in it is assimilated, is what we call in general the nation's culture. But the determinate content which this universal form acquires and which is contained in the concrete reality which constitutes the state is the national spirit itself. The real state is animated by this spirit in all its particular transactions, wars, institutions, etc. . . . Moreover, this spiritual content is the essential content of each individual, as well as of the nation. It is the sacred bond that links men and spirits together. It remains one and the same life, one great object, one great end, and one great content on which all private happiness and all private relation depend.[80]

---

79. *E*, §486.
80. G. F. W. Hegel, *Philosophy of History*, trans. H. Nisbet (Cambridge: Cambridge University Press, 1975), 96–97.

The determinate existence (*Dasein*) of right and freedom is mediated by and through recognition; it is the general *Anerkanntsein* of a people. The specific and determinate ways a people mutually recognize each other, and recognize themselves in their laws and institutions, constitute their common spirit, the spirit of their laws (to use Montesquieu's term), that is, their constitution.

> Since spirit is actual only as what it knows itself to be, and since the state as the spirit of a people, is both the law which pervades all relations within it and also the customs and the consciousness of its individuals, the constitution of a people will in general depend on the character and cultural formation of its self-consciousness. Its subjective freedom is rooted in its self-consciousness, and along with it, the actuality of its constitution.[81]

The constitution in this sense exhibits the concrete intersubjective-social rationality (or lack thereof) of a people.[82] Hegel spells out this concrete social rationality in terms of the concept of systematic organic totality.

> Freedom must be, not in the sense of contingency but of necessity. That freedom is actual belongs to its immanent organization. A people is rational only to the extent that its constitution is rational. By a people one usually understands a unity of culture, ethics, etc., and this unity is its existent substance. The people as mass pure and simple are devoid of rationality; for rationality is only the entire system. Thus the sun and the earth are, by themselves, nothing rational. However the solar system and its organization expressed in space and time is rationality. A mere mass is not rational: one cannot have respect for a people as mere people. A people that does not have noble constitution is a bad people; only the universal can be genuinely respected.[83]

Of course, such universal-social rationalism is not simply a given; it is a task to be accomplished, and the place Hegel looks to determine the degrees of development and realization of such concrete rationality is the spirit of the laws, that is, constitutional history and development.[84] The first version of Hegel's controversial assertion that the rational is actual is formulated in reference to constitutional history and development: "The spirit of a people is the [ethical] substance: what is rational must come to pass."[85] Further, "the genuine rationality is the inner authority, the correspondence to the spirit of the people."[86] Hegel makes these comments in the context of the question, Who is to make the constitution? His most direct answer to this question is found in the *Encyclopedia*.

---

81. *PR*, §274.   82. *VPR*17, §127.
83. Ibid. Hegel uses the solar system analogy in the *Aesthetik*.
84. The reader should bear in mind that Hegel's Prussia was not yet a constitutional monarchy for the simple reason that it did not yet have a constitution. In terms of the then-prevailing status quo, Hegel's *Philosophy of Right*, in calling for a written constitution, was in this regard a reformist, progressive document. So much for the myth promulgated by Popper that Hegel sold out to Prussian conservatives. See Jacques D'Hondt, *Hegel in His Time*.
85. *VPR*17, §134.   86. Ibid.

The guarantee of a constitution, i.e., of its necessity, that its laws are rational and their realization is secured, lies in the spirit of the entire people, namely in the determinate way the people has the self-consciousness of its rationality, and at the same time the guarantee is found in its actual organization as the development of its principle. The constitution presupposes the consciousness of spirit, and conversely, the spirit presupposes the constitution. . . . The question, to whom (to what authority and how is it organized) belongs the power to make a constitution, is the same as the question, who has the power to make the spirit of the people? . . . A constitution develops only from the spirit in identity with the spirit's own development. . . . It is from the indwelling spirit of a people and its history that constitutions have been made and are made.[87]

The spirit of a people expresses a determinate anthropological principle and viewpoint, a determinate shape of social rationality.[88] Consequently, the constitution is an outgrowth and expression of the spirit of a people in its historical development: "Every people has its own history, expresses its own spirit, and not the spirit or history of an alien people."[89] This concrete rationality, as constituted through an organic framework and nexus of reciprocal recognitions, is fundamentally social and historical. Such organic nexus means that there is a correlation between the subjective disposition of a people and its objective form of constitution and government, as Montesquieu pointed out.

In his 1818 lectures, Hegel expounds his theory of constitution as a determinate correlation between subjective disposition (e.g., virtue) and objective social structure (e.g., democracy).

The one-sided extremes in which the actuality of freedom is conceived are the mechanism and [corresponding] disposition of the state. The authentic actuality of freedom is its organism. . . . The living actuality of the state is the unity of [subjective] disposition and [objective] social organization. The whole must pervade everything, but in an articulated manner. The individuals must realize that in their particular labors they are active for the whole, and must have this totality for their end. This is possible only as organism—namely, the separation of powers and functions proceeds so that the separate elements become independent, and yet the whole retains absolute power. The moments, the members, must have their particular freedom and the state is brought forth out of these. The constitution is the unity of the disposition and the organism, inwardness and externality.[90]

Hegel elaborates this point by reference to Montesquieu. Montesquieu's thesis is that the state is a concrete totality and that all the particulars of its legislation, institutions, and customs are the effect and expression of its inner unity, the spirit of its laws. Montesquieu is not the first to make use of totality to explain the state; Plato had already done that. But Montesquieu is the first to take to-

---

87. *E*, §540.
88. "Every people has accordingly its determinate anthropological principle that it develops in its history and to this extent is a nation" (*VPR*17, §159).
89. *VPR*18, §121.   90. Ibid., §118.

tality as a fundamental category that makes it possible to think not just an ideal state but an actual state. At the core of states, understood as living totalities, there is a vital principle or spirit that is its center and principle of rationality.

Hegel appropriates and transforms Montesquieu's typology of constitutions and their corresponding subjective disposition or virtues. He points out that Montesquieu did not originate the threefold classification of constitutions into monarchy, aristocracy, and democracy. However, prior to Montesquieu, "the old classification of constitutions into monarchy, aristocracy and democracy presupposes a still undivided and substantial unity which has not yet attained inner differentiation as an organization developed within itself, and which consequently still lacks depth and concrete rationality. From the point of view of the ancient world, therefore, this classification is the true and correct one, for in the case of a unity which is still substantial . . . the difference is essentially external."[91] In criticism of substance metaphysics and natural law theory, Hegel observes that "it has become utterly pointless to ask which of the three is most commendable, such forms can be discussed only in a historical context."[92] When that is done, the question of the constitution ceases to be one of a pure, abstract, and ideal form or concept, and becomes rather one of a concrete intersubjective-social nexus or spirit that animates a social structure and its constituent individuals.

Montesquieu develops this conception by distinguishing three government types: republic, monarchy, and despotism.[93] Each government type or constitutional structure has a corresponding animating principle and sociohistorical condition of possibility. The republic presupposes *virtue* on the part of its members in order to be viable, monarchy presupposes *honor*, and despotism operates by instilling *terror* (*Schrecken*) and fear. The republican-democratic form functions properly only on the condition that its citizens are virtuous, that is, that they sacrifice themselves to and for the public good and prefer it to their own egoistic passions and private interests. The republic will 'go' only on virtue. Without virtue the republic will fall, just as will the monarchy without honor, or despotism without terror.

Hegel acknowledges the correctness of Montesquieu's systematic historical approach. However, he does not accept Montesquieu's particular version of holism, replacing it with an analysis of life and freedom as logical concepts and with mutual recognition as their phenomenological correlate and manifestation; he points out that Montesquieu's analysis of monarchy (honor) shows that he has only a feudal monarchy in mind, rather than a constitutional monarchy.

These criticisms do not deter Hegel from focusing on and appreciating Mon-

91. *PR*, §273. Hegel points out that the abstract substantial unity of the classical tradition reduces the difference between constitutions to mere external accidents. Thus in this traditional view, when democratic or aristocratic determinations occur in monarchy they do not retain but lose their aristocratic and democratic character.

92. Ibid.

93. For a brief but lucid account, see Althusser, *Politics and History*.

tesquieu's main contribution, namely, the systematic correlation (or the absence of such) between constitutional structure and the corresponding subjective animating principle, which is a determinate type and configuration of reciprocal recognition. He cites with evident approval Montesquieu's observations that seventeenth-century England "afforded the fine spectacle of how efforts to establish a democracy were rendered impotent by a lack of virtue on the part of the leaders, and . . . when virtue disappears from a republic, ambition takes hold of those whose hearts are susceptible to it and greed takes possession of everyone, so that the state falls prey to universal exploitation and its strength resides solely in the power of a few individuals." [94] Hegel also notes a systematic incompatibility between past constitutional forms and modern needs: "There is nothing so irrational as to appeal to the constitution of the Greeks and Romans for our constitutions, because much that was possible in these states is no longer applicable to our situation." [95] In the *Philosophy of History* he elaborates this point.

> The constitutions under which world-historical nations have blossomed are peculiar to them, and should not therefore be seen as universally applicable. Their differences do not simply consist in the particular way in which they have elaborated and developed a common basis, but in the distinct nature of the principles which underlie them. No lessons can be drawn from history for the framing of constitutions in the present. For the latest constitutional principle of our own times, is not to be found in the constitutions of world-historical nations of the past. In knowledge and art, however, it is altogether different. For in their case, the earlier principles are the absolute foundation of all that follows; for example, the philosophy of antiquity is so fundamental to modern philosophy that it is necessarily contained in the latter and constitutes its entire basis. . . . But with political constitutions, it is quite different; for ancient and modern constitutions have no essential principle in common.[96]

Hegel notes similar incompatibilities between modern liberal constitutions and heteronomous forms of religion: "It is no use to organize political laws and arrangements on principles of equality and reason, so long as in religion the principle of unfreedom is not abandoned. A free state and a slavish religion are incompatible. . . . It is nothing but a modern folly to try to alter a corrupt moral organization by altering its political constitution and code of laws without changing the religion—to make a revolution without having made a reformation." [97]

The central point that needs underscoring here is that the position that there

---

94. *PR*, §273. Hegel criticizes Montesquieu for failing to see that under modern conditions in which the power and right of particularity are developed and liberated, "it is not enough for the heads of state to be virtuous; another form of rational law is required apart from individual disposition if the whole is to have the strength to maintain its unity and to grant the forces of developed particularity their positive as well as negative rights."

95. *VPR17*, §136.

96. Hegel, *Philosophy of History*, 120.

97. *E*, §552.

is an integral correspondence between political institutions and concrete forms of recognition rests on an organic conception of the state as an articulated, organized totality. The unity of the social-political organism is not a matter of indifference. If the state really were a machine or mechanism, the parts would be indifferent to the unity of the whole. Then the seventeenth-century attempts to bring democracy to England should not have failed, Plato's *Republic* could be directly imported into modern industrial society, and any religion could be paired with any constitution. However, viewed from the perspective of historical consciousness and the concept of the state as an organic whole, some correlations are possible and some are impossible.

The Organic Correlation between Rights and Duties

For Hegel, right is the existence of all the determinations and conditions [*Bestimmungen*] of freedom.[98] But right does not become determinate or actual until it is mediated by mutual recognition. When the I becomes a We, freedom and its conditions, namely, rights, are also recognized. But when a right is recognized, then others, who co-constitute the We, have a duty corresponding to that right. "Hence duty and right coincide in this identity of the universal will and the particular will."[99] Reciprocal recognition is the underlying principle of the organic connection between rights and duties.[100]

In abstract right this correlation took a formal and abstract, yet intersubjective form: my right (e.g., to property) corresponds to a duty on someone else's part to respect and not to infringe on my freedom as a right to possession. But this correspondence between right and duty is only partial, not unlike the distinction between ought and is that is constitutive of morality. Hegel explains this correlation thus: "In abstract right I have the right and some one else has the corresponding duty. In morality it is merely an obligation [*Sollen*] that the right of my own knowledge and volition, and of my welfare, should be united with my duties and exist objectively."[101] But ethical life, reflecting the reciprocity and union of mutual recognition, overcomes the abstract individualism and formalism of abstract right and morality. "In ethical life both abstract right and morality attain their truth and unity. . . . [D]uty and right in mediation revert into each other and coincide."[102] Hence at the level of ethical life, "a right is also a duty, and a duty is also a right."[103] Hegel offers as an example: "The rights of the *Paterfamilias* over the family members are at the same time duties

---

98. Ibid., §486.   99. *PR*, §155.
100. The mere fact that Hegel conceives rights and duties to stand in an organic teleological relation shows that his conception of the state is democratic in Montesquieu's sense.
101. *PR*, §155.   102. *E*, §486.   103. Ibid.

towards them, like the child's duty of obedience is also its right to be educated to freedom and independence."[104]

This reciprocity between right and duty is a further specification of mutual recognition. Although he does not explicitly refer to Hegel's technical concept of recognition, Bosanquet nevertheless employs the term in his exposition and analysis of the concept of right.[105] Rights, Bosanquet observes, demand recognition, because they are functions and claims of one's social position within an organized, interdependent whole and are at the same time instrumental, not only to individual welfare but also to the welfare of the whole. Rights then are claims of the articulated whole operative in its parts or members. The medium through which these rightful claims are mediated and come to us is the recognition that rights are correlative to duties.

Consequently, in recognizing each other's rights, we do more than merely recognize each other as individuals. We also recognize rights as inherently universal in principle. In recognizing each other, we also recognize, at least implicitly, a system of rights. Hegel expounds the systematic connection thus: "The association of duty and right has a dual aspect in that what the state requires of individuals as a duty should also in an immediate sense be the right of individuals, for it is nothing more than the organization of the concept of freedom."[106] According to Bosanquet, "Right is a power secured in order to fill a position that is recognized as instrumental to the common good. It is impossible to argue that the position may exist and not be recognized. For we are speaking of a relation of minds, and insofar as minds are united into a single system by their attitudes towards each other, their positions and the recognition of them as minds with rights are one and the same thing."[107]

Viewed from the perspective of individuals, the state as a system of rights may appear as an external necessity to which they are subordinate. However, the state "is also their immanent end, and its strength consists in the unity of its universal and ultimate end with the particular interests of individuals in the fact that they have duties towards the state to the same extent as they also have rights."[108] Note that the duties owed the state by individuals is the way in which the state is both produced and sustained as their organic unity. Individuals and state are both productive and produced in this correlation of rights and duties.

In general, duty for Hegel is simply another dimension of right, the "other side" of right. "What is a right is also a duty, and what is a duty is also a right."[109]

104. Ibid. For an exposition of this general point of view in which rights and duties are functions of positions, see F. H. Bradley, "My Station and Its Duties," in *Ethical Studies* (London: Oxford University Press, 1876).

105. Bosanquet, *The Philosophical Theory of the State*, 195ff.

106. *PR*, §261 Zusatz.

107. Bosanquet, *The Philosophical Theory of the State*, 196.

108. *PR*, §261.   109. *E*, §486.

In ethical life, rights and duties have the same principle, namely, freedom: "there is a single principle for both duty and right, namely the personal freedom of human beings." [110] But this freedom is not freedom to do as one pleases. It is an intersubjective-ethical freedom. In short, freedom involves the correspondence between the universal or substantive will, and the particular subjective will. F. H. Bradley has expounded this multifaceted correspondence as clearly as anyone.

> Right is the universal will implying the particular will. It is the objective side implying a subjective side, i.e., duty. Duty is the particular will implying a universal will. It is the subjective side implying the objective side, i.e., right. But the two sides are inseparable. No right without duty; no duty without right and rights. Right and duty are sides of a single whole. This whole is the good. Rights and duties imply the identity, and non-identity, of the particular and universal wills. . . . The universal cannot be affirmed except in the particular, the particular only affirms itself in the universal. [111]

Thus the rights of another correspond to my duties. Duty in general designates a relation to something ethically substantial. For example, if I recognize your right to own property, your right and ownership are substantial, a limit to my freedom, and I have a duty not to infringe on your right, but also not to infringe on such rights in general. Hegel conceives the relationship, not only between individuals, but also between individuals and the state as one of reciprocal duties. The universal will of the state, or the *Anerkanntsein*, is substantial vis-à-vis its individuals; the state extends rights that protect and secure individual freedom and welfare; conversely, individuals in turn have duties toward the state.

For Hegel, this relationship is reversible: that is, the particular will and subjective freedom of its members is also something substantial for the state. The state has duties to its members to secure and protect their rights and welfare. Thus the relation of state to its members is not, in principle, one of domination and subservience.

> If we consider the concrete aspect, i.e., the Idea, we can see that the moment of particularity is essential, and that its satisfaction is therefore entirely necessary; in the process of fulfilling his duty, the individual must somehow attain his own interest and satisfaction . . . and from his situation within the state, a right must accrue to him whereby the universal cause [*Sache*] becomes his own particular cause. Particular interests should certainly not be set aside, let alone suppressed; on the contrary they should be accommodated with the universal, such that both the particular interests and the universal interest are preserved. The individual whose duties give him the status of a subject, finds that, in fulfilling his duties as a citizen, he gains protection for his person and property, consideration for his

110. *PR*, §261.
111. Bradley, "My Station and Its Duties," 208, 213.

particular welfare, satisfaction of his substantial being, and the consciousness and feeling of being a member of this whole. Moreover, through his performance of his duties as services and tasks undertaken on behalf of the state, the state itself is preserved and secured.[112]

Nevertheless, the state has a right to recognition that it must enforce; failure to do so would undermine the general system of rights and duties. Since reciprocal recognition is supposed to culminate in an organic 'We', it is important, indeed crucial, to be clear that the 'We'-organism is not a natural but rather an intersubjective, ethical, and political conception.

> In fact right and all its determinations are grounded exclusively on free personality, a self-determination which is the opposite of natural determination. The right of nature is . . . the existence of the strong and that might makes right. A state of nature is a situation of violence and injustice, of which nothing truer can be said than that it is to be left behind. In contrast, society is the sole situation in which right has its actuality. What must be limited and sacrificed in this situation is precisely the arbitrary will [*Willkür*] and the violence of the state of nature.[113]

Although the state may originate in violence (namely, the struggle for recognition), this is not its justification or its substantial principle.[114] The justification of the state is that it is necessary for human freedom and welfare and for the enforcement of rights as conditions of that freedom and welfare.

Religious and Cultural Pluralism

The general objection to the conception of the state as an organism is that it is supposed to give priority to the whole over the part, the community over the individual; that is, it tends toward totalitarian conceptions of the state.[115] Most recent studies have rejected the totalitarian reading of Hegel. Hegel's state is the reciprocal unity of its members and as such it presupposes their continued preservation and relative independence. Considering the charges of totalitarianism that have frequently been leveled against Hegel, it is important to appreciate his fundamentally antitotalitarian conception of the state as an articulated totality.[116] Hegel's logical conception of organism and his distinction between ethical-social organisms and natural organisms must be constantly borne in

---

112. *PR*, §261.   113. *E*, §502.

114. Ibid., §432 Zusatz; cf. §433: "The struggle for recognition and subjection to a master is the phenomenal manifestation out of which the social life of human beings, the beginning of states has developed. The violence present in this phenomenal manifestation is however, not the ground of right . . . It is the external or phenomenal beginning of the state, but not its substantial principle." See also *HE*, §415.

115. See Errol E. Harris, *The Spirit of Hegel* (Atlantic Highlands, N.J.: Humanities Press, 1993), 150.

116. See Karl Popper, *The Open Society and Its Enemies* (London: Routledge, 1962). Replies to charges such as Popper's range from T. M. Knox, "Hegel and Prussianism," *Philosophy* 15

mind, for these distinctions are very important to sorting out the sort of total-ity Hegel is after.

The preceding discussion allows us to explore issues of the separation of church and state, the negative consequences of nonrecognition, and the condi-tions under which the correlation of rights and duties obtains, that is, the ques-tion of the state's attitude toward those who do not recognize it or their duties to it. Taking the separation of church and state first, we note that Hegel main-tains that the state has a religious foundation. The ethical disposition constitu-tive of ethical life is grounded in religion; this is one reason why the various ethical powers and the substantial element of the state may be venerated as di-vine and sacred. The state, no less than marriage, aims at a permanent, endur-ing union that is elevated above contingencies and arbitrary vicissitudes. This enduring union is its religious dimension, its binding and enduring unity. Since the state has a religious foundation, Hegel asserts that the substantial principle of the state, including its constitution, even if the latter has an origin in time, should not be regarded as something made or produced by individuals at their discretion. "On the contrary, it is quite simply that which has being in and for itself, and should therefore be regarded as divine and enduring, and as exalted above the sphere of all manufactured things."[117] In this sense the substantive principle and the constitution have intrinsic worth and validity, "whether or not it is recognized by individuals."[118]

However, if "religion constitutes the foundation which embodies the ethical realm in general, and more specifically, the nature of the state as the divine will, it is at the same time only a foundation; and this is where the two [i.e., the state and religion] diverge."[119] While the state may have a religious founda-tion, and while this foundation must be regarded as not dependent on the recognition of particular individuals, nevertheless Hegel's state is not a theoc-racy but a secular institution. This means that the state, not the church, is for Hegel the embodiment of social and political universal rationality. The right of conscience, asserted by Protestant Christianity, is an assertion of religious freedom as a right. This right must be guaranteed, supported, and enforced by the state against sectarian domination, including domination by Protestant Christianity itself. "Indeed, since religion is that moment which integrates the state at the deepest level . . . the state ought even to require all its citizens to be-long to such a community—but any community that they please, for the state can have no say in the content of religious belief."[120]

This right of freedom of conscience, that the state must recognize and up-hold, entails the separation of church and state. This separation has been one of the most important events in the historical development of the state: "far

---

(1940): 51–63, to Avineri, *Hegel's Theory of the Modern State*, to D'Hondt, *Hegel in His Time*, to Errol Harris, *The Spirit of Hegel*, 190–207.

117. *PR*, §§ 258, 273.   118. Ibid., §258.   119. Ibid., §270.
120. Ibid.

from it being, or ever having been, a misfortune for the state if the church is divided, it is through this division alone that the state has been able to fulfill its vocation as self-conscious rationality and ethical life."[121] In the midst of sectarian conflict, the state has emerged as an independent mediator of sectarian and religious differences. Hegel observes that the state first emerged historically as an independent rationality in its mediation of sectarian religious disputes and differences. Hegel's state is thus religiously pluralistic in principle; it is supposed to be the medium of interfaith recognition and mediation. Rather than take sides in sectarian disputes, the state is supposed to be the institution that brings out and defends the universal aspects of interhuman relationships[122] and thereby maintains the fluidity and openness of the social organism. This requires a further clarification of the teleology and tendency toward unity heretofore central in Hegel's argument concerning the state.

Hegel inveighs against religious fundamentalism and authoritarianism that reject critical reflection, demand conformity, and identify the state with a particular sect or religion: "Those who 'seek the Lord' and assure themselves, in their uneducated opinion, that they possess everything immediately instead of undertaking the work of raising their subjectivity to the cognition of truth and knowledge of objective right and duty, can produce nothing but folly, outrage and the destruction of all ethical relations."[123] The dismissal of reflective and speculative thought in favor of immediate insight, authoritarian claims to exclusive revelation, and so on, amounts to fanaticism. Fanaticism seeks totality in an immediate way. The whole that is sought must be totally and indivisibly present in every part. But this view sins against ethical life as an articulated organic totality: fanaticism is the "wish to have the whole in every particular, and [it can] accomplish this only by destroying the particular, for fanaticism is simply the refusal to admit particular differences."[124] Fanaticism is the refusal to recognize the other in his difference, and leads to a totalitarian suppression of difference.

This last point needs to be underscored, in view of Ludwig Siep's claim that there is an asymmetry between individual and state in Hegel's account of recognition. Both are supposed to recognize each other, and a condition of such recognition is mutual self-limitation accompanied by release (*Freigabe*) of the other. We would expect, therefore, that the self-sacrifice on the part of the individual for the state would be matched by and correspond to a self-negation on the part of the universal will.

Here begin the problems in Hegel's doctrine of recognition. The self-negation of the universal will—institutionalized in the state and its organs—for the sake of the individual, stands in an asymmetrical relation to the individual's own self-

121. Ibid.
122. See Avineri, *HTMS*, 169–170.
123. *PR*, §270.   124. Ibid.

negation. . . . The possible distance of the individual from the enduring institutions of the general will can be . . . tolerated to a certain extent. But it cannot be willed positively . . . through self-negation, as [for example] the individual positively wills the independence of the general will through the self-negation of his exclusive particularity.[125]

In my opinion, Siep takes too negative a view of the recognition of difference inherent in toleration and fails to do justice either to the logic of reciprocity constitutive of organism or to Hegel's treatment of religious pluralism and state toleration of dissenters. If Siep were correct, the state may tolerate difference but could not will difference as difference. If that were true, the state would undermine itself as an articulated organic totality.

Hegel's discussion of religious toleration remains instructive, and significantly modifies the apparent rigid reciprocity between rights and duties constitutive of the state organism noted in the previous section of this chapter. Recall that the state rests on the reciprocal recognition, of which the reciprocity between rights and duties is a further specification. The issue of religious difference then becomes the question of the state's attitude and relation toward those communities that do not recognize their duties toward the state. The general principle is that what is a right is also a duty and vice versa. Its negative corollary is stated by Hegel thus: "Who has no rights has no duties, and who has no duties has no rights."[126] In other words, we would expect Hegel, following the logic of reciprocity and 'organic teleology', to hold that those who are different and who do not perform the appropriate duties toward the state should not—or at least need not—be accorded rights by the state.

However, Hegel does not take this position in the case of religious differences, for example, sects such as the Quakers. Instead, he favors tolerance.

> A state which is strong because its organization is fully developed can adopt a more liberal attitude in this respect, and may completely overlook individual matters which might affect it, or even tolerate communities whose religion does not recognize even their direct duties towards the state (although this naturally depends on the numbers concerned). It is able to do this by entrusting the members of such communities to civil society and its laws, and is content if they fulfill their direct duties towards it passively, for example by commutation or substitution [of an alternative service].[127]

In an important note, Hegel discusses the issue presented by Quakers and Anabaptists. Quakers, as pacifists, do not recognize any direct duty to defend the state: "Quakers have as their principle of citizenship *not* to be a citizen."[128]

125. Siep, *APP*, 279–280.
126. *E*, §486.   127. *PR*, §270.
128. *VPR*17, §136. In the 1825 lectures Hegel adds: "When piety retreats into itself and refuses to participate in the duties towards the state, and when it declares the latter godless, it

Of Quakers and Anabaptists, etc., it may be said that they are active members only of civil society, and that, as private persons, they have purely private relations with other people. Even in this context they have been exempted from taking oaths; they fulfill their direct duties towards the state in a passive manner, and although they reject outright one of the most important of these, namely the defense of the state against its enemies. Towards such sects, the state practices toleration in the proper sense of the word; for since they do not recognize their duties towards it, they cannot claim the right to belong to it.[129]

If the state extends rights to those who cannot claim the right to belong to it, the state negates itself in the very act of *Freigabe*, that is, of releasing difference from its rightful obligations. And in releasing difference from its rightful obligations and duties, does not the state, contrary to Siep, recognize, release, and affirm this difference, that is, its right to differ? Let us examine the matter more closely.

As pacifists, Quakers do not recognize a duty to defend the state. Since they do not recognize this duty toward the state, Hegel maintains that they may not claim the right to belong to the state; that is, they cannot claim the right of full membership. If the state were merely a natural organism, and if the reciprocity between it and its members were a merely conditional "tit-for-tat" reciprocity, we might expect that the state would expel the Quakers as alien and unassimilable. But in the ethical and political sphere this would amount to a return to abstract identity—the principle of totalitarianism and fanaticism. Instead, Hegel holds that the state, as an articulated social organism whose strength reflects and depends on recognition of particularity, should practice toleration toward religious minorities. This means that the state, as he conceives it, should be open to difference and consequently pluralistic rather than exclusive. Further, since the state is open to and tolerates in its midst those who do not recognize it fully, and who therefore do not perform the full range of duties required of its members, the tolerant state is not a natural but an ethical organism or totality. Toleration is a function of the ethical strength and complexity of the social organism, that is, its ability to sustain reciprocal recognition, not in spite of, but because of its diversity. The more articulated and developed a state is, the more likely it is to be tolerant of diversity.

Another group that does not recognize the religious foundation of Hegel's Christian state are the Jews. If the Jews do not recognize the state, does it follow that they should not be recognized by the state, or that they should be denied rights? Again, Hegel rejects the strict correlation or parochial position, even though the latter may be formally and technically correct in its reading of the principle of the identity of rights and duties. Hegel writes,

---

confines itself to civil society. Its members are only *bourgeois*, not *citoyens*; larger states can tolerate these sects, but not the smaller ones. A state composed solely of Quakers could not exist" (*VPR4*, 648).

129. *PR*, §270n.

Thus technically it may have been right to refuse a grant of even civil rights to the Jews on the grounds that they should be regarded not just as a particular religious group but as members of a foreign nation [*Volk*]. But the outcry against the Jews from that point of view and others, ignores the fact that the Jews are above all human beings. Being human, so far from being a mere superficial, abstract quality, is on the contrary itself the basis of the fact that civil rights arouse in their possessors the sense of counting in civil society as a person with rights, and this feeling of [recognized] selfhood, infinite and free from all restrictions, is the root from which the desired similarity in disposition and ways of thinking comes into being. To exclude the Jews from civil rights, on the other hand, would rather be to confirm that isolation with which they have been reproached and this would rightly have brought blame and reproach upon the state which excluded them. For by so refusing them, the state would thereby fail to appreciate its own principle [*sic*: freedom] as an objective institution with a power of its own. While the demand for the exclusion of the Jews claimed to be based upon the highest right, it has proven in practice to be the height of folly.[130]

The Jews are "others" whom the state should recognize as human beings, and to whom it should therefore extend civil and political rights. Failure to do so would betray the fundamental idea of the state as the institutional realization of freedom, an institution that, although it may have a religious basis, nevertheless is inclusive, nonsectarian, religiously and culturally pluralist, and independent of any particular religion. Freedom belongs to the human being as such and not just to one or to a few, or a particular religious identity; freedom itself is the principle of the state, as well as the principle underlying the correlation of rights and duties.

The question then comes down to one of recognition, not simply of rights, but of the Jews as human beings. Recognition of humanity is crucial, for humanity is "not a superficial abstract quality" but is "the basis of the fact that civil rights arouse in their possessors the sense of counting in civil society as a person with rights, and this feeling of self-hood, infinite and free from all restrictions, is the root from which the desired adjustment in disposition and ways of thinking come into being."[131] Hegel views the extension of rights to the Jews as something like a Fichtean *Aufforderung*, which presupposes a recognition of another freedom and 'alien humanity'. Hegel implies that a likely outcome of such an affirming recognition is that the alien freedom will respond and thereby cease to be utterly alien. By recognizing the Jews, therefore, the state

130. *PR*, §270 note. I have generally followed Knox's superior translation of this important passage. Hegel goes on to praise the reformist Chancellor von Hardenberg's edict of March 11, 1812, which declared that the Jews were to receive full equality of civil and political rights in Prussia. Hegel's defense of Hardenberg's edict reflects his polemic against Friess's anti-Semitic pamphlet of 1816. Friess denied that the Jews were a religious sect protected by the secular state; rather he regarded them as an alien nation, and on this basis denied their humanity and rights. Hegel rejected Friess's anti-Semitic views as the "height of folly." In contrast, Hardenberg's emancipation of the Jews, says Hegel, has "proven to be wise and honorable."
131. Ibid.

recognizes and declares that they count as persons. This recognition not only allows the Jews to be, it also accords them a sense of worth and significance that in turn gives them some sense of being at home within, and of 'having a stake' in, the state. For Hegel this sense of 'being at home' established in reciprocal recognition is not provincial, a disguised form of exclusion, but genuinely pluralistic and inclusive.

Note that Hegel's defense of toleration and inclusion is not a suppression of difference; rather it is a special, exceptional preservation of difference within the totality of recognition constitutive of spiritual-ethical organism. As Avineri has pointed out, "Arguing against the view that the Jews should first of all shed their peculiar customs and usages before being admitted into citizenship, Hegel even makes Jewish *emancipation* into a criterion of whether a state is conscious of its own universal nature."[132] Hegel's state, in recognizing the humanity of the Jews, does not simply affirm Jews in an abstract, anonymous identity with the whole; it would also affirm Jews as coequal others in their difference.[133] Contrary to Siep, this affirmation of the indivisibility of human freedom would constitute a special *Freigabe*, or release of particularity and otherness.

On the other hand, Hegel observes that if the state refused to recognize the Jews, it would contradict its own fundamental principle as an institution of right and ethical life. If it denied the Jews civil rights, it would practice the very isolation and separation from others for which it reproaches and criticizes them. Thus it would assume the posture of mastery and domination, and confirm in the Jews their isolation and separateness. It would show itself not to be a genuinely social infinite, but a false, parochial infinite, with an unassimilable other and difference. The state would not be a genuine universal, but only a parochial universal, a universal that excludes its other. The state would thus demonstrate that it does not act independently of its religious foundation but is rather subservient to parochial religious interests and/or to anti-Semitic interests. But then the state would have forgotten or misunderstood what it is supposed to be, namely, an independent and objective institution for the realization of freedom and particularity. Thus Hegel concludes that while the demand for the exclusion of the Jews claimed to be based on the highest right, it has proved in practice to be the height of folly. Here is an appreciation of the dialectical ambiguities and evils that attend a facile and dogmatic sense of 'doing the right thing', especially when the 'right thing' has as its consequence the refusal of recognition and adoption of practices of exclusion. In contrast, Hegel's state, as an articulated organic unity and totality, would affirm and preserve difference in its difference.

132. Avineri, *HTMS*, 170. My italics.
133. For Hegel's logical basis for this claim, see *E*, §§115, 119, 121, cited below in chapter 15, footnotes 16–18.

14

Sovereignty, International Relations, and War

Hegel's concept of sovereignty is an extension of his concept of social organism. Sovereignty is the ideal unity of the state, that is, its actuality as a social organism. This ideal unity of the state consists in the mutual recognition of its members and in their self-recognition in their social and political institutions. Sovereignty expresses the spirit of the laws. As such, it has two foci, an internal and an external. The internal focus or inner sovereignty of the state is located in its constitution, which provides a conception of the state as an internally differentiated and organized whole. The sovereignty of the state is maintained and renewed in the mutual recognition of its members. Sovereignty as a determinate form of mutual recognition also develops further the account of genuine conscience. For this reason Hegel is concerned to distinguish sovereignty from despotism, on the one hand, and anarchic pluralism, on the other. His thesis is that the state is a bulwark against both the wild lawlessness of the state of nature and the totalitarian dominance of the whole over individuals. Sovereignty, as an organized, internally differentiated totality of mutual recognition, is Hegel's third alternative to totalitarian despotism and anarchic individualism.

But the issue of sovereignty is not exhausted by the development of the state as an internally differentiated yet united totality. If sovereignty is a mutual recognition constitutive of the state as a living totality, the sovereign state is nevertheless not the end-station of recognition. The state as a concrete universal is not ultimate or absolute; it is exposed to contingency and can be destroyed. At the level of world history, the state turns out to be a particular individual standing over and against other states. It requires their recognition, and is exposed to the contingencies of possible nonrecognition, including war, decadence, and destruction.

Hegel conceives international relations as a struggle for recognition between states. The concept of recognition undergoes changes on this level. For while Hegel earlier rejected the state of nature (*Naturzustand*) speculations of liberal social contract theory as fiction, he now contends that sovereign states are in a state of nature in their relations to each other. What must come into existence is not communal existence but rather international order and law. Just as the original encounter between autonomous individuals was described as a life and death struggle, so also the relation between sovereign states is a comparable life and death struggle for recognition that includes the possibility of war. War ties the two foci of sovereignty together, for in wartime the ideality of members of nation, their willingness to sacrifice for the whole, becomes a far more serious matter, and the unity and sovereign independence of the state as an individual is put to the test.

Hegel regards the international level, and history, as fundamentally tragic. For on the international level, there is no mutual recognition that issues in a higher union; there is no We. For this reason Hegel claims that international law has the status of an 'ought to be'. This failure of mutual recognition on the ultimate historical level makes manifest that world history is fundamentally tragic, and it demonstrates the need for absolute spirit—art, religion, and philosophy—which is necessary to make sense of the tragic situation of freedom in history.

We shall examine first Hegel's account of internal sovereignty in terms of the organism model, as the alternative to monism and to pluralism. The mutual recognition on which the legitimacy of the state is based culminates in the organism model and is Hegel's account of genuine, as contrasted with merely formal and subjective, conscience. The highest level of mutual recognition that results in a 'We' turns out to be the state. Second, the state as a universal-individual is dialectical, in that its internal sovereignty requires recognition by other independent states. However, such recognition is contingent; it is not a given, nor can it be taken for granted. Hegel points to difficulties in achieving recognition between states. The possibility of mutual recognition is influenced and conditioned by the degree of constitutional-political development. Hegel sees a fundamental dividing line between constitutions that are based on nature and express natural relations—for example, oriental patriarchalism and theocracy that conceive the state as an extended family—and constitutions that are based on and expressions of critical rational freedom, for example, constitutional republics.[1] Between such diverse, mutually exclusive social-political systems, recognition and trust are difficult, if not impossible. Accordingly we shall consider the struggle for recognition between independent and sovereign states as an analogue to the state of nature. Finally, we shall examine briefly Hegel's account of war and peace and tragic view of world history.

---

1. *VPR*17, §135.

Sovereignty

Hegel conceives sovereignty in terms of the social-organism concept of the state. Sovereignty is the sociopolitical specification and exemplification of the objective idealism of life, namely, organism. Sovereignty designates the unity, independence, and self-perpetuation of the state organism. Sovereignty is the ideality and coinherence of the members, organs, and institutions of the state whereby the whole accomplishes and produces itself. Hegel tells us that "the state is an organism, the development of the Idea in its differences. These different aspects are accordingly the various powers with their corresponding tasks and functions, through which the universal continually produces itself in a necessary way and thereby preserves itself, because it is itself the presupposition of its own production. This organism is the political constitution; it proceeds continually from the state, just as it is the means by which the state preserves itself." [2] Again, the state is an internally "divided whole [which] exhibits a fixed and enduring determinacy which is not dead and unchanging, but continues to produce itself in its dissolution." [3] Sovereignty in part is this ability of the state to reproduce itself continuously in its dissolution, wherein the members both reflect the whole and return into the whole, while the whole perpetuates itself in their finitude and dissolution.

We have found that mutual recognition is the general intersubjective-social form of spirit and ethical life. Considered internally, sovereignty means that the struggle for recognition as well as the institution of mastery and slavery have been overcome; the I has become a We by reciprocally recognizing and being recognized by others.[4] Such reciprocal recognitions both underlie and find expression in the institutions and constitution of the state. The constitution is not a merely formal document but an expression of the social rationality and spirit of a people. It is that by virtue of which the nation preserves and renews itself.

Sovereignty is a further specification of one dimension or 'moment' of mutual recognition. Sovereignty is the element of union in the mutual recognition constitutive of the state. Just as individuals must subordinate their private wills to the common will in order to form a marriage as an enduring union, so also individuals must restrain and limit not only their "wild" lawless freedom but also their economic freedom in order to become members of a state. Sovereignty corresponds to the moment of union whereby individuals become and remain a people or nation. Sovereignty does not merely correspond to that union; it is that union, the animating vital principle constitutive of a people and present in all members of the state. As such it comes to expression in patriotism. "This disposition is one of trust . . . , or the consciousness that my sub-

---

2. *PR*, §269 Zusatz.   3. Ibid., §270 Zusatz.   4. Ibid., §57.

stantial and particular interest is preserved and included in the interest and end of another (in this case the state). . . . As a result, this other ceases to be an other for me, and in my consciousness of this, I am free."[5]

As the subjective element or specification of sovereignty, patriotism is not to be understood primarily as a willingness to make extraordinary or heroic self-sacrifices for the whole. Moreover, loud, flamboyant heroism may not be patriotic.[6] Instead Hegel links patriotism with ordinary habits of public trust and confidence: "it is that disposition which, in the normal conditions and circumstances of life, habitually knows that the community is the substantial basis and end."[7] Citizens, as members of the state, "trust that the state will continue to exist and that particular interests can be secured and fulfilled only in the state; but habit blinds us to that on which our entire existence depends. It does not occur to someone who walks the street in safety at night that this might be otherwise, for this habit of [living in] safety has become second nature, and we scarcely think that it is solely the effect of particular institutions. Representational thought often imagines that the state is held together by force; but what actually holds it together is simply the basic sense of order which everyone possesses."[8] This habitual sense of order is what underlies the willingness to make the exceptional sacrifices with which patriotism is often identified, and which may be necessary in time of war.

Patriotism is an objective idealism in Hegel's sense. The citizens of a state, as its members, suspend their merely private egoistic interests and constitute themselves as ideal, that is, as members of the larger enduring union or whole. The idea of marriage is a small-scale example of what Hegel is driving at. Marriage is an interpersonal union; it is a willingness to form a corporate identity, a new person. Hegel tells us that in the state as a spiritual being, "all the diverse elements are present only ideally and as a unity. Thus the state, as spiritual in character, is the exposition of all its moments, but individuality is also its inner soul and animating principle, its sovereignty, which includes all differences in itself."[9] Again and again Hegel underscores that the substantial unity of the state is the *ideality* of its moments. The life of the whole is present as the *ideality* of its individual members and moments. Hegel writes, "The basic determination of the political state is the substantial unity or ideality of its moments, the ideality of the moments in which . . . the particular powers and functions of the state are both dissolved and preserved. They are preserved, not as having independent justification, but a justification only insofar as they are

5. Ibid., §268.
6. Hegel observes that some "convince themselves that they possess this extraordinary patriotism in order to exempt themselves from the genuine disposition, or to excuse their lack of it" (ibid.).
7. *PR*, §268.   8. Ibid.   9. *PR*, §275 Zusatz.

determined by the Idea of the whole. Their source is the whole and they are its fluid members, just as it is their simple self."[10] This ideality does not mean that the members of the state are "swallowed up" or dissolved in some supersubject. Rather it refers to the willingness of the members to work together and make sacrifices for the common good. Parents sacrificing for the sake of their children and family, or citizens rallying to the defense of freedom and its institutions, are examples of ideality in this sense.

Hegel develops his concept of sovereignty as a normative conception; this involves the metaphors of disease and health. "The idealism which constitutes sovereignty is the same determination as that according to which the so-called parts of an animal organism are not parts, but members or organic moments whose isolation and separate existence constitute disease."[11] Hegel identifies sovereignty, so conceived, as the health of the organism. He describes health as the "proportion of the organism to its determinate existence, that is, all its organs are fluid in the universal."[12] Conversely, disease hinders this ideality and fluidity within the organism; disease is a condition opposite to such fluidity, namely, a disproportion between an irritation and the capacity of the organism to respond and overcome the irritation. In disease, the organism becomes disproportionately divided; its members decline into parts that cease to have their identity within and contribute to the whole. As a result, the vitality, fluidity, and resiliency of the organism are restricted.

Hegel points out that a stone cannot become diseased, because it is destroyed in the negative of itself. But an organism, when healthy, maintains itself in its internal self-diremption and negation; its self-preservation and self-maintenance are sovereignty. However, in disease, the organism's capacity for self-perpetuation and renewal is either overwhelmed or hindered. When its internal complexity, vitality, and fluidity are hindered, an organism declines, fails, and eventually perishes. Hegel observes that organisms, owing to their fragile complexity, are vulnerable and susceptible to disease and death, a loss of actuality in which their members revert to wholly independent, externally related parts or atoms: "It is the nature of an organism that all its parts must perish if they do not achieve identity."[13] Identity here means the vital unity and coinherence of whole and parts. "If this unity is not present, nothing can be *actual*, even if it may be assumed to have *existence*. A bad state is one which merely exists; a sick body exists, but it has no true reality. A hand which is cut off still looks like a hand, but it has no actuality."[14] Organisms contain within themselves the possibility of their own demise. Life is a continuous struggle against that possibility, and health is measured by the ability of the organism to overcome threats and sustain itself.

10. Ibid., §276.   11. Ibid.
12. *E*, §371. Hegel explicitly refers to the *Philosophy of Nature* in *PR*, §276.
13. *PR*, §269 Zusatz.
14. Ibid., §270 Zusatz. Italics in original.

Hegel believes the foregoing analysis has application to the ethical and political sphere. When the state and its sovereignty are understood on the model of an organism, there are two conditions that must be avoided if the state is to continue, namely, the suppression of all internal differentiation, as in despotism, and the suppression of union, fluidity, and vitality, as in division, anarchy, and civil war. Let us consider despotism first, because it seems to be implied by Hegel's conception of sovereignty as the ideality of every particular element and authority within the state. This question of sovereignty takes on additional significance and importance in light of the almost "standard" criticism that in the organism model, which Hegel clearly favors, the whole dominates its parts. Since the members are all internally related to the whole, they allegedly have no reality apart from or in isolation from the whole.[15] Organism appears to tend toward ontological monism, whether of a substance/accident sort such as Spinoza or its inversion, transcendental idealism, in which objects are relative to and depend for their condition of possibility on a transcendental subject.

Hegel is aware of this issue. He points out that there is an easy and very common misunderstanding that the ideality of all powers and authorities is only might and pure arbitrariness, and that sovereignty is therefore just another term for despotism. This misunderstanding arises in part from the ambiguity of the term 'idealism'. Taken in the standard sense of transcendental idealism, idealism signifies the relativity of the object of knowledge to the subject. Objects are objects for, and relative to, the transcendental subject. The transcendental subject, as the condition of objects, is not itself an object and cannot become an object. Hence the relativity of objects to it means that they are nonreciprocally, asymmetrically related to the transcendental subject. This asymmetry creates the appearance that transcendental idealism amounts to a tyranny of the subject.[16] But Hegel rejects both despotism and transcendental idealism.

The idealism he is talking about in sovereignty is the objective idealism of life itself, which we have seen is the animating principle of organism. Idealism here is synonymous with the actuality (*Wirklichkeit*) of the organism as such. This animating actuality is not itself a part or member, nor is the organism merely a maxim of reflective judgment, an 'as if' organism. Rather this ideal actuality is immanent in and constitutive of the organism itself. Apart from this objective ideal unity, the members would cease to be what they are: "The members and organs of a living body should not be considered merely as parts of it, for they are what they are only in their unity and are not at all indifferent

15. See Harris, *The Spirit of Hegel*, 150.
16. Cf. Kant's comments: "reason has insight only into that which it produces after a plan of its own. . . . [I]t must not allow itself to be kept, as it were, in nature's leading-strings, but must itself show the way, . . . constraining nature to answer questions of reason's own determining. . . . It must not, however, do so in the character of a pupil who listens to everything that the teacher chooses to say, but of an appointed judge who compels the witness to answer the questions which he has himself formulated" (Kant, preface to the second edition of the *Critique of Pure Reason*, trans. N. K. Smith [New York: St. Martin's, 1965], 20).

to that unity." [17] The living idealism of the organism depends on the articulation of the organism into real differences, on the one hand, and, on the other, the fluidity of these real differences in serving a common end or purpose, namely, the very animation and preservation of the organism itself. This fluidity of differences Hegel calls return of the members into unity.

This unity is not sheer undifferentiated unity, but depends on and is the ideality of these real differences. In asserting that the differences are ideal, Hegel does not mean that the members of the organism are obliterated. Instead, the immediacy in terms of which each appears as independent and isolated is canceled, while difference itself is preserved in that mediation by which the individual is a member of the organism. Death cancels this mediation—which is the actual vitality pervading the organism—and returns the members to mere isolated parts: "A hand which has been cut off still looks like a hand and exists, but it has no actuality." [18] Again, "This ideality of the moments [in the state] is like life in an organic body; it is present in every point, there is only one life in all of them. . . . Separated from it, each point must die." [19] Thus in organism, ideality is synonymous with actuality, and actuality presupposes and depends on the determinate negation and mediation of the real differences. This is the social-ontological significance of Hegel's famous concept of *Aufhebung*. [20] If difference is either absolute (as in anarchist atomism) or eliminated (as in totalitarianism) the organism perishes.

Sovereignty, conceived on the organic model, must not be confused with despotism. Despotism, says Hegel, "signifies the condition of lawlessness in general, in which the particular will as such, whether of a monarch or a people, counts as law, or rather replaces law." [21] Despotic freedom is sheer arbitrariness. It can only be arbitrariness (*Willkür*) because it has not yet taken account of or recognized its other. Only one will counts, and it counts immediately, refusing all mediation and qualification. Consequently there can be no law in the proper sense of the term. Others are not recognized and do not count; they are slaves or property. In despotism, therefore, there can be no genuinely social, universal consciousness mediated by reciprocal recognition, much less a lawful expression of it.

Lawfulness presupposes that the other counts and that the relation between self and other is reciprocal recognition. Law articulates this reciprocity and co-equality. Law presupposes and originates in mutual recognition, which in turn supports and sustains respect for freedom as an end in itself. This universality of law means that the only individuality that may legitimately be asserted is a 'universal individuality' of the We, or law. Despotism is either a prerecognition, pre-ethical condition, or displaces these. Moreover, despotism is ahistorical; for if only one will counts, the power dynamics are either zero or static at best. There is

---

17. *E*, §135 Zusatz.   18. *PR*, §270 Zusatz.   19. Ibid., §276 Zusatz.
20. *WL*, 5:113–114.   21. *PR*, §278.

no possibility of introducing novelty or change into the absolute position, other than despotic arbitrariness. For this reason Hegel associates despotism with those societies in which nature dominates spirit, and in which political relations are conceived as extensions of natural relations, to wit, the state is conceived as an extended family and the government is patriarchy and/or theocracy.[22]

Against despotism, Hegel defends the idea of a constitutional separation of powers.[23] Separation of powers in turn implies the recognition of difference; the other counts as a counterbalance to the power of the one. Montesquieu argued that separation of powers distinguishes modern constitutional states from despotism and classical republics.[24] But separation of powers, if it becomes total, amounts to a return of atomism and anarchy on the political level. In this case, otherness and difference can be so strong that the unity required by the social organism becomes impossible. Paralysis is often the result. Difference, when absolutized, turns a community into a mere crowd or aggregate that remains unrelated in spite of their relation. This is the centrifugal tendency of civil society that the state must oppose, rather than reflect or promote.[25]

A state is not a disorganized crowd, or externally related aggregate of absolute individuals. Hegel observes that "the state is essentially an organization whose members constitute circles within their own right [*für sich*], and no moment within it should appear as an unorganized crowd. The many as single individuals—and this is a favorite interpretation of [the term] 'the people'—do indeed live together, but only as a crowd, i.e., a formless mass whose movement and activity can consequently only be elemental, irrational, barbarous and terrifying."[26] A disorganized crowd is irrational, Hegel believes; it does not exhibit social rationality or a system of rational mediations. However, "The constitution is rational in so far as the state *differentiates* and determines its activity within itself *in accordance with the nature of the concept*. It does so in such a way that each of the powers in question is in itself the *totality*, since each contains the other moments and has them active within it, and since all of them, as expressions of the difference [*Unterschied*] of the concept, remain wholly within its ideality and constitute nothing but *a single individual* whole."[27]

Practically, on the political and constitutional level, a complete separation of powers may imply divided government, including the possibility of paralysis, civil war, or anarchy. Hegel believes these are potential dangers in Fichte's ephorate; Fichte posits an absolute separation of powers, in which the ephorate can overthrow the regime.[28] Such an absolute separation destroys the organic

---

22. Ibid., §355.   23. Ibid., §§272–273.

24. Steven B. Smith, *Hegel's Critique of Liberalism* (Chicago: University of Chicago Press, 1989), 153.

25. *PR*, §§182–184.   26. Ibid., §303.

27. Ibid., §272. Italics in original.

28. Fichte, *Grundlage des Naturrechts*, §16, III, 166–178; *SR*, 253–271. Cited by Hegel, *PR*, §273.

unity of the state: "While the powers of the state must certainly be distinguished, each must form a whole in itself and contain the other moments within it. When speaking of the distinct activities of these powers, we must not fall into the monumental error of taking this to mean that each power should exist as independently for itself and in abstraction. On the contrary, the powers should be distinguished only as moments of the concept."[29] The task is to divide the powers while retaining their functionality as a whole. This can be the case only if the whole is present throughout all its members in spite of their differences. The only conception that does justice to this requirement, while avoiding the reductive extremes of despotism (monism) and anarchism (pluralism), is organism. Each part is expressive of the whole organism, and the whole is present in each of its members. While monarch, executive, and legislature have distinct and separate functions, their continual harmony and cooperation are necessary if the state is to survive. Sovereignty is necessary for the survival of the state.

War

I shall not enter on a defense of Hegel's views on war against the manifold distortions and criticisms to which they have been subjected. On this subject I have nothing to add to Shlomo Avineri's illuminating treatment.[30] What is remarkable about Avineri's analysis is that he manages to get so much right about Hegel's views on war, without adequately appreciating the concept of sovereignty and its deep structure in the state as an organism whose ideality and unity are found in mutual recognition. War is the return, at a higher level, of the life and death struggle for recognition. Internally the struggle for recognition is in some sense over, but externally the state is a particular in relation to others. Hence externally the situation remains a struggle for recognition between nations. Just as the transcendence of freedom over nature and merely natural needs and existence is demonstrated by one's willingness to risk one's life in the struggle for recognition, so also the claim of national independence must be similarly demonstrated by confronting the possibility of war and death. War is a test of national sovereignty and, what comes to the same thing, the cohesiveness and health of the social organism in the face of threat of death, which depends on the willingness of individuals to subordinate themselves, and if necessary, sacrifice everything for the sake of the whole. Hegel observes that "the state cannot require the sacrifice of individuals simply for the sake of its honor or for the glory of God alone. The death sacrifice of the individual must be mediated through his will."[31] In war the ideality of individuals relative to the whole, easily forgotten and passed over in times of peace, becomes a serious matter.

---

29. *PR*, §272 Zusatz.   30. Avineri, *HTMS*.   31. *VPR*18, §130.

We have noted that the life of an organism is a perpetual struggle to overcome forces that oppose it and threaten it with dissolution. Hegel sees peace and war as posing different sorts of challenges to the sovereign actuality of the state. In peacetime, the forces that threaten the state come from within, namely, from civil society. In peacetime, civil society, with its strong individualist and materialistic ethos, tends to dominate the state. Civil society allows the pursuit of private interests without regard for others and thus fosters a self-centered, materialistic egoism. In peacetime, individuals come to be entrenched in their individuality and regard their material needs and interests as the ultimate perspective from which everything, including the state, ought to be measured. The state becomes subservient to individual self-interest. When that happens, self-sufficient, self-isolating individuals become entrenched in their private existence, avoid consideration of others and the public interest, and the social totality is sundered into unrelated atoms.[32] "In peace, the bounds of civil life are extended, all its spheres become firmly established, and in the long run, people become stuck in their ways. Their particular characteristics become increasingly rigid and ossified. But the unity of the body is essential to health, and if its parts grow internally hard, the result is death."[33] Thus peace tends to promote a complacent, self-indulgent individualism that undermines patriotism and fragments the whole. As Avineri observes, "A situation in which people do not hold anything beyond civil society as binding upon them, is a situation of social disintegration and *hubris*."[34] Consequently, although peace is obviously preferable to the destructive carnage of war, it nevertheless presents a situation in which the state must counter the inherent centrifugal individualist tendencies of civil society and make the competing self-interests contribute to the good of the whole.[35] If it does not succeed, then "every center of life goes its own way and establishes itself on its own; the whole falls apart. The state exists no longer."[36]

In war, the challenge to sovereignty comes from without. To meet this external challenge, the state must uproot individuals from their private interests by forcing them to confront the possibility of death and compel them to contribute to the maintenance and preservation of the whole, even if that means sacrificing their life and property. Peace and war therefore present different and opposing problems for ethical life and for sovereignty as an ethical conception.

Shlomo Avineri identifies the fundamental problem presented by war to ethical life as follows: "How can a political authority issue a command to a citi-

---

32. Hegel, *Philosophie des Geistes 1805/06*, 251; *HHS*, 172.
33. *PR*, §324 Zusatz.
34. Avineri, *HTMS*, 197.
35. *PR*, §278.
36. Hegel, *The German Constitution*, in *Hegel's Political Writings*, 146. I have modified the verb tenses of the translation. Hegel refers to the decline of the German state. "Germany is a state no longer" (p. 143). He is referring to the loss of internal sovereignty and its displacement by absolutized self-interests.

zen to serve in the army in times of war and thus expose himself to being killed or wounded, while at the same time founding the legitimacy of its authority on the postulate of preserving the individual's safety and on condemning violence?"[37] If the state were nothing more than an instrument for the protection of life and property, there would be considerable difficulty in answering this question; indeed, exposing oneself to the possibility of death would make no sense on the individualist basis of liberal social theory. If war is only for the protection of property, there may be other, less costly ways of achieving this objective. Hegel parts company with classical liberal thought on this issue and its underlying conception of the state: "It is a grave miscalculation if the state, when it requires this sacrifice, is simply equated with civil society, and if its ultimate end is seen merely as the security of the life and property of individuals. For this security cannot be achieved by the sacrifice of what is supposed to be secured. On the contrary."[38]

Consequently for Hegel the meaning and aim of war cannot be to defend property and life by sacrificing them. War has to be understood in the context of ethical life, where it relativizes the life and property of individuals in favor of the higher need of the state to secure itself collectively, even if that means that individuals must be sacrificed. War shifts attention from individuals as their own ultimate ends to sovereignty as the ideality of individuals and their property in relation to the end of the whole.

> War is a situation in which the vanity of temporal goods and things is taken seriously—a vanity which in peacetime is a theme of edifying rhetoric. War is accordingly the moment in which the ideality of the *particular attains its right* and becomes actual. The higher significance of war is that through its agency (as I have stated it elsewhere) the ethical health of peoples is preserved in their indifference towards the permanence of finite determinacies, just as the movement of the winds preserves the sea from stagnation which a lasting calm would produce— a stagnation which a lasting, not to say, perpetual peace would also produce among nations.[39]

War is a trial of national unity and sovereignty, that is, the social cohesion of the nation as a whole: "In a crisis situation—whether in internal or external affairs—it is around the concept of sovereignty that the organism and its constitutive particularities rally. It is to this sovereignty that the salvation of the state is entrusted, while otherwise legitimate functions are sacrificed; this is where the idealism of sovereignty attains its distinctive actuality."[40]

37. Avineri, *HTMS*, 195.
38. *PR*, §324.
39. Ibid. Hegel cites his earlier essay, *Natural Law* (1803). The reference to perpetual peace is a thinly veiled disagreement with Immanuel Kant. See below fn. 95.
40. Ibid., §278. Hegel also notes that in such crisis situations, edifying discourses about the vanity of temporal goods and concerns also undergoes a transformation: "We hear numerous sermons on the insecurity, vanity and instability of temporal things, but all who hear them, however moved they may be, believe that they will none the less retain what is theirs. But if this insecurity

This is not a glorification of war. Although Hegel believes that war has an ethical dimension and function, he is far from regarding war as an end in itself, or as a positive political goal of national policy. For Hegel, the function of war is to break down the materialist illusion of self-sufficient finitude and to confront the ultimate negativity of death, the absolute master. War—and it is clear that Hegel is thinking here of limited war—serves the ethical purpose of developing ethical-social freedom and communal solidarity. But this is not a neat, painless or bloodless process, for in an emergency situation such as war, "otherwise legitimate functions" and institutions must be and are sacrificed for the sake of survival of the whole. This includes the potential *voluntary* sacrifice of individual right to life and property central to civil society.

It would be an exaggeration to say that Hegel is fond of war, or that he believes that the larger ethical purpose of national sovereignty and survival can be realized only through war. For example, in his Jena *Philosophy of Spirit* (1805), he conceives war as analogous to crime and transgression. He asserts that war "is crime on behalf of the universal." [41] Just as punishment is justified only as a second coercion directed against coercion, so also war is defended by Hegel as a defensive necessity against external attack: "The end is the maintenance of the totality against the enemy who is out to destroy it." [42] Moreover, Hegel observes that although war confronts individuals and states with the possibility of death, death in war is "without individuality—death coldly received and given, not in ongoing battle where the individual has his eye on his opponent and kills him in immediate hatred; rather death emptily given and received, impersonal in the gunsmoke." [43] Although Hegel did not anticipate the destructive scale of modern warfare, he nevertheless understands the impersonal death modern weapons make possible.

Hegel's analysis of the ethical significance of war is subtle. His claim is that war is an immediate threat to national and personal existence, in which the ethical decentering of the subject and the transformation of natural individualism into the universal-ethical individualism necessary for effective national sovereignty, so often postponed or relaxed in peacetime, becomes an immediate practical imperative.

War should not be regarded as an absolute evil and as a purely external contingency. . . . It is necessary that the finite—such as property and life—should be *posited* as contingent, because contingency is the concept of the finite. On the one hand this necessity assumes the shape of a natural power; everything finite is mortal and temporary. But in ethical life, i.e., the state, nature is deprived of this power, and necessity is elevated to a work of freedom, to something ethical in character. The transitoriness of finitude now becomes a voluntary passing away,

should then actually become a serious matter in the shape of hussars with sabers drawn, the edifying and uplifting sentiments which predicted all this turns into profanity and curses against the conquerors" (*PR*, §324 Zusatz).
41. Hegel, *Philosophie des Geistes 1805/06*, 251; *HHS*, 171.
42. Ibid.   43. Ibid.

and the negativity which underlies it becomes the distinctive substantial individuality of ethical being and life.[44]

In war, both individuals and peoples must tarry with the negative and look death in the face. That is why patriotism includes an element of courage that relativizes natural egoism and accepts not only mortal finitude but also the risk of that finitude in the face of death.

Hegel claims that "the health of a state is generally revealed not so much in the calm of peace as in the stir of war. Peace is the state of enjoyment and activity in seclusion. . . . But in war the power of association of all with the whole is in evidence."[45] Or not in evidence, as Hegel observes: "Thus it was in the war with the French Republic that Germany found by its own experience that it was no longer a state."[46] For Hegel, war is a test of the vitality of a state, as a disease is a test of the health of an organism. It is only when attacked that one can determine whether the body is healthy enough to fight off or overcome disease; war provides a similar test or trial of a nation's cohesion and sovereignty. However, Hegel does not identify war directly with the health of the state, or as a necessary condition of that health; rather he claims that in war health and vitality and sovereignty are tested,[47] precisely because of the voluntary character of the sacrifices necessary to prosecute war.

It might be objected that the foregoing interpretation of Hegel's view of war overlooks an important passage from the *Phenomenology of Spirit* where Hegel appears to counsel war as an end of national policy. This text reads:

> The spirit of the universal gathering and assembly is the simple and negative being of these self-isolating systems. In order not to let them become entrenched and established in this isolation, thereby breaking up the whole and allowing the communal spirit to evaporate, government from time to time has to shake them up through war. By this means the government upsets their established arrangements and violates their independence, while the individuals who, absorbed in their own way of life, break loose from the whole and strive after the inviolable independence and security of the person, are made to feel their master, death, in the task laid upon them.[48]

Avineri finds in this passage a "radical counsel" concerning war which is problematic and to which Hegel (fortunately) never returned.[49]

It should be noted that this text occurs in a specific context of the *Phenomenology*, namely, Hegel's discussion of Greek ethical life. Hegel is discussing the

44. *PR*, §324.
45. Hegel, *German Constitution*, 143–144.
46. Ibid. Hegel refers here to the internal decline of the German Federation within the Holy Roman Empire, which conflict with France had made evident, at least to Hegel.
47. Avineri puts it this way: "War is not *the* health of a state—*in* it a state's health is put to the test" (*HTMS*, 199).
48. *PhG*, 324; *PhS*, 272.   49. Avineri, *HTMS*, 198.

contrast between human law and divine, in order to set the stage for the conflict between these ethical powers that occurs in Sophocles' tragedy *Antigone*.[50] Hegel's "radical counsel" cited above occurs in the course of expounding the logic of human law, or the law of the state, and how in the person of Creon it comes into conflict with divine law of the family as asserted by Antigone. These powers, otherwise justified, are presented here in one-sided oversimplifications and exaggerations that make conflict inevitable, as occurs in the actions of Creon and Antigone. In Hegel's interpretation of *Antigone*, the conflict between the family, represented by Antigone, and state power, represented by Creon, is not a conflict between right and wrong. Rather for Hegel, both Antigone and Creon uphold a right, namely, the right of the family and the right of the state, respectively. But Antigone and Creon fail to recognize each other, and the result is a tragic conflict, or collision of rights. The tragedy consists in the fact that these rights, which are compatible in principle, are asserted in a mutually exclusive way. According to A. C. Bradley, the end of this tragic conflict is the denial of both exclusive claims. Tragedy does not deny the rightful powers of state and family per se, "what is denied is the exclusive and therefore wrongful assertion of their right."[51] Antigone's and Creon's tragic suffering is due to the exclusive, wrongful assertion of a right.

This context of Hegel's remarks about war calls into question whether they should be construed as a radical counsel concerning war as an affirmative end of national policy as Avineri claims. It seems more plausible that these remarks are not prescriptive but descriptive in nature. As descriptive, they are not suggestions or radical counsel in any direct political sense but refer to Hegel's analysis of the historical conditions of tragic conflict, namely, the logic of a one-sided 'false consciousness' view of state power that virtually guarantees a conflict with the sacred rights of the family as the community that tarries with the negative. What precipitates the tragic conflict between family and state are the Theban wars. It is the warrior ethic at the heart of the polis that considers it acceptable policy to "shake things up" by going to war and to maintain a restrictive order in its aftermath.[52] For Hegel, the tragic suffering and downfall of Creon, who pursued such a policy, and of Antigone, who defied it,

50. Recall that the divine law is unwritten, a matter of family piety, sensed by conscience and expressive of family members' obligations to each other. For example, the family is concerned with the human being as an individual. Thus, in the case of a death of one of its members, the family tarries with the negative; i.e., it seeks to prevent him from becoming a mere nonentity and to maintain him and his memory in the human form of (family) community by seeing that he receives a proper burial. Human law, in contrast, is public, more general in that it is concerned with the individual not as a family member, but only as a citizen. It is not concerned with this particular father or brother, but only with citizens or 'universal individuals' that it intends to put in harm's way in the national defense. It does not tarry with the negative but rather flirts with it.

51. A. C. Bradley, "Hegel's Theory of Tragedy," in *Hegel: On Tragedy*, ed. A. Paolucci (New York: Anchor Books, 1962), 370.

52. See Martin Donougho, "The Woman in White: On the Reception of Hegel's Antigone," *Owl of Minerva* 21, no. 1 (Fall 1989): 65–89.

mirror and anticipate the dissolution and downfall of Greek ethical life. In spite of the controversial passage cited above, it is difficult to find in Hegel's treatment of the tragic decline and fall of Greek ethical life and its displacement by the Roman Empire, an endorsement of war as an affirmative, much less successful policy. Rather the counsel of shaking things up through war, even though it is a possible prerogative of state power,[53] seems to be both tragic hubris and folly. War is for Hegel an "aimless labor"[54] precisely because the right that is asserted falsely without qualification may not be vindicated but rather destroyed.

Finally, it is important to note that despite his pessimism, Hegel is far from the view that war settles or determines what right is. War for Hegel is never a question of right versus wrong but rather a question of right versus right, that is, a tragic collision of rights. This is clear from his early *German Constitution.*

> Wars, be they called wars of aggression or defense—a matter on which the parties never agree—would be called unjust only if the peace treaty had stipulated an unconditional peace on both sides. . . . But the potential modes of enmity are so infinite that there is no determining them by human intelligence, and . . . the more rights that are established, the more readily does a contradiction between such rights arise. . . . Each party grounds its behavior on rights and accuses the other of an infringement of right. . . . Each party claims to have right on its side, and both parties are right. It is just the rights themselves which come into contradiction with one another. . . . *Thus war . . . has now to decide, not which of the rights alleged by the two parties is the genuine right—since both parties have a genuine right—but which of the two rights is to give way. War, or whatever it may be, has to decide this, precisely because both contradictory rights were equally genuine.*[55]

Thus Hegel is not so much a cynical "realist" or pessimist as someone with a tragic view of war and history. He applies the theory of collision of rights, first worked out in his critique of Kantian morality and his analysis of Greek tragedy, to his analysis of war.

Issues of Recognition in International Relations

The sovereignty of the state, considered internally, is manifest in the ideality of its members, institutions, and authorities. All of these are relativized and

53. Avineri interprets the controversial counsel about shaking things up through war as primarily ethical in nature. On this reading Hegel does not claim that war is an end in itself; rather it has an ethical function; namely, it relativizes human existence and brings out human valor in the face of finitude, contingency, and mortality. This relativizing shows that the state is more than and transcends civil society, and that it is a higher interest. The crucial point is that the state, as the fulfillment and embodiment of the idea of freedom, is not supposed to trample freedom and its necessary institutions, but to secure these. If it calls on its citizens for the ultimate sacrifice, this final relativization must be mediated by their will, i.e., be voluntary.

54. Hegel, *System of Ethical Life*, 149.

55. Hegel, *German Constitution*, 208–210. My italics.

brought back into a living, vital social universality and unity that constitute sovereignty. Sovereignty, considered in and for itself, is the living universal will and social rationality of a people. Internal sovereignty denotes the state as the universal ideality of its particulars in the medium of mutual-reciprocal recognition or spirit. This is its domestic reciprocal recognition, patriotism, and so on. The patriotic identification of citizens with and their willingness to sacrifice for the preservation of the state are important if people are to become an enduring, self-perpetuating constitutional state.

However, a nation does not merely exist in isolation; it also exists in relation to others. Just as the will is actual only by willing something (*etwas*), so also a people, a nation, is actual only by being determinate, and as determinate, it is a particular nation among others. The sovereign state, hitherto regarded as a universal in comparison with its individual members, is now considered from the international perspective as an individual among other individuals; externally sovereignty refers to the problem of the recognition of the state by other sovereign states. Although its internal struggle for recognition whereby it becomes a sovereign state may be over, the state's struggle for recognition of its sovereignty and legitimacy vis-à-vis other states has just begun. "The state is for itself, but second, it is also for others; it must therefore be recognized, and in the modern period many collisions have arisen."[56] Not only individuals but also states require recognition and must undergo a struggle for recognition with other states.

This transition from universal dimension of the state vis-à-vis its individuals to its particular dimension vis-à-vis other states is conceived by Hegel in analogy with the initial moment of recognition, where the 'absolute' parochial self finds itself confronted by an other and thus turns out to be a *particular* in opposition to another particular. This encounter is described as a self-othering, a loss of self; the loss of self can only be overcome by mutual recognition. At the level of recognition between individuals, relation, that is, encounter, precedes the achievement of reciprocal recognition. However, at the international level, relations between states turn on recognition as their prior condition. Here recognition precedes "official" relations. Recognition thus receives further qualification on this level.

Hegel identifies three features of international recognition. First, sovereignty is not actual in isolation but rather is a claim for recognition by other states. It is as if Hegel treats sovereignty as a 'subjective certainty' that must be elevated to international recognition; only as recognized is state sovereignty legitimate. Just as recognition is a condition of the realization of an individual's freedom, so also recognition is necessary for the actualization of a state's sovereignty: "Just as little as an individual can be an actual person without relations to other persons, a state cannot be an actual individual without relations to other states."[57] Recognition is thus a condition of the state's actuality and le-

---

56. *VPR*4, §331, 740.   57. *PR*, §331.

gitimacy, as well as the condition on which all its international relations, treaties, and so on, depend.

Second, the state's external relations, or being for others, are conditioned by its internal relations, that is, the spirit and constitution of its people. In contrast to interpersonal recognition where the universal common We emerges as a result of the process of recognition, in international relations common values, political ideologies, and constitutions precede recognition as conditioning factors. International recognition depends in part on a nation's internal historical and social development at the constitutional level. A state, unlike a human being, is not entitled to be recognized simply because it exists. A people merits recognition because it has achieved internal sovereignty as reflected in its constitutional development.

> A people, as a state, is spirit in its substantial rationality and immediate actuality, and therefore is the absolute power on earth. Each state consequently stands over and against the others in sovereign independence. As such its primary, absolute entitlement is to be for the others, and this means it is entitled to be recognized by them. At the same time however this entitlement is purely formal, and the requirement that the state be recognized simply because it exists is abstract. Whether the state does in fact exist in and for itself [as an end in itself] depends on its content—its constitution and its present situation. Moreover, recognition, which implies that the two [i.e., form and content] are identical, also depends on the perception and will of the other state.[58]

Third, although states may and do reciprocally recognize each other, this reciprocal recognition does not issue or result in the formation of an international 'We' or binding supranational law. There is an important difference between interpersonal and international recognition. Although states are entitled to recognition and need the recognition of other states in order to be actual, such international recognition, even if forthcoming, does not yield any emergent universal, or supranational, institution.

Hegel cites a remark of Napoleon that gives expression to the view that the international scene is primarily power relations, to wit: "the French Republic is no more in need of recognition than the sun is."[59] This statement is plainly an assertion of an absolute sovereign independence and self-certitude for which recognition is apparently superfluous. It expresses an absolute mastery of the sort that makes the international scene a Hobbesian state of nature. However, not even Napoleon invalidates the principle that sovereign states as independent individuals nevertheless require recognition by others to be actual. Like individuals who seek to raise their subjective self-certainty and claims to freedom to public truth, nations seek international recognition of their internal principles of legitimacy: "the legitimacy of a state . . . is a purely internal mat-

---

58. Ibid.   59. Ibid., Zusatz.

ter. . . . On the other hand it is equally essential that this legitimacy should be supplemented and confirmed by recognition by other states."[60]

Moreover, to pursue a war with another state (whom one presumably refuses to recognize) involves a tacit, if not explicit, recognition of that state.[61] In spite of its destructiveness, war implies some relation to that nation which one seeks to defeat.[62] Such tacit recognition becomes an explicit issue when the question arises how and on what conditions the war is to be ended and peace established, for any peace must build on and develop the positive elements in such recognition. Hegel criticizes Napoleon's remark, observing that "it is not a question of the mere existence of the state; the state must also be recognized; it enters into the most manifold and diverse relations with other states. Those states that enter into such relations must first recognize each other."[63]

However, since sovereign states are in a state of nature vis-à-vis each other, each seeks a guarantee from the others that it will be recognized, and vice versa. "This recognition requires a guarantee that the state will likewise recognize those other states which are supposed to recognize it, i.e., that it will respect their independence. Accordingly, these other states cannot be indifferent to its internal affairs."[64] States cannot be indifferent to the internal affairs of a state that they are to recognize, since that state must guarantee to reciprocate their recognition as a condition of receiving it. The question is whether such a guarantee is credible. In the absence of supranational institutions, laws, and sanctions, is trust possible? Hegel is not optimistic; the international scene is for him the state of nature, characterized by conflict, not only between competing ideologies, but also between "modern" and "premodern" cultures. These differences make trust and recognition difficult.

Hegel notes that "the general dividing line between constitutions is between those that are based on nature and those based on freedom of the will. . . . The patriarchal and oriental systems, then the aristocratic system, and finally the democratic system mark the transition from the natural principle. . . . Whether the state coheres on the basis of nature or of freedom of the will forms the dividing line between constitutions. Every concept begins in immediacy, in nature, and strives towards rationality. Everything depends on the extent to which rationality has replaced nature."[65] Constitutions based on nature tend to conceive the state as an extension of the family, tend to be patriarchal in social structure, tend to tolerate slavery as a "natural condition" and to regard their social order as having natural or divine sanction. Patriarchy goes hand in hand with theocracy. Oriental despotism is one of Hegel's frequently mentioned ex-

---

60. *PR*, §331.

61. Ibid., §338. Hotho's version of this runs: "Even in war a bond between the states still exists, namely recognition" (*VPR3*, 836).

62. This shows that Hegel is thinking of limited war and not modern totalitarian war or nuclear war.

63. *VPR4*, §331, 741.   64. *PR*, §331.   65. *VPR17*, §135.

amples, in which only one is free.[66] But if only one is free, the others do not count; they are submerged in a single unreflective substance; consequently individuals do not count and are not recognized. Freedom here is not the freedom of mutual recognition or law but merely arbitrariness. Hegel believes that world history exhibits a development away from acceptance of natural justifications of domination such as despotic patriarchy and toward demands for liberation and freedom.[67]

Although Hegel regards the displacement of the natural by the rational as a trend in world history, this is an ongoing process. The rational is still becoming actual. Here Hegel, in spite of his *Sollenkritik*, is not far from Fichte. International relations have a complexity and "untidiness" to them that produce struggles for recognition and freedom: "Their determinate existence for each other as independent peoples derives partly from the abstract struggle for freedom, and partly from recognition. They have to show that they are cultivated, internally ordered, law abiding states, for such internal conditions are the possibility of right legal [*rechtliche*] relations with one another."[68] The relation between states is influenced in part by their internal organization and constitutional arrangements, because internal lawfulness is a condition of external lawful relations with other states. Domination of the whole over its parts is more likely to occur under conditions of undeveloped social structures and institutions (or their forcible suppression) as in despotism. Lacking respect for its own individuals and law, a despotic state might well be a threat to its neighbors. Hegel observes,

> If a state has a constitution that threatens the independence of other states, or that is incompatible with a state of peace, the other states can either refuse to recognize it or else call upon it to change its constitution in that respect. . . . The constitution is the inner life of the people, and the people should have a constitution that enables other states to live at peace with it.[69]

Again,

> The self-consciousness of a people is essentially a self-intuition in another people. They must prove that they are independent. Spirit shows itself first in reaction— the abstract struggle for freedom—in the case of savage peoples this drive to demonstrate their freedom and independence is carried out through war.[70]

Fortunately, there is another, more civilized way of demonstrating national freedom and independence.

66. *PR*, §§354–355.
67. See *PR*, §§352–358. Hegel regards Greek culture as the transition from the savagery of the state of nature to ethical life; it is a halfway house that embraces both substantial freedom and slavery. Judged by this standard, modern cultures might be regarded as transitional in the similar sense; namely, they embrace both freedom and domination.
68. *VPR*18, §131.   69. *VPR*17, §161.   70. *VPR*18, §131.

> The higher demonstration [of freedom and independence] consists in the fact that a people shows itself in its existence to be cultivated and civilized, that it has not remained at the level of natural immediacy and savagery, but has rather subdued its natural will and given it the form of universality [and law].[71]

The logic of constitutional development is a process wherein the rational displaces merely natural relations and becomes actual in and through mutual recognition. However, this logic is only partially replicated at the level of international relations.

This brings us to a difficult issue concerning international recognition, namely, recognition between states of different degrees and types of sovereignty. The internal principles and conditions of a state's sovereignty are also conditions that shape its external relations to other states, and must be taken into account by those other states as they determine whether to recognize it or not. This raises a problem for Hegel: "In the case of a nomadic people . . . the question arises how far this people can be regarded as a state."[72] If a people has not yet achieved the internal development and sovereignty of a state, can it be recognized? What would be recognized in such a case? Hegel allows that "this recognition has a concrete sense: the question 'what can be recognized' allows many levels concerning this 'what'."[73] But what would be recognized in the case of the nomads? And what would the nomads recognize in their relation to a developed state like Germany? Hegel identifies a problem in international recognition.

> In its initial stage, a people is not yet a state, and the transition of a family, tribe, kinship group, mass of people, etc., to the condition of a state constitutes the formal realization of the Idea in general within it. Without this form the people, as ethical substance—what it implicitly is—lacks the objectivity of possessing in laws a universal and universally valid existence for itself and others, and is therefore not recognized. Since its independence has no objective legality or firmly established rationality for itself, it is merely formal and does not amount to sovereignty.[74]

Here Hegel seems to suggest that a condition of international recognition is some sort of objective legality and constitutional legitimacy. Prior to a people achieving such, their internal and external recognition are problematic, or worse, because they remain on the level of master and slave.

Although Hegel is a Eurocentrist, he is not a parochial Eurocentrist. Recall his judgment that his contemporary Germany has ceased to be a state owing to its loss of internal sovereignty and its displacement by powerful private inter-

---

71. Ibid.   72. *PR*, §331.   73. *VPR*4, §331, 741.
74. *PR*, §349. Hegel adds that "even in the context of ordinary ideas we do not describe a patriarchal condition as a constitution, nor do we describe people living in this condition as a state, or its independence as sovereignty."

ests that prevent national unity.[75] Nevertheless, when it comes to the question of recognition between constitutionally developed states and those that have not yet undergone comparable constitutional development, Hegel acknowledges there are thorny issues and intractable problems. Recognition between states presupposes comparable levels of cultural development and convergence of values, especially freedom. Nevertheless, Hegel notes that "the degree of cultural development is different, so that perhaps one degree of ethical life is not recognized by the others. Thus the Europeans have not recognized the Mexicans or Peruvians. Nevertheless it must remain possible to enter into proper [*rechtliche*] relations."[76] Although Hegel's comments may appear to have a European bias or sound imperialistic,[77] we do well to keep his last sentence in mind. Recognition between nations and peoples is possible in principle, if difficult in practice.

Hegel's discussion of the Africa of his day is relevant to this issue. Hegel's knowledge of Africa was quite limited, based on newspaper accounts and reports of missionaries. Given his sources, Hegel believed that black African peoples remained in a state of nature, in a preethical, pre–world-historical condition.[78] This is evident, Hegel believes, from the acceptance of slavery, for slavery is the antithesis of freedom. Hegel addresses only in passing the European-American contribution to the slave trade, which provided a demand for this "export": "Negroes are enslaved by Europeans and sold to America. Bad as this may be, their lot in their own land is even worse, since there a slavery quite as absolute exists."[79] The issue of slavery creates major problems for recognition between European and African countries; namely, "the only essential connection that has existed and continues between the Negroes and the Europeans

75. See above fn. 36.   76. *VPR*18, §131.

77. "Inasmuch as uncivilized peoples have virtually no constitution, and the civilized peoples who live alongside them accordingly cannot rely on them and never feel secure, they take it on themselves to compel these rough peoples to accept a binding constitution" (*VPR*17, §161). This statement suggests that Hegel understands the relation between civilized and uncivilized peoples by analogy to the relation between a hero who founds a state, and the people he gathers together. In his Jena *Philosophy of Spirit 1805/06*, Hegel characterizes this relationship thus: "In this way all states were established, through the noble force of great men. It is not a matter of physical strength, since many are physically stronger than one. Rather the great man has something in him by virtue of which others may call him their lord. They obey him against their will. Against their will his will is their will. Their immediate pure will is his, but their conscious will is different. . . . This is what is preeminent in the great man, to know the absolute will and express it so that all flock to his banner. . . . In this way Theseus established the Athenian state" (*HHS*, 155). This is a benign tyranny that Hegel has in mind, a tyranny that is relatively justified as a second coercion directed against a primary coercion, in that it opposes the inherent violence of the state of nature. A benign tyranny is supposed to make tyranny superfluous by creating conditions in which it will be displaced in favor of the rule of law. This also provides a somewhat enlightened rationale for colonial development toward liberation and self-determination, rather than a perpetual condition of inequality and asymmetry.

78. *Vorlesungen über die Philosophie der Geschichte, Werke*, TWA Sk 12:119–129; English translation: *The Philosophy of History*, trans. J. Sibree (New York: Dover, 1956), 91–99.

79. Ibid., 96.

is that of slavery."[80] In short, the relation between Europe and Africa is the master/slave relation of unequal recognition.

What is troubling to Hegel is not only the master/slave relationship but also the apparent acceptance of slavery by those who are slaves: "In this the Negroes see nothing unbecoming them, and the English, who have done the most for abolishing the slave trade and slavery, are treated by the Negroes themselves as enemies."[81] Although this may sound similar to Aristotle's line that for human beings who are "suited" for slavery, slavery is no absolute injustice, that is not Hegel's view of the matter. Elsewhere Hegel observes that there is a tremendous world-historical difference between having the ontological capacity of freedom that he believes is universally constitutive of human nature and knowing that one is free. This difference Hegel expresses as freedom *an sich* and freedom *für sich*, which is usually translated as implicit and explicit freedom. Hegel explains:

> On this distinction depends the great difference in world history. Human beings are all rational; the formula of this rationality is that the human being as such is free. Freedom is human nature; it belongs to the essence of humanity. Nevertheless many peoples have practiced slavery; some continue to do so, and are content with it. Orientals are human beings and as such are free. But yet they are not really free, because they do not possess the consciousness of freedom. . . . The entire distinction between oriental peoples and peoples where slavery has been abolished is this, that the latter know that they are free. They are conscious of being free. . . . The human being is free only when he knows himself to be free.[82]

The problem Hegel is grappling with is a real one, namely, the question of recognition between peoples with fundamentally different convictions concerning freedom: those for whom freedom is fundamental, who will struggle to the death for recognition of their freedom, and those who value freedom differently, for example, as possibly subordinate to nature and natural inequalities. If international recognition requires a common element, it is difficult to see what the common element here could be, because the process of recognition is a critique, displacement, and *Aufhebung* of natural ethical life, including master/slave. The modern world and the premodern worlds appear to be the inverse of each other, and this makes recognition between them difficult.

In view of this difficulty, Hegel adopts a historical approach that seeks to

---

80. Ibid., 128; 98.

81. Ibid. Hegel mentions reports of Africans selling Africans into slavery, which he finds comparable in some respects to ancient practices of conquered peoples becoming slaves of their conquerors. However, there is a tension in Hegel's discussion between the apparent fact that Africans find slavery acceptable and his mention of a report of the "great courage" of the Africans who "allow themselves to be shot down by the thousands in war with Europeans" (12:126; 96).

82. *Einleitung in die Geschichte der Philosophie*, Hrsg. J. Hoffmeister (Hamburg: Meiner Verlag, 1966), 105–106.

mediate the differences via a concept of developmental stages in the consciousness of freedom.

> The conclusion that we draw from this condition of slavery . . . and which alone constitutes its interesting aspect, is the same conclusion we draw from the Idea, namely that the state of nature is a condition of absolute all-pervasive injustice. Every intermediate stage between the state of nature and the rational state likewise presents aspects and elements of injustice. We find slavery in the Greek and Roman states, and serfdom down to most recent times. If it exists in a state, slavery is nevertheless a moment of progress from the merely isolated sensuous existence, a phase in education. . . . Slavery in and for itself is an injustice, because the essence of human being is freedom.[83]

Given Hegel's historical approach, he refuses to reject slavery outright, but sees it as justified only in a historically relative sense, and only in this sense can there be recognition between two different cultural worlds. That is, the impossibility of direct recognition, as it were, makes indirect historical consciousness and historical recognition necessary. Indirect historical recognition is another way of practicing the *Freigabe*, or release. He tells us that "the alleged justification of slavery (with all its more specific explanations in terms of physical force, capture in time of war, . . . the slave's own acquiescence, etc.) as well as the justification of the master's status as simple lordship in general . . . depend on regarding the human being simply as a natural being."[84] As long as this conception of human being prevails, slavery will not be perceived as an injustice. On the other hand, "if we hold to the view that the human being in and for itself is free, we thereby condemn slavery. . . . Slavery occurs in the transitional phase between natural human existence and the truly human ethical condition. It occurs in a world where a wrong is still right [*wo noch ein Unrecht Recht ist*]. Here wrong still counts as valid, so that the position it occupies is a necessary one."[85] Premodern cultures and modern cultures appear to each other as inverted worlds, and for this reason mutual recognition is highly complex and asymmetrical, but not impossible. Hegel's teleological approach implies that the lower stages of development are destined to pass over into the higher. This may appear to be a disguised imperialism. However, although Europe may represent for Hegel a more highly developed consciousness of freedom, European countries, as participants in the international scene, including its slave trade, when measured against Hegel's philosophical Idea of the state, are far from exhibiting either the rationality of the actual or exhausting the actuality of the rational.

---

83. *Philosophie der Geschichte*, 12:129; *Philosophy of History*, 99.
84. *PR*, §57.
85. Ibid., Zusatz. Hegel explicitly refers to the culture of Greece as caught in this contradiction. On the one hand, the principle of personal freedom emerges there; on the other, slavery is practiced and confined to a class of laborers. See *PR*, §356.

The Deficiency
of the International 'We'

Recognition between states of comparable levels of ethical-social constitutional development might well be more likely than between peoples of different levels of cultural development. But even assuming a situation between states of comparable culture development, and assuming mutual good will, Hegel claims that reciprocal recognition between nation-states would still fall short of a We. Although there may be reciprocal recognition between states, "the final reality is lacking"; [86] that is, there is no 'We'. For Hegel, there is no supranational spirit or supranational constitution that emerges from mutual recognition. "International law is therefore a mixture of universal and positive right with contingency and power." [87] At best its normative status is that of an 'ought to be' (*Sollen*), because its normative actuality depends on distinct sovereign wills that remain independent in spite of relation.

Nations relate to each other as sovereign individuals, and the principle of their relationship is simply their individual sovereignty and self-interest: "since the sovereignty of each state is the principle governing their mutual relations, they exist in a state of nature in relation to each other, and their rights have actuality, not in a universal will with constitutional powers over them, but in their particular wills. Consequently the universal determination of international law remains only an 'ought to be', and the [normal] situation will be for relations governed by treaties to alternate with the suspension of such relations." [88] The fact that international law remains an 'ought to be' creates difficulties for those interpretations of Hegel that regard him as a historical optimist or triumphalist. On the contrary, if international law is an 'ought to be', this means that for Hegel international relations and world history are fundamentally tragic. Although Hegel previously maintained that the so-called state of nature is a fiction, he conceives the international scene as a Hobbesian state of nature, that is, as a condition where supranational laws and institutions are absent and national interests are in potential or actual conflict.

There are important differences in recognition between individuals and recognition between states. Recognition between individuals is a socioethical process in which pre- or subethical freedom is decentered and overcome. The independent subjective will is *aufgehoben* in the universal will, and the 'we', or universal consciousness, emerges and *results* from reciprocal recognition. However, Hegel notes that "states are not private persons but completely independent totalities in themselves, so that relations between them are not the same as purely moral relations or relations of private right." [89] In our examination of Hegel's concept of marriage, we found that the 'We' presupposes the surrender

86. *VPR*18, §132.   87. *VPR*17, §159.   88. *PR*, §333.
89. Ibid., §330.

of the independent subjective private will, central to ownership and property, to the corporate person. Similarly patriotism may require the surrender of freedom, property, and life for the preservation of the whole. But no such surrender of state sovereignty is contemplated or even possible. The principle and object of international recognition is individual state sovereignty. Thus a 'We' in the sense of a supranational institution or law is not the agenda, much less the telos, of international recognition. A state that subordinated its sovereignty to some supranational body would contradict its fundamental unifying principle through which it achieves sovereignty and secures freedom for its citizens. Consequently, when states enter into the process of recognition, what they seek is recognition of their independence as an end in itself. States seek recognition of their independent sovereignty as individuals, because such recognized sovereignty is the condition of entering into international relations and the condition on which all further specification of those relations turns.

Of course, states may and do enter into treaties with each other. But Hegel believes that treaties are more nearly like the property contracts of abstract right.[90] Treaties, like contracts, are a merely contingent, external convergence of wills in which the latter retain their independence and sovereignty in spite of their relation and/or convergence. To be sure, the basic principle of international law "is that treaties, on which the mutual obligations of states depend, should be observed. But since the sovereignty of states is the principle governing their mutual relations, they exist . . . in a state of nature in relation to each other, and their rights are actualized not in a universal will with constitutional powers over them, but in their own particular wills. Consequently the universal requirement of international law remains only an 'ought to be'."[91]

In abstract right contracts too can be regarded as promises that 'ought to be kept'. However, in abstract right, the contract binding two independent wills can be reviewed and enforced, if necessary, by an independent third party, for example, a court or a judge. "The position of private persons is that they are subject to the authority of a court which implements what is inherently right. To be sure, a relation between states should also be governed by what is inherently right, and in mundane affairs that which is inherently right ought to hold sway. But since no power is present to decide what is right in relation to a nation or to enforce this decision, this relation must always remain an ought to be."[92] In the mutual recognition presupposed by treaties between states, there is no self-overcoming of particular will, no union with another, and no emergent third or 'We'. The 'We' remains an 'ought to be' in the face of intractable independent national wills. Moreover, "There is no praetor to adjudicate between states, but at most arbitrators and mediators, and even the presence of these will be contingent, i.e., determined by particular wills."[93] There is no supranational insti-

---

90. Ibid., §332.   91. Ibid., §333.   92. Ibid., §330.
93. Ibid., §333.

tution or 'We' that has binding authority over sovereign states or that can enforce treaties to which they may have committed themselves. In the event that nations disagree over a treaty, there is no court or third party to mediate the dispute and effect a solution. Thus the irony is that a treaty, presumably concluded to settle a dispute short of war, can be enforced against a sovereign state only by means of war. However, war means not only the abandonment but also the destruction of international law, whose first principle is that treaties are supposed to be observed and disputes settled by peaceful means.[94]

Hegel is aware of Kant's idea of a perpetual peace that is supposed to be guaranteed by a federation of nations. Its purpose is to end, not just a particular war, but all war. Lest this sound more optimistic than it really is, it should be noted that Kant agrees with Hegel that "the positive idea of a world republic cannot be realized."[95] Kant's proposal about a league or federation of nations is something more modest than a world government. "This federation does not aim to acquire any power like that of a state, but merely to preserve and secure the freedom of each state in itself, along with that of the other confederated states, although this does not mean that they need to submit to public laws and a coercive power which enforces them, as do men in a state of nature."[96]

Hegel is critical of Kant's proposal on several grounds. One is that Kant assumes that peace is normative, and fails to appreciate that war can have ethical significance in making people aware of the limitations of civil society and their need to transcend it. A second is that "Kant's idea of a perpetual peace guaranteed by a federation of states which would settle all disputes and which, as a power recognized by each state, would resolve all disagreements so as to make it impossible for these to be settled by war, presupposes unanimous agreement between states."[97] Such unanimous agreement is practically impossible. Agreement between states will always fall short of complete universality or unanimity. But assuming that such unanimity were at least theoretically possible, "this agreement, whether based on moral, religious or other grounds and considerations, would always be dependent on particular sovereign wills, and therefore would continue to be tainted with contingency."[98] The federation would be no higher-order universal will or binding necessity that results from the determinate negation and sublation of particular sovereign wills. Instead it would be only a contingent agreement between independent sovereign wills. This agreement would be a stipulation on the part of independent states that remain sovereign over such stipulations.

The third and most important criticism of Kant targets the point that the federation does not seek any power like that of a state. One of the crucial powers that a state has is the power to enforce contracts and punish breaches of

---

94. Ibid.
95. Immanuel Kant, *Perpetual Peace, in Political Writings*, 105.
96. Ibid., 104.   97. *PR*, §333.   98. Ibid.

contract between its citizens. In denying such power to the federation, Kant apparently deprives it of what it would need to do its job, namely, keep the peace. For since the agreement represented by the federation falls short of unanimity, it would itself have to be imposed on dissenting states in order to be effective. This would not resolve the problem as Kant wishes in the direction of perpetual peace. "Kant proposed a federation of sovereigns to settle disputes between states. . . . But the state is an individual, and negation is an essential component of individuality. Thus even if a number of states join together as a family, this union, in its individual determinacy, must generate opposition and create an enemy."[99]

Thus Hegel discovers in Kant's proposal for a federation of states an ontological problem of fundamentally tragic depth and significance. Kant's federation, if it is to act and deter war, must unify itself and act as an individual, however fraught with contingency its 'individuality' may be. Action is always specific and singular. But to be individual is to be something determinate (*etwas*), and what is determinate negates something else. To be individual is thus to negate and oppose other individuals. Hegel believes that individuality is inherently tragic; the conditions of its well-being are at the same time conditions of opposition and possible conflict with others. This tragic sense of individuality pervades Hegel's understanding of action and right on both individual and sociohistorical levels.

To be sure, Hegel believes that it is possible in principle to transcend struggle and conflict, at least on the interpersonal level, but even this is not without suffering and the need for forgiveness. His accounts of forgiveness in the *Early Theological Writings* and *Phenomenology* exhibit different modalities of spirit's tragic self-realization. For Hegel, action is always particular, contingent, and variable, carried out by individuals who come into conflict. This conflict is not always a conflict between right and wrong; it is frequently a conflict between right and right, that is, tragic. Thus historical action involves conflicts and wounds. Hegel believes that the wounds of spirit can heal again, but this requires forgiveness and suffering.

Hannah Arendt makes explicit the connection between forgiveness and action.[100] Forgiving, says Arendt, is the "remedy against the irreversibility and unpredictability of . . . action."[101] Owing to irreversibility and contingency, injury or trespass against others is a virtually inevitable accompaniment of action. Thus action, to the extent it involves unavoidable injury to another, requires forgiveness. Forgiveness is the capability of undoing what has been done. Arendt observes, "The possible redemption from the predicament of irreversibility—of being able to undo what one has done though one did not,

99. *PR*, §324 Zusatz.
100. Hannah Arendt, *The Human Condition* (Chicago: University of Chicago Press, 1958), 236ff.
101. Ibid.

and could not, have known what he was doing—is the faculty of forgiving. . . . Without being forgiven, released from the consequences of what we have done, our capacity to act would, as it were, be confined to one single deed from which we could never recover; we would be victims of its consequences forever."[102] Hegel also notes that the element of reversibility, of being able to undo what one has done, is central to the concept of reconciliation. This possibility of reversing and undoing what has been done is the reason why the wounds of *Geist* can heal without leaving scars.[103]

Like Hegel, Arendt believes that forgiveness involves *Freigabe*, releasement: "Only through the constant mutual *release* from what they do can men remain free agents, only by constant willingness to change their minds and start again can they be trusted with so great a power as that to begin something new. In this respect forgiveness is the exact opposite of vengeance, which acts in the form of re-acting against an original trespassing, whereby far from putting an end to the consequences of the first misdeed, everybody remains bound to the process."[104] Hegel believes it is possible, at least at the interpersonal level and possibly at the level of the individual nation-state, to transcend tragic conflict toward community. However, for Hegel the final moment of recognition, the moment of release and allowing the other to be, that puts forth a 'We' of forgiveness, seems to be actualized, if at all, only on the interpersonal level constitutive of a religious community. Only at the interpersonal level, or at the level of absolute spirit, does it appear possible for spirit to return to itself out of otherness in spite of tragic loss.

Hegel believes world-historical action, action at the level of sovereign nation-states, cannot avoid the tragic. Kant's federation of nations, if it does what it is supposed to, namely, act to prevent war and preserve peace, will have to act as an individual. Its determinate individuality must generate a new opposition and thus bring about a situation opposite to what it intends. The attempt to avoid conflict and enforce peace may itself turn out to generate conflict and struggle for recognition.

Consequently I must part company with Avineri when he claims that "though Hegel had begun with the immanence of war—in the end he emerges with a vision of One World, united by culture and reason, progressing towards a system wherein sovereignty, though acknowledged, will wither away, and wars, though immanent, will gradually disappear."[105] In support of his conclusion, Avineri can point to Hegel's view concerning historical progress that spirit makes in its struggle for self-comprehension:

102. Ibid., 237.
103. Hegel, *PhG*, 470; *PhS*, 407.
104. Arendt, *The Human Condition*, 240. Arendt comments on the New Testament Greek terms and shows that the root meaning of *forgive* is to dismiss and release, namely, from the consequences of one's actions.
105. Avineri, *HTMS*, 207.

> The history of spirit is its own deed; for spirit is only what it does, and its deed is to make itself—in this case spirit—the object of its own consciousness, and to comprehend itself in its self-interpretation. This comprehension is its being and principle, and the completion of an act of comprehension is at the same time its alienation and transition. To put it in formal terms, the spirit which comprehends this comprehension anew and . . . returns to itself from its alienation, is the spirit at a higher stage than that at which it stood in its earlier level of comprehension.[106]

Avineri also points to Hegel's view, articulated in the *Philosophy of History*, that the modern conception of sovereignty is more highly developed and open to mediation than the ancient. This means that political independence and sovereignty on which nation-states depend are relativized within a cultural unity, predominantly European, that Hegel believed to be emerging in the modern world. He cites Hegel: "The trend of the states is, therefore, towards uniformity. There prevails among them one aim, one tendency, which is the cause of wars, friendships, and the needs of dynasties. But there also prevails among them another uniformity, which parallels the idea of hegemony in Greece, except that now it is the hegemony of spirit."[107] The question is whether the relativizing of independence and sovereignty in the hegemony of the spirit means that sovereignty becomes a merely formal element and gradually withers away. Were this the case, then Hegel would have to revise his fundamental point that international law remains an ought to be, and its implication, that nations remain in a state of nature toward each other.

My view is that whatever "progress" world history may make does not eliminate the conditions of tragic conflict. For Hegel, freedom in history and historical action are inherently tragic, because the conditions that make them possible also make for conflict and suffering. A nation must achieve and retain sovereignty to continue to exist, and this sovereignty is entitled to recognition. However, sovereign freedom, which is entitled to the 'right of rights', namely, recognition, is at the same time a condition of conflict, because at the international level it clings to a sovereign independence that precludes the emergence of supranational 'middle' or 'We'. "The highest point a people can reach is to preserve their independence and sacrifice everything to it. But this independence is nothing absolute, and it can be destroyed."[108] The nation-state and/or federation, as world-historical unities, are unavoidably parochial universalities; consequently their action is haunted by the figure of master and slave.

This does not mean that for Hegel history is simply 'might makes right'. History is the history of freedom and liberation, and there is social rationality at work in it, wherein the rational becomes actual. Nevertheless, international

106. *PR*, §343.
107. Hegel, *Vorlesungen über die Philosophie der Weltgeschichte*, ed. G. Lasson (Leipzig, 1920), 761; cited in Avineri, *HTMS*, 207.
108. *VPR*17, §163.

relations and world history also remain fraught with conflict. The final moment of recognition, at the world-historical level, remains a mere ought to be (*sollen*), and this 'ought to be' has tragic implications. Hegel alludes to and cites Schiller's poem on resignation, that world history is a court of world-judgment. This is a not a 'judgment' of a court that enforces or vindicates what is right in itself, but of the world spirit. It is world spirit that relativizes national spirits and nation-states, and in so doing brings out and demonstrates their ideality, finitude, and transitory nature.[109]

> The principles of particular national spirits are restricted. The unrestricted spirit is the universal, which exercises its absolute right over the national spirits in world history as the court of judgment—a judgment moreover that is rendered not merely by might and blind fate, but by a necessary development of its self-consciousness, whereby a single nation or people is made responsible for implementing a single moment and stage, which it receives in the form of a principle. Such and such a people is dominant in world history during such and such an epoch; and in contrast with its absolute right of being the vehicle of this present highest stage in the development of world spirit, the principles of other peoples are without rights. . . .
>
> Here spirit is striving to grasp itself in its highest form. And the highest moment is world history, the *absolute process in which the independence of peoples is displaced*; in relation to this process the independence of peoples is a nullity. . . . World history is the divine tragedy, where spirit rises above pity, ethical life, and everything that is otherwise sacred to it.[110]

Here Hegel does not embrace the proposition that might makes right, or that right is whatever happens to prevail. Rather he embraces a tragic view of history. As we have seen, Hegel's analysis of war does not support the 'might makes right' doctrine. For Hegel, war does not settle the question of right. Rather war is a tragic conflict of rights that provides no justification at all. War merely determines which national right gives way. Note too that world history undermines and displaces the sovereign independence of peoples and nations. This failure of mutual recognition and the historical displacements of sovereign national independence counterbalance any optimistic view of history as progress. Hegel, along with many of his generation, remains pained by and nostalgic over the downfall of a superior culture (ancient Greece) and its displacement by an inferior culture (the Roman Empire): "Even the finest, highest principle of a people is, as the principle of a particular people, a restricted principle, overtaken by the spirit of the age. . . . World spirit is unsparing and pitiless."[111]

109. *PR*, §341.
110. *VPR*17, §164; my italics.
111. Ibid.

15

Recent Views of Recognition and the Question of Ethics

Hegel's is not a philosophy of the subject but a post-Cartesian, post-Kantian account of ethical intersubjectivity, or philosophy of spirit (*Geist*). For both Fichte and Hegel, recognition is an account of intersubjectivity that also serves as a transcendental condition or deep structure, not only of right, but also of ethics. Despite flaws in Fichte's execution, his intention is to ground ethics and politics in the intersubjective mediation and constitution of ethical freedom. The other summons the self to responsible freedom. This priority of the other is not absolute but creates the possibility of a mutual relationship, namely, reciprocal recognition. Fichte blunts and obscures his thesis with a negative concept of freedom and the other, as well as with his coercive state mechanism aimed at security.

For Hegel, ethical life, which subsumes and transforms the traditional theory of virtues and vices, is constituted when the other comes to count and is articulated in patterns of intersubjective recognition. For Hegel, recognition constitutes the ethical sphere and relation. Recognition "is the form of consciousness of the substance of every essential spirituality: family, fatherland, state, as well as all the virtues: love, friendship, courage, honor and fame." [1] Reciprocal recognition in its various determinate types and instances is the general structure of ethical life and the embodiment of social reason that underlies and supports the concepts of law and state.

Abstract right and morality as well as the family, civil society, and state are, phenomenologically considered, determinate forms and patterns of intersubjective recognition. Ethical life embraces a plurality of levels of recognition.

1. *E*, §436.

The family is the first institution of ethical life; it is in the family that human beings first come to count for each other. But the family is ethical life in its immediacy, the initial transition from nature to spirit. This means that the family universal or 'We' is parochial. Civil society and state presuppose and require a further transcending and sublation of such parochialism. This does not occur without struggles that repeat in modification and on higher levels the patterns and stages of recognition. However, conflict and struggle are not the end-station of recognition, but only its penultimate level. The telos of recognition is reciprocal recognition constitutive of an ethical 'We', spirit, or community.

Thus mutual recognition in its fourfold structure—autonomy, union, self-overcoming, and *Freigabe*—constitutes the ethical dimension of the interhuman sphere, as well as the underpinnings of state and civil society. Against Plato and in agreement with Rousseau, Hegel believes that freedom, not nature, is the principle of the state and, further, that the ethical dimension of both civil society (corporation) and state is best understood as a recovery, extension, and transformation of the mutual recognition and ethical union constitutive of the family. Not that the state *is* a family, for that is patriarchalism, which Hegel rejects. Nevertheless, Hegel believes that the state should extend the principle of mutual recognition that underlies respect for law throughout the whole, even to those who do not reciprocate by recognizing it fully.

Hegel's ethical life embraces a plurality of levels of recognition, a plurality that encompasses such diverse offspring as dialogical philosophy and existential phenomenology. There are parallels between Hegel's analysis of the mutual recognition constitutive of the family as a sphere of love and intimacy and the dialogical philosophy of Martin Buber. In view of the not inconsiderable criticism of Hegel from Kierkegaard through Franz Rosenzweig and Levinas, it should be noted that Martin Buber identified F. H. Jacobi, Fichte, and Feuerbach as important predecessors.[2] The specific theme that Buber singles out in this literature is the "essential reciprocity" between human beings. This reciprocity is similar to the final stage of development of the concept of recognition in Hegel's analysis. Buber articulates and defends reciprocity as the basic structure of relationship in his classic *I and Thou*.

Similarly, Hegel appeals to reciprocity as a normative criterion in his critique of master/slave as a deficient, unequal form of recognition. For Hegel, reciprocity not only means that master/slave is self-subverting, it also constitutes an affirmative relation to other on which the possibility of ethics and ethical life depends. I will explore this theme of reciprocity in relation to contemporary discussions of recognition, including some of Hegel's critics. It is important to distinguish the genuine reciprocity of mutual recognition that results in *Geist*

2. Buber, *Between Man and Man*, 209–224. It is not clear how closely Buber studied Fichte. He does not mention or show any awareness of Fichte's concepts of the summons and recognition, nor does he show any appreciation of the further development of these in Schelling and Hegel. In his survey Buber jumps from Fichte to Feuerbach.

from the external "tit-for-tat" reciprocity, or reciprocity in disintegration, that is constitutive of civil society. My thesis is that the former reciprocity is constitutive of affirmative relation with other, which in turn is a condition of ethics and affirmative relation to other. The latter negative freedom is manifest in nominalism, in negative reciprocity and disintegration. The latter negative freedom and reciprocal exclusion make ethics problematic, if not impossible. Sartre's various attempts to write an ethics shipwrecked on the difficulties of negative freedom and nominalism. On the assumption of reciprocity as mutual negation, ethical responsibility and decision become "madness." Such assessments reveal how precarious ethics has become and raise nasty Nietzschean suspicions that ethics is inherently dogmatic; not only may ethics be a symptom of decline, it may also be a form of evil.[3]

Kojève

Alexandre Kojève slights or rejects reciprocal recognition in his influential lectures on Hegel. These lectures combine commentary with Kojève's own independent philosophical reflections, and produce a powerful synthesis of Hegel and Husserlian phenomenology, giving impetus to the so-called French phase of phenomenology. Largely as a result of Kojève's influence, Hegel and Hegel studies became the center of a philosophical revolution in postwar France. Maurice Merleau-Ponty was reflecting this revolution when he claimed that "all the great ideas of the past century—the philosophies of Marx and Nietzsche, phenomenology, German existentialism, and psychoanalysis—had their beginnings in Hegel; it was he who started the attempt to explore the irrational and integrate it into an expanded reason, which remains the task of our century."[4]

Judith Butler believes that Kojève does not ignore reciprocal recognition, he rejects it as a discredited ontological harmony. Kojève attributes to Hegel an optimistic, metaphysical predetermination of the interhuman, as if the latter were guaranteed of success by some sort of preestablished harmony. For Kojève and his followers, the paradigm of intersubjectivity is conflict; reciprocal recognition means reciprocal coercion. According to Butler,

> Kojève's peculiarly modern appropriation . . . occasions the questions of what in Hegel survives into the twentieth century and what is lost. Hegel's claim . . . [of] a common ontological bond between the subject and its world requires that we accept a prior set of ontological relations which structure and unify various subjectivities with one another and with the world that they confront. This presupposition of ontological harmonies that subsist in and among the intersubjective and

---

3. See Friedrich Nietzsche, *Genealogy of Morals*, trans. W. Kaufmann and R. J. Hollingdale (New York: Random House, 1967); Charles Scott, *The Question of Ethics* (Bloomington: Indiana University Press, 1990); John Caputo, *Against Ethics* (Bloomington: Indiana University Press, 1993).

4. Maurice Merleau-Ponty, *Signs*, cited in Descombes, *MFP*, 11.

natural worlds is difficult to reconcile with the various experiences of disjunction which emerge as unsurpassable in the twentieth century. . . . Kojève's refusal of Hegel's postulation of an ontological unity that conditions and resolves all experience of difference between individuals and between individuals and the external world is the condition of his own original theorizing. By rejecting the premise of ontological harmony, Kojève is free to extend Hegel's doctrine of negation.[5]

Butler's analysis shows that Kojève thinks the concept of recognition primarily on the basis of an ontology of negation and finitude. Since Kojève identifies the concept of recognition with the struggle for recognition and the deficient, asymmetrical recognition between master and slave, his theory of intersubjectivity is primarily negative. Butler claims Kojève's reading of Hegel's concept of recognition is not only suspect, it "has been deftly refuted by . . . Ludwig Siep."[6] However, she does not pursue Siep's interpretation. Vincent Descombes is more to the point in noting that Kojève's discussion was never intended to be faithful to Hegel's thought but an independent development that does violence to Hegel and Hegel's intentions.[7]

Descombes provides further clarification of the issues of identity, difference, and negation. He identifies three theses central to Kojève's project of presenting an anthropological version of Hegelian philosophy: the positivity of being, the humanity of nothingness, and the negative essence of freedom.[8] What Butler sees as Kojève's rejection of Hegel's alleged ontological harmony between human beings and the world, Descombes identifies as Kojève's assertion of a radical ontological dualism between nature and history, between being-in-itself and being-for-itself. Descombes points out that for both Kojève and Sartre, being-in-itself is understood positivistically, as a nondialectical pure identity exclusive of difference, even the difference necessary to articulate identity as $A = A$.[9] Conversely, being-for-itself, or freedom, is understood as negation, as radical instability that cannot remain the same, but is pure difference. Thus, in terms that Sartre was later to use, the human being is not what it is and is what it is not.[10]

---

5. Butler, *SD*, 63.

6. Ibid., 242n18. This important acknowledgment of recent German scholarship, and the importance of Siep's work in particular, is unfortunately buried in a footnote. It stands in stark contrast with the dominant reading of Hegel that Butler presents in this work. To be sure, her primary concern is to discuss the French reception of Hegel and thus must reflect "what Hegel is taken to be" in that reception. Butler presents a more favorable and balanced reading of Hegel vis-à-vis his French reception in her comment on Joseph C. Flay's "Hegel, Derrida and Bataille's Laughter," in *Hegel and His Critics*, ed. William Desmond (Albany: State University of New York Press, 1989), 174–178.

7. Descombes, *MFP*, 4–5. For further criticism of Kojève's interpretation, see George Armstrong Kelly, "Notes on Hegel's 'Lordship and Bondage,' " in *Hegel: A Collection of Critical Essays*, ed. Alasdair MacIntyre (Garden City, N.Y.: Anchor Books, 1972), 189–218.

8. Descombes, *MFP*, 25. Descombes believes that these theses are also upheld by Sartre.

9. Ibid., 25–37; see also Kojève, *IRH*, 212–213n.

10. Ibid., 5.

Kojève appropriates and conceives Hegel's concept of recognition on the basis of this heterogeneity, this ontological dualism. Several issues arise. Where Kojève and Sartre posit absolute opposition between being and nothingness that precludes any mediation, Hegel posits only their point of zero mediation, namely, pure indeterminacy. In the first category of his logic, Hegel shows that indeterminacy is a determination common to both pure being and nothing; that is, their determination is to have no determinations. For this reason their apparent distinction breaks down and collapses. They pass over into each other. This shows that in spite of their opposition, transition and mediation are possible. In contrast, Kojève and Sartre begin and end with the radical opposition of being and nothingness. Consequently for them mediation is impossible. This has practical implications. For Kojève and Sartre, the opposition of master and slave is final, whereas for Hegel, master/slave is the first *Aufhebung*, that is, mediation, of sheer opposition, of the life and death conflict. Master/slave is a *Gestalt* of consciousness that ends sheer violence, on the one hand, while institutionalizing it in the form of coercion and unequal recognition, on the other.

Descombes points out that Kojève's treatment of Hegel's dialectical identity of identity and difference is problematic, because for Kojève nothingness, difference, and so on, turn out to be derivative forms of identity.[11] Examining Kojève's gold ring metaphor for the ontological dualism between being and nothingness,[12] Descombes charges that the expression 'dualist ontology' is equivocal. We think that we understand being and nothingness as two types of being. But that is precisely the issue. Descombes contends that Kojève's dialectical ontology between being and nothingness is not genuinely dualist but monist. When we think through Kojève's version of dialectical unity of being and nothingness, "difference, although it is a form of nothingness—since to differ from something is not to be like it—is a part of that which is."[13] Since difference is, that is, is included in identity, it follows that difference, otherness, and negation all cease to be radically other than being. This reduces difference to identity. Descombes charges that it is not Hegel's but rather Kojève's version of the dialectic that ignores and suppresses the difference.[14] Kojève

11. To be sure, Kojève himself points out that on this issue he parts company with Hegel. Nevertheless, given the influence that Kojève's reading exerted, his position became in effect the then-contemporary statement of Hegel's philosophy. This produced further distortion and misunderstanding of Hegel's position.

12. Kojève, *IRH*, 214n.

13. Descombes, *MFP*, 36–37.

14. Descombes writes, "It could equally well have been concluded . . . that the difference between something and nothing is not, at least in the sense that 'to be' means to be something. Because if the difference between something and nothing were itself something, we would require a new difference in order to distinguish that difference, i.e., something from nothing. As a result, we must say that 'to be' need not necessarily mean 'to be something' (that is, to be identical with itself). *And this development of the argument is ignored by Kojève and his disciples*" (*MFP*, 37; italics mine).

subordinates difference to identity, or construes difference as part of or as instrumental to identity and unity.

In view of Descombes's analysis it should be noted that Hegel himself warns against such a truncation of identity. Such truncation is the way the understanding 'understands' speculative dialectic, namely, by misunderstanding and distorting it. It is the way that Parmenidean rationalism misunderstands the paradoxical dialectic of Heraclitos, the way that mechanism and substance metaphysics mishandles teleological and organic processes, the way that analytical understanding butchers life and dynamic vital processes. Hegel observes that the members and organs of a living body become mere 'parts' only under the hands of the anatomist, and for this reason he is dealing with corpses rather than with living bodies.[15] Consequently: "It is of great importance to reach an adequate understanding of the true significance of identity, and this means above all that it must not be interpreted merely as abstract identity, i.e., as identity that excludes difference. This is the point that distinguishes all bad philosophy from what alone deserves the name of philosophy."[16] Again, "Generally speaking it is contradiction that moves the world. . . . *Sublated contradiction however is not abstract identity, for that is only one side of the antithesis.*"[17] Finally, Hegel elaborates on difference and identity in a way that, as Descombes points out, Kojève and his followers ignore: "When we say that ground is the unity of identity and difference, this unity must not be understood as abstract identity, for then we would just have another name for an idea that is once more just that identity of the understanding which we have recognized to be untrue. So, in order to counter this misunderstanding, we can also say that *ground is not only the unity, but equally the difference of identity and difference.*"[18]

Kojève's negative intersubjective theory was developed at length by Sartre in *Being and Nothingness.*[19] As negative, it suppresses what for Hegel is the central point, namely, that the ethical sphere is constituted through reciprocal recognition. Ethics requires affirmative relation with other, and affirmative relation is constituted through reciprocal recognition in which union with other includes self-overcoming and *Freigabe*. For Kojève, recognition does not lead to the formation of a 'We' or ethical life in Hegel's sense. Rather he maintains the ontological primacy of individuality over community and thus reasserts an individualism that is the target of Hegel's critique. Butler puts it this way: "Recognition does not have the effect of assimilating the individual into a more

15. Hegel, *E*, §135 Zusatz.

16. Ibid., §115 Zusatz. I have followed and altered slightly the Harris translation.

17. Ibid., §119 Zusatz 2. Italics mine. This point is usually overlooked by Hegel's critics. This point separates Hegel's affirmative dialectic of the *Aufhebung* from skeptical equipollence and epochè, and from Kant's negative dialectics that reveal transcendental illusion. For further discussion, see my "Hegel and Skepticism."

18. Hegel, *E*, §121 Zusatz. Italics mine.

19. Butler, *SD*, 92–93.

inclusive community; following the tradition of classical liberalism, Kojève views recognition as a process in which individuals form communities, but these communities facilitate the development of individuality and not its transcendence."[20] It is ironic that despite his left-Hegelian leanings, Kojève develops an individualistic interpretation comparable to the political liberalism that is the target of Hegel's critique. Instead of Hegel's often comic subject who learns in the course of experience that the truth turns out to be the opposite of what he originally understood it to be—for example, the master learns that he depends on the slave whom he regards as unessential—Kojève serves up a philosophy of heroic individualism which, by treating community as external, contingent, and instrumental to individuality, takes the analysis of master and slave in a more Nietzschean direction.[21]

This is precisely the direction that French philosophy has taken since 1968. The period in which Hegel, as interpreted by Kojève, dominated the discussion (1930–1968) produced a critical reaction, and one figure who influenced this reaction is Nietzsche.[22] Nietzsche is highly influential on two figures we will examine subsequently, namely Bataille and Deleuze. Concerning the displacement of "Hegel," Judith Butler notes, "it is curious to watch the generation that follows Hyppolite, a generation largely spawned by his own seminar, which repudiates Hegel for being all the things that both Kojève and Hyppolite argued that he never really was. In other words, the immanent critique of the self-identical subject is in many ways overlooked by Derrida, Deleuze and many others who view Hegel as championing the 'subject,' a metaphysics of closure or presence, that excludes difference and is, according to his Nietzschean critics, also anti-life."[23]

In juxtaposing Hegel and Nietzsche, modern French philosophy enters an ongoing dispute. "Hegel and Nietzsche! Here is a problem yet to be solved," wrote Karl Joël in 1905.[24] Although there are a few books on this subject, the problem has not received extensive attention or discussion. It can hardly be re-

---

20. Ibid., 77.
21. As Descombes observes, Kojève's reading of Hegel highlights elements that might attract a Nietzschean, like Deleuze or Bataille. Descombes, *MFP*, 1–20.
22. The other no doubt was Heidegger. For an account of the politics of the teaching and study of philosophy in France that produces such reversals of favor and disfavor that in turn determine which philosophers are taken seriously and which are given superficial treatment, see *MFP*, 1–8. Descombes comments with apparent sarcasm, "the teaching of philosophy in France is more or less determined by the nature and function of that syllabus. Officially the syllabus, this masterpiece of rigour and coherence, is fixed by unanimous consent. In reality it is the outcome of a compromise between the various prevailing tendencies, and this is why the much celebrated masterpiece is so frequently overhauled. Charged by some with propagating a reactionary ideology, by others with eliminating whatever still remained of authentic philosophy in the preceding syllabus, successive versions reflect the momentary balance of political forces, not only within the teaching body itself, but also in the country at large" (*MFP*, 5).
23. Butler, *SD*, 176.
24. Karl Joël, *Nietzsche und die Romantik* (Jena: Diederichs, 1905), 294, cited in Daniel Breazeale, "The Hegel-Nietzsche Problem," *Nietzsche-Studien* 4 (1975): 146–164.

garded as solved, even in the peculiar sense in which philosophical disputes might be regarded as "solved." Instead of a "solution" thus far there have been two general positions staked out on this problem: (1) the rapprochement thesis, represented by Walter Kaufmann, who maintains that in spite of obvious differences there is considerable agreement between Hegel and Nietzsche: the critique of metaphysics and morality, the analysis of master and slave, as well as a terminological unity, Nietzsche's *sublimieren* and Hegel's *Aufhebung*;[25] and (2) the opposition thesis, which subdivides into those who criticize or attack Hegel from Nietzsche's standpoint and those who criticize Nietzsche from Hegel's position. Gilles Deleuze belongs to the former group. Master and slave are central to his analysis; he seeks to differentiate the Nietzschean from the Hegelian version, arguing "there is no possible compromise between Hegel and Nietzsche."[26] Stephen Houlgate belongs to the latter.[27] Houlgate's position is partly rapprochement and partly oppositional. He argues that Hegel and Nietzsche make common cause in criticizing metaphysics but adds that Nietzsche's critique is insufficiently radical or critical, and thus remains tied to what it negates. Hegel's critique of metaphysics is more radical and consistent. The criticism of metaphysics is Houlgate's central theme; he does not pursue the critique of morality, but he acknowledges that in respect to practical and social philosophy Hegel and Nietzsche are opposed to each other.

The French reception of Hegel and the Hegel-Nietzsche relation are vast topics beyond the scope of this study. In what follows, I shall critically examine only some of the issues in this reception through the lens of recognition and the interpretation of master/slave. In particular I shall focus on the influential Kojève interpretation of master/slave, first as it plays out in Sartre, then as it underlies a feminist critique of Hegel and in Deleuze's anti-Hegel polemics. Finally I shall explore the relevance of all this to the question of ethics, by examining a recent proposal for an ethics of deconstruction.[28] This will involve a brief look at Derrida, Levinas, and Hegel.

Sartre and Hegel

With the possible exception of Kojève, Sartre has done more work on the concept of recognition than any other philosopher in the twentieth century. Nevertheless, the question of Sartre's relation to Hegel is a murky one. Sartre does not follow the familiar pattern of an explicit rejection of Hegel coupled with

25. Walter Kaufmann, *Nietzsche: Philosopher, Psychologist, Antichrist*, 3d ed. (New York: Random House, 1968).
26. Gilles Deleuze, *Nietzsche and Philosophy*, trans. Hugh Tomlinson (New York: Columbia University Press, 1983), 195.
27. Stephen Houlgate, *Hegel, Nietzsche and the Criticism of Metaphysics* (Cambridge: Cambridge University Press, 1986).
28. Simon Critchley, *An Ethics of Deconstruction* (Oxford: Blackwell, 1992).

unacknowledged wholesale borrowing from him. Sartre is simultaneously a fan of Hegel and a critic. His relation to Hegel is more nearly like an ongoing discussion that is by no means a flat repudiation but a critical appropriation and further development of the starting point.

In *Being and Nothingness* (1943) Sartre was not yet acquainted with Hegel's *Phenomenology of Spirit*. What the early Sartre knows about recognition is most likely due to the influence of Kojève, who also fails to make a careful analysis of recognition while developing his own views of heroic individualism. Following Kojève, Sartre tends to identify recognition with the opposition and struggle between master and slave.[29] This is a mistake. It is well known that Sartre takes Hegel to task for being optimistic concerning the possibility of mutual recognition. The central issue is the possibility of reciprocal recognition, which Hegel affirms, in principle, while denying it in practice, at least in much of the *Phenomenology of Spirit*. For his part, Sartre denies reciprocal recognition in principle while affirming it in practice, that is, in his later determinate analyses of intersubjectivity in the *Notebooks for an Ethics*. The question is, what happens to Sartre's individualistic existential ontology in his later work? It is clear that in the *Notebooks for an Ethics*, Sartre has read and draws closer to Hegel. Although Sartre seems to allow for affirmative intersubjective relations on the level of concrete descriptions, it is not evident that he has reformulated his original ontology according to which freedom, the other, and relation to the other are fundamentally negative. The ontological status of Sartre's affirmative determinate analyses remains unclear.

Sartre's discussion of Hegel in *Being and Nothingness* is both illuminating and frustrating. On the one hand, he praises Hegel and awards him the palm over Husserl and Heidegger as far as the account of intersubjectivity is concerned.

> The "moment" which Hegel calls being-for-Other is a necessary stage in the development of self-consciousness; the road of interiority passes through the Other. . . . Hegel's brilliant intuition is to make me depend on the Other in my being. I am, he said, a being-for-self which is for itself only through another. Therefore the Other penetrates me to the heart. I cannot doubt him without doubting myself, since "self-consciousness is real only in so far as it recognizes its echo (and its reflection) in another." . . . Thus solipsism seems to be put out of the picture once and for all. By proceeding from Husserl to Hegel we have realized immense progress . . . instead of holding that my being-for-self is opposed to my being-for-others, I find that being-for-others appears as a necessary condition for my being-for-self.[30]

However, despite Sartre's appreciation of Hegel, his understanding, appropriation, and criticisms are so flawed that it may be questioned whether Sartre ac-

29. Butler, *SD*, 92–93. Butler notes, "Sartre's own formulation of human reality as a paradoxical unity of an in-itself and for-itself appears to echo almost verbatim Kojève's phrasing: 'We have to do with human reality as a being which is what it is not and which is not what it is.'"

30. Sartre, *Being and Nothingness*, 236–238.

tually read, much less understood, Hegel.[31] The questionableness of Sartre's appropriation of Hegel may be seen in his contradictory pronouncements: he praises Hegel for breaking with Cartesian idealism and solipsism in his account of intersubjectivity while criticizing his alleged idealist metaphysics for precluding an adequate account of intersubjectivity.

Following Kojève, Sartre identifies Hegel's account of intersubjectivity simply as a theory of master and slave. Although he mentions recognition in his discussion, he fails to notice Hegel's distinction between the concept of recognition and its determinate appearance in ordinary consciousness, namely, the life and death struggle culminating in the unequal recognition of master and slave. By ignoring the distinction between the ontological (eidetic) and ontic (empirical) levels and concentrating on the latter,[32] Sartre, like Kojève, fails to see that for Hegel recognition has an ontological structure capable of supporting a wider range of instantiations than master/slave, conflict, and domination.

In *Being and Nothingness*, Sartre adopts and continues the existentialist critique of Hegel that opposes the individual and decision to the abstract universal and logic, respectively. Sartre adopts a nominalist position, according to which "the particular is the support and foundation of the universal."[33] Although Sartre previously acknowledged that Hegel broke decisively with the impasse between realism and idealism, he charges that Hegel remains within metaphysical idealism. Hegel supposedly identifies being with knowing, and from this allegedly abstract identity flow Hegel's errors, namely, epistemological and ontological optimism.[34]

By epistemological optimism Sartre means (1) the assumption that reciprocal recognition in a mutual and positive sense is possible and (2) that reciprocal recognition makes possible a passage to the universal, from the I to the We.[35] Sartre denies that recognition in Hegel's sense is possible and charges Hegel with an illegitimate metaphysical attempt to overcome the ontological separation between consciousnesses. "Hegel's optimism ends in failure: between the

31. In an interview Sartre was asked whether he had read Hegel when he wrote *Being and Nothingness*. He replied, "No. I knew of him through seminars and lectures, but I didn't study him until much later, around 1945." P. A. Schilpp, ed., *The Philosophy of Jean-Paul Sartre* (LaSalle, Ill.: Open Court, 1981), 9.

32. Cf. Martin Heidegger, *Sein und Zeit* (Tübingen: Niemayer Verlag, 1984), §26, 120; cf. Sartre, *Being and Nothingness*, 9ff., 286f. Sartre himself makes similar distinctions.

33. *Being and Nothingness*, 239. As far as I can tell, Sartre never abandons this position; he calls his later theory dialectical nominalism. I shall return to this issue later.

34. Sartre misunderstands Hegel's idealism or holism. The formal absolute ego, the I am I, is precisely that idealism that Hegel criticizes in the *Phenomenology* and rejects as a pure motionless tautology (*PhG*, 175ff). This is not the first time that Hegel has been charged with holding the idealism that he was the first to attack and reject. Hegel would agree with Sartre that from such a formal conception of idealism, the pure ego as pure identity, I am I, etc., it is difficult if not impossible to understand the problem of the other or intersubjectivity. Hegel holds a different concept of identity as identity of identity and nonidentity and insists on mediation. That is why for Hegel the problem of the other and the related problem of mediation are inescapable: there is nothing in heaven or earth that does not contain mediation (*WL*, 5:66).

35. *Being and Nothingness*, 240.

Other as object and Me as subject there is no common measure. . . . I cannot know myself in the other if the other is first an object for me; neither can I apprehend the other in his true being—that is, his subjectivity. No universal knowledge can be derived from the relation of consciousnesses. This is what we shall call their ontological separation."[36] In *Being and Nothingness*, Sartre's conception of freedom is, like Fichte's, primarily negative. Hence the relation to the other is also negative, and this allows only a negative reciprocity of mutual exclusion and refusal. The result is an existential nominalism and atomism that is only temporarily suspended, for example, in the Look or in the group in fusion. This contingent, temporary suspension of atomism is not an intersubjectivity in the affirmative sense; that is, there is no positive relation to other.

We can clarify the issue and support these claims by a brief examination of Sartre's phenomenology of shame. Sartre's *phenomenology* of shame must be distinguished from his *ontological* account in *Being and Nothingness*.[37] Sartre's *phenomenological description* of shame as an essentially intersubjective consciousness employs the concept of recognition. Shame is not a reflective consciousness but is rather prereflective or nonpositional. Shame is not a state of mind one can give to oneself but shame at oneself before somebody. Sartre's starting point is an awkward or vulgar gesture. This gesture clings to me, he says, in the other's recognition.[38] The immediate presence of somebody else sends an immediate shudder through my being: "in the field of my reflection I can never meet with anything but the consciousness which is mine. But the Other is the indispensable mediator between myself and me. I am ashamed of my self as I appear to the Other."[39]

Yet such negativity of shame consciousness does not exhaust the phenomenon of shame. Significantly Sartre continues:

> By the mere appearance of the Other, I am put in the position of passing judgment on myself as an object, for it is as an object that I appear to the Other. *Yet this object which has appeared to the Other is not an empty image in the mind of another.* Such an image in fact would be imputable wholly to the Other, and so could not 'touch' me. I could feel irritation, or anger before it as before a bad

---

36. Ibid., 243. Hegel's critique of immediate knowledge makes a similar point: not only is there no direct or immediate access to the *other*, there is no immediate or privileged access of the self to *itself*. Hegel's starting point is simultaneous correlative uncertainty concerning the other and false consciousness concerning oneself. Uncertainty concerning the other is intolerable, and sets in motion the life and death struggle. Hegel's account of recognition shows that the self is for itself only through the mediation of the other's recognition. Since self-identity is mediated by other, alterity is a constitutive feature of self-identity. Moreover, Hegel's analysis of the understanding (*Verstand*) shows that abstract identity—the identity that excludes difference—is its fundamental category. The understanding's concept of abstract identity must be deconstructed and replaced by a holistic dialectical concept that relates identity and difference. The emergent universal is mediated by the other and so concrete in Hegel's sense.

37. Sartre himself draws this distinction. See *Being and Nothingness*, 268.

38. Ibid., 221.   39. Ibid., 222.

portrait of myself which gives expression to an ugliness or baseness which I do not have, but I could not be touched to the quick. *Shame is by nature recognition. I recognize that I am as the Other sees me.*[40]

Sartre's analysis of shame clearly involves recognition in Hegel's sense, a self-recognition in other. Without self-recognition in other, my appearing to the other would be merely an empty image, or an imaginative construct by the other that leaves me unaffected. But in shame I do recognize that I am this being that appears 'thus and so' to the other, and that I am as the other sees me.[41] This self-recognition in other is not a sheer negation, for I recognize that I am what the other sees. If I did not recognize that I am as the other sees me, I would not seek to evade and dissemble this fact. Here is a clear and vivid phenomenological presentation of intersubjective self-recognition in other in the Fichtean and Hegelian sense.

Sartre's *ontological analysis* of shame is something else. Sartre's ontology in *Being and Nothingness* is like an acid that dissolves the original phenomenon, namely, self-recognition in other. *Being and Nothingness* is an existential *philosophy*, a posture opposed to mediation and dialectic. Sartre distinguishes sharply between subject and object as two types of being. This ontological dualism is evident in his analysis of the certainty of being looked at by the other when there is no other empirically present.

> There is indeed a confusion here between two distinct orders of knowledge and two types of being which cannot be compared. We have always known that the object in the world can only be probable. This is due to its very character as object. It is probable that the passerby is a man; if he turns his eyes towards me, then although I immediately experience and with certainty the fact of being looked at, I cannot make this certainty pass into my experience of the other as object. In fact it reveals to me only the other as subject, a transcending presence in the world and the real condition of my being as object. In every causal state therefore it is impossible to transfer my certainty of the other as subject to the other as object which was the occasion of that certainty, and conversely it is impossible to invalidate the evidence of the appearance of the other as subject by pointing to the constitutional probability of the other as object. . . . What is certain is that I am looked at: what is only probable is that the look is bound to this or that mundane presence.[42]

The other as subject and the other as object are incomparable because they are two entirely separate orders of being.

Sartre's claim that reciprocal recognition in Hegel's sense is impossible depends on these dualist ontological premises. He writes: "Thus Hegel's opti-

---

40. Ibid. My emphasis.
41. Ibid., 261. Here Sartre claims that this is a relation of being to being, or an encounter. Recognition belongs essentially to this ontology of encounter.
42. Ibid., 276–277.

mism ends in failure: between the Other as object and me as subject there is no common measure. . . . I cannot know myself in the other if the Other is first an object for me; neither I can apprehend the Other in his true being—that is, in his subjectivity."[43] Given the gulf or ontological separation between subjects, no reciprocal recognition is possible.[44] The other and relation to the other are not structures of the for-itself; rather they are its original alienation, signifying the fall of the subject into the world.[45] Unlike Hegel, for Sartre master/slave is not a contingent historical condition but rather ontologically constitutive of inter-subjectivity: "I am a slave to the degree that my being is dependent at the center of a freedom which is not mine and which is the very condition of my being. . . . [T]his slavery is not a historical result—capable of being surmounted—of a life in the abstract form of consciousness."[46]

The absolute heterogeneity of being and nothingness implies that no media-tion is possible. This ontological position contradicts Sartre's phenomenologi-cal description of shame consciousness. Sartre confuses the negativity of shame at the vulgar gesture with the Kojèvean reading of recognition as a merely nega-tive dialectic of master and slave. He fails to see that recognition has an irreduc-ible affirmative dimension that underlies and is the condition of subsequent evasions and flight before the other. This contradiction between Sartre's phe-nomenology and his ontology of shame is due to the fact that in his phenome-nology of shame Sartre is close to Hegel's concept of recognition, but in his ontological analysis, Sartre follows and radicalizes Kojève, embracing the lat-ter's dualism between freedom and nature as well as his nominalism. The other is, ontologically speaking, an alienation: "My original Fall is the existence of the other. Shame . . . is the apprehension of myself as a nature although that very nature escapes me and is unknowable as such."[47] But if my shame is un-knowable to me, then such absolute heterogeneity makes mutual recognition impossible. I could not recognize that I am as the other sees me, for an onto-logical alienation is incapable of being overcome. Consequently, in Sartre's ontology, recognition can have only a negative significance, namely, reciprocal exclusion. Reciprocal exclusion means that recognition of self in other is im-possible. But if mutual recognition is impossible, then so is ethics, because the other is the threshold of the ethical, and the possibility of an affirmative rela-tion to other seems to be a requirement of ethics.

However, Sartre subsequently draws closer to Hegel. After 1945 he tells us he began to read Hegel; he attempted to synthesize his existentialist philosophi-cal anthropology with a social ontology, and flirts with the possibility of recip-

---

43. Ibid., 243. Here Sartre derives the plurality and ontological separation of consciousnesses from his fundamental dualistic ontology.

44. Hartmann, *Sartre's Ontology,* 115f.

45. *Being and Nothingness,* 267.

46. Ibid.   47. Ibid., 263.

rocal recognition. This move compels a reassessment of Sartre's repudiation of Hegel in *Being and Nothingness*. For a passage from the individual to the social level via reciprocal recognition is the very move that the early Sartre declared, contra Hegel, to be epistemologically optimistic and ontologically impossible. Sartre's "development" would appear to confirm the validity of Hegel's critique of Fichte in which freedom is conceived simply as negation.

Sartre's *Notebooks for an Ethics* is fascinating because of the wealth of its detailed analyses. These reflect among other things further study and appreciation of Hegel in 1945–1947, particularly his concepts of recognition and his analysis of master/slave. To be sure, Sartre continues his critical posture and ambivalence toward Hegel. On the one hand, Sartre claims that mutual recognition is a lie.[48] But this assertion is no longer a blanket rejection of reciprocity. It is as if Sartre had discovered and appropriated Fichte's and Hegel's concept of a determinate (partial) negation. On the other hand, Sartre's analysis of generosity and the appeal resemble the concept of recognition. Generosity implies an affirmative relation to the other. This suggestion is developed in Sartre's discussion of the appeal.

The appeal is a form of recognition that has nothing to do with the negativity of shame. Rather the appeal bears an uncanny similarity to Fichte's *Aufforderung*.[49] "The appeal is a request made by someone to someone in the name of something. . . . The appeal is the recognition of a personal freedom in a situation by a personal freedom in a situation."[50] In making an appeal to someone "I recognize the other's freedom without being pierced by a look. In effect, I posit that his end is my end."[51] Again, "The appeal in effect is a promise of reciprocity. It is understood that the person I appeal to may appeal to me in return."[52] Finally, and most significantly, "the appeal is the recognition of ambiguity, since it recognizes the other's freedom being in a situation, the conditioned character of his ends, and the unconditionality of his freedom. With this the appeal is itself a form of reciprocity from the moment it springs up."[53] Further, an affirmative relation to the other is explicitly acknowledged: "Through the Other I am enriched in a new dimension of being. . . . This is in no way a fall or threat. . . . [H]e enriches the world and me, he gives a meaning to my existence in addition to the subjective meaning I myself give it."[54]

Unfortunately, the *Notebooks* do not present a unified position concerning reciprocity or affirmative relation to other. Their translator, David Pellauer, ob-

48. Jean-Paul Sartre, *Notebooks for an Ethics*, trans. David Pellauer (Chicago: University of Chicago Press, 1992), 70.

49. Did Sartre read Fichte? I have no idea, and can think of no reason why he should have. Fichte's *Grundlage des Naturrechts* and his *System der Sittenlehre* were not translated into French until 1984 and 1986, respectively. If Sartre read Fichte it must have been in German.

50. Sartre, *Notebooks for an Ethics*, 274.

51. Ibid., 279.   52. Ibid., 284.   53. Ibid., 285.

54. Ibid., 499–500.

serves that "if anything is unclear it is the organizing framework that holds all these reflections together."[55] Sartre affirms generosity, but he also believes that generosity can become a new oppression. In spite of conceding affirmative character to generosity, Sartre continues to maintain that "the original relation of the other to me is already one of alienation."[56] In short, Sartre fails in the *Notebooks* to resolve the fundamental question whether mutual recognition is possible. Instead he reiterates the dualism and nominalism of *Being and Nothingness*: "Here I am with two types of consciousness: the one mediated which comes to me by way of other people, the other coming to me by way of myself. No synthesis is possible between these kinds of knowledge since the one resides in the Other and the one resides in me."[57] If no synthesis is possible, there is no 'between', and mutual recognition is ruled out. Pellauer suggests that Sartre's failure to resolve this issue may be the reason he set this project aside and why he says in a note in *Saint Genet* that today ethics is both necessary and impossible.[58]

Other commentators have pointed out that Sartre's later position, while changed, nevertheless remains unclear on the fundamental question of a possible affirmative reciprocal relation to others. Recall that this is the issue Hegel identified in Fichte as the question on which the possibility of an ethics turns. In an excellent essay "Reciprocity and the Genius of the Third," Thomas Flynn refers to the new concept of freedom Sartre develops in the *Critique of Dialectical Reason*, that the individual is free only in the group (fusion). However, Flynn warns us not to read too much into this: "if they speak of Sartre as repudiating the existentialist theory of the primacy of the individual, they have neglected to note the limitations to group integration which Sartre invokes at every turn."[59]

Sartre describes his later position, not just as nominalism but as *dialectical* nominalism. By adopting a nominalist position Sartre hopes to avoid a substantial We. But the question is, if one accepts dialectical nominalism, how is it possible to move from the individual to the social? At issue is not only the possibility of an affirmative relation to other, of the I becoming a We, but also the possibility of an ethics or ethical life in Hegel's sense. This affirmative move from the individual to the intersubjective, and from the intersubjective to

55. Ibid., xix. For an opposing view, see Thomas C. Anderson, *Sartre's Two Ethics: From Authenticity to Integral Humanity* (Chicago: Open Court, 1993). Anderson defends a more Hegelian reading of Sartre, notably on the issue of reciprocal recognition.

56. Sartre, *Notebooks for an Ethics*, xix.

57. Ibid., 451.

58. Ibid., xvii. For a different assessment, cf. Thomas Anderson, *Sartre's Two Ethics*. Anderson believes that Sartre is right to contend that a genuine humanism will be established only when we mutually recognize our common human needs. However I believe that Anderson mistakenly ascribes to Sartre Hegel's position on mutual-reciprocal recognition, a position that Sartre embraces only inconsistently and finally appears to repudiate.

59. Thomas Flynn, "Reciprocity and the Genius of the Third," in *The Philosophy of Jean-Paul Sartre*, 357.

the social, is precisely what Sartre rejected in his critique of Hegel in *Being and Nothingness*. Flynn observes that this issue surfaces again in the *Critique of Dialectical Reason*.

> Sartre hopes to arrive at a practical, non-substantial 'We.' In so arguing, he imitates those nominalists who opt for resemblance theories of universals without realizing that 'resemblance' is itself a universal. . . . Not that Sartre has created a substantial 'We' in spite of himself; but his zealous opposition to what he takes to be substantialism in social theory has blinded him to the fact that he too has assigned an ontological status to the group, namely, that of a relational entity. . . . Perhaps the chief deficiency in Sartre's theory from the ontological viewpoint is precisely this failure to offer a thoroughgoing ontology of relations. He has never undertaken a systematic analysis of relations themselves, though their distinction from substances and events has been crucial to Sartrean philosophy since *Being and Nothingness*.[60]

The ontological problem lies deeper than an omission to consider relations; it lies in dialectical nominalism itself, for, as Flynn observes, "dialectical nominalism turns out to be self-defeating, since it destroys as nominalism what it aims at establishing as dialectic, namely a real synthesis of individual actions into group praxis."[61] Sartre, says Flynn, "fluctuates between denials that the group is a hypostasis and assertions that group praxis is distinct from and irreducible to individual praxis."[62] This fluctuation means that the issue of affirmative relation, "the between," is inescapable, for "agents in relation differ from agents alone (if there could be such), and the difference is precisely the relation."[63] Sartre fails to appreciate relation, and his dialectical nominalism remains close to what Hegel calls mechanism: Subjects remain unrelated in spite of relation. This undermines intersubjectivity and ethics.

In a late interview, Sartre was asked about his views concerning the ontological separation of subjects that makes intersubjectivity and ethics problematic. Sartre replied, "In any case the separation exists, and I do not see any reason to speak of intersubjectivity once subjectivities are separated. Intersubjectivity assumes a communion that almost reaches a kind of identification, in any case a unity. It . . . thus assumes each subjectivity in relation to the others—at once separated in the same way and united in another. I see the separation but I do not see the union."[64] In affirming separation of subjects and denying any union, Sartre remains at the level of mechanism, the externality of consciousnesses that precludes any formation of a We. Sartre rejects the Hegelian 'We' and retains nominalistic individualism to the end. Hence ethics is problematic, if not impossible. I hasten to add that the substantial union that Sartre rejects is also rejected by Hegel. For Hegel, the passage from the I to the We is not a passage to abstract

60. Ibid., 356.   61. Ibid., 359.   62. Ibid.
63. Ibid.
64. Schilpp, *The Philosophy of Jean-Paul Sartre*, 44.

identity or substantiality. The I that is a We is a concrete universal, a unity of reciprocal recognition that is conditioned on the mutual free release and affirmation of the other. Where Sartre sees only separation, Hegel sees both separation and union, and the separation is a condition and requirement of the union.

Feminist Critique of Hegel

Patricia J. Mills advances several criticisms of Hegel that raise important issues concerning his concept of recognition as well as his treatment of women, marriage, and family.[65] Her criticisms raise and will help to clarify a question that has dogged the heels of Hegel's analysis, namely, whether a life and death struggle (*Kampf*) is a universal, necessary stage in the development of mutual recognition and freedom. This question becomes especially urgent in light of Kojève's reading that moves the struggle for recognition to the center of the *Phenomenology of Spirit*.

Mills begins by identifying the following antinomy in Hegel: "his account of intersubjectivity implies the equal recognition of woman even though Hegel himself is tied to a framework which prevents him from actually seeing woman as man's equal."[66] Mills is prepared to grant Hegel a theory of intersubjectivity and to grant that mutual recognition implies reciprocity and coequality of those who are recognized. Nevertheless, she maintains, Hegel remains committed to a traditional conception of family that restricts women to the domestic sphere, and this contradicts his account of recognition and intersubjectivity.[67] Mills is correct that there is a tension, if not contradiction, between the logic of reciprocal recognition and the traditional view of women that Hegel presents in *PR*, §166.

Although woman is *in principle* a coequal recognition partner with man, *in fact* she is not. In comparing women with passive plants,[68] Hegel may unwittingly undermine the worth of any recognition women might give. After all, if women are like plants, this implies that they are not only passive but also inferior to men. It implies that their recognition would be of even less importance to men than the slave's coerced and dissembling recognition of the master. If women are like plants, Mills infers that the recognition between a husband and a wife would be based more on nature than on freedom. The woman's restriction to the domestic sphere is equivalent, Mills believes, to her being in thrall

---

65. Patricia Jagentowicz Mills, "Hegel and 'The Woman Question': Recognition and Intersubjectivity," in *The Sexism of Social and Political Theory: Women and Reproduction from Plato to Nietzsche*, ed. L. Mg. Clark and L. Lange, 74–98 (Toronto: University of Toronto Press, 1979), hereafter cited as HWQ. See also Patricia Jagentowicz Mills, "Hegel's Antigone," and her *Woman, Nature and Psyche*; the chapter on Hegel is a reworked version that condenses her previous essays. I focus on HWQ because it is the most explicit treatment of the relevant issues.

66. Mills, HWQ, 75.

67. I have noted this contradiction in chapter 10.

68. *PR*, §166 Zusatz.

to nature. Hegel's account of marriage, when viewed from the standpoint of his remarks about the substantive gender roles of women appears as a de facto unequal relationship of domination, a version of master/slave. This flatly contradicts his ethical defense of monogamy as implying coequality between men and women.[69]

Mills bases her interpretation on Hegel's account of Greek ethical life in the *Phenomenology*. There Hegel expounds the traditional view that restricts woman to the domestic sphere, that is, the home and family. Of course, this is not perceived as a restriction within the traditional view. Moreover, Hegel shows that man and woman are identified with human law and divine law, respectively. The former law is man-made, and explicitly expressed in the state. The state embodies a warrior ethic. The divine law, on the other hand, has no obvious or explicit origin; no one knows its source, but it is 'older' and 'higher' than human law; it is ethical substance.[70] Hegel assigns to the family, to women, and to Antigone in particular, a special perceptivity for the unwritten divine law. Allen Wood is correct in observing that Hegel does not maintain that women are intellectually inferior to men, so much as that they have a different, but no less important, mode of perceiving and thinking.[71] In part the tragic conflict and opposition in Sophocles' *Antigone* is due to this intellectual "division of labor." Antigone's devotion to the divine law in burying her brother Polyneices leads her to defy Creon's edict that traitors are not to receive appropriate burial. Through Antigone's defiance of Creon, the divine law comes into opposition to the human law, a fact that has considerable significance for ethics and tragedy.[72]

Passing over such details and subtleties, Mills focuses instead on the issue that in the traditional view, woman has no role in the public realm; she is restricted to the domestic sphere of the family. For Mills, the traditional substantive ethical principle—which she believes Hegel accepts—makes biology women's destiny.[73] As Mills reads Hegel, women never transcend nature. The only way to transcend nature is to undergo a life and death struggle for recognition. But on Hegel's account, women do not undergo a struggle for recognition. All of her criticisms flow from this basic point. Mills argues that since woman is restricted to the domestic sphere, she never has the opportunity to undergo a struggle for recognition, and does not, Mills believes, transcend nature or come to a full consciousness of freedom. She becomes domesticated and docile.

69. This contradiction is found in *PR*, §§166–167.

70. *PR*, §144.

71. Wood, *HET*, 244–248. G. R. G. Mure made a similar observation in his *The Philosophy of Hegel* (Oxford: Oxford University Press, 1965), 92–93. Hegel's position is reflected in contemporary philosophy; see Sarah Ruddick's *Maternal Thinking* and Carol Gilligan's *In a Different Voice*.

72. *PR*, §166.

73. See chap. 9 for my critique of biological reductionism. For another critique, see Susan M. Easton, "Hegel and Feminism," in *Hegel and Modern Philosophy*, ed. David Lamb (London: Croom Helm, 1987), 30–55.

Consequently mutual recognition between husband and wife is not really mutual because it is not between equals, for transcendence of nature is, Mills believes, a male prerogative. Marriage is not an ethical relationship but remains tainted by nature and natural immediacy.

On Mills's interpretation of the traditional domestic family, it is a sphere of unfreedom that is not yet ethical life because the family members do not undergo a struggle for recognition. In contrast, for Hegel the family members do not undergo a life and death struggle for recognition against each other; they freely recognize each other without any struggle. As Siep has pointed out, Hegel identifies the family as a recognition without a conflict of wills. Hegel indicates that

> immediate ethical life is the natural in the form of feeling [*Empfindung*]; in this form it is the spirit of the family, the gods of the household and love. The chief point here is that I am no longer simply in myself as an individual, but rather have my self-consciousness in the self-consciousness of another: I am at once myself and yet another. My self-feeling is not incipient individuality, but includes just as immediately an other as myself.[74]

In identifying the family as ethical life in its immediacy, Hegel means that the family is a merely parochial universal subject. Its parochialism means that the family takes up a negative and exclusive attitude, not toward each other, but toward outsiders. It should be noted that this parochialism vis-à-vis others affects all family members, both male and female; it does not affect only women while somehow failing to affect men. In the Jena manuscripts, the life and death struggle occurs against this preethical, presocial background of the family as a parochial universal.[75] Given the immediate exclusion of other constitutive of parochial family self-consciousness, a life and death struggle is virtually inevitable. A universal consciousness, which supports and finds expression in law and justice, has not yet emerged. Master/slave represents a transitional stage toward law, in that it puts an end to sheer killing while institutionalizing inequality and coercion.

For Mills, freedom consists in transcending the private sphere of the family to the public sphere, that is, moving from the family to civil society. In Mills's reading of Hegel's assertion 'the I becomes a We', the constitution of the We requires the *transcendence* of the family. Mills locates the life of freedom not in the family but in civil society. This is precisely the freedom that the tradi-

---

74. Hegel, *Philosophie des Rechts*, 1819/20, ed. D. Henrich (Frankfurt: Suhrkamp, 1983), 55. Hegel goes on to characterize the social development beyond the family as the central social institution as *Anderswerdens*, a becoming other. This refers to the external relations of families to other families.

75. In the early, pre-*Phenomenology* accounts of the struggle for recognition, one member of a family confronts an outsider—a member of another family in a dispute over family honor, property, etc.

tional view denies women. Mills believes that this transition from family to civil society requires a struggle for recognition; that is, one enters civil society only through and by means of a life and death struggle for recognition. Such struggles and entry to public life are limited to men. Since in the traditional view, women are prevented from engaging in struggles for recognition, they remain within the undifferentiated abstract universality of family life; consequently they never achieve freedom but remain domestic, docile, and passive.

Mills's analyses of these issues depend on a particular interpretation of Hegel. She follows Kojève in identifying recognition and Hegel's entire account of intersubjectivity with the struggle for recognition on the part of master and slave. Mills follows Kojève in viewing the struggle for recognition as a universal and necessary stage in the development of freedom. She considers the struggle for recognition to be the ontogenetic principle of freedom.[76] This naturalizes the concept of recognition, because it now means that every individual must recapitulate the ontogenetic process. Moreover, the ontogenetic process includes a struggle for recognition.[77] Failure to pass through and prevail in this struggle is to fail to be free or to develop the full consciousness of freedom, that is, to remain docile, servile, and domestic. Mills's identifications of the concept of recognition with the necessity of struggle and with the public/private distinction and traditional male/female gender roles add up to the conclusion that it is only through the struggle for recognition outside the family sphere that human beings transcend immediate natural family life and achieve real freedom as particular individuals in their own right.

Note that this reading presupposes that the family is a preethical natural institution. Mills's analysis implies that the family is not a genuine form of recognition or free intersubjectivity because the family members do not recapitulate the ontogenetic struggle for recognition in their relationships with each other. This tacitly denies that the family is a valid form of freedom and recognition at all. This is close to suggesting that the family is incompatible with freedom, which Mills identifies with and locates in civil society. Hegel would find both identifications—the family with unfreedom and civil society with freedom—highly problematic.

In the case of women, the recapitulation of the ontogenetic universal and

---

76. Mills, HWQ, 77. Mills takes this 'ontogenetic principle' from Richard J. Bernstein, *Praxis and Action* (Philadelphia: University of Pennsylvania Press, 1971), 23. Bernstein simply asserts it without any textual justification or supporting argument. On the other hand, Werner Marx cautions against attributing the claim that phylogeny recapitulates ontogeny to Hegel because it misreads the *Phenomenology* as an anthropology. It is not Hegel's but Kierkegaard's view that the individual recapitulates the history of the species. "In contrast to this, the theme of Hegel's observations is not the recapitulation of the history of the species in the becoming of the individual, but rather the conditions the particular individual has to satisfy if he wishes to gain . . . the standpoint of science." Werner Marx, *Hegel's Phenomenology of Spirit: A Commentary on the Preface and the Introduction*, trans. P. Heath (New York: Harper & Row, 1975), 33.

77. Mills, HWQ, 77.

necessary struggle for recognition *outside the family* is short-circuited and prevented. Since woman is confined to the domestic sphere and excluded from the public sphere, Mills contends that the process of recognition "necessarily excludes woman."[78] Woman remains tied to first nature; that is, she is confined to natural-biological-reproductive immediacy, and unlike man, does not transcend nature or family through a struggle for recognition. Thus woman never achieves the status of an ethical subject. Mills charges that in his conception of woman's development, Hegel suspends and violates the ontogenetic principle: "the progressive movement of Spirit towards universal self-consciousness . . . is never recapitulated in woman."[79] This is a legitimate criticism of Hegel insofar as he accepts the traditional view of gender roles.[80] However, Mills has a flawed interpretation of recognition and family. I shall take up the latter issue first.

There is a tension between nature and freedom in Mills's position. On the one hand, she naturalizes recognition when she treats the struggle for recognition as the ontogenetic principle of freedom, a universal *necessary* process in which individuals "automatically" recapitulate the development of their species nature. On the other hand, she interprets recognition as a process of *free* social construction in which men dominate women and prevent them from recapitulating the universal and necessary ontogenetic process. However, Mills does not resolve this tension between necessity and freedom, or explain how an ontogenetic principle could be bypassed or short-circuited.

In view of Mills's embrace of naturalism,[81] it should be recalled that Hegel criticizes not only traditional natural law theory but also the naturalistic views of marriage and family prevalent in his own day.[82] For Hegel, marriage is both a natural and an ethical relationship in which the natural and biological are subordinate to the ethical union, the 'We', the corporate person.[83] Hegel's criticism of polygamy is an ethical critique; polygamy, he believes, is a natural inequality that betokens slavery on the part of women. For Hegel, marriage and family imply the transcendence of the state of nature. The family is both the highest institution of natural ethical life and constitutes the transition from nature to

---

78. Ibid., 80.   79. Ibid., 95.

80. However, Hegel's praise of Antigone points in another direction. Even though Antigone appears in the traditional role of representing the ethos of the family, the fact that through her action the family and state come into conflict shows that for Antigone family values are more than merely private and domestic; rather the personal here is also political. In addition, recall Hegel's point that the ethical concerns of the family for its members (but obviously not the blood or kinship relation) are supposed to be extended throughout the body politic at the level of the ethical state. Further, in Hegel's analysis of Sophocles' play, Antigone and Creon become involved in a struggle for recognition that has tragic results for both, and for Greek *Sittlichkeit* as a whole. Hegel's praise for Antigone in this struggle shows that he does not entirely accept the traditional view that Mills ascribes to him.

81. Mills embraces naturalism both in her interpretation of the family and in her view that the struggle for recognition is the ontogenetic principle of freedom.

82. See above chap. 9.   83. *PR*, §§161, 163.

ethical life, or freedom proper. In the mature *Philosophy of Right*, the family is the first institution of ethical life.

Further, Hegel observes that "the sexes are naturally different, but this *difference is rationally reconstructed* in them. Each contains both moments, but in different respects."[84] This observation shows that gender roles are not simply determined by natural ontogenesis or biology but are in principle subject to freedom, that is, rational criticism and reconstruction. This in turn implies the possibility of criticism and modification of the traditional view of marriage and family as natural, even if Hegel himself does not specifically criticize or modify the traditional family. However, his criticism of natural law theory is surely relevant and implies that Hegel would not accept Mills's interpretation of the struggle for recognition outside of the family as a universal and necessary ontogenetic principle of freedom.

The issue between Hegel and Mills can be formulated thus: 1) Whether a struggle for recognition is a universal and necessary form of the development of self-consciousness such that 2) recognition is the ontogenetic principle and process of the development of freedom; consequently 3) it must be recapitulated as a necessary stage of development in and by every individual. It is most likely that Hegel would affirm 1) and 2) but reject 3). Consider the following excerpt from his discussion of madness.

> Our interpretation of madness as a necessary form or stage in the development of the soul is naturally not to be understood as though we were asserting that every spirit, every soul, must go through this state of extreme derangement. Such an assertion would be as absurd as to assume that because in the *Philosophy of Right* crime is considered as a necessary manifestation of the human will, therefore to commit a crime is an unavoidable necessity for every individual. Crime and madness are extremes which the *human spirit in general* has to overcome in the course of its development. However, this does not mean that these appear in every individual as extremes, but only in the form of limitations, errors, follies and guilt of a non-criminal nature.[85]

Hegel here draws an important distinction between the human spirit in general, or objective *Geist*, and human beings as individuals, or subjective *Geist*. The point of this distinction is clear, namely, to limit and qualify the universality and scope of any so-called ontogenetic principle, that is, to deny that every individual necessarily recapitulates the extreme stages of development of human spirit in general. This qualification blunts, if not undermines, Mills's criticisms, to wit, that there is a necessary ontogenetic process of achieving freedom through a struggle for recognition, that women are prevented from recapitulating.

84. *VPR*17, §77. My italics. This paragraph contains the same apparent contradiction noted in *PR*, §§166–167.
85. *E*, §408 Zusatz.

Hegel identifies necessary stages in general sociocultural psychological development, for example, madness, crime, struggle for recognition, but denies that every individual necessarily recapitulates the extreme forms of these stages in his own development. Hegel rejects that view as absurd. What is true of human spirit in its development collectively is not necessarily true of human spirits distributively. In the *Phenomenology* Hegel is very careful in spelling out this relation: "The single individual must also pass through the formative stages of universal spirit *with respect to their content*, but as *shapes which spirit has already left behind*, as stages on a way that has already been worked on and made level." [86] This means that the recapitulation of the universal stages of development of spirit becomes easier for later individuals because the immediacy of the stages has been overcome, and their actuality has been reduced to possibilities that can be studied and appropriated. [87] Of course, a struggle for recognition is always possible, but it is not necessary and inevitable for all individuals.

For Hegel, the struggle for recognition is primarily about sociopolitical and cultural history, not about personal psychological development, much less relations between family members. [88] The extreme stages of development and transitions are necessary for universal objective spirit, but they are not inevitable for human beings as individuals. Given their reduction from actuality to possibility, they can fortunately be traversed in other ways besides the original violent, extremes. Education is one such way of traversal. Hegel allows for considerable contingency and variation at the level of individual development.

Where Mills identifies universal rational structures with maleness and particularity with femaleness, Hegel distinguishes his universal ontological structures and patterns from particular contingencies, including the public/private distinction and the contingencies of male and female, man and woman. Mills argues that only man dirempts himself and thus enters a dual public/private existence, while woman is restricted by traditional ethical principles to the home and domestic existence. [89] This implies that Hegel's putative universal struc-

---

86. *PhG*, 27; *PhS*, §28, 16. My italics.

87. *PhG*, 28; *PhS*, §29, 17. Cf. Werner Marx's comments in fn. 76 above.

88. As noted above, the struggle for recognition presupposes the family as a parochial universal that takes up a negative, hostile attitude toward outsiders. But this implies that such exclusivity and hostility are not *essentially* characteristic of relations between family members themselves. In this respect Hegel may appear to be innocent or naive about psychosocial development. But his point is difficult to reject without at the same time rejecting the family altogether as unreformable.

89. Cf. Allen Wood's remarks concerning the problem of reconciling the substantive and subjective-reflective principles or elements of freedom (*HET*, 246). Wood formulates this problem in terms of an antinomy between putatively feminine, prereflective feelings, dispositions, and personal relationships and putatively masculine, reflective, autonomous self-determination. It is puzzling that Wood identifies the substantive ethical principle with women and the reflective principle of subjective freedom with men. No doubt it is because Hegel himself makes this identification in *PR*, §166. However, the issue of the relation of ethical substance to ethical subjectivity is not just a gender issue. As Ilting has shown, it is the central systematic problem of the *Philosophy of Right*, namely, the reconciliation of subjective freedom (abstract right and morality) with ethical substance (*Sittlichkeit*). But classical ethical substance in Hegel's view is a parochial universality.

tures, and so on, are implicitly identified with the male gender. This identification blurs the important distinction between ontic and ontological.

In contrast, Hegel maintains the ontic/ontological distinction. While the universal human spirit dirempts itself and has to run through and result from certain universal and necessary stages of development, including national development, the life and death struggle, and master/slave, this is not necessarily true for individuals. Hegel explicitly rejects the idea that individual persons must necessarily go through all the conflicts of the universal consciousness. In light of the distinction between ontological and ontic dimensions, Hegel can assert that domination and oppression are issues that affect potentially all human beings and are not to be simply reduced to or equated with male domination or patriarchalism. To be sure, male domination, or patriarchalism, is one form such oppression can take,[90] but it is not the only form. Moreover, in retaining the ontic/ontological distinction rather than collapsing it as do Mills and Kojève, Hegel makes it clear that unequal, oppressive forms of recognition are historical *contingencies* that can and must be overcome.

Since Mills accepts and depends on Kojève's reading, she has difficulty in dealing with Hegel's account of love: "If we consider this exposition on love in the light of the analysis of self-consciousness as the desire for recognition we find a critical inconsistency. While it is clear that love is a desire for recognition, for the lover desires the desire of the other, *the dialectic of love is not*

That is, the entire traditional view of gender difference—male and female—is prereflective and not just the "woman" side of that difference. In Wood's terms, the organic relation between ethical substance and subjective freedom means in one sense everything is immediate, prereflective, namely, a given, including gender identity and roles, and in another sense everything is reflective, namely, a posited product, and thus subject to criticism and revision. For Hegel, such positing, which includes mutual recognition as a critical principle, is the way in which the rational becomes actual. Despite ongoing criticism, Hegel believes that there are certain institutional constants, which can be continuously re-formed and modified. Criticism and liberation from merely traditional gender differentiation are always possibilities. If this turns everyone into an instance or representative of the reflective principle of subjective freedom, so be it, for this is the critical process wherein substance becomes subject, the actual becomes rational. As Hegel observes, both male and female gender roles are not simply natural givens but are subject to rational criticism and reconstruction (*VPR*17, §77). Where Hegel's conservatism vis-à-vis ethical substance becomes evident is not in his determination that women have aptitude only for home and family (for here he betrays his fundamental views concerning mutual recognition and equality), but in his claim that institutions like family, civil society, and state are fundamental conditions of human freedom and consequently should not simply be abandoned but reformed.

90. In this connection it should be noted that Hegel has his own critique of patriarchy, as an attempt to impose the structure, not only of the family, but also of theocracy, on the state. The patriarchal principle that the state is a family retains a parochial universality that is the basis of racist, ethnic, and sectarian prejudices. Patriarchy represents a form of domination and tyranny that must be overcome, in Hegel's view, by the constitutional state as the objective realization of freedom. How this can be done without extending women full political membership, and the right to vote, is another question. Hegel's argument against patriarchy can certainly be turned against some of Hegel's own residual patriarchalist views of family. However, this "turn" is not the development of a new argument unheard of by Hegel; rather it extends Hegel's own arguments made against polygamy, and at the sociopolitical level against patriarchalism, to the level of the family. It cites Hegel "against Hegel" in an effort to make his position consistent with his own best insights.

grounded in the hostility of a life and death struggle."[91] I am not sure what this means, but the reasoning seems to be something like this: (1) the universal ontological pattern of recognition grounds everything in the hostility of a life and death struggle; (2) love is a particular instance of recognition; (3) therefore love must be grounded in hostility, life and death struggle, and so on; (4) but love does not exhibit such structures and/or patterns; (5) therefore Hegel is inconsistent. Hegel would reject such reasoning as absurd, *sinnlos*, because it grasps recognition at a subordinate level and treats that subordinate level as foundational for higher levels. It fails to appreciate that love, as a higher form of recognition, is supposed to overcome and reconcile the conflicts of the lower levels.

For his part, Hegel is emphatic that the violent struggle for recognition, while universal and necessary at the level of objective spirit, that is, in the life of a people, is nevertheless not foundational for, much less immanent in, all forms of recognition. The life and death struggle for recognition that Mills, following Kojève, presents as foundational is for Hegel characteristic of the state of nature.[92] Hegel's claim is that the state of nature must be overcome if there is to be such a thing as a human community or a state and that recognition is the process in which the state of nature is overcome and freedom actualized in the world. Hegel's *Philosophy of Right* is based on the proposition that the state of nature and the struggle for recognition can be and/or are being transcended. The public realm in modern states—to the extent that it has not disintegrated into the excesses and contradictions of civil society—is not inherently a struggle for recognition. In his *Encyclopedia Philosophy of Spirit*, he addresses this issue.

> In order to prevent possible misunderstandings with regard to the standpoint just outlined, we must note that the struggle for recognition pushed to the extreme here indicated can occur only in the state of nature [*Naturzustande*] where human beings exist only as separate individuals. But such a struggle is far removed from civil society and the state, because there the recognition for which the combatants fought already exists. *Although the state may originate in violence, it does not rest upon it. Violence, in producing the state, has brought into existence something that is justified in and for itself, namely law and constitution.* In the state what prevails is the spirit of the people, custom and law. Here the human being is recognized and treated as a rational being, as free, as a person; and the individual for his part makes himself worthy of this recognition by overcoming the natural state of self-consciousness and obeying a universal, a will existing in and for itself, the law. He behaves towards others in a manner that is universally valid, recognizing them as he wishes to have others recognize him, namely as free, as person. In the state, the citizen derives his honor from the position he fills, from the trade he follows and from his laboring activity. His honor thereby has a substantial content that is universal and objective, and no longer dependent on an empty subjectivity. Honor of this kind is lacking in the state of nature where individuals,

91. Mills, HWQ, 89. My italics.
92. *PR*, §§57, 331, 349, 351.

wherever they may be and whatever they may do, want to compel others to recognize them.[93]

Hegel maintains that the struggle for recognition, while necessary on the level of the state of nature, becomes contingent on a higher level of mutual recognition: "In a spirit that is more developed than another, the lower concrete existence has been reduced to an inconspicuous moment; what used to be the heart of the matter [*die Sache selbst*] has become now but a trace."[94] Thus mutual recognition is possible without any life and death struggle. This is precisely Hegel's position. In the 1825 *Lectures on the Philosophy of Spirit*, he flatly asserts that "in the civilized condition, particularly family, civil society and the state, I recognize everyone and am recognized without any struggle whatsoever [*ganz ohne Kampf*]."[95]

Given Hegel's critique of natural law, his sense of historical relativity, and the flexibility and variability he allows in the process of mutual recognition at the individual level, it would be a most precarious interpretation to hold that for Hegel women cannot be recognized as equals, or that the mutual recognition of husband and wife cannot be ethical but is merely natural. Hegel's ethical critique of polygamy, that in it women do not receive their rights, and his defense of monogamy as that form of marriage proper to the equal right and recognition of husband and wife, presuppose and express the fundamental point that in mutual-reciprocal recognition the state of nature is not normative or foundational and that men and women are capable of recognizing each other "not merely as natural but as free beings."[96] This position articulates the main thrust of Hegel's thought concerning ethical life as the telos and result of mutual recognition. His traditional views about the inferiority of women in *PR*, §166, not only contradict his high praise of Antigone and his defense of monogamy but also betray the historical consciousness and teleological development of freedom and liberation that are central to his thought.

Hegel, Nietzsche, and Deleuze

In her study of the French appropriation of Hegel, Judith Butler notes a curious pattern of simultaneous rejection of and dependence on Hegel in Kojève's and Hyppolite's students such as Deleuze, Foucault, and Derrida: "The difference from Hegel is a vital and absorbing one, and the act of repudiation more often than not requires the continued life of that which is to be repudiated, thus paradoxically sustaining the 'rejected Hegel' in order to reconstitute contem-

93. *E*, §432 Zusatz. My italics.
94. *PhG*, 26; *PhS*, §28, 16.
95. Hegel, *The Berlin Phenomenology*, ed. and trans. M. J. Petry (Boston: D. Reidel, 1981), 78.
96. *E*, §431 Zusatz.

porary identity in and through the act of repudiation again and again. It is as if Hegel becomes a convenient rubric for a variety of positions that defend the self-sufficient subject, even those positions that defend a Cartesian view of consciousness which Hegel himself clearly rejects."[97] These philosophers overlook Hegel's critique of subjectivity and instead willfully characterize Hegel as "championing 'the subject', a metaphysics of closure or presence, that excludes difference and is, according to his Nietzschean critics, anti-life."[98]

For Deleuze, Hegel and dialectic are the target of Nietzsche's philosophy: "Anti-Hegelianism runs through Nietzsche's work as its cutting edge."[99] Nietzsche's philosophy is best understood as antidialectical, as asserting a nondialectical difference that has hierarchical pluralism as its ontological correlate. Deleuze's preference for hierarchical pluralism might be derived from Kojève's identification of recognition with master and slave, as well as from his reading of Nietzsche. The interpretation of recognition, master and slave, is at the heart of Deleuze's polemics against Hegel. Descombes observes that the way Deleuze makes his case against Hegel and dialectic "is a further confirmation that, since Kojève, the master-slave relationship has been a constant in French thought. . . . In post-Kojèvean discourse we witness some curious exchanges. Sometimes the 'dialectic of mastery and slavery' takes on Marxist connotations: the master is exploitative, he enjoys his privileges without working. . . . Elsewhere it has a Nietzschean flavor: the modern bourgeois is considered a despicable being because he is no more than an emancipated slave, a freedman who has interiorized the master."[100]

Deleuze rejects what he takes to be the "Hegelian" version of master and slave because he believes it is fundamentally servile. Not just Hegel's slave, but Hegel's 'subject' and Hegelianism as a totality, is a servile morality, an expression of the ascetic ideal. This charge is most plausible if it is understood as directed not at Hegel but at Kojève's reading of Hegel. Against the Hegelian master and slave, Deleuze articulates and defends a Nietzschean version. His distinction between the two turns on a further distinction between *differential* self-affirmation (Nietzsche) and *dialectical* self-affirmation.[101]

Differential affirmation is pure self-affirmation, an affirmation of difference as such. This conception of affirmation is based on Nietzsche's master morality. Deleuze expresses it thus: *I am good, therefore you are evil.* The assertion has the sense of a primary affirmation with no internal negation. "We ask, who is it that begins by saying 'I am good'? It is certainly not the one who com-

97. Butler, *SD*, 176.   98. Ibid.

99. Deleuze, *Nietzsche and Philosophy*, 8.

100. Descombes, *MFP*, 158.

101. Two interpreters have called attention to this distinction. See Daniel Breazeale, "The Hegel-Nietzsche Problem," and Murray Greene, "Hegel's 'Unhappy Consciousness' and Nietzsche's 'Slave Morality'," in *Hegel and the Philosophy of Religion*, ed. Darrel E. Christensen (The Hague: Martinus Nijhoff, 1970), 124–141.

pares himself to others, or the one who compares his actions and works to superior and transcendent values. . . . The one who says 'I am good' does not wait to be called good." [102] The ethics of the master is self-glorification, and, unlike Hegel, mastery does not contain within itself its own negation, nor does it subvert itself. It is pure self-affirmation without any inherent negativity. According to Deleuze, the negativity of mastery is purely external; that is, it exists only from the slave's perspective.

In contrast, *dialectical* self-affirmation is dependent, derivative, and servile. Deleuze finds it in both Hegel's master and slave. Servile self-affirmation begins with a negation: *You are evil, therefore I am good.* Here the affirmation of self is based on and derivative from a comparison with and negation of something else. The servile self needs to say no to the other, in order to be able to affirm itself as good. Its goodness is derivative and dependent on what it negates. Consequently this self-affirmation is a weak one, lacking creativity; its creativity and affirmation consist in saying no to something else. Deleuze believes that dialectical self-affirmation is really negative, a form of servile morality or *ressentiment.* "It is an exhausted force which does not have the strength to affirm its difference, a force which no longer acts, but reacts to the forces that dominate it—only such a force brings to the foreground the negative element in its relation to the other. Such a force denies all that it is not and makes this negation its own essence and the principle of its existence." [103]

Further, since such a self-affirmation presupposes, requires, and depends on an other, it seeks recognition. For Deleuze, the desire for recognition is inherently servile:

What the wills in Hegel want is to have their power *recognized.* . . . This is the slave's conception, it is the image that the man of ressentiment has of power. *The slave only conceives of power as the object of recognition . . . the stake in a competition, and therefore makes it depend, at the end of a fight, on a simple attribution of established values.* If the master-slave relationship can easily take on the dialectical form, to the point where it has become an archetype or school exercise

102. Deleuze, *Nietzsche and Philosophy,* 119.
103. Ibid., 9. Charles Scott identifies this pattern as constitutive of the ascetic ideal, thereby connecting the ascetic ideal with servile morality: "the discipline of the ascetic ideal is self-denial in the form of continuous correction and submission of the animal, the chaotic, the meaningless. It is a discipline that subtly humiliates the meaninglessness of life by imposing a meaning for life under the transcending authority of pure life/pure being. . . . The ascetic ideal is both an articulation of an unbridgeable breach in human existence, a breach that is bordered by what our tradition names spirit and animal, as well as an expression of will to power. As unconscious will to power, the ascetic ideal is a forceful affirmation of the human meaning that enables the human organism to affirm itself in the face of no meaning at all. It is an affirmation that radically denies its own occurrence, and that sickens itself by willing its own denial in the very illusion of its self-affirmation. Nietzsche's way of stating this paradox is that all willing that takes its direction from the ascetic ideal longs to get away from appearance, change, becoming and death, and in denying the very elements of life it denies its own happening and willing nothingness in the illusion of spirituality: the idea wills the void—death—in spite of itself." *The Question of Ethics,* 36–37.

for every young Hegelian, it is because the portrait of the master Hegel offers us is, from the start, a portrait that represents the slave . . . as at best a successful slave. Underneath the Hegelian image of the master, we always find the slave.[104]

For Deleuze, the desire for recognition is servile, betraying a weak if not impotent will that can affirm only on the basis of a prior negation. Hegel's master is merely a successful slave.

Deleuze's interpretation of master and slave undermines the concept of recognition and intersubjectivity. According to Deleuze, not only are Hegel's slave and master servile in Nietzsche's sense, so is the very concept of recognition itself. On Deleuze's reading, recognition is either a sign of servile dependence or superfluous. The master has no need of recognition, because differential self-affirmation dispenses with recognition. This last point becomes evident when Deleuze interprets differential self-affirmation on pluralist assumptions. Affirmation is *self*-affirmation, the affirmation of difference and the enjoyment of the play of its own difference.[105] But if self-affirmation is pure affirmation of difference, then relation to others and recognition by others are unnecessary and even a hindrance. Moreover, for Deleuze relation implies comparison with others, and comparison betokens dependence and need. But the Nietzschean master is completely independent of the slave and has no need of the slave. He delights in being who he is and affirms himself differentially, that is, without any need to compare himself with others. Differential self-affirmation has no need of recognition, and no need of others.[106]

For Deleuze, master and slave do not share a common human identity, for the master does not share the slave's mediated, dependent identity and existence. To be sure, the master's "difference" from the slave negates the slave; the slave experiences this negation as evil and terrifying. However, the negation of the other (slave) is a secondary consequence of the primary and full affirmation, a conclusion from positive premises.[107] The eagle that devours the lamb does so because its nature as a bird of prey is to devour lambs. But this is not a *ressentiment*-laden negation that expresses a derivative, weak self-affirmation. It is an assertion of pure difference, which is not experienced as an opposition or dependent on opposition. Deleuze's interpretation of differential self-affirmation highlights nondialectical difference and leads to a *hierarchical* pluralism. From this perspective, the interhuman and the social are a hindrance, a herd morality that must be overcome by the *Übermensch*. The *Übermenschen* themselves do not need recognition; they affirm difference, and difference undercuts identity:

104. Deleuze, *Nietzsche and Philosophy*, 10. Italics in original.
105. Ibid., 189.
106. Such differential self-affirmation is also found in a remark of Napoleon, cited by Hegel, that the French republic was no more in need of recognition than the sun (*PR*, §331 Zusatz).
107. Deleuze, *Nietzsche and Philosophy*, 119–121.

there is nothing, that is, no common element, to be recognized. Pure self-affirmation implies and leads to nominalism.

The slave's negation of mastery, on the other hand, creates morality, and morality transforms the master's self-affirmation into evil. "Slaves are like sheep that ascribe the predatory behavior of their enemies to a malicious will, an intent to do them harm; they demand that the eagle behave as a lamb. Such is the revolt of slaves in morality, as a result of which they succeed in persuading masters of their guilt. Whoever is able to devour the other . . . and yet refrains, is good. Strength is thus separated from its potential, turned against itself and drawn into becoming reactive."[108] The servile consciousness interprets difference as oppositions. That is why, according to Deleuze, dialectic, which thrives on opposition, is symptomatic of servility. Dialectical opposition presupposes or brings to light an underlying identity that dissolves difference. For Deleuze, dialectic is a vehicle whereby what is other and different is reduced to the same, thus abolishing hierarchical pluralism and nominalism.

We can now appreciate why Deleuze repudiates recognition. The desire for the other and the demand for reciprocal recognition are all servile. The other is invoked only to be negated, that is, to serve as a foil for the weak self-affirmation. The latter cannot tolerate real difference, but reduces the other to the same. Moreover, mutual recognition abolishes Deleuze's preferred hierarchical pluralism. It appears to abolish affirmative values and does not create any values save negative, *ressentiment*-laden, life-denying values. For Deleuze, nothing new emerges from recognition, there is no transformation or self-overcoming. In recognition the other is negated for the sake of imposing established, conventional values, the values of the herd.[109]

However, it should be noted that Deleuze thinks recognition only within the framework of an opposition between master and slave. The opposition between them is taken to be absolute: no mediation or reconciliation is possible. Mastery is purely affirmative (its negation is secondary and derivative) and servility is purely negative (its affirmation is secondary and derivative). Deleuze's attempt to think recognition within the exclusive opposition between master and slave comes right out of Kojève: the concept of recognition is completely identified with opposition, which in turn is conceived as absolute and incapable of mediation. Deleuze fails to note that it is Kojève, not Hegel, who substitutes opposition for difference and thereby provides the negations that *ressentiment*

---

108. Descombes, *MFP*, 161.

109. Incidentally, Hegel also described something like *ressentiment* and herd morality in his aphorism: "No man is a hero to his valet; not however because the man is not a hero, but because the valet is only a valet" (*PhS*, §665, 404). Hegel observes that this game of *ressentiment* is played by juxtaposing the universal aspect of the hero's action with the particularity of the hero as a finite fallible individual, thus negating that universal dimension by reducing it to the level and dimension of mere contingent particularity. In addition, *ressentiment* denigrates heroic accomplishments as self-serving.

needs in order to thrive.[110] For Deleuze, the alternatives are *either* the pure nondialectical self-affirmation of mastery that affirms difference *or* the dialectical, negative self-affirmation of the slave that negates and undermines difference and alterity in favor of the herd. Thus Deleuze believes Hegel and Nietzsche are irreconcilable.

But this betrays a failure to understand reciprocal recognition in Hegel's sense. The Hegelian 'We' is no herd morality but involves its own critique of morality and 'the subject'. The 'We' is constituted, not by saying 'no' to an other, but to oneself, that is, to the self-aggrandizement that Deleuze appears to favor. The union of selves in the 'We' is not an expression of a blind will to power but conditional on *Freigabe* that allows selves to be and affirms them in their individuality as members. It cannot be overemphasized that for Hegel the 'We' arises from an ethically transformed individuality that allows the other to be and affirms the other in its difference. Hegel's 'We' and ethical life are determinate, articulated universals and not herd morality in Nietzsche's sense. The herd morality reflects a homogeneity that reflects the abstract universal that excludes particularity and difference, rather than Hegel's determinate universal. There is no equivalent in Kojève, Deleuze, or Nietzsche to Hegel's 'We' or his intersubjective concept of a mediated ethical self-overcoming.[111] Lacking such a determinate social universal, Deleuze and Nietzsche reinforce or reinstate the individualism that they criticize.

Moreover, Deleuze's attempt to think master and slave differently from Hegel, that is, without relation or comparison, ultimately fails. For Deleuze, differential self-affirmation affirms pure difference; that is, the master supposedly does not relate to or compare himself with the slave. There is no internal negation, and mastery does not contain within itself the seeds of its own subversion. Hence mastery is supposed to issue in sheer difference and hierarchical pluralism. This means that "the relation of master to slave should not be superimposable upon that of slave to master. In one it is a relation of difference; in the other a relation of opposition. But if this is so, then . . . there can be no relationship between master and slave. . . . The worlds of master and slave being separate, the master will never be obliged to question his difference from the slave, nor the slave his opposition to the master. The master must not even be capable of recognizing the slave, like Aristotle's God who is ignorant of matter."[112]

Deleuze's attempt to separate the master from the servile morality fails, be-

110. Deleuze, *Nietzsche and Philosophy*, 196. Breazeale notes that "Deleuze seems to have little appetite for actually reading Hegel" and that the way Deleuze draws his contrast between Hegel and Nietzsche raises "serious questions concerning his competence as a student of Hegel" ("The Hegel-Nietzsche Problem," sec. 4). Butler also wonders how, if Deleuze were correct in his assessment that Hegel and dialectic are weighed down by the spirit of gravity, the bacchanalian revel Hegel mentions in the preface to the *Phenomenology* could have gotten under way (*SD*, 209).
111. See Greene, Hegel's 'Unhappy Consciousness' and Nietzsche's 'Slave Morality'."
112. Descombes, *MFP*, 164–165.

cause, as several interpreters have pointed out, even for Nietzsche, master morality and servile morality constitute an opposition and thus are relative to each other. Keith Ansell-Pearson maintains that, contrary to Deleuze, "the active forces require the opposition of the reactive forces in order to define and assert themselves as active. . . . Unlike Deleuze's thought, Nietzsche's rests on principles of domination and hierarchy. It is only through a comparison of values that the master's affirmation of noble values can take place."[113] Hierarchy is a relation of sorts, namely, an aristocratic relation. It presupposes an opposition drawn from competition and comparison. This tacit reference and relation to other is inherent in Deleuze's very terminology, to wit, *differential* self-affirmation. Descombes rightly wonders whether it is possible to conceive of an evaluation of a noble sort that is not inherently comparative, that does not imply a comparison with and relation to an other or others. Difference itself is a form of relation. If it were really possible to have done with the other, such that the other is not a presupposition of or present in differential self-affirmation, "then Deleuze ought not to say that 'the master affirms his difference,' but that 'he affirms his *identity.*'"[114] But there is more: in taking difference in the direction of aristocratic hierarchical pluralism, Deleuze, following Kojève and Nietzsche, provokes the very *ressentiment* and servile revolt that is supposed to be overcome.[115] Deleuze not only undermines his own project, he also falls short of Hegel's account of the overcoming of mastery and slavery in reciprocal recognition and liberation.[116]

This ensemble of criticisms confirms that Deleuze conceives recognition only at a subordinate or penultimate level, the level of opposition between master and slave. It also confirms Houlgate's assessment of Nietzsche, to wit, "Nietzsche fails to free philosophy from the metaphysical conception of the subject as something isolated and independent because he fails to free philosophy from the form of oppositional thinking, and thus conceives the 'true' subject as confronting and asserting itself against—that is, in opposition to— . . ."[117] In short, Deleuze's and Nietzsche's conceptions of self-overcoming and differential self-affirmation fall back into the very bourgeois individualism and evoke the *ressentiment* that they seek to overcome. In spite of Nietzsche's criticism of romanticism, he has not overcome it but only offered another version of it.[118] Deleuze's nominalism only further entrenches such individualism.

113. Keith Ansell-Pearson, *An Introduction to Nietzsche as Political Thinker* (Cambridge: Cambridge University Press, 1994), 115.

114. Descombes, *MFP*, 166.

115. See William E. Connolly, *Political Theory and Modernity* (Oxford: Blackwell, 1988), 159–160; on Nietzsche's aristocratism and its social-political problems, see Ansell-Pearson, *An Introduction to Nietzsche.*

116. *E*, §436 Zusatz.

117. Houlgate, *Hegel, Nietzsche, and the Critique of Metaphysics*, 184.

118. R. F. Beerling argues that Nietzsche, while a critic of romanticism, fails to overcome it. See his "Hegel und Nietzsche," *Hegel Studien* 1 (Bonn: Bouvier Verlag, 1961), 244–245.

Hegel's comment on Fichte and romantic irony may also serve as his comment on Nietzschean aristocratic self-overcoming and Deleuzian differential self-affirmation.

> Every content which is to have value for the ego is only posited and recognized by the ego itself. Whatever is, is only by the instrumentality of the ego, and what exists by my instrumentality I can equally well annihilate again. . . . The ego can remain lord and master of everything, and in no sphere of morals, law, things human and divine, profane and sacred, is there anything that would not first have to be laid down by the ego and could not equally well be destroyed by it. Consequently everything genuinely and independently real becomes only a show, not true and genuine on its own account or through itself, but a mere appearance due to the ego in whose power and caprice and at whose free disposal it remains.[119]

For Hegel, Deleuzian differential self-affirmation would imply the vanity, the emptiness of everything other than itself. "If the ego remains at this standpoint, everything appears to it as null and void, except its own subjectivity, which therefore becomes hollow and empty and itself mere vanity."[120] It is but a short step to the aesthetic play of differences so prized as an antidote to moralism's seriousness and gravity. While rejecting the seriousness of morality as the point where conscience becomes evil, Hegel also notes that the reduction of everything to the play of differences, especially aristocratic differences, has problems of its own because it empties everything of value save the self, and then it empties the self. The self is insufficient to serve as the source or foundation of normative culture and ethics.

In contrast to the aesthetic play of differences, Hegel believes that there is a proper sense of seriousness: "Genuine seriousness comes about only through a substantial interest, a matter that has intrinsic worth, [such as] truth, ethical life, etc., such that I become something essential for myself only insofar as I immerse myself in such intrinsic value and become conformed to it in my knowing and acting."[121] Further, Hegel criticizes aristocratic aestheticism for looking down on the rest of humanity for whom right and ethical life count as something solid, obligatory, and essential, and explaining such attitudes away as "restrictive," "trivial," and "banal."[122] To Hegel's eyes, such aristocratic difference that shuns all determinacy and relation as herd morality is not genuine freedom but the hell of inescapable, solipsistic individualism: "In the poets . . . we find Hell and damnation expressly identified as being bound forever to one's subjective deed, being alone with what is most peculiarly one's own; it is a deathless consideration of this possession."[123] Liberation from such a hell is

---

119. Hegel, *Aesthetik*, 13:93–94; *Aesthetics*, 64–65.
120. Hegel, *Aesthetik*, 13:93–94; *Aesthetics*, 66.
121. Hegel, *Aesthetik*, 13:94; *Aesthetics*, 66.
122. Hegel, *Aesthetik*, 13:94–95; *Aesthetics*, 66.
123. Hegel, *FK*, 146–147. Hegel refers to Dante's *Inferno* and Goethe's *Orestes* as well as to Jacobi's *Woldemar*.

found in relationships of reciprocal recognition and intersubjectively mediated self-overcoming that come as an unexpected gift and deliverance.

Daniel Breazeale has pointed out a contradiction in Deleuze's critique of mutual recognition.[124] On the one hand, Deleuze treats recognition as inherently servile, in contrast with the master's differential self-affirmation. On the other hand, Deleuze argues that genuine self-affirmation demands recognition by another, which of course is Hegel's point. In his final chapter, Deleuze returns to the question of affirmation. He writes,

> Affirmation is the enjoyment and play of its own difference. . . . What is the play of difference in affirmation? Affirmation is posited for the first time as multiplicity, becoming and chance. For multiplicity is the difference of one thing from another, becoming is difference from self and chance is difference 'between all' or distributive difference. Affirmation is then divided in two, difference is reflected in the affirmation of affirmation: the moment of reflection where a second affirmation takes the first as its object. . . . [I]n this way affirmation is redoubled: *as object of the second affirmation it is affirmation itself affirmed, redoubled affirmation, difference raised to the highest power.*[125]

Note that according to Deleuze affirmation is doubled. This recalls the theme of the doubling of consciousness we have found in Fichte and Schelling and with which Hegel's analysis of recognition begins. This doubling is an affirmation of affirmation, in which difference (the first affirmation) is raised to the highest power.

It is difficult to know what this means. If difference is really raised to the highest power, does it require recognition? If not, why the double affirmation? And if it does require recognition, what is left of the earlier polemics against Hegel and, in particular, Deleuze's claim that the need for recognition is inherently servile? Deleuze would have failed, fortunately in my view, to maintain the utter separation between Nietzschean and Hegelian accounts of master/slave on which his anti-Hegelian reading of Nietzsche depends.

Further, how would the affirmation of difference differ, if at all, from Hegel's *Freigabe*? Deleuze asserts that "to affirm is not to take responsibility for, to take on the burden of what is, but to release, to set free what lives."[126] This seems to be a restatement of Hegel's point, camouflaged by the rhetoric of opposition. However, does this assertion have an intersubjective sense for Deleuze? I doubt that it does. To set free what lives is an act of self-overcoming of the *Übermensch*; such self-affirmation, as pure affirmation of difference, if taken radically, seems to end in radical separation and nominalist atomism that undermine recognition. On the other hand, if release is understood within the context of recognition and the doubling of selves, Deleuze's talk about re-

---

124. Breazeale, "The Hegel-Nietzsche Problem," n. 15.
125. Deleuze, *Nietzsche and Philosophy*, 188–189. Italics mine.
126. Ibid., 185.

leasing and setting free what lives would be similar, if not indistinguishable, from Hegel's account of the *Freigabe*. Once again Deleuze would have failed to maintain his separation and opposition between Hegel and Nietzsche.

However, Deleuze's remarks about doubling and affirmation of affirmation probably fall short of a reciprocal recognition in Hegel's sense. There remains an asymmetry in that 'Ariadne' seems to affirm Dionysius, but her affirmation of his affirmation seems unrequited. It is as if she remains a fiancée who never consummates a relationship; her relationship, as expounded by Deleuze, is without reciprocity or common identity.

Derrida and the 'Ethics of Deconstruction'

In the previous sections we have established that, owing in no small measure to the Hegel renaissance in France led by Kojève and Hyppolite which since 1968 has entered an anti-Hegel phase, Hegel has been at the center of contemporary philosophical debates and disputes about intersubjectivity and the possibility of ethics. Further, although Kojève placed the struggle for recognition at the center of his Hegel interpretation and theory of action, recognition was grasped at a penultimate level of incomplete mediation, or, as conflict, struggle, that is, as essentially master and slave. Kojève produced a distorted but influential reading of Hegel that falls back into the romantic individualism that was the target of Hegel's critique. Although Sartre repeatedly flirted with both Hegel and the concept of recognition, especially in his *Notebooks for an Ethics*, his dialectical nominalism undermined the possibility of an ethics and led him to remark that today ethics is both necessary and impossible. Kojève's oppositional, heroic individualist reading in turn facilitated the turn from Hegel to Nietzsche and the claim that the desire for recognition is fundamentally servile, and that such servility taints not only Hegel's master and slave but also Hegel himself.

What needs to be underscored here is that none of these studies has appreciated the full significance of recognition as a topic in its own right, much less explored its significance for ethics and for Hegel's ethics in particular. Given their misidentification of recognition with master/slave, Kojève and his followers have simply passed over the question whether recognition could have and does have any significance for ethics besides a negative one. Thus they have passed over the affirmative significance mutual recognition has for both Fichte and Hegel in their ethical and political theories. Instead, the anti-Hegel movement in recent French philosophy has continued a trajectory begun by Kojève by aligning itself with Nietzsche and Heidegger. This alignment keeps a certain interest in ethics alive but takes it in an increasing critical and skeptical direction. Ethics has become more a question, an exposure and interruption of "dangerous" fascistic tendencies toward unity in traditional modes of thought, including traditional 'ethics'.[127]

This 'ethics of interruption' appears to rest on a suspicion of all unities and communities, and ethics itself, as inherently dangerous. Beneath such suspicion may well be a view of the other and of relationship as inherently negative. Translating the 'hermeneutics of suspicion' into the language of intersubjectivity, it is as if the other functions only negatively as an *Anstoß*. No affirmative relation to the other-*Anstoß* is possible; or if possible, affirmative relations are nevertheless suspicious or "dangerous." Without wishing to appear innocent or naive concerning dangers, it should be pointed out that danger here seems to function as a sign for potential problems inherent in all intersubjective-social unions, communities, and institutions. However, it is one thing to acknowledge the possibility of problems in communities and institutions—such as Hegel does in his account of master slave—and quite another to maintain that intersubjectivity, community, and institutions are themselves problems, dangers, and so on. Such is the view of extreme self-sufficient individualism inherent in Nietzschean mastery and Deleuzian differential self-affirmation.

In light of these issues, and in view of the positive significance of reciprocal recognition in Hegel's ethics and ethical life, I want to examine Simon Critchley's recent proposal for an ethics of deconstruction, that, like Hegel, seeks to bring together a negative critical aspect (represented by Derrida) and a positive constructive proposal (represented by Levinas). I will seek to show that the elements of Critchley's proposal not only reiterate Hegel's constructive moves but also presuppose the concept of recognition.

Critchley begins with a problem: how can there be an ethics of deconstruction if ethics belongs to the philosophical tradition that deconstruction deconstructs? If ethics, traditionally conceived, is founded on and derivative from ontology, and ontology as metaphysics of presence falls under deconstruction's *Differance* and correlative double reading, can there be an *ethics* of deconstruction at all? Critchley's first task is to defend Derridean deconstruction against the charge that its double reading based on the play of *Differance* is a form of ethical skepticism and nihilism. He begins by conceding that Derridean deconstruction does indeed make ethics problematic. As traditionally understood, ethics is founded on philosophy and ontology, both of which fall under deconstruction. However, Critchley argues that the deconstructive double reading of texts, the clotural reading, is motivated by an unconditional ethical imperative, namely, openness to what is other: "Clotural reading is history read from the standpoint of the victims of that history."[128] The ethical imperative places text in a larger interhuman context.

127. In addition to the work of Foucault and Derrida, see Scott, *The Question of Ethics*, and Critchley, *An Ethics of Deconstruction.*
128. Critchley, *Ethics of Deconstruction*, 30.

Critchley acknowledges that the concept of an unconditional ethical imperative is close to Kant's categorical imperative. However, Kant's categorical imperative embodies the claim that reason by itself is practical, capable of generating its own ends. The imperative of deconstruction is the duty to be open to alterity.[129] This could be read as a simple elaboration of Kantian respect for humanity, whether in oneself or in another, always as an end in itself and never merely as a means. However, in a move similar to the post-Kantian development of the concept of recognition from Fichte to Hegel, Critchley argues that respect for law presupposes a more concrete respect for the other person. The encounter with the other is "the condition of possibility for an experience of the law."[130] Like Fichte and Hegel, Critchley acknowledges intersubjectivity as the condition and threshold of ethics.

This turn to an introduction of the other as the condition and criterion of ethics means that Derridean deconstruction must be supplemented with Levinas. Critchley defends such a move by citing Derrida's own acknowledgment of substantive agreement with Levinas's ethics.[131] While traditional Kantian ethics falls under deconstruction, Levinas's proposals concerning the face of the other involve an alternative conception of ethics as a nonontological, or anti-ontological, first philosophy. The event of the face establishes for Levinas the priority of ethics over ontology. Thus Levinas makes common cause with Derridean deconstruction in criticizing and disrupting Western ontology and logo-centrism. The goal of deconstruction is to locate a point of otherness within a philosophical conceptuality and then to deconstruct this conceptuality from the position of alterity.[132]

Derrida can identify such a point of otherness only negatively through a double reading and the experience of undecidability. Thus deconstruction can interrupt the metaphysics of presence and closure, but it cannot provide any affirmative ethical criterion of its own. For then it would abandon the strategy of double reading and undecidability. On the other hand, Levinas provides this point of otherness in an affirmative sense: the interhuman is not neutral or undecidable; it is asymmetrically structured by the priority of the other over the subject (the same). The event of the face provides the ethical norm and imperative for deconstruction, as well as the criterion of practical decision that suspends Derridean undecidability.

The critical issue raised by Critchley's proposal is the problem of moving from Derridean undecidability, which suspends decision, to Levinasian responsibility, which implies affirmativity that suspends undecidedness in decision.

---

129. Ibid., 41.   130. Ibid., 48.

131. In a 1986 interview on the subject of ethics, Derrida asserts, "Faced with a thinking like that of Levinas, I never have an objection. I am ready to subscribe to everything that he says. That does not mean that I think the same thing in the same way, but in this respect the differences are very difficult to determine" (*Altérités*, 74, cited in Critchley, *Ethics of Deconstruction*, 9–10).

132. Critchley, *Ethics of Deconstruction*, 26.

In the double reading, the alterity that is invoked is a negative alterity that interrupts and suspends the dominant reading of the text. Double reading is a contemporary version of the principle of equipollence of ancient skepticism: that to every argument an opposing argument of equal validity can be constructed. This produces an equipollence or antinomy that undermines immediate dogmatic certainty.[133] Equipollence thus leads to the skeptical epoché, or suspension of judgment.

In bringing together Derridean deconstruction and Levinas, Critchley can point to the fact that both operate skeptically vis-à-vis the logocentric tradition. In fact, they can be seen as complementary forms of skepticism about that tradition. Derridean double reading has a negative critical function, not unlike Kant, of preserving a possible opening for alterity.[134] The positive normative sense of alterity is provided by Levinas. However, as Critchley concedes, the problem remains, how to move from Derridean undecidability to Levinasian decision and responsibility for the other?[135] The difficulty lies in the fact that deconstruction provides no adequate account of decision in the affirmative sense; how could it and remain true to double reading? Critchley apparently subordinates deconstructive double reading and questioning to a prior responsibility; that is, he sides with Levinas against Derrida.[136] But if this so, then Derridean undecidability does not, as Critchley maintains, provide a prior condition of possibility for the event of the face. Rather deconstructive undecidability is something that must be overcome, and is overcome, *aufgehoben*, in the face to face. In this respect, Critchley's proposal is close to Fichte and Hegel.

This shows that the concept of recognition in Hegel's sense remains relevant to the contemporary interest in constructing an ethic. The issue that Hegel

133. Hegel's important essay "Relationship of Skepticism to Philosophy" (1802) (in *Between Kant and Hegel: Texts in the Development of Post-Kantian Idealism*, ed. George Di Giovanni and H. S. Harris, 313–362 [Albany: SUNY Press, 1985]) is overlooked by those who seek to portray Hegel as the philosopher of the subject and as the culmination of the metaphysics of presence. In this essay Hegel maintains the superiority of ancient to modern skepticism, since the latter is only a partial skepticism directed against reason while remaining dogmatic about sense perception. Ancient skepticism turned its critical arsenal against sense perception as well. Further, Hegel believes that Kant's antinomies of pure reason represent a modern statement of the principle of equipollence. The same equipollence procedure is followed by Fichte in his first introduction to the *Wissenschaftslehre* (1794), in the theoretically undecidable antinomy between dogmatism and idealism. Hegel's dialectic has its origins in his appreciation of ancient skepticism and equipollence. However, for Hegel the target of skepticism is not philosophy but dogmatism. The skeptical tropes, including equipollence, are effective against dogmatism but powerless against philosophy because the demands that they embody are rational demands. The rational demand is to allow the other that dogmatism suppresses to come on the scene and to qualify and mediate the original dogmatic standpoint. In his *Encyclopedia* he presents skepticism as the 'inhibited' negative side of an affirmative dialectic. See Forster, *Hegel and Skepticism*; Williams, *Recognition*, chaps. 5–6; Williams, "Hegel and Skepticism."

134. Critchley, *Ethics of Deconstruction*, 96.

135. Ibid., 95–96, 189–200.

136. Ibid., 195: "The liberty and choice of the questioning attitude are subordinated to a prior responsibility."

identified in Fichte—the contradiction between the concept of reciprocal recognition and the loss of trust and confidence that undermines recognition and legitimates coercion—continues in different versions and shapes in contemporary philosophy. Hegel identified recognition as the threshold of the ethical, namely, when the other comes to count; he went on to identify mutual-reciprocal recognition as the condition of possibility on which ethics and ethical life depend. Without affirmative self-recognition in other, ethics and ethical life would be impossible. The only alternative to ethical life would be a reduction of ethics to the question of ethics, or a critical-negative ethics of interruption and deconstruction. A rejection of affirmative self-recognition in other would undermine not only Hegel but also Levinas and the dialogical tradition.

Having injected Hegel's concept of recognition into this discussion, I want to examine briefly both Derrida's and Levinas's discussions of Hegel. In the first case the critical question is whether Derrida reads Hegel in such a way that the concept of recognition might have plausibility for Derrida. In the second case, the question is whether Levinas's account of the face is opposed to Hegel's concept of recognition.

In his essay "Differance" [137] Derrida identifies a radical difference, a difference that he claims is not dialectical or oppositional, a difference not subject to but beyond dialectics, which he calls *differance*. [138] *Differance* eludes direct communication. As Derrida "expounds" it, it both is and is not a transcendental concept. *Differance* is both the quasi-transcendental condition of possible universal structures and the impossibility of such structures ever fulfilling their transcendental foundational role. It is difficult to know how to take such assertions, because to the extent that differance is a transcendental concept, it invokes as its condition of possibility the very thing it criticizes, namely, transcendental grounding. On the other hand, if *differance* were a transcendental condition of possibility, it would be subject to its own criticism; that is, it would be prevented from filling its peculiar transcendental role of disrupting universal structures. These difficulties mean that differance can be discussed only indirectly and is "demonstrated" chiefly in the reading, that is, double reading, of philosophical texts. *Differance* is not so much a principle as a movement of dissociation, or errancy. It is not a concept, or category of being; it is not a realm but the subversion of every realm. [139] Derrida identifies "the enigma of difference" thus:

137. Jacques Derrida, "Differance," in *Speech and Phenomena*, trans. D. Allison (Evanston: Northwestern University Press, 1973), 129–160.

138. He notes that the verb *differ* (*differer*) differs from itself. On the one hand, it can mean difference, distinction, inequality, and discernibility; on the other, it can mean deferral, i.e., the interposition of a delay, the interval of spacing and temporalizing that puts off until later the possible that is presently impossible. These two senses of difference, differ and defer, have a common root. This common root is a sameness that is nevertheless not identical, and which Derrida names differance.

139. Derrida, "Differance," 153.

How can we conceive of differance as a systematic detour which, within the element of the same, always aims at either finding again the pleasure or presence that had been deferred . . . and at the same time, how can we, on the other hand, conceive of difference as the relation to an impossible presence, as an expenditure without reserve, as an irreparable loss of presence, an irreversible wearing down of energy, or indeed as a death instinct and relation that apparently breaks up any economy? It is evident—it is evidence itself—that system and non-system, the same and the absolutely other, etc., cannot be conceived together.[140]

Derrida raises anew and radicalizes the problem of the difference first formulated by Fichte and Hegel. He is not unaware of this historical background, for he tells us that in pursuing differance he continues the project of philosophy under the privileged heading of Hegelianism.[141] This does not mean that Derrida agrees with Hegel; far from it. He believes that Hegel seeks to "tame" the difference and master it. Difference is both recognized and yet refused in its radicality. Hegel overlooks or represses alterity, when he regards difference as a moment of identity. To counter what he takes to be Hegel's reductionism, Derrida both seeks and asserts a difference that is an impossible presence and thus is antisystem.

Derrida develops his critique of Hegel in another essay, "From Restricted to General Economy: A Hegelianism Without Reserve,"[142] in which he pursues a reading of Hegel and the difference, through a reading of Georges Bataille.[143] Bataille is an important figure for Derrida and for our understanding of Derrida's deconstruction of Hegel, not least because he focuses on Hegel's account of master and slave and, following Kojève and Nietzsche, takes the servile consciousness as central to Hegel's view. In Bataille's reading, the "laboring" of the Hegelian servile consciousness is motivated by a demand for meaning. Bataille's reading of Hegel appeals to Derrida because by conflating the Hegelian and Nietzschean servile consciousness, Bataille "gets underneath" and displaces Hegel by demonstrating an excess, a difference, a negation, that resists the preservation of meaning in the *Aufhebung*.

Derrida makes this case in a section entitled "The Epoch of Meaning: Lordship and Sovereignty."[144] He focuses on the life and death struggle that precedes the emergence of master and slave. "Putting life at stake is a moment in the constitution of meaning. . . . It is an obligatory stage in the history of self-consciousness."[145] But there are two conditions that must obtain for this to work. The first is that the master must stay alive in order to enjoy what he has

---

140. Ibid., 150–151.   141. Ibid., 151.
142. This essay has been translated in *Writing and Difference*, trans. A. Bass (Chicago: University of Chicago Press, 1978), 251–277.
143. Derrida, "Differance," 151. For a critical discussion of this essay, see Flay, "Hegel, Derrida and Bataille's Laughter."
144. Derrida, "From Restricted to General Economy," 254.
145. Ibid.

won by risking his life. The second is that at the end of this progression, the truth of the independent consciousness is the consciousness of the slave. Derrida comments, "When servility becomes lordship, it keeps within it the trace of its repressed origin. . . . It is this dissymmetry, this absolute privilege given to the slave that Bataille did not cease to meditate. The truth of the master is in the slave; and the slave become a master remains a 'repressed' slave. Such is the condition of meaning, of history, of discourse, of philosophy, etc."[146] On this reading, therefore, Hegel's *Phenomenology of Spirit* is a history of the servile consciousness and its ascetic ideal.

Derrida believes that, having raised the demand that philosophy tarry with negative, namely, death, Hegel backs away from both death and the negative because they threaten the epoch of meaning. To rush headlong toward death is to risk the absolute loss of meaning. This is not what those entering the struggle for recognition had hoped to win. Like the slave, Hegel is unwilling to risk this loss. Consequently, says Derrida, in part selectively quoting Hegel, "Hegel called this mute and unproductive death, this death pure and simple, abstract negativity, in opposition to 'the negation characteristic of consciousness which cancels in such a way that it preserves and maintains what is sublated, and thereby survives its being sublated."[147] In backing away from death, negativity, and meaninglessness, and opting for determinate negation, Derrida believes that Hegel shows his own servility and adherence to the ascetic ideal: better any meaning than none at all.

Derrida next proceeds to identify the critical issues raised by Bataille's concept of sovereignty, which is another version of Deleuze's differential self-affirmation.

> Burst of laughter from Bataille. Through a ruse of life, that is, of reason, life has stayed alive. Another concept of life has been surreptitiously put in its place, to remain there, never to be exceeded, any more than reason is ever to be exceeded. This life is not natural life, the biological existence put at stake in lordship, but an essential life that is welded to the first one, holding it back, making it work for the constitution of self-consciousness, truth, and meaning. Through this recourse to the *Aufhebung*, which conserves the stakes, remains in control of the play, limiting it and elaborating it by giving it form and meaning, this economy of life restricts itself to conservation, to circulation and self-reproduction as the reproduction of meaning; henceforth everything covered by lordship collapses into comedy. The independence of self-consciousness becomes laughable at the moment when it liberates itself by enslaving itself, when it starts to work, that is, when it enters dialectics. Laughter alone exceeds dialectics and the dialectician; it burst out only on the basis of an absolute renunciation of meaning, an absolute risking of death.[148]

Derrida believes that Bataille has correctly identified Hegel's blind spot. Hegel raises the issue of death and abstract negation, only to back away into determi-

---

146. Ibid., 254–255.   147. Ibid., 255.   148. Ibid., 255–256.

nate negation for the sake of preserving meaning. This is to show, without acknowledging it, that death is a radical negativity that can no longer be determined as negativity within a process or system. Within systematic discourse, Derrida believes, negativity is not genuinely negative but simply a dialectical resource; it is always the underside and accomplice of positivity and meaning. "In naming the without-reserve of absolute expenditure 'abstract negativity', Hegel, through precipitation, blinded himself to that which he had laid bare under the rubric of abstract negativity. And did so through precipitation towards the seriousness of meaning and the security of knowledge." [149]

However, to take the negative seriously "is convulsively to tear apart the negative side, that which makes it the reassuring other surface of the positive; and it is to exhibit within the negative . . . that which can no longer be called negative . . . precisely because it has no reserved underside, because it can no longer permit itself to be converted into positivity, because it can no longer collaborate with the continuous linking up of meaning, concept. . . . Hegel saw this without seeing it, showed it while concealing it." [150] For Derrida, the "explanation" of Hegel's simultaneous showing and concealing death is his servility and acceptance of the ascetic ideal. "In interpreting negativity as labor, in betting for discourse, meaning, history, etc., Hegel has bet against play, against chance. He has blinded himself to the possibility of his own bet, to the fact that the conscientious suspension of play was itself a phase of play." [151]

Instead of "Hegelian" mastery, which is servility, Bataille and Derrida speak of a sovereignty that has Nietzschean roots. This sovereignty differs from "Hegelian" servile mastery in that it accepts Nietzsche's critique of the ascetic ideal and gives up the demand for meaning. However, as Derrida notes, the renunciation of meaning is highly problematic: "In sacrificing meaning, sovereignty submerges the possibility of discourse." [152] How then can sovereignty as the alternative to meaning and the ascetic ideal communicate itself? Derrida notes that there is only one discourse, and it is significative; here one cannot get around Hegel. To adopt a discourse that is play without rules simply allows discourse about the excess of discourse to be domesticated and subordinated better than ever. To avoid this risk, which is the modern risk, "poetry must be 'accompanied by an affirmation of sovereignty' which provides, Bataille says in an admirable, untenable formulation which could serve as the heading for everything we are attempting to reassemble here as the form and torment of his writing, 'the commentary on its absence of meaning.'" [153] However, Derrida is not willing to follow Bataille all the way. He offers a Hegelian self-reflexive criticism that Bataille's position is untenable because sovereignty seems to end, like skepticism, in silence and self-erasure. Bataille obviously backs away from sheer nonassertion and silence. But then his position turns out to be Hegelian of sorts because it attributes a meaning, within discourse, to the absence of meaning.

149. Ibid., 259.   150. Ibid., 259–260.   151. Ibid., 260.
152. Ibid., 261.   153. Ibid.

Bataille's sovereignty is supposed to be a liberation from 'servile mastery'. But this "liberation" can only be expressed negatively, as Derrida proceeds to do in a series of quite important negations. Sovereignty has no identity, is not self for itself; it does not govern itself or anything else, it does not subordinate anything, nor is it subordinate to anything. It must forget itself as opposed to *Erinnerung*. From our perspective the most important negation of all is that "it must no longer seek to be *recognized*."[154] Sovereignty must renounce recognition because to seek recognition is servile.[155] Thus Bataille writes: "If one goes to the end, one must erase oneself, undergo solitude, suffer harshly from it, renounce being recognized: one must be there as if absent, deranged and submit without will or hope, being elsewhere. Thought . . . must be buried alive. I publish this knowing it misconstrued in advance, necessarily so."[156] Clearly mutual recognition and relationship are excluded from Bataille's sovereignty, just as they are excluded by Deleuze's differential self-affirmation. In short, "sovereignty is absolute only when it is absolved from every relationship and keeps itself in the night of the secret."[157]

Derrida comments that "sovereignty dissolves the values of meaning, truth. . . . This is why the discourse that it opens is not true, truthful or sincere."[158] He echoes and cites Sartre's comment on Bataille: "Here then is an invitation to lose ourselves without forethought, without counterpart, without salvation. Is it sincere? . . . For after all, M. Bataille writes, occupies a position at the Bibliotheque Nationale, reads, makes love, eats."[159] It is ironic that Sartre, who went to considerable trouble to show that sincerity is in bad faith, should raise this issue concerning Bataille. Moreover, in view of Sartre's rejection of Hegel, it is doubly ironic that Sartre's questioning of Bataille's sincerity and consistency is an essentially Hegelian self-reflexive criticism.

Derrida's essay ends inconclusively. Yet he seems to tilt toward Bataille against Hegel, even as he charges him with Hegelian tendencies, because Bataille's concept of sovereignty helps to formulate a nondialectical difference. From the standpoint of this difference, Hegel's treatment of death and the need for recognition appear to be servile, because, Derrida believes, both present different versions of the demand that difference be assimilated to identity. In apparently siding with Bataille against Hegel in regarding recognition as servile, Derrida embraces a radical difference.

Nevertheless, it is difficult to determine the extent of Derrida's agreement with Bataille, particularly Bataille's reading of Hegel. On the one hand, Derrida surely 'knows' that Bataille is following Kojève's reading because it is im-

154. Ibid., 265. Italics mine.
155. As the translator asserts in his note, p. 336.
156. Derrida, "From Restricted to General Economy," 266.
157. Ibid.
158. Ibid., 270.
159. Sartre, *Situations* I, cited in Derrida, "From Restricted to General Economy," 337.

possible to miss. Apparently Derrida endorses this reading in his plea contra Hegel for a Hegelianism without reserve. On the other hand, in another essay, "Violence and Metaphysics," Derrida discusses Levinas and attacks Levinas's criticism of Hegel. Here Derrida *defends* Hegel against Levinas. The crucial point to be noted is that this defense requires a reading of Hegel quite different from Kojève's, and from the reading Derrida offers in the Bataille essay. A different reading of Hegel is necessary if for no other reason than that the "Hegel" Levinas seems to attack is Kojève's "Hegel": that is, the fundamental inequality of recognition reduces the other to the same. There are three points to be noted. (1) Derrida observes that to construe the other as a mere mundane entity, as the same, is the basic gesture of violence.[160] (2) The interhuman relation of the dialogical tradition is not to be found in Husserl but requires a posttranscendental move. Derrida formulates this post-Husserl, posttranscendental move as an intersubjective economy. He says that the intersubjective 'economy' is a transcendental symmetry of two empirical asymmetries. Specifically, the other, for me, is an ego that I know to be in relation to me as to an other.[161] This intersubjective 'economy' is championed by Levinas, for whom relation to other is ethical, and ethics is first philosophy, and as such takes priority over ontology. (3) However, Derrida then goes on to ask, "Where have these movements been better described than in *The Phenomenology of Mind*?"[162] This remark suggests that Derrida regards Hegel's concept of recognition and intersubjectivity as at least on par with, if not superior to, Levinas's account of the interhuman relationship. Moreover, Derrida identifies the issue of reciprocal recognition in Hegel, and, unlike his position in the Bataille essay, he defends it while charging that Levinas has not appreciated it sufficiently.

There is little doubt that Derrida 'knows better' than to accept uncritically Kojéve-Bataille's interpretation of Hegel, master/slave, and so on. His reference to Hegel as formulating Levinas's vision of the interhuman relation better than Levinas himself has done suggests that he understands the difference between Kojève's and Hegel's understanding of recognition, and that for Hegel recognition is not simply identifiable with the master/slave relation. Derrida also understands the significance of reciprocal recognition as the symmetry of two asymmetries and regards it as an acceptable alternative to Levinas's formulation. Perhaps Derrida "saw this without seeing it, showed it while concealing it," and this is *his* blind spot vis-à-vis Hegel. If Derrida is serious in his positive appraisal of Hegelian mutual recognition, that is, if he is not just doing another double reading, this positive assessment of Hegel, and specifically Hegel's concept of recognition, would at the same time constitute a significant step on Derrida's part toward the possibility of intersubjectivity and ethics.

---

160. Jacques Derrida, "Violence and Metaphysics," in *Writing and Difference*, 125.
161. Ibid., 126.   162. Ibid.

Levinas:
Reciprocity and Totality in Question

Levinas is critical of Hegel, following the influential lead of Franz Rosenzweig.[163] He undoubtedly had Hegel in mind when he opposed infinity (the Other) to totality. He believes that in the passage from particular to universal that is central, not only to Buber's, but also to Hegel's concept of reciprocity, the other is leveled and reduced to the same. This leveling leads to the homogeneous state and totalitarianism.[164] Levinas repeats the familiar charge that Hegel's 'We' is a community that suppresses individuality and leads to totalitarianism.

A Levinasian line on reciprocal recognition might run as follows: Hegel's reciprocal recognition is insufficient. It merely reinscribes the individual within a whole, and thus self and other are reduced to the same. Further, the classical priority of the whole over the parts leads to totalitarianism. This charge depends on a concept of the whole as abstract identity that we have found Hegel criticizes and rejects. For Levinas, however, the other must take absolute priority over the subject, and such priority is expressed in an essential asymmetry and nonreciprocity, even heteronomy. Levinas does not discuss the issue of reciprocity explicitly in reference to Hegel. Nevertheless, the issue can be clarified somewhat by examining Levinas's critical response to Martin Buber. As noted above, Buber believes that relation involves an "essential reciprocity" between man and man. Buber extends and reformulates Hegel's point that spirit is not a subject that stands in contrast to an object; rather spirit, constituted by reciprocal recognition, is an intersubjectivity, an interhuman (*Zwischenmenschliche*) or 'between'. "In the beginning is not a substantial subject, but relation."[165] Relation for Buber is synonymous with reciprocity: "One should not try to delete the meaning of the relation: relation is reciprocity."[166]

Levinas both appreciates and criticizes Buber. It is difficult to determine precisely Levinas's relation to Buber because he has written two essays that reach contradictory assessments of Buber's position.[167] On the one hand, he praises

163. See Emmanuel Levinas, "Franz Rosenzweig: A Modern Jewish Thinker," in *Outside the Subject*, trans. Michael B. Smith (Stanford: Stanford University Press, 1993). Levinas told one interviewer that he simply borrowed Rosenzweig's critique of Hegel (Salomon Malka, *Lire Lévinas*, 2d ed. [Paris: Editions du Cerf, 1989], 105, cited in translator's introduction, *Outside the Subject*, xxii).

164. Levinas, "Outside the Subject," 15; cf. p. 50.

165. Buber, *I and Thou*, 69.

166. Ibid., 58; cf. pp. 67, 79.

167. Levinas, "Martin Buber and the Theory of Knowledge." This essay, which is highly critical, claiming that Buber, by his tacit acceptance of the traditional philosophy of the subject, undermined the I-Thou as an ethical relationship, was written in 1958. Levinas offers a strikingly different, more positive assessment of Buber in a later essay, "Martin Buber, Gabriel Marcel and Philosophy," that appears in *Martin Buber: A Centenary Volume*, ed. H. Gordon and J. Bloch (n.p.: KTAV, 1984). For a discussion of Levinas's complex and often changing relation to Buber, see Robert Bernasconi, "Failure of Communication as a Surplus," in *Provocation of Levinas*, ed. R. Bernasconi and D. Wood (New York: Routledge, 1988), 100–136.

Buber with originating dialogical philosophy and developing the theme of the interhuman. Levinas believes that dialogical philosophy breaks with classical philosophy of subjectivity. "The relation cannot be identified with a 'subjective' event because the I does not represent the Thou but meets it. . . . [T]he I-thou meeting does not take place in the subject but in the realm of being."[168] Thus dialogical philosophy is postmetaphysical and postfoundational.

On the other hand, Levinas criticizes Buber. The chief problem, he believes, is that Buber remains too close to classical philosophy of subjectivity with its substance metaphysics. For example, when Buber writes that in the beginning is the relation, his concern is to break with the view that individuals are unrelated atoms, complete in themselves. But Levinas would be cautious about assigning priority to the relation as such, because this might suggest not only that the relation is prior to the *relata*, it might lead to the dissolution of the *relata* themselves. In other words, assigning priority to the relation might be another version of the priority of the whole over its parts. Totality or holism might undermine the priority of the ethical. Levinas believes this is what happens in Hegel, Heidegger, and the Western tradition.

There are several issues here. First is the reciprocity of the interhuman relationship. Robert Bernasconi observes that Levinas is not always consistent in criticizing reciprocity and that his relation to Buberian reciprocity is complex and undergoes change.[169] Levinas does not want to make responsibility conditional on reciprocity and seeks to avoid a "tit-for-tat" external reciprocity. His criticism of external, conditional tit-for-tat reciprocity is similar to Hegel's criticism of the exploitative, atomistic ethos of civil society. Second, Levinas is critical of the concept of love, fearing that it involves or implies fusion, loss of limits and boundaries. Thus he would be suspicious of the We, the emergent universal consciousness or totality. Third, Levinas believes that the relation to the other is fundamentally asymmetrical and nonreciprocal. The face as event cannot be cognitively or emotionally mastered. The face is transcendent. "The way in which the other presents himself, exceeding the idea of the other in me, we here name face. . . . The notion of the face . . . brings us to a notion of a meaning prior to my *Sinngebung*, and thus independent of my initiative and power."[170] Whatever intersubjectivity may be, it does not mean a direct knowledge of or fusion with others. Consequently, separation is not eliminated but remains in intersubjective relations. Separation means that the intersubjective relation is "a relationship within an independence."[171]

At first glance, there appears to be a serious antinomy here. Hegel believes that reciprocal recognition is the telos of intersubjective and social relationships. Levinas believes, on the contrary, that if asymmetry is transcended, the resulting reciprocity implies a coequality that in turn implies that self and

---

168. Levinas, "Martin Buber and the Theory of Knowledge," 65.
169. Bernasconi, "Failure of Communication as a Surplus."
170. Levinas, *Totality and Infinity*, 51–52.
171. Ibid., 102.

other are leveled and totalized. When totalized, the other is denied, or reduced to the same; the other is neutralized by ontological universality and totality.

Levinas's rejection of reciprocity remains problematic. On the one hand, if the intersubjective relation is nonreciprocal and asymmetrical as Levinas claims, then the face commands and summons us from an irreducibly transcendent height. However, from such a "height" the face also remains pre-worldly and formal; like Kant's categorical imperative, it lacks determinate content.[172] Moreover, if intersubjectivity is asymmetrical, then love and friendship, insofar as these require reciprocity, appear to be impossible. But it seems wrong to deny that these are possible or that they are ethical. On the other hand, if intersubjectivity is characterized by reciprocity, then love and friendship, the enlarged mentality and *Geist*, are all possible.

Levinas believes that the ethical dimension of interhuman relation requires and is constituted by asymmetry. Hegel would agree that this asymmetry is the starting point of encounter but deny that it is permanent. Levinas's requirement of permanent asymmetry makes it appear as if the other who summons us to responsibility would lose his authoritative appeal as soon as he were to enter into relation or as soon as an affirmative reciprocal response is made or as soon as a We, community, or totality is constituted. Such a view presupposes that to enter into relation cancels independence and ethics. This presupposition is rejected by Hegel in his account of ethical life, including love, honor, and patriotism. Far from canceling independence, relation can enrich and strengthen independence. Further, for Hegel an asymmetrical, one-sided relation is no relation at all. Relation, if genuine, must be reciprocal. If relation is reciprocal, this means that the *relata* do not persist unchanged or unqualified in spite of relationship. If the *relata* remain absolute in relationship as Levinas asserts, such relation can only be something external to the *relata*. This is precisely the view of relation that dialogical philosophy seeks to overcome. Levinas also rejects this view of relation as external in his critique of tit-for-tat reciprocity that makes 'my' responsibility conditional on the other's responsibility.[173]

Does entering into reciprocal relation imply relativizing, loss of value, and/or freedom? Levinas apparently believes that it does. For this reason he continues to insist on the asymmetry of ethical/intersubjective relation. But he softens the asymmetry a bit. The asymmetry of intersubjectivity means that "the same and the other at the same time maintain themselves in relationship and absolve themselves from this relation, remain absolutely separated."[174] The 'whole' that

---

172. Levinas's insistence on radical asymmetry appears to resemble Sartre's position concerning the other as the subject of the look, the Other who looks at me. As Theunissen has observed, for Sartre the other as subject of the look is and remains preworldly; that is why the other-subject cannot be connected up with anything mundane or to which the *cogito* stands in a cognitive relation. See Theunissen, *The Other.*

173. Levinas, *Ethics and Infinity*, 96–98.

174. Levinas, *Totality and Infinity*, 102. Levinas charges Hegel and the tradition with favoring unity over multiplicity and difference. Thus he appropriates deconstruction and skepticism to criti-

is formed by I and Thou is a whole in which each remains independent and from which each can absolve itself. Levinas believes that Hegel denies this when he totalizes self and other. However, we have seen that Derrida criticizes and corrects Levinas's interpretation of Hegel on just this issue. The absolution of *relata* that Levinas wants, claims Derrida, is already there in Hegel. Derrida is correct.

Levinas's polemics against Hegel overlooks the latter's concept of recognition. Reciprocal recognition is possible only if each side renounces its attempt to steal the other's possibilities, acknowledges the other, and allows her to be. Release means allowing the other to be and accepting the other as she wants to be accepted, gives herself out to be, and so on. Allowing the other to be means to renounce attempts to control and master. The totality that is accomplished through reciprocal recognition is one in which its members are mutually accepted and allowed to be. Such relation is not something wholly external that leaves the *relata* unaffected. The self, in its relation to itself, is affected by the other. For Hegel, genuine community is not the abrogation but the realization of freedom: *bei sich im anderen zu sein*. In such a community recognition is not coerced as in master/slave but freely offered, and only because freely offered can it satisfy the need for recognition. Genuine mutual recognition cannot be coerced; and it can be freely given only if persons remain free in relationship.

When Levinas formulates his own conception of the interhuman against Buber's putative relational holism, he writes, "It should be observed that the act whereby the I withdraws and thus distances itself from the Thou or 'lets it be' in Heidegger's terms, is the same act which renders a union with it possible. In effect, there is no union worthy of the name except in the presence of this sort of otherness: union, *Verbundenheit*, is a manifestation of otherness." [175] This is Hegel's point. The similarity between Levinas's absolution and Hegel's *Freigabe* is obvious. Union with other presupposes that coercion and violence have been renounced and the other is allowed to be. For Hegel too intersubjective union—reciprocal recognition—is a manifestation of otherness. So understood, reciprocal recognition and relation are not the nemesis of freedom but the conditions within which responsible freedom is evoked and realized.

In view of recent interest in the question of ethics, as well as Simon Critchley's proposal for an ethics of deconstruction that grounds ethics normatively in affirmative relation to and responsibility for other, a Levinasian appreciation and appraisal of Fichte and Hegel are long overdue. This is not to deny important differences between deconstructive ethics and Hegel's. Derridean deconstruction appeals to the other as nonassimilable in order to prevent closure; hence it maintains the skeptical equipollence stance in order to interrupt the dogmatic move that levels the other and reduces it to immanence. Hegel would

---

cize metaphysics and totality while nevertheless presenting his own ethical views as if they are unaffected by this critique.

175. Levinas, "Martin Buber and the Theory of Knowledge," 66.

have understood this point, given his analysis of skepticism, as well as his defense of political toleration of dissenters. Derridean deconstruction makes an opening for the other but, according to Critchley, never gets beyond the opening. Hence its undecidability is a de facto ethical skepticism that must be supplemented by affirmative reference and relation to other, in Critchley's case, by Levinas. But in attempting to combine Derrida and Levinas, Critchley may only create an antinomy of 'decided undecidability' in which the moment of decision is "madness." That ethics appears as a kind of madness is a telling commentary on the plight of contemporary ethical thought; it is a version of Sartre's despairing comment that ethics is both necessary and impossible.

Hegel, on the other hand, believes that if ethics is possible, then the threshold of the ethical must not only be open toward the other as the horizon of decision, but also crossed in actually making decisions and commitments consistent with ethical life and freedom. When that threshold is crossed, self and other both must count, mutually recognize each other, and be ethically transformed. The result of a mutual recognition that includes union, self-overcoming, and *Freigabe* is a relationship and community in which freedom is not only preserved but also enhanced and enriched, namely, ethical life. Ethical life is a non-totalitarian, articulated totality that liberates, preserves, and safeguards freedom and alterity.[176] Ethical life in Hegel's sense is not totalitarianism but a bulwark against it. Hegel's ethics of recognition not only remains relevant to contemporary concerns as a counterdiscourse to modernity; as a correction to both the ancients and the moderns it still has much to offer our disrupted and fragmented cultural situation at the end of the twentieth century.

176. Ibid., 218. Critchley's alternative to 'organic totality' is virtually identical to Hegel's concept of community as a social organism. See also Houlgate, *Freedom, Truth and History*, chap. 3, pp. 123–125.

Bibliography

Works by Fichte

Fichtes Werke. Hrsg. I. H. Fichte. Berlin: Walter de Gruyter, 1971. This is a reprint of Johann Gottlieb Fichte's *Sämmtliche Werke*, Herausgegeben von I. H. Fichte, Band 8. Berlin: Veit, 1845–1846. All of the following entries are included in this edition.

Erste Einleitung in die Wissenschaftslehre (1797), Fichtes Werke 1. Hrsg. I. H. Fichte. Berlin: Walter de Gruyter, 1971. English translation in *Science of Knowledge*, trans. and ed. Peter Heath and John Lachs. New York: Appleton Century Crofts, 1970.

Grundlage des Naturrechts nach Principien der Wissenschaftslehre (1796), *Werke* 3. Hrsg. I. H. Fichte. Berlin: Walter de Gruyter, 1971. Pp. 1–385. English translation: *Science of Rights*, trans. A. E. Kroeger (1889). Reissued London: Routledge & Kegan Paul, 1970.

"Review of Anesidemus." In George Di Giovanni and H. S. Harris, eds., *Between Kant and Hegel: Texts in the Development of Post-Kantian Idealism.* Albany: SUNY Press, 1985. Pp. 136–157.

System der Sittenlehre nach Principien der Wissenschaftslehre (1798), *Werke* 4. Hrsg. I. H. Fichte. Berlin: Walter de Gruyter, 1971. English translation: *The Science of Ethics*, trans. A. E. Kroeger. London: Kegan Paul, 1897, 1907.

Tatsachen des Bewusstseins (1810). *Fichtes Werke.* Band 2. Berlin: Walter de Gruyter, 1971.

Über die Bestimmung des Gelehrten (1794). *Werke* 6. Hrsg. I. H. Fichte. Berlin: Walter de Gruyter, 1971. English translation: *Some Lectures Concerning the Scholar's Vocation.* In *Fichte: Early Philosophical Writings*, ed. and trans. Daniel Breazeale. Ithaca: Cornell University Press, 1988. Pp. 137–184. Reprinted in *Philosophy of German Idealism*, ed. Ernst Behler, *The German Library*, vol. 23, Ed. Volkmar Sander. New York: Continuum, 1987. Pp. 1–38.

Wissenschaftslehre 1794. Fichtes Werke. Band 1. Hrsg. I. H. Fichte. Berlin: Walter de Gruyter, 1971. English translation: *Science of Knowledge*, ed. and trans. Peter Heath and John Lachs. New York: Appleton Century Crofts, 1970.

Wissenschaftslehre novo methodo. 1796–1799. English translation: *Foundations of Transcendental Philosophy*, trans. Daniel Breazeale. Ithaca: Cornell University Press, 1992.

Works by Hegel

Werke in zwanzig Bänden, Theorie Werkausgabe. Frankfurt: Suhrkamp Verlag, 1971. This is a reprint based on the *Werke 1832–1845*, edited by Eva Moldenhauer and Karl Markus Michel. When this edition is cited, it is abbreviated TWA, followed by the publisher Sk and volume number in the Suhrkamp edition; thus TWA Sk 3.

Differenz des Fichte'sche und Schelling'sche System der Philosophie. Werke, TWA Sk 2. English translation: *The Difference between Fichte's and Schelling's System of Philosophy*, trans. H. S. Harris and W. Cerf. Albany: SUNY Press, 1977.

Einleitung in die Geschichte der Philosophie. Hrsg. Johannes Hoffmeister. Hamburg: Felix Meiner Verlag, 1940.

Enzyklopädie der philosophischen Wissenschaften im Grundrisse. Heidelberg, 1817. Reprinted in *Sämtliche Werke*, Band 6, Jubliäumsausgabe in zwanzig Bänden, Hrsg. H. Glockner. Stuttgart: Frommann-Holzboog, 1968. English translation: *Encyclopedia of the Philosophical Sciences in Outline*, trans. Stephen A. Taubeneck, *The German Library*, vol. 24, ed. E. Behler. New York: Continuum, 1990.

Enzyklopädie, Werke, TWA Sk 8–10. English translation: *Hegel's Logic, Hegel's Philosophy of Nature, Hegel's Philosophy of Mind*, trans. W. Wallace together with the *Zusätze* in Boumann's text (1845), trans. A. V. Miller. Oxford: Clarendon Press, 1971. New translation: *The Encyclopedia Logic*, trans. T. F. Geraets, W. A. Suchting, and H. S. Harris. Indianapolis: Hackett, 1991.

Foreword to H. Fr. W. Hinrichs Die Religion im inneren Verhältnisse zur Wissenschaft (1822), TWA Sk 11. English translation: *Beyond Epistemology: New Studies in the Philosophy of Hegel*, ed. F. Weiss, trans. A. V. Miller. The Hague: Martinus Nijhoff, 1974.

Geschichte der Philosophie, Werke. TWA Sk 18–20.

Glauben und Wissen. Werke. TWA Sk 2. English translation: *Faith and Knowledge*, trans. W. Cerf and H. S. Harris. Albany: SUNY Press, 1977.

Grundlinien der Philosophie des Rechts. TWA Sk 7. English translation: *Elements of the Philosophy of Right*, ed. Allen W. Wood, trans. H. Nisbet. Cambridge: Cambridge University Press, 1991. Older translation: *Hegel's Philosophy of Right*, trans. T. M. Knox. Oxford: Clarendon Press, 1952.

Hegel: The Letters, trans. C. Butler. C. Seiler. Bloomington: Indiana University Press, 1984.

Hegels theologische Jugendschriften. Hrsg. H. Nohl. Tübingen: J. C. B. Mohr (Paul Siebeck), 1907, reprinted 1966. This has been partially reprinted in *Hegels Werke*, TWA Sk 1; English translation: *Early Theological Writings*, trans. T. M. Knox. Chicago: University of Chicago Press, 1948.

Jena Realphilosophie (1805/1806), in *Jenaer Systementwürfe III: Naturphilosophie und Philosophie des Geistes*, Hrsg. Rolf-Peter Horstmann. Hamburg: Felix Meiner Verlag, 1987. English translation: *Hegel and the Human Spirit*, trans. Leo Rauch. Detroit: Wayne State University Press, 1983.

Phänomenologie des Geistes, Hrsg. Johannes Hoffmeister. Hamburg: Felix Meiner Verlag, 1952. English translations: *Phenomenology of Mind* (J. B. Baillie). New York: Macmillan, 1910. *Phenomenology of Spirit* (A. V. Miller). Oxford: Oxford University Press, 1977.

Philosophie des Geistes 1803/1804. Fragment 21 (*Jenaer Systementwürfe I: Das System der spekulativen Philosophie*, Neu herausgegeben von Klaus Düsing und Heinz Kimmerle. Hamburg: Felix Meiner Verlag, 1986). English translation: *First Philosophy of Spirit*, trans. H. S Harris, in *G. W. F. Hegel, System of Ethical Life (1802/03) and First Philosophy of Spirit (1803)*. Albany: SUNY Press, 1979.

Philosophy of Subjective Spirit, ed. and trans. M. J. Petry. 3 vols. Dordrecht: D. Reidel, 1979. Volume 3 contains the Griesheim transcript of the 1825 lectures. This transcript has also been published by Petry as *G. W. F. Hegel: The Berlin Phenomenology*. Boston: D. Reidel, 1981.

"Review of C. F. Göschel's Aphorisms," trans. Clark Butler, *Clio* 17, no. 4 (1988): 369–393.

System of Ethical Life (1802/03) and First Philosophy of Spirit, trans. H. S. Harris and T. M. Knox. Albany: SUNY Press, 1977.

The Critical Journal. In George Di Giovanni and H. S. Harris, eds., *Between Kant and Hegel: Texts in the Development of Post-Kantian Idealism*. Albany: SUNY Press, 1985.

Über die wissenschaftlichen Behandlungsarten des Naturrechts, TWA Sk 2. English translation: *Natural Law*, trans. T. M. Knox. Philadelphia: University of Pennsylvania Press, 1975.

Verhältnis Skeptizismus zur Philosophie, Werke. TWA Sk 2. English translation: *On the Relationship of Skepticism to Philosophy*, trans. H. S. Harris, in George Di Giovanni and H. S. Harris, eds., *Between Kant and Hegel: Texts in the Development of Post-Kantian Idealism*. Albany: SUNY Press, 1985. Pp. 311–362.

Die Verfassung Deutschlands, Werke. TWA Sk 1; English translation: *The German Constitution*, in *Hegel's Political Writings*, trans. T. M. Knox. Oxford: Oxford University Press, 1964.

Vorlesungen über die Aesthetik, Hegels Werke. TWA Sk 13–15; English translation: *Aesthetics: Lectures on Fine Art*, trans. T. M. Knox. Oxford: Clarendon Press, 1975.

Vorlesungen über die Beweise vom Dasein Gottes, Hrsg. G. Lasson. Hamburg: Felix Meiner Verlag, 1930, 1973.

Vorlesungen über die Philosophie der Religion, Werke. TWA Sk 16–17.

Vorlesungen über die Philosophie der Religion. Teil 1: *Der Begriff der Religion*; Teil 2: *Die bestimmte Religion*; Teil 3: *Die vollendete Religion*, Hrsg. von Walter Jaeschke. Hamburg: Felix Meiner Verlag, 1983, 1985, 1984. English translation: *Lectures on the Philosophy of Religion*. Vol. 1: *The Concept of Religion*; Vol. 2: *Determinate Religion*; Vol. 3: *The Consummate Religion*, ed. Peter C. Hodgson, trans. R. Brown, P. Hodgson, and J. Stewart, with the assistance of H. S. Harris. Berkeley: University of California Press, 1984, 1986, 1985.

Vorlesungen über die Philosophie der Weltgeschichte. Band 1. Die Vernunft in der

Geschichte, Hrsg. Johannes Hoffmeister. Hamburg: Felix Meiner Verlag, 1955. English translation: *Philosophy of History*, trans. H. Nisbet. Cambridge: Cambridge University Press, 1975.

Vorlesungen über Naturrecht und Staatswissenschaft (Wannenman Nachschrift, 1817, Heidelberg), Hrsg. Staff of the Hegel Archive. Hamburg: Felix Meiner Verlag, 1983. English translation: *Lectures on Natural Right and Political Science*, trans. J. M. Stewart and P. C. Hodgson. Berkeley: University of California Press, 1995.

Vorlesungen über Naturrecht (Homeyer Nachschrift), Hrsg. Karl-Heinz Ilting. Berlin, 1818.

(Vorlesung über die) Philosophie des Rechts, 1819, ed. D. Henrich. Frankfurt: Suhrkamp, 1983.

Vorlesungen uber Rechtsphilosophie, 1818–1831, Hrsg. Karl-Heinz Ilting. Stuttgart: Frommann-Holzboog, 1973.

"Wer Denkt Abstrakt?" *Werke.* TWA Sk 2; translated as "Who Thinks Abstractly?" in *Hegel: Texts and Commentary,* trans. and ed. Walter Kaufmann. Notre Dame: University of Notre Dame Press, 1977.

Wissenschaft der Logik, Werke. TWA Sk 5 and 6. English translation: *Hegel's Science of Logic,* trans. A. V. Miller. Atlantic Highlands, N.J.: Humanities Press, 1969.

General Works Consulted

Aboulafia, Mitchell. *The Mediating Self.* New Haven: Yale University Press, 1986.

Allison, Henry. *Kant's Theory of Freedom.* Cambridge: Cambridge University Press, 1990.

Althusser, Louis. *Politics and History: Montesquieu, Rousseau, Marx.* London: Verso, 1982.

Anderson, Thomas C. *Sartre's Two Ethics: From Authenticity to Integral Humanity.* Chicago: Open Court, 1993.

Angehrn, Emil. *Freiheit und System bei Hegel.* Berlin: Walter de Gruyter, 1977.

Ansell-Pearson, Keith. *An Introduction to Nietzsche as Political Thinker.* Cambridge: Cambridge University Press, 1994.

Arendt, Hannah. *The Human Condition.* Chicago: University of Chicago Press, 1958.

Aristotle. *Metaphysics, Introduction to Aristotle.* Ed. R. McKeon. New York: Modern Library, 1947.

Aristotle. *Politics.* Trans. E. Barker. Oxford: Oxford University Press, 1958.

Aschenberg, Reinhold. "Der Wahrheitsbegriff in Hegel's 'Phänomenologie des Geistes.'" In *Die ontologische Option,* hrsg. Klaus Hartmann. Berlin: Walter de Gruyter, 1976.

Avineri, Shlomo. "The Discovery of Hegel's Early Lectures on the Philosophy of Right." *Owl of Minerva* 16, no. 2 (Spring 1985): 199–208.

———. *Hegel's Theory of the Modern State.* Cambridge: Cambridge University Press, 1972.

Baumanns, Peter. *Fichtes Ursprungliches System: Sein Standort zwischen Kant und Hegel.* Stuttgart: Frommann-Holzboog, 1972.

Beck, Lewis White. *A Commentary on Kant's Critique of Practical Reason.* Chicago: University of Chicago Press, 1960.

Beerling, R. F. "Hegel und Nietzsche." *Hegel Studien* 1. Bonn: Bouvier Verlag, 1961. Pp. 244–245.

Beiser, Frederick C. *Enlightenment, Revolution and Romanticism.* Cambridge, Mass.: Harvard University Press, 1992.

―――. *The Fate of Reason.* Cambridge, Mass.: Harvard University Press, 1987.

Beiser, Frederick C., ed. *The Cambridge Companion to Hegel.* Cambridge: Cambridge University Press, 1993.

Benhabib, Seyla. *Critique, Norm and Utopia: A Study of the Foundation of Critical Theory.* New York: Columbia University Press, 1986.

Bernasconi, Robert. "Failure of Communication as a Surplus." In *Provocation of Levinas*, ed. R. Bernasconi and D. Wood, 100–136. New York: Routledge, 1988.

Bernstein, J. M. "From Self-Consciousness to Community: Act and Recognition in the Master-Slave Relationship." In *The State and Civil Society: Studies in Hegel's Political Philosophy*, ed. Z. A. Pelczynski. Cambridge: Cambridge University Press, 1984.

Bernstein, Richard J. *Praxis and Action.* Philadelphia: University of Pennsylvania Press, 1971.

Berthold-Bond, Daniel. *Hegel's Theory of Madness.* Albany: SUNY Press, 1995.

Bosanquet, Bernard. *The Philosophical Theory of the State.* London: Macmillan, 1899.

Bradley, A. C. "Hegel's Theory of Tragedy." In *Hegel: On Tragedy*, ed. A. Paolucci, 367–389. New York: Anchor Books, 1962.

Bradley, F. H. "My Station and Its Duties." In *Ethical Studies.* London: Oxford University Press, 1876. Pp. 160–213.

Breazeale, Daniel. "The Hegel-Nietzsche Problem." *Nietzsche-Studien* 4 (1975): 146–164.

Buber, Martin. *Between Man and Man.* Trans. R. G. Smith and Maurice Friedman. New York: Macmillan, 1965.

―――. *I and Thou.* Trans. W. Kaufmann. New York: Scribners, 1970.

Butler, Judith. Comment on Joseph C. Flay's "Hegel, Derrida and Bataille's Laughter." In *Hegel and His Critics*, ed. William Desmond. Albany: SUNY Press, 1989.

―――. *Subjects of Desire: Hegelian Reflections in Twentieth-Century France.* New York: Columbia University Press, 1987.

Caputo, John. *Against Ethics.* Bloomington: Indiana University Press, 1993.

Carr, David. *Interpreting Husserl.* Boston: Martinus Nijhoff, 1987.

Clark, Malcolm. *Logic and System: A Study of the Transition from Vorstellung to Thought in the Philosophy of Hegel.* Loewen: Universitaire Werkgemeenschap, 1960.

Connolly, William E. *Political Theory and Modernity.* Oxford: Blackwell, 1988.

Critchley, Simon. *An Ethics of Deconstruction.* Oxford: Blackwell, 1992.

Cullen, Bernard. *Hegel's Social and Political Thought.* New York: St. Martin's Press, 1979.

Dallmayr, Fred. *G. W. F. Hegel: Modernity and Politics.* Newbury Park, Calif.: Sage, 1993.

Daniel, Klaus. *Hegel Verstehen: Einführung in sein Denken.* Frankfurt: Campus Verlag, 1983.

Deleuze, Gilles. *Nietzsche and Philosophy.* Trans. Hugh Tomlinson. New York: Columbia University Press, 1983.

Dent, N. J. H. *Rousseau.* Oxford: Oxford University Press, 1988.

―――. *A Rousseau Dictionary.* Oxford: B. H. Blackwell, 1992.

Derrida, Jacques. "Differance." In *Speech and Phenomena*, trans. D. Allison. Evanston: Northwestern University Press, 1973. Pp. 129–160.

————. "From Restricted to General Economy: A Hegelianism Without Reserve." In *Writing and Difference*, trans. Alan Bass. Chicago: University of Chicago Press, 1978. Pp. 251–277.

————. "Violence and Metaphysics." In *Writing and Difference*, trans. Alan Bass. Chicago: University of Chicago Press, 1978. Pp. 79–153.

Descombes, Vincent. *Modern French Philosophy*. Trans. L. Scott-Fox and J. M. Harding. Cambridge: Cambridge University Press, 1980.

Desmond, William. *Art and the Absolute*. Albany: SUNY Press, 1986.

————. *Beyond Hegel and Dialectic*. Albany: SUNY Press, 1992.

————. *Desire, Dialectic and Otherness*. New Haven: Yale University Press, 1987.

D'Hondt, Jacques. *Hegel in His Time*. Trans. J. Burbidge. Lewiston, N.Y.: Broadview Press, 1988.

Di Giovanni, George, ed. *Essays on Hegel's Logic*. Albany: SUNY Press, 1990.

Di Giovanni, George, and H. S. Harris, eds. *Between Kant and Hegel: Texts in the Development of Post-Kantian Idealism*. Albany: SUNY Press, 1985.

Donougho, Martin. "The Woman in White: On the Reception of Hegel's Antigone." *Owl of Minerva* 21, no. 1 (Fall 1989): 65–89.

Duesberg, Hans. *Person und Gemeinschaft: Philosophische-Systematische Untersuchungen des Sinnzusammenhangs von personaler Selbstständigkeit und interpersonaler Beziehung an Texten von J. G. Fichte und M. Buber*. Bonn: Bouvier Verlag, 1970.

Düsing, Edith. "Genesis des Selbstbewusstseins durch Anerkennung und Liebe: Untersuchungen zu Hegels Theorie der konkreten Subjektivität." In *Hegels Theorie des subjektiven Geistes* [*Spekulation und Erfahrung II/14*], hrsg. Lothar Eley, 244–279. Stuttgart: Frommann-Holzboog, 1990.

————. *Intersubjektivität und Selbstbewusstsein*. Köln: Dinter Verlag, 1986.

Düsing, Klaus. *Hegel und die Geschichte der Philosophie, Erträge der Forschung*. Band 206. Darmstadt: Wissenschaftliche Buchgesellschaft, 1983.

————. *Das Problem der Subjektivität in Hegels Logik*. Hegel Studien 15. Bonn: Bouvier Verlag, 1976.

Easton, Susan M. "Hegel and Feminism." In *Hegel and Modern Philosophy*, ed. David Lamb, 30–55. London: Croom Helm, 1987.

Eley, Lothar. *Hegels Theorie des subjektiven Geistes* [*Spekulation und Erfahrung II/14*]. Stuttgart: Frommann-Holzboog, 1990.

Fackenheim, Emil. *The Religious Dimension in Hegel's Thought*. Chicago: University of Chicago Press, 1967.

Ferry, Luc. *Rights: The New Quarrel Between the Ancients and the Moderns*. Chicago: University of Chicago Press, 1990.

Feuerbach, Ludwig. *The Essence of Christianity*. Trans. G. Eliot. New York: Harper & Row, 1957.

————. "Towards a Critique of Hegel's Philosophy" (1839). In *The Fiery Brook: Selected Writings of Ludwig Feuerbach*, trans. Zawar Hanfi. New York: Doubleday Anchor, 1972. Pp. 53–96.

Fichtes Lehre vom Rechtsverhältniss: Die Deduktion der SS 1–4 der Grundlage des Naturrechts und ihre Stellung in der Rechtsphilosophie. Frankfurt am Main: Vittorio Klostermann, 1992.

Findlay, J. N. *Hegel: A Re-Examination*. New York: Collier Macmillan, 1962.

———. "Reflexive Asymmetry: Hegel's Most Fundamental Methodological Ruse." In *Beyond Epistemology: New Studies in the Philosophy of Hegel*, ed. F. Weiss, 154–173. The Hague: Martinus Nijhoff, 1974.

Fink, Eugen. "Operative Concepts in Husserl's Phenomenology," trans. William Mc-Kenna. In *A Priori and World: European Contributions to Husserlian Phenomenology*, ed. W. McKenna, R. M. Harlan, and L. E. Winters, 56–701. The Hague: Martinus Nijhoff, 1981.

Flay, Joseph C. "Hegel, Derrida and Bataille's Laughter." In *Hegel and His Critics*, ed. William Desmond, 163–173. Albany: SUNY Press, 1989.

———. *Hegel's Quest for Certainty*. Albany: SUNY Press, 1984.

———. "Hegel's *Science of Logic*: Ironies of the Understanding." In *Essays on Hegel's Logic*, ed. George di Giovanni, 153–169. Albany: SUNY Press, 1990.

Flynn, Thomas R. "Reciprocity and the Genius of the Third." In *The Philosophy of Jean-Paul Sartre*, ed. P. A. Schilpp, 345–370. LaSalle, Ill.: Open Court, 1981.

———. *Sartre and Marxist Existentialism*. Chicago: University of Chicago Press, 1984.

Forster, Michael N. *Hegel and Skepticism*. Cambridge, Mass.: Harvard University Press, 1989.

Foster, Michael B. *The Political Philosophies of Plato and Hegel*. Oxford: Clarendon Press, 1935; New York: Garland, 1984.

Foucault, Michel. *Discipline and Punish*. Trans. Alan Sheridan. New York: Vintage, 1979.

———. "The Discourse on Language." In *Archeology of Knowledge*, trans. A. M. Smith. New York: Pantheon Books, 1972. Pp. 215–237.

Fry, Christopher Martin. *Sartre and Hegel: The Variations of an Enigma in l'Etre et le Neant*. Bonn: Bouvier Verlag, 1988.

Fulda, H. F. "Der Begriff des Geistes bei Hegel und seine Wirkungsgeschichte." In *Historisches Wörterbuch der Philosophie*, hrsg. Joachim Ritter, Band 3, 191ff. Stuttgart: Schwabe, 1971.

Gadamer, Hans-Georg. "Hegel and Heidegger." In *Hegel's Dialectic: Five Hermeneutical Studies*, trans. P. Christopher Smith. New Haven: Yale University Press, 1976. Pp. 100–116.

———. *Hegel's Dialectic: Five Hermeneutical Studies*. Trans. P. Christopher Smith. New Haven: Yale University Press, 1976.

———. "Hegel's Dialectic of Self-Consciousness." In *Hegel's Dialectic: Five Hermeneutical Studies*, trans. P. Christopher Smith. New Haven: Yale University Press, 1976. Pp. 54–74.

———. *Truth and Method*. New York: Seabury Press, 1975.

Gasché, Rudolphe. *The Tain of the Mirror: Derrida and the Philosophy of Reflection*. Cambridge, Mass.: Harvard University Press, 1986.

Goossens, Wilfried. "Ethical Life and Family in the *Phenomenology of Spirit*." In *Hegel on the Ethical Life, Religion and Philosophy*, ed. A. Wylleman, 163–194. *Louvain Philosophical Studies 3*. Dordrecht: Kluwer, 1989.

Greene, Murray. "Hegel's 'Unhappy Consciousness' and Nietzsche's 'Slave Morality'." In *Hegel and the Philosophy of Religion*, ed. Darrel E. Christensen, 125–141. The Hague: Martinus Nijhoff, 1970.

Habermas, Jürgen. "Arbeit und Interaktion: Bemerkungen zu Hegels Jena Philosophie des Geistes." Cited in *Frühe politische Systeme*, hrsg. G. Göhler, 786–814. Frankfurt: Ullstein, 1974. English translation: "Labor and Interaction: Remarks on Hegel's *Jena Philosophy of Mind*. In *Theory and Practice*, trans. John Viertel. Boston: Beacon Press, 1974. Pp. 142–169.

———. *The Philosophical Discourse of Modernity*. Trans. F. Lawrence. Cambridge, Mass.: MIT Press, 1987.

———. *Theory and Practice*. Trans. J. Viertel. Boston: Beacon Press, 1973.

Halper, Edward. "Hegel and the Problem of the Differentia." In *Essays on Hegel's Logic*, ed. G. di Giovanni, 191–211. Albany: SUNY Press, 1990.

Harris, Errol E. "The Contemporary Significance of Hegel and Whitehead." In *Hegel and Whitehead: Contemporary Perspectives on Systematic Philosophy*, ed. George R. Lucas, Jr., 17–28. Albany: SUNY Press, 1986.

———. *Formal, Transcendental and Dialectical Thinking: Logic and Reality*. Albany: SUNY Press, 1987.

———. "Hegel's Theory of Political Action." In *Hegel's Philosophy of Action*, ed. L. S. Stepelevich and D. Lamb, 157–174. Atlantic Highlands, N.J.: Humanities Press, 1983.

———. *The Spirit of Hegel*. Atlantic Highlands, N.J.: Humanities Press, 1993.

Harris, H. S. "The Concept of Recognition in Hegel's Jena Manuscripts." *Hegel-Studien* 20 (Bonn: Bouvier Verlag, 1979): 229–248.

———. *Hegel's Development: Night Thoughts*. Oxford: Clarendon Press, 1983.

Hartmann, Klaus. "On Taking the Transcendental Turn." *Review of Metaphysics* 20, no. 2 (December 1966): 223–249.

———. *Politische Philosophie*. Freiburg: Karl Alber Verlag, 1981.

———. *Sartre's Ontology: A Study of Sartre's Being and Nothingness in the Light of Hegel's Logic*. Evanston: Northwestern University Press, 1966.

———. "Towards a Systematic Reading of Hegel's *Philosophy of Right*." In *The State and Civil Society*, ed. Z. A. Pelczynski, 114–136. Cambridge: Cambridge University Press, 1984.

Hartmann, Nicolai. *Philosophie des deutschen Idealismus*. Zweite Auflage. Berlin: Walter de Gruyter, 1960.

Harvey, Irene E. *Derrida and the Economy of Différance*. Bloomington: Indiana University Press, 1986.

Hegel: Einführung in seine Philosophie. Ed. Otto Pöggeler. Freiberg/München: Karl Alber Verlag, 1977.

Heidegger, Martin. *Hegels Begriff der Erfahrung, Holzwege*. Frankfurt: Vittorio Klostermann, 1950. English translation: *Hegel's Concept of Experience*. Trans. K. R. Dove. New York: Harper & Row, 1971.

———. *Hegel's Phenomenology of Spirit*. Trans. P. Emad and K. Maly. Bloomington: Indiana University Press, 1988.

———. *Holzwege*. Frankfurt: Vittorio Klostermann, 1950.

———. *Sein und Zeit*. Tübingen: Niemayer Verlag, 1984.

Heimsoeth, Heinz. *Fichte*. Munich: Reinhardt, 1923.

Henrich, Dieter. "Fichtes ürsprungliche Einsicht." In *Subjektivität und Metaphysik*, ed. D. Henrich and H. Wagner, 188–232. Frankfurt: Suhrkamp, 1966.

———. "Hegel und Hölderlin." In *Hegel im Kontext*. Frankfurt: Suhrkamp, 1967.

———. "Hegels Theorie über den Zufall." In *Hegel im Kontext*. Frankfurt: Suhrkamp, 1967.

Heinrichs, Johannes. *Die Logik der Phänomenologie des Geistes*. Bonn: Bouvier Verlag, 1974.

Honneth, Axel. *The Struggle for Recognition*. Trans. Joel Anderson. Cambridge, Mass.: Polity Press, 1995.

Horowitz, Asher. *Rousseau, Nature and History*. Toronto: University of Toronto Press, 1987.

Horstmann, Rolf-Peter. *Ontologie und Relationen: Hegel, Bradley, Russell und die Kontroverse über interne und externe Beziehungen*. Hain: Athenäum, 1984.

Hösle, Vittorio. *Hegels System: Der Idealismus der Subjektivität und das Problem der Intersubjektivität*. 2 vols. Hamburg: Meiner Verlag, 1987.

———. "Zur Interpretation von Fichtes Theorie der Intersubjektivität." In *Fichtes Lehre von Rechtsverhältniss: Die Deduktion der §§1–4 der Grundlage des Naturrechts und ihre Stellung in der Rechtsphilosophie*. Frankfurt: Vittorio Klostermann, 1992.

Houlgate, Stephen. *Freedom, Truth and History: An Introduction to Hegel's Philosophy*. London: Routledge, 1991.

———. "Hegel and Fichte: Recognition, Otherness, and Absolute Knowing." *Owl of Minerva* 26, no. 1 (Fall 1994): 3–19.

———. *Hegel, Nietzsche and the Criticism of Metaphysics*. Cambridge: Cambridge University Press, 1986.

———. "Hegel's Ethical Thought." In Symposium on Wood, *Bulletin of the Hegel Society of Great Britain*, no. 25 (Spring/Summer 1992): 1–17.

Hunter, C. K. *Der Interpersonalitätsbeweis in Fichtes früher angewandter praktischer Philosophie*. Meisenheim am Glan: Anton Hain Verlag, 1973.

Husserl, Edmund. *Cartesian Meditations*. Trans. Dorion Cairns. The Hague: Martinus Nijhoff, 1960.

———. *The Crisis of European Science and Transcendental Phenomenology*. Trans. David Carr. Evanston: Northwestern University Press, 1970.

———. *Ideen I, II, III*, Hrsg. Marly Biemel. The Hague: Martinus Nijhoff, 1969.

Hyppolite, Jean. "Anmerkungen zur Vorrede der Phänomenologie des Geistes und zum Thema: das Absolute ist Subjekt." In *Materialien zu Hegels Phänomenologie des Geistes*, Hrsg. H. F. Fulda and D. Henrich, 45–53. Frankfurt am Main: Suhrkamp Taschenbuch Verlag, 1973.

———. *Genesis and Structure of Hegel's Phenomenology of Spirit*. Trans. S. Cherniak and J. Heckman. Evanston: Northwestern University Press, 1974.

———. "Life and the Consciousness of Life in the Jena Philosophy." In *Studies on Marx and Hegel*, ed. and trans. John O'Neill, 3–21. New York: Harper & Row, 1969.

Ilting, Karl-Heinz. "The Structure of Hegel's *Philosophy of Right*." In *Hegel's Political Philosophy*, ed. Z. A. Pelczynski, 90–110. Cambridge: Cambridge University Press, 1971.

Jacobi, F. H. *Brief an Fichte* (1799). English translation: "Open Letter to Fichte," 1799, trans. Diana I. Behler. In *Philosophy of German Idealism*, ed. Ernst Behler, 119–142. *The German Library, vol. 23*. New York: Continuum, 1987.

Janke, Wolfgang. *Fichte: Sein und Reflexion*. Berlin: Walter de Gruyter, 1970.

Joël, Karl. *Nietzsche und die Romantik*. Jena: Diederichs, 1905.

Jonas, Hans. "Spinoza and the Theory of Organism." In *Philosophical Essays: From Ancient Creed to Technological Man*. Chicago: University of Chicago Press, 1974.

Jurist, Eliot. "Hegel's Concept of Recognition." Ph.D. dissertation, Columbia University, 1983.

Kainz, Howard. *Paradox, Dialectic and System: A Contemporary Reconstruction of the Hegelian Problematic.* University Park: Pennsylvania State University Press, 1988.

Kant, Immanuel. *Critique of Practical Reason.* Trans. Lewis White Beck. New York: Library of Liberal Arts, 1956.

————. *Critique of Pure Reason.* Trans. Norman Kemp Smith. New York: St. Martin's Press, 1965.

————. *Foundations of the Metaphysics of Morals.* Trans. Lewis White Beck. New York: Library of Liberal Arts, 1959.

————. *Metaphysics of Morals.* Trans. H. B. Nisbet. In *Political Writings*, ed. H. Reiss, 131–175. Cambridge: Cambridge University Press, 1991.

————. *Kritik der Urteilskraft. Werke 5*, Akademie Textausgabe. Berlin: Walter de Gruyter, 1968. English translation: *Critique of Judgment*, trans. J. H. Bernard. New York: Hafner, 1961.

————. "What Is Enlightenment?" In *Foundations of the Metaphysics of Morals*, trans. Lewis White Beck, 83–90. New York: Library of Liberal Arts, 1959.

Kaufmann, Walter. *Nietzsche: Philosopher, Psychologist, Antichrist.* 3d ed. New York: Random House, 1968.

Kelly, George Armstrong. *Idealism, Politics and History: Sources of Hegelian Thought.* Cambridge: At the University Press, 1969.

————. "Notes on Hegel's 'Lordship and Bondage.'" In *Hegel: A Collection of Critical Essays*, ed. Alasdair MacIntyre, 189–218. Garden City, N.Y.: Anchor Books, 1972.

Kierkegaard, Søren. *Fear and Trembling.* Trans. H. Hong. Princeton: Princeton University Press, 1983.

Kojève, Alexandre. *Introduction to the Reading of Hegel.* Ed. Allan Bloom, trans. J. H. Nichols, Jr. New York: Basic Books, 1969.

Kolb, David. *The Critique of Pure Modernity: Hegel, Heidegger, and After.* Chicago: University of Chicago Press, 1986.

Kroner, Richard. *Von Kant Bis Hegel.* Tübingen: J. C. B. Mohr, 1921–1924.

Landau, Peter. "Hegels Begrundung des Vertragrechts." In *Materialien zu Hegels Rechtsphilosophie*, hrsg. Manfred Riedel, 2:176–200. Frankfurt: Suhrkamp, 1975.

Lauth, Reinhard. "Le probleme de l'interpersonalite chez J. G. Fichte." *Archives de Philosophie 26* (1962): 325–344.

Levinas, Emmanuel. *Ethics and Infinity.* Trans. Richard Cohen. Pittsburgh: Duquesne University Press, 1985.

————. "Franz Rosenzweig: A Modern Jewish Thinker." In *Outside the Subject*, trans. Michael B. Smith, 49–66. Stanford: Stanford University Press, 1993.

————. "Martin Buber and the Theory of Knowledge." In *The Levinas Reader*, ed. Sean Hand, 57–74. Oxford: B. H. Blackwell, 1989.

————. "Martin Buber, Gabriel Marcel and Philosophy." In *Martin Buber: A Centenary Volume*, ed. H. Gordon and J. Bloch, KTAV, 1984.

————. *Otherwise than Being or Beyond Essence.* Trans. A. Lingis. The Hague: Martinus Nijhoff, 1981.

————. "Substitution." In *The Levinas Reader*, ed. Sean Hand, 88–125. Oxford: Basil Blackwell, 1989.

———. *Time and the Other.* Trans. Richard Cohen. Pittsburgh: Duquesne University Press, 1987.

———. *Totality and Infinity.* Trans. A. Lingis. Pittsburgh: Duquesne University Press, 1969.

Litt, Theodor. *Hegel:Versuch einer kritischen Erneurung.* Heidelberg: Quelle & Meyer, 1961.

Lucas, George, Jr. *The Rehabilitation of Whitehead: An Analytical and Historical Assessment of Process Philosophy.* Albany: SUNY Press, 1989.

———. *Two Views of Freedom in Process Thought.* Missoula, Mont.: Scholars Press, 1979.

Lucas, Hans-Christian. "The Identification of *Vernunft* with *Wirklichkeit* in Hegel." *Owl of Minerva* 25, no. 1 (Fall 1993): 23–45.

Lukàcs, Georg. *The Young Hegel.* Trans. Robert Livingstone. Cambridge, Mass.: MIT Press, 1976.

Marcuse, Herbert. *One Dimensional Man.* Boston: Beacon Press, 1964.

Marx, Werner. *Hegel's Phenomenology of Spirit: A Commentary on the Preface and the Introduction.* Trans. P. Heath. New York: Harper & Row, 1975.

———. *Heidegger and the Tradition.* Trans. Theodore Kisiel. Evanston: Northwestern University Press, 1971.

McCumber, John. "Contradiction and Resolution in the State: Hegel's Covert View." *Clio* 15, no. 4 (1986): 379–390.

———. *Poetic Interaction: Language, Freedom, Reason.* Chicago: University of Chicago Press, 1989.

Mills, Patricia Jagentowicz. "Hegel and 'The Woman Question': Recognition and Intersubjectivity." In *The Sexism of Social and Political Theory: Women and Reproduction from Plato to Nietzsche,* ed. L. Mg. Clark and L. Lange, 76–98. Toronto: University of Toronto Press, 1979.

———. "Hegel's Antigone." *Owl of Minerva* 17, no. 2 (Spring 1986): 131–152.

———. *Woman, Nature and Psyche.* New Haven: Yale University Press, 1987.

Mohanty, J. N. *The Possibility of Transcendental Philosophy* [*Phaenomenologica* 98]. Dordrecht: Martinus Nijhoff, 1985.

Mure, G. R. G. *A Study of Hegel's Logic.* Oxford: Oxford University Press, 1950.

Nietzsche, Friedrich. *Genealogy of Morals.* Trans. W. Kaufmann and R. J. Hollingdale. New York: Random House, 1967.

Pannenberg, Wolfhart. "Der Geist und sein Anderes." In *Hegels Logik der Philosophie,* ed. D. Henrich and R. P. Horstmann, 151–160. Stuttgart: Klett-Cotta, 1984.

Philolenko, Alexis. *La liberté humaine dans la philosophie de Fichte.* Paris: Vrin, 1966.

Plato, *Republic* 351d. Trans. G. M. A. Grube. Indianapolis: Hackett, 1992.

Pöggeler, Otto. *Grundprobleme der grossen Philosophen,* hrsg. Josef Speck. UTB 464. Göttingen: Vandenhoeck & Ruprecht, 1982.

———. *Hegels Idee einer Phänomenologie des Geistes.* Freiburg: Alber Verlag, 1973.

Popper, Karl. *The Open Society and Its Enemies.* London: Routledge, 1962.

Priest, Stephen, ed. *Hegel's Critique of Kant.* Oxford: Clarendon Press, 1987.

Primoratz, Igor. *Banquo's Geist: Hegels Theorie der Strafe. Hegel-Studien Beiheft* 29. Bonn: Bouvier Verlag, 1986.

———. *Justifying Legal Punishment.* Atlantic Highlands, N.J.: Humanities Press, 1989.

Prokopczyk, Czeslaw. *Truth and Reality in Marx and Hegel.* Amherst: University of Massachusetts Press, 1980.

Ravven, Heidi M. "Has Hegel Anything to Say to Feminists?" *Owl of Minerva* 19, no. 2 (Spring 1988): 149–168.

Redding, Paul. *Hegel's Hermeneutics.* Ithaca: Cornell University Press, 1996.

Reinhold, K. L. *The Foundation of Philosophical Knowledge (1794).* Trans. George di Giovanni. In *Between Kant and Hegel.* Albany: SUNY Press, 1985.

Reyburn, Hugh. *The Ethical Theory of Hegel: A Study of the Philosophy of Right.* Oxford: Oxford University Press, 1921. Reprint 1970.

Ricoeur, Paul. *Husserl: An Analysis of His Phenomenology.* Evanston: Northwestern University Press, 1967.

———. *The Symbolism of Evil.* Trans. E. Buchanan. Boston: Beacon Press, 1969.

———. *Time and Narrative,* vol. 3. Trans. K. Blamey and D. Pellauer. Chicago: University of Chicago Press, 1988.

Riedel, Manfred. *Zwischen Tradition und Revolution: Studien zu Hegels Rechtsphilosophie.* Stuttgart: Klett-Cotta, 1982. English translation: *Between Tradition and Revolution: The Hegelian Transformation of Political Philosophy.* Trans. W. Wright. Cambridge: Cambridge University Press, 1984.

Riley, Patrick. *Will and Political Legitimacy.* Cambridge, Mass.: Harvard University Press, 1982.

Rockmore, Tom. *Hegel's Circular Epistemology.* Bloomington: Indiana University Press, 1986.

Rosen, Stanley. *The Ancients and the Moderns: Rethinking Modernity.* New Haven: Yale University Press, 1989.

———. "Freedom and Spontaneity in Fichte." *Philosophical Forum* 19, no. 2–3 (Winter-Spring 1988).

———. *G. W. F. Hegel: An Introduction to the Science of Wisdom.* New Haven: Yale University Press, 1974.

Rousseau, Jean-Jacques. *Social Contract.* Trans. and intro. G. H. D. Cole. London: Everyman's Library, 1975.

Royce, Josiah. *Lectures on Modern Idealism.* New Haven: Yale University Press, 1919.

———. "The Possibility of Error." In *The Philosophy of Josiah Royce,* ed. John K. Roth, 44–76. New York: Crowell, 1971.

———. *The Problem of Christianity.* Chicago: University of Chicago Press, 1968.

Röttges, Heinz. *Dialektik und Skeptizismus: Die Rolle des Skeptizismus für Genese, Selbstverständnis und Kritik der Dialektik [Monographien zur philosophischen Forschung].* Hain: Athenäum, 1986.

Sartre, Jean-Paul. *Being and Nothingness.* Trans. Hazel Barnes. New York: Philosophical Library, 1956.

———. *Notebooks for an Ethics.* Trans. David Pellauer. Chicago: University of Chicago Press, 1992.

Scheler, Max. *The Nature and Forms of Sympathy.* Trans. Peter Heath. Hamden, Conn.: Shoe String Press, 1970. Translation of *Vom Wesen der Sympathiegefühl (1923).*

Schelling, F. W. J. *Philosophical Letters on Dogmatism and Criticism.* Trans. Fritz Marti. In *The Unconditional in Human Knowledge.* Lewisburg: Bucknell University Press, 1980.

Schilpp, P. A., ed. *The Philosophy of Jean-Paul Sartre.* LaSalle, Ill.: Open Court, 1981.

————. *System des Transzendentalen Idealismus*. Hamburg: Meiner Verlag, 1962. English translation: *System of Transcendental Idealism* (1800). Trans. Peter Heath. Charlottesville: University Press of Virginia, 1978.

Schmidt, Dennis J. *The Ubiquity of the Finite: Hegel, Heidegger and the Entitlements of Philosophy*. Cambridge, Mass.: MIT Press, 1988.

Schulz, Walter. "Das Problem der absoluten Reflexion." In *Wissenschaft und Gegenwart Heft 24*. Frankfurt am Main: Klostermann, 1963.

————. *Die Vollendung des Deutsche Idealismus in der Spätphilosophie Schellings*. Pfullingen: Neske Verlag, 1975.

Schutz, Alfred. "The Problem of Transcendental Intersubjectivity in Husserl." In *Collected Papers*, vol. 3, ed. I. Schutz. The Hague: Martinus Nijhoff, 1966.

————. *Reflections on the Problem of Relevance*. New Haven: Yale University Press, 1977.

————. "Scheler's Theory of Intersubjectivity." In *Collected Papers. Vol. 1: The Problem of Social Reality*, ed. M. Natanson. The Hague: Martinus Nijhoff, 1967.

————. "Type and Eidos in Husserl's Late Philosophy." *Collected Papers*, vol. 3, ed. I. Schutz, 92–115. The Hague: Martinus Nijhoff, 1966.

Schürmann, Reiner. *Meister Eckhart [Studies in Phenomenology and Existential Philosophy]*. Bloomington: Indiana University Press, 1978.

Scott, Charles. *The Question of Ethics*. Bloomington: Indiana University Press, 1990.

Seidel, George J. *Fichte's Wissenschaftslehre of 1794*. West Lafayette, Ind.: Purdue University Press, 1993.

Sextus Empiricus. *Outlines of Pyrrhonism* I. Trans. R. G. Bury. *Loeb Classical Library*. Cambridge, Mass.: Harvard University Press, 1976.

Siep, Ludwig. *Anerkennung als Prinzip der praktische Philosophie: Untersuchungen zu Hegels Jenaer Philosophie des Geistes*. Freiburg: Karl Alber Verlag, 1979.

————. "The *Aufhebung* of Morality in Ethical Life." In *Hegel's Philosophy of Action*, ed. L. Stepelevich and D. Lamb, 137–155. Atlantic Highlands, N.J.: Humanities Press, 1983.

————. *Hegels Fichtekritik und die Wissenschaftslehre von 1804*. Freiburg: Karl Alber Verlag, 1970.

————. "Intersubjektivität, Recht und Staat in Hegels *Grundlinien der Philosophie des Rechts*." In *Hegels Philosophie des Rechts: Die Theorie der Rechtsformen und ihre Logik*, Hrsg. D. Henrich and R–P Horstmann. Stuttgart: Klett-Cotta, 1982.

————. "Kampf um Anerkennung: Zu Hegels Auseinandersetzung mit Hobbes in den Jenaer Schriften." *Hegel-Studien* 9 (Bonn: Bouvier Verlag, 1974), 155–207; English translation in *Hegel's Dialectic of Desire and Recognition*, ed. John O'Neill, 273–288. Albany: SUNY Press, 1996.

————. *Praktische Philosophie im Deutschen Idealismus*. Frankfurt: Suhrkamp, 1992.

Smith, John. "Hegel's Critique of Kant." *Review of Metaphysics*, 26 (1973): 438–460.

Smith, Steven B. *Hegel's Critique of Liberalism*. Chicago: University of Chicago Press, 1989.

Smith, Steven G. "Reason as One for Another: Moral and Theoretical Argument in the Philosophy of Levinas." In *Face to Face with Levinas*, ed. Richard Cohen, 53–72. Albany: SUNY Press, 1986.

Solomon, Robert C. "Hegel's Concept of *Geist*." In *Hegel: A Collection of Critical Essays*, ed. A. MacIntyre, 125–149. New York: Doubleday Anchor, 1972.

Taminiaux, Jacques. "Dialectic and Difference." In *Dialectic and Difference: Finitude in Modern Thought*, trans. R. Crease and J. Decker. Atlantic Highlands, N.J.: Humanities Press, 1985.

Taylor, Charles. *Hegel*. London: Cambridge University Press, 1976.

Theunissen, Michael. "Begriff und Realität: Hegels Aufhebung des metaphysischen Wahrheitsbegriffs." In *Seminar: Dialektik in der Philosophie Hegels*, Hrsg. Rolf-Peter Horstmann. Frankfurt am Main: Suhrkamp, 1978.

————. *Hegels Lehre vom absoluten Geist as theologisch-politischer Traktat*. Berlin: Walter de Gruyter, 1970.

————. "The Repressed Intersubjectivity in Hegel's Philosophy of Right." In *Hegel and Legal Theory*. London: Routledge, 1991. Original in German: "Die verdrängte Intersubjektivität in Hegels Philosophie des Rechts." In *Hegels Philosophie des Rechts*. Hrsg. v. Dieter Henrich und Rolf-Peter Horstmann. Stuttgart: Klett-Cotta, 1982.

————. *The Other: Studies in the Social Ontology of Husserl, Heidegger, Sartre and Buber*. Trans. Christopher Macann. Cambridge, Mass.: MIT Press, 1984.

————. *Sein Und Schein: Die kritische Funktion der Hegelschen Logik*. Frankfurt am Main: Suhrkamp, 1980.

Tuschling, Burkhard. "*Rationis societas*: Remarks on Kant and Hegel." In *Kant's Philosophy of Religion Reconsidered*, ed. Philip J. Rossi and Michael Wren, 181–205. Bloomington: Indiana University Press, 1991.

Walsh, W. H. *Hegelian Ethics*. London: Macmillan, 1969.

Weischedel, Wilhelm. *Der frühe Fichte: Aufbruch der Freiheit zur Gemeinschaft*. Stuttgart: Frommann-Holzboog, 1973.

Westphal, Kenneth. "The Context and Structure of Hegel's *Philosophy of Right*." In *The Cambridge Companion to Hegel*. Cambridge: Cambridge University Press, 1993. Pp. 234–270.

————. *Hegel's Epistemological Realism*. Dordrecht: Kluwer, 1989.

White, Alan. *Absolute Knowledge: Hegel and the Problem of Metaphysics*. Columbus: Ohio University Press, 1983.

Whitehead, Alfred N. *Process and Reality*. New York: Macmillan, 1929.

Wildt, Andreas. *Autonomie und Anerkennung: Hegels Moralitätskritik im Lichte seiner Fichte-Rezeption*. Deutscher Idealismus Band 7. Stuttgart: Klett-Cotta, 1982.

Widman, Joachim. *Fichte* [Sammlung Göschen]. Berlin: Walter de Gruyter, 1982.

Williams, Robert R. "The Concept of Recognition in Hegel's Jena Philosophy." *Philosophy and Social Criticism* 9:1 (Fall 1982): 101–113.

————. "Discernment in the Realm of Shadows." *Owl of Minerva* 26, no. 2 (Spring 1995): 133–148.

————. "Hegel and Heidegger." In *Hegel and His Critics*, ed. W. Desmond, 135–157. Albany: SUNY Press, 1989.

————. "Hegel and Skepticism." *Owl of Minerva* 24, no. 1 (Fall 1992): 71–82.

————. "Hegel and Transcendental Philosophy." *Journal of Philosophy* 82, no. 11 (November 1985): 595–606.

————. "Hegel's Concept of *Geist*." In *Hegel's Philosophy of Spirit*, ed. Peter G. Stillman, 1–20. Albany: SUNY Press, 1986.

————. *Recognition: Fichte and Hegel on the Other*. Albany: SUNY Press, 1992.

————. "The Other: F. H. Jacobi and German Idealism." In *Hegel on the Modern World*, ed. Ardis Collins, 73–92. Albany: SUNY Press, 1995.

Winfield, Richard D. *Reason and Justice*. Albany: SUNY Press, 1988.

Wood, Allen W. *Hegel's Ethical Thought*. Cambridge: Cambridge University Press, 1991.

————. Reply, Symposium on Wood, *Bulletin of the Hegel Society of Great Britain*, no. 25 (Spring/Summer 1992): 34.

Yovel, Yirmiahu. *Kant and the Philosophy of History*. Princeton: Princeton University Press, 1980.

Index